Aristotle's Metaphysics

ARISTOTLE'S METAPHYSICS

*Translated with Commentaries
and Glossary by*
HIPPOCRATES G. APOSTLE

INDIANA UNIVERSITY PRESS
Bloomington and London

FOURTH PRINTING 1975

Copyright © 1966 by Indiana University Press

Library of Congress catalog card number: 66–22451

Manufactured in the United States of America

cl. ISBN 0-253-30920-4
pa. ISBN 0-253-30921-2

To my father

Contents

Preface   ix

Aristotle's Metaphysics   3

Commentaries   253

    Summary of the Metaphysics   3

Book	Text	Commentaries
A	12	254
α	35	268
B	39	272
Γ	54	281
Δ	73	296
E	102	317
Z	108	322
H	137	348
Θ	146	353
I	160	365
K	176	378
Λ	197	393
M	213	409
N	236	434

Glossary
    English-Greek   449
    Greek-English   479

Index   485

Preface

When a great and fertile thinker has much to say in a limited time and without the present speedy means of having it recorded in detail, he chooses, if he has a sense of proportion, a condensed form of expression in order to cover the important points and so state the maximum. Aristotle would seem to have been writing under such circumstances, and, of course, he was writing for mature thinkers. In his works, one notices subjects, predicates, verbs, and important premises are often omitted; and to understand one part of his works one often finds it necessary to have gone through another part, since there is very little repetition. Arguments for or against a thesis are often given by mention of a phrase (like "*the third man*") or some other abbreviated expression, whose full meaning is not available to us; and some works which could throw light on the extant works are irretrievably lost. There are many key terms each of which is given many meanings, but since the specific meaning in a given context is usually not indicated, various interpretations may arise.

There is also the claim advanced by some, W. Jaeger for example, that the works we possess of Aristotle indicate a development in his thought, and this would imply a certain amount of inconsistency. If we add to this some deviation or corruption in the Greek texts handed down to us, and also some expected inconsistency, in terminology and thought, in any thinker who attempts to give a comprehensive and detailed account of the various fields of knowledge, the problems of translating the thought through the text become even more acute. In fact, some have gone so far as to say that certain parts attributed to Aristotle are notes taken down by students or that they are spurious works.

Our aim is to translate Aristotle's thought into English as accurately as possible under the circumstances. The difficulties indicated above can be minimized by adherence to certain principles of translation, some of which are concerned with terminology and others with thought. The translation must correspond to the Greek text as far as possible, and this requires a terminology which is consistent, adequate, familiar, and clear. The text is highly condensed, and to bring out the thought, whether inductively or by proof or in some other way, commentaries are required and references to the other works are advisable whenever possible. Since bringing out the thought is of primary importance within the limits of one volume, historical, philological, grammatical, and other such considerations, and also a discussion of other commentators, will be reduced to a minimum. We shall translate the *Metaphysics* first, for it is by nature prior to the other sciences and its principles are assumed by the other sciences. Then *Physics* will follow, and the others, as time allows.

Something should be said about the principles of translation.

(1) The terms should be consistent, for the first aim of these translations is knowledge and not something else, such as a work of art or a display of erudition. If in some cases synonyms should be used for linguistic propriety, they should be listed.

(2) The terms should be adequate. Consistency does not imply adequacy. One English term may be used consistently for a number of Greek terms differing in meaning, as in the case of "knowledge", but such simplification destroys important distinctions and so clouds or misleads thought. The unnecessary use of English synonyms, it may be added, does not contribute to adequacy and should be avoided.

(3) The terms should be familiar, that is, commonly used and with their usual meanings. If such terms are available, the use of strange terms, whether in English or in some other language, adds nothing scientific to the translation but unnecessarily strains the reader's thought and often clouds or misleads it. For example, the term ποιότης should be translated as "quality" and not as "quale", and the expression τὸ μόριον τῆς ψυχῆς as "the part of the soul" and not as "the departmental power of the soul"; "Concerning Youth and Old Age" is a better title than "De Iuventute et Senectute", and expressions like *"hypatê"*, *"eo ipso"*, *"terminus ad quem"*, and *"ceteris paribus"* should be avoided.

(4) The terms should be clear. Clarity is aided by definition, by the use of analogy or example or induction, or in some other way. When one is aware of distinctions for which no different terms exist, he should introduce new terms or use existing terms but indicate the various meanings of each. Aristotle chose the latter way, and a commentary indicating the meaning intended in a context is often advisable for the sake of the student. To beginners, for example, the specific meaning intended by "prior" or "cause" or "substance" is not always clear.

(5) Commentaries are time-saving and instructive. Premises needed to make the conclusion evident are not always mentioned in the text;

many of them are distributed throughout the existing works, and others are not available at all, for some of the works are lost.

(6) The translation should be definite in meaning; if cloudy, aside from its uselessness, it may not even be subject to correction.

The above principles of translation are sufficient for the present, though subsidiary ones might be added. The key philosophical and other important terms, along with the definitions of most of them or references, appear in the Glossary. The Commentaries are restricted mainly to details; occasionally they contain alternatives to the given translation, whenever these appear to have some plausibility. Aside from the Summary for each Book, no systematic attempt has been made to give, as St. Thomas Aquinas did, a detailed organization of each Book and Section.

The success of a translation depends, of course, largely on the extent to which the translator understands the thought, especially in the case of Aristotle's works, which, though condensed and difficult, are fortunately highly consistent.

We have tried to adhere to the above principles so far as practicable. Along with these, we have adopted the following conventions for the sake of clarity.

To distinguish in writing a vocal or written expression from what it signifies, we enclose it with double quotation marks. For example, "Socrates" is a term and not a man; it signifies Socrates, who was a man and not a term. Similarly, "four is a square integer" is an expression and it signifies a fact. Thoughts are analogous to expressions, and they too are enclosed with double quotation marks. For example, we may say that the thought "five is an even number" is false. We also use the conjunction "that" instead of quotation marks, as in "the thought that five is even is false". Expressions in Greek are not enclosed by quotation marks, for this is not necessary. For example, we may write: The word ποσόν is a Greek term and is translated as "quantity".

Whenever an object is under dialectical consideration, and there is a problem as to whether it is a thing or an expression (or thought) of that thing, single quotation marks are used. For Plato, for example, 'a man' as a universal and an Idea is not an expression but has independent existence, but for Aristotle this is not the case; and there may be a discussion concerning this issue. Single quotation marks are also used for the parts of Platonic Numbers, as explained in the Commentaries of Book M, and whenever we are not sure whether Aristotle is speaking of an object or of the term which signifies that object.

Terms in italics with initial capital letters signify principles posited by philosophers other than Aristotle. For example, the *One* and the *Dyad* are posited by Plato as the two principles from which all the other things are generated; *Water* is posited as the material principle by Thales; and the *Odd* and *Even* are posited as the two principles by some of the Pythagoreans.

Expressions in italics without initial capital letters are used in three ways. (1) For emphasis. (2) For some standard expressions used by Aristotle, such as *"the third man"*. (3) For terms used also in roman type, and for two reasons: (a) Aristotle uses some terms in two senses, generically and specifically; for example, αὐτόματον is used as a genus and also as a species, and we use "chance" for the genus but *"chance"* for the species. (b) Rather than use a strange term or introduce a new one, we often use a term in roman type for one meaning and the same term in italics for a meaning somehow allied to the first or narrower than the first. For example, we use "desire" and *"desire"*, "form" and *"form"*, "composite" and *"composite"*. The distinct meanings of such terms appear in the Glossary.

Expressions appearing in brackets are added for the sake of the reader and are not translations from the Greek. For example, in "for that which exists potentially may not be existing [actually]", the term "actually" in brackets is added merely for clarity and is not a translation of a corresponding Greek term. Brackets are also used to indicate English synonyms, when these are translations of only one Greek term, as in line 1012b34, in which "principle", "beginning", and "starting-point" are synonyms of ἀρχή.

Students who are interested in getting the thought accurately are urged to make full use of the Glossary. Many Greek terms, such as προαίρεσις, ὕδωρ, ἐμπειρία, and πρακτική are used with accurate meaning by Aristotle but have no exact equivalents in English, and the English terms chosen for them (*"choice"*, "water", "experience", and "practical", respectively), though close in meaning, still leave room for apparent inconsistency or falsity and unfair criticism, unless the reader is aware of the meaning given to them in the Glossary. In addition, in the case of a few terms, we have chosen the terms used by most or all of the translators, even if more technical terms could have been used. For example, for the term ἀριθμός we are using "number" instead of "natural number" or "whole number", although the usual meaning of "number" is closer to the term ποσόν than to the term ἀριθμός.

The texts used for the translation were those of I. Bekker, W. Christ, W. Jaeger, and W. D. Ross, along with the variants presented in the footnotes of those texts. In the margins of the translation we have inserted the pages and lines of the Bekker text, which are standard. The various works of Aristotle and the Bekker pages containing each of them are listed at the beginning of the Commentaries. The meanings given to a few terms in the Glossary were arrived at by induction, comparison, deduction, or in some other way, for no definitions of those terms appear in the Greek text. Whenever we disagreed with all of the Greek texts and their variants, we translated as we thought best, and a commentary was added giving our alternative in Greek and the reasons for it.

I am grateful to Professors John P. Anton, Paul G. Kuntz, Richard P. McKeon, and Henry B. Veatch for their help in discussing with me the general aspects of this translation; to Father William H. Kane and Father Joseph Owens for a number of important corrections of a philosophical nature; to Professor Richard Cole, Professor Sheldon Zitner, Mr. James Holbrook, and Mr. Michael Young for their help in the choice of an appropriate English terminology and for many philosophical and linguistic corrections in the manuscript; to Professor John M. Crossett, who was most kind and generous with his time in discussing with me in detail the various phases of the translation since it began and in making numerous suggestions and corrections; and to Misses Linda Fiene, Eva Gardebring, and Jan A. Thomas for their faithful secretarial and other assistance.

In view of the magnitude of this task, I will welcome suggestions or corrections, which may be sent to me directly.

H. G. A.

Grinnell College

Aristotle's Metaphysics

Summary of the Metaphysics

Book A

1. Philosophy is a science of certain principles and causes. 980a21–982a3.
2. Philosophy is a theoretical science and is concerned with the most universal principles and causes. 982a4–983a23.
3. The early philosophers put forward only material principles or causes of things. 983a24–984a23.
4. Later thinkers added in some sense also moving causes, or formal causes, or final causes, but vaguely or inadequately. 984a18–988a17.
5. Criticism of predecessors. 988a18–993a10.
6. No one mentioned any cause other than the four (material, moving, final, and formal) given in the *Physics*. 993a11–27.

Book a

1. Philosophy is the science of the highest truth, and so of the highest principles or causes, and these are eternal. 993a30–993b31.
2. The causes are finite, both in series and in kind, and in series there is always a first cause. 994a1–994b31.
3. Each science should use the method appropriate to its subject. 994b32–995a20.

Book B

1. Philosophy should list and discuss the problems well, both those considered by others and those neglected. 995a24–995b4.
2. The problems of philosophy. 995b4–996a17.
    (1) Whether the causes are investigated by one or many sciences.

3

(2) Whether philosophy investigates only the principles of substances or also the principles of demonstration.

(3) Whether it is one science which investigates all substances, or more than one.

(4) Whether only sensible substances exist, or also others.

(5) Whether philosophy investigates substances, or also their essential attributes.

(6) Whether the principles of things are the genera or the ultimate constituents into which they are divisible.

(7) If the principles are the genera, whether these are the ultimate or the proximate.

(8) Whether there is, besides matter, another principle existing in virtue of itself, and if so, whether it is separate or not.

(9) Whether the principles, both material and formal, are definite in number or in kind.

(10) Whether the principles of both destructible and indestructible things are (a) the same or distinct and (b) destructible or indestructible.

(11) Whether unity and being are the substances of things or just predicates of underlying subjects.

(12) Whether the principles are universal or individuals.

(13) Whether the principles exist potentially or actually.

(14) Whether the mathematical objects (points, lines, planes, etc.) are substances or not, and whether they exist separately or not.

3. Discussion of the problems. Arguments for and against each side of each problem. 996a18–1003a17.

Book Γ

1. Philosophy investigates being qua being and the essential attributes of being; and although "being" has many senses, there is a main sense to which all the others are somehow related. 1003a21–5a18.

2. It is the task of philosophy to investigate also the principles of demonstration, for these are principles of all being. 1005a19–b8.

3. The principle of contradiction is the most certain of all. 1005b8–34.

4. Criticism of those who deny the principle of contradiction. 1005b35–1011b15.

5. The principles of contraries. 1011b15–22.

6. The principle of the excluded middle. 1011b23–2a28.

7. The one-sided positions, such as "everything is true", "everything is false", "everything moves", etc., are necessarily false. 1012a29–b31.

Book Δ

Meanings of philosophical terms

1. Principle. 1012b34–3a23.
2. Cause. 1013a24–4a25.
3. Element. 1014a26–b15.
4. Nature. 1014b16–5a19.
5. Necessary. 1015a20–b15.
6. Unity. 1015b16–7a6.
7. Being. 1017a7–b9.
8. Substance. 1017b10–26.
9. Same. 1017b27–8a19.
10. Opposite. 1018a20–b8.
11. Prior, posterior. 1018b9–9a14.
12. Potentiality. 1019a15–1020a6.
13. Quantity. 1020a7–32.
14. Quality. 1020a33–b25.
15. Relation. 1020b26–1b11.
16. Complete. 1021b12–2a3.
17. Limit. 1022a4–13.
18. In virtue of. 1022a14–36.
19. Disposition. 1022b1–3.
20. Having or habit. 1022b4–14.
21. Affection. 1022b15–21.
22. Privation. 1022b22–3a7.
23. Having or holding. 1023a8–25.
24. From. 1023a26–b11.
25. Part. 1023b12–25.
26. Whole. 1023b26–4a10.
27. Mutilated. 1024a11–28.
28. Genus or race. 1024a29–b16.
29. Falsity. 1024b17–5a13.
30. Accident or attribute. 1025a14–34.

Book E

1. Generically, the theoretical sciences are mathematics, physics, and theology (first philosophy); and of these, theology is first, most universal, and most honorable, for its object is separate, immovable, eternal, most divine, and a cause most of all. 1025b3–6a32.
2. The nature of accidental being, and why no science of it is possible. 1026a33–7a28.
3. Arguments for the existence of accidental being as a cause or a principle. 1027a29–b16.
4. Being as existing in the soul, whether as truth, or falsity, or as whatness. 1027b17–8a6.

Book Z

1. The primary investigation of being is that of substance, for it is prior to all others in formula, in knowledge, and in time. 1028a10–b7.
2. The objects which are thought to be substances by other thinkers. 1028b8–32.
3. The kinds of objects which thinkers call "substances" are essence, universal, genus, and especially subject (matter, or form, or a *composite*). However, matter as a subject is not a substance, for it is not separate. 1028b33–9a34.

4. Essence, like whatness or definition, belongs primarily to substances and secondarily to the others. 1029b1–1030b14.
5. Difficulties in attributing essence to essential attributes and so considering them as definable. 1030b15–1a14.
6. Of things stated primarily and by themselves, each is one and the same as its essence. 1031a15–2a11.
7. Generation takes place by nature, art, or chance. The principles or causes of generation. 1032a12–3a23.
8. That which is generated is not the form or the matter, but the *composite*, and it is generated by a mover who has the same form in some sense and puts the form in the matter. 1033a24–4a8.
9. The matter of that which is generated both by art and chance has within it a moving principle in a sense the same as, or related to, the form of the thing generated. 1034a9–b7.
10. A composite which is generated may also be a subject with an attribute (like a healthy Socrates). 1034b7–19.
11. The conditions under which a part of a thing is part of the definition of the thing or is prior to the thing. 1034b20–6a25.
12. The kind of parts of a thing which are parts of its form, and the kind of parts which are not such parts. 1036a26–7b7.
13. The cause of unity in a definition of a thing; and, in defining, the kind of terms which should be included, and their appropriate order. 1037b8–8a35.
14. A universal cannot be a substance, but as a common predicate it signifies suchness; hence, the Ideas cannot exist, for they are posited as universals, and also as substances, which are individuals. 1038b1–9b19.
15. Since definitions and demonstrations are of what is universal and necessary, an individual qua such is not definable or *known*. The same applies to Ideas, for they are individuals. 1039b20–1040b4.
16. The parts of sensible substances and whatever has no definite unity (like air and fire) are not substances but rather potentialities or matter, and what belongs commonly to things, like unity and being, are not substances but rather principles of knowledge. 1040b5–1a5.
17. The form (or essence, or *substance*) of a *composite* is the primary cause and the principle, but not an element, of the unity and existence of the *composite*. 1041a6–b33.

Book H

1. In a sensible thing there is a substance in the sense of an underlying subject, and this differs for each kind of change. 1042a3–b8.
2. In sensibles there is also a substance as the *actuality* of the thing, and there are kinds of *actualities*. 1042b9–3a28.

3. The *actuality* of a sensible thing is not an element of it, but as the cause of its unity and existence it is a principle, either eternal, or not generable in the manner a *composite* is generable. 1043a29–4a14.

4. Proximate and ultimate matter are distinct, and in a definition the proximate causes should be given. 1044a15–b20.

5. Matter exists in that and only that which is generated and which is therefore a *composite*; and in generation, a *composite* A becomes a *composite* B by first returning to its matter. 1044b21–5a6.

6. The cause of unity in a definition is its differentia, which is the form or actuality, and genus is the matter or potentiality. 1045a7–b23.

Book Θ

1. Of potentialities with respect to motion, those of acting are prior to those of being acted upon, and the others follow. 1045b27–6a35.

2. Rational and nonrational potencies. 1046a36–b28.

3. The doctrine of the Megaric school is false; for, in holding that a thing has potency only when it acts, it destroys the possibility of generation and of other changes. 1046b29–7b2.

4. The view that everything is possible is necessarily false. 1047b3–30.

5. Conditions under which rational and nonrational potencies are *actualized*. 1047b31–8a4.

6. What potentiality and *actuality* are in general, and their analogous nature. 1048a25–b17.

7. *Actuality* is distinct from motion. 1048b18–36.

8. Conditions under which something is potentially another thing, and the naming of the latter derivatively from their matter or accidents. 1048b37–9b3.

9. *Actuality* is prior to potentiality in formula, in substance, and, in a sense, in time; and no indestructible or necessary substance has potentiality, except in some cases (Moon, Sun, etc.) but with respect to place or quality. 1049b4–1051a3.

10. A good *actuality* is better than the corresponding potentiality, but a bad *actuality* is worse; and nothing eternal is bad or in error. 1051a4–21.

11. Knowledge of what is potential comes to be through the *actuality* of that potential by thought. 1051a21–33.

12. Truth and falsity, whether in things or in the soul, is about a composite or what is divided, and truth in the soul is caused by truth or falsity in things. As for what is simple, there is no truth or falsity, but either apprehension or no apprehension of it. 1051a34–2a11.

Book I

1. To be essentially one is to be indivisible either (a) by being continuous, or (b) by being a whole, or, if having one formula, (c) by being numerically one or (d) by being one in kind. 1052a15–b18.
2. Also, to be one is to be a measure of a number in each genus but primarily in quantity, and this measure is a principle. Thus, if the measure is a foot, the number is a number of feet. 1052b18–3b8.
3. Just as "being" has many senses, so does "unity"; so a unity is no single nature but may be a quality, or a quantity, or a substance, etc. 1053b9–4a19.
4. How unity is opposed to plurality; the kinds of unity are sameness, equality, likeness, and the corresponding pluralities are otherness, inequality, unlikeness. Difference is a kind of otherness. 1054a20–5a2.
5. Contrariety is complete difference, and it is a kind of privation. Contrariety is posterior in existence to contradiction. 1055a3–b29.
6. The equal is opposed to the great and the small, taken together, as the privative negation of them. 1055b30–6b2.
7. The many are opposed to the one also as the measure to the measurable, and they are opposed to the few as excessive plurality to deficient plurality, for "many" is not univocal. 1056b3–7a17.
8. Intermediates lie between contraries, are within the same genus as contraries, and are composed of contraries. 1057a18–b34.
9. Otherness in species, and sameness in species. 1057b35–8a28.
10. Otherness in species is caused by contrariety or contrast in the form and not in the matter of a thing. 1058a29–b25.
11. The destructible and the indestructible are in distinct genera. 1058b26–9a14.

Book K

1. Statement and discussion of the problems of philosophy. They are almost identical with those considered in Book B, but their disdiscussion here is less thorough. See *Commentaries*, Book B. 1059a18–1060b30.
2. Philosophy investigates being qua being and the essential attributes of being; and although "being" has many senses, there is a main sense to which all the others are related. 1060b31–1b17.
3. It is the task of philosophy to investigate also the principles of demonstration, for these are principles of all being. 1061b17–33.
4. The principle of contradiction is the most certain of all. 1061b34–2a5.
5. Criticism of those who deny the principle of contradiction. 1062a5–3b35.
6. Generically, the theoretical sciences are mathematics, physics, and

theology (first philosophy); and of these, theology is the first, the most universal, and the most honorable, for its object is a principle which is first, separate, immovable, and eternal. 1063b36–4b14.

7. The nature of accidental being, why no science of it is possible, and why there is an accidental cause, though posterior to nature. 1064b15–5b4.

8. Motion does not exist apart from physical objects, and it is the *actuality* of the potential qua potential. 1065b5–6a34.

9. The infinite is not a substance but an attribute of a quantity, and it can exist only potentially; thus, no actual infinite body exists. 1066a35–7a37.

10. The three kinds of change. 1067b1–8a7.

11. The three kinds of motion. 1068a8–b25.

12. Definition of togetherness in place, apart in place, touching, between, contrariety in place, succession, contiguity, and continuity. 1068b26–9a14.

Book Λ

1. Separate substances are of three kinds: sensible which are destructible, sensible but eternal, and immovable. 1069a18–b2.

2. The principles or causes of changeable or movable objects are three: the two contraries (form and privation), and matter. 1069b3–34.

3. What is generated is neither matter nor form but a *composite,* and it is generated by a fourth cause, a moving cause, which may be external. 1069b35–1070a30.

4. The principles or causes of distinct things are distinct, and if the same, they are so by analogy, i.e., there is form, privation, and matter. 1070a31–1a3.

5. In another manner, potentiality and actuality are also principles, and they are causes; and they may be distinct for distinct things, or the same (whether in kind or by analogy). 1071a3–b2.

6. An immovable and eternal substance necessarily exists; and it must be without potentiality but only an *actuality,* moving eternally and in the same way the first heaven around the center of the universe. 1071b3–2a26.

7. The prime mover moves like the primary object of desire or of thought; He is simple, indivisible, without part or magnitude, most noble, and a final cause in Himself; and He is Intellect, unaffected and unalterable, whose *activity* is eternal, the best, and the most pleasant of all, and whose object of contemplation is Himself. 1072a26–3a13.

8. Since, besides the locomotion of the first heaven, there are other locomotions to account for those of the planets, there must be

other unmoved movers besides the prime mover. In all, there are probably 55 unmoved movers, or some such number of them. 1073a14–4a21.

9. There is only one universe. 1074a31–b14.

10. Some difficulties concerning the nature of the Intellect and the object which He thinks. The Intellect is not a potency but an *actuality*, and He is thinking of Himself. 1074b15–5a10.

11. Goodness in the whole universe is primarily in the prime mover and secondarily in the order in it. Criticism of other doctrines. 1075a11–6a4.

Book M

1. Some thinkers posit as nonsensible and immovable substances the Ideas and the Mathematical Objects, others say that these two are identical, and still others posit only the Mathematical Objects. 1076a8–37.

2. Mathematical objects cannot exist *with* sensible objects. 1076a38–b11.

3. Mathematical objects cannot exist as separate substances. 1076b11–7b14.

4. Mathematical objects are inseparable from sensible substances, but they can be separated in thought and investigated qua separate from sensible objects. 1077b14–8a31.

5. Since order, symmetry, and definiteness are species of beauty and are attributes of mathematical objects, mathematics does investigate beauty even if the term "beauty" is not mentioned. 1078a31–b6.

6. Plato's first theory of Ideas, reasons for positing it, and criticism of the theory. 1078b7–1080a11.

7. The possible ways in which mathematical objects, especially numbers and their units, may be the substances of things; most of these ways were actually posited by various thinkers. 1080a12–b36.

8. Whether (a) all units are comparable, or (b) all incomparable, or (c) some comparable and others not, difficulties follow in positing the Ideas as Numbers; moreover, neither in fact, nor according to the theory of Ideas, can units differ in quantity or in quality. 1080b37–3a20.

9. Those (Speusippus and followers) who posit only the Mathematical Objects as separate substances are likewise faced with difficulties. 1083a20–b1.

10. The position of Xenocrates is the worst, for in identifying the Ideas with the Mathematical Objects it commits two errors in a single doctrine. 1083b1–8.

11. The Pythagoreans are right in not positing the numbers as separate from sensible objects, but wrong in saying that sensible magnitudes are composed of numbers and that indivisible magnitudes exist. 1083b8–23.
12. Difficulties and impossibilities result in the generation of units and Numbers, whether finite or infinite, in the generation of Magnitudes from their principles, and in positing the *One* as indivisible and as both form and matter. 1083b23–6a21.

   Lines 1086a21–7a25 do not belong here. Perhaps they are an earlier draft of the beginning of Book M.
(13.) The Platonists say that the Ideas are separate nonsensible substances and objects of *knowledge,* but they err in positing them both as universal and as individual. 1086a21–b13.
(14.) Whether the Ideas or the Mathematical Objects are posited as nonsensible substances, difficulties are faced with regard to the existence or knowledge of their principles, whether these be universal or individual. 1086b14–7a25.

Book N

1. All thinkers err in saying that the principles (matter and form) of immovable substances are contraries; for contraries are attributes, and these are inseparable and so not principles. 1087a29–8b13.
2. But immovable substances, qua eternal, cannot change, while substances with matter can and sometime will change. 1088b14–35.
3. These thinkers erred especially in not distinguishing the senses of "being," so to explain the plurality of things, they posited nonbeing or falsity, which, together with being, made a plurality of things possible. 1088b35–1090a2.
4. Why should the Numbers or the Mathematical Objects exist? For Plato, they are at least the causes of sensibles; for the Pythagoreans, they are the sensibles or in the sensibles; but other difficulties arise in these doctrines. But for Speusippus, they are not even the causes of the sensibles, and yet mathematical *attributes* exist in the sensibles. 1090a2–1a29.
5. How are the principles related to the good and the noble? Difficulties follow if the principles are contraries, if the *One* is an element and also a principle, and if Numbers are separate, prior, forms, and objects of *knowledge,* whether Numbers are Ideas or just mathematical, and whether the good is assigned to the first principle or appears later in generation. 1091a29–2a17.
6. It is not stated how Numbers are composed of or come from the principles, or how they are the causes of the *substances* or of the existence of things, and each possibility leads to difficulties. 1092a17–3b29.

Book A

1

All men by nature desire understanding.[1] A sign of this is their liking of sensations; for, even apart from the need of these for other things, they are liked for their own sake, and of all sensations those received by means of the eyes are liked most. For, not only for the sake of doing something else, but even if we are not going to do anything else, we prefer, as the saying goes, seeing to the other sensations. The cause of this is the fact that, of all the sensations, seeing makes us know in the highest degree and makes clear many differences in things.[2]

By nature, animals are born with the power of sensation, and from sen- sation memory comes into being in some of them but not in others. Because of this, animals which can remember are more prudent or more teachable than animals which cannot remember. Of the former, those which cannot hear sounds are prudent but cannot be taught, such as the bee or any other species of animals like it, but those which can hear can also be taught.

All animals, except men, live with the aid of appearances[3] and memory, and they participate but little in experience; but the race of men lives also by art and judgment.[4] In men, experience comes into being from memory;[5] for many memories[5] of the same thing[6] result in the capacity for one experience. And experience seems to be almost similar[7] to science and art, but science and art come to men through experience;[8] for, as Polus rightly says, "experience made art, but inexperience, luck."[9] Now art comes into being when out of many notions[10] from experience we form one universal belief concerning similar facts. For, to have a belief that when Callias was having this disease this benefited him, and similarly with Socrates and many other individuals, is a matter of ex- perience; but to have a belief that this benefited all persons of a certain kind who were having this sickness, such as the phlegmatic or the bilious or those burning with high fever, is a matter of art.

15 Experience does not seem to differ from art where something is to be done; in fact, we observe that men of experience succeed more than men who have the theory[11] but have no experience. The cause of this is that experience is knowledge of individuals but art is universal knowledge, and all *actions* and productions deal with individuals. The doctor does not cure 'a man' universally taken, except accidentally, but Callias

20 or Socrates or someone else to whom also the essence of man happens to belong.[12] If, then, someone without experience has the theory and knows the universal but is ignorant of the individual included under this universal, he will often fail to cure; for it is rather the individual that is

25 curable. Nevertheless, we regard understanding and comprehension as belonging to art more than to experience, and we believe that artists are wiser than men of experience; and this indicates that wisdom is attributed to men in virtue of their understanding rather than their experience, inasmuch as men of understanding know the cause but men of experience do not. For men of experience know the fact but not the

30 *why*[13] of it; but men of art know the *why* of it or the cause. It is because of this that we regard also the master-artists of a given craft as more

981*b* honorable, as possessing understanding to a higher degree, and as wiser than the manual workers, since the former know the causes of the things produced, but the latter are like certain inanimate things which act but do so without understanding that action, as in the case of fire which burns. Inanimate things bring about the effects of their actions by some

5 nature, while manual workers do so through habit which results by practicing.[14] Thus, master-artists are considered wiser not in virtue of their ability to do something but in virtue of having the theory and knowing the causes. And in general, a sign of a man who understands is the ability to teach, and because of this we regard art more than experience to be science; for those who have the art can teach, but those who

10 do not have it cannot teach. Again, we do not consider any of the sensations to be wisdom, although these are the most authoritative in the knowledge of individuals; but they do not tell us the *why* of anything, as for example why fire is hot, but only the fact that it is hot.

The first who arrived at any art that went beyond the ordinary sen-

15 sations was probably admired by men, not only because there was some usefulness in the objects arrived at, but also as being wise and superior to others. As more arts were arrived at, some for the necessities of life and others as the only ends of *activity*, those who arrived at the arts for the latter purpose were always believed to be wiser than those who

20 did so for the former because their sciences were not instrumental to something else. Now when all such arts were already developed, the sciences[15] concerned neither with giving pleasure to others nor with the

necessities of life were discovered, and first in such places where men had leisure. Accordingly, it was in Egypt that the mathematical arts were first formed, for there the priestly class was allowed leisure.

In the *Ethics* we have stated the difference between art and science and the others which come under the same genus.[16] But the purpose of our present discussion is to bring out this: all men believe that what is called "wisdom" is concerned with the first causes and principles; so that, as stated before, a man of experience seems to be wiser than a man who has any of the sensations, a man of art wiser than a man of experience, a master-artist wiser than a manual worker, and theoretical sciences to be wisdom to a higher degree than productive sciences.[17] Clearly, then, wisdom is a science of certain causes and principles.

2

Since this is the science we are seeking, we must inquire what are the kinds of causes and principles whose science is wisdom. If we were to go over the beliefs which we have about the wise man, this might perhaps make the answer more evident. We believe (a) first, that the wise man *knows* all things in a manner in which this is possible, not, however, *knowing* them individually;[1] (b) second, that a wise man can acquire knowledge of what is hard and not easy for any man to know (ability to have sensations is common to all, and therefore easy, but not a mark of wisdom); (c) third, that he who is more accurate and more able to teach the causes in each science is wiser; (d) fourth, that of the sciences, the one pursued for its own sake and for the sake of understanding is wisdom to a higher degree than the one pursued for the sake of what results[2] from it; (e) fifth, that the superior science is wisdom to a higher degree than the subordinate science, for the wise man must not be placed in rank by another but must set the ordering, and he must not obey another but must be obeyed by the less wise.

These, then, are the beliefs in kind and in number which we have concerning wisdom and wise men. Of the attributes listed, that of *knowing* all things must belong to him who has universal *knowledge* in the highest degree; for he understands in a sense[3] all the underlying subjects. And the most universal things are on the whole the hardest for men to know, for they are most removed from sensations. Also, the most accurate of the sciences are those which are concerned mostly with the first causes, for the sciences with fewer principles are more accurate than those which use additional principles; for example, arithmetic is more accurate than geometry.[4] Moreover, the science which investigates causes is more capable of teaching than the one which does not; for

30   those who teach are those who state the causes of each thing. Further,
      to understand things or *know* them for their own sake belongs in the
      highest degree to the science of that which is *known* in the highest de-
      gree; for he who pursues *knowing* for its own sake will pursue most of all
982b the science taken in the highest degree, and such is the science of that
      which is *knowable* in the highest degree; and that which is *knowable* in
      the highest degree is that which is first or the causes, for it is because of
      these and from these that the other things are known, and not these
      because of the underlying subjects. Finally, the supreme science, and
5   superior to any subordinate science, is the one which knows that for the
      sake of which each thing must be done, and this is the good in each case,
      and, in general, the highest good in the whole of nature.

      From all that has been said, then, it is evident that the name which is
      sought applies to the same science; for it is this science which must in-
10   vestigate the first principles and causes, and the good or final cause is
      one of the causes.

      That it is not a productive science[5] is also clear from those who began
      to philosophize, for it is because of wondering that men began to philos-
      ophize and do so now. First, they wondered at the *difficulties* close at
15   hand; then, advancing little by little, they discussed *difficulties* also
      about greater matters, for example, about the changing attributes of the
      Moon and of the Sun and of the stars, and about the generation of the
      universe. Now a man who is perplexed and wonders considers himself
      ignorant (whence a lover of myth, too, is in a sense a philosopher, for a
      myth is composed of wonders), so if indeed they philosophized in order
20   to avoid ignorance, it is evident that they pursued science in order to
      understand and not in order to use it for something else. This is con-
      firmed by what happened; for it was when almost all the necessities
      of life were supplied, both for comfort and *activity,* that such thinking[6]
25   began to be sought. Clearly, then, we do not seek this science for any
      other need; but just as a man is said to be free if he exists for his own
      sake and not for the sake of somebody else,[7] so this alone of all the
      sciences is free, for only this science exists for its own sake.

      Accordingly, the possession of this science might justly be regarded
30   as not befitting man; for human nature is servile in many ways, and so,
      as Simonides says, "God alone should have this prerogative," and it
      would be unworthy of a *man* not to seek the science proper to his nature.
      If, then, there is something in what the poets say and the Deity is by
983a nature jealous, he would most probably be so in this case, and all men
      of intellectual eminence would be unfortunate.[8] But neither is it possible
      for the Deity to be jealous[9] (nay, according to the proverb, "bards tell
      many a lie"), nor need we suppose that there is a science more honorable

5   than this one. For the most divine science is the most honorable, and a
science would be most divine in only two ways: if God above all would
have it, or if it were a science of divine objects. This science alone
happens to be divine in both ways; for God is thought by all to be one
10   of the causes and a principle, and God alone or in the highest degree
would possess such a science. Accordingly, all the other sciences are
more instrumental[10] than this, but none is better.

However, the acquisition of this science must in a sense bring us to
a state which is contrary to that when we began our inquiries. For all
men begin, as we said, by wondering that things are as they are when
the cause has not been investigated, as in the case of marionettes or of
15   the solstices or of the incommensurability of the diagonal of a square
with respect to its side; for all seem to wonder at the fact that no least
unit of magnitude exists which can measure both the side and the diagonal of a square. But we must end with the contrary and, according to
the proverb, the better state, as is also the case in these instances when
one has learned the cause; for nothing would make a geometrician
20   wonder so much as this, namely, if a diagonal were to be commensurable
with the side of a square.

We have stated, then, the nature of the science we are seeking, and
the aim of our concern and of our entire *inquiry*.

3

It is evident, then, that we must acquire *knowledge* of the first causes[1]
25   (for we say that we understand each thing when we think that we know
its first cause),[2] and causes are spoken of in four senses. In one sense, we
say that *the substance*[3] or the essence is a cause (for the *why*[4] leads us
back to the ultimate formula,[5] and the first *why* is a cause and a prin-
30   ciple); in another, it is the matter or the underlying subject; in a third,
the source which begins motion; and in a fourth, the cause opposite to
the previous, namely, the final cause or the good (for this is the end of
every generation and every motion).[6] We have investigated these causes
983*b*   sufficiently in the *Physics;*[7] however, let us examine the contributions of
others before us who attempted the investigation of being and philosophized about truth. For clearly they, too, speak of certain principles
and causes, and so there will be some profit in our present *inquiry* if we
5   go over what they say; for either we shall discover some other genus
of cause, or we shall be more convinced of those we just stated.

Most of those who first philosophized regarded the material kinds of
principles as the principles of all things; for that of which things consist,

and the first[8] from which things come to be and into which they are
finally resolved after destruction (this being the persisting *substance* of
the thing, while the thing changes in its affections), this they say is the
element and the principle of things; and because of this they think that
nothing is generated and nothing perishes, since such a nature is always
preserved. Just as in the case of Socrates when he becomes noble or
musical, we do not say that he is generated in the full sense,[9] nor that he
perishes in the full sense if he loses these habits, because Socrates himself as an underlying subject still persists, so it is in the other cases; for
there must be some nature, either one or more than one, which is preserved and from which the others are generated.

However, these thinkers do not all agree as to the number and kinds
of such principles. Thales, the founder of such philosophy, says that this
principle is *Water* (and on account of this he also declared that the earth
rests on water), perhaps coming to this belief by observing that all food
is moist and that heat[10] itself is generated from the moist and is kept
alive by it (and that from which things are generated is the principle of
all); and he came to this belief both because of this fact and because the
seeds of all things have a moist nature, and water is the principle of
the nature of moist things.

Some think that even the ancients, who lived long before the present
generation and were first to speculate about divine things, had similar
beliefs about nature, for they represented Ocean and Tethys as fathers
of generation, and the oath of the Gods as being by *Water* or *Styx* (as
the poets called it); for that which is most ancient is most honorable,
and that which is most honorable is that by which one swears. Perhaps
it may not be clear whether this doctrine about nature happens to be
primitive and ancient; at any rate, Thales is said to have spoken out in
this manner concerning the first cause. As for Hippo, one would not consider him worthy of being included among these thinkers because of
the shallowness of his *thought*.

Anaximenes and Diogenes posit *Air* as being prior[11] to *Water* and as
being in the highest degree a principle of simple bodies; but Hippasus
of Metapontium and Heraclitus of Ephesus posited *Fire* as the principle.
Empedocles posited four principles, adding to the principles already
stated a fourth, *Earth;* for he says that these always persist and are not
generated but combine into a unity or are separated out of a unity in
varying numbers of parts.

Anaxagoras of Clazomenae, older than Empedocles but later in philosophical works, says that the principles are infinite;[12] for he says that
almost all homogeneous things (as in the case of water and fire)[13] are
generated and perish only in this sense, namely, by combination and

10

15

20

25

30

984a

5

10

15

separation, and neither are they generated nor do they perish in any other sense but stay eternally the same.

From what has been said one might think that the only cause is the kind which is called "material". But as philosophers progressed in this manner, the facts themselves opened the way for them and contributed in forcing them to make further inquiries. However true it may be that every generation and destruction proceeds from some one principle, or even more than one, why does this happen and what is the cause?[14] For, indeed, the underlying subject itself does not cause itself to change. What I mean, for example, is this: neither the wood nor the bronze causes itself to change; the wood does not make a bed, nor the bronze a statue, but some other thing is the cause of the change. Now to seek this is to seek another principle, namely, as we might say, the source which begins motion.

Now those who were the very first to take up this kind of *inquiry* and to say that the underlying subject is one were not dissatisfied with themselves; but some of those who say that the underlying subject is one, as if defeated by this inquiry,[15] say that the *One* and the whole of nature is immovable not only with respect to generation and destruction (for this was an old belief and agreed upon by all) but also with respect to every other change, and this belief is peculiar to them. Of those who said that the universe is one, then, none happened to discern also a cause of this kind, except perhaps Parmenides, and to this extent, that he posits not only one cause but in some sense two causes.[16] But those who posit more than one,[17] such as the *Hot* and the *Cold*, or *Fire* and *Earth*, are more able to state the second cause; for they regard *Fire* as having a nature which can move things, but *Water* and *Earth* and such things as having a contrary nature.[18]

Following these thinkers and their principles, since such principles were not sufficient to generate the nature[19] of things, later thinkers, forced once more by truth itself as we said, sought the next principle. For it is perhaps unlikely that *Fire* or *Earth* or any other such should cause things to be or become good or noble[20] or that those thinkers should have thought so; nor again was it right to entrust a matter of such importance to *chance* or to luck.[21] When someone said that *Intelligence* exists in nature, as in animals, and that He is the cause of the arrangement and of every kind of order in nature, he appeared like a sober man in contrast to his predecessors who talked erratically. We know that Anaxagoras openly made these statements, but Hermotimus of Clazomenae is credited with having made them earlier. Those who had such beliefs, then, posited as principles of things both the cause of what is noble and the moving cause.

4

One might suspect that Hesiod was the first to seek such a cause, or
someone else who posited *Love* or *Desire*[1] as a principle in things, as
Parmenides does also; for the latter says, in describing the generation
of the universe,

> Love first of all the Gods she planned.

And Hesiod says,

> First of all was Chaos made,
> And then broad-breasted Earth
> And Love 'mid all the Gods supreme.

And these suggest that there must be in things some cause which will
move them and bring them together. As to how we are to assign priority
to these thinkers concerning these beliefs, let this await later *judgment*.[2]

Now since in nature there appeared to exist also the contraries of
good things, not only order and what is noble but also disorder and what
is base,[3] and bad things appear to be greater in number than good
things, and base than noble things, accordingly, another thinker introduced *Friendship* and *Strife*, each as the cause of each of the two genera
of things, respectively. For if one were to follow up and attend to the
thought intended rather than to the vague expression of Empedocles, he
would find *Friendship* as the cause of good things and *Strife* as the cause
of bad things. Thus, if we were to say that in a sense Empedocles both
mentions and is the first to mention *Badness* and *Goodness* as principles,
we might perhaps be right, if indeed the cause of all good things is
Goodness itself and of all bad things *Badness* itself.

As we said, then, the thinkers up to the time of Empedocles appear
to have touched upon two of the causes which we distinguished in the
Physics,[4] the material cause and the moving cause, but lightly and not
at all clearly, as untrained men box in fights; for, also these go around
their opponents and often strike fine blows, but neither do these box
scientifically, nor do the above thinkers seem to understand what they
are saying, for they appear to use the two causes occasionally and to a
small extent. For Anaxagoras uses *Intelligence* as an artificial device for
the arrangement of the universe, and when faced with the problem of
giving the cause for the necessary existence of something, then he drags
in *Intelligence;* and in other things which are generated he uses as a
cause any other thing rather than *Intelligence*.

As for Empedocles, although he uses the causes more frequently than
Anaxagoras, he does so neither adequately nor consistently.[5] At any

25   rate, he often makes *Friendship* separate the elements and *Strife* combine them. For when the elements in the universe are separated by *Strife*, the parts of fire combine into one unity, and so do the parts of each of the other elements; and again when the elements are brought together into one unity by *Friendship*, the parts of each element are of necessity separated from their corresponding unity. Now, in contrast

30   with his predecessors, Empedocles was the first to introduce this cause with further differentiation, positing not one but distinct and contrary principles[6] of motion. Moreover, he was the first to speak of the four so-

985*b*   called material elements, not using them as four, however, but only as two, *Fire* by itself, and the elements opposed to it (*Earth, Air,* and *Water*) as of one nature.[7] One may gather this by studying his verses. This, then, is our version of this thinker concerning the manner of his expression and the number of principles he posited.

5   Leucippus and his associate Democritus declare that the *Full* and the *Void* are the elements, calling the one "being" and the other "nonbeing", that is, the *Full* or the *Solid* is being but the *Void* or *Rare* is nonbeing[8] (hence, they say that being exists no more than nonbeing, inasmuch as a body exists no more than void), and that these are the material causes

10   of things. And just as those thinkers, who posit one underlying substance, generate all other things by its *attributes,*[9] positing the *Rare* and the *Dense* as the principles of all other changing attributes, so these thinkers say that the differentiae are the causes of all other differences

15   in things. These differentiae are three: *Shape, Order,* and *Position.*[10] For they say that things differ only in contour, arrangement, and turning; and of these, contour is shape, arrangement is order, and turning is position. For A differs from N in shape, AN from NA in order, and Z from N in position. As for motion, what its source is or how it belongs to

20   things, they casually neglected as the other thinkers did. Such, then, I say, seems to be the extent of the inquiries which the earlier thinkers made into the two causes.

5

    Contemporaneously with these thinkers, and even before them, the so-called Pythagoreans, who were engaged in the study of mathematical

25   objects, were the first to advance this study, and having been brought up in it, they regarded the principles of mathematical objects as the principles of all things. Since of mathematical objects numbers[1] are by nature first,[2] and (a) they seemed to observe in numbers, rather than in fire or earth or water, many likenesses to things, both existing and in generation (and so they regarded such and such an attribute of num-

30   bers as justice,[3] such other as soul or intellect,[4] another as opportunity,[5]
        and similarly with almost all of the others), and (b) they also observed
        numerical *attributes* and ratios in the objects of harmonics;[6] since, then,
        all other things appeared in their nature to be likenesses of numbers, and
986a   numbers to be first in the whole of nature, they came to the belief that
        the elements of numbers are the elements of all things and that the
        whole heaven is a harmony and a number. And whatever facts in num-
5   bers and harmonies could be shown to be consistent with the *attributes*,
        the parts, and the whole arrangement of the heaven, these they collected
        and fitted into a system; and if there was a gap somewhere, they readily
        made additions in order to make their whole system connected. I mean,
        for example, that since ten is considered to be complete and to include
10   every nature in numbers,[7] they said that the bodies which travel in
        the heavens are also ten; and since the visible bodies are nine, they
        added the so-called "Counter-Earth" as the tenth body.

            We have discussed these matters more accurately elsewhere;[8] but
        we are going over them here in order to learn from these thinkers what
        principles they posit and how these principles fall under the causes we
15   have named. Indeed, these thinkers appear to consider numbers as
        principles of things, and in two senses: as matter and also as affections
        or possessions[9] of things. The elements of a number are the *Even* and the
        Odd, the *Odd* being finite and the *Even* being infinite; the *One* is com-
20   posed of both of these (for it is both even and odd);[10] a number comes
        from the *One*; and, as we said, the whole heaven is numbers.

            Other members of the same school declare that the principles are ten,
        that is, ten pairs arranged in two columns, opposite against opposite:

Finite-Infinite	Resting-Moving
Odd-Even	Straight-Curved
One-Many	Light-Darkness
Right-Left	Good-Bad
Male-Female	Square-Rectangular

        Alcmaion of Croton seems to have come to such belief, and either he got
30   it from them or they got it from him. For Alcmaion was in the prime of
        life when Pythagoras was old, and he expressed himself just about as
        they did; for he says that a great many things relating to men come to
        two, meaning any chance contraries (not a specific list like that given
        by the others),[11] for example, white and black, sweet and bitter, good
        and bad, great and small, etc. Thus, Alcmaion gave indefinite hints
986b   about the rest, but the Pythagoreans stated both how many and which
        are the contrarieties.

            From both of these schools,[12] then, we can gather this much, that the
        principles of things are the contraries, and from the Pythagoreans we

5   are told how many and which the contraries are. But these schools have not been clearly articulate as to how their principles can be grouped and related to our list of causes;[13] however, they seem to place the elements under the material kind of cause; for they say that substances consist of or are fashioned out of these elements as out of constituents.

10   This account, then, is sufficient to give us a view of the *thought* of those early thinkers who declared the elements of nature to be more than one. There are some, however, who spoke of the universe as if it were of one nature; but not all of them were alike, either in expressing themselves well,[14] or in speaking in accordance with the nature of things.[15] Our discussion of them, then, is in no way relevant to the present inquiry into the causes; for, unlike some natural philosophers

15   who assume being to be one [16] and yet generate things from it as from matter, these thinkers speak in another way. For the former posit also motion (at any rate, they generate the universe), but these say that the universe is immovable. However, this much is pertinent to our present inquiry. Parmenides seems to conceive the *One* with respect to formula[17]

20   but Melissus conceives it with respect to matter; hence, the former says that it is finite but the latter says that it is infinite. Xenophanes, who was the first among these to speak of the *One* (Parmenides is said to have become his disciple), said nothing clearly, nor does he seem to have touched upon the nature of the *One* in any of these two senses; but gazing at the whole heaven, he said, "the *One* is God."

25   As we said, these thinkers need not be considered in our present inquiry. Two of them, Xenophanes and Melissus, may be completely ignored as being somewhat immature; but Parmenides, being more observant, seems to be saying something. For, claiming that nonbeing, in contrast to *Being*, does not exist, he thinks it is necessary that *Being*

30   be one and that nothing else be (we spoke more clearly about this in the *Physics*).[18] But being forced to conform to phenomena, and believing that these are one according to formula but many according to sensation, he now posits two causes or two principles, the *Hot* and the *Cold*,

987a   as if speaking of fire and earth; and he classifies the *Hot* as the principle with respect to being but the *Cold* as the principle with respect to nonbeing.

From what has been said, then, and from the wise men whose account concerning these matters has by now been considered, we gather this

5   much: the first philosophers posit a corporeal principle (for water and fire and such things are bodies), some of them using only one corporeal principle and the others more than one, but both place these principles under one kind, the material principle; other philosophers, however, posit as a cause both the material principle and the source of motion, and the latter cause is regarded as one by some but as two by others.

10   Down to the Italian school,[19] then, and apart from them, philosophers
expressed themselves rather weakly concerning the causes of things,
except that, as we said, they have in fact used two kinds of causes, one
of which, the source of motion, was regarded as one by some but as
two by others. The Pythagoreans, however, spoke of two principles in
15   the same manner[20] but added this much (which is peculiar to them),[21]
that the *Finite* and the *Infinite* and the *One* are not to be regarded as
being other natures, such as fire or earth or some other thing of this sort,
but that the *Infinite* itself and the *One* itself are the *substances* of the
things of which they are predicated, and hence that numbers are the
20   *substances* of all things. Concerning principles, then, they spoke in this
manner, and concerning the whatness of a thing, they began to discuss
and give definitions but gave too simple a treatment. For they were defining superficially and thought that the *substance* of what is defined
is the *substance* of the first[22] thing to which the definition belongs, as
25   if one were to think that the double is the same as two, because two is
the first thing which is double of some other thing. But to be double and
to be two are not equally the same; otherwise, one thing will be many,
and this was indeed happening with these thinkers.[23] This much, then,
may be gathered from the earlier philosophers and the ones that
followed.

                                    6

30   After the philosophies named came the system of Plato, which followed these philosophies[1] in many respects but also had its own pe-
culiarities distinguishing it from the philosophy of the Italians.[2] For,
having in his youth become familiar first with Cratylus and the Heraclitean doctrines (that all sensible things are always in a state of flux and
that no science of them exists), he continued to believe these even in
987*b*   his later years. Now Socrates was engaged in the study of ethical matters,
but not at all in the study of nature as a whole, yet in ethical matters he
sought the universal and was the first to fix his *thought* on definitions.
Plato, on the other hand, taking into account the *thought* of Socrates,
5   came to the belief that, because sensible things are always in a state of
flux, such inquiries were concerned with other things and not with the
sensibles; for there can be no common definition of sensible things when
these are always changing. He called things of this other sort "Ideas"
and believed that sensible things exist apart from Ideas and are named
according to Ideas. For the many sensibles which have the same name
10   exist by participating in the corresponding Forms.[3] The only change
he made was to use the name "participation"; for the Pythagoreans say

that things exist by imitating numbers, but Plato, changing the name, says that things exist by participating in the Forms. As to what this imitation of or participation in the Forms might be, they left this an open question.

15   Further, he says that besides the sensible things and the Forms, and between these, there exist the Mathematical Objects, differing from the sensible things in being eternal and immovable, and from the Forms in that there are many alike whereas the Form itself corresponding to these is only one.[4]

    Since the Forms are the causes of all other things, he thought the
20   elements of the Forms are the elements of all things. As matter, the *Great* and the *Small* are the principles; as *substance*, it is the *One*. For from the *Great* and the *Small* and by participation in the *One* come the Forms, and these are Numbers.

    In saying that the *One* is a substance, and not that it is something else of which "one" is predicated,[5] he spoke like the Pythagoreans, and like them he believed that the Numbers are the causes of the *substance* of
25   all other things. But he was unlike the Pythagoreans, (a) in making the *Infinite* not one principle but a *Dyad*, consisting of the *Great* and the *Small*, (b) in saying that the Numbers exist apart from the sensible things and not that these are numbers, and (c) in positing the Mathematical Objects between the Numbers and the sensible things; and this is peculiar to him. Now Plato, unlike the Pythagoreans, posited
30   the *One* and the Numbers as existing apart from things and introduced the Forms because he was making logical inquiries[6] (for earlier thinkers had no knowledge of dialectics), and he made the other nature a *Dyad* because the Numbers, except those which are first,[7] could be generated
988a   with natural ease from it as from some plastic material. Yet what really happens is the contrary; for this sort of generation is not reasonable. For these thinkers make many things out of the matter, and the Form generates only once; but what we observe is that from one piece of matter one table is made, while he who puts the form upon the matter,
5   although he is one, makes many tables.[8] The relation of the male to the female is similar, for the female is impregnated by one copulation, while the male impregnates many females.[9] But these are imitations of those principles.

    This, then, is how Plato described the causes we are seeking. It is evident from what has been said that he uses only two causes, the cause
10   of the whatness and the cause according to matter (for the Forms are causes of the whatness of the other things, and the cause of the whatness of the Forms is the *One*). It is also evident what the underlying matter is, in virtue of which the Forms are predicated of the sensible things, and the *One* is predicated of the Forms; this is the *Dyad*, or the *Great*

and the *Small*. Further, he assigned the cause of goodness and the
15   cause of evil to the elements, one to each of them, just as some of the
earlier philosophers (for example, Empedocles and Anaxagoras) sought
to do.[10]

7

We have given a concise and summary account of those who spoke
20   and the manner in which they spoke concerning the principles and the
truth; yet we have gathered only this much from them, that not one of
those who spoke of a principle or a cause mentioned any other than
those we described in the *Physics*,[1] but all appear to have touched upon
them in some sense, although lightly.

Some speak of the principle as being matter, whether they assume it
25   to be one or many, and whether they posit it to be a body or incorporeal;
for example, Plato speaks of the *Great* and the *Small*, the Italians[2] of
the *Infinite*, Empedocles of *Fire* and *Earth* and *Water* and *Air*, Anaxagoras of the infinitude of homogeneous things. All these thinkers did
30   touch upon this kind of cause, and so did those who spoke of *Air*, or of
Fire, or of *Water*, or of something denser than fire but thinner than air
(for some spoke of the first element as being of this kind). The latter
thinkers touched upon this cause only;[3] others, however, touched upon
the source which begins motion, as for example those who posited
Friendship and *Strife*[4] or *Intelligence*[5] or *Love*[6] as a principle.

35   As for the essence or the *substance*, no one expressed it *clearly*, but
988*b*   those who posit the Forms[7] speak of it more than anyone else; for, it is
not as matter that they posit the Forms as causes of the sensible things,
and the *One* as a cause of the Forms, nor do they believe that the Forms
and the *One* are causes in the sense of a source which begins motion (for
they are rather causes of motionlessness and of rest, so they say), but the
5   Forms furnish the essence in each of the other things, and the *One* fur-
nishes the essence in each of the Forms.

As for that for the sake of which *actions* and changes and motions take
place, they speak of it as a cause in some sense, but not as it is stated
here or in the sense in which it is in its nature a cause. For, those who
speak of *Intelligence* or of *Friendship*, although they posit each of these
causes as a good in a sense, do not nevertheless do so in the sense that
10   some things exist or are generated for the sake of these but speak as if
motions proceed from these. In a similar way, those who say that the
One or *Being* is of such a nature say that it is the cause of the *substance*
of other things[8] but not that those things exist or are generated for the
sake of the *One* or of *Being*. So the fact is that in one sense they speak

15   of the good as a cause but in another sense they do not; for they speak of it not essentially but accidentally.[9]

All these thinkers, then, being unable to touch upon another cause, seem to confirm the fact that we have described the number and kinds of causes rightly. Moreover, it is clear that, if we are to seek the causes, we must either seek all of them in the ways stated or seek them in some

20   of the ways stated. Let us next go over the possible *difficulties* with regard to the way in which each of these thinkers has spoken and also state what the situation is concerning the principles.

8

Those who say that the universe is one and posit as matter some one nature which is corporeal and has magnitude clearly err in many ways;

25   for they posit the elements of bodies only, but not of incorporeal things, even though incorporeal things exist.[1] Also, in trying to state the causes of generation and destruction, although they speak as natural philosophers about all things, they leave out the cause of motion.[2] Moreover, they do not posit the *substance* or the whatness as a cause of anything;[3]

30   and besides, they easily call any of the simple bodies, except earth, a principle without examining how these are generated from each other (I mean fire, water, earth, and air). For things are generated from each other by combination, or by separation, and it makes the greatest difference as to which of these is prior and which is posterior.[4] For, (1) on the

35   one hand, the most elementary of all would seem to be the first things

989a   out of which the others are generated by combination, and of the bodies such would be the ones which have the smallest parts and which are most fine. Hence, those who posit fire as the principle would be most consistent with this statement. Each of the other thinkers, too, agrees

5   that the element of bodies is of this sort. At any rate, none of those who posited only one element claimed that earth is that element, clearly because its parts are great, but each of the other three elements has found an advocate; for some say that fire is that element, others water, still others air. (But why do they not ever name earth, as common people

10   do? For these say that all things are earth. Hesiod, too, says that of the bodies earth was generated first; so, this happened to be an old and a popular belief.[5]) According to this argument, then, he who says that the element is any one of the simple bodies other than fire, or posits

15   that it is denser than air but finer than water, would not be speaking rightly. But, (2) on the other hand, if that which is posterior in generation is prior in nature, and that which is concocted or made into a compound is posterior in generation,[6] the contrary would be the case: water

would be prior to air, and earth would be prior to water.[7] Let this, then, be our account of those who posited one cause such as we have stated.

20   The same might be said even if one posits more than one element; for example, Empedocles speaks of matter as being the four bodies. For he too is faced with consequences, some of which are the same as those we have just given, while others are peculiar to him. For we observe that these bodies are generated from each other, and in this way no one of them, such as fire or earth, stays always the same body[8] (we spoke

25   about these matters in the *Physics*);[9] and as for the cause of things in motion, whether one or two should be posited, he must be thought to have spoken neither altogether rightly, nor altogether reasonably.[10] In general, those who speak in this manner are of necessity discarding alteration; for cold will not come from heat, nor heat from cold. For how can the contraries themselves be affected, and what single nature would

30   become now fire and now water?[11] Empedocles says there is no such single nature.

          If we were to believe that Anaxagoras spoke of two elements, we would most certainly do so from his statements, which he himself did not articulate, but which he would have accepted of necessity as indicating two elements if one were to induce him to see this. To say that the principle was a blend of all things is absurd not only in many other

989*b*   respects, but also (a) because it follows that they must not have been blended before, (b) because no chance thing can by nature be blended with any chance thing,[12] and (c) in view of the fact that *attributes* and accidents would be separable from substances[13] (for it is the same things

5   that can be blended and be separated); however, if one were to follow him up by putting together closely what he intends to say, perhaps he would appear to be more modern in his statements. For when nothing was separated, clearly nothing could be truly asserted of that substance; I mean, for example, that it was neither white, nor black, nor grey, nor otherwise colored, but necessarily without color, for otherwise it would

10   have had one of these colors. Similarly and by the same argument, it would have been without taste and without any other similar attribute. Thus, it could have neither any quality, nor any quantity, nor be an instance of a *this*, otherwise, some one thing expressed by a species would have belonged to it. But this would be impossible if indeed all were blended together, for otherwise a thing of some one species would have

15   been separated from the other species; but he said that all were blended except *Intelligence*, and that this alone is unblended and pure. From these statements, then, it follows that he was speaking of two principles, the *One* (for this is simple and unblended) and the *Other*, which we posited as being indefinite before it becomes definite and participates in some form. Thus, while he spoke neither rightly nor clearly, he meant

20   to say something like what later thinkers were saying and what now appears more and more to be the case.[14]

But these thinkers happen to be at home only with discussions regarding generation and destruction and motion; for it is almost of substances of this kind alone that they seek the principles and causes. However,

25   those who investigate all things, positing some of them to be sensible and others nonsensible, are clearly examining both genera; consequently, we should dwell on them at greater length and gather what they say well and what not well with reference to our present inquiry.

30   The so-called Pythagoreans use principles and elements which are more foreign than those which the natural philosophers use. The cause of this is that it was not from sensible things that they took them; for the mathematical objects, with the exception of those of astronomy, are without motion.[15] Yet all their discussions and studies are concerned

990a   with nature; for they generate the heavens,[16] retain the facts as regards the parts, *attributes*, and operations within the heavens, and use up the principles and the causes for these facts, as if agreeing with the other natural philosophers that being is just this, namely, that which is sensible

5   and is contained in the so-called heavens. But, as we said, they claim that the causes and the principles are sufficient to rise up to the higher of beings,[17] and that they are more suited to these than to the discussions about physics. However, these thinkers say nothing as to how there can be motion if only the *Limit* and the *Unlimited* or the *Odd* and the

10   *Even* are assumed,[18] or how, without motion and change, there can be generation and destruction and the operations of the bodies which are carried[19] within the heavens.

Moreover, whether it is granted to them that a magnitude is composed of these principles or this is shown to be so, still, we may ask, how will some bodies be light and others heavy?[20] If we consider what

15   they assume and say, they are speaking no more of mathematical bodies than of physical bodies;[21] and this accounts for the fact that they have said nothing whatever about fire or earth or the other bodies of this sort, just as they have nothing to say, I suppose, which is peculiar to sensible bodies.

Further, how are we to accept, on the one hand, that the *attributes*

20   of numbers and the numbers themselves are the causes of what exists and is generated in the heavens both in the beginning and now, and on the other, that no numbers exist other than the ones of which the universe consists? For, when they say that opinion and opportunity lie in a certain region and injustice and separation (or blend) a little above

25   or below, stating that a demonstration of this is the fact that each of them is a number, but it then turns out that already a plurality of magnitudes exists together in this place because these *attributes* follow the

corresponding places, we may then ask: Are these numbers the same as the numbers in the heaven which must be accepted as being these things, or are they distinct from them? Plato at least says that they are distinct from them,[23] although he, too, regards all of them as numbers, both these things and their causes, but the latter as intelligible while the former as sensible numbers.

9

Let us leave the Pythagoreans for the present, for to have touched upon them as much as we did is sufficient. Those who posited the Ideas as causes, first, in seeking to find the causes of the things about us, introduced other things equal in number to these, as if a man who wished to count but, thinking that he could not do so with the few things at hand, created more. In seeking the causes of these things, they proceeded from these to the Forms, which are about equal to or not less than these;[1] for, there exists a Form having the same name as that which is predicated of many sensibles, of substances as well as of non-substances,[2] and of these things[3] as well as of eternal things.[4]

Yet none of the ways which are used to show that the Forms exist appears convincing; for, from what is laid down, in some cases a syllogism is not necessarily formed, and in others it follows that there will be Forms even of things of which we[5] think that no Forms exist. For, according to the arguments from the sciences there will be Forms of all things of which there are sciences;[6] according to the "one predicated of many" argument there will be Forms even of denials;[7] and according to the argument, that we can think of something which has been destroyed, there will be Forms of destructible things, for an image of what has been destroyed can exist.[8]

Again, of the most accurate statements, some posit Ideas of relations, yet we[9] deny that a genus of relations exists by itself,[10] and others speak of the *third man*.[11] And in general, the statements concerning the Forms discard those things[12] whose existence we[13] prefer to the existence of the Ideas; for what follows is that Number is first and not the *Dyad*,[14] that the relative is prior to that which exists by itself,[15] and all other conclusions which, drawn by some believers in the doctrine of Ideas, are contrary to the principles of that doctrine.

Again, according to the belief in virtue of which we[13] say that Ideas exist, there will be Forms not only of substances but also of many other things (for not only of a substance is a concept one but also of any other thing, and not only of substances are there sciences but also of other things; and a countless number of other such difficulties follow).

30

991a

5

10

15

20

25

30

991b

According to what necessarily follows and the doctrine of Forms,[16] if Forms can be shared, only of substances must there be Ideas; for Ideas are not shared as attributes, but each Idea must be shared in this sense, namely, qua not being said of a subject.[17] I mean, for example, that if a double participates in Double Itself, it does so also in eternity, but as in an attribute, for eternity is an attribute of the Double.[18] Accordingly, the Forms will be of substances;[19] and the same names signify substances whether applied to these things or to the Ideas, otherwise, what will be the meaning of saying that there exists something apart from the many things here, the one over the many? And if each Idea and the things that participate in it have the same form, there will be something common to all; for, why should the form of two be one and the same in the perishable two's and the many eternal Two's[20] any more than in Two Itself and any perishable two? But if that form is not the same for all, they would be equivocally named, and this would be similar to calling both Callias and a piece of wood "a man", although we observe nothing common in them.

Above all, one might go over the difficulties raised by this question: What do the Forms contribute to the eternal things among the sensibles[21] or to those which are generated and destroyed? For, they are not the causes of motion or of any other change in them. And they do not in any way help either towards the *knowledge* of the other things[22] (for, they are not the *substances* of them, otherwise they would be in them) or towards their existence[23] (for they are not constituents of the things which share in them). It might perhaps seem that they are causes in the way in which whiteness is a cause when it is blended in the white thing. But this argument, first used by Anaxagoras and then by Eudoxus and some others, can easily be upset;[24] for it is easy to collect many statements contradicting such a doctrine. Moreover, all other things do not come to be from the Forms in any of the usual senses of "from". And to say that the Forms are patterns and that the other things participate in them is to use empty words and poetic metaphors. For, if we look up to the Ideas, what will their function be? Any chance thing may be or become like another thing even without being copied[25] from it, so that, whether Socrates exists or not, a man like Socrates might be born. Likewise, it is clear that this might be the case even if there were to be an eternal Socrates.[26] Moreover, there will have to be many patterns of the same thing, and so many Forms; of a man, for example, there will be Animal, Two-footed, and at the same time Man Himself.[27] Also, Forms will be patterns not only of sensible things but also of other Forms; for example, this is how the genus will be related to a species of it among the Forms. Thus, the same Form will be both a pattern and a copy.[28]

Again, it would seem impossible for a *substance* to exist apart from that of which it is the *substance*. Accordingly, how could the Ideas, being the *substances* of things, exist apart from them? In the *Phaedo* this is stated in this manner: The Forms are the causes of the existence as 5   well as of the generation of things. But even if the Forms do exist, still no thing which participates in something is generated unless there is a mover. And many other things are generated, such as a house or a ring, of which we[29] say no Forms exist. Clearly, then, also the rest may be generated by such causes as the ones which produce the two things just mentioned.[30]

10   Again, if the Forms are Numbers, how will they be causes? Is it in view of this, that the things themselves are other numbers, for example, that one man is this number, Socrates is that number, and Callias is another?[31] Why then are the Numbers causes of the latter? If the former are eternal but the latter are not, this difference too would not account for it at all.[32] On the other hand, if it is in view of this, that the things about us are ratios[33] of numbers, like a harmony, clearly there is still some one thing in each of the numbers which form that ratio. If this 15   thing then is the matter, it is evident that the Numbers themselves will be certain ratios of something to something else.[34] I mean, for example, that if Callias is a numerical ratio of fire and earth and water and air, his Idea too will be a Number of certain underlying things; and Man Himself, whether it is a Number of a sort or not,[35] will still be a nu-20   merical Ratio and not just a Number. Because of all this, then, none of these will be just a Number.

Again, from many numbers one number is formed, but how can one Form be formed from many Forms?[36] And if it is not from them[37] but from the Units in them that a Number is formed, such as 10,000 for example, how are the Units related to each other in the Number formed? Many absurdities will follow whether the Units (a) are all alike in kind,[38] 25   or (b) are not alike in kind, either in the sense that, prior to the forma-tion of this Number, the Units of each Number are alike in kind but not alike in kind with those of any other Number, or in the sense that no one Unit is alike in kind with any other Unit. For, having no attri-butes,[39] with respect to what will the Units differ? These alternatives are neither reasonable nor in agreement with our thinking.

Again, these thinkers must set up another genus of number as the subject of arithmetic, and also other genera, all of which are simply called "Intermediate Objects" by some of them. But how is this to be 30   done, and from what principles will these objects come?[40] Or, why will these be between the things about us and the Ideas? Again, each 992a   of the Units in Two is generated from a prior *Dyad*, although this is impossible.[41] Again, why is a Number, taken as a whole, one?[42]

Again, in addition to what has been said, if the Units are different, these thinkers should have spoken like those who say that the elements are four or two, for each of those thinkers does not call the elements by a common name, such as "body", but calls them "fire" and "earth", whether body is common to both fire and earth or not; but as it is, these thinkers speak of the *One* as if it were homogeneous, like fire, or like water. But if this is so, the Numbers will not be substances;[43] but it is clear that, if there is a *One Itself* and this is a principle, the term "one" is used in many senses, for no other way is possible.

When we[29] wish to reduce substances to their principles, we[29] posit lengths as being formed from the *Long* and *Short* (a sort of species of the *Great* and *Small*), planes from the *Wide* and *Narrow*, and bodies from the *Deep* and *Shallow*.[44] But then, how will a plane have a line, or a solid have a line and a plane? The *Wide* and *Narrow* is a genus distinct from the *Deep* and *Shallow*.[45] Accordingly, just as a number does not belong to these, in view of the fact that the *Many* and *Few* is distinct from them, so it is clear that none of the higher will belong to any of the lower.[46] Nor yet is the *Wide* a genus of the *Deep*, for then the body would have been a species of the plane.[47] Further, from what principles are the points, which are present in magnitudes, generated?[48] Even Plato was struggling against this genus of things as being geometrical suppositions, and he called the point "principle of a line";[49] however, he often posited the indivisible lines as this genus, although such lines must have limits. Thus, if from an argument the existence of a line follows, from the same argument follows also the existence of a point.[50]

In general, although philosophy seeks the cause of visible things, we[29] have left out such a cause (for we[29] say nothing about the cause which begins change), and thinking that we[29] state the *substances* of these things, we[29] assert the existence of other *substances;* but as to how the latter are *substances* of the former, our[29] statements say nothing, for "participation", as we said, means nothing. Nor do the Forms touch upon that which we observe in the sciences to be indeed the cause, for whose sake each intellect and each nature acts, and which we claim to be one of the principles;[51] but philosophy has become mathematics for modern thinkers, although they say that mathematics should be studied for the sake of other things.[52]

Moreover, one would come to the belief that the underlying substance as matter is too mathematical, and that it is a predicate and a differentia of a substance and of matter rather than matter, that is, I am speaking of the *Great* and the *Small;*[53] and this is like the *Rare* and the *Dense*, of which the natural philosophers speak as being the first differentiae of the underlying subject, for these are species of *Excess* and *Deficiency*. As for motion, if the *Great* and the *Small* are motion,[54] it is clear that the Forms will be moved;[55] if not, whence did motion come?[56] Indeed, the whole inquiry into nature is discarded.[57]

10   Also, what seems to be easy is not done, namely, to show that all things are one;[58] for, if we grant all their assumptions, what follows from the examples they use is not that all things are one but that there is a *One Itself*. And even this is not shown, unless we grant that the universal is a genus; but this is impossible in some cases.[59]

Nor are there any arguments to show how Lengths and Planes and
15   Solids, which come after the Numbers, exist or will exist,[60] or what power they have;[61] for these can neither be Forms (for they are not Numbers), nor Intermediates (for these are Mathematical Objects), nor yet destructible, but they appear to be another and a fourth genus of objects.[62]

In general, the search for the elements of all beings, without distinguishing the many senses of the term "being", makes discovery impos-
20   sible, especially if the manner of proceeding is by seeking the kinds of elements out of which things are composed. For it is indeed impossible to find the elements out of which acting, being acted upon, or straightness are composed, but if at all, those of substances alone can be found; consequently, it is not true to think that one is seeking or has found the elements of all things.[63] And how would one be taught
25   the elements of all things?[64] Clearly, it is not possible for him to start with previous knowledge of them. For, just as a man who is learning geometry, although he may have previous understanding of other things, has no previous knowledge at all of what that science is concerned with and what he is about to learn, so is it also in other cases; so if there is a
30   science of all things, as some say,[65] he who is learning it could have no previous knowledge of it at all, although all instruction received proceeds by means of previous knowledge of some or all of the elements, whether by means of demonstration or by means of definition; for one must have prior understanding of the elements from which a definition is to be formed and these must be known; and learning by induction
993a   proceeds similarly. But if, on the other hand, the science under consideration happens to be innate, it is strange that we are not aware of possessing the best of all sciences.[66]

Again, how will one know in that science the elements out of which its objects are composed, and how will this be made clear? This, too, presents a *difficulty,* for there might be disagreement, as there is about
5   certain syllables; for some say that *za* is composed of *s*, *th*, and *a*, but others say that it is a distinct sound and is none of those which are known. Moreover, how could one come to know the objects of sensation without the corresponding power of sensation? But if indeed the

elements of which things are composed are the same for all, one should be able to do so, as one does in the case of the composite sounds which have elements proper to sound.[67]

10

It is clear, then, also from what has been said before, that all thinkers seemed to seek the causes named in *Physics*,[1] and that besides these we have no other that might be named. But they talked about these vaguely; and in one sense they stated them all, but in another they did not state them at all.[2] For philosophy about all things at the start seems to falter, inasmuch as it is at first both new and just beginning.[3] For example, this is how Empedocles speaks of bone, as existing by virtue of a ratio, and this would be the essence or the *substance* of a thing. But then, it is likewise necessary that flesh and each of the others have a ratio, or else none at all; and it is because of this ratio that also flesh and bone and each of the others will exist, and not because of the matter (which he calls "fire" and "earth" and "water" and "air"). But while he would have necessarily agreed if someone had pointed this out to him, he himself did not state it *clearly*.[4]

These matters were pointed out before. But let us return to them once more and list the problems that might be raised; for these might perhaps help us somewhat in solving some of the later problems.

Book α

1

30
993*b*
   The investigation of truth is in one sense difficult, in another easy. A sign of this is the fact that neither can one attain it adequately, nor do all fail, but each says something about the nature of things; and while each of us contributes nothing or little to the truth, a considerable amount of it results from all our contributions. Thus, if the truth seems
5 to be like the door in the proverb "Who would miss it?", in this sense it would be easy; but to have some of the whole truth and not be able to attain the part we are aiming at,[1] this indicates that it is difficult. Perhaps the cause of this difficulty, which may exist in two ways, is in
10 us and not in the facts.[2] For as the eyes of bats are to the light of day, so is the intellect of our soul to the objects which in their nature are most evident of all.[3]

   It is just to be grateful not only to those with whose opinions we might agree, but also to those who have expressed rather superficial opinions; for the latter, too, have contributed something, namely, they have
15 handed down for us the habit of thinking. If there had been no Timotheus, we would not have much lyric poetry; and if there had been no Phrynis, there would have been no Timotheus. The same may be said of those who spoke about the truth; for some of them handed down to us certain doctrines, but there were others before who caused them to be what they were.

20   It is also right for philosophy to be called "a science of truth". For the end of a theoretical science is truth, but the end of a practical science is performance;[4] for even if practical scientists examine how things are, they investigate what is relative to something else and what exists at the moment, and not what is eternal.[5] Now we do not understand a truth without its cause; also, of things to which the same predicate belongs, the one to which it belongs in the highest degree is that in
25 virtue of which it belongs also to the others. For example, fire is the hottest of whatever is truly called "hot", for fire is the cause of hotness

35

in the others.[6] Likewise, therefore, that is most true which is the cause of truth in whatever is posterior to it.[7] Accordingly, the principles of eternal things are of necessity always the most true; for they are true not merely sometimes, nor is there anything which is the cause of their existence, but they are the cause of the existence of the other things; accordingly, as each thing is related to its existence, so is it related to its truth.[8]

2

But clearly there is a beginning, and the causes of things are not infinite, either as a series[1] or in kind. For neither can one thing come from something else as from matter ad infinitum[2] (for example, flesh from earth, earth from water, water from fire, and so on without an end), nor can the source which begins motion (for example, a man is moved by air, air by the sun, the sun by *Strife*,[3] and so on without limit) be such. Similarly, the final cause cannot proceed to infinity; for example, walking for the sake of health, health for the sake of happiness,[4] happiness for the sake of something else, and in this manner always one thing being for the sake of another. And the case of the essence is similar. For of the intermediates, of which there is a last and also a prior, the prior must be the cause of the posterior.[5] For if we had to say which of the three is the cause, we should say the first; certainly not the last, for this is the cause of none, nor yet the middle, for it is the cause of only one (and it makes no difference whether it is one or many, or whether infinite or finite in number).[6] But of things which are infinite in this manner[7] (and of the infinite in general) all the parts are alike intermediate, except the last; so that if there is no first, there is no cause at all.[8]

Nor can the process go on to infinity in the downward direction, with a beginning at the top, so that from fire should come water, from water, earth, and in this manner always a coming to be of something in another genus. For something comes to be from something else in two ways (excluding the sense in which "from" means after, as in "the Olympic games come from the Isthmian games"), either as a *man* comes to be from a boy by a change in the latter, or as air from water. By "a *man* comes to be from a boy" we mean, in general, that which has come to be from that which is coming to be, or the completed thing from that which is in the process of being completed; for there is always something between, as in the case of generation,[9] which is between existence and nonexistence, so in the case of that which is being generated, which

is between being and nonbeing. Now a learner is a man who is coming
30   to be a scientist, and this is the meaning of saying "from a learner he
is becoming a scientist". On the other hand, when we say "water comes
to be from air", in this case the air is destroyed. On this account, in the
former case the process is not reversible, and the boy does not come to
994*b*   be from the *man;* for from the generation it is not that which is in the
process of becoming that is coming to be, but that which exists after that
generation. It is in this way, too, that the day comes to be from the morning, namely, that it comes after the morning; on this account, the morning does not come from the day either. But in the other case the process
is reversible.[10] In both cases, however, the number cannot go on to
5   infinity. For in the one case, those which are between must have an end;
in the other, things change back and forth, for the destruction of either
one is the generation of the other.[11] At the same time, what is first,[12]
being eternal, cannot be destroyed; for since generation does not proceed upwards to infinity,[13] it is necessary, when something is generated
with the destruction of something else, that that which is first, in the
sense *that from which,* should be eternal.[14]
Moreover, the final cause is an end, and as such it does not exist for
10   the sake of something else but others exist for its sake. Thus, if there is
to be such one which is last, the process will not be infinite; but if there
is no such, there will be no final cause. But those who introduce an infinite series are unaware of the fact that they are eliminating the nature
of the good, although no one would try to do anything if he did not
15   intend to come to a limit. Nor would there be intellect in the world; for,
at any rate, he who has an intellect always *acts* for the sake of something,
and this is a limit, for the end is a limit.
But the essence, too, cannot always be reduced to another definition
longer than the preceding one. First, if such reduction were possible,
each definition in the resulting series would be a definition to a higher
degree than the one which precedes it; but if there is no final definition
20   which is first, neither will any of the others be such as stated.[15] Second,
those who speak in this manner eliminate *knowing;* for it is not possible
for us to understand unless we come to the indivisibles.[16] Nor is it possible to know[17] a thing; for how can we think of an infinite number of
parts in this sense?[18] For the situation here is not similar to that with the
line which, being divisible without a stop, cannot be conceived unless
25   we stop[19] (for here, one who is to traverse the infinite line[20] will not
count the sections). But the matter in a moving object must also be
conceived.[21] Moreover, no object can be infinite;[22] and if it is, at least
the essence of infinity is not infinite.[23] Again, if the kinds of causes were
infinitely many, knowing[17] would still be impossible; for we think we

30   have understanding when we know the causes, but the infinite by addi-
      tion cannot be gone through in a finite time.

3

995*a*   The way we receive à lecture depends on our custom; for we expect
      a lecturer to use the language we are accustomed to, and any other
      language appears not agreeable but rather unknown and strange be-
      cause we are not accustomed to it; for the customary is more known. The
      power of custom is clearly seen in the laws, in which the mythical and
5   childish beliefs prevail over our knowledge about them, because of cus-
      tom. Some people do not accept statements unless they are expressed
      mathematically; others, unless they are expressed by way of examples;
      and there are some who demand that a poet be quoted as a witness.
      Again, some demand accuracy in everything, while others are annoyed
10   by it, either because they are unable to follow connections or because
      they regard it as petty. For accuracy is sometimes petty, and as in busi-
      ness transactions, so in discussions it seems mean to some people.
          Therefore, one should already be trained in how to accept statements,
      for it is absurd to be seeking science and at the same time the way of
15   acquiring science; and neither of them can be acquired easily. The
      accuracy which exists in mathematical statements should not be de-
      manded in everything but only in whatever has no matter. Accordingly,
      the manner of proceeding in such cases is not that of physics; for perhaps
      all nature has matter. (Hence, we should first inquire what nature is;
      for in this way, too, it will become clear what the objects of physics are,
      and in addition, whether one science or more than one should investi-
20   gate causes and principles.[1])

Book **B**

1

With regard to the science which is the subject of our inquiry, we
must first state the problems which should be discussed first. They are
concerned with matters about which some thinkers expressed different
beliefs, and besides them, with some other matters which may happen to
have been overlooked. Now those who wish to succeed in arriving at
answers will find it profitable to go over the *difficulties* well; for answers
successfully arrived at are solutions to *difficulties* previously discussed,
and one cannot untie a knot if he is ignorant of it. The *difficulties* raised
by *thought* about its object reveal this fact: insofar as *thought* is in
difficulties, it is like those who are bound; and in both cases one cannot
go forward. Accordingly, one should first study all the difficulties both
for the purposes stated and because those who inquire without first
going over the *difficulties* are like those who are ignorant of where they
must go; besides, such persons do not even know whether they have
found or not what they are seeking, for the end is not clear to them,
but it is clear to those who have first gone over the *difficulties*. Further,
one who has heard all the arguments, like one who has heard both
parties in a lawsuit or both sides in a dispute, is necessarily in a better
position to *judge* truly.

The first problem, which is concerned with the objects discussed in
our introduction,¹ is (1) whether it belongs to one or to many sciences
to investigate the causes, and (2) whether that science should attend
only to the first principles of substances or also to the principles from
which all men proceed to prove something, for example, whether it is
possible at the same time to assert and deny one and the same thing
or not, and other such principles; and (3) if that science is about substances,² whether it is one science that deals with all substances or more
than one, and if more, whether all are of the same rank or some of them
should be called "wisdom" and the others something else. And we must
also inquire into this, (4) whether sensible substances alone should be

Margin line numbers: 25, 30, 35, 995*b*, 5, 10, 15

said to exist or besides these also others, and if others also, whether such substances are of one genus or of more than one; for example, some thinkers[3] posit the Forms and also the Mathematical Objects between the Forms and the sensible things. As I say, then, we must examine these, and (5) whether our investigation is concerned only with substances or also with the essential attributes of substances; and in addition, concerning sameness and otherness and likeness and unlikeness and contrariety, and with regard to priority and posteriority and all other such, about which the dialecticians are trying to inquire, conducting their inquiry from accepted opinions only, to what science does it belong to investigate all these? To these we must also add their own essential attributes,[4] for we must inquire not only what each of these is, but also whether there is only one contrary to a contrary. And (6) are the principles and the elements the genera or the constituents into which a thing is divisible?[5] And (7) if the genera, are they those which are proximately[6] predicated of the individuals or ultimately; for example, is it 'an animal' or 'a man' that is a principle of, and exists to a higher degree than, an individual man? Also, (8) we must inquire and discuss most of all whether there is, besides matter, something[7] which is a cause in virtue of itself or not, and whether this is separable[8] or not, and whether it is one in number or more than one; and whether there is something apart from the *composite* or not (by "a *composite*" we mean what exists, when something is predicated of matter),[9] or in some cases there is but not in others, and in what sort of things there is. Again, (9) we must inquire whether the principles are definite in number or in kind,[10] both in the formulae and in the underlying subject; and (10) whether the principles are the same in both indestructible and destructible things, or distinct, and whether all principles are indestructible, or those of destructible things are destructible. Again, (11) there is the most difficult and most perplexing problem, whether the *One* or *Being*, as the Pythagoreans and Plato used to say, is not some other thing but is itself the *substance* of things, or this is not so but the underlying subject is something else, for example, *Friendship*, as Empedocles says, or *Fire*,[11] or *Water*,[12] or *Air*,[13] as others say. Again, (12) we may inquire whether the principles are universal or like individual things; and (13) whether they exist potentially or *actually*, and further,[14] whether they exist in some other manner[15] or with respect to motion, for these problems might cause much *difficulty*. Moreover, (14) are numbers and lines and figures and points substances in any sense or not, and if substances, are they separate from sensible things or are they constituents of them?[16]

Concerning all these problems, not only is it difficult to arrive at the truth, but it is not even easy to discuss the problems well.

2

(1) First, then, we shall discuss the first of the problems raised, whether it belongs to one or to more sciences to investigate all the
20   genera of causes.

Now how could it belong to one science to know the principles if these are not contrary?[1] Besides, there are many things which do not have all the principles. For in what manner can a principle of motion or the nature of the good exist in immovable things, if indeed every thing
25   which is a good essentially and through its own nature is an end and is such a cause, that the others are generated or exist for the sake of this thing, and if the end or the final cause is an end of some *action* and all *actions* exist with motion? Accordingly, this principle could not exist in immovable things, nor could there be a *Good Itself*. For this reason,
30   nothing in mathematics is shown through this cause, nor is there any demonstration stating "because it is better, or worse", and no one even mentions anything of this sort. And so because of this, some sophists, Aristippus for example, used to speak of mathematics with contempt; for in the other arts, even the ones requiring manual skill, such as
35   carpentry and cobbling, people always say "because it is better, or
996*b*   worse", but in mathematics no one speaks about the good or bad.

But if there are many sciences of the causes and each of them is con- cerned with a distinct principle, which of these sciences should be spoken of as the one we seek, or who of those possessing each science
5   has *knowledge* of the object of inquiry in the highest degree? For the same thing may have all the kinds of causes; for example, in the case of a house, the source of motion is the art or the builder, the final cause is its function,[2] the matter is earth and stones, the form is its structure. From our previous description[3] of the sciences which should be called
10   "wisdom", there is reason for each of them to be so called. For inasmuch as it is the supreme and highest in rank, and the other sciences, like servants, cannot with justice contradict it, such should be the science of the end or of the good (for the others are for the sake of the end or the good); but inasmuch as it was described as dealing with the first causes and with what is most *knowable*, such should be the science of sub- stance. For as one may have *knowledge* of the same thing in many ways,
15   we say that he who knows that the thing is something has understanding to a higher degree than he who knows that it is not something,[4] and in the kinds of knowing that the thing is something there is the more and the less, and it is he who knows the whatness of the thing who has under- standing in the highest degree, and not he who knows that the thing has

by nature a quantity or a quality or can act or be acted upon.[5] Moreover, in the other cases, too, we think there is understanding of each
20   thing, and of those things of which there is demonstration, when we
understand what it is.[6] For example, what is the squaring of a rectangle?
It is the finding of the mean. It is similar with all other cases. As for
generations and *actions* and every other change, we think we understand each when we understand the source of motion; and this is distinct
from and opposed to the end. Thus, it would seem that it belongs to dis-
25   tinct sciences to investigate the distinct causes.

(2) There is disagreement, too, as to whether it belongs to one or more
sciences to investigate also[7] the demonstrative principles. By "demonstrative principles" I mean the common doctrines from which all men
prove something; for example, the principle "In every case one must
30   either assert or deny", and "It is impossible to be and not to be at the
same time", and all other such premises. Is it the same science or a distinct science which is concerned with these principles and also with
substances, and if it is not the same science, which of the two is the one
we are seeking?

It is not reasonable that one science should be concerned with these
principles; for why should the comprehension of these principles be
35   peculiar to geometry more than to any other science? If indeed it belongs to every science alike to be concerned with these principles, but if
997a   it is impossible for all the sciences to be concerned with them, then, as
with these sciences, so it cannot be peculiar to the science of substances
to be concerned with the knowledge of them. We might also add, in
what manner can there be a science of these principles? For we already
5   know what each of them is; and even other arts use them as principles
which are known. If they come under a demonstrative science, the subject of that science will have to be some one genus, and some things in
that science will be *attributes*[8] and the others axioms (for a demonstration of all things is impossible); for a demonstration proceeds *from*
something, is *about* something, and is *of* something.[9] So it turns out that
10   all things which are to be proved will come under some one genus; for
all the demonstrative sciences use the axioms.

On the other hand, if the science of substances is distinct from that
dealing with the demonstrative principles, which of them is by nature
more authoritative and prior? For these axioms are most universal and
are principles of all objects. And if it is not the concern of the philos-
15   opher, whose concern is it to investigate what is true and what is false
about them?

(3) In general, is there one science of all substances or more than
one? If more than one, what sort of substances come under the science
we seek? On the other hand, it is not reasonable that there should be one

20   science of all substances; for, if every demonstrative science investigates
the essential attributes of some subject from the common doctrines,
then there would have to be one demonstrative science of all the attributes.[10] Certainly, the investigation of the essential attributes of the
same genus from the same doctrines[11] belongs to the same science. For
the subject belongs to one science, and so do the axioms, whether to
the same or to another science;[12] consequently, so do the attributes,
25   whether investigated by these sciences or by one of them.

(5) Further, is our investigation concerned only with substances[13]
or also with their attributes? I mean, for example, if solids and lines
and planes are substances,[13] is it the concern of the same science to
30   know these and their attributes (which are proved by the mathematical
sciences) for each genus, or of another science? If of the same, then the
science of substances,[13] too, would be a demonstrative science; but it
seems that there is no demonstration of whatness. But if of another
science, what science will be the one to investigate the attributes of
substances? It is extremely difficult to answer this question.

35   (4) Again, are we to say that only sensible substances exist, or be-
997*b*   sides these also others?[14] And if others also, are they of one kind or are
there many genera of substances, such as, for example, the Forms and
the Intermediate Objects as some say,[15] the Intermediate Objects being
the subject of the mathematical sciences? The manner in which we[16]
speak of the Forms as being both causes and substances by them-
5   selves has been stated in our first discussion of them.[17] There are many
difficulties in this doctrine, but none is less absurd than to say, on the
one hand, that there exist certain natures apart from those in the heavens, and on the other, that these are the same as the sensible things
except that they are eternal while sensible things are destructible. For
they say just this, that there exists Man Himself and Horse Itself and
10   Health Itself, and in this they resemble those who say that there exist
Gods but that they are like men. But just as the latter were positing none
other than eternal men, so these thinkers are positing the Forms as being
none other than eternal sensible things.[18]

Moreover, if besides the Forms and the sensible things one posits the
Intermediate Objects, he will be faced with many *difficulties*. For
15   clearly, just as there will be Lines besides Lines Themselves and the
sensible lines, so the situation with each of the other genera will
be similar. Accordingly, since astronomy is one of the mathematical
sciences, there will be also a Heaven besides the sensible heaven,[19] and
similarly a Sun and a Moon and the other heavenly objects. Yet how
are we to be convinced of all this? It is not reasonable that this Heaven
20   among the Intermediates should be immovable, and it is utterly impossible that it should be in motion.[20] Concerning the objects discussed

by optics and mathematical harmonics, the case is similar; for they, too, cannot exist apart from the sensible objects for the same *reasons;* for if there exist Intermediate sensible objects and sensations, clearly there will also exist Animals between Animals Themselves and destructible animals.

One might also raise this question: What kinds of things should be sought by these sciences? If geometry is to differ from geodesy only in this, that the latter is concerned with things we sense but the former with non-sensible things, clearly in the case of medical science, too, there will be a science between Medical Science Itself and medical science which is concerned with sensible health, and similarly with each of the other sciences. Yet how is this possible? For there will have to be also Healthy Objects besides the sensible healthy objects and Health Itself. At the same time, it is not even true that geodesy is concerned with sensible and destructible magnitudes; for it would be destroyed if these are destroyed.[21] Nor would astronomy be concerned with sensible magnitudes or with this heaven. For neither are sensible lines such as the geometrician speaks of (for no sensible thing is straight or round in the sense in which he uses the terms "straight" and "round"; for the circle touches the ruler not at a point, but in the way in which Protagoras used to say in refuting the geometricians), nor are the motions and the orbits of the heavenly bodies similar to those discussed by astronomy, nor do points have the same nature as the stars.[22]

There are some thinkers[23] who say that the so-called Intermediate Objects between the Forms and the sensible things do exist, but they exist in the sensible things and not apart from them. It would take too long to go through all the impossible consequences of this doctrine, but it is enough to consider even such as the following: It is not reasonable that this should be so only in the case of the Intermediate Objects, but clearly it would be possible also for the Forms to be in the sensible things; for both come under the same argument.[24] Moreover, two solids will necessarily be in the same place, and the Intermediate Objects will not be immovable while they are in moving sensible things.[25] In general, for what purpose would one posit the Intermediate Objects to exist, but to exist in the sensible things? The same absurdities will result as those previously mentioned; for there will be a Heaven besides this heaven, except that it will not exist separately but in the same place, and this is indeed more impossible.

3

(6) There is a great *difficulty* concerning these matters as to how one should state the case in order to arrive at the truth, and also concerning

the principles as to whether it is the genera that one should believe to be the elements and principles or rather the primary constituents of each thing. For example, the elements and principles of voice seem to be the

25   primary constituents out of which all voices are composed and not 'voice' which is common to all;[1] and of geometrical demonstrations we call those "elements" whose demonstrations are present in the demonstrations of all or of most of the other geometrical theorems.[2] Moreover, in the case of bodies, both those who posit many elements and those who posit only one say that the principles are those of which things are

30   composed or consist. For example, Empedocles says that it is *Fire* and *Water* and the other elements of which things are constituted, and he does not speak of the elements as being the genera of things. Further,

998b   if one wishes to observe the nature of other things also, a bed for example, he will know its nature when he knows the parts out of which it consists and how these parts were put together.[3] From these arguments it would seem that the principles of things are not the genera.

5   On the other hand, insofar as we know each thing through its definition, and the genera are principles of definitions, the genera must be principles of the things defined.[4] And if to gain *knowledge* of things is to gain *knowledge* of the species according to which things are named, still the genera are principles of the species. Also, some of those who

10   posit the *One* or *Being* or the *Great* and *Small* as the elements of things appear to use them as genera.[5]

But we should not speak of the principles in both ways. For there is only one formula[6] of the *substance* of a thing; but the definition by means of genera is distinct from the formula which states the constituents of a thing.[7]

15   (7) Further, however much the genera may be principles, should we regard the first genera as principles or those which are lastly predicated of the individuals?[8] This, too, is a matter of dispute. For if the universals are principles to a higher degree, evidently the highest genera will be the principles; for these are said of all things. Accordingly, there will be as

20   many principles of things as there are first genera, and so both 'being' and 'unity' will be principles and substances; for these most of all are said of all things. But it is not possible for either 'unity' or 'being' to be a genus of things; for each differentia of any genus must *be* and also

25   be *one*, but it is impossible either for the species of a genus or for that genus alone to be a predicate of the *proper* differentiae of the species.[9] Thus, if 'unity' or 'being' is indeed a genus, no differentia will be either a being or one. But if 'being' and 'unity' are not genera, neither will they be principles if the genera are indeed principles. Moreover, those which lie between and result by the addition of differentiae to a genus will also

30   be genera,[10] down to the indivisibles;[11] but some of these are thought to be genera and others not. Moreover, the differentiae are principles

to a higher degree than the genera;[12] and if also the differentiae are principles, the principles become infinite,[13] so to speak, especially if one were to posit the ultimate genus as a principle.[14]

999a

Again, if unity is a principle of a sort to a higher degree, and unity is indivisible, and that which is indivisible is so either with respect to quantity or in species, and the indivisible in species is prior,[15] and the genera

5 are divisible into species, then the lowest predicate[16] would have unity to a higher degree; for "a man" is not a genus of individual men. Again, among things in which there is priority and posteriority, what is a predicate of them cannot exist as something apart from them. For example, if two is first among the numbers, no number will exist as something apart from the species of numbers; and similarly, no figure will exist apart

10 from the species of figures.[17] And if no such genus will exist apart from its species, still much less will the other genera exist apart from their own species; for it is thought that genera exist of these above all.[18] As for the indivisibles, no priority or posteriority exists among them.[19] Again, where one thing is better and another worse, that which is better is always prior; so no genus of these would exist either.

15 From all this, then, it appears that the species which are predicates of indivisibles are principles to a higher degree than the genera. But again, it is not easy to say in what manner we are to believe these to be principles. For the principle or cause should exist apart from the things of which it is the principle, or be capable of existing separately from them. But why should we believe such an object to exist apart from

20 each thing if not for the fact that it is a predicate universally and of all? But if it is because of this, the more universal objects should be posited as being principles to a higher degree; so the first genera would be principles.[20]

4

(8) A problem, which follows the preceding ones and is most difficult

25 of all and needs investigation above all, awaits our discussion now.

If nothing exists apart from individual things, and these are infinite, how is it possible to get *knowledge* of an infinite number of individuals? For insofar as something is one and the same and belongs to things uni-

30 versally, to this extent we know them all. But if this is necessary and something must exist besides the individuals, it would also be necessary that the genera, whether the lowest[1] or the ultimate, exist apart from the individuals. But we have just discussed the impossibility of this.[2]

Moreover, however much something exists besides the *composite*, whenever something is a predicate[3] of matter, must it, if it exists, be

999*b* apart from them in all cases, or in some but not in others, or in none?[4] If nothing exists besides the individuals, there would be no intelligible object, but all things would be sensible and there would be no *knowledge* of anything, unless by *"knowledge"* one means sensation.[5]

Further, nothing would be eternal or immovable, for all sensible things are destructible and are in motion.[6] But if there is nothing eternal, neither is generation possible; for there must be something which is in the process of becoming and from which something else is being generated, and the last of these must be ungenerable, if indeed there is a stop and generation out of nonbeing is impossible.[7] Further, if generation and motion exist, there must also be a limit; for no motion is infinite but every motion has an end, and nothing is being generated if the generation cannot be completed, and that which has been generated must exist when it has first been generated.[8]

Again, if matter exists because it cannot be generated, it is even more reasonable for the *substance*, which that matter at any time is coming to be, to exist;[9] for if neither *substance* nor matter exist, nothing will exist at all. But if this is impossible, something must exist besides the *composite*, namely, the *shape* or form. But again, if one posits this, there is this *difficulty:* for what things should he posit it and for what should he not? Evidently, we should not posit it for all; for we should not posit the existence of some house apart from the individual houses.[10]

Moreover, is the *substance* of all individuals one, for example, of all men? But this is absurd; for all things whose *substance* is one are one. But they are many and different. This, too, is unreasonable.[11] At the same time, how does matter become each of the individuals and how is the *composite* these two?

(9) Again, one might raise also this question about the principles. If they are one in kind, nothing will be numerically one, not even *One Itself* or *Being Itself*. And how will *knowing* exist, if there will not be some one thing about the many?

On the other hand, if the principles are numerically one,[12] and each of the principles is one, and not, as in sensible things, other principles for other things (for example, if one individual syllable is the same in kind as another, their principles will be also the same in kind; for, numerically, the principles are distinct just as the syllables are), if, to repeat, unlike the case of the syllables, the principles of things are numerically one, there will be nothing else besides the elements (for the expressions "numerically one" and "individual" do not differ in meaning; in fact, by "the individual" we mean that which is numerically one, and by "the universal", the one about the many). Accordingly, just as in the case of voice, if its elements were numerically definite,[13] the letters would necessarily be as many as the elements, so it would be in the case of things and their elements if no two or more of the latter were the same.

(10) A *difficulty* which is not smaller than any of the others has been neglected by both present thinkers and their predecessors, namely, whether the principles of destructible and indestructible things are the same or distinct. Now, if they are the same, how is it that some things are destructible and others indestructible, and through what cause?

The school of Hesiod and all the theologians thought only of what was plausible to themselves and paid little attention to us [as philosophers]. For, positing gods as the principles, and all else as generated by gods, they say that those beings which did not taste of nectar and ambrosia became mortal—clearly, using names known to themselves. But the use they make of these causes is beyond us. For if those who taste nectar and ambrosia do so for pleasure, their existence is in no way caused by them; but if nectar and ambrosia are the causes of their existence,[14] how could those who taste them be eternal and still be in need of food?

However, it is not worthy of us to pay serious attention to those who indulge in mythical subtleties; but by pressing our inquiry we must ask those who proceed by demonstration why it is that things which are composed of the same principles are some of them eternal in nature but others destructible. Since these thinkers mention no cause, and since it is not reasonable that what they say should be the case, clearly the principles and causes could not be the same. For even Empedocles, who indeed might be considered as expressing himself most consistently, is subject to the same error; for as a principle he posits *Strife* as the cause of destruction, yet it would seem that *Strife* is no less the cause of generating things, excluding the *One*,[15] since all things except *God*[16] come from *Strife*. At any rate, he says:

> From which come all that was and is,
> And is to be in time beyond,
> Both trees, and men and women grew,
> Beasts, trees, and water-nurtured fish,
> And above all the long-aged Gods.

And even apart from this, from what he says it is clear that if *Strife* had not been in things, all these would have been one; for when these came together, then *Strife* stood outermost. And because of this it also follows from his doctrine that the most happy God is less wise[17] than all others since he does not know all the elements; for he possesses no *Strife*,[18] and knowledge of the like is by the like.[19] He says,

> For earth by earth is known, water by water,
> By ether god-like ether, by fire scorching fire,
> And love by love, and strife by woeful strife.

10   But, to resume the argument, at least this is evident, that a consequence
of his doctrine is that *Strife* is no more a cause of destruction than of
existence. Similarly, *Friendship* is no more a cause of existence than of
destruction; for in combining things into one, it destroys the others.
Besides this, he does not even mention the cause of change, but he says
that things are by nature this way:

15   But when Strife waxed great among the members of the Sphere,
And rose to claim its honor when the time came round
Which, in turn, is fixed for them by a mighty oath.

From this it appears that the existence of change is necessary, but he
indicates no cause at all for this necessity. However, he alone speaks
consistently, at least to some extent; for he does not posit both destruc-
20   tible and indestructible things but makes them all destructible, except
for the elements. The *difficulty* we are speaking of now is, why it is that
some things are destructible but others are not, if indeed they are
formed from the same principles.

Concerning the fact that the principles could not be the same, let
the foregoing discussion suffice. If, on the other hand, the principles of
destructible things are distinct from those of indestructible things, one
problem is whether the former principles will also be indestructible or
25   destructible. If they are destructible, clearly, they too must be composed
of something else, for in all cases things are destroyed into what they
are composed of; and so it follows that there are other principles prior[20]
to these principles. However, this is impossible, whether the process
stops or goes on to infinity.[21] Moreover, how would destructible things
exist, if their principles were to be annihilated? But if the principles are
30   indestructible, why is it that the things composed of these principles
are destructible while those composed of the other principles are indestructible? For this is not reasonable but is either impossible or requires
1001a   lengthy argument. Further, no one has even tried to posit distinct principles,[23] but all posit the same principles for all things. And so they
swallow the *difficulty* we first raised as if they consider it of little importance.

(11) Of all the problems, the one which is most difficult to investigate
5   and most necessary for knowing the truth is this: whether being and
unity are *substances* of things or not, and whether each of them, without being something else, is being and unity respectively, or whether we
should inquire what is that which is a being or one, as if there were
some other nature underlying each of them;[24] for some thinkers take
the former but others the latter position concerning the nature of being
10   and unity. Plato and the Pythagoreans believe that neither *Being* nor
the *One* is some other thing, but that such is their very nature, that is,

the *substance* of the *One* is to be *One* and that of *Being* to be *Being*. But the natural philosophers believe otherwise. Empedocles, for example, as if reducing the *One* to something more known, states what the *One* is; for it would seem that by *"One"* he means *Friendship;* it is this, at any rate, which for him is the cause of unity in all things. Others say that this *Unity* or *Being*,[25] of which things consist or from which they have been generated, is *Fire,* and others say that it is *Air.* Those who posit more than one element speak in a similar way; for they must also say that *Unity* or *Being* are exactly as many as there are principles.[26]

If we do not posit 'unity' or 'being' to be a substance, it also follows that none of the other universals is a substance; for 'unity' and 'being' are the most universal of all.[27] And if *Unity Itself* or *Being Itself* is not something, scarcely will any of the others be something, except for the so-called individuals. Moreover, if 'unity' is not a substance, clearly neither could a number exist as a separate nature of things; for a number is units, and a unit is just a 'unity.'[28]

If, however, unity itself or being itself is something, unity or being must be the *substance* of each, respectively; for there is nothing else which is universally a predicate of what is or is one, respectively, but only each of them. But if being itself and unity itself were something, there is much *difficulty* as to how there can be something else besides these, that is, how things can be more than one. For what is distinct from being does not exist, so the statement of Parmenides must follow, namely, that all things are one and this is *Being*.[29]

There are objections to both positions. For whether unity is not a substance or unity itself is something, a number cannot be a substance. If unity is not a substance, we have stated earlier why a number cannot be a substance;[30] but if unity itself is something, the same difficulty arises as that concerning being. For from what will another unity,[31] besides unity itself, come? It must be from non-one; but all things are either one or many, and of the many each is one.

Further, if unity itself is indivisible, according to Zeno's axiom it will be nothing. For he says that that which neither makes the sum greater when added nor the remainder less when subtracted is not one of the beings, clearly believing that being is a magnitude, and if a magnitude, then corporeal; for this is a being in all dimensions. The others, the plane and the line for example, will increase the result when added in one way but not when added in another way,[32] but the point or the unit will not increase it at all. But since Zeno's arguments are crude, and the existence of something indivisible is possible, so that there is a defense both for this latter[33] and against Zeno (for when such a thing is added the result will be greater in number though not in magnitude), still, how can a magnitude come from such a unity or such unities?[34] For this is like saying that a line consists of points.

20   But even if one believes, as some say, that a number is generated from unity itself and something else which is not-one,[35] we must inquire none the less why and how the thing generated will be sometimes a number and sometimes a magnitude, if indeed the not-one is *Inequality* and is of the same nature. It is not clear how magnitudes could be gen-
25   erated either from the *One* and *Inequality* or from some Number and *Inequality*.[36]

5

(14) A *difficulty* which follows the preceding is whether numbers and bodies[1] and planes and points are substances or not. If they are not, it baffles us to say what being is and what the *substances* of things are.
30   For affections and motions and relations and dispositions and ratios do not seem to indicate the *substance* of anything;[2] for all of them are said of some subject and none of them is a *this*.[3] As for objects which most of all might seem to indicate substances, such as water and earth and
1002a   fire and air, of which the composite bodies consist, their heat and cold- ness and such are affections and not substances, but the body alone which is affected by these persists as a sort of a thing and a substance.
5   What is more, a body is a substance to a lesser degree than a surface, and a surface than a line, and a line than a unit or a point; for a body is de- fined in terms of these, and these seem to be capable of existing without a body, but a body cannot exist without these.[4] It is because of these arguments that (a) the common people and the earlier thinkers consid-
10   ered a body to be a substance and a being, and the rest as *attributes* of it, and hence the principles of bodies to be the principles of things, but that (b) the later and wiser thinkers[5] considered numbers to be sub- stances.

As we said, then, if these are not substances, there is no substance and no being at all; for indeed the attributes of these do not deserve to
15   be called "beings". Yet if it is agreed that lines and points are substances to a higher degree than bodies, but we do not see in what kind of bodies these can exist (for they cannot exist in sensible things),[6] a substance could not exist at all. Further, these appear to be divisions[7] of bodies,
20   one in width, another in depth, and another in length. Besides this, any figure is as much in a solid as any other figure, or else no figure is in it at all; accordingly, if Hermes is not in the stone,[8] neither will half of the cube be in the cube as something definite, and so, neither will the sur- face[9] be in the cube; for if any sort of surface were in it,[10] the surface
25   which marks off the half cube would be in it too. The same argument applies to any line or point or unit. Accordingly, if bodies are in the highest degree substances but planes and lines and points are substances

to a higher degree than bodies, and if the latter do not exist or are not substances, we are baffled as to what being is and what the *substance* of things is.

30 In addition to what has been said, unreasonable consequences follow even in matters concerning generation and destruction. For it seems that a substance, if it did not exist before but it now does, or if it existed before but now it does not, undergoes these changes by being in the process of becoming or of being destroyed,[11] respectively; however, points and lines and surfaces cannot be in the process of becoming or of being destroyed, but at one moment they exist and at another they do

1002b not.[12] For whenever bodies come into contact or are divided, the limits become instantaneously one when the bodies come into contact, or instantaneously two when they are divided; so, when the limits are together they do not exist but have been destroyed, and when the parts of a body are divided, limits now exist which did not exist before. For, certainly, the indivisible point within the line was not divided into two.

5 And if they are in the process of generation or destruction, from what are they generated?[13] It is likewise with the moment in time; for neither can this be in the process of generation or destruction, but, not being a substance, it always seems to be distinct. Clearly, it is likewise with

10 points and lines and planes, and for the same reason; for all are alike either limits or divisions.

6

In general, one might raise also this problem:[1] Why, besides the sensibles and the Intermediate Objects, should we seek other things, such as the Forms which we[2] posit?

15 It may be because of this: while the Mathematical Objects differ from those in this world in some other respect,[3] they do not differ from them in there being many of the same kind (and so their principles will not be definite in number; for just as the principles of all language in this world are not definite in number, although they are definite in kind[4]—unless

20 one considers the principles of an individual syllable or an individual voice whose principles are definite in number—so is it in the case of the Intermediate Objects, for things of the same kind there are also infinite), and so if besides the sensible things and the Intermediate Objects there were no other things (such as Forms posited by some), neither would a given substance be one both in number and in kind, nor would the prin-

25 ciples of things be definite in number although they would be definite in kind; but if the principles are to be definite both in number and in kind, it is also necessary because of this to posit the Forms.[5] Even if

these thinkers do not articulate their doctrine well, still this is what they mean; and it is necessary for them to say this, that each of the Forms is a substance and that none of them exists as an attribute.

30   But if we posit the Forms to exist and each of the principles to be one numerically and not in kind, we have previously stated the impossible consequences which necessarily follow.[6]

(13) Closely connected with these, we should discuss whether the elements exist potentially or in some other way.[7] If in some other way,
1003a   something else will be prior to the principles; for potentiality is prior to that other cause,[8] and it is not necessary for every potentiality to be that of which it is the potentiality.[9] But if the elements exist potentially, then no thing may exist at all.[10] For even that which does not yet exist is po-
5   tential, since it is not-being that is becoming a being but none of what is impossible to be.[11]

(12) We must raise these problems, then, concerning the principles, and also whether the principles are universal or, as we call them, in-dividuals. For if they are universal, they will not be substances; for none of what is common signifies a *this* but only a *such*, and a substance is a
10   *this*. And if a common predicate is a *this* and can be exhibited, Socrates will be many things: Socrates himself, and a man, and an animal, if indeed each of these indicates a *this* and a unity.[12]

If the principles are universal, then, these results follow; if they are
15   not universal but exist as individuals, they will not be *known;* for all *knowledge* is universal. So, if there is to be *knowledge* of them, there will be, besides these principles, others which are prior[13] and are predi-cated of them universally.

Book Γ

1

There is a science which investigates being qua being and what belongs essentially to it. This science is not the same as any of the so-called "special sciences"; for none of those sciences examines universally being qua being, but, cutting off some part of it, each of them investigates the attributes of that part, as in the case of the mathematical sciences.[1] Now since we are seeking the principles and the highest causes, clearly these must belong to some nature in virtue of itself. If, then, also those who were seeking the elements of things were seeking these principles, these elements too must be elements of being, not accidentally,[2] but qua being. Accordingly, it is of being qua being that we, too, must find the first causes.[3]

2

The term "being" is used in many senses, yet not equivocally, but all of these are related to something which is one and a single nature.[1] It is like everything that is called "healthy", which is related to health by preserving health, or by producing health, or by being a sign of health, or by being receptive of health. And what is called "medical" is similarly related to the medical art; for it is so called by possessing the medical art, or by being naturally adapted for it, or by being something done by it. And we can find other terms which are used in the same way as "healthy" and "medical".[2] Thus, also "being" is used in many senses, but all of these are related to one principle, for some are called "being" in view of the fact that they are substances, others by being *attributes*[3] of substances, others by being on their way to becoming substances,[4] or else by being destructions or privations or qualities of substances, or productive or generative either of substances or of whatever is related

10   to substances, or negations of any of these or of substances. On account
        of this, we even say that nonbeing *is* nonbeing.

        Now, just as there is one science of all that is healthy, so it is with the
        others. For not only does the investigation of objects which are named
        according to one nature belong to one science,[5] but also of objects
        which are named in relation to one nature; for the latter, too, are in some
15   sense named according to one nature.[6] Clearly, then, the investigation
        of all things qua things belongs to one science. Now in every case a
        science is concerned mainly with that which is first, both as that on
        which the others depend, and as that through which the others are
        named.[7] Accordingly, if this is a substance, it is of substances that the
        philosopher should possess the principles and the causes.

20   For each genus of things there is both one power of sensation and one
        science; grammar, for example, which is one science, investigates all
        kinds of speech. Accordingly, it belongs to one generic science to in-
        vestigate all the kinds of being,[8] and it belongs also to one specific
        science to investigate each kind of being.

        If, now, being and unity are the same and are one nature in the sense
        that they follow each other in the same way in which a principle and a
        cause do, but not in the sense that they are signified by one formula[9]
25   (however, it makes no difference even if we were to believe the latter;
        in fact, it would be even more suitable),[10] seeing that *one man* and *being
        a man* and *a man* are the same and that the added word in "one man
        exists" does not make it signify something other than what "a man exists"
        does (this is clear from the fact that unity and being are not separated
30   in generation or in destruction),[11] and similarly with "unity", then it is
        evident that the same thing is indicated by the addition of any one of
        these, and what is one is not distinct[12] from what is a being. Moreover,
        the *substance* of each individual[13] is one not by accident, and similarly
        it is essentially[14] a being; so that there are as many kinds of being as
35   there are of unity. And the investigation of the whatness of these belongs
        to the same generic science; I mean, for example, the investigation of
        sameness and likeness[15] and the others of this sort as well as of their
1004*a* opposites. And nearly all the contraries are referred to this principle.
        Let us regard these as having been investigated in the *Collection of
        Contraries.*[16] And there are as many parts of philosophy as there are
        substances,[17] so that there must be among them a first[18] and one which
5   follows; for there are immediate genera which have being and unity.
        Therefore, the corresponding sciences will follow these genera. For the
        philosopher is like the so-called mathematician, for also mathematics
        has parts, and in it there is a first and a second science and others which
        follow.[19]

10   Since it belongs to one science to investigate opposites, and plurality is opposed to unity, and since it belongs to one science to investigate also denial and privation because unity is investigated in both ways, that is, with respect to its denial as well as to its privation[20] (for we say that something does not exist either without qualification or in some genus; thus, in the former case, from the denial of unity no[21] differentia

15 is added to it, for the denial of it[22] is its absence; but in privation there is also an underlying nature of which the privation is asserted);[23] to repeat, since plurality is opposed to unity, it belongs to the same science to know also the opposites of the kinds of unity which we mentioned, for example, otherness and unlikeness and inequality[24] and all the others which are named either according to these or according to plurality

20 and unity. One of them is contrariety, for contrariety is a kind of difference, and difference is a kind of otherness.[25] Since, then, "unity" has many senses, all these will also have many senses,[26] yet it belongs to one science to know them all; for terms belong to different sciences not if they just have many meanings, but if neither are they asserted of one

25 nature nor have their formulae reference to one nature. Now since all things are referred to that which is primary, as for example all things which are called "one" are referred to what is primarily one, we must say that the case is similar with sameness and otherness and the contraries; so that after distinguishing the various senses of each, we must give a similar account of how the others are related to that which is

30 primary in each category; for some are referred to what is primary in the sense that they possess it, others in the sense that they produce it, and others in other such ways.[27]

    It is evident, then, that it belongs to one science to discuss these things as well as substance[28] (this was one of the problems we listed);[29] and so,

1004*b* it is the philosopher's task to be able to investigate all of them. For if it is not the philosopher, then who will examine whether Socrates and sitting Socrates are the same, or if a given contrary has only one contrary to it, or what is a contrary, or the various senses of the term "contrary"? And similarly with all other such questions.

5   Since, then, these are essential *attributes* of unity qua unity and of being qua being, but not qua numbers or qua lines or qua fire, clearly it belongs to this science also to know both the whatness of these and their attributes. And those who inquire into these matters err not in the sense that they do not philosophize, but in not considering substances,[28]

10 of which they comprehend nothing, as prior[30] to attributes. For just as there are proper *attributes* of numbers qua numbers, such as oddness and evenness, commensurability and equality, excess and deficiency, whether these belong to numbers essentially or in relation to one

another,[31] and likewise other proper *attributes* belonging to solids, whether motionless or in motion, and whether without weight or with weight,[32] so there are proper *attributes* belonging to being qua being, and it is the task of the philosopher to examine the truth about these. A sign of this is the following: dialecticians and sophists put on the same appearance as the philosopher (for sophistry only appears to be wisdom, and dialecticians discuss everything) since being is common to all. But clearly they discuss all things because these are *proper* to philosophy. Now sophistry and dialectics busy themselves with the same genus[33] of things as philosophy, but philosophy differs from dialectic in the manner of its capacity, and from sophistry in the kind of life *chosen*. Dialectics is tentative concerning things which philosophy knows, sophistry makes the appearance of knowing without knowing.[34]

Again, one of the two columns of contraries is a privation, and all objects are referred to being and not-being, and to unity and plurality; for example, rest is referred to unity, motion to plurality.[35] Now almost all thinkers agree that things and substances are composed of contraries; at any rate, all say that the principles are contraries, some positing the *Odd* and the *Even*, others the *Hot* and *Cold*, others the *Limit* and the *Unlimited*,[36] others *Friendship* and *Strife*.[37] All the other objects, too, appear to be referred to unity and plurality (let us assume this reference), and the principles posited by the other thinkers fall indeed entirely under these as if these were their genera. So it is evident also from this discussion that it belongs to one science to investigate being qua being; for all these objects are either contraries or composed of contraries,[38] and the principles of contraries are unity and plurality. And these belong to one science, whether they are named according to one nature or not; perhaps the truth is that they are not so named.[39] But even if "unity" has many meanings, the other meanings are stated by being referred to the primary meaning, and likewise for the contraries of these; and even if being or unity is not universal and the same or not separable when applied to all things (as perhaps it is not),[40] still some things are referred to one primary object and the others to those which follow the primary. Because of this, it is not the task of the geometer to investigate what a contrary is, or completeness, or being, or unity, or sameness, or otherness, except by hypothesis.[41]

It is clear, then, that it belongs to one science to investigate being qua being and whatever belongs to it qua being, and that the same science investigates not only substances,[28] but also whatever belongs to substances,[28] both the attributes mentioned and also priority and posteriority, genus and species, whole and part, and the others of this sort.[42]

3

20 We must state whether it belongs to one or to a distinct science to inquire into what in mathematics are called "axioms"[1] and into substances.[2] It is evident that the inquiry into these belongs to one science and to the science of philosophy; for the axioms belong to all things and are not proper to some one genus apart from the others. And all men use them, since they belong to being qua being, and each genus is a being.

25 However, they use them only to the extent that they need them, that is, as far as the genus extends, in which [genus] they use demonstrations.[3] So, since it is clear that the axioms belong to all beings qua beings (for this is common to them), the investigation of these axioms belongs also to him who is to know being qua being. On account of this, no one who

30 examines only a part of being, such as the geometer or the arithmetician, tries to say anything about them, whether they are true or not, except for some physicists who have done so for a good reason; for these thought that they alone were inquiring about the whole of nature or about being.[4] But since there is a scientist who is yet above the physicist

35 (for nature is only one genus of being), the inquiry into these axioms, too, should belong to him who investigates universally and about first

1005b substances.[5] Physics, too, is a kind of wisdom, but not the primary one.

The attempts of some of those who state how truth should be received

5 show a lack of training in analytics; for they should have this *knowledge* before coming to the present inquiry and not inquire while learning it.[6]

Clearly, then, it is the task of the philosopher, that is, of the one who investigates all substances[7] insofar as they by nature come under his science, to examine also the principles of the syllogism. Now, it is fitting for him who is to have knowledge in the highest degree concerning each genus to be able to state the most certain principles of

10 things in that genus,[8] so that he who is to have such knowledge of being qua being, too, must be able to state the most certain principles of all things. This is the philosopher, and the most certain principle of all is that about which it is impossible to think falsely; for such a principle must be most known[9] (for all men may be mistaken about things which

15 they do not know) and be also non-hypothetical.[10] For a principle which one must have if he is to *understand* anything is not an hypothesis; and that which one must know if he is to know anything must be in his possession for every occasion.

Clearly, then, such a principle is the most certain of all; and what this principle is we proceed to state. It is: "The same thing cannot at the

20 same time both belong and not belong to the same object[11] and in the

same respect";[12] and all other specifications that might be made, let
them be added to meet logical objections.[13] Indeed, this is the most
certain of all principles; for it has the specification stated above. For it
is impossible for anyone to believe the same thing to be and not to be,
25   as some think Heraclitus says; for one does not necessarily believe what
he says.[14] If, then, contraries cannot at the same time belong to the
same subject (and let the usual specifications be added also to this
premise), and if the contrary of an opinion[15] is the negation of that
30   opinion, it is evident that the same person cannot at the same time believe the same object to be and not to be; for in being mistaken concerning this he would be having contrary opinions. It is because of this that
all those who carry out demonstrations make reference to this as an
ultimate doctrine.[16] This is by nature a principle also of all the other
axioms.[17]

4

35   There are some who,[1] as we said, say that it is possible for the same
1006a   thing to be and not to be and also to believe that this is so. Even many
physicists[2] use this language. We, on the other hand, have just posited
that it is impossible to be and not to be at the same time, and through
5   this we have shown[3] that it is the most certain of all principles. Some
thinkers demand a demonstration even of this principle, but they do so
because they lack education; for it is a lack of education not to know of
what things one should seek a demonstration and of what he should
not. For, as a whole, a demonstration of everything is impossible; for
the process would go on to infinity, so that even in this manner there
10   would be no demonstration.[4] If, then, there are some things of which
one should not seek a demonstration, these thinkers could not say which
of the principles has more claim to be of this kind.[5]

That the position of these thinkers is impossible can also be demonstrated by refutation, if only our opponent says something; and if he
says nothing, it is ridiculous to seek an argument against one who has
15   no argument insofar as he has no argument, for such a man qua such[6]
is indeed like a plant. Demonstration by refutation, I may say, differs
from demonstration[7] in this, that he who demonstrates might seem to
be begging the question,[8] but if the other party is the cause of something posited, we would have a refutation but not a demonstration.[9] The
principle for all such arguments is not to demand that our opponent
20   say that something is or is not (for one might believe this to be a
begging of the question), but that what he says should at least mean
something to him as well as to another; for this is necessary, if indeed

he is to say anything. For if what he says means nothing, such a man could not argue either by himself or with another.[10] But if he grants this, there will be a demonstration; for there will already be something definite. But he who is the cause of something granted is not he who demonstrates but he who takes a stand; for while he denies argument he listens to argument. Besides, he who has granted this has granted that something is true without a demonstration, so that not everything can be so and not so.[11]

First, then, at least this is clearly true, that each of the expressions "to be" and "not to be" has a definite meaning; so that not everything can be both so and not so.[12] Again, if "a man" has one meaning, let this be a two-footed animal. By "has one meaning" I mean this: if "a man" means X, then, if something is a man, to be a man would be to be X. It makes no difference even if one says that "a man" has many meanings, provided that they are definite in number; for he might use a distinct name for each formula—for example, if he were to say that "a man" does not have one meaning but many, one of which would have the formula "a two-footed animal", and that there are also other formulae, but definite in number; for he could then posit a distinct name for each of these formulae. And if he did not so posit but were to say that the meanings of "a man" are infinite in number, it is evident that there would be no formula. For not to signify one thing is to signify nothing, and if names have no meanings, then discussion with one another, and indeed even with oneself, is eliminated; for it is not possible for anyone to conceive of anything if he does not conceive of one thing,[13] and if it is possible, he could then posit one name for this one thing.

Let a name, then, as stated in the beginning, mean something and have one meaning. Then it is not possible for "to be a man" to have the very same meaning as "not to be a man", if "a man" not only signifies something predicable of one thing but also has one meaning; for we do not use "having one meaning" in the sense of "predicated of one thing", since in such a sense "the musical" and "the white" and "the man" would also have one meaning, and so all of them would be one, for they would be synonymous.[14] And "to be" and "not to be" will not be the same except by equivocation, just as what we call "a man" others would call "not a man."[15] But the problem is not whether the same thing can at the same time be a man and not be a man in name, but whether he can be and not be so in fact. Now if the meanings of "a man" and "not a man" are not distinct, clearly, neither will those of "to be a man" and "to be not a man" be distinct; and so to be a man will be to be not a man, for they will be one.[16] (For "to be one" means, as in the case of "a garment" and "a coat", that their formula is one.) And if they are one, "to be a man" and "to be not a man" will have one meaning.

But it was shown that they signify distinct things. Accordingly, if it is
30   true to say "X is a man", it is necessary for X to be a biped animal, for
this was what "a man" was posited as signifying; and if this is necessary,
it is not possible for X not to be a biped animal (for "to be necessarily
a man" means this, namely, to be impossible not to be a man). Hence it
is not possible at the same time to truly say of a thing that it is a man
1007a   and that it is not a man. The same argument applies to being a not-
man;[17] for "to be a man" and "to be a not-man" have distinct meanings,
if indeed also "being white" and "being a man" have distinct meanings,
for the former two terms are much more opposed, so that they must
5   have distinct meanings.[18] And if one were to say that "white" and "a
man" signify one and the same thing, we shall again say just what we
said earlier, that not only the opposites but all things will be one.[19] And
if this cannot be, what follows is what we have stated, if our opponent
answers our question. But if, when asked a single question, he adds
10   also the denials, he is not answering the question. For nothing prevents
the same thing from being a man and white and a great many other
things; yet when asked if it is true or not true to say that X is a man, he
should give an answer with one meaning, but he should not add that X
is also white and great. Besides, it is impossible to list an infinite number
15   of accidents[20] anyway; so, he should either list them all or none. Similarly, even if X is a countless number of times a man and not a man,[21]
one should not, when answering the question "Is X a man?", say that X
is at the same time not a man, unless he lists also all the other accidents[20]
20   which belong or do not belong to X. But if he were to do this, he would
not be arguing.

In general, those who say this eliminate substances and essences.[22]
For they must say that all things are attributes, and that the essence of
being just[23] a man or an animal does not exist. For if something is to be
an essence of just a man, this will not be the essence of not-man or will
25   not be not the essence of a man, and these are indeed the negations of
"the essence of a man"; for what this[24] signified was one thing, and this
was the *substance* of something. But to signify the *substance* of something is to signify that its essence is not something else. And if the
essence of being just a man were to be the essence of just being a not-
man or just being not a man, it would be something else. And so these
30   thinkers must say that there can be no such formula of anything but that
everything is an attribute of a thing, for it is in this way that the *substance*
of a thing is distinguished from an attribute of it;[25] for example, whiteness is an accident of a man, in view of the fact that he is white, but he is
not just whiteness. If every thing were an attribute of something, there
would be no first subject of which something would be attributively a
35   predicate[26] (that is, if "an attribute" always signifies that something is

1007b   attributively a predicate of a subject). Such predication, then, must go on to infinity.[27] But this is impossible, since not even more than two terms are combined in accidental[28] predication. For an accident is not an accident of an accident unless both are accidents of the same thing. I mean, for example, that the white is musical, and the musical is white,

5   and this is so in view of the fact that both are accidents of a man. But Socrates is accidentally musical not in the sense that both Socrates and the musical are accidents of some other thing.[29] So, since some things are said to be accidents in the latter sense and others in the former sense, those in the latter sense (like the write in Socrates) cannot be infinite in

10   the upward direction; for example, there can be no other accident to white Socrates, for no unity is formed out of all of them.[30] Nor can the white have some other accident, such as the musical; for the latter is no more an accident of the former than the former of the latter, and we have already made the distinction that some are accidents in this sense and others in the sense in which the musical is an accident of Socrates. In

15   this last sense, the accident is not an accident of an accident, but in the other sense it is, and so it is not in every case that something will be an accident of an accident.[31] So there will be something which signifies a substance.[32] And if this is so, we have shown that contradictories cannot be predicates at the same time.

  Again, if all contradictories are true at the same time about the same

20   thing, clearly all things will be one. For the same thing will be a trireme and a wall and a man, if of anything one may truly affirm or truly deny anything, and this necessarily follows for those who use the argument of Protagoras.[33] For if it seems to someone that a man is not a trireme, it is clear that he is not a trireme; but then he is also a trireme, if indeed

25   the contradictory is also true. And then what results is the doctrine of Anaxagoras, "All things are together"; and so no thing truly exists.[34] Accordingly, they seem to be speaking of the indeterminate, and although they think that they are speaking of being, they speak of not-being; for the indeterminate is potential being and not actual being. But

30   of any thing they must assert the affirmation or the denial of every thing; for it is absurd if the denial of a thing belongs to that thing but the denial of something else not belonging to the thing does not belong to it. For example, if it is true to say of a man that he is not a man, clearly it is also true to say of him that he is not a trireme. Accordingly, if the

35   affirmation "he is a trireme" belongs to him, so must the denial. If, however, that affirmation does not belong to him, then the denial of it will

1008a   belong to him at least more than his own denial belongs to him. So, if his own denial also belongs to him, the denial "he is not a trireme" will also belong to him; and if this belongs to him, so does the affirmation "he is a trireme".[35]

  These [absurdities] then follow for those who maintain this doctrine,

and it also follows that it is not necessary either to affirm or to deny
something. For if it is true that X is a man and not a man, it is clear that
X will neither be a man nor not a man; for the latter two are the denials
of the former. And if the former two are combined into one, the latter
two would also be combined into one as opposed to the other.[36]

Again, either the doctrine applies to all cases, and any X is both white
and is not white and also a being and not a being, and likewise with the
other assertions and denials, or it does not apply to all but it does to
some and not to others. And if it does not apply to all, they should have
stated which are the exceptions. But if it applies to all, again either (1)
the denial is true if the assertion is true, and the assertion is true if the
denial is true, or (2) the denial is true if the assertion is, but the assertion is not always true if the denial is. And if (2) is the case, there will be
some definite and permanent nonbeing,[37] and the doctrine concerning
it will be certain; and if nonbeing is something certain and known, the
opposite assertion will be more known.[38] But (1) if the assertion is likewise true whenever the denial is true, then it is necessary that either (a)
each is true when separately stated (for example, "X is white" is true,
and again "X is not white" is true), or (b) this is not the case. And if (b) it
is not true to state each separately, he who is saying these things is also
not saying them, and also nothing exists. But how can nonbeing talk
or think?[39] Also, all things will be one, as we said before,[40] and the
same thing will be a man and God and a trireme and the denials of these.
For if all assertions and denials are truly predicated alike of each thing,
one thing will not differ from another.[41] For if it does differ, to say this
will be true and peculiar in this case. Similarly, (b) if each can be true
whenever it can be stated separately, what we have said still follows. In
addition, everyone will be speaking truly and also falsely, and the same
man will admit that he is speaking falsely.[42] It is evident at the same
time that to question him is to inquire about nothing, since he is not saying anything. For he says neither that it is so [definitely], nor that it is
not so [definitely], but that it is both so and not so; and again he denies
both by saying that it is neither so nor not so, for otherwise there would
be something definite.

Again, if the denial is false whenever the assertion is true, and the
affirmation is false whenever the denial is true, it would not be possible
truly to assert and deny the same thing at the same time. But perhaps
they would say that this is just what they posit at the start.[43]

Again, if anyone believes that something is so, or that it is not so,
does he believe falsely, but he who believes both does so truly? If the
latter believes truly, what does it mean to say that such is the nature of
things?[44] If he does not believe truly, but he believes more truly than
he who believes that something is so, or that it is not so, then things in
some sense do possess something; and it would be true to say that this is

so,[45] but it is not at the same time true to say that it is not so. But if one says that all speak alike falsely and truly, then such a man can neither
10　speak nor mean anything; for he says that this is so and not so at the same time. If he has no belief of anything but is equally thinking and not thinking, how would he differ from a plant?[46]

It is most evident that no one of those who posit this doctrine, or anyone else, is disposed in his actions in the same way.[47] For why does a man walk to Megara and not stay where he is with the thought that he
15　is walking to Megara? And why does he not walk straight into a well or over a precipice, if such happens to be in his way, but appear to guard himself against it, with the thought that it is not equally good and not good to fall in? Clearly, then, he believes one course of action to be better and the opposite not better. And if this is so, then he must also
20　believe one thing to be a man and another not a man, one thing to be sweet and another not sweet. For, when he thinks that it is better to drink water and see a man and then makes inquiries about them, he does not equally seek and believe everything; yet he should, if the same
25　thing were alike a man and not a man. But as we said, no one who appears to guard himself against some but not against other things believes or acts according to such doctrine. Thus, as it seems, all men have beliefs in one way, if not about all things, at least about what is better and what is worse. And if it is not *knowledge* but opinion that they have, they should be all the more concerned about the truth, just as those who are sick are more concerned to be healthy than those who
30　are healthy; for compared to a man with *knowledge*, a man with opinion, too, is not healthily disposed towards the truth.

Again, however much things may be so and not so, at least the more and the less are still present in the nature of things; for we should not
35　say that both two and three are alike even, nor that both he who regards four to be five and he who regards one thousand to be five are alike mistaken. And if they are not alike mistaken, it is clear that the first man is
1009*a*　less mistaken and so thinks more truly. Accordingly, if that which has more of something is nearer to it, there should be a truth to which the more true is nearer.[48] And even if there is not,[49] still there exists at least something which is more certain and more true, and this would free us
5　from the unconditional doctrine which prevents a thing from being made definite by *thought*.

5

The saying of Protagoras, too, comes from the same doctrine, and both he and they are alike in positing that a thing must both be and not

be. For if all opinions and all appearances are true,[1] all of them must
10   be both true and false at the same time. For many men have contrary
beliefs, and they regard those whose opinions are contrary to theirs as
mistaken; consequently, the same thing must both be and not be. And if
this is so, all opinions must be true; for those who are mistaken[2] and
those who think truly have opposite opinions, and if this is the way
15   things are, then all men think truly.

It is clear, then, that both doctrines come from the same *thinking*. But
the manner of dealing with them is not the same for all these thinkers;
for some need persuasion by *thought* while others by verbal arguments.
Those who came to such belief from the *difficulties* they have raised can
easily be cured of their ignorance; for our reply will be directed not to
20   their vocal statements but to their *thought*. But those who state such a
doctrine for its own sake can be cured by a refutation of that doctrine
as expressed in speech and in words.

To those who have reflected on the *difficulties*, the doctrine came from
the sensation of things. (1) The belief that contradictions and contraries
belong to the same thing at the same time arises from observing that
25   contraries are generated from the same thing. Accordingly, if nonbeing
cannot become being,[3] the thing was alike with both contraries earlier,
just as Anaxagoras says that everything is blended in everything, and
also Democritus; for he too says that the *Void* and the *Full* exist alike
in every part, although he says that the *Full* is being and the *Void* is
30   nonbeing. To those, then, whose belief comes from these sensations we
shall say that in one sense they speak rightly but in another sense they
are mistaken.[4] For "being" has two senses, so that in one way something
can be generated from nonbeing but in another it cannot,[5] and the same
thing can be at the same time both a being and a nonbeing, but not in
35   the same respect;[6] for the same thing can be potentially both contraries
at the same time, but it cannot be so in actuality. Moreover, we shall
also require them to believe that among things some other substance
exists to which neither motion nor destruction nor generation belongs
at all.[7]

1009*b*   (2) The truth concerning appearances, too, came to some thinkers in
a similar way from sensible things. For they think that truth should
not be *judged* by the majority or the minority; the same thing seems
sweet to some who taste it but bitter to others, so that if all men were
5   sick or insane, except two or three who were healthy or sane, the latter
would seem to be sick or insane and not the others. Again, they say that
many animals have of the same things appearances which are contrary
to ours, and that even to the same person the same things do not always
seem to be the same with respect to sensation. Thus, it is not clear which
10   of these appearances are true and which are false; for the ones are no

more true than the others, but both are alike true. It is at least on account of this that Democritus says that either nothing is true, or that truth, to us at least, is not clear.

In general, then, it is because these thinkers believe thought to be sensation, and sensation to be alteration, that they say that what appears according to sensation must be true; for it is from these arguments that also Empedocles and Democritus and, one might say, each of the others came to possess such doctrines. For Empedocles, too, says that as the habits of men change, so do their thoughts:

> For thought in men increases with what is before them.

And elsewhere he says:

> And thought in them always alters as much as does their nature.

And Parmenides expresses himself in the same manner:

> For, as each is formed of many-jointed limbs,
> So is the mind of men; for that which
> Thinks in each and every man is but the
> Nature of his limbs; and what is more of
> This is also more of thought.

And Anaxagoras is reported to have expressed to some of his companions that things to them would be such as they would believe them to be. And they say that Homer, too, appeared to have had this doctrine, in view of the fact that he made Hector, when the latter was lying stunned by the blow, think other thoughts, the implication being that even the deranged are thinking, but not the same things. So it is clear that if both these are instances of thought, then things, too, are both so and not so at the same time. What results from all this, however, is most distressing. For if those who most of all have observed what the truth may be (and these are the ones who seek and cherish it most) have such doctrines and say these things about the truth, should we not expect beginners in philosophy to lose interest in it? For to seek the truth would be but to chase birds in the air.

These thinkers came to this doctrine because of the fact that, though seeking the truth about things, they believed that only sensible things exist; and it is in these that the nature of the indeterminate and of being, in the sense in which we have stated, exists to a great extent. And so what they say does seem to be the case, but it is not true; for it is more fitting to state it this way than the way Epicharmus did about Xenophanes.[8] Moreover, observing that all this nature is in motion, and thinking that nothing is true of that which changes, they came to the belief that nothing indeed may be truly said of that which changes altogether

10   and in every way.[9] Now it was from this belief that blossomed the most
extreme of the doctrines we have mentioned, namely, that of the followers of Heraclitus, and also such doctrine as was held by Cratylus,
who finally thought that nothing should be spoken but only moved his
finger,[10] and who criticized even Heraclitus for saying that one cannot
15   step into the same river twice, for he himself thought that one could
not do so even once.[11]

However, our reply to this argument, too, will be that when the
changing thing changes, there is some reason for these thinkers to truly
think that the changing thing is not. Yet even this is disputable; for
that which is losing an attribute still retains something of that which is
being lost, and some part of that which the changing thing becomes is
20   already there.[12] And in general, while something is being destroyed,
there exists[13] yet something; and if something is being generated, there
must be something out of which it is being generated[14] and something
by which it is being generated,[15] and the process in each case cannot go
on to infinity. But leaving these arguments aside, we maintain that to
change with respect to quantity is not the same as to change with respect
to quality.[16] Let us grant that the object does not remain the same with
25   respect to quantity; still it is with respect to form that we know each
thing.[17] Moreover, those who have such beliefs deserve criticism also
in view of the fact that from their observation of sensible things, small
in number, they have expressed themselves similarly about the entire
heaven. For it is only in the place of sensible things around us that
30   destructions and generations constantly occur, but this place is, in a
manner of speaking, not even a part of the whole universe; so that it
would be more just to reject the sensible things in this place for the sake
of the things in the rest of the universe than to condemn the latter for the
sake of the former. Moreover, it is clear that our reply to them, too,
will be the same as that made earlier[18] to the others; for we shall have
35   to show and convince them that some immovable nature exists. Moreover, in saying that things both are and are not, these thinkers are even
faced with the consequence that all things are at rest rather than in motion; for there is nothing to which they can change, since everything
1010b already belongs to every thing.[19]

Concerning the truth regarding the fact that not every appearance
is true, first, it is a fact that no sensation[20] of its proper sensible is false;[21]
but appearance[22] is not the same as sensation. Then we are justly sur-
5   prised if these thinkers raise the question whether the size of the magnitudes and the kinds of colors are such as they appear to those at a distance or to those who are near, whether things are such as they appear to
the sick or to the healthy, whether those things are heavy which so
appear to the weak or to the strong, and whether those things are true

which appear to those who are asleep or to those who are awake. For it
10   is evident that they themselves do not think so; at least no one in Libya,
believing at night that he is in Athens, starts walking to the Odeum.
Again, with regard to the future, as Plato too says, the opinion of a
doctor and that of an ignorant man are indeed not equally reliable, that
is, as to whether the sick will get well or not. Again, with regard to the
15   powers of sensation themselves, the power of the non-proper object is
not so reliable as the power of the proper object, or, that of the object
nearby is not so reliable as that of its own object;[23] but in the case of
colors it is sight that *judges* and not taste, and in the case of flavors it is
taste and not sight. And no power of sensation ever says about its proper
object that it is so and not so at the same time.[24] But not even at an-
20   other time does it doubt about that affection, but it may doubt about
the thing to which the affection belongs. For example, the same wine,
either due to its own change or due to a change of one's body, might
seem sweet at one time but not at another; but at least sweetness, such as
25   it is when it exists, never changes, and one always thinks truly of it
as such, and that which will be sweet will of necessity be of this kind.[25]
Yet all these doctrines do away with this; and just as they deny the existence of a *substance* of anything, so they deny that anything exists
of necessity; for the necessary cannot be now this and now that, and
30   so if something exists of necessity, it will not be so and not so.[26]

In general, if indeed only what is sensible exists, nothing would exist if
things with a soul did not exist, for then there would be no power of
sensation.[27] For one thing, it is equally true that the sensibles[28] and the
effects of the sensibles would not exist (for the latter are affections of
that which senses), but for another, it is impossible that the underlying
subjects which cause the sensations should not exist, even if there is no
35   sensation of them. For a sensation is surely not a sensation of itself, but
there is also something else besides that sensation which must be prior
1011a to the sensation;[29] for that which moves is by nature prior to that which
is moved. And even if the two are spoken of in relation to each other,
this is no less true.[30]

6

There are some, among both those who are convinced of these doctrines[1] and those who only profess them, who raise the problem by
5   asking who is to be the *judge* of the healthy man, and, in general, who
is to *judge* rightly any thing. But raising such problems is like raising the
problem whether we are now sleeping or awake. All such problems

amount to the same thing, for they demand a reason for everything; they
10 ask for a principle but they demand a demonstration of it, although
from their actions it is obvious that they are not convinced.[2] But as we
just said, their trouble is this: they seek a reason for that which has no
reason; for the starting-point of a demonstration is not a demonstration.[3]
Now the former may be easily convinced of this fact, for it is not difficult
15 to grasp. But those who seek to be persuaded by verbal argument alone
are asking for the impossible; for they claim the right of stating the contraries, and so they begin by stating them.

Now if not all things are relative, but there are some things which exist
in virtue of themselves,[4] not every appearance would be true;[5] for an
20 appearance is an appearance to someone, so he who states that all appearances are true makes all things relative.[6] For this reason we should
guard ourselves against those who seek persuasion by verbal arguments
and who at the same time claim to be defending their position, by requiring them to say, not that an appearance just exists,[7] but than an appearance exists *for him* to whom it appears, and *when* it appears, and *in the
respect*[8] in which it appears, and *in the manner* in which it appears. And
25 if they are giving a defense of their position, but not in this manner, they
will soon turn out to be making contrary statements. For it is possible for
the same thing to appear to be honey to sight but not to the sense of taste,
and for the same thing to appear unlike to the sight of each of two eyes, if
these are unlike. So against at least those who say that what appears is
30 true (for the reasons stated formerly) and that because of this everything
is alike false and true (for things do not appear the same to all, nor
always the same to the same person, but often contrary at the same time;
for the sense of touch says that there are two objects when the fingers are
crossed, but sight says that there is one), we reply "yes, but not to the
35 same power of sensation and in the same respect and in the same man-
1011*b* ner and at the same time"; so that it is with these qualifications that the
appearance is true.[9] But perhaps it is because of this that those who
argue not because of the *difficulty* of the case but for the sake of verbal
argument are compelled to say, not that what appears is true, but that
it is true to whomever it so appears. And as we said before, they are also
5 compelled to say that everything is relative to opinion and sensation, so
that nothing has occurred and nothing will be unless someone has first
formed an opinion about it.[10] But if something did occur or will be,[11]
it is clear that not everything will be relative to opinion.

Again, if something is one, as a relative it will be so to one thing or to
something definite;[12] and if the same thing is both a half and an equal,
nevertheless it is not in relation to the double that it is an equal. If, then,
10 in relation to a thinking[13] object, a man and the object thought are the

same,[14] it is not a thinking object which is a man but the object thought.[15] And if each thing is relative to a thinking object, then the thinking object will be relative to an infinite number of kinds of things.[16]

Concerning the fact that of all doctrines the most certain is the doctrine that opposite assertions are not true at the same time, the consequences which confront those who say that they are so true, and why they say so, let the foregoing discussion suffice.

Since it is impossible for contradictories to be truly said of the same object at the same time, it is evident that neither can contraries belong to the same object at the same time. For one of the contraries is not less[17] a privation of the other contrary, and a privation of the *substance* of a thing is a denial in some definite genus. Accordingly, if it is impossible to truly affirm and deny something at the same time, it is also impossible for contraries to belong to an object at the same time, unless both belong in a qualified way,[18] or one of them in a qualified way and the other without qualification.[19]

7

What is more, there cannot be anything between two contradictories, but of any one subject,[1] one thing must either be asserted or denied. This is clear if we first define what is truth and what is falsehood. A falsity is a statement[2] of that which is that it is not, or of that which is not that it is; and a truth is a statement of that which is that it is, or of that which is not that it is not. Hence, he who states of anything that it is, or that it is not, will either speak truly or speak falsely. But of what is neither being nor nonbeing it is not said that it is or that it is not.[3] Moreover, the intermediate between two contradictories[4] would be either as the grey is between the black and the white, or as that which is neither a man nor a horse is between a man and a horse. If it were like the latter, it could not change[5] (for not-good changes into good, and this into not-good), but an intermediate[6] always appears to change; for there is no change except into the opposites and the intermediates. But if it were an intermediate like the former, then even in such a case the generation into the white would have to be not from the not-white; but such change, too, is not observed.[7]

Again, *thought* either affirms or denies every object of *thought* or intelligible object;[8] and this is clear from the definition when *thought* thinks truly or falsely. When it connects in one way by asserting or denying, it thinks truly, when in the other way, it thinks falsely.

Again, there would have to be an intermediate for every pair of contradictories, if one is not arguing for the sake of argument; and so a man could also say something which is neither true nor not-true. And there will be an intermediate between being and nonbeing, and so also a change between generation and destruction.[9]

10   Again, there will also be an intermediate in all genera in which the denial of one contrary implies the other contrary; in numbers, for example, there will be a number which is neither odd nor not-odd. But this is impossible, and this is clear from the definition.

Again, the process of getting intermediates will go on to infinity, and things will be not only half as many again, but even more.[10] For there will again be the denial of the combination of the assertion and denial

15   of an intermediate, and this [denial of both] will be something; for the *substance*[11] of this will be distinct from the combination of the assertion and the denial of that intermediate.

Again, if a man said "no", when asked whether something is white, he denied nothing else but that it is white; and that denial is the non-being of whiteness.

Some people gave in to this doctrine just as they did to other paradoxical doctrines; for when they cannot refute eristical arguments, they

20   give in to them and agree that the conclusion is true. Thus, it is because of this that some men take that position, but others do so because they demand a reason for everything. Now in dealing with all these men, our starting-point is from definition. To form a definition it is necessary for them to mean something by a term; for then the formula, of which the name is a sign, becomes a definition.

25   The statement of Heraclitus, that every thing is and is not, seems to make everything true,[12] but that of Anaxagoras, that an intermediate exists between two contradictories, makes everything false; for when things are blended, the blend is neither good nor not-good, so that it is not possible to say anything truly.[13]

8

30   Having settled these matters, it is also evident that the one-sided statements made by some thinkers and about all things cannot be true. Some say that nothing is true (for, they say, nothing prevents everything from being like the commensurability[1] of the diagonal with the side of a square), others say that everything[2] is true; and these statements are

35   about the same as those of Heraclitus. For he who says "everything is
1012*b*   true and also false" also states each part of this separately, so that if each of these parts is impossible, so is the combination of the two. Moreover, it is evident that there are pairs of contradictories in each of which both parts cannot be true at the same time, nor false at the same time, al-

though in the latter case this might seem more possible from what has been said.[3]

Now in meeting all such arguments we should demand, as we stated above,[4] not that something be or not be, but that it should have a meaning; so that we should argue with these thinkers from a definition, after the meaning of the terms "falsity" and "truth" has been laid down. And if falsity is none other than the denial of truth, then it is impossible for everything to be false; for one part of the contradiction must be true.[5] Again, if it is necessary with regard to anything[6] either to assert or to deny it, it is impossible for both contradictories to be false; for just one part of the contradiction is false. Indeed, such statements even lead to the common objection that they annihilate themselves;[7] for he who says that everything is true makes also true the statement which is contrary to his own, and so he makes his own statement not true (for the contrary statement says that his is not true),[8] and he who says that everything is false makes also his own statement false. But if the former thinker makes the exception by saying that only the contrary of his own statement is not true, and the latter that only the contrary of his own is not false,[9] it follows none the less that they would have to require an infinite number of statements to be false and true respectively; for in saying "this statement[10] is true", the latter thinker makes this statement itself true, and this goes on to infinity.[11]

It is also evident that neither those who say that all things are at rest speak truly, nor those who say that all things are in motion. For if all things are at rest, whatever is true will always be true and whatever is false will always be false, yet there appears to be a change; for there was a time when he who says this did not exist, and again there will be a time when he will not exist.[12] And if all things are in motion, nothing will be true, and so everything will be false;[13] but this has been shown to be impossible. Besides, it is being that must change, for it is from something that there is a change to something else.[14] Finally, it is not the case that all things are sometimes at rest or sometimes in motion, and that nothing is always in the same way; for there is something which always moves the things which are in motion, and the first mover is itself immovable.[15]

Book Δ

1

"A principle" [or "a beginning", or "a starting-point"] means (1) that
part of a thing from which one would first move; for example, of a line
or a road, there is a principle from which one moves in one direction,
and also another principle from which one moves in the contrary direction.

(2) Also, it means that from which each thing would best be generated; for example, in learning, sometimes we should not begin from
what is first and the principle of a thing, but from what one would learn
most easily.[1]

(3) Also, that from which as a first constituent a thing is generated;
for example, the keel of a ship, the foundation of a house, and of an
animal some believe it is the heart,[2] others the brain, and others some
other such thing, whatever this may be.

(4) Also, the first from which, not as a constituent, a thing is generated, or the first from which motion or change by nature begins; for
example, a baby is generated from its father and mother,[3] and a fight
from abuse.

(5) Also, that in accordance with whose *choice* that which is in motion
moves or that which is changing changes; for example, the magistracies
in cities and the dynasties and kingships and tyrannies are called "principles", and so are the arts, and of these the master-arts most of all.

(6) Also, that from which a thing is first knowable is also said to be
a principle of the thing, for example, the hypotheses[4] in demonstrations.

(7) The term "a cause" has as many senses as the term "a principle";[5]
for all causes are principles.

It is common to all principles, then, to be the first from which a thing
either exists or is generated or is known; and of these, some are constituents of the thing[6] and others are outside. Therefore, nature is a
principle, and so is an element,[7] and also *thought* and *choice*,[8] and a

substance and a final cause;[9] for the good or the noble [10] is a principle of the knowledge and of the motion of many things.

2

"A cause" means (1) that from which, as a constituent,[1] something is generated; for example, the bronze is a cause of the statue, and the silver of the cup, and the genera of these [are also causes].

(2) Also, the form or the pattern, this being the formula[2] of the essence, and also the genera of this; for example, in the case of the octave, the ratio 2:1, and in general, a number[3] and the parts in the formula.

(3) Also, that from which a change or a coming to rest[4] first begins; for example, the adviser is a cause, and the father is a cause of the baby, and in general, that which acts is a cause of that which is acted upon, and that which brings about the change is a cause of that which is being changed.

(4) Also, the end, and this is the final cause [that for the sake of which]; for example, walking is for the sake of health. Why does he walk? We answer, "In order to be healthy"; and having spoken thus, we think that we have given the cause. And those which, after that which started the motion, lie between the beginning and the end, such as reducing weight or purging or drugs or instruments in the case of health, all of them are for the sake of the end;[5] and they differ in this, that some of them are instruments while others are operations.

Causes, then, are spoken of in about so many senses; and since they are spoken of in many senses, there may be many non-accidental causes of the same thing (for example, in the case of a statue, both the art of sculpture and the bronze are causes of it, not in virtue of something else, but qua a statue, though not in the same manner, but the bronze as matter and the art as the source of motion); and there may be causes of each other (for example, exercise is a cause of good physical condition, and good physical condition is a cause of exercise, although not in the same manner, but good physical condition as an end, and exercise as a moving principle); and again, the same thing may be a cause of contraries, for that which when present causes something, when absent it is sometimes said to be the cause of the contrary (for example, we say that the absence of the pilot was the cause of the capsizing, while his presence was the cause of safety, and both presence and privation[6] are moving causes.

All the causes already mentioned fall into four most evident types. For,

the letters in the case of the syllables, the matter in the case of manu-
20   factured articles, fire and earth and all such in the case of bodies, the
parts in the case of the whole, the hypotheses[7] in the case of the conclusion,[8] all of these are causes in the sense that they are *that of which*
the latter consist; and of these,[9] those first mentioned in each case are
causes in the sense that they are the underlying subject, as in the case
of the parts,[10] but the other[11] in each case is a cause in the sense of
essence, and this is the whole[12] or the composition or the form. As for
the seed and the doctor and the adviser and, in general, that which acts,
25   all these are causes in the sense of the source of change or of stopping.
Finally, each of the rest is a cause in the sense that it is the end or the
good of the others; for that for the sake of which the others exist or are
done tends to be the best or their end. Let there be no difference here
between calling this "the good" or "the apparent good".[13]

These, then, are the causes and their number in kind, but their modes
30   are numerically many, although when summarized they are fewer. For
causes are spoken of in many ways even within the same kind, since one
cause may be prior[14] and another posterior. For example, the cause of
health is the doctor, or the artist, and the cause of the octave is the
ratio 2:1 or a number; and whatever includes[15] each is always a cause.
35   Again, there are accidental causes and their genera; for example, the
cause of a statue is Polyclitus in one way and a sculptor in another, in
1014*a*   view of the fact that the sculptor is by accident Polyclitus.[16] Also,
whatever includes the accident is a cause; for example, a man is a
cause of the statue, or in general, even an animal, in view of the fact
that Polyclitus is a man, and a man is an animal. Even of accidents,
5   some are more remote or more near than others, for example, if the
white or the musical were to be called "a cause" of the statue, and not
only Polyclitus or a man.[17]

Of all causes, both those which are said to be *proper*[18] and those by
accident, some are said to be causes potentially and others *actually;* for
example, the cause of the house to be built is the builder and of the
10   house that is being built the builder who is building. Similar remarks
will apply to the things caused by the causes already listed; for example,
the cause may be a cause of this statue or of a statue or, in general, of
a portrait,[19] and it may be a cause of this bronze or of bronze or of
matter in general.[20] Similar remarks may be made in the case of accidents. Again, both accidental and *proper* causes and objects caused
may be spoken of in combination; for example, not Polyclitus, nor the
15   sculptor, but Polyclitus the sculptor.

However, all these are six in number, and each of them is spoken of
in two ways. For as causes or objects caused they are stated either as

individuals, or generically, or as accidents, or as the genera of accidents, or as combined, or singly taken, and in each of these either in *actuality* or according to potency. And there is this much difference, that causes which are in *actuality* and are taken as individuals exist, or do not exist, at the same time as those of which they are the causes, for example, as in the case of this doctor who is healing and this man who is being healed, and this builder who is building and that building which is being built. But with respect to potentiality this is not always so; for the house is not destroyed at the same time as the builder.

3

By "an element" we mean (1) the first[1] constituent of which a thing is composed and which is indivisible in kind into other kinds; for example, the elements of speech are those of which speech is composed and into which it is ultimately divisible, while they can no longer be divided into other parts of speech distinct in kind from them. And even if they are divisible, but the parts are of the same kind, they are called "elements"; for example, a part of water is water,[2] while a part of a syllable is not a syllable.[3] Similarly, those who speak of the elements of bodies mean the parts into which the bodies are ultimately divided, while those parts are no longer divisible into other parts differing in kind; and whether such parts are one or more, they are called "elements". In a somewhat similar way we speak of the elements of geometrical demonstrations and, in general, the elements of demonstrations; for the first demonstrations, which are also present in many later demonstrations, are called "elements of demonstrations", and these are the first syllogisms each of which has three terms and proceeds by means of a middle term.

(2) Also, by a transfer of meaning men call "an element" that which, being one and small, is useful for many things;[4] and so the small and the simple and the indivisible is called "an element". Hence it comes about that the most universal objects are elements,[5] in view of the fact that each of them, being one and simple, belongs to many or to all or to most; and on this account, unity and the point are thought by some to be principles.[6] Since, then, the so-called genera[7] are universal and indivisible (for there is no formula[8] for them), some call these genera "elements", and more so than the differentiae, in view of the fact that the genus is more universal than the differentia; for that to which the differentia belongs, the genus also follows, but that to which the genus belongs, the differentia does not always belong.[9]

Common to all the senses is this: An element of each thing is a primary constituent of it.

4

"Nature" means (1) the generation of growing[1] objects, as if one were
to pronounce the letter "υ" in "φύσις" long.

(2) Also, the first constituent[2] from which a growing object grows.

(3) Also, the source,[3] from which motion first begins in each natural
thing, and which belongs to that thing qua that thing.

Objects are said to grow if they increase by means of something else
by contact and also by growing together or by adhering together by
nature, as in the case of embryos. A growing together differs from contact; for in the latter case nothing else besides touching is necessary, but
in things growing together there is something, one and the same in both,
which, instead of touching, makes them grow together and is one with
respect to continuity and quantity, but not with respect to quality.[4]

(4) Also, the first constituent,[5] which is in a natural thing or from
which a natural thing is generated, and which is without shape or incapable of changing from its own potentiality; for example, the bronze
in a statue and in bronze articles is called "a nature", and so is the wood
in wooden things. And similarly with all other cases; for each of them
comes from such a nature which persists as first[5] matter. And it is in this
sense that men say that the elements of natural objects are natures, some
calling it "fire", others "earth", others "air", others "water" or some other
such object, some using some of these and others using them all.

(5) Also, the *substance*[6] of natural things, as with those who say that
the nature is the first composition of a thing: for example, Empedocles
says:

> Nothing that is has a nature,
> But only a blend and parting of things blent,
> And "nature" is a name bestowed on these by men.

Thus, in things which exist or are generated by nature, although there
is already a constituent in them from which by nature they are generated or exist, we say they do not yet have a nature unless they have
a form or a *shape*.

That which is a composite of the two[7] is said to exist by nature; for
example, such are the animals and their parts.

Nature, then, is either the first matter (and this in two senses: either
first in relation to the thing, or first in general; for example, in works of
bronze, bronze is first in relation to them, but first in general would be
perhaps water,[8] if all things that can be melted are water), and the form
or the *substance*, and this latter is the end of generation.[9]

(6) By extending the latter meaning of "nature", we now call "nature"

every *substance*[10] in general, in view of the fact that nature, too, is a *substance* of a sort.[11]

From what has been said, nature spoken of in the primary and main sense is the *substance* of things which have a principle of motion in themselves qua what they are; for the matter is called "a nature" by the fact that it is receptive of nature in the primary and main sense, and generations and growth are called so by the fact that they are motions from the point of view of nature in that sense.[12] And the principle of motion in things existing by nature is also this nature somehow present in those objects, either potentially or actually.[13]

5

"Necessary" means (1) that without which as a joint cause a thing cannot live; for example, breathing and food are necessary for an animal, for it cannot exist without them.

(2) Those without which the good cannot be or come to be, or those without which we cannot get rid of or be deprived of the evil; for example, drinking the medicine is necessary if one is to stop being sick, and sailing to Aegina is necessary if the man is to get the money.

(3) The compulsory, or force[1], and this is that which obstructs or prevents[2], contrary to tendency or *choice;*[3] for the compulsory is said to be necessary, and hence painful, as Evenus says:

For all the necessary did nature grievous make.

And force is a necessity of a kind, as Sophocles says,

But force makes me of necessity act thus.

And it seems that necessity cannot be persuaded to change, and rightly so; for it is contrary to the motion in accordance with *choice* or with judgment.

(4) That which cannot be otherwise is said to be necessary. And it is in virtue of this necessity that all the others, too, are somehow said to be necessary; for the compulsory is said to be that which necessarily acts or suffers when action according to tendency[4] is not possible because of that which compels, as if force were a necessity because of which something cannot be otherwise. It is similar with joint causes in the case of living and the good; for when the good or life or existence is not possible without certain things, these are necessary, and this cause[5] is a kind of necessity. Again, a demonstration[6] is necessary in view of the fact that, if something has been demonstrated without qualification,[7] it cannot be otherwise; and the causes of this are the first premises,[8] if these, from

which a syllogism proceeds, cannot be otherwise. Accordingly, of some
10   things which are necessary, the cause is something distinct from them;
but of other things there is no cause distinct from them, but because
of them other things are necessary.[9] Hence, the necessary in the primary
and main sense is the simple;[10] for this cannot be in many ways so as to
be now in one way and now in another, for if the latter were the case
it would have been in many ways. If, then, there are things which are
15   eternal and immovable, there is nothing compulsory for them and nothing against their nature.[11]

6

"One" means (1) one by accident, (2) one essentially.
(1) For example, Coriscus and the musical, and musical Coriscus, are
accidentally one; for it is the same thing that is called "Coriscus" and
20   "musical" and "musical Coriscus".[1] Also, the musical and the just, and
musical Coriscus and just Coriscus, are one in each case by accident;
the just and the musical are one in view of the fact that they are accidents of one substance, the musical and Coriscus are one in view of the
fact that the former is an accident of the latter. And similarly, in a
sense, musical Coriscus is one with Coriscus in view of the fact that one
25   part in the formula of the former is an accident of the other part, that
is, the musical is an accident of Coriscus; and musical Coriscus is by
accident one with just Coriscus, in view of the fact that the former part
of each is an accident of the latter part, which is one. The case is similar even if the accident is stated in the case of a genus or of some one
of the universal names;[2] for example, if one asserts that a man is the same
30   as a musical man; for this is so either in view of the fact that the musical
is an accident of a man who is one substance, or in view of the fact that
it is by accident that both "musical" and "a man" are predicates[3] of some
one individual, such as Coriscus. However, the two belong to him not in
the same way, but the one perhaps[4] as a genus and in the *substance*, the
35   other as a habit or an affection[5] of the substance. All things that are said
to be one by accident, then, are so said in this way.
(2) Of things that are said to be one essentially, (a) some are said to
1016a   be one by being continuous; for example, a fagot tied by a string is one
by continuity,[6] and so are pieces of wood glued together. And a line,
even if bent, is said to be one if it is continuous, just as each part of the
body, such as a leg or an arm. Of these themselves, what is continuous
5   by nature is one to a higher degree than what is continuous by art.[7] A
thing whose motion is one in virtue of itself and cannot be otherwise is
said to be continuous,[8] and a motion is one if it is indivisible, that is, in-

divisible in time.[9] Things[10] are essentially continuous if they are one not by contact; for if you place pieces of wood in contact with one another, you would not say that they are one continuous piece of wood or one continuous body or one continuous thing of a sort. In general, then, things which are continuous are said to be one, even if they are bent;[11] and they are said to be one to a higher degree if they are not bent; for example, the shin or the thigh is one to a higher degree than the leg, in view of the fact that the motion of the leg may not be one.[12] And the straight line is one to a higher degree than the bent line; and if a bent line has an angle, we call it both "one" and "not one", in view of the fact that its motion may or may not be simultaneous.[13] The motion of a straight line is always simultaneous, and no part of it which has magnitude is at rest while another part moves, as would be the case of a straight line bent at an angle.

(b) In another sense, things are called "one" if their underlying subject does not differ in kind; and things do not so differ in kind if their kind cannot be subdivided by sensation.[14] The underlying subject meant is either the first or the last[15] in relation to the end. For, on the one hand, qua indivisible in kind, wine is said to be one and water is said to be one;[16] and on the other hand all flavory liquids, such as oil and wine and things that can be melted, are said to be one in view of the fact that the ultimate underlying subject is the same, for all these are water or air.[17]

Also those things are called "one" whose genus is one, although they differ by opposing differentiae; and all these are said to be one in view of the fact that the genus underlying the differentiae is one.[18] For example, a horse and a man and a dog are one in this sense: they are all animals. This meaning of "one" is in a way similar to the previous, as if the matter were one. Now these are sometimes called "one" in this manner but sometimes they are called "the same" according to the higher genus, if they are finally the species of their next genus. For example, the isosceles and the equilateral are one and the same figure, in view of the fact that both are triangles, but they are not the same triangles.[19]

(c) Things are called "one" if the formula which states their essence[20] is indivisible into another formula which signifies the essence of the thing (of course, every formula in virtue of itself is divisible).[21] For it is in this way that what increases or decreases is one, namely, in view of the fact that its formula is one, just as the formula of a species of plane figures is one.[22] In general, those things are one in the highest degree if the thinking of their essence is indivisible and cannot separate them either in time or in place or in formula, and of these the substances above all.[23] For universally, those things which cannot be divided, insofar as they cannot be divided, are said to be one; for example, if a man qua a man cannot be divided, he is one man, if qua an animal, he is one animal, if qua a magnitude, one magnitude. Most things are called "one" in view of the fact that they act on, or are affected by, or have, or are related to, some other thing which is one, but things which are primarily called "one" are those whose *substance* is one, either by continuity, or in kind, or in formula; for we count as many either things which are not continuous, or things which are not one in kind, or things whose formula is not one.

Again, in one sense we say that anything is one if it is a quantity and continuous, but in another sense we do not say so unless the object is a whole of some kind, that is, unless it has one form; for example, we would not say that the parts of a shoe which are put together haphazardly are one (except in the sense that they are one because of continuity), unless they are so put together that they form a shoe and so have some one form.[24] On this account, the circular line[25] is one in the highest sense, in view of the fact that it is a whole and complete.

(3) *To be one* is to be a principle of some number. For the first measure is a principle; the first object by which we know is the first measure in each genus; accordingly, the principle of the knowable in each case is the one.[26] But the one is not the same in all the genera. For in one case it is the quarter-tone, in another it is the vowel or the consonant; in weight it is another, and in motion still another. But in every case the one is indivisible, either in quantity or in kind. That which is indivisible according to quantity and qua quantity is called "a unit" if it is indivisible in every dimension and has no position, "a point" if it is indivisible in every dimension and has position, "a line" if it is divisible only in one dimension, "a plane"[27] if it is divisible only in two dimensions, and "a body" if it is divisible according to quantity in all or three dimensions. And reversing the order, that which is divisible only in two dimensions is a plane,[27] if divisible only in one it is a line, and if in no way divisible according to quantity it is a point or a unit, a unit if it has no position but a point if it has position.

Again, some things are one according to number, others are one according to species,[28] others are one according to genus, and others are one according to analogy. They are one numerically if the matter[29] is one, they are one in species if the formula is one, they are one in genus[30] if they are under the same category, and they are one according to analogy if they are related as a third to a fourth.[31] What is one in any of the senses after the first always follows what is one in any of its preceding senses. For example, things which are one numerically are also one in species, but things which are one in species are not all one numerically;[32] and things which are one in species are also one in genus, but things which are one in genus are not all one in species although they are one by analogy; and things which are one by analogy are not all one in genus.

It is also evident that "many" will have meanings opposite to those of "one". For things are many if they are not continuous; they are many if their matter, either their first or their last, is divisible in kind; and they are many if their formulae which signify the essence are many.

7

The term "being" is used[1] either (1) accidentally or (2) essentially.

(1) For example, we say that the just *is* musical by accident, and the man *is* musical or the musical *is* a man by accident, and this is much like saying that the musician builds, in view of the fact that the builder is by accident a musician or the musician is by accident a builder; for here the expression "this is that" means that one thing is an accident of the other. And so it is in the examples given; for when we say that the man is musical or that the musical is a man, or that the white is musical, or that the musical is white, in the latter two cases the fact is that both the musical and the white are accidents of the same thing; in the first case the fact is that the musical is an accident of a thing, and in "the musical is a man" the fact is that it is of the man that the musical is an accident.[2] And it is in this last sense that we say "the not-white is", the fact being that that of which the not-white is an accident *is*.[3] Accordingly, things are said to be by accident, as in "A *is* B", either because both A and B belong to the same thing, which *is*, or in view of the fact that the latter, B, belongs to the former, which *is*, or in view of the fact that the latter *is*,[4] to which belongs the former, of which the latter is predicated.

(2) Those things are said to be essentially which are signified by the various ways of predication; for these are as many as there are meanings of "being". Since some predicates signify whatness, others a quality, others a quantity, others a relation, others acting or being acted upon, others whereness, others whenness, "being" has the same significance as each of these. For there is no difference in significance between "a man is recovering" and "a man recovers", or between "a man is walking" and "a man walks", or between "a man is cutting" and "a man cuts"; similarly with the rest.[5]

(3) Again, "to be" and "is" mean that something is true, and "not to be" that it is not true but false, these meanings being alike in the case of affirmation and denial. For example, in "Socrates *is* musical", the "is" means that it is true[6] that Socrates is musical, and in "Socrates *is* not-white", that this is true; but in "the diagonal *is not* commensurate

with the side" the "is not" means that it is false[7] that the diagonal is commensurate with the side.

1017*b*   (4) Again, "to be" or "being" in each of the cases mentioned means, in one sense, that the thing is potentially as stated, and, in another, that it is actually as stated. For we say "it is seeing" both of that which can see and that which is actually seeing, we say "to *know*" both of that which can use *knowledge* and that which is using it, and we say "the thing that rests" both of that which is at the time resting and that which can rest. In substances the situation is similar; for we say "Hermes *is* in the marble", and "half of the line *is* in the line",[8] and "it *is* corn" even if it is not yet ripe. However, as to when a thing exists potentially and when it does not yet so exist, this must be determined elsewhere.[9]

8

10   By "a substance" we mean (1) the simple bodies, such as earth and fire and water and all such,[1] and in general the bodies and whatever consists of these, such as animals and divine things,[2] and also the parts of these. All these are called "substances" in view of the fact that they are not predicated of a subject, but the others are predicated of these.

15   (2) It also means that which, being a constituent in such things as are not predicated of a subject, is the cause of their being, as the soul in an animal.[3]

        (3) Substances are also the parts which are constituents in substances taken in the first sense, which limit these substances and indicate a *this*, and without which the whole is annihilated;[4] for example, some say[5] that this is the plane in the case of a body, and the line in the case

20   of a plane, and in general, a number is thought by some thinkers to be such a substance, for if this is annihilated nothing is thought to exist, and it is thought to limit[6] everything.

        (4) The essence, whose formula is a definition, is also said to be the substance[7] of each thing.

        The term "a substance", then, has two senses:[8] it means the ultimate subject[9] which is not predicated of something else, and also that which

25   is a *this* and is separable,[10] such being the *shape* or the form of each thing.

9

        (1) Things are called "the same" by accident;[1] for example, the white and the musical are the same in view of the fact that they belong to the same thing by accident, and the man and the musical are the same in

30   view of the fact that the latter belongs to the former by accident. And the musical is the same as the man, in view of the fact that the musical belongs to the man by accident. Also, the musical man is by accident the same as each of the preceding two, and each of those two is by accident the same as the musical man; for the man or the musical is said to be the same as the musical man, and the musical man is said to be the same as either the man or the musical. On this account,[2] all these are not said[3] to be the same universally; for it is not true to say

35
1018a   that every man is the same as the musical; for what is truly said universally belongs essentially, but the accidents do not belong essentially but are predicates simply of individuals. For Socrates and musical Socrates are thought to be the same, but "Socrates" is not a predicate of many things; and so we do not say "every Socrates" as we say "every

5   man". These, then, are the ways we speak of those things which are the same by accident.

    (2) Things are also called "the same" essentially, just as they are called "one"; for things whose matter is one, either in kind or in number, are called "the same", and so are things whose *substance* is one. Thus, it is evident that sameness is a kind of unity, either of things which are many, or of what is treated as many, as for example when a man says that a thing is the same as itself, treating it as if it were two.[4]

10   Things are called "other" [or "distinct"] if either their kinds or their matter or the formula of their *substance* are more than one; and in general, the meanings of "the other" are the opposite of those of "the same".

    Things are called "different" which, (1) being distinct, are the same in some respect, only not in number, but in kind or in genus or by analogy. (2) Also they are called "different" if their genus is distinct,

15   or if they are contraries, or if they have otherness in their *substance*.

    Things are called "like" [or "similar"] which are affected[5] in the same way in every respect, or if they are affected in the same way in more respects than they are affected in a distinct way, or if their quality[6] is one. Also one thing is said to be like another if, with respect to those contraries in it which can alter, it has the majority of or the more important contraries which the other thing has. The term "unlike" has meanings which are opposite to those of "like".[7]

10

20   We call "opposites" the contradictories, the contraries, the relatives, privation and possession; and also the extremes from which and to which,[1] as in generations and destructions, and those which cannot be present at the same time in that which admits of both are said to be

opposed, either these themselves or those out of which they are made[2] (for grey and white do not belong to the same thing at the same time, hence, those out of which they are made are opposed).

25

We call "contraries" (1) those which differ according to genus and cannot at the same time be present in the same thing,[3] and (2) those which differ most in the same genus,[4] and (3) of those which admit of being in the same subject, the ones which are most different,[5] (4) and those which differ most and come under the same power,[6] and (5) those whose difference is greatest either without qualification,[7] or according to genus, or in kind.

30

The others are called "contraries" either by having contraries such as those just mentioned, or by being receptive of them,[8] or by having the capability of producing or of being affected by them, or by [actually] producing or by [actually] being affected by them,[9] or by being in the process of losing them or acquiring them, or by possessing them or by being deprived of them.

35

Since "one" and "being" have many meanings, all the other objects which are called according to these must also follow, and so sameness and otherness and contrariety must be distinct in each category.[10]

1018*b*

By "other in kind" we mean things which, being of the same genus, are not subordinate the one to the other,[11] or things which are in the same genus and have a difference,[12] or things which have a contrariety[13] in their *substance*. Contraries, too, are distinct in kind from one another, either all or those which are called so in the primary sense;[14] and so are those whose formulae in the last species of their genus are distinct, as a man and a horse, which are indivisible in genus[15] but whose formulae are distinct. Also things which have the same *substance* but have a difference are called "other in kind".[16] The expression "the same in kind" is used in as many senses as, but opposed to, those of "other in kind".

5

11

"Prior" and "posterior" have the following senses: (1) When there is something which is first or a principle in each genus, we call "prior" that which is nearer[1] to some definite principle which either exists without qualification and by nature, or is relative to something or somewhere, or is posited by some,[2] but we call "posterior" that which is farther.

10

(a) With respect to place, for example, the prior is nearer either to some definite place by nature, such as the center or the outermost limit of the universe, or to some chance place, than the posterior.

15

(b) With respect to time, of past events we call "prior" that which is farther from the present (thus, the Trojan war is prior to the Persian war, in view of the fact that the time interval from the present is greater), but of future events we call "prior" that which is nearer to the present (thus, the Nemean are prior to the Pythian games, in view of the fact that they are nearer to the present, which we use as a principle and as something first).

20   (c) With respect to motion, that which is nearer to the first mover is called "prior"; for example, the boy is nearer[3] to the man. The first mover, here, is a principle in an unqualified sense.

    (d) With respect to power, that which exceeds in power or is more powerful is called "prior", and such is that according to whose *choice* the other which is called "posterior" must follow; so that if the prior

25 does not move the posterior is not moved, but if the prior moves then the posterior is moved, and *choice* here is a principle.

    (e) With respect to order, when there is some definite thing relative to which other things are arranged at intervals according to some formula, that which is nearer to that thing is called "prior". For example, in the chorus the second man is prior to the third, and the next to the lowest string is prior to the lowest; in the first case, the principle is the leader, in the second, it is the middle string.[4]

30   The term "prior" in these cases, then, is used in the senses just stated, but in another sense (2) a thing is said to be prior in knowledge, either in a qualified sense or without qualification, and of these, those which are prior according to formula are distinct from those which are prior according to sensation.[5] For, according to formula the universals are prior, but according to sensation the particulars are prior.[6] And accord-

35 ing to formula, the accident[7] is prior to the whole, for example, the musical is prior to the musical man; for the formula of the whole cannot exist without that of the part,[8] although musicality cannot exist unless something exists which is musical.[9]

    (3) Again, the *attributes* of prior things are called "prior"; for ex-

1019a ample, straightness is prior to planeness. For the first is an essential *attribute* of a line, the second of a surface.[10]

    Objects, then, are called "prior" and "posterior" in the manner stated, but (4) others are called so with respect to nature or *substance*, when some things can exist without the others, but not conversely—a distinc-

5 tion used by Plato. Since "to be" has many senses, first the underlying subject is prior, and hence a substance is prior.[11] Second, in another sense objects are called "prior" and "posterior" with respect to potentiality and actuality; for some objects are prior with respect to potentiality, others with respect to actuality. For example, with respect to potentiality, the half line is said to be prior to the whole line, the part prior to the whole, and matter prior to substance, but with respect to

10 actuality they are posterior; for they will actually exist after decom-

position.[12] Indeed, in some sense all objects which are said to be prior and posterior are called so according to these last senses;[13] for with respect to generation some objects can exist[14] without others, such as the whole without the parts, and with respect to destruction it is otherwise, such as the part without the whole. Similarly with the rest.[15]

12

15 "Potency"[1] means: (1) the principle of motion or of change which is in a thing other than the thing moved or changed, or in the thing moved or changed but qua other; for example, the art of building is a potency which does not exist in the thing built, but the medical art is a potency which could be in the man who is being healed, but not qua being healed. In general, then, the principle of change or of motion,
20 which [principle] exists in another thing or in the same thing qua other, is called "potency".

(2) "Potency" also means the principle of being moved or of being changed by another thing or by the thing itself qua other. For in virtue of the principle by which a thing is acted upon in some way, we say that the thing is capable of being acted upon: sometimes we say so if (a) the thing can be acted upon in any way, but sometimes (b) if it can be acted upon not in any way but for the better.

(3) Again, "potency" means the principle in virtue of which one accomplishes something well or according to *choice*. For sometimes we
25 say of those who merely walk or speak, but not well or not as they *choose* to, that they are not capable of speaking or of walking.

(4) The term "potency" is similarly used also for the principle of being acted upon, which is in the thing.[2]

(5) Again, those habits are called "potencies" in virtue of which things cannot at all be affected or changed, or cannot be easily moved for the worse; for things are broken or crushed or bent or altogether destroyed
30 not by being capable, but by not being capable or by lacking something, and they are unaffected in this way if they are so affected only with great difficulty or only slightly because they have a potency or are able or are somehow disposed.

Since "potency" has so many meanings, so too "the capable"[3] in one sense means (1) that which has a principle of moving or of changing (for
35 even that which brings about a stop[4] is in one sense capable) another
1019b or itself qua other; in another, (2) if it has a potency of being changed by another thing[5] [in the preceding sense]; in another, if it has a potency of changing in a certain way, either for the worse or for the better (for even that which is destroyed is thought to be capable of being destroyed, for it would not have been destroyed if it were not capable of it. As

5   it is, it has some disposition as a cause or a principle of being so affected.[6] Sometimes it is thought to be such[7] by having something, but sometimes by being deprived of something;[8] and if a privation is in some sense a having, everything will be capable by having something, so that it will be capable by having either a possession as a principle, or the privation

10   of this if it can have it; but if a privation is in no way a possession, then "capable" will be equivocal);[9] in another, (3) if the thing has no potency or principle of being destroyed by another or by itself qua other.[10] Again, all of these are called "capable" either if changing, or being changed, or not being changed just happen to take place, or if they do so well.[11] For such potency exists even in inanimate things such as in-

15   struments; for they say that one lyre is capable of being played, but another not, if the latter's tone is not good.

     "Incapacity" means the privation of a potency or of such a principle as stated before, either in the sense that there is no such potency at all in the thing,[12] or in the sense that the thing does not have the potency which it should have by nature, or even in the sense that it does not have it at the time when it should by nature have it; for we would not use the expression "incapable of begetting" similarly for a child, a man,

20   and a eunuch.[13] Again, to each kind of capacity there is an incapacity which is opposite, both to that which can just move and to that which can move well.

     Also, some things are called "incapable" according to the incapacity just stated, but there is another sense of "capable" and "incapable" [or, "possible" and "impossible"]. "Impossible" means that whose contrary is necessarily true;[14] for example, it is impossible for the diagonal of

25   a square to be commensurate with the side; that is, "the diagonal is commensurate with the side" is false,[15] and "the diagonal is incommensurable with the side", which is its contrary, is not only true but also necessary. So, "the diagonal is commensurable with the side" is not only false, but also necessarily false. The contradictory[16] of the impossible, which is the possible, occurs when it is not necessary that the contrary of the possible[17] be false; for example, if "a man sits" is possible,

30   then "a man does not sit" is not of necessity false. As we said, then, one sense of "the possible" is that which is not of necessity false,[18] another, that which is true,[19] a third, that which may[20] be true. Also, it is by a change in meaning that the term "potency" or "power" is used in geometry.[21]

35   The senses of "the possible" just given are not according to potency.[22]

1020a   But all the senses according to potency are related to the first potency,[23] and this is the principle of change in another thing or in the same thing qua other. For the others are called "capable" in view of the fact that something else has a potency, or does not have a potency, or has a

potency in a certain manner, over them. The term "incapable" is similarly used. Thus, the main definition of the primary potency would be:
a principle of change in another thing,[24] or in the same thing qua other.

13

"Quantity"[1] means that which is divisible into constituents, either[2]
of which or each of which is by nature one and a *this*.[3] A plurality is a
kind of quantity if it is numerable, a magnitude is a kind of quantity
if it is measurable. It is called "a plurality" if it is divisible potentially
into parts which are not continuous, but "a magnitude" if it is divisible
potentially into continuous parts. Of magnitudes, that which is continuous in one dimension[4] is called "length", if in two it is called "width",
and if in three, "depth". Of these, a limited plurality is called "a number", a limited length is called "a line", a limited width is called "a
surface", and a limited depth, "a body".[5]

Again, some quantities are said to be essential, others accidental; for
example, a line is an essential quantity, but the musical is an accidental
quantity. Of what is essential in quantities, some are so in virtue of
their *substance*, as a line for example, which is a quantity of some kind
(for in its formula, which states the whatness, "quantity"[6] is present);
others are *attributes* or possessions[7] of such a *substance*, for example,
much and little,[8] long and short, wide and narrow, deep and shallow,
heavy and light, and the others of this sort. Also, the great and the small,
and the greater and the less, whether in virtue of themselves or in relation to one another,[9] are essential *attributes* of quantity; and by an
extension of meaning, these names are applied also to other things.[10]

Of quantities which are spoken of accidentally, some are said to be
quantities in the way in which the musical and the white are said to
be quantities, in the sense that the subject to which they belong is a
quantity;[11] others are said to be quantities like motion and time, for
these too are said to be quantities in a way and are continuous in view
of the fact that the subjects of which these are *attributes* are divisible.
By "subject" here I mean not the moving object but the interval through
which the object has moved; for, in view of the fact that the interval
is a quantity, the motion too is called "a quantity", and in view of the
motion, the time too is called "a quantity".[12]

14

"Quality" means (1) the differentia of the *substance*.[1] For example, a
man is an animal of a certain quality, that is, he is two-footed, and like-

35   wise a horse, being four-footed; and a circle is a figure of a certain
1020b quality, that is, non-angular.[2] Thus, the differentia of the *substance* is
       considered as being a quality.

       One meaning of "quality", then, is the differentia of the *substance*,
       but (2) there is another meaning which applies to immovable and mathe-
       matical objects[3] as in the case of numbers which are said to be of a
       certain quality; for example, the numbers which are composite[4] and
5   not one-dimensional, of which the plane and the solid are imitations[5]
       (these are numbers which have two and three factors, respectively),
       and in general, that which belongs to the *substance* of a quantity be-
       sides quantity itself. For the *substance* of each is what it is once; for
       example, six is not what it is twice or thrice, but what it is once, for
       six is six[6] once.

       (3) Also, the affections of substances that move, such as heat and
10   cold, whiteness and blackness, heaviness and lightness, and other such,
       with respect to which bodies are said to alter as they change, are called
       "qualities".

       (4) The term is also used for the virtues and vices with respect to
       which things move and, in general, goodness and badness.

       In a way, then, "quality" has two meanings, of which one is most
15   important. For, the primary quality is the differentia of the *substance*,
       and a part of this is the quality which exists in numbers;[7] for the latter
       is a kind of differentia of *substances*, which are either not in motion or
       not qua in motion.[8] Secondly, the affections of moving things qua mov-
       ing and the differences of motions[9] are called "qualities". Virtues and
20   vices are a part of those affections, for they indicate differentiae of mo-
       tion and of activity, according to which things in motion act or are acted
       upon well or badly; for that which can be moved or be active in one way is
       good, but that which can do so in another or contrary way is bad. "Good"
       and "bad" signify a quality most of all in things having a soul, and of
25   these most of all in those which have *choice*.[10]

15

       Things are called "relative" (1) as the double to the half, the triple
       to the third, and in general, the multiple to the submultiple, and that
       which exceeds to that which is exceeded;[1] (2) as that which can heat
30   to that which can be heated, that which can cut to that which can be
       cut, and in general, that which can act to that which can be acted upon;
       (3) as the measurable to the measure, the *knowable* to *knowledge*, and
       the sensible to sensation.

       (1) Relatives in the first sense are spoken of with respect to numbers

either without specification or in a definite way, whether in relation to
themselves or to unity. For example, that which is a double in relation
to unity is a definite number;[2] that which is a numerical multiple in
relation to unity is not definite, and it may be this or that.[3] That which
is half again as much as that to which it is so related is numerically
definite relative to a given number, but the superparticular in relation
to the subparticular is numerically indefinite,[4] as in the case of a multiple
in relation to one. As for that which exceeds to that which is exceeded,
it is altogether indefinite with respect to number; for numbers are commensurate, but these are named without reference to numerical commensurability; for that which exceeds, relative to that which is exceeded,
is equal to what is exceeded and more, and the additional part is indefinite, for it may be' anything, that is, equal or unequal to what is
exceeded.[5] All these relatives, then, are spoken of with respect to number and the *attributes* of number, but in another way there are also the
equal and the like and the same; for all these are named according
to oneness. For those things are called "the same" whose *substance* is
one, those are called "like" whose quality is one, and those are called
"equal" whose quantity is one.[6] The one[7] in a number, however, is a
principle and a measure, so that all these are called "relatives" with
respect to number, but not in the same way.

(2) Things that can act and be acted upon are called "relative" by
virtue of a potency to act and a potency to be acted upon, and so are
the *actualities* of those potencies. For example, that which can heat is
relative to that which can be heated, in view of the fact that each is so
capable; and again, that which heats is relative to that which is heated,
and that which is cutting is relative to that which is being cut, in the
sense that the potencies are being *actualized.* There are no *actualities*
of relatives with respect to number except in a manner stated elsewhere;[8] for *actualities* with respect to motion do not exist there. Relatives with respect to potency are also spoken of with respect to time;
for example, that which has acted is relative to that which has been
acted upon, and that which will act is relative to that which will be
acted upon. Thus it is in this way that a father is said to be the father
of his son; for the former has acted and the latter has been acted upon
in some way. Again, some are relatives according to the privation of a
potency, as in the case of the incapable and whatever is spoken of
in this manner, for example, the invisible.

Every thing which is said to be a relative with respect to number
or potency is a relative in view of the fact that its being is such that it
is said of something else, but not that something else is related to it.[9]
But (3) the measurable or the *knowable* or the *thinkable* is said to be
relative in the sense that something else is said to be related to it. For

"the *thinkable*" signifies that a *thought* of it is possible; but the *thought* is not relative in the sense that it is stated as related to that of which it is the *thought*, for then the same thing would be stated twice. Simi-

larly, sight is the sight of something, not of that of which it is the sight (although it would be true to say this),[10] but it is related to a color or to some other thing of this sort. In the other case, the same thing will be stated twice, namely, that sight is of that of which it is the sight.

Relatives which are essentially so spoken, then, are spoken of in this manner, but others are said to be relatives if their genera are relatives in the sense just stated; for example, medical science is a relative in view of the fact that its genus, 'science', is thought to be a relative.[11] Further, relatives are said to be also those things in virtue of which things which have them are called "relatives"; for example, equality is a relative in view of the fact that the equal is a relative, and likeness is a relative in view of the fact that the like is a relative.[12] Things are called "relative" also by accident. For example, a man is a relative, in view of the fact that by accident he is a double [of something], and to be a double is to be a relative; and the white is a relative, if by accident the same thing is both a double and white.

16

"Complete" [or "perfect"] means (1) that outside of which it is not possible to find even one of its parts; for example, the complete time of each thing is that outside of which it is not possible to find any time which is a part of that time.[1] (2) Also, that which with respect to virtue or goodness cannot be exceeded within its genus;[2] for example, a perfect doctor or a perfect fluteplayer is one who lacks nothing with respect to the form of his *proper* virtue. In this manner, by transferring the mean-ing to even bad things, we speak of a perfect slanderer and a perfect thief, as indeed we even say that they are good, that is, a good thief and a good slanderer. Virtue, too, is a perfection; for each thing or *substance* is complete when with respect to the form of its *proper* virtue it lacks no part of its natural magnitude.[3] (3) Things which have an end which is good are called "perfect";[4] for it is in virtue of having that end that they are said to be perfect. And so, since the end is something ultimate, by transferring the meaning even to bad things we use the expressions "a complete loss" and "complete destruction" when no thing escaped destruction or badness but the ultimate was reached. And be-cause of this, by a transfer of meaning, even death is called "the end",[5] in view of the fact that both are ultimate. The ultimate final cause is also an end.

Things are essentially called "complete", then, in so many senses, some in the sense that with respect to goodness they lack nothing or they cannot be exceeded or no part of them can be found outside, others in the general sense that within their genus nothing exceeds them or 1022*a* nothing can be found outside, and the rest are so called according to these senses, by producing something complete, or by having it, or by being adapted to it, or by being related to the primary senses of "complete" in some way or other.

17

5   "Limit" means (1) the ultimate part of each thing, or the first[1] part outside of which no part can be found, or the first part inside of which all parts exist; (2) the form of a magnitude or of that which has magnitude; (3) the end[2] of each thing, such being that towards which, but not that from which, a motion or an *action* is directed, although sometimes it is both that from which and that towards which; (4) the final cause; (5) the *substance* of each thing, or the essence of each thing, for 10   this is said to be the limit of knowledge; and if of knowledge then of the thing also.

It is evident, then, that "limit" has as many senses as "principle", and yet more; for a principle is a limit, but not every limit is a principle.[3]

18

15   "That in virtue of which"[1] has many meanings. (1) The form or the *substance* of each thing; for example, that in virtue of which the good is good is goodness itself. (2) The first subject in which a thing comes to be by nature; for example, color is in the surface.[2] "That in virtue of which", then, in the primary sense means the form, and in a secondary sense it means the matter of each or the first underlying subject of each. 20   In general, "that in virtue of which" has as many senses as "cause"; for we say indifferently (3) "in virtue of what has he come?" or "for the sake of what has he come?", and (4) "in virtue of what has he proved, or proved falsely?", or "what is the cause of the syllogism, or the false syllogism?"

Again, (5) we use "that according to" with respect to position, as in the expressions "according to where he stands" and "according to where he walks"; for all such expressions signify position or place.[3]

25   Accordingly, "that in virtue of itself" must have many senses. For "that in virtue of itself" means the essence of each thing; for example, Callias is Callias in virtue of himself and the essence of Callias. Also, whatever is present in the whatness of a thing; for example, Callias

is an animal in virtue of himself; for in his formula "animal" is present,
for Callias is an animal of a certain kind. Again, the subject of an
attribute, provided that the subject or a part of it is the first to have
the *attribute*. For example, the surface is in virtue of itself white; and
a man lives in virtue of himself, for the soul, which is the first in which
living belongs, is a part of the man. Again, that of which there is no
other cause; for of a man there are many causes: animal, two-footed,[4]
yet a man is a man in virtue of himself. Again, whatever belongs[5] to a
thing alone and qua alone does so belong in virtue of that thing; consequently, that which is separate exists in virtue of itself.[6]

19

"Disposition" means the order of that which has parts, either with
respect to place,[1] or with respect to potency,[2] or with respect to kind;[3]
for there must be a position[4] of a sort, as the word "disposition"
indicates.

20

"Having" [or "habit"] means (1) a sort of *actuality* of that which has
and that which is had, as if it were an *action* of a sort or a motion. For
when one thing makes and another is made, there is a making between
them; so too between the man who has[1] a garment and the garment
which is had there is a having. Evidently, it is impossible to have this
having; for the process would go on to infinity if it is possibe to have a
having of that which is had.[2]

(2) "Habit" means a disposition according to which that which is
disposed is well or ill disposed, and is so disposed either in itself or in
relation to something else;[3] for example, health is a habit, for it is such
a disposition.

(3) We call "a habit" that which is a part of a disposition such as we
just described; consequently, the virtue of any part is a disposition.[4]

21

"Affection" means (1) a quality in virtue of which a thing can be
altered; for example, whiteness and blackness, sweetness and bitterness,
heaviness and lightness, and all others of this sort are affections.

(2) The *actualities* or alterations of these.[1]

(3) Of the latter, the alterations or motions[2] which are rather harmful,
and of these most of all those which are painful.

(4) Also, misfortunes and pains of considerable magnitude are called "affections".[3]

22

"Privation" means (1) not having something which can be had by nature, even if that which does not have it would not by nature have it; for example, the plant is said to be deprived of eyes.

25 (2) Not having something which a thing, either itself or its genus, should by nature have. For example, in one sense a blind man is said to be deprived of sight, and in another sense a mole is said to be so deprived; for the latter is deprived with respect to its genus, the former with respect to himself.

(3) Not having something if and when a thing should by nature have it; for blindness is a privation, yet one is not called "blind" at every age 30 but if he has no sight when he should by nature have sight. Similarly, a thing is said to be deprived of something if it does not have it, although it should by nature have it, in something or[1] with respect to something or in relation to something or in a certain manner.

(4) The taking away of something by force is called "privation".

"Privation" has as many senses as there are negations of terms which are prefixed by *"un"* or *"in"* or *"im"* or suffixed by *"less"*.[2] For a thing is called "unequal" if it does not have equality although it can by 35 nature have it; a thing is called "invisible" if it has no color at all or if it has a faint color; and a thing is called "footless" if it has no feet at all or if it has them but badly. Again, a thing is said to be deprived of 1023*a* something if it has it to a small degree, as in the case of the seedless fruit; for this somehow comes under the heading of having something badly. Again, a thing is said to be deprived of something if the latter belongs to the thing but not easily or well; for example, by "uncuttable" we mean not only that which cannot be cut, but also that which cannot be cut easily or well. Again, a thing is said to be deprived if it lacks all; 5 for it is not he who has only one eye that is called "blind", but he who has no sight at all. According to this, it is not true that every man is either good or bad, either just or unjust, but there is also an intermediate state.[3]

23

"To have" [or "possess", or "hold"] has many meanings. (1) To treat 10 according to one's own nature of tendency; accordingly, fever is said to possess the man, the tyrants are said to have the cities, and the wearers of clothes to have the clothes.

(2) That in which a thing exists, as in something[1] receptive of it, is said to have the thing; for example, the bronze has the form of the statue, and the body has the disease.

(3) That which contains is said to have the things contained. For the thing contained is said to be had by that in which it exists; for example, we say that the vessel has the liquid, that the city has men, and that the ship has sailors. And it is in this way that the whole has the parts.[2]

(4) That which according to its own tendency prevents a thing from moving or *acting* is said to hold that thing; for example, the pillars hold the weight on them, and, as the poets maintain, Atlas holds the heavens, which would otherwise fall to the earth, and some natural philosophers speak similarly about the heavens.[3] In this way, too, that which keeps things together in one continuous whole is said to hold them, for these would otherwise disperse in virtue of their respective tendencies.[4]

"To be in something" has similar meanings and follows those of "to have something" [or "to hold something" or "possess something"].[5]

24

"To be from[1] something" [or "to come from something"] means (1) to be from something as from matter, and in two ways, either with respect to the first genus[2] or with respect to the last species; for example, in one sense all things that can be melted are formed from water,[3] but in another sense a statue is formed from bronze.

(2) Also, it means to come from the first moving principle. For example, "from what did the fight come?"; we say from abusive language, in view of the fact that this was the starting-point of the fight.

(3) Also, it means to be from the composite of matter and *form*, as the parts are from the whole, and the verse from the *Iliad*, and the stones from the house; for the *form* is an end, and that which has an end is complete.[4]

(4) Also, it means to be formed, as the form or species is formed from its parts; for example, "a man" is formed from "two-footed",[5] and a syllable from its elements.[6] For this sense is distinct from that in which the statue is formed from the bronze; for the composite substance comes from sensible matter, but the species comes from the matter of the species.[7] Some objects, then, are said to come from something in these senses.

(5) Also, it means to come from a part, in any of the previous senses; for example, we say the baby comes from the father and the mother,

and the plants come from earth, in view of the fact that in each case the former comes from a part of the latter.

(6) It also means to come after it in time; for example, night is said to come from day and the storm from the calm, the fact being that the former comes after the latter in each case. Of these, some are so said by changing one into the other, as in the examples given,[8] but others only by being successive in time. For example, the voyage was made from the equinox, in view of the fact that it was made after the equinox; and the Thargelian festival comes from the Dionysia, that is, after the Dionysia.

25

"A part" means (1) that into which a quantity can be in any way divided; for that which is subtracted from a quantity qua quantity is always called "a part" of that quantity, as for example two, which is said to be in some sense[1] a part of three.

(2) It also means only those parts, in the sense just considered, which measure the quantity of which they are such parts;[2] consequently, in the first sense two is said to be a part of three, but in the second sense it is said not to be a part.

(3) Also, those into which a kind can be divided,[3] without reference to quantity, are also said to be parts of that kind; and so they say that the species are parts of the genus.

(4) Also, it means those into which a whole is divided or of which it is composed, whether this whole is a form or that which has a form. For example, the bronze is a part of the bronze sphere or the bronze cube, and this is the matter in which the form exists; and the angle is a part.[4]

(5) Also, those are said to be parts of a whole which exist in the formula which signifies the thing; and so in this sense it is the genus that is said to be a part of the species,[5] although in another sense it is the species that is said to be a part of the genus.[6]

26

"A whole" means (1) that from which is absent none of the parts of which it is said to be by nature a whole.

(2) That which contains the objects contained in such a way that they are one, either in the sense that each of them is some one thing,[1] or in the sense that what is composed of them is one. For (a) the uni-

30 versal, or what in general is taken as being such when we say "as a whole", is universal in this manner: it contains many in the sense that it is a predicate of each, and they are all one in the sense that each is one; for example, a man, a horse, and God[2] are all animals. And (b) what is continuous and limited is said to be a whole when it is some one thing consisting of many constituents, especially when these exist potentially,

35 and if not, then even if they exist actually.[3] And of these, those which are one by nature are said to be wholes to a higher degree than those which are one by art, just as we spoke in the case of oneness, and in this sense a whole is a kind of unity.

1024a (3) In the case of a quantity which has a beginning and a middle and what is last, if position in it makes no difference, it is called "all" [or "a total"], but if position makes a difference, it is called "a whole"; and if both are possible[4], then it is called both "all" and "a whole". The latter

5 is such that its nature stays the same by a change in position, but not its *shape*, as in the case of wax or a coat; for each of these is called both "a whole" and "all", since it has both a form that changes and a nature which remains the same by a change in position. But water and wet objects and numbers are called "totals", and we do not speak of a number or of water as being a whole except metaphorically. We predicate the term "all" in the plural of those things if "all" in the singular is a predi-

10 cate of each of them separately; for example, we say "all these numbers"[5] and "all these units".

27

It is not any chance quantity that is called "mutilated" but only the one which is divisible into parts and is a whole.[1] For two is not called "mutilated" when one of the units is taken away (for the part removed by mutilation is never equal to what is left), and in general no number

15 is called "mutilated", for the *substance* of the thing must remain after mutilation.[2] If a cup is mutilated, it must still be a cup; but the number is no longer the same. Further, even if a thing consists of unlike parts, it is not always that it is said to be mutilated; for, in a sense, even a number has unlike parts, such as two and three.[3] And in general, things in which position makes no difference, such as water and fire, are not

20 said to be mutilated; but in order to be mutilated, things must be such that according to their *substance* position makes a difference. Besides, they must be continuous; for a harmony is composed of unlike parts which have position, but it does not become mutilated. Further, even if the things are wholes, they do not become mutilated by the privation of any part. For the parts removed must neither be the main parts[4] of the *substance* nor be in any chance place; for example, if a hole is

25   made in a cup, we do not have something mutilated,⁵ but we do have
        a mutilated cup if the handle or some projecting part is removed. And a
        man is mutilated not if the flesh or the spleen is removed but if an ex-
        tremity is removed, not any extremity, but one which when completely
        removed does not grow again. Because of this, people with shaven⁶
        heads are not said to be mutilated.

28

        "Genus" [or "race"] means (1) a continuous generation of things¹
30   which have the same form; for example, we say "as long as the human
        race exists", which means: as long as the generation of men continues.
            (2) That from which as from a first mover things come into existence;²
        for it is in this sense that some are called "Hellenes" by race and others
        "Ionians", in view of the fact that the former come from Hellen as their
35   first begetter and the latter from Ion. And the race is called after the
        male begetter more than after the matter,³ although it is also called
        after the female, as in the case of the race of Pyrra.
1024*b*   (3) Of plane figures and of solid figures we call the plane "a genus"
        and also the solid "a genus"; for each of the figures is, say, such-and-such
        a plane, and such-and-such a solid; and this is the subject which under-
        lies the differentiae.⁴
5   Again, (4) the first constituent which is stated in the formula of the
        whatness is called "a genus", whose qualities are called "differentiae".
            The term "genus", then, is used as follows: (1) with respect to a con-
        tinuous generation of things of the same species; (2) with respect to the
        first mover, which is of the same species as the things moved; (3) as
        matter⁵, for that which has a differentia or a quality is the underlying
        subject, which we call "matter".
10   Things are called "other in genus" [or "distinct in genus"] (1) if their
        first⁶ underlying subjects are distinct and cannot be analyzed⁷ one into
        the other or both into the same subject; for example, matter and form
        are distinct in genus.⁸ (2) Also, if they come under distinct categories of
        being. For some things indicate a whatness, others a quality, others
15   some other one of the senses of "being" listed earlier;⁹ for of these no
        one can be analyzed into another, nor can they be analyzed into
        something else which is one.

29

        "False" means: (1) false as a fact, and in two ways: (a) in the sense
        that two things are not together or cannot be together,¹ as when we say

20   that the diagonal is commensurable with the side or that you are sitting; for of these, the former is always false but the latter only sometimes, and in this way they are not beings; (b) in the sense that the false facts are beings but appear by nature to be either not such as they are[2] or what does not exist, as for example a sketch or a dream; for these are
25   something but not that of which they create the appearance. We call "a false fact", then, either what does not exist or an existing thing which creates the appearance of being what it is not.

2(a) A false formula[3] qua false[4] is a formula which is not of the thing in question. Consequently, every formula is false if it is of something other than of that of which it is true; for example, the formula of a circle is false if given as the formula of a triangle. The formula of each thing is in one sense unique, and this is the formula of the essence,[5] but in
30   another sense there are many formulae of a thing, since the thing itself is in some sense the same as the thing with an attribute;[6] for example, Socrates and musical Socrates are the same. 2(b): A false formula, without qualification, is a formula of no thing whatsoever.[7] Consequently, Antisthenes was naive in claiming that a thing can be expressed only by the formula *proper* to itself, that is, that for each thing there is just one formula.[8] From this position the conclusion was drawn that contradiction is impossible, and that falsehood is almost impossible. But
35   it is possible to call each thing not only by its own formula, but also by the formula of another, whether falsely[9] and even completely so,[10] or to
1025a   call it in a qualified way but truly,[11] as when we call eight "a double" by using the formula of two.

Things, then, are called "false" in the senses stated, but (3) a man is called "false" if he readily or by *choice* makes false statements, not for the sake of something else[12] but for its own sake, or if he creates false
5   beliefs in others with false statements,[13] just as in the case of things which are called "false" by creating a false appearance. From this it follows that the argument in the *Hippias,* that the same man is false and true, is misleading; for it assumes that a man is false if he has the ability to speak falsely, such a man being one who understands and is prudent,[14] and it also assumes that he who is willingly bad is better.
10   This assumption is falsely made by induction, for a man who willingly limps is better than one who does so unwillingly, if by "limping" Plato means imitating a limp; but one who is willingly lame is perhaps worse than one who is unwillingly so, as in the case of moral habits.

30

"Accident" means that which belongs to something and can be truly
15   said of it, but which belongs to it neither necessarily nor for the most

part; for example, if someone, while digging a hole for a plant, found a treasure, the finding of a treasure is an accident of the digger of a hole; for the former comes from the latter or after the latter neither necessarily,[1] nor is it for the most part that the digger finds a treasure

20   while planting. And a musical man might be pale; but since this happens neither necessarily nor for the most part, we say that paleness is an accident of the musical man. Thus, since something can exist which may belong to something else (and some things do so somewhere and sometimes), whatever so belongs (but not because this subject exists at a certain time or place) is an accident. There is indeed no definite

25   cause of an accident, but only a chance cause; and this is indefinite. Arriving in Aegina was an accident for a man, if he arrived not because he set out to arrive there but because he was carried out of his course by a storm or was captured by pirates. The accident took place or exists, not qua the subject to which it belongs but qua some other thing; for the storm is the cause of his arriving where he was not sailing

30   for, that is, arriving in Aegina.[2]

   "Accident" [we will use "attribute" for this sense] has also another sense, namely, whatever belongs to a thing in virtue of that thing[3] but is not in the *substance* of that thing; for example, the equality of the angles to two right angles so belongs to a triangle. And such accidents [attributes] may be eternal,[4] but accidents of the first kind can never be. The argument for this is stated elsewhere.[5]

Book **E**

1

We are seeking the principles and causes of things, but clearly, qua things. For there is a cause of health and of good physical condition, and there are principles and elements and causes of mathematical objects, and in general, every science which proceeds by *thinking*[1] or which participates in *thought* to some extent[2] is concerned with causes and principles, whether these are very accurate[3] or rather simplified.[4] But all these sciences, marking off some being or some genus, conduct their investigations into this part of being, although not into unqualified being nor into their part of being qua being,[5] and they say nothing concerning whatness; but starting from the whatness of their subject, which [whatness] in some sciences is made clear by sensation but in others is laid down by hypothesis,[6] they thus proceed to demonstrate more or less rigorously the essential attributes of their genus. Consequently, it is evident by such induction[7] from these sciences that there is no demonstration of *substance* or of whatness but that these are made known in some other way. Similarly, they say nothing as to the existence or non-existence of the genus they investigate, and this is because it belongs to the same power of *thought* to make known both the whatness and the existence of a genus.

Now physical science, too, happens to be concerned with some genus of being (for it is concerned with such a substance which has in itself a principle of motion and of rest), and it is clear that this science is neither practical nor productive.[8] For in productive sciences the principle[9] of a thing produced is in that which produces, whether this is intellect or art or some power, and in practical sciences the principle of *action* is in the doer, and this is *choice;* for that which is done and that which is *chosen* are the same thing.[10] Thus, if every *thought* is practical or productive or theoretical,[11] physics would be a theoretical science, and theoretical about such being as can be moved,[12] and about *substances* which according to formula are for the most part non-separable[13] only.

We must not fail to notice how the essence and the formula of an object of physics exists, for inquiry without this leads nowhere. Now of things defined and of the whatness of things, some are considered in the manner in which snubness exists, others in the manner in which concavity exists. These differ by the fact that "snubness" is *understood* with matter (for a snub is a concave nose) but "concavity" without sensible matter. If, then, all physical things are named in a manner like the snub (as for example a nose, an eye, a face, flesh, bone, and in general an animal, and also a leaf, a root, a bark, and in general a plant; for what is signified by the formula of each of these is not without motion but always has matter), it is clear how we must seek and define the whatness in physical things and why it belongs to the physicist to investigate even some part of the soul, namely, that which does not exist without matter.[14] From what has been said, then, it is evident that physics is a theoretical science.

Mathematics, too, is a theoretical science; but whether its objects are immovable and separate is not at present clear. It is clear, however, that some mathematical sciences investigate their objects qua immovable and qua separate.[15] But if there is something which is eternal and immovable and separate, the knowledge of it evidently belongs to a theoretical science, not however to physics (for physics is concerned with certain movable things)[16] nor to mathematics, but to a science which is prior to both. For physics is concerned with separable[17] but not immovable things, and mathematics is concerned with some immovable things although perhaps not separable but as in matter.[18] The first science, however, is concerned with things which are both separate and immovable. Now all causes[19] must be eternal, and these most of all;[20] for these are the causes of what is visible among things divine.[21] Hence, there should be three theoretical philosophies, mathematics, physics, and theology.[22] For it is clear that if the divine is present anywhere, it would be present in a nature of this sort, and the most honorable science should be concerned with the most honorable genus of things.[23] So, the theoretical sciences are to be preferred over the other sciences, but theology is to be preferred over the other theoretical sciences.[24]

One might raise the question whether first philosophy is in any way universal[25] or is concerned merely with some genus and some one nature. In the case of the mathematical sciences, their objects are not all treated in the same manner; geometry and astronomy are concerned with some nature, but universal mathematics is common to all.[26] Accordingly, if there were no substances other than those formed by

30 nature, physics would be the first science; but if there is an immovable substance, this would be prior, and the science of it would be first philosophy and would be universal in this manner,[27] in view of the fact that it is first. And it would be the concern of this science, too, to investigate being qua being,[28] both what being is and what belongs to it qua being.

2

35 But since the unspecified term "being" has many senses,[1] one of which is being by accident, another is that which is true (and nonbeing is that which is false), and besides these senses there are the various categories (for example, whatness, quality, quantity, whereness, whenness, and
1026b similarly any other meaning which the term may have), and in addition to these there is potential being and also *actual* being—since "being", then, has many senses, we must first speak of accidental being, in view of the fact that there can be no investigation of it.

5 A sign of this is the fact that no science, be it practical or productive or theoretical, takes the trouble to consider it. For the builder who is building a house is not producing at the same time the attributes which are accidental to the house when built, for these are infinite; for nothing prevents the house built from being pleasant to some men, harmful to some others, useful to still others, and distinct so to speak from any
10 other thing, but the art of building produces none of these attributes. In the same way, the geometer does not investigate the attributes which are in this manner accidental to figures,[2] nor the problem whether a triangle is distinct from a triangle whose angles are equal to two right angles.[3] And this happens with good reason; for an accident is a mere
15 name, as it were. And so in a sense Plato was not wrong when he ranked sophistry as being concerned with nonbeing.[4] For the discussions of the sophists deal most of all with what is accidental, so to speak; for example, whether the musical and the grammatical are the same or distinct,[5] and likewise for musical Coriscus and Coriscus, and whether everything which exists, but not always, has come to be, so that if he
20 who was musical became grammatical, then also he who was grammatical became musical, and all other such arguments.[6] For accidental being appears to be somewhat close to nonbeing.[7] This is also clear from such arguments as the following: of things which exist in another manner, there is generation and destruction, but of accidental being there is no generation or destruction.[8] Nevertheless, concerning
25 accidental being we must state, as much as can be stated, what its nature

is and through what cause it exists; for perhaps it will be at the same time clear also why there is no science of it.

Now since, among things, some exist always in a certain way and of necessity so (by "necessity" we do not mean the one according to force, but the impossibility of being otherwise), while others exist neither of necessity nor always but for the most part, this latter existence is the principle and the cause of the existence by accident;[9] for that which exists neither always nor for the most part we call "an accident". For example, if in the dog-days we have storm and cold weather, this we say is an accident, but not if we have sultry heat, in view of the fact that the latter occurs always or for the most part, but the former does not. And a man is pale by accident (for he is neither always so nor for the most part), but he is an animal not by accident. And the builder produces health by accident, in view of the fact that it is by nature a doctor and not a builder who produces health, but it is an accident that the builder is a doctor. And a cook, who aims at making tasty food, may make something which produces health,[10] but he does so not in virtue of the art of cooking; so, we say that this occurred by accident, and in a qualified sense the cook produces health, but in an unqualified sense he does not. For in some of the cases of things which happen always or for the most part there exist productive capacities,[11] but in the case of accidents there is no art and no definite capacity at all; for of things which exist or are generated by accident the cause is accidental too. Thus, since not all things are or are generated of necessity or always, but most of them are so for the most part, accidental being must exist. For example, it is neither always nor for the most part that the pale is musical, but since this occurs sometimes, it is an accident; if such things never occur, all things will exist of necessity. So, matter[12] is an accidental cause, capable of being otherwise than for the most part.

We must begin, then, by raising the problem whether there is nothing besides what exists either always or for the most part, or is this impossible? Since this is impossible,[13] there is something besides what exists either always or for the most part, and this is what exists by chance or by accident. Again, do things exist for the most part without anything existing always at all, or are there things which exist eternally?[14] We must examine this later.[15] However, it is evident that there is no science of accidental being; for every science is of that which is always or for the most part. For how else will one be instructed or instruct another; for it must be definitely stated that this is so either always or for the most part, for example, that for the most part honey-water is beneficial to a patient with fever. But science cannot state the exception to what occurs for the most part; for example, it cannot say "this benefit will not occur on the day of the new moon", for then the non-occurrence of benefit on the day of the new moon will itself be a thing which is either always or for the most part, and an accident is something other than what is always or for the most part.[16] We have stated, then, what an accident is, through what cause it exists, and that there is no science of it.

3

That there exist principles and causes which are generable and destructible but which are not in the process of being generated and destroyed, is evident. For if this is not the case, everything will exist of necessity, that is, if there must be a non-accidental cause for whatever is being generated or is being destroyed.[1] Will A exist or not? Yes, if B occurs; otherwise it will not. And B will exist if C occurs. And in this manner it is clear that as one always subtracts time from a given finite time he will come to the present.[2] Thus, this man will die by disease or violence, if he goes out; and he will go out if he gets thirsty; and he will get thirsty if something else happens; and in this manner we shall come to something which now exists, or to something which occurred in the past. For example, if he is thirsty; he will be so if he eats pungent food, and this either is the case or is not. Thus of necessity he will die, or he will not die. And similarly if one crosses over to past events, the argument is the same; for the last thing to which we come already exists in something, I mean the occurrence in the past. All future things, then, will be of necessity. For example, he who lives will die; for something already happened, for example, the presence of contraries in the same body. But whether he will die by disease or violence is not yet definite, unless so-and-so occurs.[3] It is clear, then, that the process goes back to a principle, but this no longer goes back to something else. This, then, will be the principle of what occurs by chance, and no other thing will be the cause of this. But to what kind of principle or what kind of cause we are thus led back, whether to a principle in the sense of matter or in the sense of final cause or in the sense of moving cause, is something which requires the utmost consideration.

4

So much for accidental being, then, for we have described it sufficiently. As for being in the sense of true, and nonbeing in the sense of false, these are about a combination and a division,[1] and taken

30

1027b

5

10

15

20   together they are about the two parts of a contradiction. For in the
case of truth, affirmation is of objects which are combined, and denial
is of objects which are divided, but in the case of falsity, affirmation is
of objects which are divided and denial of objects which are combined.
How it happens that we think things together or apart is another problem. By "thinking things together or apart" I do not mean thinking them
25   in succession one after another, but so thinking them that they become
a unity of a sort;² for falsity and truth are not in things (for example,
it is not the good that is true, nor the bad by itself that is false), but in
*thought.*³ As for the simple things and the whatness of them, not even
in *thought* is there truth or falsity of them.⁴ What should be investigated
with regard to being and nonbeing in this sense, then, is something to
be considered later.⁵

30   But since combining and dividing exist in *thought* and not in things,
and being in this sense is distinct from being in the main sense (for
thought attaches to or detaches from the subject⁶ either a whatness⁷ or
a quality or a quantity or something else), we must leave aside accidental being and being in the sense of truth. For in the first case the
1028a cause is indefinite, in the second it is an affection of *thought;* both are
about the remaining genus of being, and they do not make clear any
nature of being as existing outside.⁸ And so, leaving these aside, we
should examine the causes and principles of being itself qua being. It
5   is evident from our account of the various senses of terms, then, that
the term "being" has these many senses.

Book **Z**

1

10   The term "being" is used in several senses, as we pointed out previously in our account of the various senses of terms.[1] In one sense, it signifies whatness and a *this;*[2] in another, it signifies a quality or a quantity or one of the others which are predicated in this way. Although "being" is used in so many senses, it is evident that of these the primary

15   sense is whatness, and used in this sense it signifies a substance. For when we state that this has some quality, we say that it is good or bad but not that it is three cubits long[3] or a man; but when we state what it is, we say that it is a man or a god but not white or hot or three cubits long. The others are called "beings" in view of the fact that they are quantities of being which is spoken of in this primary sense, or

20   qualities of it, or affections of it, or something else of this kind. Because of this, one might even raise the problem whether walking, being healthy, sitting, and the others of this kind are beings or not beings;[4] for by nature each of these does not exist by itself and cannot be sepa-

25   rated from a substance, but rather, if anything, it is that which walks or that which sits or that which is healthy that is a being. These latter appear to be beings to a higher degree, because there is something definite in each of them, namely, the underlying subject; and this is the substance and the individual, which is indicated in the corresponding predication, for we do not use the terms "the good" and "that which

30   sits"[5] without including the substance. It is clear, then, that each of the others exists because substances exist.[6] Thus, being in the primary sense, not in a qualified sense but without qualification,[7] would be a substance.

    Now the term "primary" [or "first", or "prior to all others"] is used in many senses, yet a substance is primary in every sense: in formula, in knowledge, and in time. For of the other categories no one is sepa-

35   rable, but only substance.[8] And in formula, too, substance is primary; for in the formula of each of the other categories the formula of a

substance must be present.[9] And we think we understand each thing
to the highest degree when we know, for example, what a man is or
1028*b*   what fire is, rather than their quality or their quantity or their whereness,[10] and even of these latter, we understand each when we know
what a quantity is or what a quality is.[11] And indeed the inquiry or
perplexity concerning what being is, in early times and now and always,
is just this: What is a substance? For it is this that some assert to be
5   one,[12] others more than one,[13] and some say that it is finite, while others
that it is infinite.[14] And so we, too, must speculate most of all, and first
of all, and exclusively, so to say, concerning being which is spoken of
in this sense. What is being?

2

Substance is thought to belong most evidently to bodies; and so we
10   say that animals and plants and their parts are substances, and also
the natural bodies, such as fire and water and earth and each one of
this sort, and also parts of these, and composites of these (either of
parts or of all of them), such as the heavens and its parts, the stars and
the Moon and the Sun. We must inquire whether these alone are sub-
15   stances or also others, or some of these and some others, or none of
these but some others.
Some thinkers[1] are of the opinion that the limits of bodies are substances, such as surfaces and lines and points and units, and that they
are substances to a higher degree than bodies or solids. Moreover,
some[2] think that no such as the ones just mentioned exist, but only
sensible objects; but others[3] think that such do exist, and that they are
many[4] and are eternal and are beings to a higher degree, as in the case
20   of Plato, who posits two [kinds of] substances, the Forms and the
Mathematical Objects, and also the sensible bodies as the third kind.
Speusippus spoke of yet a greater number [of kinds] of substances, and
of distinct principles for each kind; he starts from the *One* as a principle
for numbers, posits another principle for magnitudes, still another for
soul, and in this manner he extends the kinds of substances.[5] Still
25   others[6] say that the Forms and the Numbers have the same nature, and
that from these follow all the others, such as the lines, the planes, and
so on, all the way down to the substances of the universe and the sensible substances.
Concerning these matters we must examine what is stated well and
what is not, which are the substances, whether there are other sub-
30   stances besides the sensible or not and how these exist,[7] whether there
exist separate substances other than sensible substances or not, and if

yes, then why such exist and how. But first, we must sketch out what a substance is.

3

The term "substance" is spoken of, if not in more,[1] still in four main senses; for the essence is thought to be the substance[2] of an individual, and the universal, and the genus, and fourthly the underlying subject. The subject is that of which the others are said, but the subject itself is not said of anything else.[3] And so we must describe first the subject; for the primary[4] subject is thought to be a substance in the highest degree.

In one sense, the subject is said to be the matter; in another sense, it is said to be the *form;* in a third, it is said to be the composite of these. By "matter" I mean, for instance, bronze;[5] by "*form*", the shape of its outward appearance; and by "the composite of these", the statue as a *composite*. Thus, if the form[6] is prior[7] to matter and is a being to a higher degree than matter, for the same reason it will be prior to the composite of form and matter.

We have now stated sketchily what a substance is, that it is that which is not said of a subject but of which the others are said. But we must not state it only in this manner, as this is not enough. The statement itself is not clear,[8] and further, matter becomes a substance. For if this is not a substance, we are at a loss as to what else is a substance. If the others are taken off, nothing appears to remain. For, of the others, some are affections and actions and potencies of bodies, while length and width and depth are quantities and not substances (for a quantity is not a substance), but that to which as first[9] these belong is a substance to a higher degree. Yet if length and width and depth are removed, we observe nothing left, unless there is something bounded by these; so matter alone must appear to be a substance, if we inquire in this manner. By "matter" I mean that which in itself is not stated as being the whatness of something, nor a quantity, nor any of the other senses of "being". For there is something of which each of these is a predicate, whose being[10] is other than that of each of the predicates; for all the others are predicates[11] of a substance, while a substance[12] is a predicate[11] of matter. Thus, this last is in itself neither a whatness nor a quantity nor any of the others; and it is not a denial of any of these, for even a denial belongs to something accidentally.[13]

From what has been said, it follows that matter is a substance. But this is impossible; for to be separable and a *this* is thought to belong most of all to a substance. Accordingly, the form or the *composite*

30   would seem to be a substance to a higher degree than matter.[14] The
       composite substance, that is, the composite of matter and *shape*, may
       be laid aside; for it is posterior[15] and clear. Matter, too, is in a sense
       evident.[16] But we must examine the third, for this is the most perplexing.
           It is agreed that there exist substances[17] among the sensibles, so we
1029*b*3   must first inquire into the sensibles. For, it is useful to proceed from the
       less to the more known. Instruction is acquired by all in this manner:
5   through the less known by nature to the more known by nature; and
       just as in conduct, in which the purpose is to start from what is good
       to each individual[18] and make good to each individual that which is
       good in general, so here, the purpose is to start from what is more
       known to the individual and proceed to make known to the individual
       what is known by nature. Now what is known and first to each individual
10   is often known slightly and has little or no being.[19] Nevertheless, from
       what is poorly knowable but knowable to oneself one must make an
       effort to know what is generally knowable, proceeding, as we stated,
       from what is knowable to oneself.

           4

1   Since we have specified in the beginning[1] the number of ways in
2   which the term "substance" is used, and one of these was thought to
13   be the essence, we must investigate this. And first let us make some
       logical remarks[2] about it. The essence of each thing is what the thing
15   is said to be in virtue of itself.[3] The essence of you is not the essence
       of a musician; for, it is not in virtue of yourself that you are a musician.
       Your essence, then, is what you are in virtue of yourself; but not in every
       sense of the expression "in virtue of yourself", for, it is not in this sense
       that a surface is white in virtue of itself, since to be a surface[4] is not to
       be white.[5] Moreover, the essence of a surface is not the essence of both,
       that is, of a white surface. Why not? Because "surface" reappears in
20   the expression of its own essence. In the expression of the essence of a
       thing, in other words, the term signifying the thing must not appear
       as a part. Thus, if to be a white surface is to be a smooth surface, then
       to be white[6] and to be smooth are one and the same.
           Since composites exist also with respect to the other categories (for
       there is some underlying subject in each case, as in quality, quantity,
25   whenness, whereness, and in motion),[7] we must inquire whether there
       is a formula of the essence for each of them and whether essence belongs
       to them; for example, whether to a white man belongs an essence of a
       white man. Let the term "a cloak" signify a white man. What is the
       essence of a cloak? But "a cloak" does not signify something which is

30　said to be in virtue of itself.[8] Perhaps "not in virtue of itself" has two senses, one by addition, the other not by addition. In the first sense, that which is being defined is stated by being attached to something else, for example, if, in defining the essence of white, one were to state the formula of a white man; in the second sense, if to something something else is attached, for example, if "a cloak" were to signify a white

1030a　man, and one were to define a cloak as white. Now a white man is white, indeed, yet his essence is not the essence of white.

But is to be a cloak an instance of an essence at all, or not? But an essence is just a *this*,[9] whereas if something is said of[10] something else we do not have just a *this*; for example, a white man is not just a *this*,

5　if a *this* belongs only to substances. Thus, there is an essence only of those things whose formula is a definition. However, there is a definition, not if a name and its formula merely have the same meaning (for then all formulae will be definitions, since there can be a name having the same meaning as any given formula, and so even the *Iliad*[11] would be

10　a definition), but if the name and its formula signify something primary;[12] and in the formula of such a primary being it is not the case that something is said of[10] something else. Essence, then, will belong to nothing which is not a species of a genus, but only to a species[13] of a genus; for it is these that are thought to be stated neither in virtue of participation, nor with an attribute, nor with an accident.[14] As for

15　the others, if there is a name for each of them, there will be a formula signifying that this belongs to that, or instead of a simplified formula one that is more accurate;[15] but there will be no definition and no essence.

Or else, the term "definition" like the term "whatness" has many senses; for in one sense the term "whatness" signifies a substance and

20　a *this*, in another it signifies each of the other categories, a quantity, a quality, and the like. For, just as existence belongs to all although not similarly, but to some[16] primarily and to others[17] secondarily, so whatness belongs to substances in the full sense but to the others in a qualified way. We might even ask of a quality "What is it?", so that a

25　quality, too, is an instance of whatness, although not in the full sense[18], but just as, in the case of nonbeing, some use the verbal expression "nonbeing is", not that nonbeing simply exists but that nonbeing is nonbeing, so with the whatness of a quality.

Thus, we must also consider how we should express ourselves on each point, but we must not allow our expression to go beyond the facts.[19] And so now, since what we have said is evident, in a similar

30　manner an essence will belong primarily and in the full sense to a substance; and it will belong also to the others, just as the whatness will, not as an essence in the full sense, but as an essence of a quality,

or of a quantity, or etc. For we must say that these latter are beings
either by equivocation, or by adding and subtracting (as when we say
that the unknowable is knowable),[20] although it is in a way right to
35   call them "beings" neither equivocally nor in the same sense, seeing
that they are like what we call "medical", which are neither one and
1030b   the same thing nor called "medical" equivocally, but are called so in
view of the fact that they are related to one and the same thing; for
the materials and the operation and the instrument are called "medical"
neither equivocally nor with one meaning, but in relation to one thing.

Anyway, it makes no difference whichever way one wishes to speak
5   about these things; what is evident is the fact that definitions and
essences, in the primary and unqualified sense, are of substances alone.
There are also definitions and essences of the others[21] in a similar manner, but not in the primary sense. If we posit this, it is not necessary
that there be a definition of a term if the term and its formula have the
same meaning, unless the formula is of a certain kind, namely, a formula
which signifies one thing,[22] not one by continuity as in the case of the
10   *Iliad*[23] or of things which are bound together,[24] but one in any of the
main senses of "one". The senses of "one" correspond to those of "being", and "being" signifies a *this,* or a quantity, or a quality.[25] And so
there will be a formula and a definition even of a white man, but in a
sense distinct from that of whiteness and that of a substance.

5

If one denies that a formula by addition is a definition, a *difficulty*
15   arises as to whether there can be a definition of anything which is not
simple but is a combination, for this must be indicated by an additional
term. What I mean, for example, is this: there is a nose and concavity,
and also snubness, which is stated in terms of the two, since one of
them is in the other, and concavity[1] or snubness is an *attribute* of a
20   nose not by accident but essentially; and it is in the nose not as whiteness is in Callias or in a man (by the fact that Callias is white, to whom
the essence of man happens to belong), but as the male is in the animal
and as the equal is in quantity and as all the attributes are in things to
which they are said to belong essentially. And each of these *attributes*
(a) has in its formula the formula or the name of the subject of which
it is the *attribute* and (b) cannot be signified apart from that subject.
For example, whiteness can be signified apart from the man, but the
25   female cannot be signified apart from the animal.[2] Thus, either there
is no essence and no definition of any of these *attributes,* or if there is,
it is in another way, as we said.[3]

But there is also another *difficulty* concerning such *attributes*. For if a snub nose and a concave nose are the same, snubness and concavity will be the same; but if the latter two are not the same (because one cannot speak of snubness apart from the thing of which it is an essential *attribute*, for snubness is concavity in the nose), then either one should not say "a snub nose" or he will be saying the same thing twice, namely, "a concave nose nose"; for "a snub nose" will be "a concave nose nose". And so it is absurd that such things should have an essence; otherwise, there is an infinite regress, for in "a snub nose nose" there will be still another "nose".[4]

Clearly, then, only of a substance is there a definition. For if there is a definition of the other categories also, it must be by addition, as in the case of a quality or oddness; for oddness cannot be defined without a number, nor a female[5] without an animal. In saying "by addition", I mean an expression in which the same term is stated twice, as in the examples cited. And if this is true, neither can there be a definition of a combined pair, such as an odd number. Yet we fail to see that the formulae are not stated accurately. But if there are definitions of these, too, then either they are definitions in another sense, or, as we stated,[6] we should say that "a definition" and "an essence" have many senses. Thus, in one sense, a definition and an essence can belong to nothing but substances, but in another sense, they can belong also to other things.

It is clear, then, that a definition is a formula of an essence, and that there are essences either of substances alone, or of substances in the highest sense and primarily and in the full sense.

6

We should inquire whether each thing and its essence[1] are the same[2] or distinct. This is useful for our inquiry into *substance;*[3] for each thing is thought to be nothing else but its own *substance*, and the essence is said to be the *substance* of each thing.

Now of a thing which is stated accidentally,[4] it would seem that the thing is distinct from its essence, for example, a white man is distinct from the essence of a white man; for if these were the same, the essence of a man and the essence of a white man would be the same, for a man and a white man are the same, as people say, and so the essence of a white man would be the same as the essence of a man.[5] Or, it is not necessary for accidental being to be the same as its essence.[6] For it is not in such a way that the outer terms become the same, since what would perhaps happen is this, namely, that the outer terms which are accidental to the same term would be the same; for example, the essence of white and the essence of musical[7] would be the same, and this seems not to be the case.[8]

As for things which are stated by themselves,[9] is it necessary for them to be the same as their essences? For example, this would be the
30   case if some substances exist, like the Ideas posited by some thinkers, prior to which other *substances* or natures exist.[10] For if Good Itself were distinct from the essence of Good,[11] Animal Itself from the essence
1031*b*   of Animal, and Being from the essence of Being, then besides the ones posited there would be other substances and natures and 'Ideas', and these latter would be also prior to the former, that is, if an *essence* is a substance. And if the two kinds were severed from each other,[12] there would be no science of the former,[13] and the latter would not be be-
5   ings.[14] (By "being severed" I mean this, that neither the essence of Good belongs to Good Itself, nor Good Itself to the essence of Good).[15] For there is a science of each thing only when we know its essence. And as it is with the Good, so it is with the others. So if the essence of Good were not Good, neither would the essence of Being be Being, nor would the essence of *One* be *One*.[16]

10   Now all essences exist alike in this manner, or else none of them does so exist; so that if the essence of being is not a being, neither will any of the others be in the same way.[17] Moreover, if the essence of good does not[18] belong to something, this will not be good. Conse- quently, the good and the essence of good must be one,[19] the beauti- ful[20] and the essence of beautiful must be one, and so with all others which are stated not of something else but by themselves and are pri-
15   mary.[21] For if this is so, it is also adequate, even if no Forms exist;[22] and perhaps more so even if Forms do exist.[23] At the same time it is clear that if indeed there exist Ideas such as some assert, the underlying subject[24] will not be a substance; for these would of necessity be sub- stances but could not be predicated of a subject; otherwise, they would exist by being participated in.[25]

From these arguments it is clear that each thing and its essence are
20   one and the same[26] but not by accident,[27] and that to *know* each thing is to *know* its essence, and so even by exhibiting particular instances,[28] it is clear that a thing and its essence must be one.

As for the thing which is stated accidentally,[29] such as the musical and the white, since the terms "the musical" and "the white" have double meanings, it is not true to say that the thing and its essence are the same;
25   for both the subject to which the attribute belongs and the attribute itself are called "white", so in one sense the thing and its essence are

the same, but in another sense they are not the same; for the essence of white is not the same as the man or the white man, but it is the same as the attribute white.[30]

The absurdity would be apparent also if one were to use a name for each essence; for there would be an essence also of an essence, for example, there would be an essence also of the essence of a horse. If so, why should not some things[31] be their essences from the start, if indeed an essence is a *substance*? Moreover, not only a thing and its essence are one,[32] but also the formula of each is the same, as is clear also from what has been said; for it is not by accident that the essence of unity and unity are one.[33] Further, if unity and the essence of unity were distinct, the process would go on to infinity; for, there would be the essence of unity and also unity, so that according to the same argument there would again be the essence of the essence of unity and also the essence of unity, etc.

Of things which are primary and are stated by themselves, then, it is clear that each of them and its essence are one and the same. Evidently, the sophistical refutations of this position and the problem whether Socrates and the essence of Socrates are the same are solved in the same way; for in solving a problem successfully, it makes no difference whether one is answering another's questions or is using the arguments for the solution of that problem. We have stated, then, how each thing and its essence are the same and how they are not the same.

7

Of things which are generated,[1] some are generated by nature,[2] others by art,[3] still others by chance;[4] but every thing generated is generated by something,[5] and out of something,[6] and it becomes something. By "becomes something" I mean that it becomes something according to each[7] of the categories; for it becomes either a *this*,[8] or a quantity, or a quality, or it comes to be somewhere. A natural generation is a generation of something which is generated from nature; that out of which something is generated is what we call "matter"; that by which it is generated is a thing which exists by nature; and that which is generated is a man or a plant or something else of this kind, which we call "a substance" in the highest degree. Now all things which are generated, whether by nature or by art, have matter; for there is a potentiality for each of them to be, and also not to be, and this potentiality is the matter in each. Universally, that out of which something is generated is a nature, that with respect to which it is generated is a nature[9] (for, that which is generated, such as a plant or an animal, has a nature),

and that by which something else is generated is a nature, the so-called
"nature according to form", and this is of the same kind as the nature
of the thing generated but exists in another thing, for a man gives birth
to a man.[10]

This is the way, then, in which things are generated through nature,
and the other generations are called "productions". All productions are
generations by art, or by a power, or by *thought*.[11] However, some of
these are also generations by *chance* or by luck, and in this manner
they resemble the generations by nature; for, among things generated,
there are some which are the same [in species], whether generated from
seed or without seed.[12] We shall examine these matters later.[13]

Things generated by art are those whose form is in the soul.[14] By
"form" I mean the essence of each thing and the first *substance*,[15] for
even contraries have in some sense the same form; for the opposite
substance is the privation of the other *substance*, as in the case of disease
and health, for disease is made known by the absence of health, and
"health" is the formula in the soul and in *knowledge*.[16] Now the healthy
is generated when a man thinks as follows: since health is so-and-so, if
the subject is to be healthy it must have such-and-such, let us say uniformity, and if uniformity, then warmth; and he always thinks in this
manner until he arrives at something final which he himself can produce. Then the motion from this instant onward, which here is a motion
towards health, is called "production". Thus, it turns out that in a sense
health is generated from health,[17] and a house from a house (that is,
the material house from the house without matter), for the medical art
and the building art are the forms, respectively, of health and of the
house. By "substance without matter" I mean the essence.

Of the generations and motions just considered, one of them is called
"thinking" and the other "production"; thinking occurs from the principle or the form,[18] production from the end of thinking and thereafter.
The intermediate steps take place in a similar manner. What I mean,
taking an example, is this: If one is to be healthy, his body must be
made uniform. What is uniformity? It is so-and-so. And this will come
to be if the body is made warm. What is warmth? It is so-and-so. Now
this is potentially in the body, and it is up to the doctor to make it
actual in the body. Now if the generation is from art, that which produces and from which the motion towards health begins is the form in
the soul; but if the generation is by chance, it is whatever begins the
production in a manner in which production would begin by him who
produces by art, as in healing which begins perhaps by warming, and
the doctor does this by rubbing.[19] Accordingly, warmth in the body
is either a part of health or is followed, directly or through a number
of stages, by such a thing which is a part of health. This is the last

thing that acts and is a part in this sense,[20] but in another sense that part is the materials, as the stones of a house,[21] and similarly for the others.

So, as the saying goes,[22] nothing could be generated if nothing were existing before. It is evident, then, that some part of the thing generated must exist before, for matter is a part; for matter is present during the generation and it is this matter that is becoming something.[23] But is this matter also a part in the formula of the thing? In stating what bronze spheres are, we do so in both ways; that is, we may include the matter of the sphere by saying that it is bronze, or by saying that the form is such-and-such a figure; and "figure" is the first genus in which the bronze circle is placed.[24] The bronze sphere, then, has matter in its formula.

In some cases, after the thing has been generated, it is called, when referred to the matter out of which it was generated, not "that" but "that-y" [or "that-en"];[25] for example, the statue is called not "stone" but "stony". However, a healthy man is not called after that from which he becomes healthy; the cause of this is the fact that he comes to be healthy from the privation as well as from the subject which we call "matter" (that is, both the man becomes healthy and the sick becomes healthy), but we speak of him as becoming healthy from the privation rather than from the subject, that is, he becomes healthy from being sick rather than from being a man. Thus, it is not the sick that is called "healthy", but the man, and he is called "a healthy man".[26] But if the privation is unclear and nameless, and such would be any chance figure of bronze, or of bricks and timber for a house, the generation from these with such privation seems to be like the generation from the sick.[27] So, just as we do not say of a healthy man, who became so from being sick, that he is a sick man, so of the statue we say not that it is wood[28] but (by varying the word) that it is wooden, not bronze but brazen, not stone but stony, and of the house not bricks but brick-en; for, if we look at the situation very carefully, we would not say without qualification that the wood becomes a statue, or the bricks a house,[29] since that which becomes must change and not remain. It is because of this fact that we speak in this manner.

8

Since that which is generated is generated by something (by "something" here I mean the source which begins generation), and out of something (let this be not the privation but the matter; we have already specified[1] the sense in which we use the term "matter"), and it becomes

something (this is a sphere or a circle or whatever else it may happen
to be), just as one does not make the underlying subject (for example,
the bronze),[2] so he does not make the sphere, except accidentally; that
is, what he makes is the bronze sphere, and since the bronze sphere is
a sphere, he makes the sphere accidentally. For, to make a *this* is, in
short, to make it out of an underlying subject. I mean that to make the
bronze round[3] is not to make the roundness or the sphere but some other
thing, namely, to make this form in something else. For, if one were to
make the form, he would have to make it out of something else; for
this was assumed.[4] For example, one makes a bronze sphere in this
manner: out of this, which is bronze, he makes that,[5] and this is a sphere.
If, then, he were to make also the sphere itself, clearly he would have
to make it in the same manner, and the generations would have to go
on to infinity.[6]

It is evident, then, that the form (or whatever we ought to call the
shape in the sensible thing) is not being generated, nor is there a generation of it,[7] nor is an essence[8] generated; for this is that which is
generated in something else by art or nature or a power. What one
makes is an existing bronze sphere, for he makes it from bronze and
a sphere;[9] he produces the form in the matter, and the result is a bronze
sphere. But if the essence of a sphere is to be generated at all, it will
have to be so out of something. For that which is generated must always
be divisible, and one part must be this and another that; that is, one
part must be matter and the other form. Accordingly, if a sphere is a
figure equidistant from the center, one part of this would have to be
that-in-which and this part he would not make, the other part would
have to be that which he produces in the first part, and the whole would
have to be the thing generated,[10] as in the case of the bronze sphere.
So it is evident from what has been said that what is called "a form"
or "a *substance*" is not generated, but what is generated is the *composite* which is named according to that form, and that there is matter[11]
in everything that is generated, and in the latter one part is this and
another that.[12]

Does a sphere, then, exist apart from the individual material spheres,
or a house apart from those made of bricks?[13] Or, if the form existed
apart as a *this,* is it not the case that no generation of it would ever be
possible?[14] But "form" signifies a *such*[15] and this is not a *this* and a
definite[16] thing; and what the artist makes or the man begets is a *such*
from a this,[17] and what is generated is a *such* this.[18] Thus, the entire *this*
is Callias, or Socrates, just as in the other case it is the individual bronze
sphere; and in general, a man or an animal is like a bronze sphere.

It is evident, then, that the causes of forms,[19] if we take these to be
what some thinkers are in the habit of calling "Forms", if such[20] exist

apart from the individuals, are of no use in the generation and the *sub-stances* of things; and at least because of this, Forms need not exist as substances by themselves.[21] Indeed, it is even evident in some cases that that which generates another is like that which is generated, not numerically one and the same but one in species, as in natural genera-tions; for a man begets a man, unless something is generated contrary to nature, as for example a mule by a horse. And even in such cases a similarity exists; for that which would be common to a horse and an ass, the genus next above them, has no name, but both a horse and an ass would come equally under that genus as if under the genus "mule". So it is evident that there is no need at all of setting up a Form as a pattern (for we should have looked for such forms [or Forms] in physical substances above all, since these are substances in the highest degree); but that which begets is sufficient to produce and to be the cause of the form in the matter. And when the whole has been generated, such a form in this flesh and these bones, this is Callias or Socrates; and this is distinct from that which generated it because the matter is distinct,[22] but it is the same in species since the species is indivisible.

9

We might inquire why some things, such as health, are generated both by art and by chance while others, such as a house, are not so generated. The cause is this: In the making and the generation of things by art, the matter which is the starting-point of the generation, in which[1] part of the thing generated exists, is in some cases such that it can be moved by itself, but in other cases it cannot be so moved; and if it can, in some cases it can be moved by itself in some special way, but in other cases it cannot be so moved. For many things can be moved by them-selves, but not in a special way like dancing. Accordingly, things whose matter is of the latter kind, stones, for example, cannot be moved in some special way except by something else, but they can be moved in some other way by themselves.[2] Fire, too, is a thing of this kind. It is because of this that some things will not come to be without that which possesses the art, but others will;[3] for, in the latter case, the matter will be moved by that which does not have the art but which can be moved by itself, or by another thing which does not have the art, or by a part of the thing.[4]

From what we have said it is also clear that, as in things generated by nature, so here, if a thing is not generated by accident, then it is generated by something which, or by a part of it which, has in some sense the same name as the thing itself (for example a house is generated

by a house),[5] or by the intellect,[6] for the art here is the form[7] of the
25   house in the intellect; or, by a part with the same name,[8] or by something
having such a part, for the first essential cause[9] of producing is a part.
For the heat in the motion produces the heat in the body, and this heat
is either health, or a part of health, or is followed by a part of health or
30   by health itself. And so it is the heat in motion that is said to produce
health; that is, the heat in motion, followed by the heat which results
in the body, makes health. Thus, as in syllogisms, the beginning of all
is the *substance*. For syllogisms proceed from the whatness of things,
and so do these generations.[10]

Things which are formed by nature are like the generations just considered. For the seed acts just like things which act by art since it has
1034b the form potentially, and that from which the seed proceeds has the
same name as that which the seed becomes, but only in a sense (for we
must not expect the same name in every generation as in "a man from
a man", since we also have "a woman from a man"; and this is why, if
what is generated is not abnormal, a mule is not generated by a mule).[11]
But things by nature which are generated by chance are, as in the case
5   of things generated by art, those whose matter can be moved also by
itself in the way in which it can be moved by the seed;[12] but things
whose matter cannot be so moved by itself cannot be generated otherwise than by things like themselves.[13]

It is not with respect to substance alone that our argument reveals
that the form is not generated;[14] the argument is alike common with
10   respect to all primary[15] forms, such as those of quantity, of quality, and
of the other categories. For just as it is the bronze sphere that is generated, but not the sphere or the bronze, and likewise for the bronze
itself if this is generated[16] (for the matter and the form[17] must always
pre-exist), so also in the case of whatness, and of quality, and of quantity,
and of the other categories, the situation is similar; for it is not a certain
15   quality that is generated but the wood with that quality, and it is not a
certain quantity but the wood or the animal with that quantity. But a
property of substances alone may be observed from what has been said,
namely, that there must actually pre-exist, other than what is generated,
a substance which is acting, for example, an animal, if what is generated
is an animal; but this is not necessary in the case of a quality or a
quantity, except potentially only.[18]

10

20   Since a definition is a formula, and every formula has parts, and since
a formula is related to the thing in a similar way as a part of the

formula to the corresponding part[1] of the thing, we may now raise the question whether the formulae of the parts should be present in the formula of the whole or not. For they appear to be present in some
25 cases, but not in others. The formula of a circle does not have the formula of the segments of the circle, but the formula of a syllable does have the formula of its letters; yet the circle is divisible into segments just as the syllable into its letters. Moreover, if the parts are prior to the whole, and the acute angle is a part of the right angle and the finger
30 is a part of the animal, the acute would be prior to the right angle and the finger would be prior to the man. But the latter are regarded as prior[2] to the former; for in each case, the formula of the part has the formula of the whole, and the whole is prior in existence to the part since it can exist without it.[3]

In fact, the term "a part" has many meanings, and in one sense it means: that which measures with respect to quantity.[4] But let us dis-
1035a miss this and inquire about the parts of the *substance* of a thing. If, then, there is matter, and form, and the *composite* of the two, and each of them is a substance, in one sense even matter is called "a part" of a thing, while in another sense this is not so, but the only parts are the elements out of which the formula of the form consists. For example,
5 flesh is not a part of concavity (for flesh is the matter in which concavity comes to be), but it is a part of snubness; and of the *composite* statue the bronze is a part, but it is not a part of that which is called "the form" of the statue.[5] For what should[6] be stated is the form, or the thing qua having that form, but the material part should[6] never be stated by itself.
10 This is why the formula of the circle does not have the formula of its segments,[7] but the formula of the syllable does have the formula of its letters; for the letters are parts of the formula of the form and are not matter,[8] but the segments are parts in the sense that they are the matter which receives the form of a circle. Yet the segments of the circle are nearer to the form than the bronze is, that is, when the bronze takes on the form of roundness.[9]
15 In a sense, however, not all sorts of letters of a syllable are in the formula of the syllable, if, for example, these are individuals made of wax or are sounds in the air; for these are now parts of the syllable as sensible matter. For even if a line is destroyed into its halves when divided, and a man is likewise destroyed into bones and muscles and flesh, the line and the man, because of this, are not composed of these
20 in the sense that these are parts of the *substance* of a line and of a man, respectively, but in the sense that these are parts as matter;[10] and they are parts of the *composite* but in no way parts of the form or of what is signified by the formula; and this is why these are not present in each formula.

The formula, in the case of some things, then, will have the formula
of such parts,[11] but the formula in the case of other things should not,
that is, if the formula is not of a *composite*.[12] It is because of this that
some things are composed of those elements as their principles[13] into
25   which they are destroyed, but others are not. Things which are *composites* of form and matter, then, such as the snub or the bronze circle,
are reduced, when destroyed, to those elements and have matter as a
part; but things which do not include matter but are without matter,
and whose formulae are of the form only, are not destroyed, either not
30   at all or at least not in this way.[14] So in the former case those elements
are principles and parts of the things, but they are neither parts nor
principles of their form. And it is because of this that a clay statue is
reduced to clay when destroyed, and a bronze sphere to bronze, and
Callias to flesh and bones, and, we may add, the circle[15] is reduced to
1035b   segments, since this circle is something which includes matter; for the
term "the circle" is equivocally used to name any circle without qualification and also an individual circle, because there are no proper names
for individual circles.[16]

Although the truth has just been stated, let us state it still more
clearly, taking up the problem once more. Those which are parts of the
5   formula, and into which the formula is divisible, are prior, either all or
some of them.[17] However, the formula of the right angle is not divisible
into[18] the formula of the acute angle, but the formula of the acute angle
does have that of the right; for in defining the acute angle one uses the
right angle, since an acute angle is an angle less than a right angle.[19]
10   The situation is similar in the case of the circle and the semicircle, for
the semicircle is defined in terms of the circle; and the finger, too, is
defined in terms of the whole, for a finger is such-and-such a part of a
man. Thus, such parts which exist as matter and into which the whole
is divisible as into its matter, are posterior;[20] but those which are parts
of the formula or of the *substance* (that is, substance according to the
formula) are prior, either all or some of them.[17] And[21] since the soul of
15   an animal (for this is the *substance* of an ensouled body) according to
formula is the *substance* or the form or the essence of such a body, each
part of the latter,[22] if defined well, will not be defined without its function, and this [function] cannot exist in that part without sensation;[23]
and so, while the parts of the soul, either all or some of them,[24] are
prior to the *composite* animal (and similarly in other individual cases),
20   the body[25] and its parts are posterior to this *substance*, and it is not
this *substance* but the *composite* that is divided into these parts[26] as into
its matter. Accordingly, in one sense these parts are prior to the *composite,* but in another sense they are not.[27] For they cannot exist if
separated from the whole; for it is a finger of an animal not in any man-

25   ner whatsoever, since it is equivocally called "a finger" if it is dead. However, in some cases the part is simultaneous[28] with the whole, and this is a principal part and is the first part in which the formula[29] or the *substance* of the thing is present, as for example the heart or the brain, if one of them happens to be such a part, although it does not matter which one of the two it is. But a man or a horse or any individual considered in this manner, but universally, is not a *substance* but a *com-*
30   *posite* of this formula and this matter, universally[30] taken; but a specified individual composed of this individual matter, this is now Socrates, and similarly in other cases.

    A part, then, may be a part of the form[31] (by "form" I mean essence), or of the *composite* of form and matter.[32] But the parts of the formula
1036a   are parts only of the form, and the formula is of the universal; for the essence of a circle and a circle are the same, and so are the essence of a soul and a soul. As for the *composite,* such as this circle, which is an individual, either sensible or intelligible (by "intelligible" I mean the
5   mathematical circle,[33] and by "sensible" I mean the bronze or wooden circle), of these there is no definition, but they are known by being thought[34] or sensed; and when the actuality of this knowledge ceases, it is not clear whether they exist any longer or not, but they are always spoken of and known by the universal formula.[35] As for matter, it is
10   unknowable in itself.[36] Some matter is sensible and some is intelligible; examples of sensible matter are bronze and wood and any movable matter,[37] but intelligible matter exists in sensible things but not qua sensible, as in the mathematical objects for example.

    We have discussed, then, the whole and the part, and also priority and posteriority concerning them. So if anyone asks whether it is the right
15   angle and the circle and the animal that are prior, or the parts into which these are divisible or of which they consist, we must say that a single answer cannot be given. For if also the soul is the living animal, or the soul of each individual is the individual, and the essence of a circle is the circle, and the essence or *substance* of the right angle is the right angle, then in some sense we should say that the whole is posterior to
20   the parts; for example, the right angle is posterior to the parts in its formula, and the individual right angle is posterior to its individual parts (both in the case of the bronze right angle which is with matter, and in the case of the one which is included by individual lines). On the other hand, while the right angle which is without matter is posterior to the parts in its formula, it is prior to each individual part.[38] So the answer cannot be given without qualification. And if the soul is not the
25   animal but is distinct from it, even so, some parts must be said to be prior and others posterior, as we stated.[39]

11

It is also reasonable to raise this problem, namely, what kind of parts are parts of the form and what are parts not of the form but of the *composite*. Indeed, if this is not clear, it is not possible to define a thing; for a definition is of the universal and of the form. If, then, it is not evident what kind of parts are parts as matter and what are parts not 30   as matter, neither will the formula of the thing be evident.

Now, in the case of things that appear to exist in subjects which are distinct in kind, as a circle may exist in bronze and stone and wood, it seems clear that the bronze and the stone are not parts of the *substance* of the circle, because the circle is separable from them.[1] But in the case 35   of things which are not seen to be separable, nothing prevents these 1036*b*   from being like the circle, as if all the circles that had been seen were of bronze; for the bronze would none the less be no part of the form, although it would then be difficult for *thought* to leave it out. For 5   example, the form of a man appears to exist always in flesh and bones and other such parts. Are these, then, parts of the form and of the formula? No, they are matter; but because the form does not exist in other kinds of matter, we are unable to separate the two.

Since this is thought to be possible,[2] although it is not clear in which cases, some thinkers raise a doubt even in the case of the circle and the triangle and regard it as not right to define these in terms of lines 10   and continuity, taking the position that we speak of lines and continuity in the case of triangles and circles just as we speak of flesh and bones in the case of a man, and of bronze and stone in the case of a statue; and they reduce all things to numbers and say that the formula of a line is the formula of two.[3] And of those who posit the Ideas, some say that 15   Two is Line Itself; but others say that Two is the form of Line, for these say that in some cases a thing is the same as the form of it, as in the case of Two and the form of Two, but that this is not so in the case of Line.[4] And so for these thinkers it turns out that there is one form for many things whose forms appear distinct, as it was indeed also for the 20   Pythagoreans;[5] and it is possible for them to make only one object, Form Itself, as the form of all things, and regard all the rest as not being forms, and in this way all things would indeed be one.[6]

We have stated, then, that there is some *difficulty* with regard to definitions, and why this is so. And so to try to reduce all things and to do away with matter is useless effort; for surely[7] some things are of a distinct form in a distinct matter, or they are such subjects disposed in 25   such-and-such a manner. And the comparison which Socrates the

younger used to make is not stated well; for it departs from the truth
and attempts to create the belief that a man may exist without his parts
just as a circle does without the bronze. But the two cases are not
similar; for an animal is sensible and cannot be defined without motion,
and so it cannot exist without its parts existing in a certain manner.
For it is not in any manner whatsoever that a hand is a part of the body,
but only when it can perform its function, so it must be alive; if not, it is
not a part.[8]

As for the mathematical objects, why are the formulae of the parts
not parts of the formulae of the wholes? For example, why are the
formulae of the semicircles not parts of the formula of the circle? For
these objects are not sensible. But does this make a difference? For even
some non-sensible things can have matter; for there is some matter in
every thing which is not just an essence and a form by itself but is a
this.[9] Accordingly, as we said before, the semicircles will not be parts
of a circle universally taken, but they will be parts of the individual
circles; for some matter is sensible and some is intelligible.

It is also clear that the soul is the first *substance*,[10] the body is the
matter, and a man or an animal, universally taken, is a *composite* of the
two; and "Socrates" or "Coriscus", if each term signifies also the soul of
the individual, has two senses (for some say that it is the soul that is the
individual, others that it is the *composite*), but if it signifies simply this
soul and this body,[11] then such an individual term is like the corresponding universal term.[12]

Whether there exists, besides the matter of such substances, another
kind of matter,[13] and so whether we should look for other substances as
the *substances* of these,[14] such as numbers or something of this sort,
should be considered later.[15] For it is for the sake of this that we are
also[16] trying to describe sensible substances, although in some sense
the investigation of sensible substances belongs to physics or second
philosophy; for the physicist must know not only about matter, but also
about *substance*[17] according to formula, and even more so about the
latter.[18] As for definitions, how the elements in a formula are parts and
why[19] a definition is one formula (for clearly the thing is one, and since
it has parts, it is one by virtue of something), these should be considered
later.[20]

What essence is and how it exists by itself, has been universally stated
for all cases;[21] and we have also stated why the formula of the essence
of some things has the parts of the thing defined but that of other things
does not have them, and that in the formula of the *substance* of a thing
the parts of the thing which exist as matter are not present, for these
are parts not of that *substance* but of the *composite* substance.[22] And
of the latter substance there is a formula in one sense, but in another

sense there is not. For there is no formula of it with its matter,[23] since this is indefinite, but there is a formula of it with respect to its first *substance*, for example, a formula of the soul in the case of a man. For this

30 *substance* is the form which is in the thing, and this form along with the matter is the *composite* thing, also called "a substance", as in the case of concavity; for from this and the nose a snub nose or snubness is composed ("nose" is present twice in "snub nose" or "snubness"); but in the *composite* substance, that is, in the snub nose or in Callias, matter is also present.[24] And we have stated that in some cases the

1037*b* essence of a thing and the thing are the same, as in first *substances*;[25] for example, curvature and its essence are the same, if curvature is a first *substance*. (By "first *substance*" I mean one which is not stated as being in something else or in an underlying subject as in matter). But

5 things which exist as matter, or which include matter, are not the same as their essence; nor are those things which are one by accident, such as Socrates and the musical, since these are the same by accident.[26]

12

Let us now deal first with definition, to the extent that we have not

10 done so in the *Analytics;* for the *difficulty* raised there[1] has a bearing upon our discussion of substance. The *difficulty* which I am refering to is this: Why is it that a thing, whose formula we call "a definition", is one? For example, let "a two-footed animal" be the formula of a man. Why then is this[2] one and not many, such as an animal and two-footed?

15 For in the case of "a man" and "white" we have many if whiteness does not belong to the man,[3] but we have one thing if it does belong and if the man, who is a subject, is affected[4] by the attribute; for then the two become one, and we have a white man. But in the former case, an animal does not participate in two-footedness; for the genus is not thought to participate in the differentiae,[5] otherwise the same thing

20 would be participating in contraries at the same time (since the differentiae by which the genus becomes different are contrary). Even if the genus does participate in them, the same argument exists, if indeed the differentiae are many, as for example, 'terrestrial', 'two-footed', and 'wingless'. For why are these one and not many? Not in view of the fact that they are present in the thing, for in this way there would be

25 a unity out of all.[6] But it is the elements in the definition that should be one;[7] for a definition is one formula and a formula of a *substance*, so that this formula must be of something which is one (for, in our manner of speaking, a *substance* is something which is one and indicates a *this*).

We should first examine definitions according to the way in which they are divided. Now there is nothing else in a definition but what is called "the first genus" and "the differentiae"; however, there are also other genera, the first genus and those formed when the differentiae are added to the first genus, for example, the first genus may be "animal",[8] the next "two-footed animal", then again "wingless two-footed animal", and similarly if a definition is stated with more terms. In general, it makes no difference whether the definition is stated with many or few terms, and so, whether with few or just two; and if with two, the one will be a differentia and the other a genus, as in "two-footed animal" for example, in which "animal" is the genus and "two-footed" the differentia.

If then a genus does not exist unqualifiedly apart from its species,[9] or if it exists but does so as matter[10] (for the 'voice' is a genus and[11] is matter, but the differentiae make the species or the letters out of it), it is evident that a definition is a formula composed of the differentiae.[12] Moreover, a differentia should be subdivided by its own differentiae. For example, if 'footed' is a differentia of 'animal', then again the differentiae of 'a footed animal' should be understood qua footed.[13] Therefore, if we are to state the subdivision correctly we should say, not that of footed animals some are winged but others are wingless (since we would be saying this through incapability), but that some are cloven-footed and others are not, for it is these that are the differentiae of a foot; for it is cloven-footedness that is a footedness.[14] And we should always proceed in this manner till we come to the differentiae which have no differentiae. When this is done, there will be as many species of footedness as there are [ultimate] differentiae, and the kinds of footed animals will be equal in number to these differentiae.

If this is so, then it is evident that the last differentia will be the *substance* of the thing and its definition,[12] if indeed one is not to state the same thing many times in the definition, for this would be redundant. And this does happen; for when one says "two-footed footed animal",[15] he is saying nothing else than "an animal, having feet, having two feet", and if he continues subdividing *properly* each differentia, he will be stating the same thing many times, as many as there are differentiae.[16] If then the differentia of the differentia is taken each time, the last one will be the form and the *substance;* but if one subdivides according to accidents, as in the subdivision of footedness into white and black, there will be as many differentiae as subdivisions.[17]

So it is evident that a definition is a formula composed of the differentiae, and of the last of these if the definition is right. This would be clear if the order of the terms in a definition were to be changed; for example, if one were to say that "a footed two-footed animal" is the definition of a man. For when "two-footed" has been stated, the term "footed" becomes redundant. But there is no order in the *substance* of a thing; for how are we to conceive one part posterior and another prior?[18]

35   Concerning definitions with respect to their manner of subdivision, then, let this preliminary statement as to what sort of things they are suffice.

13

1038*b*   Since our inquiry is about substance, let us return to it once more. Just as the underlying subject is called "a substance", and also the essence and the *composite* of the two, so too is the universal. We have
5   discussed two of them, the essence and the underlying subject; and a subject may underlie in two ways, (a) either by being a *this*, as an animal underlies its attributes, (b) or as matter underlies actuality.[1] The universal, too, is thought by some[2] to be a cause in the highest degree and to be a principle, so let us discuss also the universal; for it seems that it is impossible for any of the so-called "universals" to be a substance.

10   First, the *substance* of a thing is peculiar to it and does not belong to another thing,[3] but a universal is common; for by "a universal" we mean that whose nature is such that it may belong to many.[4] Of which of these, then, will the universal be the *substance*? Either of all or of none. But it cannot be the *substance* of all.[5] And if it is of one of them, this one will also be the others;[6] for things whose *substance* is one have
15   also one essence and are themselves one.[7]

            Again, that which is called "a substance"[8] is not said of a subject, but a universal is always said of some subject. But while a universal cannot be a *substance* in the manner[9] in which an essence is, can it not be present in a substance as 'animal' is in a man and a horse?[10] But clearly there is a formula of a universal. And it makes no difference
20   even if there is no formula of everything that is in the *substance;*[11] for this[12] will none the less be the *substance* of something,[13] as 'man'[14] is the *substance* of a man in whom it is present. If so, then again the same result will arise; for it will be, as 'animal' for example, the *substance* of that in which it is present as something peculiar to it.[15] More-over, it is impossible and absurd that what is a *this* and a substance, if
25   composed of parts, should not be composed of substances or of *this-es* but of a quality, for a non-substance or a quality would be prior to a substance and to a *this*.[16] This is indeed impossible; for neither in formula nor in time nor in generation[17] can the *attributes* of a substance

be prior to that substance, since otherwise they would be separable. Further, to Socrates, who is a substance, another substance[18] will be present, and so a substance will exist in two things.

In general, if 'man' or any other thing spoken of in this manner is a substance, it follows that neither is any part of its[19] formula a *substance* of anything nor does it exist apart from it or in something else;[20] I mean, for example, that neither does 'animal' exist apart from individual animals, nor does any other part of the formula so exist.

From these theoretical considerations, then, it is evident that none of the things that belong[21] universally is a substance, and that none of the common predicates signifies a *this*, but only a *such*.[22] Otherwise, many difficulties follow, and also the *third man*.[23]

Again, this is clear also from the following. No substance is composed of substances which exist in actuality; for two objects which exist thus in actuality are never one in actuality, but if they are two potentially, they can be one.[24] For example, the double line[25] is composed of two halves, but these latter exist potentially; for the actuality of each would make them separate.[26] Thus, if a substance is one, it cannot consist of substances which are present in it.[27] And in this sense Democritus speaks rightly; for, he says, it is impossible for one thing to consist of two things or for one thing to become[28] two things (for, he takes the position that substances are indivisible magnitudes). It is clear, then, that the situation with numbers is similar, if indeed a number is a composite of units, as is said by some; for, either the number two is not one thing, or no unit in the number two exists in actuality.

But there is a *difficulty* in this result. For, if no substance can be composed of universals because a universal indicates a *such* but not a *this,* and if no substance can be a composite of substances which exist in actuality, every substance would be incomposite,[29] and so there could be no formula of any substance. But it is the opinion of all and it has been stated earlier[30] that either of a substance alone is there a definition, or of a substance most of all; and now, even of the latter there seems to be no definition. If so, then there can be no definition of anything; or else, in a sense there can be, and in a sense there cannot. This statement will be clearer from what will be said later.[31]

14

From this discussion it is also evident what consequences confront those who posit the Ideas as substances[1] and as existing separately, and who at the same time posit the species as being composed of the genus and the differentiae.[2] For if the Forms exist, and Animal is in Man and

in Horse, then Animal is either one and the same numerically in both
of them or is distinct in them. It is clear that it is one in formula; for in
30   each case one would give the same formula for it. If then there exists
Man Himself, who in virtue of himself is a *this* and exists separately,
then each of the parts of which he is composed, such as Animal and
Biped, must indicate a *this* and be separate and a substance;[3] so also
Animal must be a *this* and exist separately and be a substance.

Now, if one[4] and the same Animal is in Horse and in Man, just as you
1039b   are one and the same with yourself, how will it be one[4] while being
in separate things, and why will this Animal not be also separate from
itself?[5] Further, if it is to participate in Biped and Many-footed, something impossible results; for contraries will belong to it at the same time
although it is one and a *this.*[6] But if it does not so participate, how can
5   one truly say that an animal is biped or terrestial?[7] Perhaps the two are
in combination, or in contact, or blended.[8] But all these alternatives
are absurd.

Then is Animal distinct in each case? But there will be an infinity[9]
of Forms, so to say, whose *substance* is Animal;[10] for it is not by accident that Man has Animal as a part. Moreover, Animal Itself will be
10   many things. For Animal is a substance in each of its species, for it is
not a predicate of other things, or if not, Man will have Animal as a part,
and the latter will be a genus of Man; and further, all the parts of Man
will be Ideas. Indeed, each of them cannot be the Idea of one thing
and the *substance* of another, for this is impossible. Each Animal in
the specific Ideas, then, will be Animal Itself. Further, of what is this
15   Animal composed, and how is each specific Idea composed of it? Or,
how can this Animal, whose *substance* is just Animal, exist apart from
Animal Itself?

Again, these and other more absurd consequences follow in the case
of sensible things.

If, then, all these are impossible, clearly no Forms of sensible things
exist in the way in which some thinkers say they do.

15

20   Since a substance as a *composite* is distinct from that as a formula[1]
(that is, in one way, a substance exists as a *composite* of the formula
with the matter, while in another, as the formula in general), substances
which are stated in the former sense can be destroyed, for they can also
be generated, but the formula does not exist in a way so as to be capable
25   of being destroyed, for neither can it be generated[2] (for it is not the
essence of a house that is generated but the essence of *this* house),[3] but

formulae exist and do not exist without being generated or destroyed, for it has been shown that no one generates or makes these.[4] And it is because of this that there is neither definition nor demonstration of individual sensible substances,[5] in view of the fact that they have mat-
30   ter whose nature is such that it can both be and not be these substances; and this is why all these individual substances are destructible. Accordingly, if a demonstration is of that which necessarily is and a definition is scientific,[6] and if, like *knowledge* which cannot be sometimes *knowledge* and sometimes ignorance[7] (but it is opinion that can be sometimes knowledge and sometimes ignorance), neither a demonstra-
1040a   tion nor a definition can be otherwise than it is[8] (for it is opinion which is of that which can be otherwise), it is clear that there can be neither a definition nor a demonstration of individual sensible substances. For, when destructible things are removed from sensation, their existence is uncertain to those who possess *knowledge;*[9] and although their for-
5   mulae[10] are retained in the soul, there can no longer be any definitions or demonstrations of them. For this reason, in matters relating to definitions, if someone is defining[11] an individual, we should not ignore the fact that such a definition may always be refuted; for no individual can be defined.[12]

Nor indeed can any Idea be defined; for, as they say, an Idea is an
10   individual and is separate.[13] Now a formula must consist of names; and he who is defining should not introduce a new name, for this would be unknown.[14] As for the names already available, each of them is common to all of a kind, and so it can belong to other things besides that which is defined; for example, if, in defining you, one were to say that you are a lean animal, or a white animal, or something else, such a formula may also belong to another thing. And[15] if one were to say that nothing
15   prevents each name by itself from belonging to many things, but that it may belong only to the thing defined when all of them are taken together, we would reply first, that they belong[16] also to both,[17] for example, that "two-footed animal" belongs to an animal and to what is two-footed.[18] And in the case of eternal things this is even necessary,[19] since at least the elements are prior[20] to and[21] are parts of the composite, and they are also separate, if indeed Man is separate. For either
20   none is separate, or both are. If neither,[22] the genus cannot exist apart from the species; but if the genus can exist apart, so can the differentia.[23] Also, these are prior in existence to the species;[24] for if the species exists, so do the genus and the differentia, but if each of the latter exists, the species does not necessarily exist. Again, if the Ideas are composed of Ideas[25] (for the parts are more incomposite than the whole), each of the parts of an Idea, such as Animal or Two-footed in
25   the case of Man, will have to be predicated of many;[26] but if not of

many, how will the Idea be known?[27] For there will be an Idea which cannot be predicated of more than one thing. But this does not seem to be the case, since every Idea is regarded as being capable of being shared.

As we said, then, these thinkers are unaware of the fact that it is impossible to define individuals among eternal things, especially if each of them is unique, such as the Sun or the Moon. Thus, not only do some err by adding such attributes by the removal of which the Sun will still exist, as for example its going around the Earth or its hiding at night (for if it were to stop or be visible,[28] it would no longer be the Sun,[29] although this would be absurd since "the Sun" signifies a certain substance),[30] but also by using attributes which may belong to another individual. For example, if some other individual with such attributes were to come into existence, clearly it would be the Sun; and so the formula would turn out to be common. But the Sun which was to be defined is an individual, like Cleon or Socrates. And we might add, why does not any of these thinkers produce a definition of Idea?[31] It would become clear, if they tried, that what we have just said is true.

16

It is also evident that most of what are regarded as substances are potentialities. These are the parts[1] of animals (for none of them exists separately, and when separated, even then, they all exist as matter), and earth, and fire, and air;[2] for none of them is one, but they exist like a heap until they are transformed and a unity is produced out of them.[3] One might be led to believe that, most of all, the parts of living things and[4] those[5] which are near the soul exist both actually and potentially, in view of the fact that they have their principles of motion somewhere in their joints; and on account of this, some animals continue living after they are divided. Yet, when the animal is one and is continuous by nature, and not by force or even by being grown together,[6] every part exists potentially; for that which is one by force or by being grown together is abnormal.

Since the term "unity" is used like the term "being", and the *substance* of what is one is one, and things whose *substance* is one numerically are numerically one, it is evident that neither unity nor being can be the *substance* of things,[7] just as neither the essence of an element nor that of a principle can be that *substance;* but we ask "What is the principle of the thing?" in order to go back to something more known.[8] Of these, however, being and unity would be *substances* to a higher degree than a principle or an element or a cause,[9] but even unity and being are not *substances,* if indeed nothing else that is common is a *substance;* for a *substance* belongs to nothing but to itself or to that which has it[10] (of which it is the *substance*). Moreover, what is one cannot exist in many ways[11] at the same time, but what is common can exist in many ways at the same time; hence, it is clear that no universal exists apart from the individuals.[12] But those who posit the existence of Forms are in one respect right, that is, by separating them, if these are indeed substances, but in another respect they are not right, that is, when they posit one Form as the form of many things.[13] The cause of this is the fact that they cannot say what such indestructible substances are which exist apart from individual and sensible substances. Accordingly, they posit them as being the same in kind as the destructible substances[14] (for these we do know); for example, they posit Man Himself and Horse Itself,[15] adding the word "Itself" to the names of sensible things. Yet, even if we had not seen the stars, I should think that eternal substances would none the less exist apart from the substances we would know. So now, too, if we cannot say what they are, it is just as necessary that some eternal substances exist.[16]

It is clear, then, that none of the so-called "universals" is a substance,[17] and that no substance is composed of substances.[18]

17

Let us again continue the discussion from another starting-point, so to say, and state what should be called "a substance" and what kind of thing it is;[1] for perhaps from this also the substance which is separate[2] from sensible substances will be clear to us.

Since a substance, then, is a principle and a cause, let us proceed from here. Now the *why* is always sought in this manner: "Why does something belong to something else?" For to inquire why a musical man is a musical man is either to inquire into the fact already stated, namely, why a musical man is a musical man, or into something else. But to ask why something is itself is to inquire into nothing, for the fact or the existence of something must be clear;[3] for example, the fact that the moon is eclipsed must be clear. Thus, *the fact that something is itself,*[4] this is the one *answer*[5] and the one cause in all cases, as, for example, in the questions "Why is a man a man?" and "Why is the musical musical?", unless one were to answer that each thing is indivisible from itself, since to be one for each thing is to be indivisible from itself. But this[6] is common to all things and a short answer for all of them. On the other hand, we might ask why a man is an animal of such-and-such a kind. Here, however, it is clear that we are not asking why he who

is a man is a man. We are asking, then, why something belongs to something else. That it does belong, this must be evident; otherwise,
25   the inquiry is about nothing. For example, "Why does it thunder?", that is, "Why is sound generated in the clouds?" In such an inquiry something is said of something else. And why are these things (for example, bricks and stones) a house?[7] It is evident, then, that we are seeking the cause (logically[8] speaking, this is the essence), which is in some cases the final cause (as perhaps in the case of a house or a
30   bed) and in others the first mover (for this too is a cause); but while we seek the latter kind of cause in generations and destructions, we seek the former kind also in cases of existence.[9]

      The object now sought escapes notice especially when the question
1041*b* raised is not properly expressed, as in the question "What is a man?", and this is because it is expressed simply and does not specify that something belongs to something else. But we should articulate the question properly before raising it, otherwise, it will be on the borderline between an inquiry into something and about nothing. Since, then, something must have something else[10] and the existence must be as-
5   sumed, clearly the question is "Why is the matter some one thing?"; for example, "Why are these materials a house?" Because to them belongs this,[11] which is the essence of a house; and because a man is this,[11] or, this body has this.[11] Thus, we are seeking the cause (and this is the form) through which the matter is a thing; and this cause is the *substance* of the thing. Concerning that which is simple, however, it is
10   evident that there is no inquiry and no teaching, but there is another manner of inquiring about such a thing.[12]

      Now since that which is composed of something exists in such a way as to be one in its totality, not like a heap but like a syllable (the syllable is not the letters, and so "*ba*" is not the same as "*b*" and "*a*", nor is the flesh the same as fire and earth; for after disintegration the flesh and
15   the syllable no longer exist, but their elements, which are the letters for the latter and fire and earth for the former, do exist), the syllable is not only its letters (the vowel and the consonant) but something else besides,[13] and the flesh is not only fire and earth or the hot and the cold but something else besides. If, further, that additional something must
20   also be (a) an element or (b) a composite of elements, (a) in case it is an element, the same argument will apply again, for flesh will then be composed of this element and of fire and of earth and of something else yet, and in this way the process will go on to infinity;[14] (b) but in case it is composed of elements, clearly it is composed not of one element (for we will have the previous case) but of many, so that again
25   the same argument will apply to the result, whether in the case of flesh or of the syllable.[15] It would seem, however, that this additional some-

thing is not an element but something else, and that it is the cause[16] through which this is flesh and that is a syllable; and similarly in all other cases. And this is the *substance* of each thing; for this is the first cause[17] of the thing's existence. Since some objects are not *substances* of things, but those that are substances[18] are formed according to nature or by nature, the *substance* of these would appear to be this nature, which is not an element but a principle.[19] As for an element, it is that which is present as matter in a thing and into which the thing is divisible, as the syllable "*ba*" is divisible into "*a*" and "*b*".

30

Book **H**

1

1042*a*   From what has been said we must draw conclusions, and, after sum-
ming these up, we must bring our inquiry to a close. We have said that it
5   is of substances that we seek the causes and principles and elements.[1]
As to what objects are substances, some are agreed upon by all thinkers,
but also certain others are advocated by some thinkers. Those agreed
upon are physical substances, such as fire, earth, water, air, and the
10   other simple bodies, and next, plants and their parts, and animals and
parts of animals, and finally, the heavens and its parts,[2] but some thinkers say that also the Forms and the Mathematical Objects are substances.[3] From certain arguments it turns out that the essence and the
underlying subject are also substances. Moreover, from other arguments the genus is to a higher degree a substance than the species,
15   and the universal is to a higher degree a substance than the individual;[4]
and to the universal and the genus we may attach also the Ideas, for
these are thought to be substances according to the same argument.

Since the essence is a substance, and the formula of this is a definition, for this reason we have given a description of a definition and of
that which exists in virtue of itself.[5] Since a definition is a formula, and
20   a formula has parts, it was also necessary with respect to parts to examine what sort of objects are parts of *substances* and what are not,
and also if to a part of a *substance* there is a corresponding part in the
definition of the *substance*.[6] Moreover, we have shown that neither a
universal nor a genus is a substance;[7] as for the Ideas and the Mathematical Objects, we must examine them later,[8] for some thinkers say
that these exist in addition to the sensible substances.

Let us now proceed to discuss those which are agreed upon as being
25   substances. These are the sensible substances, and all sensible substances have matter. Now a substance is an underlying subject; and
in one sense, this is matter (by "matter" I mean that which is not a *this*
in *actuality* but is potentially a *this*[9]); in another sense, it is the formula

or the *form*, which is a *this* and separable in formula; in a third sense,
30   it is the composite of the two, of which alone there is generation and
destruction, and which is separate without qualification, for of substances according to formula some are separable[10] but others are not.[11]

It is clear that also matter is a substance, for in all opposite changes
there is some subject which underlies the changes; for example, with
35   respect to place there is something which is now here but after elsewhere; with respect to increase[12] there is something which is now of a
certain quantity but after less or greater; with respect to alteration there
1042b   is something which is now healthy but later sick; and similarly with
respect to substance, there is something which is now in generation but
later in destruction, and something which is now a subject as a *this* but
later a subject with respect to a privation.[13] And the other changes
follow this change[14] [with respect to substance], but one or two of the
5   other changes is not followed by this change; for if something has matter which can change with respect to place, it is not necessary for it
to have matter which can change with respect to generation or destruction.[15] The difference between unqualified and qualified generation has
been stated in the *Physics*.[16]

2

Since the existence of a substance as an underlying subject and as
10   matter is agreed upon, and this is what exists potentially, it remains
for us to state what a substance as the *actuality* of a sensible thing is.
Democritus seems to think that there are three differentiae; that the
underlying body, which is matter, is one and the same, but that it
differs either in contour, which is shape, or in turning, which is position,
15   or in arrangement, which is order.[1] But many differences appear to exist.
For example, some things are spoken of as being combinations of matter, as in the case of things formed by fusion, such as honey-water,
others as being bound together, such as a bundle, others as being glued
together, such as a book, others as being nailed together, such as a
casket, others in more than one of these ways; and some things differ
20   in position, such as a threshold and a lintel (for these differ by lying in
a certain way), others in time, such as dinner and breakfast, others in
place, such as winds; and some things differ in sensible attributes, such
as hardness or softness, density or rarity, dryness or wetness, and they
25   differ either in some or in all of these, and in general, some differ by
excess and others by deficiency. Hence it is clear that the "is" has as
many senses [as there are differences]; for a thing *is* a threshold in view
of the fact that it lies in a certain position, and "to be" for this thing

means to lie in that position, and "to be ice" means to be condensed
in a certain way. In some cases, the being of a thing will be defined
even by all of these attributes, since the thing may be partly blended,
partly fused, partly bound together, partly condensed, and partly
formed by the use of other differentiae, as in the case of a hand or
a foot. Accordingly, we should posit the genera of differentiae (for these
will be the principles of existence), that is, those in virtue of which
things differ by being more or less dense or rare, or the others of this
sort; for all these come under excess and deficiency. And if anything
differs in shape, or smoothness or roughness, then it differs in straightness or curvature. And for other things, *to be* will be *to be blended,*
and *not to be* will be the opposite.

It is evident from these that if the *substance*[2] is the cause of the
being of each thing, then it is in these differentiae that we must seek
the cause of the being of each of these things. Now none of these differentiae is a substance,[3] not even if combined,[4] but in each case it is
something analogous to *substance;* and just as in substances that which
is a predicate of matter is the *actuality* itself, so also in the other definitions, that which is a predicate is to the highest degree the *actuality.*[5]
For example, if we are to define a threshold, we should say "wood or
stone in such-and-such a position", and we should define a house as
"bricks and timber in such-and-such a position" (or, also the final cause
is present in some cases), and ice as "water frozen or condensed in
such-and-such a way"; and we should define a harmony as "such-and-
such a combination of high and low", and the rest in the same manner.

It is evident from these that there is a distinct *actuality* for distinct[6]
matter, and a distinct formula; for in some cases it is the combination,
in others the blend, and in others some one of the others which we have
named. On account of this,[7] in defining what a house is, those who say
that it is stones and bricks and wood speak of what is potentially a
house, for these are matter; those who say that it is a receptacle for
sheltering animals or goods, or some other such thing, speak of the
actuality of the house. But those who combine both, speak of the
third kind of substance, the one composed of matter and form (for it
seems that the formula by means of the differentiae is that of the form
and of the *actuality,* but the formula of the constituents is rather that
of the matter); and this is similar to the kind of definitions which
Archytas used to accept, for they are of both matter and form. For
example, what is windlessness? Stillness in a large expanse of air. Air
is the matter, stillness is the *actuality* and the *substance.* What is a
calm? Smoothness of the sea. The underlying subject as matter is the
sea, the *actuality* or the *shape* is smoothness.

From what has been said it is evident what a sensible substance is and how it exists; in one sense it is matter, in another it is the *form* or *actuality,* and in a third it is the composite of these two.

3

We should not ignore the fact that sometimes we are unaware of whether a name signifies the composite substance, or the *actuality* or *shape,* for example, whether "a house" signifies the composite, that is, a covering made of bricks and stones laid in such-and-such a manner, or, the *actuality* or form, that is, a covering, whether "a line" signifies twoness in length[1] or twoness, and whether "an animal" signifies a soul in a body or a soul; for it is the soul which is the *substance* or the *actuality* of a certain body. The name "an animal" may also be applied to both, not as having the same formula when asserted of both, but as being related to one thing.[2] But, although these distinctions contribute something to another inquiry,[3] they contribute nothing to the inquiry into sensible *substances;* for the essence belongs to the form or *actuality.* For a soul and the essence of a soul are the same, but the essence of a man is not the same as the man, unless also the soul is called "a man"; accordingly, in some cases a thing and its essence are the same,[4] in others this is not so.

From our inquiry it appears that the constituents of a syllable are not its letters plus their combination, nor, in the case of a house, are they bricks and combination.[5] And this is right; for a combination or blend does not consist of those objects of which it is the combination or the blend.[6] And in the other cases, it is similar; for example, if a threshold exists by virtue of its position,[7] the position does not consist of the threshold,[8] but it is rather the threshold which is composed[9] of the position. Nor is a man an animal plus two-footedness, but there must be something which exists besides these, if these are matter,[10] and this something is neither an element, nor does it consist of elements, but is the *substance;* and it is this that some thinkers leave out and state only the matter. So if this is the cause of the existence and of the substance, then it is this that they should be calling "a substance".

Now this *substance*[11] must either be eternal or be destructible without being in the process of being destroyed and generable without being in the process of being generated. It was shown and made clear elsewhere that no one makes or generates the form,[12] but what is made is a *this,*[13] and what is generated is something from these.[14]

It is not yet clear if the *substances* of destructible things can exist apart, but it is clear that in some cases they cannot, for example, in cases where they cannot exist apart from the individuals, as in a house

30

35

1043*b*

5

10

15

20

or utensil. Perhaps these things themselves are not substances, nor anything else except the things which are formed by nature;[15] for one might
posit only nature[16] as a *substance* in destructible things.

The problem which the followers of Antisthenes and other such uneducated men used to raise has some value here, namely, that it is not
possible to define the whatness of a thing, for a definition according to
them is a long rigmarole, but that it is possible to state and even teach
what kind of a thing something is; for example, in the case of silver,
that it is not possible to define its whatness, but that one may say that
it is like tin. If so, then there can be a definition and a formula of a
substance, if it be composite,[17] whether sensible or intelligible; but
there can be no such of its primary constituents,[18] if the defining formula signifies that something is attributed to something else, where one
part is to be like matter and the other part like *shape*.[19]

It is also evident, if *substances* are in a sense numbers, why they are
numbers in this sense and not composed of units as some say.[20] For (1) a
definition is a number of a sort; for it is divisible and into indivisibles,[21]
since no formula is infinite,[22] and a number is a thing of this sort.[23] And
(2) just as, if anything which is a part of a number is subtracted from
or added to a number, even if that part is the smallest, the number
formed is no longer the same but distinct, so the definition or the essence will not be the same but distinct if something is added to or
subtracted from it.[24] And (3) there must be something in a number by
which the number is one, but these thinkers say nothing about what it
is that makes a number one, if indeed it is one. For either it is not one
but a heap as it were, or if it is indeed one, they should state what it
is that makes a unity out of many.[25] And a definition is one, but similarly
they have nothing to say about its unity.[26] And this is to be expected;
for a *substance* is one in this way for the same reason, not one as a sort
of unit or point, but as an actuality and a nature of some kind.[27] And
(4) just as a number does not admit the more or the less, so neither does
a substance in the sense of form; and if a substance does so admit, it
will be a substance which includes matter.[28]

Concerning the generation and destruction of the so-called substances,[29] how they are possible and how they are not, and also the
reference of substances to numbers, let the discussion up to now suffice.[30]

4

Concerning material substance, we must not forget that even if all
generated things are generated from the same primary constituent or

constituents[1] and if the matter as a principle is the same for all, still there is matter which is *proper* to each thing; for example, for phlegm the proximate matter is the sweet or the fatty, for the bile it is the bitter or some others, and perhaps all these come from the same matter.[2] And the same thing comes from many matters, if among these one comes from the other;[3] for example, phlegm comes from the fatty and the sweet, if the fatty comes from the sweet; and it comes from the bile when this is decomposed into its ultimate matter. For one thing may come from a second in two ways, either when the second is earlier on the way to generation, or when it is analyzed into its principles.[4]

If the matter is one, distinct things may be generated because of distinct moving causes; for example, from wood a chest and a bed may be made. In some cases, if the things are distinct their matter must be distinct; for example, a saw could not be made of wood, nor is this up to the moving cause; for no such cause could make a saw out of wool or wood. But if it is at all possible for the same thing to be made from distinct matters,[5] it is clear that the art or the moving principle must be the same; for if both the matter and the moving principle are distinct, so will be the thing generated.

So when one seeks the cause of something, since "cause" has several senses, all the possible causes in each case should be stated. For example, what is the material cause of a man? Let us say, the menses. What is the moving cause? Let us say, the seed. What is the cause as form? It is his essence. What is the final cause? His end. Perhaps the latter two are the same.[6] But we should state the proximate causes. What is the material cause? Not fire or earth, but what is proper to the thing. Accordingly, with regard to physical and generable substances we should proceed in this manner, if we are to proceed rightly, that is, if indeed the causes are these and so many and if we are to know the causes.

As for the physical but eternal substances, this requires another discussion.[7] For perhaps some of them have no matter, or not matter of this kind but only matter which is movable with respect to place.[8] Nor is there matter in those things which exist by nature but are not substances; however, their underlying subject is a substance. For example, what is the cause of an eclipse, and what is its matter? There is no matter, but it is the Moon which is affected by the eclipse. What is the moving cause which has destroyed the light? The Earth. Perhaps there is no final cause. The cause as form is the formula, but this is not made clear unless it includes the cause.[9] For example, what is an eclipse? A privation of light. But if we add "caused by the Earth moving in between", what results is the formula which includes the cause.[9] In the case of sleep it is not clear what is the primary part that is affected. Is it the animal? Yes, but in virtue of what part, or which is the primary part? The heart, or some other part. Next, by what moving cause? Next, what is the affection of the primary part, but not of the whole animal? Let us say, such-and-such immobility. Yes, but this occurs in virtue of 20 what affection[10] of the primary part?

5

Since some things now exist and now do not exist but are not in the process of being generated or of being destroyed, as for example points, if they exist indeed, and in general forms[1] and *shapes*[2] (for it is not whiteness that is generated but it is the wood that becomes white, if everything generated comes to be from something and comes to be 25 something[3]), not all contraries can be generated from each other, but the generation of a light man from a dark man is distinct from that of lightness from darkness.[4] Nor have all things matter,[5] but only those which are generated from or change to each other. Those things which exist and do not exist, without being in the process of changing, have no matter.

There is a *difficulty* as to how the matter of each thing is related to 30 the contraries. For example, if the body is potentially healthy, and disease is contrary to health, is the body potentially both? And is water potentially both wine and vinegar? Or is it that, in the one case, it is matter with respect to a possession or a form, and in the other, with respect to privation or destruction, which are contrary to nature?[6]

35   There is also the *difficulty* as to why wine is not the matter of vinegar nor potentially vinegar, although vinegar is generated from wine, and 1045*a* why a living animal is not potentially dead. Indeed they are not, but destructions are accidental,[7] and it is the animal's matter itself which, in virtue of the destruction, is the potency and matter of a corpse, and it is water which is the matter of vinegar. For generation in these cases is like generation of night from day. And all things which change to each other in this manner must go back to their matter; for example, 5 if a corpse is to become an animal, it must first go back to its matter and then in this way become an animal,[8] and vinegar must first go back to water and then become wine.

6

Returning to the *difficulty* stated earlier concerning definitions and numbers,[1] we may ask: What causes each of them to be one? For in 10 anything which has many parts and whose totality is not just a heap but is some whole besides just the parts, there is some cause, inasmuch as in bodies, too, the cause of unity is in some cases contact, in others viscosity, or some other such affection. Now a definition is one formula not by the placing of things together, as in the *Iliad*, but by being a formula of one thing.[2] What is it, then, that makes a man one, and why is he one and not many, such as an animal and also a biped, if indeed there exists, as some say,[3] Animal Itself and Biped Itself. For why are these two not Man, so that men may exist by participating not in Man[4] or one Idea but in two, Animal and Biped? And, in general, a man would then be not one but more than one, an animal and a biped. It is evident, then, if we proceed in this manner, as these thinkers are accustomed to define and speak, we cannot answer or solve the *difficulty*. But if, as we maintain, the one is matter and the other *form*,[5] and the former exists potentially but the latter as *actuality*, what we seek no longer seems to be a *difficulty*. For this is the same *difficulty* as the one which would arise if the definition of a *cloak* were to be "a round bronze"; for the name would be a sign of this formula, so that we would be inquiring into the cause of the unity of roundness and bronze.[6] The difficulty indeed no longer appears, in view of the fact that the one is matter and the other form. What causes[7] that which exists potentially to be in *actuality*, then, aside from that which acts in the case of things which are generated? Doubtless, nothing else causes that which is potentially a sphere to be a sphere in actuality, but this is the essence in each.[8]

Of matter, some is intelligible and some sensible,[9] and in a formula it is always the case that one part is matter and one part is *actuality*; for example, in the case of a circle, "a plane figure."[10] But of the things which have no matter, whether intelligible or sensible, each is immediately just a unity as well as just a being, such as a *this*, or a quality, or a quantity.[11] And so in their definitions, too, neither "being" nor "one" is present, and the essence of each is immediately a unity as well as a being. Consequently, nothing else is the cause of oneness or of being in each of them;[12] for each is immediately a being and a unity, not in the sense that "being" and "unity" are their genera, nor in the sense that they exist apart from individuals.

It is because of this *difficulty* that some thinkers speak of participation but are perplexed as to what causes participation and what it is to participate, and others speak of communion with the soul, as when Lycophron says that *knowledge* is the communion of *knowing* with the soul, and still others call life a composition or connection of soul with body. However, the same argument applies to all; for being healthy, too, will be a communion or a connection or a composition of soul and health, and the being of a triangular bronze[13] will be a composition of

15

20

25

30

35

1045b

5

10

15

bronze and a triangle, and being white will be a composition of surface and whiteness. They are speaking in this manner because they are seeking a unifying formula of, and a difference between, potentiality and actuality. But, as we have stated, the last matter and the *form* are one and the same; the one exists potentially, the other as *actuality*. Thus, it is like asking what the cause of unity is and what causes something to be one; for each thing is a kind of unity, and potentiality and actuality taken together exist somehow as one. So there is no other cause, unless it be the mover which causes the motion from potency to *actuality*. But all things which have no matter are without qualification just unities of one kind or another.

Book Θ

1

We have discussed primary being,[1] which is substance, and to which
the other categories of being are referred. For it is in virtue of the
formula of substance that each of the others, such as quantities and
qualities and the like, is called "a being"; for all of these will have the
formula of substance, as we said in the beginning of our discussion.[2]
Now since "being" means whatness or quality or quantity, but it is also
used with respect to potentiality and actuality and function,[3] let us
also describe potentiality and actuality. And first, let us take up what
is called "potentiality" [or "potency", or "power", or "capacity", or "capability"] in the most proper sense of that term, although it is not useful
for our present purpose. For "potentiality" and *"actuality"* are predicates of more objects than those in which there is motion. But after
discussing this sense of "potentiality", we shall also make clear the
other senses when we describe *actuality*.

We have explained elsewhere[4] the various senses of "potentiality" and
"to be capable". Of these, we may dismiss the ones which are called
"potencies" by equivocation; for some are called so by some similarity,
as in geometry when we say that certain things are or are not powers
by being or not being so and so in some way or other.[5] As for the so-
called "potencies" which are related to the same kind,[6] they are all principles of one sort or another and are related to the primary one, and
this is a principle of change in another thing or in the thing itself qua
other. For one of them is a potency of being acted upon, and this is in
the thing which is acted upon and is a principle of change by being
acted upon by another or by itself qua other. Another is a habit of not
being acted upon for the worse or to destruction by a principle of
change in another thing or in the thing itself qua other. Now in all these
definitions there is the formula of the primary potency. Again, these
are said to be potencies either by merely acting or by merely being acted
upon, or by acting or being acted upon well, and so even in the formulae

of the latter the formulae of the former potencies are somehow present.[7]

It is evident, then, that in a sense the potency of acting and of being acted upon is one (for a thing is capable either if it itself has the potency of being acted upon or if something else can be acted upon by it), but in another sense it is a distinct potency.[8] For one potency is in that which is acted upon; for it is because this thing has some principle, and also because matter is a principle, that the thing is acted upon, or one thing is acted upon by another. For that which is oily can be burned, and that which yields in a certain way is malleable, and similarly with the others. But another potency is in that which acts, as heat and the art of building, the former being in that which can heat, the latter in that which can build. Hence, insofar as something is by nature united, it is never acted upon by itself; for it is one and not another thing.[9] Also, incapability or the incapable is a privation which is the contrary of a potency of this sort, and so to every potency there is a contrary potency in the same subject and with respect to the same thing.[10] But "privation" has many senses; for a thing is said to be deprived (1) if it does not have something,[11] or (2) if it does not have what it should by nature have,[12] either (a) not at all, or (b) not when by nature it should have it, whether in a certain way (for example, if it lacks it entirely) or in any way at all. In some cases, we say that things are deprived if by nature they would have something but by force they do not have it.

2

Since of such principles[1] some are present in inanimate things, but others are present in living things and in the soul and also in that part of the soul which has reason,[2] it is clear that of the potencies, too, some will be nonrational but others will be with reason. Hence, all the arts or the productive sciences are potencies; for they are principles which can cause a change in another thing or in the artist himself qua other. And every potency with reason is capable of causing both contraries, but every nonrational potency can cause only one; for example, heat can cause only heating, but the medical art can cause sickness as well as health. The cause of this is the fact that *knowledge* is reason, and the same reason makes known both the thing and its privation, although not in the same way;[3] and in a sense it is a reason of both, but in another sense it is a reason of the thing rather than its privation.[4] And so such sciences[5] must be potencies of both contraries, yet they are essentially[6] of the thing but not essentially of the privation of that thing; for reason, too, is essentially of the thing but in a sense accidentally of its privation.[7]

15 For, it is by denial and removal that the formula makes known the contrary; for a contrary is the primary privation, and this privation is the removal of the other contrary.

Since contraries cannot exist at the same time in the same thing, but science is a potency by having reason, and the soul has a principle of motion, then whereas the healthy produces only health and that which can heat produces only heat and that which can cool produces only 20 cold, the scientist can produce both. For reason is of both, although not in the same way,[8] and it is in the soul which has a principle of motion; and so the scientist can produce both contraries[9] from the same principle of motion by connecting it to the same thing.[10] Hence, things which are capable with respect to reason produce contraries in things without reason;[11] for the contraries are included in a single principle, in reason.

25 It is also evident that the potency of merely acting or being acted upon follows from that of acting or being acted upon well, but that the latter does not always follow from the former; for he who acts well necessarily acts, but he who merely acts does not necessarily act well.

3

There are some, such as the thinkers of the Megarian school, who say 30 that a thing has a potency only when it is active, but that when it is not active it has no potency for that activity; for example, he who is not building is not able[1] to build, but he can build only when he is building, and similarly with the others. It is not difficult to perceive the absurdities which follow from these statements; for it is clear from this that if a man is not building then he will not be a builder, since to be a builder 35 is to be able to build, and similarly with the other arts. If, then, it is impossible for a man to have such arts without learning them and having acquired them at some time, and also impossible for him not to have 1047a them without having lost them at some time (either through forgetfulness or through some affection or through lapse of time; for certainly the objects[2] cannot have been destroyed, since they always exist), when the builder ceases to build, he will no longer have the art; and when he will immediately start building again, how will he have acquired the 5 art?[3] And similarly with regard to lifeless things. For no thing will have the potency of being cold or hot or sweet or, in general, of being sensed unless it is being sensed; and so these thinkers would turn out to be asserting the doctrine of Protagoras.[4] What is more, nothing will have the power of sensation if it is not sensing or active. Accordingly, if a blind man is one who has no sight, although it is his nature to have sight

10   and to have it at that time of his existence, the same people will be blind
      many times during the day,[5] and likewise deaf.
          Again, if that which is deprived of potency is incapable, that which
      is not now in the process of generation will be incapable of being
      generated; but he who says of that which was incapable of generation
      that it now exists or that it will exist would be speaking falsely (for this
      was the meaning of "incapability"[6]). Thus the statements of these
15   thinkers eliminate both motion and generation.[7] For that which is
      standing will always stand and that which is sitting will always sit;
      for that which sits will not get up, since it will be impossible for it to
      get up if it does not have the power to get up. If, then, the statements
      of these thinkers cannot be true, it is evident that potentiality and
      actuality are distinct; but their statements make potentiality and
20   *actuality* the same, and so it is no small matter that they are seeking to
      eliminate. Consequently, a thing may[8] be capable of being something
      else and yet not be it, or, it may be capable of not being something
      else and yet be it;[9] and similarly in the other categories, a thing may
      be capable of walking and yet not be walking, and capable of not
      walking and yet be walking. What is capable of something, then, is such
25   that nothing will be impossible if to it will belong the *actuality* of that of
      which it is said to have the potency. I mean, for example, if a thing is
      capable of sitting and may[10] sit, if sitting will belong to it there will be
      nothing impossible;[11] and similarly in the case of a thing capable of being
      moved or of moving, of standing or of making something else stand, of
      existing or of becoming, of not existing or of not coming to be.
30   The term *"actuality"*, which is placed along with the term "actuality",
      has been extended to other things from motions,[12] where it was mostly
      used; for *actuality* is thought to be motion most of all. And this is why
      people do not attribute motion to what does not exist but some other
      predicates; for example, they say that nonbeings are thinkable or
35   *desirable*, but not that they are in motion. And this is in view of the
      fact that, while they do not exist in *actuality*, they may exist in
1047*b* *actuality*. For some nonbeings exist potentially; but they do not exist,
      in the sense that they do not exist actually.

                    4

          If the possible is what we have stated it to be and what follows from
5   it,[1] evidently one cannot truly say "so-and-so is possible, but it will
      not be" in a way so as to eliminate the impossible.[2] I mean, for example,
      one might say, without taking into account[3] the impossible, that it is pos-
      sible for the diagonal and the side of a square to be measured by the

10 same unit, but that it will not be measured, seeing that nothing prevents what is possible to be or to become from not being or not coming to be. But it follows from what we laid down, if we were to assume also that what is possible, though not existing, exists or has become, that nothing will be impossible; yet in this case something will be impossible, for it will be impossible for a common unit to measure both the diagonal and the side. Indeed, the false and the impossible are not the same; for although it is false that you are now standing, nevertheless it is not impossible.

15 At the same time it is clear that, if it is necessary for B to exist when A exists, then it is also necessary for B to be possible when A is possible. For if it is not necessary for B to be possible, nothing prevents B from being not possible.[4] Now let A be possible. Then when A is possible,
20 nothing impossible results if we lay down A as existing; and then it is necessary for B to exist. But B was taken as impossible. So let it be impossible; then, if B is impossible, so must A be. But A was taken as possible; so, B also must be possible. If, then, A is possible, B also will be possible, if indeed they were so related that, if A exists, it is necessary for B to exist. If, then, A and B being laid down as related in this way,
25 B is not possible in this way, neither will A and B be related as laid down. Also, if, when A is possible, it is necessary for B to be possible, then, if A exists, it is necessary for B to exist also. For, the statement "If A is possible, it is necessary for B to be possible" means this: if A exists at the time when and in the manner in which it is possible for it to
30 exist, it is necessary also for B to exist then and in that manner.

5

As all potencies are either innate, like the senses, or come by practice, like that of flute-playing, or by study, like those of the arts, one acquires
35 potencies by practice or by discourse from previous activity,[1] but this is not necessary in the case of potencies which are not of this sort and which are potencies over that which is acted upon.

1048a Since that which is capable is capable of something and at some time and in a certain manner (and all the other specifications must be added to make this definite), and some things can cause motion according to formula and their potencies include a formula while other things are nonrational and their potencies are without reason, and since the former
5 potencies must be in living things but the latter[2] may be in both, then, in the case of the latter potencies, when the agent and the patient approach each other, the former must act and the latter must be acted upon, each in the manner in which it is capable,[3] but in the case of the

former potencies this is not necessary. For each of the nonrational
potencies can produce only one effect, while each of the rational potencies can produce contrary effects.[4] Will the latter, then, produce contraries at the same time? But this is impossible. So in the case of the
rational potencies there must be something else which decides, and by
this I mean desire or *choice*. For whichever of two things an animal
desires by decision, this it will bring about when it has the potency to
do so and approaches that which can be acted upon. Thus, every thing
which is capable according to formula must act on that which it desires,
whenever it desires that of which it has the capability and in the
manner in which it has that capability. And it has the capability of so
acting when the patient is present and is disposed in a certain manner;
otherwise, the agent will not be able to act. And to add the further specification "if nothing external prevents" is no longer needed; for the
agent has the potency in the manner in which this is a potency of acting,
and the potency is such not in any way whatsoever but in a certain way
which also takes care of the external hindrances, since these are barred
by some of the specifications present. And so, even if one wishes or
desires to do two things or contrary things at the same time, he cannot
do them; for it is not in this manner that he has the potency of doing
them, nor is it a potency of doing them at the same time, since he can
do things only in the manner in which he has the potency.

6

Since we have discussed[1] what is called "a potency" with respect to
motion, let us explain what *actuality* is and what sort of object it is.
For if this is distinguished, the potential [or capable], too, will be at the
same time clear in view of the fact that by "potential" we mean not only
that whose nature is to move another or to be moved by another
(whether without qualification or in some manner[2]), but also something
else; and it is because of our inquiry into the latter sense of "potential"
that we have discussed the former senses.

Now *actuality* is the existence of a thing, not in the way in which we
say that something exists potentially. For example, we say that Hermes
is potentially in the wood and that the half-line is in the whole line,
in view of the fact that in each case what exists potentially can be
separated from the whole; and we say that a man is a scientist even if
he is not in the process of investigating something, provided that he is
capable of doing this; but Hermes and the line when separated, and the
scientist in the process of investigation, these exist in *actuality*. What we
mean is clear by induction from individual cases, and we should not

seek a definition of everything[3] but should also perceive an object by means of an analogy; thus, as that which builds is to that which is capable of building, so is that which is awake to that which is asleep, or that which is seeing to that which has its eyes shut but has the power to see, or that which is separated from matter to matter itself, or the finished product to the raw material. Let the term *"actuality"* signify the first part of each of these differences and "the potential" signify the second part.[4]

Things which are said to be in *actuality* are not all called so in the same manner but by analogy, that is, as A is in B or is related to B, so C is in D or is related to D; for, in some cases, *actuality* is to the potential as motion is to the power to move, in others, as a *substance* to some matter. But the infinite and the void and all other such objects are said to exist potentially and in *actuality* in a sense distinct from many other things, such as that which sees or walks or is seen. For the latter may sometimes be truly stated as existing so even without qualification, for of a thing we say that it is seen sometimes if it is actually being seen and sometimes if it is capable of being seen; but the infinite is potential not in such a way that it will be separate in *actuality*, but it is potential in knowledge.[5] For, to a never-ending process of division we attribute an *actuality* which exists potentially, but not a separate existence to the infinite.[6]

Since of the actions which have a limit[7] none is an end[8] but each is for the sake of an end, as in the process of losing weight, whose end is thinness, and since that which loses weight while in motion does not have that for the sake of which its motion exists, such an action is not an *action*, or at least it is not complete, for it is not an end. But the end and *action* belong to that other kind.[9] For example, we are seeing[10] and at the same time we have seen, we are engaged in acts of prudence and have been so engaged, we are thinking and have thought;[11] but it is not a fact that we are learning and have learned or that we are being cured and have been cured. Also, we live well and at the same time have lived well, and we are happy and have been happy.[12] If not, the action should have come to an end sometime, as in the process of losing weight; but in these cases it is not so, since we are living and have lived. Of these, the former should be called "motions," the latter *"actualities"*. For every motion is incomplete, as in losing weight, learning, walking, and building. These, then, are motions, and they are incomplete; for one is not walking and at the same time has walked, nor is he building and has built, nor is a thing being generated and has been generated, nor is it being moved and has moved, but they are distinct; and moving another thing is distinct from having moved another thing. On the other hand, the same thing has seen and is seeing at the same time,[13] and likewise it is thinking and has thought. I call each of the latter "an *actuality*", but

1048*b*

5

10

15

20

25

30

35

each of the former "a motion". From these and other similar statements it is clear what an *actuality* is and what kind[14] of an object it is.

7

We must now specify when something is potentially another thing
1049a and when it is not; for it is not potentially another at any time. For example, is earth potentially a man? No, but rather when it has already become a seed, and perhaps not even then.[1] This is similar to being healed, since not everything can be healed by the medical art or by luck,[2] but only something which has this capability, and it is this thing which is potentially healthy. A definition of that which becomes actual by *thought* from existing potentially is this, that it becomes actual when *thought* wishes it and nothing external prevents this, and, in the case of that which is being healed, when nothing in it[3] prevents the healing. Similarly with that which is potentially a house; if nothing in its parts, which are its matter, prevents them from becoming a house, and if nothing need be added or be taken away or be changed,[4] then this is potentially a house. It is likewise with the others if the principle[5] of generation is external,[6] or even if this principle is in that which is potential and nothing external obstructs it from becoming by itself[7] what it can be. For example, the seed is not yet potentially a man; for it must be placed in something else and change.[8] And when it is already such that it can be moved by its own principle,[9] it is then potentially a man; but prior to this it has need of another principle.[10] It is like the earth, which is not yet potentially a statue, for it needs to be changed and become bronze.

It seems that in naming something after its material principle we say not that it is a *this* but that it is a *that-en;*[11] for example, the box is not wood but wooden, the wood is not earth by earthen, and again, earth is likewise not *that* (if this is its material principle) but *that-en;* and that from which the derivative name comes is always potentially and without qualification the object from which the thing generated is derivatively named. For example, the box is neither earthen nor earth, but wooden; for it is wood that is potentially a box or the matter of the box, wood universally taken of a box universally taken, and this individual wood of this individual box. If there is something first which is in no way called "that-en" according to something else, then this is primary matter, for example, if earth is airy, and air is not fire but fiery, then fire is primary matter;[12] but if this last is a *this,* then it is a substance.[13] For the universal and the underlying subject differ in this, that the latter is a *this* and the former is not;[14] for example, a man and a body and a soul are subjects to which affections belong, and the musical and the pale

are affections. That which acquires music is called not "music" but "musical", a man is called not "paleness" but "pale", and not "a walk" or "a motion" but "walking" and "moving", and these are like the word "that-en". And whenever such predicates are used, the ultimate subject
35   is a substance; but if a predicate[15] is not of this sort but is a form or a *this*, the ultimate underlying subject is matter and a material sub-
1049*b* stance. And it is indeed right[16] that an object should be called "that-en" according to its matter and its affections,[17] for both are indefinite. We have stated, then, when something should be called "potential" and when not.

8

5   As we have distinguished earlier[1] the various senses of "prior", it is evident that *actuality* is prior to potentiality. By "potentiality" I do not mean only the specific one which is said to be a principle of change in another thing or in the same thing qua other, but in general every prin- ciple of change or of rest. For nature, too, is in the same genus of poten-
10 tiality;[2] for it is a moving principle, not in another thing, but in the same thing qua itself. To every such potentiality, then, *actuality* is prior both in formula and in substance [or *substance*]; and in one sense it is prior in time, but in another sense it is not.

Clearly, it is prior in formula; for that which is primarily capable is capable by virtue of the fact that it may be in *actuality*; for example,
15 the constructive is that which can construct, the able-to-see is that which is capable of seeing, and the visible is that which can be seen. The same thing may be said of the others, so that the formula or knowledge of that which is in *actuality* must be prior to the formula or knowledge of that which is potential.[3]

Actuality is prior in time to potentiality in this sense, that there exists another thing of the same species, but not numerically the same as the thing in question, which is prior in time to the latter. What I mean is
20 this, that prior in time to this individual man who now exists in *actuality* and to this corn and to this animal that sees, there was the matter and the seed and that which could see, and these were potentially this man and this corn and this seeing animal, but not yet in *actuality*; but prior in time to these potential things there existed in *actuality* other things
25 from which these things were generated. For it is always by a thing in *actuality* that another thing becomes *actualized* from what it was potentially; for example, a man by a man and the musical by the musi- cal, as there is always a first mover, and this mover already exists in *actuality*.[4] We have stated in our discussion of substance that everything which is being generated is being generated from something and by

something,[5] and the latter is the same in species as that which will be
30   generated. This is why it is also thought that no builder can exist if he
has not built anything or a lyre player if he has never played the lyre;
for he who learns to play the lyre learns to play it by playing it, and
similarly in all other cases. From cases like the latter arose a sophistical
objection, namely, one which claims that a man who possesses no science
35   will do that which is the object of science.[6] Doubtless, a learner does
not possess the science, but because of that which is being generated a
part has been generated, and, in general, of that which is in motion a
1050a   part has been moved (this is clear in our discussion of motion),[7] it
would seem that the learner, too, must possess some part of the science.[8]
It is clear, then, that here, too, *actuality* in this sense is prior in generation
and in time to potentiality.

But it is also prior in substance. First, things which are posterior[9]
5   in generation are prior in form or in substance;[10] for example, an adult
is prior to a child, and a man is prior to seed; for the former in each case
already has the form, the latter does not. Also, everything which is
being generated proceeds towards a principle and an end. For the final
cause [or, that for the sake of which] is a principle, and generation is for
the sake of an end; and the end is an *actuality*, and potentiality is viewed
10   as being for the sake of this.[11] Animals do not see in order to have sight,
but they have sight in order to see. Likewise, men have the art of building in order to build, and men have the power of investigation in order
to investigate, but they do not investigate in order to have the power
of investigating, unless they are learning; yet these are not investigating
except in a qualified sense[12] or in view of the fact that they are in no
need of speculating.[13]

15   Further, matter exists potentially in view of the fact that it might
come to possess a form;[14] and when it exists *actually*, then it exists in
a form.[15] And it is likewise with the other cases, even with those whose
end is motion.[16] And so just as teachers think that they have achieved
their end when they have exhibited their pupils at work, it is likewise
20   with nature.[17] For if this is not so, we shall be faced with Pauson's
Hermes;[18] and as in this case, so with *knowledge* it is not clear whether
it is inside or outside. For performance is an end, and *actuality* is performance.[19] And so even the name "*actuality*" (ἐνέργεια) is derived from
the name "work" (ἔργον) and points to "actuality" (ἐντελέχεια).[20]

Since in some cases the ultimate end is the use of something (such as
25   seeing in the case of sight, and sight has no other function besides
seeing)[21] but in other cases something else is generated, such as (in
addition to the act of building) a house, which proceeds from the art
of building, nevertheless in the former case the use is the end and in
the latter it is an end to a higher degree than the potency.[22] For the act
of building is in the thing which is being built, and that act progresses

30 and has come to be simultaneously with the house. Accordingly, in those cases where that which is generated is something other than the use of the potency, the *actuality* of that potency is in the thing that is being made; for example, the act of building is in the thing which is being built, weaving is in the thing which is being woven, and similarly in the other cases, and, in general, motion is in the thing that is in

35 motion.[23] But in those cases in which there is no other function besides the *actuality*, the *actuality* exists in that which has it; for example, seeing is in that which sees, investigating is in a man who investigates,

1050b and life[24] is in the soul, and so happiness, too, is in the soul (for happiness is a kind of life). And so it is evident that the *substance* or the form is an *actuality*. According to this argument, then, it is evident that

5 *actuality* is prior in substance to potency; and as we said, one *actuality* always precedes another in time, until we come to the *actuality* of the eternal prime mover.[25]

What is more, *actuality* is prior in substance to potentiality in the more dominant sense;[26] for eternal things are prior in substance to destructible things, but nothing which exists potentially is eternal. The argument is as follows. Every potency is at the same time a potency for the contradictories; for, while that which is not capable of existing could

10 not exist at all, anything which is capable of existing may not be in *actuality*. Thus, that which is capable of existing may or may not exist; and so the same thing is capable of existing and of not existing. And that which has the capability of not existing may not be; and that which may not be is destructible, either without qualification, or with respect

15 to that which it may not be; for example, if in the latter case, it is with respect to place or quantity or quality,[27] but if without qualification, it is with respect to substance.[28] Hence, no thing which is indestructible without qualification exists potentially without qualification; but nothing prevents such a thing from being potential in some respect, for example, with respect to quality or place.[29] Indestructible things, then, exist in *actuality*.[30] Nor can things which exist of necessity exist potentially; and these are indeed primary, for if they did not exist, nothing

20 would exist.[31] Nor does motion exist potentially, if it exists eternally; nor is anything, which is in motion eternally, moved potentially except from place to place, and nothing prevents such things from having matter.[32] And so the Sun and the stars and the whole heaven are always active, and there is no fear that any of them will ever stop (although natural philos-

25 ophers do fear this). Nor are they worn out by this activity, for their motion does not come from a potentiality of two contradictories, as in destructible things, so as to make the continuity of such motion subject to wear; for the cause of weariness is substance in the sense of matter or potency,[33] and not in the sense of *actuality*.

30   Indestructible things are imitated by changing things, such as fire
and earth. For these, too, are always in activity; for they move in virtue
of themselves and have motion in themselves.[34] The other potencies,[35]
which have been distinguished, are all potencies for contradictories; for
that which can move something in a certain way can also move it not
in that way, that is, if it is a potency according to formula,[36] but if it is
a nonrational potency, the same one is a potency for contradictories by
being, respectively, present with or absent from that which it can move.[37]

35   If, then, there exist such natures or substances[38] as in various discussions
are called "Ideas", there will be something much more scientific than

1051a   Science Itself and also something much more in motion than Motion
Itself; for the former in each case is an *actuality* to a higher degree than
the latter, since the latter is only a potency for the former.

It is evident, then, that *actuality* is prior to potency and to every principle of change.

9

That a good *actuality* is better and more honorable than the poten-
5   tiality for it is clear from what follows.[1] If a thing is named according
to its capability, the same thing is capable of both contraries; for example, that which is said to be capable of being healthy is at the same
time capable of being sick, for the potentiality of being healthy is the
same as that of being sick, and likewise for the potentiality of being
10   at rest and in motion, of building and of demolishing, and of being built
and of being demolished. Now the potentiality for both contraries is
present at the same time, but the contraries cannot be present at the
same time; and the *actualities* of those contraries cannot be present in
a thing at the same time, as for example being healthy and being sick.
Thus, one of the two *actualities* must be good, but the corresponding
potentiality is alike a potentiality for both *actualities* or for neither of
15   them.[2] Hence, a good *actuality* is better than the potentiality for it.[3] It
is also necessary that the end and the *actuality* of what is bad is worse
than the potentiality for it; for that which is capable of a bad *actuality*
is capable of both contraries.

From this it is also clear that the bad does not exist apart from things;
for the bad is by nature posterior to the potentiality for it.[4] And so
20   nothing bad or defective or corrupt exists in the first principles and
eternal things; for corruption is a kind of badness.[5]

Also, geometrical demonstrations are discovered in *actuality;* for it
is by dividing that we discover them.[6] If the divisions were already
made, the theorems would be evident; as it is, they[7] exist potentially.

Why are the angles of a triangle equal to two right angles? In view of the fact that the angles about a point on a line are equal to two right angles. If the line parallel to one side had already been drawn, to the

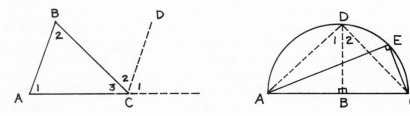

one who saw this the cause would be at once clear.[8] Why is the angle inscribed in a semicircle universally[9] a right angle? Because if the three lines are equal, two of them being the radii BA and BC from the center B and forming the base AC, and the other being the perpendicular BD, the theorem is clear to him who sees this[10] and understands the earlier theorem.[11] Thus it is evident that potential things are discovered by being brought to *actuality*. The cause of this is the fact that thinking is an *actuality*.[12] And so it is by *actuality*[13] that the potential becomes *actual;* and because of this we come to know by acting, for numerical *actuality*[14] is posterior in generation to its potentiality.

10

Since "being" and "nonbeing" have senses according to the types of categories and also according to the potentiality or *actuality* of these categories and their contraries,[1] but being in the most proper sense is the true and the false,[2] and this concerning[3] things is in view of the fact that they are united or separated, so that a man thinks truly if he thinks that what is separated is separated and what is united is united, but falsely if his thought is contrary to the way in which things exist, we may raise this question: When does truth or falsity[4] as expressed exist or not exist? Concerning this matter we must examine what our position is.

Now it is not because we think truly of your being white that you are white, but it is because you are white that we speak truly in saying that you are white.[5] If, then, some things are always united and cannot be separated, others are always separate and cannot be united, and still others can have both contraries[6] (and here *to be* is to be united and to be one, and *not to be* is not to be united but to be more than one), as regards those things which may have both contraries, the same opinion or the corresponding statement becomes false and true, and at one time

15   it may be true but at another time false.[7] But as regards things which
         cannot be otherwise,[8] the same belief or the corresponding statement
         does not become true at one time and false at another time, but it is
         always true or always false.

         Concerning things which are incomposite, what does "to be" or "not
         to be" or "truth" or "falsity" mean for them. Each of them is not a
         composite, like the white wood or the incommensurable diagonal, so
20   as *to be* when two things are united and *not to be* when they are sepa-
         rated; nor can truth and falsity belong to them as they do in the previous
         cases.[9] Or, just as truth about these is not the same, so *to be* is not the
         same for them; but truth about each of these is to apprehend it or to
25   assert it[10] (for affirmation and assertion are not the same), and ignorance
         of it is not to apprehend it.[11] For it is not possible to be mistaken about
         the whatness of something except accidentally.[12] Similar remarks may
         be made with regard to non-composite *substances,* for it is impossible
         to be mistaken about them. And all of them exist in *actuality,* not po-
         tentially, for otherwise they could be generated or destroyed; but as it
30   is, being itself is neither generated nor destroyed, for it would have to
         be generated from something.[13] Thus one cannot be mistaken concern-
         ing that which is just a being and in *actuality,* but either he conceives
         it or he does not. But we do inquire about the existence of them, namely,
         whether such things exist or not.[14]

         Concerning being as truth and nonbeing as falsity, being is true if
35   it is a united being but false if it is not united.[15] But in the case of what
1052a   is one, if it is just a being, it exists in just this way, and if not in this
         way, it does not exist;[16] and the truth about each such being is the
         conception of it, and there is neither falsity nor mistake about it but
         only ignorance, yet not the kind of ignorance which is like blindness,
         for blindness exists as if one were to have no power to conceive of it
         at all.

5   It is also evident, with regard to immovable things, that if anyone
         believes [truly] that they are immovable, he cannot be mistaken with
         respect to time. For example, if anyone thinks that a triangle does not
         change, he will not think that at one time the sum of its angles is equal
         to two right angles but at another time this is not so (for the triangle
         would then change). However, it is possible to think that some instances
         of an immovable thing have an attribute but others do not have it;[17]
         for example, one may think that no even number is prime, or that some
         even numbers are prime but other even numbers are not prime. But it
10   is not possible to think thus in the case of what is numerically one,[18] for
         one will no longer think that some instances have an attribute and others
         do not have it, but he will think either truly or falsely that something
         is always so.

Book I

1

That "one" is used in many senses has been stated previously in our account of the various meanings of terms.[1] Although "one" has many meanings, things which are called "one" primarily and essentially, but not accidentally, can be summarized under four heads.

20 (1) Things are one if they are continuous, either simply[2], or in the highest degree by nature, and not by contact or by being tied together; and of these, those whose motion is more indivisible and more simple are one to a higher degree and are prior.[3]

(2) As in the previous case, if the thing is a whole and has some *shape* or form, it is said to be one to a higher degree; and most of all, if it is 25 by nature of this sort and has something in itself which is the cause of its being continuous, and not by force as in things which are glued together or nailed together or tied together.[4] A thing is of this sort if its motion is one and is indivisible in place and time; so it is evident that if some magnitude has by nature a principle of motion, which motion is of the first kind, and of this kind it is the primary (that is, if this is locomotion[5] and it is circular[6]), then this magnitude[7] is primarily one. Some things, then, are one in this way, either continuous or wholes.

30 (3, 4) Others are called "one" if their formula is one. Such are those things of which the thinking is one, that is, they are such that the thinking of each is indivisible;[8] and it is indivisible if they are indivisible in kind or in number. (3) What is indivisible in number is the individual, (4) and the indivisible in kind[9] is [or are] the indivisible in knowledge or *knowledge*[10] so that that which causes a substance to be one[11] would be the primary one.[12]

35 The term "one", then, has these many senses: what is continuous by nature, and the whole, and the individual, and the universal. All these 1052*b* are one in view of the fact that they are indivisible, some in motion, and others in the thinking of them or in their formula.

We should keep this fixed in mind that the questions "What sort of

things are said to be one?" and "What is the essence of one?" and "What
is its formula?" must not be taken as if they were the same. For "one"
5   has the various senses just given, and each thing will be one if it comes
under some one of those senses; but "the essence of one" will sometimes mean to be one in some one of these senses, but sometimes it
will mean something else, which is closer to the meaning of the name
"one" and is potentially each of those senses.[13] This is so also with the
terms "element" and "cause", if, on the one hand, one were to state
definitely which are the things of which each term is predicated, and
10   if, on the other, he were to define each term. For in one sense the element is *Fire*[14] (perhaps it is the *Infinite* by itself,[15] or some other such
object), but in another sense it is not; for the essence of fire and the
essence of an element are not the same, so while the element may be
fire as a certain thing and a nature, yet the name "element" signifies
that so-and-so belongs to something, namely, that something else consists of it as a primary constituent.[16]
15   Similarly with "cause", "one", and all such terms. Thus, too, to be
one is to be indivisible, and this is to be a *this* and separable by itself
either in place or in kind or in *thought*, or, in addition, to be a whole and
indivisible. Most of all, it is to be the first measure of each genus, and
most properly, of quantity, for it is from this that it has been extended
to the others.
20   Now a measure is that by which a quantity is known; and a quantity
qua quantity is known either by a unity or by a number,[17] and every
number is known by a unity. Thus, every quantity is known qua quantity by a unity, and that by which, as first, quantities are known is
that which is one. And so a unity is the principle of a number qua num-
25   ber. Hence, also in other things we speak of a measure as being something by which as first they are known, and the measure of each is
a unity, whether in length, or in width, or in depth, or in weight, or in
speed. The terms "weight" and "speed" here mean what is commonly
possessed by both contraries in each case, for each of the terms has two
senses. For example, "weight" means either any tendency whatever to
go down[18] or an excessive tendency to go down, and a thing is said to
30   have speed either if it has any motion whatever or if it has excessive
motion; for, in one sense, even what is slow has speed, and even what
is lighter has weight. Now in all these, the measure and the principle
is something which is one and indivisible, since even in lines we treat
the length of one foot as indivisible.[19] For everywhere we seek as a
measure something which is one and indivisible; and this is something
35   which is simple either in quality or in quantity.
         Now where it is thought impossible to subtract or add, there we have
1053*a* a measure which is accurate.[20] Consequently, the measure of a number

is the most accurate; for a unit is posited as indivisible in all respects. In all other cases, we imitate such a measure. For in the case of a stade or a talent or anything which is comparatively large, the addition or subtraction of something might escape notice more than in the case of something comparatively small. And so the first thing to or from which, according to sensation, nothing can be added or subtracted without being noticed, this is made by all the measure,[21] whether of liquids, or of solids, or of weight, or of magnitudes; and we think we understand the quantity of something only when we understand it through this measure.

Indeed, we understand motion too by the simple[22] and fastest motion; for this occupies the least time.[23] And so in astronomy we posit as a principle and a measure something which is one of this sort; for such we assume to be the motion of the heavens, which is uniform and fastest,[24] and we *judge* other motions by relating them to this.[25] And in music we have the quarter-tone, in view of the fact that it is the least interval, and in voice we have the letter. And each of these is one in this sense, not that what is one is something common to them,[26] but as we said.

However, the measure is not always one numerically, but sometimes more than one; for example, we have two quarter-tones as measures (not with respect to hearing but with respect to ratio[27]), and the measures of voice are many,[28] and the diagonal and the side of a square are measured by two quantities, and similarly with all other magnitudes.[29] Thus, then, the one is the measure in all cases, in view of the fact that we know the constituent principles of the *substance* of something by dividing either with respect to quantity or with respect to kind.[30] And the one is indivisible because of the fact that the first in each genus is indivisible. But it is not in a similar way that the one is indivisible in all the cases; for example, in the case of one foot and one unit, the latter is indivisible in every respect, while the former tends to be indivisible when referred to sensation,[31] as we have already stated; for, perhaps[32] everything continuous is divisible.

The measure is always of the same kind as that which is measured; for the measure of magnitudes is a magnitude, and specifically, the measure of length is a length, that of width is a width, that of voice is a voice, that of weight is a weight, and that of units is a unit. For we must state the matter as we did, but we must not say that the measure of numbers is a number, although we should have, if we were to use similar language. But the claim in the case of number is not similar to that of the other cases, for it is similar to the claim that the measure of units is units and not a unit; but a number is a plurality of units.[33] And for the same *reason* we call also *knowledge* and sensa-

tion "a measure of things", in view of the fact that we know something
by them,[34] although they are measured rather than they measure.[35] In
fact, it is as if someone else measured us and we came to know how
35   big we are by observing the extent to which he applied the foot-rule
to us. Yet Protagoras says "man is the measure of all things", as if he
1053b   had said "the man who *knows*" or "the man who *senses*", seeing that
the first man has *knowledge* and the second has sensation, which people
say are the measures of things. Indeed, he is saying nothing, although
he appears to be saying something remarkable.

It is evident, then, that to be one, if we are to describe it especially
5   according to the name, is to be some measure, most properly of quantity, and then of quality.[36] And it will be such if, in the first case, it is
indivisible with respect to quantity, and in the second, indivisible with
respect to quality. Hence, the one is indivisible, either simply, or qua
one.[37]

2

With respect to the *substance* and nature of oneness we must inquire,
10   as we did in the discussion of *difficulties*,[1] what oneness is and how we
should consider it, whether it is a substance of a sort, as the Pythagoreans
said first and Plato later, or rather there is some nature underlying it,
in which case we should make this more known and speak more in the
15   manner of the physical philosophers; for one of these says that the one
is *Friendship*,[2] another that it is *Air*,[3] another that it is the *Infinite*.[4]

If indeed no universal can be a substance, as we have stated in our
discussion of substance and of being,[5] and if being itself cannot exist
as a substance and as something which is one and is apart from the
20   many (for it is common to all) but only as a predicate, then neither can
unity be a substance; for "being" and "unity" are the most universal
of all predicates. Thus, neither are the genera natures of some kind and
substances separable from other things, nor can "unity" be a genus for
the same reasons for which "being" and "*substance*" cannot be genera.[6]

Further, the situation with unity is similar to that of all the others.
25   Now "unity" has as many senses as "being"; so since in qualities the
one is a certain thing and a certain nature, and similarly in quantities,
it is clear that we should inquire in general what unity is,[7] just as we
should inquire what being is, as it is not enough to say that the nature
of unity is just unity. But in colors that which is one is a color; for ex-
30   ample, whiteness, that is, if the other colors appear to be generated
from white and black, black being the privation of white just as darkness
is the privation of light.[8] Thus, if things were colors, they would be a

certain number, but of something, evidently of colors indeed; and the one would be one something, namely, whiteness. Similarly, if things were tones, there would be a number, but a number of quarter-tones, and their *substance* would not be just a number; and the one would be something whose *substance* would be not unity but a quarter-tone. Similarly in the case of articulate voice, all things would be a number of letters, and unity in letters would be a vowel. And if all things were rectilinear figures, there would be a number of figures, and the one would be a triangle.[9] The same argument may be used in the other genera of things. Hence, since there are numbers and also a unity of some kind in affections, and in qualities, and in quantities, and in motions, and since in each of them the number is a number of certain things and the corresponding unity is a certain thing but the *substance* of that unity is not just unity, the situation must be similar also with substances; for the situation is similar for all cases.

It is evident, then, that in every genus unity is a certain nature, and that the nature of unity is in no case just unity itself; but just as in colors we must seek that unity as one color, so in substances we must seek it as one substance. That "unity" has in some sense[10] the same meaning as that of "being" is clear (a) from the fact that it follows the categories equally and is not within just one of them (for example, unity is neither within the category of whatness only, nor within that of quality only, but is related to them just as being is), (b) from the fact that nothing more is predicated by using "one man" rather than "man", just as in the case of "being" when added to "whatness" or to "quality" or to "quantity",[11] and (c) from the fact that to be one[12] is to be some one of these latter.

3

The one and the many are opposed in many ways. In one way, the one is opposed to plurality as the indivisible to the divisible;[1] for what is either divided or divisible is called "a plurality", and what is indivisible or not divided is called "one". Now since there are four kinds of opposition, and since of the two opposites one of them is said to be opposed according to privation,[2] one and plurality must be contraries, but neither contradictories nor relatives.[3] Now unity is named after and made known from its contrary, that is, the indivisible from the divisible, because plurality or the divisible is more sensible than the indivisible, so that plurality is prior in formula to the indivisible because of sensation.

Under unity there is sameness and likeness and equality, as we have specified in our *List of Contraries*,[4] and under plurality there

is otherness and unlikeness and inequality. The term "the same" has
several meanings. (1) Sometimes we speak of that which is the same
numerically.[5] (2) That which is one in formula as well as in number; for
example, you are one with yourself both in form and in matter. (3) If
the formula of the first *substance* of a thing is one.[6] For example, equal
straight lines are the same, and so are equal and equal-angled quad-
rangles although they are many;[7] but in these equality[8] is a unity.

Things are called "similar" or "alike" (1) if they are not the same
without qualification, nor without a difference with respect to their
composite *substance*,[9] although they are the same in kind. For example,
the greater square is similar to the smaller square, and unequal straight
lines are alike; for these are similar, but not the same without qualification.[10] (2) Things are said to be similar if, having the same form and
admitting a difference of degree, they do not differ in degree.[11] (3) Also,
if they have the same affection which is one in species; for example,
things which are white, whether bright or dim, are said to be alike, in
view of the fact that they are one in species. (4) Also, if things are in
more respects the same than they are distinct, either without qualification or with respect to their obvious attributes; for example, tin is like
silver, and gold is like fire qua yellow or flame-colored.[12]

It is clear, then, that "the other" (or "the distinct") and "the unlike"
have many meanings. In one sense, the distinct is opposed to the same,
and so one thing is either the same as or distinct from another thing.[13]
In another sense, two things are distinct if not both their matter and
formula are one;[14] and so you and your neighbor are distinct. In a third
sense, things are distinct corresponding to the mathematical examples
given.[15] Now it is because of this[16] that sameness and otherness relate
only objects each of which is one and a being, whatever these may
be. For "otherness" is not the contradictory of "sameness". Thus, "the
other" is not a predicate of nonbeing; however, "not the same" is a
predicate of nonbeing,[17] and it can be a predicate of every being, for
any being or unity is by nature either one or not one with another being
or unity.

Otherness and sameness, then, are opposed in the manner stated, but
difference is distinct from otherness. For the distinct and that from
which it is distinct are not necessarily distinct in some respect; for any
thing is either distinct from or the same as any thing whatsoever. But
that which is different is different from something else in some respect,
so that there must be something which is the same with respect to which
there is a difference.[18] And that which is the same is the genus or the
species; for that which differs does so with respect to a genus or a
species, with respect to a genus if the things do not have a common
matter and if no generation exists from the one to the other (for

Line markers in left margin:
35
1054*b*
5
10
15
20
25

30 example, if they come under distinct categories), and with respect to
a species if they are under the same genus. By "genus" we mean the
same predicate of both things which differ according to *substance*. As
for contraries, they are things which are different, and contrariety is a
kind of difference. That this hypothesis is well taken is clear by in-
35 duction. For all these[19] appear to be different, not being just distinct;
but some are distinct in genus, while others are distinct within the
1055a same category and so are in the same genus or are the same in genus.[20]
We have specified elsewhere[21] what sort of things are the same or distinct in genus.

4

Since things which differ from one another may do so to a greater
5 or less degree, there exists also a greatest[1] difference, and this I call
"contrariety". That there is a greatest difference is clear by induction.
For things which differ in genus have no way of proceeding to each
other but are far removed and noncomparable.[2] As for things which
differ in species, their generations proceed from contraries as from
10 extremes; and the interval from extremes is the greatest, and so the
interval between contraries is also the greatest. But surely what is
greatest in each genus is complete. For that is greatest which cannot
be exceeded, and that is complete beyond which nothing can be found.
For complete difference has an end (just as in the case of other things
which are said to be complete by having an end), and beyond the end
15 there is nothing; for in everything the end is an extreme and includes
all, and therefore, beyond the end there is nothing, and the complete
needs nothing more.[3]

It is clear from what has been said, then, that contrariety is complete
difference. Since we speak of contraries in many senses, the senses of
"complete" will follow these senses in the manner in which the essence
of contrariety will belong to the contraries.[4]

20 This being so, it is evident that each contrary cannot have more than
one contrary; for neither can there be anything more extreme than the
extreme, nor can there be more than two extremes for one interval. And
in general, if contrariety is a difference, and a difference is between
two things, then complete difference will also be between two things.[5]

The other definitions of contraries must also be true of contraries.[6]
25 For (1) a complete difference is the greatest difference since nothing
beyond it can be found, whether things differ in genus or in species.
For it has been shown that there is no difference in relation to things
outside of a genus,[7] and in things within a genus complete difference

is the greatest; and (2) things in the same genus which differ most are contraries, for complete difference between these is the greatest;[8] and (3) contraries are things which differ most in the same subject which can receive them, for it is the same matter that is receptive of contraries;[9] and (4) the most different things which come under the same faculty are contraries; for it is one science that deals with one genus of things, and among these complete difference is the greatest.[10]

The primary contrariety is that of possession and privation, and not every privation (for "privation" has many senses) but that which is complete.[11] The others are called "contraries" according to these contraries, in the sense that some have these contraries, others produce or can produce these, others are processes of acquiring or of losing these or other contraries.[12] Now if the oppositions are contradiction, privation,[13] contrariety, and relatives, and since of these contradiction is primary,[14] and nothing can exist between two contradictories but something may exist between contraries, it is clear that contradictories and contraries are not the same.[15] But a privation is a kind of contradiction; for either that which cannot have something at all, or that which does not have what it would by nature have, is said to be deprived, either altogether or in some determinate way[16] (for the term "privation" here has many senses, which we have distinguished elsewhere[17]). Thus, a privation is a contradiction or an incapacity which is determinate or included in the subject which can have it. Therefore, although there is nothing between two contradictories, in some cases of a privation there is something between; for, every object is equal or is not equal, but not everything is equal or unequal, but if so, only in the case of a thing which is receptive of the equal.[18] If, then, generations in matter take place from contraries, and if they proceed either (a) from the form or the possession of the form, or (b) from some privation of the form or of the *shape*, it is clear that every contrariety would be a privation but not every privation would be equally a contrariety. The cause of this is the fact that that which is deprived may be deprived in many ways.[19] For it is only the extremes from which changes proceed that are contraries. This is also evident by induction. For every contrariety has a privation of one of the contraries. But not all cases are similar; for inequality is the privation of equality, unlikeness is the privation of likeness, and vice is the privation of virtue. And privations differ as we have stated; for, in one case we have a privation if the thing is only deprived,[20] in another, if it is deprived at a certain time,[21] or in a certain part (for example, at a certain age, or in the main part), or entirely.[22] Therefore, in some cases there is something between (there are men who are neither good nor bad[23]), but in other cases there is nothing between (a number must be either odd or even). Further, some contraries have a definite underlying subject, others do not.[24] Thus, it is evident that one of the contraries is always called according to privation; but it is enough if this is so of the primary or generic contraries, for example, the one and the many, for the rest are led back to these.

5

30 Since each contrary has only one contrary, one might raise the question how the one is opposed to the many, and the equal to the great and the small.

We use the term "whether" in a disjunction of two opposites; for example, "whether white or black", and "whether white or not white".
35 But we do not say "whether a man or white", except in a hypothetical way or by way of inquiry, as for example in "whether it was Cleon or Socrates that came". In the latter case, the two parts of the disjunction need not be in any genus. However, this usage of "whether" here is an extension of the former usage; for only opposites cannot belong at
1056a the same time to the same thing, and "whether" is so used here as to exclude the possibility of the arrival of both Cleon and Socrates, for otherwise the phrase "whether it was Cleon or Socrates that came" would be ridiculous.[1] Even if the coming of both Cleon and Socrates was granted as one part of the disjunction, we would still have a disjunctive opposition in a similar way, a disjunction of the one and the many, for example, "whether both came or just one of them".[2]

If, then, we use the word "whether" always when our inquiry is about
5 opposites, and we do ask "whether it is greater or less or equal", what is the opposition of the equal to the greater and the less? For the equal cannot be contrary to just one of them or to both; for why should it be contrary to the greater rather than to the less?[3] Moreover, the equal is contrary to the unequal. So, it would be contrary to more than one thing.[4] But if "the unequal" means the same for both [the greater and
10 the less] at the same time, it would be opposed to both;[5] and this perplexity supports those who say that the *Unequal* is a *Dyad*.[6] But the consequence is that one of a pair of contraries has two opposing contraries, and this is indeed impossible.[7]

Again, the equal appears to be an intermediate between the great and the small, but neither does a contrariety appear to exist between, nor is such possible from the definition; for it would not be complete
15 if it were between something, but rather, it is always something else that is between it.[8]

It remains, then, that the equal is opposed to the great and the small either as a denial or as a privation.[9] But it cannot be so opposed to either of the two; for why should it be opposed to the great rather than to the small? It is opposed to both of them, then, as a privative denial. This is why the word "whether" is referred to both, and not to just one of them (for example, not "whether greater or equal" and not "whether equal or less"), but all three are included.[10] There is a privation of necessity;[11] for not everything which is not greater or less is equal, but only the things which can by nature be greater or less. The equal, then, is that which is neither great nor small but can by nature be great or small, and it is opposed to both as a privative denial;[12] and this is why it is between them.[13] And that which is neither good nor bad is so opposed to both good and bad, but it has no name; for "good" and "bad" have many meanings, and the subject which can receive them is not unique.[14] But that which is neither white nor black is unique to a higher degree than that which is neither good nor bad; yet even this is not uniquely stated, although the colors of which this privative denial is asserted are somehow limited (for they must be grey or yellow or something else of this sort).[15]

Therefore, those who think that all such expressions have similar meanings, so that between a shoe and a hand there should be that which is neither a shoe nor a hand if between the good and the bad there is that which is neither good nor bad (as if there should be something intermediate in all cases), are not right in their criticism of others. Their conclusion does not necessarily follow. For in the one case, the joint denial is of those opposites which have something between, and there is some interval by nature; but in the other case no differentiae exist, for the two things which are jointly denied are in distinct genera, and so the underlying subject is not one.[16]

6

One might raise similar questions about the one and the many. For if the many are opposed to the one without specification, certain impossibilities will follow. For, (1) the one will be a little or few,[1] since the many are opposed also to the few. Moreover, (2) two will be many if the double, which derives its name from two, is indeed a multiple. So, the one will be few; for relative to what will two be many if not relative to the one and the few? For there is nothing else which is less than two.[2] Further, (3) as the long and the short are in length, so the much and the little are in plurality, and whatever is much is also many, and the many are much. Then, if no difference arises in the continuous which can easily be bounded,[3] the little will be an instance of a plurality. Therefore, the one will be an instance of a plurality, if indeed it is a little; and this follows necessarily, if two are many.[4]

Perhaps the many are in some sense also called "much", yet with a difference, as in the case of water which is called "much", but not "many".[5] But "many" is asserted of whatever is divisible;[6] and (a) in one sense, if it is a plurality in excess, either without qualification or in relation to something[7] (and likewise "little"[8] is asserted of a plurality which is deficient[9]), but (b) in another sense, if it is asserted of a number,[10] and a number

20   is opposed only to the one. For it is in the latter sense that we speak of one and many, as if someone were to say "one and ones", or "the white and the whites", or "the measured or measurable in relation to the measure".[11] It is also in this manner that we speak of multiples; for each number is said to be many in view of the fact that it is unities, and

25   measurable by a unity, and it is many as opposed to the one and not to the little. Thus, it is in this sense that also two is many, not as a plurality in excess, whether relative to something or without qualification, but as a plurality, although the first plurality.[12] Now two is few without qualification; for two is the first plurality which is deficient (and for this reason Anaxagoras was not right in leaving the subject by saying

30   "all things were together, infinite both in plurality and in smallness" [and he should have used "in fewness"[13] and not "in smallness"], for things are not infinite in fewness), since it is not because of the one, as some say, but because of two that something is a little.

       In numbers, the one is opposed to the many as the measure to the measurable; and these are opposed as relatives, that is, those which are relatives not in virtue of themselves. Elsewhere we have distinguished

.35   two senses in which things are called "relative":[14] (1) some as in the case of contraries, (2) others as in the case of *knowledge* to the *knowable*,

1057a in the sense that something else is asserted in relation to a thing. But nothing prevents the one from being less than something, for example, less than two; for if it is less, it is not therefore a little.[15] As for plurality, it is as if it were a genus of number;[16] for a number is a plurality measurable by the one.[17] And in some sense the one and a number are op-

5   posed, not as contraries, but, as we have said, as some relatives; for the one, qua a measure, is opposed to a number qua measurable. This is why not everything that is one[18] is a number, for example, if there is something which is indivisible. Although *knowledge* is similarly related to the *knowable*, this is not so represented; for it would seem that *knowl-*

10   *edge* is a measure and the *knowable* is that which is measured, yet all *knowledge* is *knowable* but not all the *knowable* is *knowledge,* so that in some sense *knowledge* is measured by the *knowable*.[19] As for plurality, it is neither the contrary of the little (but it is that which is much that is contrary to that which is little, in the sense that plurality in excess is contrary to plurality which is deficient), nor the contrary of

15   unity in every sense. But as we said, in one sense it is a contrary as the divisible[20] to the indivisible, and in another sense, as a relative to

its correlative (as in the case of *knowledge* to the *knowable*), provided that plurality is a number and the one is a measure.

7

Since there may be an intermediate between contraries, and in some cases there is, intermediates must consist of contraries.[1]

Now all intermediates are in the same genus as the contraries between which they are. For we call "intermediates" those into which that which changes into something must change before.[2] For example, if one were to pass from the highest string to the lowest by the smallest intervals, he would come to the intermediate tones before; and if in colors he were to pass from white to black, he would come to crimson and grey before coming to black; and similarly with the others. But it is not possible to change from one genus to another except accidentally, as from color to shape for example.[3] All intermediates, then, as well as the things between which they are, must be in the same genus.

Moreover, all intermediates are between certain opposites; for things which change essentially can only do so from these opposites. This is why it is impossible for intermediates to be between things which are not opposites; for there would then be a change even from non-opposites. Now of opposites, in the case of contradictories there is nothing between; for a contradiction is this, namely, an opposition, of which only one of its two parts is present in a thing, and which has nothing between. Of the remaining opposites, some are relatives, some are privations,[4] and some are contraries. Those relatives which are not contraries[5] have nothing between. The cause of this is the fact that they are not in the same genus. For what is between *knowledge* and the *knowable*?[6] But between the great and the small there is something.[7]

If the intermediates then are in the same genus, as has been shown, and are between contraries,[8] they must consist of these contraries. For either there will be a genus of these contraries or not. And if there will be a genus in such a way that there will then be something prior to the contraries, the differentiae of that genus, which caused the contrary species of that genus, will be contraries prior to the contrary species of that genus; for a species is a composite of a genus and a differentia. For example, if whiteness and blackness are contraries, and whiteness is a piercing color but blackness is a compressing color, the differentiae 'piercing' and 'compressing' will be prior; so that these are the prior contraries of one another.[9] Moreover, things which differ in a contrary manner are contrary to a higher degree,[10] and the others which are intermediate will be composed of the genus and the differentiae. For

example, each color which is between whiteness and blackness must
15 be said to be composed of the genus (the genus here is 'color') and a
certain differentia. But this differentia will not be a primary contrary;
otherwise, each intermediate color will be either whiteness or blackness.
Hence, it will be distinct from the primary contraries;[11] and so it will
be between the primary contraries (and the latter are the primary
differentiae, the 'piercing' and the 'compressing'). Thus, our first con-
20 cern should be with these primary contraries which are not in a genus,[12]
and we must ask of what their intermediates are composed. For things
which are in the same genus[13] must be composed of incomposites which
exclude the genus, or else be incomposites. Now the contraries are not
composed of each other,[14] and so they are principles; as for the intermediates, either all of them are incomposite or none. But there is a thing
which comes to be from a contrary,[15] so that a change into this thing
25 will precede the change into the other contrary; and this thing will be
more of one contrary and less of the other. This thing, then, will be
between contraries. And so all the other intermediates, too, will be
combinations; for that which has more of one contrary and less of the
other is somehow a combination of those of which it is said to have
more of the one and less of the other.[16] Since, then, there are no other
30 things which are of the same genus as, but prior to, the contraries, all
the intermediates must consist of contraries. Hence, all the lower ones,
too, both contrary and intermediates,[17] will be composites from the primary contraries.[18] It is clear, then, that all the intermediates are in the
same genus, that they are between contraries, and that they all consist
of[19] contraries.

8

35 That which is other [or distinct] in species than something must be
some thing which is other, and this thing must be in both. For example,
if a certain animal is other in species than something else, both must
be animals. Things which are other in species, then, must be in the
same genus. By "genus" I mean that which, being one and the same, is
1058a asserted of both, and which is not accidentally differentiated,[1] whether
as matter[2] or in some other way. For not only must this which is common
belong to both, for example, not only must both be animals, but this
animality must also be distinct in each of the two,[3] for example, the
one must be a horse and the other a man; and because of this, that which
5 is common is said to be other in species in the two cases. One thing,
then, will be in virtue of itself one sort of animal, and the other another
sort of animal; for example, the one will be a horse, the other a man.

This difference, then, must be an otherness of the genus. For this otherness of the genus, which makes the genus itself distinct, I call "differentia". Accordingly, this differentia will be a contrast,[4] and this is clear
also by induction. For everything is divided by opposites, and it has
been shown that it is contraries that are in the same genus. For contrariety was shown to be complete difference,[5] and every difference in
a species is an otherness of something, so that this something is the
same and is the genus of both. That is why all contraries which are
different in species[6] but not in genus are in the same line of predication
and are most distinct; for the difference of contraries is complete, and
these cannot exist together[7] in the same thing.[8] A difference, then, is a
contrast. This, then, is what it is to be distinct in species, namely, to
possess contrast while being in the same genus and being indivisible.[9]

Things are said to be the same in species if they are indivisible and
possess no contrast; for it is in division[10] and in the intermediates[11] that
contrasts arise before we come to the indivisibles.[12] Therefore, it is
evident that no species of a genus is either the same in species or other
in species if it is related to its so-called "genus"[13] (and this is as it should
be; for matter is made known by denial, and the genus is the matter of
that of which it is called the genus, not in the sense in which we speak
of the genus [or race] of the Heracleidae, but in the sense in which genus
exists in the nature of the thing), or if it is related to something not in
the same genus; but it will differ in genus from the latter,[14] and in
species from other species in the same genus as itself. For the difference
of that which differs in species must be a contrast;[15] and this belongs
only to things in the same genus.

9

The question might be raised as to why a woman does not differ
from a *man* in species, although male and female are contraries and
their difference is a contrast, and why a female animal and a male
animal are not distinct in species. Yet this is an essential difference of
animals and not like whiteness and blackness,[1] and female and male
belong to animals qua animals. This question is about the same as the
following: "Why does one contrast make things distinct in species, but
another does not?" For example, footed-ness and winged-ness make
animals distinct in species, but whiteness and blackness do not.

Is it in view of the fact that the former are *proper attributes* of the
genus, but the latter are less[2] so? Also, since one part of the thing is the
formula and the other the matter, contrarieties[3] which are in the formula
do make a difference in species, but those which are in the *composite*,

which includes matter, do not. This is why whiteness and blackness in men do not cause a difference in species, and a white man does not differ according to species from a black man, not even if one name[4] is posited for each. For a man here is like matter,[5] and matter does not bring about a difference. And because of this, men are not species of "man", although the flesh and the bones of which this man and that man consist are distinct. And although the *composites* are distinct, they are not distinct in species in view of the fact that there is no contrast in their formula; and this[6] is the ultimate indivisible. But "Callias" is the formula with the matter.[7] And a man is white in view of the fact that Callias is white; accordingly, a man is by accident white.[8] Nor does a bronze circle differ in species from a wooden circle.[9] Nor do a bronze triangle and a wooden circle differ in species because of their matter, but in view of the fact that there is contrast in their formulae.

If matter is somehow distinct, then, is it a fact that it does not make things distinct in species, or is there a sense in which it does? For why is this horse distinct in species from this man? Yet their formulae include matter.[10] Or is it in view of the fact that it is in their formulae that there is contrast? But there is also contrast in a white man and a black horse. And these are distinct in species, but not qua white (in the case of the man) and qua black (in the case of the horse), since a man and a horse would be distinct in species even if they were both white. As for the male and the female, although *proper attributes* of animals,[11] they are in their matter or body and are not attributes according to their[12] *substance*. This is why the same seed, being affected in one way or another, becomes male or female.

We have stated, then, what it is to be distinct in species, and why some things differ in species but others do not.

10

Since contraries are distinct in kind, and the destructible[1] and the indestructible are contraries (for a privation is a definite incapacity),[2] the destructible and the indestructible must be distinct in genus.[3]

So far we have spoken in universal terms, so that it might not seem necessary for any indestructible and destructible things to be distinct in species, just as in the case of what is white and black.[4] For the same thing may be both and at the same time, if it is universally taken, just as a man so taken might be white and black;[5] and the same may be said of individuals, for the same individual may be now white and now black,[6] although not at the same time. Nevertheless the white is contrary to the black.

But of contraries some belong to some things by accident, like the
ones just mentioned and many others as well, other contraries cannot
so belong, and the destructible and the indestructible are among them;
for nothing is destructible by accident. For that which belongs to something by accident may not belong to it; but destructibility belongs of
necessity to that to which it belongs,[7] otherwise, one and the same thing
would be destructible and indestructible if destructibility may not belong to it. Thus, destructibility must either be the *substance* of each
destructible thing or belong to that *substance*. The argument is the same
for indestructibility, for each of them belongs to a thing of necessity.
Therefore, those[8] qua which, or in virtue of which as first, one thing is
destructible and another thing is indestructible, are opposite, and so
they must be distinct in genus.

Accordingly, it is evident that Forms, such as some thinkers posit,
cannot exist; for otherwise there would be a destructible man and an
indestructible man.[9] Yet the Forms are said (a) to be the same in species
as the corresponding individuals, and (b) to be called by the same name
not equivocally; but things which are distinct in genus are more distinct
than things which are distinct in species.

Book K

1

That wisdom is a science of principles is clear from our first remarks[1] in which we discussed the problems confronted by other thinkers who spoke about principles; but one might raise the problem as to whether wisdom should be believed to be one science or many. For if one, the fact still remains that it is always one science which deals with contraries; but the principles are not contrary.[2] And if it is not one, what kind of sciences should we posit them to be?[3]

Again, does it belong to one or to more sciences to investigate the principles of demonstration? If to one, why should it belong to this rather than to any other?[4] If to more, what kind of sciences should we posit them to be?[5]

Again, does wisdom deal with all substances or not?[6] If not with all, it is difficult to say what kinds of substances it deals with. If one science deals with all substances, it is not clear how the same science can deal with all of them.[7]

Again, does wisdom deal only with *substances* or also with their attributes?[8] If with both, there is a demonstration of attributes, but not of *substances*. If one science deals with *substances* and another with the attributes, what science is each and which of them is wisdom? For the science dealing with the attributes will be demonstrative wisdom, but the science of *substances* will be dealing with what is first.[9]

But the science sought should not be posited as dealing with the causes stated in the *Physics*.[10] For it is not concerned with final cause, since such is the good, and this is found in the field of *action* and in things which are in motion; and this is the first thing that causes motion (for such is the end), and the first thing that causes motion is not found in immovable things.[11]

In general, there is this problem, whether the science we now seek is concerned at all with sensible substances or not, but with some other substances.[12] If with others, it would be either with the Forms or with

Mathematical Objects.[13] Now clearly the Forms do not exist.[14] There is
still a *difficulty* even if one posits their existence, namely, why the same
is not the case with the other things of which there are Forms as it is
with the mathematical objects. What I mean is this, that these thinkers
place the Mathematical Objects between the Forms and the sensible
things as if a third kind besides the Forms and those[15] among the
sensibles; but there is no third man and no third horse besides the
corresponding Ideas of them and individual men and horses.[16] If, on
the other hand, it is not as they say, with what sort of things should we
posit the mathematician to be concerned? Certainly not with the things
of this world; for none of these is such as the mathematical sciences
seek.[17] Nor is the science which we now seek concerned with mathematical objects; for none of them is separable. Nor yet is it concerned
with sensible substances; for they are destructible.[18]

In general, one might raise the question as to what kind of science
should discuss the *difficulties* about matter in the mathematical
sciences.[19] For it belongs neither to physics, because the whole inquiry
of the physicist is about things which have in themselves a principle of
motion and of rest, nor yet to the science which is concerned with demonstration and scientific knowledge, for this science inquires into just
this genus. It remains, then, that it is the philosophy which we proposed
which should inquire into these matters.[20]

One might discuss the problem whether the task of dealing with
the principles, which are called "elements" by some, should be assigned
to the science we are seeking. All thinkers take the position that these
principles are present in composite things. But it would seem that the
science we are seeking should be concerned rather with universals; for
all discussions and all sciences are about universals and not about the
last things[21] of which universals are predicated, and so in this sense
the science we are seeking would be concerned with the first genera.[22]
These, then, would turn out to be 'being' and 'unity'; for these most
of all would be believed to include all things and to be like principles
most of all, because they are first by nature; for, if these are destroyed,
all the rest disappear also, since every thing is a being and is one. However, if one posits these as genera, then, inasmuch as their differentiae
would necessarily share in them while no differentia could share in a
genus, for this reason it would seem that we should posit them neither
as genera nor as principles.[23]

Again, if the more simple is a principle to a higher degree than the
less simple, and the ultimate subdivisions[24] of the genus are simpler than
the genera (for they are indivisible, but the genera are subdivided into
many and different species), the species would seem to be principles to
a higher degree than the genera. On the other hand, inasmuch as the

species are annihilated if the genera are annihilated, the genera would seem to be principles more than the species;[25] for an object is a principle of other objects if its annihilation means also the annihilation of the others.[26] These, then, and other such *difficulties* arise.

2

Again, should we posit something[1] besides the individuals, or, if not, is the science we are seeking concerned with these?[2] But these are
5   infinite.[3] At least, besides the individuals, there are the genera and the species;[4] but the science we are now seeking is concerned with neither of them. We have stated why this is impossible.[5] And in general there is this problem, whether or not we should believe that there exists a separate substance[6] other than the sensible substances or the substances
10   in this world, or that these are the objects that exist and these are the concern of wisdom. For we seem to be seeking another substance, and the issue before us is this, namely, to see whether there is something separate by itself and belonging to no sensible thing.

Further, if there is some other substance besides the sensible substances, to what kind of sensible things should we posit this substance
15   to correspond? For why should one posit this substance to correspond to men rather than to horses or to other animals or even to inanimate things in general?[7] Even so, to construct eternal substances equal in number to sensible and destructible substances would seem to go beyond what is reasonable?[8] But if the principle we are now seeking
20   is not separable from bodies, what other principle, more than matter, would one posit it to be? Matter, to be sure, does not exist in *actuality*, yet it does exist potentially. But it would seem that the form or *shape* is more entitled to be a principle than matter;[9] yet this [form or *shape*] is destructible, and so there is no eternal substance at all which is separate and by itself. But this is absurd, for such a principle or a sub-
25   stance seems to exist and is sought by almost all distinguished men; for how can there be order if there is nothing eternal and separate and permanent?

Again, if indeed there is a substance and a principle of such a nature as that which we are now seeking, and if this is one and the same for all things, eternal as well as destructible, a *difficulty* arises as to why it is
30   that, although this principle is the same, some things coming under it are eternal but others are not;[10] for this is absurd. But if there is one principle of destructible and another principle of eternal things, if the principle of destructible things is also eternal, a similar *difficulty* arises; for why, if this principle is eternal, are not the things under it also
35   eternal?[11] But if this principle is destructible, there will be of this prin-

ciple another principle, and of the latter principle still another principle, and this will go on to infinity.[12]

Moreover,[13] if one posits being and unity as the objects which are thought to be immovable principles most of all, first, if each of the terms "being" and "unity" does not signify a *this* and a substance, how will being and unity be separate and by themselves?[14] But such are the eternal and first principles which we seek. But if each of those terms does signify a *this* and a substance, all things will be substances;[15] for "being" is a predicate of every thing, and of some of them also "unity" is a predicate.[16] But it is false to think that all things are substances. Further, as for those[17] who say that the first principle is the *One* and that this is a substance, and who generate first Numbers from the *One* and matter and say that these are substances, how can their statements be true? For how are we to conceive of Two and each of the other composite[18] Numbers as being *One*?[19] They neither say anything about this, nor is it easy to say anything.

If, however, one posits as principles lines and what follows them[20] (I mean the primary surfaces[21]), these are not even separate substances, but sections or divisions, the former of surfaces and the latter of bodies (and points are sections or divisions of lines), and further, they are limits of these same things; and all of them exist in something else and none is separable.[22]

Further, how are we to believe that the *One* and the point[23] are substances? For, there is a generation of every substance but there is none of a point; for a point is a division.[24]

A further *difficulty* arises from the fact that every science is of universals and of the *such*, while a substance is not a universal but rather a *this* and a separate thing;[25] so that if a science is concerned with principles, how are we to believe that these are substances?[26]

Again, does anything exist apart from the *composite* or not? By "the *composite*" I mean the matter and what exists with it.[27] For if not, all things in matter are destructible.[28] But if something does exist apart, this would be the form or the *shape*. But it would be difficult to state definitely in which cases this exists apart and in which it does not; for in some cases it is clear that the form is not separable, as is the case of a house.[29]

Again, are the principles in kind or numerically the same?[30] For if numerically, all things will be the same.

3

Since the science of the philosopher is concerned with being qua being universally and not with respect to some part of being, and since

1060b (margin)
5 (margin)
10 (margin)
15 (margin)
20 (margin)
25 (margin)
30 (margin)

"being" has many senses and is not used only in one sense, then if things are called "being" equivocally and not with respect to something common, being will not come under one science (for there will be no one genus of the various senses of "being"), but if things are called "being" with respect to something common, they might come under one science.[1]

Now the term "being" is used in the way we have stated, like the terms "medical" and "healthy"; for we use each of these, too, in many senses. Each thing which is called "medical" or "healthy" is called so in view of the fact that it somehow refers to medical science in the first case, to health in the second, to something else in another case, and in each case to some thing which is the same. For a statement and a knife are called "medical" in view of the fact that the statement comes from medical science and the knife is useful in medical science. Similarly with the term "healthy"; for one thing is called "healthy" in view of the fact that it is a sign of health, and another in view of the fact that it produces health. Things are called in this way in the other cases too.

It is in this way, too, that things are called "being"; for each of them is called "being" in view of the fact that it is an affection of being[2] qua being, or a habit of it, or a disposition, or a motion, or something else of this sort. And since in everything which is called "being" a reference is made to something which is one[3] and is common, each of the contrarieties, too, will be referred to the primary differences and contrarieties[4] of being, whether the primary differences of being are plurality and unity, or likeness and unlikeness, or some others; let these be taken as already investigated. It makes no difference if that which is called "being" is referred to being or to unity. For even if these are not the same but are distinct,[5] at least they are convertible; for what is one is somehow also a being, and that which is a being is one.

So since in every case the investigation of all contraries belongs to one and the same science, and in each pair one of the contraries is named as being the privation of the other (although one might raise the question regarding some contraries, in which there is something intermediate, how this can be said to be a privation, as in the case of the unjust and the just), in all such cases we must posit as the privation not the privation of the whole formula but of the last species. For example, if a just man[6] is a man who obeys the laws in accordance with some habit, an unjust man will not be totally deprived of the whole formula, if he is only in some respect deficient in obeying the laws, but the privation will belong to him only in that respect;[7] and similarly with the other cases.

Now just as the mathematician pursues the investigation of his objects[8] by abstraction (for he pursues his investigation after leaving out all that is sensible, such as heaviness and lightness and hardness

and their contraries, and besides these, also heat and cold and the other
sensible contrarieties, and keeping only things which have quantity and
are continuous, some in one dimension, others in two, others in three,
35   he investigates the *attributes* of these qua quantities and continuous,[9]
and not with respect to something else; and in the case of some objects
he is concerned with their relative positions and what belongs to them,
1061b   but in the case of others, with their commensurabilities or incommen-
surabilities, and in still others, with their ratios, yet for all of these we
posit the science of geometry to be one and the same), so it is with the
investigation of being. For it belongs to none other than to philosophy
to investigate the attributes of being, to the extent that it is being, and
5   also the contrarieties of it qua being. To physics one would assign the
investigation of things not qua things, but rather qua participating in
motion. Although dialectics and sophistry deal with the attributes of
things, they do not do so qua things, nor with being itself to the extent
that it is being. So it remains that it is the philosopher who is capable of
10   investigating the things we have named to the extent that they are
things. Thus, since everything which is called "a being", even if the
term has many senses, is called so with respect to something which is
one and common, and since the contraries are called so in the same
way (for they are referred to the primary contrarieties and differences
15   of being), all such things can come under one science, and the problem
stated in the beginning[10] may be taken as solved, that is, the problem
as to how there can be one science of things which are many and
different in genus.

4

Since the mathematician, too, uses the common axioms but in a specific way, it must be the concern of first philosophy to investigate also
20   the principles of these. The fact that if equals are subtracted from equals
the remainders are equal[1] is common to all quantities; but mathematics, cutting off a part of its *proper* subject matter, proceeds to
investigate this part[2] (for example, lines or angles or numbers or any of
the other quantities) not, however, qua being, but qua continuous in
25   one or two or three dimensions, whatever each of them may be. But
philosophy does not inquire into the attributes which belong to a part
of being qua a part of being;[3] it investigates each of such parts but
only qua being. The science of physics pursues its investigations in the
same manner as mathematics; for physics investigates the attributes
30   and the principles of things qua in motion and not qua being. But we
said that the first science is concerned with the objects of physics to the

extent that they are beings, and not qua some other thing.[4] For this reason, both physics and mathematics should be posited as being parts of wisdom.[5]

5

There is a principle in things about which we cannot be mistaken but must always be disposed in the contrary way, that is, to think truly; and the principle is this, that the same object cannot at one and the same time be and not be,[1] or admit of any other opposites in the same manner. And although there is no demonstration of such principles in an unqualified sense, there is a demonstration against anyone who denies them. For it is not possible to have a syllogism of the principle[2] from a more convincing principle, yet if indeed one is to demonstrate it without qualification, one should have at least such a syllogism.[3] But to show the asserter[4] of opposites why he speaks falsely, one must obtain from him such a statement which is the same as "it is not possible for the same thing to be and not to be at one and the same time" but which does not seem to be the same; for only thus can a demonstration be given against the one who says that opposite assertions may be truly made of the same thing.

Now those who are to have a discussion with each other must also *understand* each other; for if this does not happen, how can they communicate with each other? Accordingly, each name used must be known and signify something, but only one thing and not many; and if it signifies many things, it must be made evident to which one of them it applies. So, in saying "it is this" and also "it is not this", that which he says it is he denies that it is, so what a given name signifies he denies that it does so signify; and this is impossible. So, if indeed "it is so-and-so" signifies something, it is impossible for its contradictory to be true of the same thing.[5]

Again, if the name[6] signifies something and this is truly asserted, it is necessary for that which is asserted to be;[7] and if it is necessary that it be, it cannot at that time not be; hence, it is not possible for opposite assertions to be true of that same thing.

Again, if an assertion is no more true than its denial, he who calls something "a man" will be speaking no more truly than he who calls it "not a man".[8] But it would seem that even in calling a man "not a horse"[9] one would be speaking either more truly or not less truly than if he were to call him "not a man";[8] yet he will be speaking also truly if he calls him "a horse", for contradictory assertions are taken as alike true. Accordingly, the same man turns out to be a horse, or any other animal.[10]

Now none of the above arguments is an unqualified demonstration of the principle in question, nevertheless they are demonstrations against those who posit contrary opinions.[11]

Perhaps Heraclitus himself, if he were questioned in this manner, would have been quickly persuaded to admit that contradictory asser-
35   tions can never be true of the same things; but as it is, he adopted this doctrine without an *understanding* of what he was saying.[12] Univer-
1062b   sally,[13] if his statement is true, neither will this itself be true,[14] namely, the statement "it is possible for the same thing to be and not to be at one and the same time". For just as, when separated, the affirmation is no more true than the denial, so the denial of the combination of these
5   two, if the combination is taken as if a single affirmation, is no more true than that combination taken as an affirmation.[15] Further, if nothing can be affirmed truly, this statement itself, namely, "nothing can be affirmed truly" would also be false.[16] But if a true affirmation does exist, this
10   would refute what is said by those who oppose such statements[17] and eliminate discourse completely.

6

The saying of Protagoras is almost like the doctrines we have men-
tioned;[1] for he, too, said that man is the measure of all things, and this is saying none other than that what a thing is thought to be by each man
15   is precisely what the thing is. If this happens to be the case, then it fol-
lows that the same thing both is and is not, so that it is both good and bad, and likewise with the other so-called "opposite assertions"; and this is because a thing often appears to be beautiful to some but the contrary to other people, and that which appears to each man is the
20   measure. This *difficulty* may be solved if we examine the source of this belief. For it seems to have come to some people (a) from the doctrine of the natural philosophers, and to others (b) from the fact that not all men have the same knowledge about the same things, but that a given thing appears pleasant to some and the contrary of this to others.

25   Now, a view common to almost all those[2] who are concerned about nature is that nothing is generated from nonbeing and that everything is generated from being.[3] Accordingly, since from being completely white and in no way nonwhite something is becoming not-white (and is now not-white), that which is becoming not-white does so from what must have been not-white; so, according to them, it must have been generated
30   from nonbeing if that thing[4] did not exist as both not-white and white. But it is not difficult to solve this *difficulty;* for we have stated in the *Physics*[5] how things which are generated do so from nonbeing and how from being.

Moreover, it is foolish to attend alike to the opinions and imaginations
35   of disputing parties, for clearly those on one side must be mistaken.[6]
      This is evident from what happens with respect to sensations; for the
1063a same thing never appears sweet to some people and the contrary of this
      to others, unless in the one case the sense organ which *judges* the said
      flavors is injured or defective. In such a case, we should believe those
5   on one side to be the measure but not those on the other. My statement
      applies alike to the good and the bad, the beautiful and the ugly, and
      all other such. For the claim of our opponents does not differ from that
      of those who make each thing appear two by pressing below the eye
      with their finger, and say that there are two things, because two things
10   appear, and again that there is one, for each thing appears as one to
      those who do not press the finger.

      In general, it is absurd to form our *judgment* of the truth from the
      fact that the things about us appear to change and never to stay the
      same. For, in seeking the truth, we should start from things which are
15   always the same and suffer no change. Such are the heavenly bodies,
      for these do not appear to be now of one kind and now of another but
      are always the same and share in no change.[7]

      Again, if there is motion, there is also something which is in motion,
      and every thing in motion is moved from something and into some-
      thing. So, the thing in motion must exist in that from which it will be
20   moved and not be in itself, must then be moving into another thing,
      and must finally become[8] that other thing; but then two contradictories
      cannot be true of it in each of these at the same time.[9]

      And if the things about us are continuously flowing and in motion
      with respect to quantity, as one might posit this although it is not true,[10]
      why should they not remain the same with respect to quality? These
25   thinkers appear not least to predicate contradictories of the same thing
      from their belief that the quantities of bodies do not remain the same,
      for example, because they believe that a thing both is and is not four
      cubits long. But a substance exists in virtue of its quality,[11] whose
      nature is definite, while quantity has an indefinite nature.[12]

      Again, when the doctor prescribes a certain food, why do they take it?
30   For, according to them, why should the food be bread any more than
      not bread, and so what difference would it make if they ate it or not?
      But as it is, they take this food as if they are thinking truly about it and
      as if this is the food prescribed. Yet there was no need for them to do so
      if no fixed nature at all remained the same in sensible things but all of
35   them were always in motion and flowing.[13]

      Again, if we are always altering and never remain the same, in what
      way are we better off than the sick, if things never appear the same to
1063b us?[14] For to the sick, because they are not disposed as they were when
      they were well, things do not appear alike with respect to the senses; and

these sensible things, at any rate, did not share in any change because of the disposition of the sick, although they produce not the same but distinct sensations in them.[15] Indeed, if the change mentioned occurs also in us, it is equally necessary for us to be disposed in the same manner. If, on the other hand, we are not changing but are remaining the same, then there is something which remains the same.[16]

A solution of the *difficulties* mentioned is not easy for those who possess them from verbal arguments, unless they posit something for which they no longer demand a reason, for this is how all arguments and all demonstrations take place; for if they posit nothing, they eliminate discussion with others and any discourse whatever.[17] Hence, there is no argument against such men.[18] But it is easy to answer those who are perplexed by the *difficulties* as handed down and to put an end to the causes of their perplexity.[19] This is evident from what has been said.

From this discussion, then, it is evident that opposite assertions cannot be true of the same thing at one time; nor can contrary assertions, because every contrary is asserted in virtue of a privation. This is clear if we analyze the formulae of contraries to their principles.[20] Similarly, it is not possible to predicate truly an intermediate[21] of one and the same thing. For if the subject is white, in saying that it is neither white nor black we shall be speaking falsely; for the subject will turn out to be white and not white, and the second of the two terms which are put together, which is the contradictory of "white", will be truly asserted of that subject.[22]

Nor indeed is it possible to speak truly in the manner in which Heraclitus does, or Anaxagoras.[23] If we do, we will be predicating contraries of the same thing; for when the latter says that in any given thing there is a part of every thing, what he is saying is that the thing is no more sweet than it is bitter (and likewise for any other pair of contraries), if indeed in any thing everything is present not only potentially but *actually* and as separate from the other parts.[24]

Similarly, neither can all assertions be false, nor can all be true, both because of many other objections that might be brought forward through this thesis, and because of this, namely, that if all statements are false, he who says "all statements are false" will not be speaking truly,[25] while if all statements are true, he who says "all statements are false" will not be speaking falsely.[26]

7

Every science seeks certain principles and causes of each *knowable* thing coming under it;[1] for example, medical science and gymnastics do this, and so does each of the other productive and mathematical sci-

1064*a*

ences. For each of these, having marked off some genus of things for itself, concerns itself with it as with something which exists and is a being, although it does so not qua being, since there is a science distinct from these which concerns itself with any genus of being qua being. Each of the sciences just mentioned accepts in some way the whatness of things in its genus and tries to show the rest more or less accurately. Some of them accept the whatness through sensation, others take it by hypothesis; and so it is clear from such induction that there is no demonstration of the *substance* or the whatness of things.

Since there is a science about nature, clearly it must be distinct from both a practical and a productive science. For the principle of motion in a productive science is in that which produces and not in that which is produced, and this is either some art or some other power. Similarly, the principle of motion in a practical science is not in the thing done but rather in the doers. But the science of the physicist is concerned with things which in themselves have a principle of motion.[2] It is clear from what has been said, then, that physics must be neither a practical nor a productive science, but a theoretical[3] one; for it must come under one of these genera of sciences.

Now since each of the sciences must understand in some way the whatness and must use it as a principle, we must not forget how the physicist should define things and how he must accept the formula of the *substance* of a thing, whether as in the case of the snub or rather as in the case of the concave. For of these, the formula of the snub states also the matter of the thing, but that of the concave does not state the matter. For snubness comes to be in the nose, and therefore the formula of snubness is investigated so as to include the nose; for the snub is a concave nose. Accordingly, it is evident that the formula of flesh, too, and of the eye and of the other parts must always be stated so as to include the matter.

Since there is a science of being qua being and separate, we must inquire whether we should posit this to be the same as physics or rather distinct from it. Physics is concerned with things having in themselves a principle of motion, while mathematics is a theoretical science and one that is concerned with things which remain the same but are not separable. Thus, there is a science distinct from these which is concerned with separate and immovable being, if indeed there exists such a substance, that is, one which is separate and immovable, as we shall try to show.[4] And if indeed there is such a nature in things, the divine, too, would be here if anywhere, and this nature would be the primary and most dominant principle. Accordingly, it is clear that there are three genera of theoretical sciences: physics, mathematics, and theology.[5] The genus of the theoretical sciences is the best; and of these sciences, the

5   last one named is the best, for it is concerned with the most honorable
     of things, and each science is said to be better or worse in virtue of
     its *proper knowable* object.

         One might raise the question whether, if in any way, we should posit
     the science of being qua being as a universal science or not.[6] Now each
     of the mathematical sciences is concerned with some one definite genus,
10   but universal mathematics is common to all. If, then, natural substances
     are the first of things, physics will be the first of the sciences, too; but if
     there is another nature or substance which is separate and immovable,
     the science of it, too, must be distinct from and prior to physics, and
     also universal[7] by being prior.

                              8

15   Since the unspecified term "being" is used in many ways, one of
     which is the so-called "accidental being", we must first inquire into
     such a being.[1] It is clear that none of the traditional sciences busies
     itself with accidents. For neither does the science of building inquire
20   into the accidents which will belong to those who will use the house
     (for example, whether they will live painfully or in the opposite way),
     nor does the science of weaving or of making shoes or of cooking; but
     each of these sciences inquires only into that which is essentially proper
     to that science; and this is its *proper* end. And neither do any of the
     recognized sciences, except sophistry, inquire into arguments such as
25   this: "If he who is musical is becoming grammatical, he will be both at
     the same time, not having been both before; and since that which exists,
     but not always, was in the process of becoming, it follows that he was
     becoming musical and grammatical at the same time";[2] for sophistry
     alone busies itself with accidents, and so Plato was not wrong in saying
30   that the sophist wastes his time with nonbeing.[3]

         That no science of accidents is possible will be evident if we try to
     see what, after all, an accident is. We say that everything exists either
     always or of necessity (by "necessity" we do not mean by force, but the
35   one which we use in demonstrations[4]), or for the most part, or neither
     for the most part, nor always or of necessity, but by chance; for ex-
     ample, there might be cold in the dog-days, but this occurs neither
1065a always, nor of necessity, nor for the most part, but it might happen
     sometimes. An accident, then, is that which occurs, but not always nor
     of necessity nor for the most part. We have now stated what an acci-
     dent is, and it is clear why there is no science of such a thing; for every
5   science is of that which exists always or for the most part, but the acci-
     dent does not come under either of these.

So it is clear that of things by accident there are no causes or principles such as there are of things existing essentially; for otherwise all things will exist of necessity. For if A exists when B exists, and B exists when C exists, and if C exists not by chance but of necessity, that of which C was the cause will also exist of necessity, and so on down to the last thing which is said to be caused (yet this was stated as existing by accident). So all things will exist of necessity, and both that which exists as it chances and that which may become or may not become will be entirely eliminated from things which are generated. The same results will follow even if the cause is assumed not as existing but as being generated; for everything will be generated of necessity. For tomorrow's eclipse will occur if this occurs, and this will occur if that occurs, and that will occur if something else occurs; and in this manner if we keep on subtracting time from the finite time between now and tomorrow, we shall sometime come to what exists now. So since this exists, everything after this will occur, and so all things will occur of necessity.

Now, as regards being in the sense of truth and not by accident, it exists as something combined by *thought* and is an affection of *thought,* and so the principles of such a being are not sought,[5] but only of being which is outside of thought and is separate; and as regards the other (I mean being by accident), it exists not of necessity and is indefinite, and the causes of such being are unordered and infinite.

Final cause exists in things generated by nature[6] or by *thought.* When some[7] of these things are generated by accident, there is luck. For just as there is essential being and accidental being, so it is with cause. Luck is an accidental cause in things generated by *choice* for the sake of something. Therefore, luck and *thought* are concerned with the same thing; for *choice* does not exist without *thought.* The causes of things which might occur by luck are indefinite;[8] and this is why luck is inscrutable to human judgment and is an accidental cause, but in an unqualified sense it is a cause of nothing.[9] Luck is good or bad when the result is good or bad; it is good fortune or misfortune if the goodness or badness is of considerable magnitude.[10]

Since no accidental being is prior to essential being, it is likewise with [accidental and essential] causes. So, if luck or *chance* is the cause of the heavens, *Intelligence*[11] and nature are prior causes.[12]

9

A thing may exist in *actuality* only, or potentially, or potentially and in *actuality;*[1] and it may be a *this,* or a quantity, or any of the others. But motion does not exist apart from things; for that which changes

does so always with respect to the categories of being, and there is
nothing common to these which is in any one category.[2] In all cases,
10   a category may belong to its individuals in two ways. For example, in
the case of a *this,* it may be the *shape* of the thing or a privation of the
shape; with respect to quality, a thing may be white or black; with
respect to quantity, it may be complete or incomplete; and with respect to locomotion, it may be up or down, or, light or heavy. Thus,
there are as many kinds of motion or of change as there are of being.[3]
15   If a division is made in each genus into the potential and the actual, the
actuality of the potential qua potential I call "motion".

That what we say is true, is clear from what follows. For when the
buildable, in so far as it is what we mean by "buildable", is in *actuality,*
then it is [in the process of] being built, and this is building.[4] Likewise,
20   there is learning, healing, walking, jumping, aging, ripening. Motion
takes place, then, while this actuality exists, and neither earlier nor
later. So motion is the actuality of that which exists potentially when
it is in activity not qua itself but qua movable.[5] By "qua" I mean the
25   following. The bronze is potentially a statue; however, motion is not the
actuality of the bronze qua bronze. For, to be bronze and to be potentially something[6] are not the same, since if they were without qualification the same according to formula, the actuality of the bronze
would be a motion. But they are not the same. This is clear in the case
of contraries; for to be capable of being healthy and to be capable of
30   being sick are not the same; otherwise, being healthy and being sick
would be the same. It is the underlying subject, be it moisture or blood,
which is one and the same, whether in health or in sickness. Since, then,
to be bronze and to be potentially something are not the same, just as
to be a color and to be visible are not the same,[7] it is of the potential
qua potential that the actuality is motion.

It is clear, then, that it is this, and that an object happens to be
35   in motion when this actuality exists, and neither before nor after.
1066a For each [such] thing may sometimes be in *actuality* and sometimes
not, as in the case of the buildable qua buildable; and it is the *actuality*
of the buildable qua buildable that is [the process of] building. For
this *actuality* is either the [process of] building or the house. But when
5   the house exists, it is no longer buildable; and it is the buildable that
is being built. This *actuality,* then, must be [the process of] building,
and [the process of] building is a motion. The same argument applies
to the other motions.

That we have stated the facts well is clear from what the other thinkers say about motion and from the fact that it is not easy to describe
10   it in another way. Nor could one place it in some other genus.[8] This is
clear from the fact that some call it "otherness" or "inequality" or "non-

being",[9] none of which is necessarily in motion. Besides, change is no more into these or from these than into or from their opposites. The cause of positing motion as being some one of these is the fact that motion seems to be something indefinite; and the principles in one of the two columns of contraries are indefinite because they are privative, for none of them is either a *this* or a *such* or any of the remaining categories. And motion seems to be indefinite because of the fact that it can be placed neither under the potentiality of things nor under the *actuality* of them; for neither that which is potentially a quantity is necessarily moved, nor that which is *actually* a quantity. And although motion is thought to be an *actuality* of a sort, yet it is incomplete; and the cause of this is the fact that the potential, of which this is the *actuality,* is incomplete. And it is because of this that it is difficult to grasp its whatness; for it must be placed either under privation or under potentiality or under unqualified *actuality,*[10] but none of these alternatives appears possible. It remains, then, that motion is what we said it is, both an *actuality* and not an *actuality* in the way stated, difficult to grasp, but capable of existing.

It is also clear that motion is in the movable; for it is the actuality of the movable caused by that which can move another. And the *actuality* of that which can cause motion is no other; for the actuality must be in both. For it[11] can cause motion by being capable of doing so, and it is causing motion by *actually* doing so, but it can *actualize* itself on that which can be moved; so the *actuality* for both will be one,[12] just as the interval from one to two is the same as that from two to one, and that uphill is the same as that downhill, although the essence of each of the two in each case is not one. The case of that which moves and that which is moved is similar.

10

The infinite is either (1) that which cannot be gone through since it does not by nature admit of being gone through, as in the case of a voice which is invisible,[1] or (2) that which admits of being traversed but without an end, either (a) almost so,[2] or (b) by nature admitting of being traversed,[3] it cannot be traversed or has no limit. Further, the infinite exists by addition or by subtraction[4] or by both.[5]

The infinite cannot be something which is separate and sensible.[6] For if it is neither a magnitude nor a plurality, but its *substance* is to be infinity itself, and not an attribute, it will be indivisible;[7] for that which is divisible is either a magnitude or a plurality. But if it is indivisible, it is not infinite, except in the sense in which voice is invisible.[8] But this is not the sense in which people use the term nor

that which we are seeking, but that which is untraversable. Moreover, how can the infinite exist by itself, if not even numbers or magnitudes, of which the infinite is an *attribute*, exist by themselves?[9] Further, if the infinite exists as an attribute,[10] it will not be qua infinite an element
10   of things,[11] just as the invisible is not an element of speech, although voice is invisible.

It is also clear that the infinite does not exist in *actuality*. For otherwise any part of it that might be taken would be infinite; for to be infinite and the infinite are the same, if indeed the infinite is a substance and not an attribute of an underlying subject.[12] Thus, it is either in-
15   divisible, or, if it can have parts, it is divisible into parts each of which is infinite. But the same infinite cannot be many infinites; for, if it is a substance and a principle, a part of it will be infinite in the same sense in which a part of air is air.[13] It can have no parts, then, and it is indivisible. But the actually existing infinite cannot be indivisible;[14] for
20   it must be a quantity. Then it exists as an attribute.[15] But if this is so, we have stated that it cannot be a principle, but that of which it is an attribute will be a principle, *Air* or the *Even*.[16]

The preceding inquiry is universal; but it will be clear from what follows that the infinite does not exist in sensible things. If the formula of a body is "that which is bounded by surfaces", no infinite sensible or intelligible body could exist; nor could a number exist as something
25   separate and infinite, for a number or that which has a number is numerable.

This is also clear from the following considerations from physics. The infinite can be neither composite nor simple. It cannot be a composite body, seeing that the elements are finite[17] in plurality. For the con-
30   traries must be balanced and no one of them must be infinite; for if one of the two bodies falls in any given way short of the other in potency, the finite will be destroyed by the infinite.[18]

Also, it is impossible for each body to be infinite. For a body is that which has extension in every direction, and the infinite is infinitely extended, so that if the infinite is a body, it will be infinite in all direc-
35   tions.[19] Nor can the infinite be one and a simple body, either (a) as some say,[20] as something apart from the elements, from which they generate those elements (for such a body does not exist apart from the elements; for everything can also be decomposed into that of which it
1067a   consists, but this is not observed in the case of elements[21]), or (b) as fire or any other of the elements. For apart from the difficulty of how any of the elements could be infinite,[22] the total cannot, even if it is finite, either be or become any one of them, as Heraclitus says that all
5   things at times become fire.[23] The same argument applies also to the *One*, which the physicists posit besides the elements. For everything changes from a contrary, for example, from hot to cold.[24]

Again, a sensible body is somewhere, and the place[25] of the whole and of the part is the same, as in the case of the earth.[26] So (a) if the infinite body is all of the same kind, either it will be motionless or it will always be in motion with respect to place.[27] Now this is impossible; for why should it move up rather than down or to any other place, or rest at one rather than at another of these places? For example, if there is a clod in the infinite body, where will it move or stay? For its place is the infinite place of the homogeneous body of which it is a part. Will the clod then occupy the whole place? But how? What, then, will its rest or motion be? It will either rest everywhere, in which case it will not be in motion, or it will be moving everywhere, in which case it will not be resting.[28]

But (b) if the whole[29] has unlike parts, the places of the parts will also be unlike; and first, the whole body will not be one except by contact,[30] and second, the parts will be either finite or infinite in kind. They cannot be finite;[31] for, if the whole is infinite, some of them will be infinite[32] but others will not, for example, fire or water will be infinite. But such a part or an element will be the destruction of the contrary elements.[33] But if the parts are infinite and simple,[34] the places will be infinite also, and the elements will be infinite; and if this is impossible and the places are finite,[35] the whole will of necessity be limited also.

In general, there cannot exist an infinite body and also a place for bodies if every sensible body[36] is either heavy or light. For it will move either towards the center or upwards, but the infinite, either the whole of it or half of it, can do neither; for how will one make any distinctions in it,[37] or how will one part of the infinite be up and another part down, or one part at the extreme and another at the center? Further, every sensible body is in place, and there are six kinds of place;[38] but these cannot exist in an infinite body. In general, if an infinite place cannot exist, neither can an infinite body; for that which is in place is somewhere, and this means that it is either up or down or in some one of the others, and each of these is a boundary.

The infinite[39] is not the same in magnitude and in motion and in time in the sense that it is one nature, but the posterior is named in accordance with the prior; for example, a motion is called "infinite" in virtue of the magnitude over which an object moves or alters or increases, and time is called "infinite" because of the motion which is infinite.[40]

11

1067*b* That which changes may do so accidentally,[1] as when the musical walks; or it is said to simply change if something in it changes, as when

a part changes (for we say that the body becomes healthy, if the eye
becomes healthy). But there is something which is primary that is essentially moved, and this is the essentially movable. It is the same with
the mover; for that which moves another does so either accidentally,[2]
or in virtue of a part of itself, or essentially itself. There is, then, something primary which moves; and there is something which is moved, also
the time during which, and that from which, and that to which it is
moved. But the forms[3] and the affections and the place towards which
things are moved are immovable, as for example *knowledge* and heat;[4]
thus, it is not heat that is motion, but heating.

Now non-accidental change belongs not to all things, but only to
contraries, and to their intermediates, and to contradictories.[5] We may
be convinced of this by induction. That which can change may[6] do
so either from a subject to a subject, or from what is not a subject to
what is not a subject, or from a subject to what is not a subject, or from
what is not a subject to a subject. By "a subject" I mean that which is
signified by an affirmative term.[7] Consequently, there must be three
changes; for there is no change from what is not a subject to what is not
a subject, since, in view of the fact that there is no opposition, these are
neither contraries nor contradictories.[8]

A change from what is not a subject to a subject, with respect to
contradiction, is said to be a generation, and it is a generation without
qualification if it is of a subject which exists without qualification,[9] but
it is qualified if it is of a qualified subject.[10] A change from a subject to
what is not a subject is said to be a destruction, and it may be without
qualification or qualified.

Now if "nonbeing" has many senses, and neither that which exists
by combination or separation[11] can be in motion, nor that which exists
potentially and is opposed to unqualified being[12] (for the not-white or
the not-good can still be in motion accidentally, for the not-white could
be a man;[13] but the unqualified non-*this*[14] cannot be in motion at all),
it is impossible for nonbeing to be in motion. And if this is so, a generation cannot be a motion; for that which is becoming something is
a nonbeing. For however much something is generated by accident,
still it is true to say that nonbeing belongs to that which is becoming
[something] without qualification. Similarly, nonbeing cannot be at
rest.[15] These difficulties follow, then, and also this, that if everything
in motion is in place, although nonbeing is not in place, it would have
to be somewhere. A destruction, too, is not a motion; for the contrary
of a motion is a motion or rest, but a destruction is the contrary of a
generation.

Since every motion is a change, and the three kinds of change have
been stated, and of these those with respect to generation and destruc-

tion are not motions but are changes with respect to contradiction,[16] motion must be a change only from a subject to a subject. The subjects may be contraries,[17] or intermediates; for even a privation may be posited as a contrary, and it is made known by means of an affirmative term, as in "naked", "toothless",[18] and "black".

12

If the categories are divided into substance, quality, place, acting, being acted upon, relation, quantity, there must be three motions, of quality, of quantity, and of place. There is no motion with respect to substance, because there is nothing contrary to a substance.[1] Nor is there motion of a relation; for, when one of the relatives is changing, the other relative may cease to be true although it is not changing, and so motion of relatives is accidental.[2]

Nor is there a change of an acting thing or of that which is acted oń, or of a mover or of that which is being moved, in view of the fact that there is no motion of a motion, no generation of a generation, and in general, no change of a change. For there may be a motion of a motion in two ways, either (1) when a motion is taken as a subject, as when a man [as a subject] is moved if he changes from white to black, so that in this sense a motion, too, might be heated or cooled or change place or increase (but this is impossible, for a change is not a subject), or (2) when some other subject changes from one change to another kind,[3] as when a man changes from sickness to health. But this too is not possible except accidentally. For every motion is a change from something to something else, and it is likewise with a generation and a destruction (except that the latter are changes into opposites in one way,[4] but motion is such a change in another way[5]). Accordingly, a man will be changing from health to sickness and at the same time from this change to another change. So it is clear that if he has become sick, he will have changed into some other kind of change (of course, he may also rest), but always not into a chance change;[6] and this change will be from something to something else. Hence, this opposite change will be that of becoming healthy.[7] But this will be by accident; for example, in changing from recollection to forgetfulness, it is that[8] to which these belong that changes now into something with *knowledge* and now into something with ignorance.

Moreover,[9] this would go on to infinity, if there were a change of a change or a becoming of a becoming. For if of the latter, so must it be of the former.[10] That is, if the unqualified becoming was sometime generated, what is unqualifiedly generated was also generated. So, that which is unqualifiedly becoming did not yet exist, but something was being generated or was already generated. And this, too, was at one time being generated, so that it was not yet at that time something which was being generated. Now since in an infinite series there is no first, there will be no first here either, nor something that follows the first. Accordingly, no thing can be generated or be moved or change.

Further, it is the same object that can have a contrary motion and a coming to rest, or a generation and a destruction. So, when that which is a becoming has become, it is then being destroyed; for neither is it then a becoming, nor is it afterwards, since it must be a process of being destroyed.[11]

Again, matter must underlie that which is being generated and that which is changing. What matter would this be which would become a motion or a generation in a manner in which a body or a soul changes with respect to quality?[12] And, in addition, into what will they be moving? For, that into which a motion proceeds from something must be a thing and not a motion. But how can this be? Surely, learning is not of learning; so, neither is there a generation of a generation.

Since there is no motion with respect to a substance or a relation or with respect to acting or being acted upon, it remains that there is a motion only with respect to quality, quantity, and place; for it is in each of these that contrariety exists. Now by "quality" I mean not what is in the *substance*[13] of the thing (for, also the differentia is called "a quality"), but the affective quality, that with respect to which a thing is acted upon or is incapable of being acted upon. Now the immovable is either (a) that which can in no way be moved,[14] or (b) that which moves with difficulty in a long time or begins slowly, or (c) that which has a nature of being moved but cannot do so either when, or where, or in the manner in which[15] it should by nature be in motion. And it is only that which is immovable in sense (c) that I call "being at rest"; for rest is contrary to motion, so that it is the privation of motion in that which can receive motion.[16]

Things are said to be together in place if they are in one primary[17] place, and they are said to be apart if they are in distinct primary places. Things are said to touch if their boundaries are together. An intermediate[18] is said to be that to which a changing thing by nature arrives prior to arriving at its extreme, if it changes by nature continuously. A thing is said to be contrary in place if it is at the maximum distance away along a straight line. A thing is said to be successive if, being after[19] the principle,[20] and being separated in position or in kind or in some other way, there is no other thing in the same genus between it and that which it succeeds;[21] for example, there are no lines between one line and another that succeeds it, and the same applies to units and to houses. (However, nothing prevents something else from being between[22]). For that which is successive is successive of a certain thing;[23] and it is posterior, for it is not one that succeeds two, nor the first day of the month which succeeds the second. That which is successive and touches that which it succeeds is said to be contiguous to it.

Since every change is between opposites, and these[24] are contraries or contradictories, and since there is no middle between contradictories, it is clear that what is an intermediate is between contraries. The continuous is an instance of the contiguous or the touching. We call something continuous if the limits of two objects which are touching and are held together contiguously become one and the same; so that it is clear that the continuous is found in those objects out of which some unity by nature results in virtue of a contact that holds them together. And it is clear that the successive is first;[25] for the successive does not necessarily touch, but that which touches is successive; and if something is continuous, it touches, but if it touches, it is not necessarily continuous; and in things which cannot be in contact,[26] there can be no natural unity. Hence, a point is not the same as a unit, for contact belongs to points and not to units, but units may be in succession; and something can be between two points,[27] but not between two units.

Book Λ

1

The subject of our investigation is substance; for it is of substances that we are seeking the principles and causes. For even if the universe were a kind of a whole, so to say, substance would be the first part;[1] and if it were a succession of parts,[2] even then, substance would be first, then quality, then quantity. At the same time the others which follow are not even beings in an unqualified sense, so to speak, but are qualities and motions;[3] otherwise, even the not-white and the not-straight would be beings[4] (since we do say even of these that they exist, as for example in "there exists a not-white").[5] Moreover, none of the others is separable. Even the ancient philosophers would confirm this in view of what they were doing; for they were seeking the principles and the elements and the causes of substances. Now present-day thinkers are more inclined to posit the universals as substances;[6] for the genera are universal, and they say that these are principles and substances to a higher degree, because they make logical inquiries into things.[7] The early thinkers, on the other hand, posited the individuals as substances, such as fire and earth, but not what is common to them, 'body'.[8]

There are three kinds of substances. One genus of substances is the sensible, of which (1) one kind is eternal,[9] and (2) the other is destructible (agreed upon by all thinkers), like plants and animals, and it is of the latter that we must find the elements, whether these be one or many. Another kind is (3) the immovable substances,[10] and certain thinkers say that these are separate, some[11] dividing them into two kinds, the Forms and the Mathematical Objects, others positing these two as of one nature,[12] and others[13] positing only one of these, the Mathematical Objects. The sensible substances[14] are the subject of *physics*, for they are in motion; but immovable substances are the subject of another science, if no principle is common to these and to sensible substances.

Now sensible substances are changeable. If change proceeds from

20

25

30

35

1069*b*

5   opposites or from intermediates, and not from all kinds of opposites (for also voice is non-white[15]) but from contraries, there must be something underlying which changes to contraries; for it is not the contraries that change.[16]

2

Moreover,[1] this underlying object remains during the change, but the contrary does not remain. There is, then, some third object besides the contraries: matter.[2]

10   If changes are of four kinds, with respect to either whatness[3] or quality or quantity or whereness, and if unqualified generation and destruction are changes with respect to a *this*,[3] increase and decrease with respect to quantity, alteration with respect to an affection, locomotion with respect to place, then changes would proceed from a contrary to the corresponding contrary in each case.[4] It is matter, then, which can

15   have each of the contraries, that is changing.[5] Since "being" has two senses, everything changes from potential being to *actual* being, for example, from the potentially white to the *actually* white; and it is likewise with increase and decrease. So, it is not only from nonbeing as an attribute[6] that things can be generated, but all things are generated

20   also from being, but from being which is potential, although this is not a being in *actuality*. And the *One*[7] of Anaxagoras (which is better than saying "all things were together"), and the *Blend* of Empedocles and Anaximander, and what Democritus calls "all things were together", this in each case is what exists potentially, not in *actuality*. Thus, these thinkers could have been thinking of matter.

25   Now all things which change have matter, but there is distinct matter in distinct things.[8] And even of eternal things, those which are not generable but are movable with respect to place also have matter, not generable matter, but matter which changes from place to place.[9]

One might raise this question: "From what kind of nonbeing does generation proceed?", for "nonbeing" has three senses.[10] If indeed there exists something potentially, nevertheless it is not potentially any chance thing, but distinct things come from distinct subjects.[11] Nor is

30   it sufficient to say "all things were together"; for there are differences in matter, since otherwise why were an infinity[12] of things generated but not one? For there is just one *Intelligence*, so that if also matter were one,[13] only that would have come to be in *actuality* which matter was potentially.[14] The causes and the principles, then, are three; two of them are the contraries, of which one is the formula or the form and the other is the privation, and the third is the matter.

3

35

1070*a*

Next,[1] neither the matter nor the form is generated, and I mean the ultimate matter and form.[2] For everything that changes does so in some respect, and by something, and into something, and out of something. That by which it is changed is the first mover,[3] that which changes is the matter,[4] and that to which it is changed is the form.[5] The process will go on to infinity if not only the bronze becomes round, but also roundness or the bronze[6] is generated; there must be a stop.

5

Next, each substance[7] is generated by something which has the same name (for man begets man), both in the case of natural substances and in the others;[8] for a thing is generated either by art, or by nature, or by luck, or by *chance*. Art is the principle[9] in a thing other than that which is generated, nature is a principle in the thing itself,[10] and the remaining causes are privations of these.[11]

10

There are three kinds of substances. (a) One kind is matter, which is a *this* in appearance,[12] for what exists by contact and not by organic unity is matter and an underlying subject; (b) another is nature, which is a *this*, and it is that to which something changes, and a possession;[13] and (c) a third is the composite of the two, which is an individual, as for example Socrates or Callias.

15

In some cases, that which is a *this* does not exist apart from the composite substance,[14] as in the case of the form of a house, unless it be the art of building;[15] and of these there is no generation or destruction, but the house without the matter, and health, and also everything according to art exist and do not exist in some other way.[16] But if something does exist apart, it is in cases of natural substances.[17] And in this respect Plato did not speak wrongly when he said that there are as many Forms as there are things by nature (if indeed there are Forms at all), but that there are no Forms of such things as fire, flesh, and head; for all these are matter, and the last of these is matter of a substance in the highest degree.[18]

20

25

Moving causes exist prior to what they generate, but a cause in the sense of a formula[19] exists at the same time as that of which it is the cause.[20] For when a man is healthy, it is at that time that also health exists; and the shape of a bronze sphere exists at the same time as the bronze sphere. But if there is something that remains after, this should be considered. For in some cases there is nothing to prevent this; for example, if the soul is such, not all of it but only the intellect,[21] for it is perhaps impossible for all of the soul to remain. It is evident, then, at least because of all this, that there is no necessity for the Ideas to exist; for it is a man that begets a man, an individual that begets an individual,

30 and similarly in the case of the arts, for the art of medicine is the formula of health.[22]

4

In one sense, the causes and principles of distinct things are distinct,
but in another sense, if one is to speak universally and analogically,
they are the same for all. For one might raise the question whether the
principles and elements of substances and of relations are distinct or
35 the same, and similarly in the case of each of the categories.[1] But it
would be absurd if they were the same for all; for both relations and
1070b substances would then come from the same elements. What would these
be, then? For there exists nothing common to substances and the other
categories, but the elements are prior to the things of which they are
the elements.[2] Moreover, neither are substances the elements of relations, nor are any of these the elements of a substance.[3] Further, how
5 can the same elements be the elements of all things? For, none of the
elements can be the same as that which is composed of elements; for
example, B or A cannot be the same as BA; nor is any of the intelligibles
an element, such as unity or being, for these belong also to each of the
composites.[4] No element, then, can be either a substance or a relation.
10 But it must be one or the other. Hence, not all things have the same
elements.

Or else, as is our way of putting it, in one sense they do have the
same elements but in another sense they do not. For example, in the
case of sensible bodies, perhaps the elements are, the hot as form,[5]
then again the cold as privation, and as matter, that which in virtue
of itself and proximately[6] is potentially hot or cold; and all these, as well
as the *composites* of these as principles, are substances, and so is any
15 unity which is generated from the hot and the cold, such as flesh or
bone (for that which is generated must be distinct from its elements).
These then are the elements and principles of things just stated, but of
other things there are other elements and principles; and so, in view of
the manner in which we have stated the case, the principles and elements cannot be the same for all things, except by analogy, that is, in
the sense in which one might say that there are three principles, form,
20 privation, and matter. But each of these is distinct for each genus; for
example, in colors, they are white, black, and a surface, but in day and
night, they are light, darkness, and air.[7]

Since not only the constituents in a thing are causes but also what is
outside, such as the mover, it is clear that a principle is distinct from
an element, but both are causes,[8] and principles are divided into these

25   two kinds; and the mover or that which causes rest is a principle and a
       substance. Thus, there are three elements, analogically taken, but there
       are four causes or principles; but the elements are distinct for distinct
       things, and the first⁹ cause is distinct for distinct things. For example,
       health and disease and body are the elements, and the medical art is
       the mover; form and disorder of some kind and bricks are the elements,
30   and the art of building is the mover; and it is into these that the prin-
       ciples are subdivided. And since in physical things the mover may be,
       for example, a man in the case of a man, while in things which come to
       be from *thought* the mover is the form or the contrary of the form, the
       causes are in one sense three but in another sense four.¹⁰ For the medi-
       cal art is in some sense health, the art of building is in some sense the
       form of the house, and it is a man that begets a man. Again, besides
35   these there is that which, as first of all things, moves all things.¹¹

                          5

1071a   Since some things are separate and others are inseparable, it is the
       former that are substances. And because of this, the causes of all things
       are the same,¹ and this is so in view of the fact that *attributes* and mo-
       tions cannot exist if substances do not exist. Next, these² would be per-
       haps soul and body, or intellect and desire and body.
           Next, there is another sense in which the principles are by analogy
5   the same, namely, as *actuality* and potentiality; but even these are dis-
       tinct for distinct things and exist in distinct ways. For, in some cases,
       the same object exists sometimes in *actuality* and sometimes potentially,³
       as in the case of wine or flesh or a man; and these, too, fall under the
       causes already named. For, what exists *actually* is the form, if separable,
10   and the *composite*, and also privation, as for example, darkness or dis-
       ease; but what exists potentially is matter, for it is this that is capable
       of becoming both.⁴ But in another way, in things whose matter is not
       the same, to be in *actuality* and to be potentially differ in that the form
       is not the same but distinct. Thus, in the case of a man, the causes are
       the elements, which are fire and earth as matter and the form proper
15   to the man as form, and in addition something else outside, such as
       the father, and also the Sun and the *oblique course*, and these latter
       are neither the matter of the man nor the form or its privation nor yet
       something of the same kind but are moving causes of him.⁵
           Again, it should be noted that in some cases causes may be stated
       universally but in others this cannot be. But in all cases the primary⁶
       principles⁷ are the primary⁸ *this* which exists *actually* and something
20   else which exists potentially.⁹ Accordingly, universals do not exist in

this manner,[10] for it is an individual that is the principle of an individual; for, although the principle[11] of a man, universally speaking, is a man, universally speaking (even if a universal man does not exist), the principle of Achilles is Peleus, of you it is your father, and of this BA it is this B, and in general the principle of BA is B without qualification. Then, with regard to the kinds of *substances*,[12] as we said, the causes and elements are distinct for things not in the same genus, for example, for colors, sounds, substances, and quantities, and they are the same only by analogy; and they are distinct even in the same species, not distinct in species, but numerically distinct, as in the case of your matter and your form and your moving cause, on the one hand, and mine, on the other, although universally and in formula they are the same.

Thus, to inquire what are the principles[13] or the elements[14] of substances and of relations and of qualities, or whether they are the same or distinct, clearly this is possible for each of these in view of the fact that the terms are used in many senses;[15] but when the senses have been distinguished, the principles and the elements are not the same but distinct, unless they are taken in a certain sense and are to include all things. In one sense, they are the same by analogy, in view of the fact that there is matter, form, privation, and a moving cause; and in another sense, the causes of substances are in some manner the causes of all, in view of the fact that when substances are destroyed all other things are destroyed.[16] Moreover, the first thing[17] which exists as *actuality* is the cause of all. On the other hand, there are first[18] causes which are distinct if, being contraries, they are spoken of neither as genera nor in many senses;[19] and, in the same way, there are first causes which are distinct as matter. We have stated, then, what the principles of sensible things are and how many they are, and in what sense they are the same and in what sense distinct.

6

Since three kinds of substances were named,[1] two of them physical and one immovable, we should discuss the latter, in view of the fact that there must be some eternal substance which is immovable. For substances are the first of all things,[2] and if they are all destructible, all things are destructible. But it is impossible for motion either to be generated or to be destroyed; for it always existed.[3] The same applies to time; for if there is no time, neither can there be a *before* and an *after* in time.[4] And so motion, too, is continuous in the same manner as time is; for either motion and time are the same,[5] or time is an *attribute* of motion.[6] But motion cannot be continuous except with respect to place, and of this motion, only the one which is circular.[7]

Moreover, if there is a thing which can move other things or can act upon them but which will not *actually* do so, then there will be no motion;[8] for that which has a potency may not be *actualizing* it. So there

15   is no gain even if we posit eternal substances, like those who posit the Forms,[9] unless there is in them a principle which can cause a change. But even such a principle is not enough (nor is any substance other than the Forms[10]), for, if this principle will not be in activity, there will be no motion. Moreover, if the substance of such a principle is a potency, still this is not enough even if this principle is in activity, for motion will not be eternal; for that which exists potentially may not be

20   existing [*actually*].[11] Hence, there must be a principle of such a kind that its *substance* is *actuality*. Moreover, such substances must be without matter; for they must be eternal, if indeed something else is also eternal.[12] They must exist, then, as *actualities*.

Yet there is a *difficulty;* for it seems that whatever exists in *actuality* also has the potency for it, but that whatever has a potency need not

25   *actualize* it, and so potency seems to be prior[13] to *actuality*. But if this is so, nothing will exist;[14] for something may have the potency to be and still not be. And indeed, the same impossibility follows from the statements of the theologians who generate the universe from *Night,* or of the physicists who say that all things were together. For how will anything be moved if no cause exists in *actuality?*[15] Matter itself will

30   certainly not move itself, but carpentry[16] will move it; and neither the menses nor the earth will move themselves, but the seeds[17] will act on the earth and the semen on the menses.

This is why some thinkers, like Leucippus and Plato,[18] posit eternal activity; for they say that motion is eternal. But they do not state why[19] this exists nor which[20] it is, nor yet its manner[21] or the cause of it.[22] For

35   nothing is moved at random, but there must always be something, just as it is at present with physical bodies which are moved in one way by nature but in another by force or by the intellect or by something else. Then again, which of them is first?[23] For this makes a great difference.

1072a Plato cannot even state what it is that he sometimes considers to be the principle, that is, that which moves itself; for, as he himself says, the soul came after,[24] and it is generated at the same time as the universe.

Now to regard potency as prior to *actuality* is in one sense right and in another sense not right; and we have already stated[25] how this is so.

5   That *actuality* is prior is confirmed by Anaxagoras (for *Intelligence* according to him exists in *actuality*), by Empedocles (who posits *Friendship* and *Strife*), and by others, such as Leucippus, who say that motion always exists. If so, then *Chaos* or *Night* did not exist for an infinite time, but the same things existed always, whether passing through cycles or in some other way,[26] if indeed *actuality* is prior to potency. So

10   if the same things always take place in cycles, there must be something,

say A, which always remains and is in activity in the same way.[27] But if there is to be generation and destruction, there must be something else, say B, which is always in activity now in one way and now in another. So it is necessary for it to be active in one way according to itself and in another according to something else; then the latter is either still another thing, say C, or the first thing. Surely, it must be the first thing; for otherwise C would still be its own cause and the cause of B. So it is better to say that it is the first, for it is this that is the cause of being in activity always in the same way, and it is something else that is the cause of being in activity in another way; and so it is evident that that which is always active in distinct ways requires two causes.[28] And, in fact, it is in this way that motions take place. So why should we seek other principles?

7

Since the account given in this manner is possible, and if it were not, the universe would have been generated from *Night* or from the *togetherness of all things*[1] or from nonbeing,[2] the *difficulties* may be regarded as solved, and so there is something which is always moved with an unceasing motion, which is circular; and this is clear not only by arguments but also from the facts.[3] So, the first heaven must be eternal; and further, there is also something which this moves.[4] And since that[5] which is moved and is a mover is thus an intermediate, there is something which causes motion without being moved,[6] and this is eternal, a substance, and an *actuality*.[7] And this is the way in which the object of desire or the intelligible object moves, namely, without itself being moved.[8] Of these, the primary objects are the same;[9] for the object of *desire* is that which *appears* to be noble, and the primary object of wish is that which *is* noble.[10] We desire because it seems[11] rather that it seems because we desire; and thinking is the starting-point. Now the intellect is moved by the intelligible, and things which are intelligible in virtue of themselves are in one of the two columns of opposites;[12] and of these, substances are primary, and of substances, that which is simple and in *actuality* is primary.[13] Oneness is not the same as the simple; for "one" signifies a measure, but "simple" signifies the manner in which something exists.[14] Moreover, both the noble and that which is chosen for its own sake are in the same column of opposites;[15] and that which is primary is always the best,[16] or by analogy so.[17]

That the final cause exists in immovable things is clear by distinguishing the two meanings of "final cause". For the final cause may be (a) for some thing or (b) that for the sake of which,[18] and of these the one may

exist[19] but the other may not; and it [the final cause] causes motion as
something which is loved, and that which is moved moves the others.
5   If, then, something is moved, it can be otherwise than as it is; so even
if the primary locomotion[20] exists as an *actuality*, still that[21] which is
moved qua being moved can be otherwise with respect to place, even
if not with respect to its *substance*. And since there is some mover which
causes motion but is itself immovable and exists as *actuality*,[22] this can
in no way be otherwise than as it is. Now of all changes locomotion is
10   primary, and of locomotions the circular is primary;[23] and it is this
motion which the immovable mover causes.[24] This mover, then, exists
of necessity; and if so, then nobly, and as such, it is a first principle. For
"necessity" has the following senses: (a) by force, which is contrary to
a thing's tendency, (b) that without which the good is impossible, and
(c) that which cannot be otherwise but exists without qualification.[25]
        Such, then, is the principle upon which depends the heaven and na-
15   ture. And its *activity* is like the best which we can have but for a little
while.[26] For it exists in this manner eternally (which is impossible for
us[27]), since its *actuality* is also pleasure.[28] And it is because of this
[activity] that being awake, sensing, and thinking[29] are most pleasant,
and hopes and memories[20] are pleasant because of these. Now thinking
according to itself is of the best according to itself,[31] and thinking in
20   the highest degree is of that which is best in the highest degree. Thus,
in partaking of the intelligible, it is of Himself that the Intellect is thinking;[32] for by apprehending and thinking it is He Himself who becomes[33]
intelligible, and so the Intellect and its intelligible object are the same.[34]
For that which is capable of receiving the intelligible object and the
substance is the intellect,[35] and the latter is in *actuality* by possessing
the intelligible object;[36] so that the possession of the intelligible is more
divine than the potency of receiving it, and the contemplation of it is
25   the most pleasant and the best.[37] If, then, the manner of God's existence
is as good as ours sometimes is,[38] but eternally, then this is marvelous,
and if it is better,[39] this is still more marvelous; and it is the latter. And
life belongs to God, for the *actuality* of the intellect is life,[40] and He is
actuality; and His *actuality* is in virtue of itself a life which is the best
and is eternal. We say that God is a living being which is eternal and
30   the best; so life and continuous duration and eternity belong to God,
for this is God.
        Those who believe, as the Pythagoreans and Speusippus do, that the
most noble and the best are not in the principle, because the principles
of plants and of animals are also causes but nobility and completeness
35   are in what comes from them, do not think rightly. For the seed comes
1073*a*   from other things which are prior[41] and complete, and that which is first
is not the seed but the complete thing. One might say, for example,

that prior to the seed is the man, not the man who comes from this seed but the man from whom this seed comes.

It is evident from what has been said that there exists a substance which is eternal and immovable and separate from sensible things. It has also been shown that this substance cannot have any magnitude but is without parts and indivisible.[42] For it causes motion for an infinite time, but no finite thing has infinite potency. Since every magnitude is either infinite or finite, this substance cannot have a finite magnitude because of what we said, and it cannot be infinite in view of the fact that there exists no infinite magnitude at all.[43] Moreover, it cannot be affected or altered; for all the other motions are posterior to locomotion.[44] It is clear, then, why these facts are so.[45]

8

We should not neglect to consider whether we should posit one such substance or more than one, and if the latter, how many; but with regard to the statements made by other thinkers, we should mention the fact that concerning the number of such substances they said nothing that can be even *clearly* stated. The doctrine of Ideas does not inquire specifically into this problem, for those who speak of the Ideas speak of them as Numbers, and concerning Numbers they sometimes speak as if these were infinite but at other times as if they were limited to ten;[1] but as to why there should be so many Numbers, nothing is stated seriously enough to amount to a demonstration. We, however, should discuss this problem by starting with the assumptions and distinctions already made.

Now the principle[2] and the first of beings is immovable, both in virtue of itself and accidentally,[3] and it causes the primary motion,[4] which is eternal and one.[5] But since that which is moved must be moved by something, and the first mover is of necessity immovable in virtue of itself, and an eternal motion must be caused by an eternal being and one motion by one being, and since we also observe that, besides the simple locomotion of the universe which we say is caused by the first and immovable substance, there are other locomotions[6] (those of the planets) which are eternal (for a body with a circular motion is eternal and is never at rest, and we have shown this in the *Physics*[7]), then each of these locomotions, too, must be caused by a substance which is in virtue of itself immovable and eternal.[8] For a star is by its nature an eternal substance, and the mover is eternal and prior[9] to that which is moved, and that which is prior to a substance must be a substance.[10] So it is evident that there must be as many substances as there are

locomotions and that in their nature they are eternal and immovable
1073*b* in virtue of themselves and without magnitude, and the cause of this
has been stated earlier.[11]

' It is evident, then, that the movers are substances, and that of these
there is a first, a second, etc., according to the same order as the locomotions of the stars. Now as regards the number of locomotions,[12] this
should be the concern of the mathematical science which is closest to
5 philosophy, and this is astronomy; for it is this science which is concerned with the investigation of sensible but eternal substances, while
the others, such as arithmetic and geometry, are not concerned with
any substances.[13] That there are many locomotions of heavenly bodies
is evident also to those who have studied the matter to some extent; for
10 each of the planets has more than one locomotion.[14] But as to the
number of these, we may for the present give an indication by quoting
what some mathematicians are saying, so that there may be in our
thought a belief in some definite number; as for the rest, we should
partly investigate ourselves and partly inquire from those who investi-
15 gate the subject, and if those who are investigating this subject have
opinions contrary to those just stated, we should respect both views
but accept the more accurate.

Eudoxus held[15] that each of the locomotions of the Sun and of the
Moon is in three spheres, of which the first is that of the fixed stars,
20 the second along the circle which bisects the Zodiac, and the third
along the circle inclined across the breadth of the Zodiac, but the
circle along which the Moon moves is inclined at a greater angle than
that along which the Sun moves. The motion of each of the planets
is in four spheres, and of these the first and second are the same as
25 those in the previous case (for the locomotion of the sphere of the
fixed stars belongs to all the spheres, and that of the sphere next under
it which moves along the circle bisecting the Zodiac belongs to all),
the poles of the third sphere of each planet are in the circle bisecting
30 the Zodiac, and the locomotion of the fourth sphere is in the circle
inclined at an angle to the equator of the third; and the poles of the
third sphere are different for different planets, except for Venus and
Mercury which have the same poles.

Callippus posited the same position of the spheres as that held by
Eudoxus, that is, with respect to the order of the intervals, but while
35 he assigned to Jupiter and Saturn the same number of spheres as Eudoxus did, he thought that two more spheres should be added to the
Sun and also to the Moon, if one is to account for the observed phenomena, and one more to each of the other planets.

1074*a* But if all the spheres combined are to account for the observed phenomena, there must be other spheres for each planet, one less in number

than those assigned to it, which would counteract these and restore to the same position the first sphere of the star which in each case is next
5 in order below; for only thus can the motion of the combined spheres produce the motion of the planets. Since, then, the spheres in which the planets are carried are eight for Jupiter and Saturn and twenty-five for the others, and of these only those need not be counteracted in which the lowest-situated planet is carried, the spheres which counteract
10 those of the first two planets will be six, those of the next four planets will be sixteen, and the total number of spheres which includes both those which carry the planets and the ones which counteract those spheres will be fifty-five. If we are not to add to the Moon and to the Sun the motions we mentioned, all the spheres will be forty-seven.
15 Let, then, this be the number of spheres, and if so, it is reasonable to believe that the immovable substances or principles are also as many. As to what is necessarily the case, this may be left to more competent thinkers.

If there can be no locomotion[16] which does not contribute to the locomotion of a star, and if moreover every nature or substance[17] which
20 is unaffected and which in virtue of itself attains its best should be regarded as an end, then there can be no other nature besides those mentioned, but this must be the number of substances. For if there were others, they would be movers as ends of locomotions; but there can be no other locomotions besides those mentioned. And in view of the heavenly bodies which are in locomotion, this is a reasonable
25 belief. For if each thing that carries[18] something does so by nature for the sake of that which is carried,[19] and every locomotion is likewise for the sake of something which is so moved, no locomotion can exist for its own sake or for the sake of another locomotion, but each must exist for the sake of a star. For if every locomotion exists for the sake of another locomotion, the latter too will exist for the sake of a third;
30 and so, since it is impossible to proceed to infinity, the end of each locomotion in the heavens must be some of the divine bodies which are so moved there.[20]

It is evident that there is only one heaven. For if there are more than one,[21] like men, the principle[22] for each will be one in species but many in number. But things[23] which are many in number have matter; for the
35 formula is one and the same for the many, as in the case of the formula of a man, while Socrates is only one. But the primary essence[24] has no matter, for it is actuality. Thus, the first immovable mover is one both in formula and in number; and so, that which[25] is always and continuously in motion is only one. Hence, there is only one heaven.[26]

1074*b* The ancients of very early times bequeathed to posterity in the form of a myth a tradition that the heavenly bodies are gods and that the

divinity encompasses the whole of nature. The rest of the tradition has
5 been added later as a means of persuading the masses and as something
useful for the laws and for matters of expediency; for they say that
these gods are like men in form and like some of the other animals, and
also other things which follow from or are similar to those stated. But
if one were to separate from the later additions the first point and attend
to this alone (namely, that they thought the first substances to be gods),
10 he might realize that this was divinely spoken and that, while probably
every art and every philosophy has often reached a stage of development as far as it could and then again has perished, these doctrines
about the gods were saved like relics up to the present day. Anyway,
the opinion of our forefathers and of the earliest thinkers is evident to
us to just this extent.

9

15 Certain problems arise with regard to The Intellect [God]; for He
seems to be the most divine of things manifest to us, yet there are certain difficulties as to how He can exist as such. For if He is not thinking
of anything, why the veneration of Him? He is like a man who sleeps.
And if He is thinking, but what decides this thinking is something else[1]
20 (for the *substance* of that which decides thinking is not thinking, but a
potency[2]), then He cannot be the best substance.[3] For it is because of
[the act of] thinking that honor belongs to Him. Moreover, whether
His *substance* is intellect[4] or thinking,[5] of what does He think? Either
He thinks of Himself or of something else; and if something else, then
either always of the same thing or sometimes of one thing and sometimes of another. But does it make any difference or not whether He is
25 thinking of that which is noble rather than of any chance thing? Would
it not be absurd to be *thinking* of certain things?[6] Clearly, then, He is
thinking of that which is most divine and most honorable, and He is
not changing; for change would be for the worse,[7] and this change
would then be a motion.[8]

First, then, if He were not thinking[9] but a potency, it is reasonable
that the continuity of His thinking would be fatiguing Him.[10] Moreover,
30 it is clear that something else would be more honorable than The Intellect, namely, the object of thought; for to think or thinking may
belong even to that which thinks of the worst objects, so that if this is
to be avoided (for there are even things which it is better not to see
than to see), Thinking would not be the best of things.[11] It is of Himself,
then, that The Intellect is thinking, if He is the most excellent of things,
and so Thinking is the thinking of Thinking.

35 But it appears that *knowledge* and sensation and opinion and *thought* are always of other objects, and only incidentally of themselves. Moreover, if thinking and being thought are distinct, in virtue of which of these does goodness belong to The Intellect? For to be thinking and to

1075*a* be an object of thought are not the same.[12] Or is it not that in some cases *knowledge* and its object are the same?[13] In the productive sciences, this object is the *substance* or the essence[14] but without the matter, in the theoretical sciences it is the formula and the thought. Accordingly, since the intellect and the object of thought are not distinct in things

5 which have no matter, the two will be the same, and so both thought[15] and the object of thought will be one.

Further, there remains the problem whether the object of Thinking is composite;[16] for if so, Thinking would be changing in passing from one part of the whole to another part.[17] Is it not the case that what has no matter is indivisible, like the human intellect,[18] or even that[19] which is thinking of a composite object[20] in an interval of time? For it does not possess goodness in this part or in that part but possesses the highest

10 good in the whole,[21] though it is distinct from it. It is in this manner that Thinking is the thinking of Himself through all eternity.[22]

10

We must also inquire in which of two ways the nature of the whole has the good and the highest good, whether as something separate and by itself,[1] or as the order of its parts. Or does it have it in both ways, as in the case of an army? For in an army goodness exists both in the order

15 and in the general, and rather in the general; for it is not because of the order that he exists, but the order exists because[2] of him. Now all things are ordered in some way, water-animals and birds and plants, but not similarly; and they do not exist without being related at all to one another, but they are in some way related.[3] For all things are ordered

20 in relation to one thing. It is as in a household, in which the freemen are least at liberty to act at random but all or most things are ordered, while slaves and wild animals contribute little to the common good but for the most part act at random;[4] for such is the principle of each of these, which is their nature. I mean, for example, that all these must come together if they are to be distinguished; and this is what happens in

25 other cases in which all the members participate in the whole.[5]

We must not fail to notice how many impossible or absurd results face those who speak otherwise, what sort of views are put forward by subtler thinkers, and what sort of views are faced with the least difficulties. Now all thinkers posit all things as coming from contraries. But

neither "all things" nor "from contraries" is right.[6] Nor do these thinkers
30   say, of things to which contraries belong, how those things are composed
of contraries; for contraries cannot be acted upon by each other.[7] For
us, however, the problem is reasonably solved by the positing of a third
object.[8] But these thinkers posit one of the contraries as being matter,
as in the case of those who posit the *Unequal* as the matter for the
Equal[9] or those who regard the *Many* as the matter for the *One*.[10] This
difficulty, too, is solved in the same manner; for the matter, for us, is not
35   contrary to anything. Moreover, for these thinkers all things except the
One will participate in badness; for *Bad Itself* is one of the two elements.[11] As for the other thinkers,[12] they do not even regard the principles as being the *Good* and the *Bad;* yet in all things the good is in the
highest degree a principle.[13] Now the former thinkers rightly regard the
1075*b*   *Good* as a principle, but they do not say how it is a principle, whether
as an end or as a mover or as form.

Empedocles, too, speaks absurdly, for he posits *Friendship* as the
good; and as a principle, it is posited both as a mover (for it brings things
together), and as matter (for it is a part of the *Blend*). Indeed, even if the
5   same thing happens to be a principle both as matter and as a mover,
nevertheless to be matter is not the same as to be a mover. In which
sense, then, is *Friendship* a good?[14] It is also absurd that *Strife* should
be indestructible, since *Strife,* for him, is the nature of the bad.[15]
Anaxagoras posits the *Good* as a principle in the sense of a mover,
since for him *Intelligence* moves things; but it moves for the sake of
something, so that the *Good* should be something else (unless it is so
10   posited in another sense, as used by us; for, the medical art is in some
sense health[16]). It is also absurd that he should posit no contrary of
the *Good* or of *Intelligence*.[17] As a matter of fact, all those who posit
contraries do not use them, unless we reshape their views into a system.

Again, no one states why some things are destructible but others are
indestructible; for all things are posited by these thinkers as being com-
15   posed of the same principles.[18] Again, some thinkers posit things as
coming from nonbeing; others, to avoid this necessity, say that all things
are one.[19]

Again, no one states why there will always be generation and what is
the cause of generation.[20] And those who posit two principles[21] need
another principle which is more authoritative.[22] And those who posit
the Forms also need a more authoritative principle; for why did things
20   participate in the Forms or do so now?[23] And for all other thinkers there
must be something which is the contrary of wisdom or of the most
honorable science; but for us this is not necessary, for there is nothing
contrary to that which is first. For, in all cases, contraries have matter
which is potentially these contraries, and ignorance, which is the con-

trary of knowledge, should be of the contrary object; but there is nothing contrary to what is first.[24] Again, if there were nothing besides the sensible things, there would be no principle or order or generation or heavenly objects, but of a principle there would always be another principle,[25] as all the theologians and the physicists say. And if the Forms or Numbers were to exist, they would not be the causes of anything; or if they were, at least not of motion.[26] Again, how can magnitude or what is continuous come from things which have no magnitude? For no number, either as a mover or as a form, can make what is continuous.[27] Moreover, no contrary is just a potency of acting or of moving, for it would then be possible for it not to exist, and besides, action is posterior to the potency of it;[28] and if so, no things would be eternal.[29] But there are such; so some of their premises must be rejected. We have stated how this should be done.[30]

Again, in virtue of what is a number one, or a soul, or a body, or in general, each form or thing? No one says anything at all; nor can any of them say anything, unless they do in the way we do, that it is the mover that makes each one.[31] As for those who assert that Mathematical Numbers are first and, following these, posit one kind of substances after another with distinct principles for each kind, they represent the substances of the universe as a plurality of unrelated parts (for substances of one kind, whether existing or not, contribute nothing to those of another kind) and with many principles;[32] but things do not wish to be governed badly.

"The rule of many is not good; let one the ruler be."[33]

Book M

1

We have stated what is the substance of sensible things in two
places, first in the *inquiry* concerning physical things, where we dealt
with substance in the sense of matter,[1] and later with substance with
respect to *actuality*.[2] Since our concern is whether, besides the sensible
substances, there exists an immovable and eternal substance or not,
and if it does exist, what it is, first we must examine what is said by
others, so that, if there is anything which they do not state well, we may
not be liable to the same error, and, if there is any view common to
them and us, we too may not be privately dissatisfied with ourselves;
for one should be content to state some things better than one's predecessors and the rest not worse.

There are two doctrines concerning immovable and eternal substances. Some say that the Mathematical Objects are such substances,
that is, Numbers and Lines and the rest of this kind, and also that the
Ideas are such substances. Since some thinkers put forward two genera
of these,[3] the Ideas and the Mathematical Numbers, and others say
that these two have the name nature,[4] and still others say that only the
Mathematical Objects exist as such substances,[5] we must first attend
to the mathematical objects,[6] without positing any additional nature
as belonging to them, that is, without inquiring whether they happen
to be Ideas or whether they are the principles and substances of things,
but only whether as mathematical objects they exist, and if they exist,
how they exist. After this, we must restrict our attention to the Ideas
themselves in general and as much as is demanded by the occasion;[7]
for this topic has been much discussed in our *Popular Writings*.[8] Finally,
the greater part of our discussion must be directed to that other inquiry
in which we examine whether the substances and principles of things
are Numbers[9] and Ideas; for, after attending to the Ideas, this remains
as our third concern.

If the mathematical entities exist, then, they must be either in the sensible things, as some say,[10] or separate from sensible things (and this is what others say[11]). Or, if they exist in neither of these ways, either they do not exist, or they exist in some other manner; and in the latter case, the point at issue will not be with their existence but with the manner of their existence.

2

It has been already stated in our discussion of *difficulties*[1] that mathematical objects cannot exist in sensible things and that the account of these thinkers is also fictitious, for it is impossible for two solids to be in the same place; moreover, for the same reason the other powers and natures would have to be in sensible things and not exist separately. These statements have been made earlier.[2] In addition, it is evident from their doctrine that no body[3] could be divided; for a body would have to be divided at a plane, a plane at a line, and a line at a point, so that if a point could not be divided, neither could a line, and if not a line, neither could a plane or a body. Now what difference does it make whether sensible things are such natures or, without being themselves such natures, have in themselves other such natures? The result will be the same; for if the sensible things are divided, so will the other natures, or if these latter cannot be divided, neither can the sensible things.[4]

On the other hand, such natures cannot even exist separately.[5] For, if besides the sensible solids there exist other solids which are separate and also prior to the sensible, it is clear for the same reason[6] that besides the sensible planes there must exist other planes which are separate,[7] and also other points and lines. If so, then again, besides the planes and lines and points of the mathematical solids there exist, respectively, other planes and lines and points which are separate;[7] for the incomposites are prior to the composites.[8] And if there exist non-sensible bodies which are prior to[9] the sensible bodies, for the same reason there exist also planes which are prior to the planes in the immovable solids and which exist by themselves.[10] Thus, these planes (and this applies also to lines) will be distinct from the planes which are in the separate solids;[11] for the latter planes are with the mathematical solids, but the former planes are prior to[9] the mathematical solids. Once more, in these prior planes there will be lines, and for the same reason there must be other lines and points prior to these lines; and those prior lines will have points, and prior to these points there will be other points, beyond which no other prior points exist.

Indeed, the accumulation becomes absurd. For the result will be

30   one set of solids besides the sensible solids; three distinct sets of planes
        besides the sensible planes, that is, one set existing apart from the
        sensible set, another existing in the mathematical solids, and a third
        existing apart from the mathematical solids; four distinct sets of lines;
        and five distinct sets of points.[12] If so, with which set in each case will
        the mathematical sciences be concerned? Certainly not with the planes
35   and lines and points in the immovable solid, for a science is always
        concerned with what is prior.[13] The same arguments may be used in the
        case of numbers; for there will be a set of units besides the points,
        another set besides the sensible beings, still another besides the in-
        telligible beings, so that the genera of mathematical numbers will be
        infinite.[14]

1077a   Moreover, how is it possible to solve the *difficulties* raised in our list
        of problems?[15] For, as in the case of geometry, astronomy will be con-
        cerned with things existing apart from sensible things; but how can
        a heaven and its parts (or anything which has motion) exist apart from
5   the sensible heaven and its parts?[16] Similarly with the objects of optics
        and harmonics; for there will exist a voice and a sight apart from the
        sensible and individual voices and sights. Clearly, then, the same will
        apply to the other sensations and sensible things; for why should some
        of them[17] exist apart from the sensibles and not the others? If this is so,
        then there will exist also animals apart from the sensible animals, as
        indeed in the case of sensations.

        Again, some mathematical propositions are universally expressed by
10   mathematicians in such a way that the objects signified are distinct from
        these mathematical substances.[18] Accordingly, there will be other sub-
        stances which are separate, which lie between the Ideas and the Inter-
        mediates,[19] and which are neither specific numbers nor points nor spe-
        cific magnitudes nor time. If this is impossible, it is clear that the others,
        too, cannot exist separate from the sensible substances.

15   In general, if one posits the mathematical objects as natures which
        are separate,[20] conclusions contrary both to truth and to the accepted
        beliefs will follow. For these natures, because they are posited as such,
        must be prior[21] to the sensible magnitudes, but with respect to truth
        they must be posterior; for the incomplete magnitude is prior in gen-
20   eration[22] but posterior in substance to the complete magnitude. For
        example, this is how the lifeless is related to the living.[23]

        Again, by virtue of what, and when, will a Mathematical Magnitude
        be one? A sensible magnitude is one by virtue of a soul or part of a soul[24]
        or something else which is reasonable,[25] otherwise, it will be many and
        disintegrate. In the case of a Mathematical Magnitude, which is a
        quantity and divisible, what causes it to be one and to hold together?[26]
25   Again, the way generation proceeds may clarify the matter. For what

is generated first is something with length, then with width, lastly with depth, and completion has been attained. Accordingly, if that which is posterior in generation is prior in substance, the body would be prior to the plane and the line, and as such it would be complete and a whole in a higher degree than they are, seeing that it can also become ani-
30   mate.[27] But how can a line or a plane be animate? Such an axiom[28] is beyond our senses.

Again, a body is in some sense a substance, for it is somehow already complete.[29] But how can lines be substances? Neither as form or *shape*, if such is the soul for example, nor as matter, like the body for example;
35   for we observe that no body can consist of planes or lines or points. If these latter were material substances of some kind, we would have
1077b   observed them capable of being put together to form a body.[30] Let it be granted that they are prior in formula to the body.[31] But it is not always the case that what is prior in formula is also prior in substance. For A is prior in substance to B if A surpasses B in existing separately, but A is prior in formula to B if the formula of A is a part of the formula of B; and the two priorities do not belong to the same thing together.[32]
5   For if attributes, as for example a motion of some kind or whiteness, do not exist apart from substances, whiteness is prior in formula to the white man but not prior in substance; for whiteness cannot exist separately but exists always in the *composite*. By "the *composite*", here, I
10   mean the white man. So, it is evident that neither is the thing abstracted prior, nor is what results by addition posterior;[33] for it is by addition of whiteness that we speak of a white man.

That the mathematical objects are not substances to a higher degree than bodies, nor prior in existence to sensible things but prior only in formula, nor yet capable of existing separately anywhere, has been
15   sufficiently stated. But since it was shown they cannot exist in sensible things,[34] it is evident that, either they do not exist at all, or they exist in some sense and because of this they exist not without qualification;[35] for "existence" has many senses.

3

Now, just as certain universal propositions in mathematics, which are about things not existing apart from magnitudes and numbers, are
20   indeed about numbers and magnitudes but not qua such as having a magnitude or as being divisible,[1] clearly, so there may be propositions and demonstrations about sensible magnitudes, not qua sensible but qua being of such-and-such a kind.[2] For just as there are many propositions concerning sensible things but only qua moving, without reference to the whatness of each of these and the attributes that follow

25   from it³—and it is not necessary because of this that there should exist
       either a moving⁴ of a sort which is separate from the sensible thing or
       is some definite nature in the sensible thing⁵—so also there will be
       propositions and sciences about things in motion, not qua in motion but
       only qua bodies, or only qua planes,⁶ or qua lengths, or qua divisible,⁷
30   or qua indivisible with position, or just qua indivisible.⁸
            Thus, since it is true to say, without specifying, that not only what is
       separate exists but also what is not separate (for example, that the mov-
       ing⁹ exists), it is also true to say, without specifying, that the mathe-
       matical objects exist, and to be indeed such as mathematicians say they
35   are. And just as it is true to say, without specifying, that each of the
       other sciences is concerned with certain things—not with what is acci-
       dental to those things (for example, not with the white, if the healthy is
       white and if the science is concerned with the healthy) but only with
1078a those things qua such, that is, with the healthy qua healthy if it is the
       science of the healthy, and with a man qua man if it is the science of
       man—so it is with geometry. If the objects of the mathematical sciences
       also happen to be sensible but are not investigated qua sensible, this
       does not mean that those sciences will not be concerned with sensible
5   things,¹⁰ or that they will be concerned with other things separated
       from the sensibles.
            If A belongs to a thing, many other essential attributes of A will also
       belong to that thing qua A. For example, proper *attributes* belong to the
       female animal qua female, or to the male animal qua male, although no
       female or male¹¹ exists separate from animals. So, proper *attributes*
       belong also to sensible things qua having lengths or qua having surfaces.
10   And to the extent that we are investigating what is prior in formula and
       is simpler, to that extent the result will be more accurate, and by
       "accurate" I mean simple. Thus, the science which leaves out magnitude
       is more accurate than the one which includes it, and the science which
       leaves out motion as well as magniture is the most accurate of the
       three.¹² And if a science is concerned with motion, it is most accurate
       if it is concerned with the primary¹³ motions; for these are the simplest,
       and of the primary motions the even motion is yet the simplest.¹⁴ The
15   same statements apply to optics and harmonics; for they investigate
       sight and sound, respectively, no qua sight or qua sound, but qua lines
       and numbers, which, however, are *proper attributes* of sight and sound
       respectively.¹⁵ Mechanics, too, proceeds in the same way. So, if one
       lays down as separate certain attributes and inquires into these qua what
       they are, he will not by so doing inquire into what is false, just as he
20   will not speak falsely when he draws a line on the ground and calls it a
       foot long when it is not a foot long; for this latter falsehood is not in
       the premises.
            A thing can best be investigated if each attribute which is not

separate from the thing is laid down as separate,[16] and this is what the arithmetician and the geometrician do. Thus, a man qua a man is one and indivisible. The arithmetician lays down this: to be one is to be indivisible, and then he investigates the attributes which belong to a man qua indivisible. On the other hand, the geometrician investigates a man neither qua a man nor qua indivisible, but qua a solid. For it is clear that the attributes which would have belonged to him even if somehow he were not indivisible can still belong to him if he is indivisible.[17] Because of this fact, geometers speak rightly, and what they discuss are beings, and these are beings; for "being" may be used in two senses, as actuality and as matter.[18]

Now since the good is distinct from the beautiful[19] (for the good is always in *action* but the beautiful may also be in what is immovable), those[20] who assert that the mathematical sciences say nothing about the beautiful or the good speak falsely. For they do speak about and show these, and in the highest degree. The fact that they do not use the names, while they do exhibit constructions and theorems about them, does not mean that they say nothing about them. Now the most important kinds of the beautiful are order, symmetry, and definiteness, and the mathematical sciences exhibit properties of these in the highest degree.[21] And since these (that is, order and definiteness) appear to be causes of many things, it is clear that the mathematical sciences must be dealing in some way with such a cause, that is, the cause in the sense of beauty. However, we shall speak about these matters at greater length elsewhere.[22]

4

Concerning the mathematical objects, that they are beings and how they exist, and also in what sense they are prior and in what sense they are not, let the foregoing discussion suffice. As for the Ideas, we must first examine the doctrine of the Ideas itself, in the manner first believed by those[1] who first spoke of the existence of the Ideas, without connecting the doctrine in any way with the nature of numbers. These thinkers came upon this doctrine of Ideas because they were convinced about the truth of the Heraclitean arguments which state that all sensible things are always in a state of flux, so that if there is to be a science or *knowledge* of anything, there must exist apart from the sensible things some other natures which are permanent, for there can be no science of things which are in a state of flux.[2]

Now Socrates occupied himself with the moral virtues, and in connection with these he was the first to seek universal definitions. For, of the

20   physicists, only Democritus touched upon the subject of definition a
little,[3] and in some way he defined the hot and the cold; while the
Pythagoreans before him considered definitions of a few things, raising
such questions, for example, as "What is opportunity?",[4] "What is justice?",[5] "What is marriage?",[6] and the formulae[7] they gave to these were
in terms of numbers. But Socrates had a good reason in seeking the
whatness of a thing, for he was seeking to prove something, and the
25   whatness of a thing is a principle of syllogisms; for dialectical ability
in his day did not yet exist so as to enable men, even without the
knowledge of whatness, to speculate about contraries[8] and about the
problem whether contraries come under the same science or not. It is
just to give credit to Socrates for two things, inductive arguments and
defining universally; and both these are concerned with principles of
science.
30   But Socrates did not posit the universals as separate, nor the definitions;[9] these thinkers, however, regarded them as being about other
things, separate from sensible things, and called such things "Ideas".
And so, almost by the same argument, they came to the conclusion that there are Ideas of all things of which we speak universally;[10]
35   and this resembles the case of a man who wished to count and who,
thinking he could not do so with the few things at hand, created more.
1079a For, in seeking the causes of the sensibles, these thinkers proceeded
from these to the Forms, which are more numerous, so to say, than the
individual sensibles;[11] for there exists a Form bearing the same name
as that which is predicated of many sensibles, of substances as well as
of non-substances,[12] and of these things[13] as well as of eternal things.[14]
5   Yet none of the ways which are used to show that the Forms exist
appears convincing; for, from what is laid down, in some cases no
syllogism is necessarily formed, and in others it follows that there will
be Forms even of things of which they think that no Forms exist. For
according to the arguments from the sciences there will be Forms of all
things of which there are sciences;[15] according to the argument "one
10   predicated of many", there will be Forms even of denials;[16] and according to the argument that we can think of something which has
been destroyed, there will be Forms of destructible things, since an
image of what has been destroyed can exist.[17]
Again, of their most accurate statements, some introduce Ideas of
relations, though a genus of relations is denied by them as existing by
itself,[18] while others speak of *the third man*.[19] And in general, the
statements concerning the Forms eliminate those things[20] whose ex-
15   istence the believers in the Forms would prefer to the existence of the
Ideas; for what follows from their statements is that Number is first
and not the *Dyad*,[21] that a relation is prior to a number,[22] that the rela-

tive is prior to what exists by itself,[23] and all other conclusions which, drawn by some believers in the doctrine of Ideas, are contrary to the principles put forward concerning Ideas.

20   Again, according to their belief in virtue of which Ideas are said to exist, there will be Forms not only of substances but also of many other things; for not only of a substance is a concept one, but also of what is not a substance, and not only of substances will there be sciences.[24] A great many other difficulties like the ones considered also follow.

25   According to what necessarily follows and to the doctrine of Forms,[25] if these can be shared in, there must be Ideas only of substances; for Ideas are not shared in as attributes, but each Idea must be shared in this sense, namely, qua not being said of a subject.[26] I mean, for example, that if something shares in Double Itself, it shares also in eternity, but
30 as in an attribute; for eternity is an attribute of the Double.[27] Accordingly, the Forms will be of substances;[28] and the same names signify substances whether applied to the sensibles or to Ideas,[29] otherwise, what will be the meaning of saying that there exists something apart from the many sensible individuals, the one over the many? And if each Idea and the things that share in it have the same form, there will be something common to them all; for why should the form of two be
35 one and the same in the perishable twos and the many eternal Twos[30]
1079b any more than in Two Itself and any perishable two? But if that form is not the same for all, they would be equivocally named, and this would be similar to calling both Callias and a piece of wood "a man", although we observe nothing common in them.[31]

    Also, if we posit that in other respects the usual formulae are to apply to the Forms, that in the case of a circle, for example, "a plane figure"
5 and the remaining parts of the formula are to apply to Circle Itself, and that to each such formula is to be added something indicating that the resulting formula applies to an Idea, we must consider if this is not entirely meaningless. To what will this be added? To the "Center", to the "Plane", or to all the parts? All the parts in a substance are Ideas, as for example Animal and Biped. Moreover, Itself must be something
10 also, just as the plane is some nature which as a genus is present in all its species.[32]

5

    Above all, one might go over the *difficulties* raised by this question: What do the Forms contribute to the eternal beings among the sensibles[1] or to those which are generated and destroyed? For they are not the
15 causes of motion or of change in them.[2] And they do not in any way

help either towards the *knowledge* of the other things[3] (for they are not *substances* of them; otherwise they would be in them[4]) or towards their existence[5] (for they are not present in the things which share them). It might perhaps seem that they are causes in the way in which

20 whiteness is a cause when it is blended in the white thing. But this argument, first used by Anaxagoras and then by Eudoxus and others in discussing the *difficulties,* can easily be upset; for it is easy to infer many statements contradicting such a doctrine.[6] Moreover, all other things

25 are not from the Forms in any of the usual senses of "from".[7] And to say that the Forms are patterns and that the other things share in them is to use empty words and poetic metaphors.[8] For if we look up to the Ideas, what will they do? Any chance thing can be or become like another without being copied[9] from it, so that, whether Socrates exists or

30 not, a man like Socrates might be born.[10] Likewise, it is clear that this might be the case even if there were to be an eternal Socrates. And there will be many patterns of the same thing, and so many Forms; of a man, for example, there will be Animal, Two-footed, and at the same time Man Himself.[11] Moreover, the Forms will be patterns not only of sensible things but also of other Forms; for example, this is how the

35 genus will be related to its species among the Forms. Thus, the same Form will be both a pattern and a copy.[12]

Again, it would seem impossible for a *substance* to exist apart from

1080a that of which it is the *substance.* Accordingly, how could the Ideas, being the *substances* of things, exist apart from them?[13] In the *Phaedo* this is stated in this manner: the Forms are the causes of the existence[14] as well as of the generation[15] of things. But even if the Forms do exist,

5 still no thing is generated unless there is a mover;[16] and many other things are generated, such as a house or a ring, of which, as they themselves say, no Forms exist. Clearly, then, the other things, of which they say there are Ideas, can also exist and be generated through such causes which cause the things just mentioned, but not through the Forms.[17]

Concerning the Ideas, then, it is certainly possible both in this way

10 and by means of more logical[18] and more accurate arguments to collect many objections similar to those we have considered.

6

Having stated our position concerning the Ideas, it is well now to examine what follows from the statements concerning numbers made by those who say that the numbers are separated substances and the first causes of things.

If a number is indeed a nature and if its *substance* is not some other nature but is itself just a number, as some say,[1] it is necessary that either (1) there is something first[2] in it, something else that follows, etc., these being distinct in kind,[3] and this priority begins immediately with the units, so that no unit is comparable with any other unit;[4] or (2) all units are merely successive and any of them is comparable with any of the others, as mathematicians speak of the mathematical number, for in this number no one unit differs from another;[5] or (3) some units are comparable but others are not; for example, if Two is first[6] after *One*, and Three follows Two, and so on with the other Numbers, and the units within each Number are comparable (for example, the two units in the first Two are comparable with each other, the three units in the first Three are likewise comparable, and so on with the rest of the Numbers), but the units of Two Itself are not comparable with those of Three Itself, and similarly for any two such Numbers[7] (and so, mathematical number is counted thus: one, and then two, the latter resulting by the addition of another unit to one, and three results by the addition of another unit to two, and similarly with the other numbers; but these Numbers are counted thus: *One*, and then Two, the latter being composed of units distinct from *One*, and then Three, without including Two as a part, and so on with the other Numbers); or (4) one kind of number is the first kind we stated, a second is the one mathematicians speak of, and a third is the one we have named last.[8]

Again, the kinds of numbers listed must (A) be all separated from things, or (B) none of them be separated but exist in the sensible objects, not existing in them, however, in the manner we first considered,[9] but in the sense that sensible objects consist of numbers as their constituents,[10] or (C) some of them be separated but others not separated.[11]

These, then, are of necessity the only ways in which numbers can exist. And of those who said that the *One* is a principle and a substance and an element of all things, and that a number is made out of the *One* and of something else,[12] almost everyone spoke of numbers as existing in some one of these ways, except for this, that no one said that all the units are noncomparable. And this happened with good reason; for no other way is possible besides the ones stated. Thus, some[13] say that both kinds of numbers exist, those of one kind which have the prior and the posterior being the Ideas, and those of the second kind being the Mathematical Numbers and that the latter are distinct from the Ideas and the sensible objects; and both kinds are separate from the sensible objects. Others[14] say that only Mathematical Numbers exist, and that of all things these are first[15] and are separate from sensible objects. The Pythagoreans, too, posit numbers of only one kind; and they say that these do not exist separately, but that the sensible substances consist of these. For they posit the whole universe as constructed out of numbers, but not numbers consisting of units in the usual sense,[16] for they believe that units have magnitude. But these thinkers are unable to say how the first *One* was constructed so as to have magnitude. Another thinker[17] says that numbers of the first kind alone exist, those of the Forms; and some[18] say that mathematical numbers are the same as these.

A similar situation exists in the case of lengths, planes, and solids. For some[19] say that the Mathematical Objects[20] exist and are distinct from those[21] which come after the Ideas; but those who speak differently say that the Mathematical Objects exist and they do so in a mathematical way,[22] and these thinkers do not regard Ideas as Numbers and deny the existence of Ideas; still others[23] say that the Mathematical Objects exist but not in a mathematical way, for, according to them, neither is every Magnitude divisible into Magnitudes, nor is it the case that any two units taken at random make a Dyad. All those who say that the *One* is an element and a principle of things posit numbers as consisting of units taken in the usual sense,[16] except the Pythagoreans who, as we said before, say that units have magnitude.

It is evident, from what has been said, in how many ways it is possible to speak of numbers, and that all the views taken concerning numbers have been stated. But all these doctrines are impossible, and some[24] are perhaps more so than others.

7

First, then, we must consider if the units are comparable or noncomparable, and if noncomparable, in which of the two ways we distinguished. For it may be that any unit is noncomparable with any other; and it may also be that any unit in Dyad Itself is noncomparable with any in Triad Itself, and, among the first Numbers[1] in general, that any unit in one Number is noncomparable with any unit in another Number.

Now, if all units are comparable and without difference, we get the mathematical numbers and of one kind only, and the Ideas cannot be these numbers.[2] For what kind of a number will Man Himself or Animal Itself or any other Form be? There is only one Idea in each case, that is, there is only one Man Himself and only one Animal Itself; but there are infinitely many numbers which are similar and without difference, so that one triad will no more be Man Himself than another triad.[3] But if the Ideas are not numbers, neither can they exist at all. For from what principles will the Ideas be formed? From the *One* and

224

15   the *Indefinite Dyad* it is Numbers that are formed, and the principles and elements[4] are spoken of as being of just these Numbers, but the Ideas cannot be ranked as either prior or posterior to the Numbers.[5]

But if the units are noncomparable[6] in the sense that any unit is noncomparable with any other unit, what are formed can be neither mathematical numbers[7] (for mathematical numbers consist of units which do 20 not differ, and the properties shown to belong to numbers are adapted to numbers with such units) nor the Numbers which are Forms. For they speak of Numbers as following in succession,[8] the Dyad, the Triad, Four, etc., yet neither will the first dyad [or Two] be formed from the *One* and the *Indefinite Dyad,* nor will the other Numbers that follow; for the units in the first dyad are generated simultaneously, either from 25 the *Unequals* (the generation of Two took place when the *Unequals* were equalized) as the first exponent of the Ideas stated,[9] or in some other way.

Moreover, if one of the units is prior[10] to the other, it will also be prior to the Dyad since this consists of the two units; for, if something is prior and something else posterior, the composite of the two will be prior to the latter but posterior to the former.[11] Further, since *One Itself* 30 is first, there will also be another One which is first among the others but second after *One Itself,* and also a third One which is second after the latter One but third after *One Itself.* Thus, the units would be prior to the Numbers after which they are named; that is, in Two there will 35 be a third unit prior to the existence of Three, and in Three there will be a fourth and a fifth unit prior to the existence of Four and of Five. Now none of these thinkers spoke of the units as being noncomparable in this manner, but according to their principles it is also reasonable 1081*b* that the units should be so,[12] although according to truth this would be impossible.[13] For, if there is a first unit or a first *One,* it is reasonable that there should be priority and posteriority among the units, and similarly for the Dyads if there is a first Dyad; for after what is first 5 it is reasonable and necessary that there should be a second, and if a second, then a third, and so on with the others that follow. However, it is impossible to say[14] both at the same time, namely, that after the *One* there is a first unit and a second, and also that there is a first Dyad. But they posit a first unit or a first *One,* but not also a second and a 10 third, and they posit a first Dyad, but not also a second and a third.

It is also evident that, if all the units are noncomparable, the Dyad Itself and the Triad Itself and the other Numbers cannot exist. For whether the units are not different or are all different, each number 15 must be counted by addition as follows: two, by adding to one another one; three, by adding to two another one; and likewise for four.[15] If this is so, then the Numbers cannot be generated in the manner in

which these thinkers generate Numbers from the *Dyad* and the *One;*
20 for the Dyad becomes a part of the Triad, the Triad a part of Four, and
the same happens with the Numbers that follow. But according to these
thinkers Four was generated from the first Dyad and the *Indefinite
Dyad;* and the result is two 'Dyads'[16] besides the Dyad Itself, or if
not, then Dyad Itself will be a part of Four, and another 'Dyad' will be
added. Similarly, the Dyad Itself will be generated from *One Itself* and
25 another One; but if this is so, the other element cannot be the *Indefinite
Dyad,* for, it would have to generate a unit [the extra One] and not
the definite Dyad.[17]

Again, how will there be other 'Triads' and 'Dyads' besides the
Triad Itself and the Dyad Itself,[18] and in what manner will they consist
30 of prior[19] and posterior units? Now all these are fictitious,[20] and there
cannot be a first Dyad and then Triad Itself. Yet there must be, if indeed the *One* and the *Indefinite Dyad* are to be elements. Thus, if the
results are impossible, the principles cannot be those which they put
35 forward. If all the units are different, then, these and other such results
necessarily follow.

But if the units of one Number differ from those of another, while
the units in the same Number do not differ, even so the difficulties
1082a which follow are not fewer. In Ten Itself, for example, there are ten
units, and Ten Itself consists of ten units as well as of two 'Fives'.
But since this Ten is not any chance Number and is not composed of
5 any chance 'Fives'[21] (just as it is not composed of any chance units), the
units in this Ten must differ. For, if they do not differ, the two 'Fives'
of which this Ten is composed will not differ either; but since these
differ,[22] the units also will differ.[23] But if they differ, will there be no
other two 'Fives' in this Ten besides these two, or will there be other
10 two 'Fives'? If not, this would be unreasonable; and if there will be,
what kind of Ten will be composed of them? Certainly, no Ten other
than Ten Itself exists in the latter. Moreover, Four cannot be composed
of any chance 'Dyads'; for, as they say, the *Indefinite Dyad* received
15 the definite Dyad and made two 'Dyads', since its function was to
double what it received.[24]

Again, how is it possible for the Dyad to be a nature besides its
two units and for the Triad to be a nature besides its three units? For
this may be either when one thing shares in another, as a white man
shares in whiteness and in a man, or when one is a differentia of the
20 other, as a man in the case of being an animal and two-footed. Moreover, some parts are one by contact, others by being blended, still others
by position; yet none of these ways can apply to the units to form the
Dyad or the Triad; but just as two men are not a unity apart from both,
so must it be with the units.[25] And the fact that units are indivisible

25 is no cause for any difference in them; for points too are indivisible, yet a pair of them is nothing other apart from the two.[26]

In addition, we must not forget this which results, the existence of prior and posterior 'Dyads', and similarly for the other 'Numbers'. For, though we may allow the 'Dyads' in Four to be simultaneous, yet
30 these are prior to the 'Dyads' in Eight which they have generated; that is, just as the first Dyad generated the 'Dyads' in Four, so the latter 'Dyads' generated the 'Fours' in Eight Itself. Thus, if the first Dyad is an Idea, the other 'Dyads' too will be Ideas.[27] The same argument applies also to the units; for the units in the first Dyad generate
35 the four units in Four, so that all the units become Ideas, and an Idea will be composed of Ideas.[28] It is clear, then, that those things of which these happen to be Ideas will also be so composed; for example, one
1082b might say that animals are composed of animals, if the corresponding Ideas are so related.[29]

In general, to posit units as being different in any manner is absurd and fictitious (by "fictitious" I mean that which is forced to agree with a hypothesis); for neither with respect to quantity nor with respect to
5 quality do we observe one unit as differing from another unit, and one number must be either equal or unequal to another number, this being so in all cases but most of all when the ultimate parts of a number are indivisible units.[30] So if one number is neither greater nor less than another, then it must be equal to it; and in numbers, things which are equal and do not differ at all are believed to be the same.[31] If not, neither
10 will the 'Dyads' in Ten Itself be without difference, though they are equal; for what reason will one have in saying that they are without difference?

Again, if any unit and another unit are two, then a unit from the Dyad Itself and one from the Triad Itself will be a 'Dyad' composed of differing units; and will this 'Dyad' be prior or posterior[32] to the
15 Triad? It rather seems that it must be prior;[33] for one of the units is simultaneous with the Triad and the other is simultaneous[34] with the Dyad. We, too, believe universally that one and one, whether these are equal or unequal,[35] are two, as for example, the good and the bad, or a man and a horse; but those who put forward the views under consideration deny this even if the two ones are units.[36]

20 It would be strange if the Triad Itself as a number were not greater than the Dyad; and if it is greater, clearly in the Triad Itself there is a part equal to the Dyad, so that this part will not differ from the Dyad Itself.[37] But this cannot be so, if there is a first Number and a second;
25 nor will the Ideas be numbers.[38] Now, if there are to be Ideas, those who require the units to be different are right on this point, as we said earlier, for each Form is unique;[39] but if the units are not different, the

'Dyads' and the 'Triads' too will not be different. So, this is why they
find it necessary to say that in counting thus, "one, two", we do so not
30   by adding a unit to what precedes;[40] for if we count by so adding, there
will be no generation from the *Indefinite Dyad,* nor can there be Ideas,[41]
since one Idea will then be a constituent of another Idea, and all the
Forms will be parts of one Form. Consequently, relative to their hypothesis they speak rightly, but on the whole they do not speak rightly;[42]
for they eliminate many facts, since they would admit that there is a
35   *difficulty* here, namely, whether in counting and saying "one, two,
three" we do so by adding a unit each time or by considering the numbers separately. But we do count in both ways; so, it is ridiculous that
this *difficulty* should be referred to so great a difference in *substance.*[43]

                              8

1083*a*   First of all it is well to determine what the differentiae of numbers
and of units are, if such exist. Now units must differ either with respect
to quantity or with respect to quality; yet it appears that neither of
these differentiae can belong to units. But numbers qua numbers may
5   differ according to quantity.[1] Now if units, too, differed in quantity,
one number would also differ from another number even if both were
equal in their multitude of units.[2] Also, are the first units larger or
smaller, and do units which are posterior increase or diminish? All these
alternatives are unreasonable.[3] Moreover, neither can units differ with
10   respect to quality; for no affection can belong to them, and, as these
thinkers themselves say, even in Numbers[4] quality is an attribute posterior to quantity. Further, neither from the *One* nor from the *Dyad*
could quality come to the units; for the former has no quality,[5] and the
function of the latter is to generate quantity since its nature is to be the
cause of the existence of many things.[6] On the other hand, if somehow
15   there is another alternative, they should state this most of all at the
beginning, and of the units they should specify the differentiae and,
most of all, why these differentiae must belong to the units; otherwise,
what differentiae are they talking about?[7]
        It is evident, then, that if the Ideas are indeed Numbers,[8] neither can
20   all the units be comparable,[9] nor can they be noncomparable in either
of the two ways.[10] But neither is the manner in which some others speak
about numbers stated well. These are those[11] who think that Ideas do
not exist, either simply as Ideas[12] or as being certain Numbers;[13] that
there exist Mathematical Objects; that the Numbers are first[14] of all
things; and that the principle of these Numbers is the *One Itself.*[15] Now
25   it is absurd that *One* should be the first among the ones, just as the other

thinkers say,[16] but not a first Dyad among the dyads, nor a first Triad among the triads; for the same argument applies to all. If, then, these are the facts concerning the Numbers and if anyone posits the existence of Mathematical Numbers only, the *One* is not a principle; for if it is,
30 it must differ from the other units, and if so, there must also be a first Dyad differing from the other dyads, and similarly with the other Numbers which follow.[17] So if the *One* is a principle, the facts concerning Numbers must rather be as Plato used to say, and there must be a first
35 Dyad, and a first Triad, and the Numbers must not be comparable with one another. But if, as before, one posits this, we have said that many impossbile consequences follow.[18] But either this or the other must
1083b be the case; so, if neither is the case, the Numbers cannot be separate.[19]

It is also evident from what has been said that the third version,[20] according to which the Numbers as Ideas are the same as the Mathematical Numbers, is the worst. For two errors must follow from a single
5 doctrine: first, Mathematical Numbers cannot exist in this manner, and, as other hypotheses proper to this doctrine are required,[21] longer arguments become necessary; second, the consequences that follow from the doctrine which considers Numbers as Ideas must follow also here.

The Pythagorean version[22] has in one sense fewer difficulties than those stated before, but in another sense it has other difficulties peculiar
10 to itself. For by the positing of numbers as not separate,[23] many of the impossible consequences are removed; on the other hand, impossible consequences follow from the fact that bodies are posited as composed of numbers which are mathematical numbers.[24] For it is not true to say that indivisible magnitudes exist;[25] and, however true it may be to say
15 that indivisible magnitudes exist, at least units have no magnitude. But how is it possible for a magnitude to be composed of indivisibles?[26] Arithmetical numbers, to be sure, are composed of units which are indivisible. But these thinkers say that things are numbers; at least, they attach to bodies properties demonstrated of numbers as if bodies were composed of numbers.
20 If a number, then, in order to exist as a being by itself, must indeed exist in some one of the ways which have been stated, and if it cannot exist in any of these ways, evidently it has no nature such as is attributed to it by those who make it separate.[27]

Again, does each unit consist of the *Great* and the *Small* after these
25 have been equalized, or does one unit consist of the *Small* and the other of the *Great*? If the latter, neither does each thing consist of all the elements,[28] nor are the units without difference;[29] for in one unit there is the *Great*, and in the other the *Small*, the latter being contrary in nature to the *Great*. Besides, how is the Triad composed of units? There

30   will be an odd unit. But perhaps it is because of this that in odd Numbers .
they put the *One Itself* in the middle.[30]

If, however, each of the two units consists of both, after these have
been equalized,[31] how will the Dyad, being one nature, consist of the
Great and the *Small*? Or how will it differ from a unit?[32] Moreover, the
unit will be prior to the Dyad; for, if it is destroyed, the Dyad is
35   destroyed.[33] Accordingly, it must be an Idea of an Idea,[34] since it is at
least prior, and it must have been generated before it. Out of what,
then?[35] The function of the *Indefinite Dyad* was merely to double.

Again, the Numbers must be either infinite or finite;[36] for they posit
1084a the Numbers as separate, so it is not possible that neither of these
attributes belong to Numbers.[37] Now, clearly, an infinite number cannot
exist; for an infinite number is neither odd nor even, but the generation
of Numbers is always that of an odd or that of an even Number,[38]
5   thus: (1) an odd Number results when the *One* is added to an even
Number, (2) an even Number results (a) when the *Dyad* receives the
One, and what results from this in succession,[39] and (b) when the *Dyad*
receives an odd Number.[40] Further, if each Idea is of something, and the
Numbers are Ideas, an infinite Number will likewise be an Idea of
something, either of a sensible thing or of some other thing. Yet this is
10   impossible, either in view of their thesis,[41] or according to formula,[42]
if this is how they form the Ideas.

On the other hand, if the Numbers are finite, how far do they go? In
stating their answer, they must give not only the fact but also the cause
of it. Now if the Numbers end with Ten, as some say,[43] in the first place
the Forms will soon fall short. For example, if the Triad is Man Him-
15   self, what Number will be Horse Itself? It is only up to Ten that each
Number will be something Itself. Then it must be some 'Number' within
these,[44] for these too are substances and Ideas. But these will still fall
short, for the species of animals will be greater in Number.[45] It is at
the same time clear that if a 'Triad' is Man Himself in this manner, so
will the other 'Triads' be, for all such within the same Number are
20   similar;[46] so, if each 'Triad' is an Idea, this being Man Himself, there
will be an infinite[47] number of instances of Man Himself, or if not, then
at least an infinite number of instances of 'Man'.[48] And if the smaller
'Number' is a part of the greater Number, when the former is composed
of some of the comparable units of the latter, then, if Four Itself is the
Idea of something, say, of a horse or of whiteness, 'Man' will be a part
25   of the Idea of a horse if, say, 'Man' is a 'Dyad'.[49]

It is also absurd that there should be an Idea of ten, but not of
eleven or of the numbers that follow.[50]

Again, some things exist and are generated even if no Forms of them exist; why are there no Forms of them also? It is not the Forms, then, that are their causes.[51]

30   Again, it is absurd that the Number-series up to Ten should be a being and a Form to a higher degree than Ten Itself, even though there is no generation of the Number-series as one thing while there is so of Ten.[52] But they proceed to develop their doctrine as if the Number-series up to Ten were complete. At any rate, they generate the things that follow, for example, the void, analogy, the odd, and the others of 35 this kind, within the Number-series; for they attribute some of these things, such as motion, rest, goodness, and badness, to the principles,[53] and the others to the Numbers. And so they attribute oddness to the *One*; for if they were to attribute it to Three, how could Five be odd?[54]

1084b   Then the magnitudes and the like are likewise attributed to Numbers up to a certain Number; for example, first the Indivisible Line, then the Dyad, then the rest up to Ten.[55]

    Again, if the Numbers exist separately, one might raise the question whether the one[56] is prior[57] or the Triad and the Dyad. Inasmuch as a 5 Number is a composite, the one is prior;[58] but inasmuch as the universal[59] or the Form[60] is prior, a Number[61] is prior, for each of the units is a part of a Number as its matter, and the Number is the form. And in one sense the right angle is prior to the acute, for the latter is defined in terms of the former;[62] but in another sense the acute angle is prior to the right, for the acute angle is a part, and the right angle is divided into acute angles. As matter, then, the acute angle and the elements 10 and the unit are prior, but with respect to form or to *substance* according to formula, the right angle and the whole as composite of matter and form are prior; for the composite is nearer to the form and to what is signified by the formula, but it is posterior in generation.[63]

    How, then, is the one a principle?[64] By not being divisible, they say. 15 But both the universal and the part or element are indivisible, although in different senses: the former with respect to formula,[65] the latter with respect to time.[66] In which of the two senses, then, is the one a principle? As we said, both the right angle is thought to be prior to the acute, and the latter to the former,[67] and each of these angles is one. In fact, they posit the one as a principle in both senses.[68] Now this is impossible; for 20 the universal is one[69] as form or substance, but the element is one as a part or as matter. For each part is in some sense one, in fact potentially one, if for example a Number is one thing and not like a heap and is thus composed of units distinct from those in any other Number, as it is said; but each unit does not exist actually as one.[70]

    The cause of the error into which these thinkers fell is the fact that they were conducting their inquiry from the point of view of mathe-25 matics and at the same time from universal expressions, so that, on the one hand, from the former they posited the *One* and the principle as if it were a point, for a unit is a point[71] without position; and, just like some other thinkers,[72] they made things by putting together the smallest elements. Thus, the unit becomes the matter of Numbers and at the same time prior[73] to the Dyad, and it also becomes posterior[74] to it since the Dyad is a whole and one thing and a Form.[75] On the other hand, because of their inquiry into universals, they spoke of oneness as a predicate and as a part in this sense.[76] But these two senses of "one" cannot belong to the same thing at the same time.[77]

If we allow the *One Itself* just this, namely, to be without position (for it differs in no way from being a principle[78]), and the Dyad to be divisible but each unit indivisible, a unit would be more similar to the *One Itself* than to the Dyad.[79] If so, then conversely, the *One Itself* would be more similar to a unit than to the Dyad. Consequently, each of the two units in the Dyad would be prior[80] to the Dyad. But they deny this; at least they generate the Dyad first.[81] Again, if the Dyad Itself is one thing and the Triad Itself is also one thing, the two together will form a 'Dyad'. From what, then, is this 'Dyad' formed?[82]

9

Since there is no contact[1] but there is succession in numbers between whose units there is nothing (for example, there is nothing between the units of a dyad or a triad), one may also raise the question whether it is the *One Itself* that the Numbers succeed or not, and whether the Dyad or either of its two units is prior to the Numbers that succeed the Dyad.[2]

Similar difficulties result also with the genera of things which follow the Numbers,[3] that is, with the Line and the Plane and the Solid. Some thinkers generate these from the species of the *Great* and the *Small,* that is, Lengths from the *Long* and *Short,* Planes from the *Wide* and *Narrow,* and Volumes from the *Deep* and *Shallow;*[4] these are species of the *Great* and the *Small.*[5] As for the principle which corresponds to the *One,* different thinkers take different positions.[6] Here too, however, there appear to be a great many instances of the impossible, the fictitious, and what is contrary to all that is reasonable. For (a) the kinds of Magnitudes turn out to be severed from each other,[7] unless their principles are so related that, for example, the *Wide* and *Narrow* is also *Long* and *Short;* but if this is so, the Plane will be a Line and the Solid will be a Plane.[8] Moreover, from what principles will Angles and Shapes and such things come?[9] And (b) the same happens here as in the case of Numbers; for the long, the short, the wide, and the rest are *attributes* of magnitudes, but magnitudes do not consist of these any more than a line consists of the straight and the curved, or a solid of the smooth and the rough.[10]

A common *difficulty* may be discussed in all these doctrines, the very same as that we discussed in connection with the various species of a genus, namely, if one posits the universals, whether [for example] Animal Itself or something distinct from Animal Itself exists in a particular animal. If the universal does not exist separately, no *difficulty* will arise; but if the *One* and the Numbers exist separately, as these thinkers say, it is not easy to solve the *difficulty*, if we are to call the impossible "not easy". For when one conceives the one[11] in a dyad or in any individual number whatsoever, does he conceive the *One Itself* or something else?[12]

Some, then, generate magnitudes from matter of this sort, but others[13] generate them from the *Point* (the *Point* seems to these thinkers to be not the *One* but something like the *One*[14]) and from some other matter like *Plurality*, but not from *Plurality Itself*; yet the *difficulties* with these principles are none the less the same. For if the matter is one, a Line and a Plane and a Solid will be the same; for from the same principles one and the same thing will be generated.[15] But if the matters are more than one, and there is one [kind of] matter for a Line, another for a Plane, and still another for a Solid, either they follow each other or not, so that the same results will follow even in this manner; for either the Plane will have no Line, or it will be a Line.[16]

Again, no attempt is made to show how Numbers are generated from the *One* and *Plurality*; but however they express themselves, the resulting difficulties are the same as in the case of those who generate Numbers from the *One* and the *Indefinite Dyad*. For one thinker generates Numbers from a universal Plurality but not a specific Plurality, another thinker generates them from a specific Plurality, the primary Plurality; for the *Dyad* is regarded as a primary Plurality.[17] Thus, the two views do not differ at all, so to speak, and the same *difficulties* will follow, namely, those with regard to blending, position, fusion, generation, and the others of this sort.[18]

Above all, one might press this question: "If each unit is one, from what does it come?" Certainly, it is not the *One Itself*. It must come, then, from the *One Itself* and *Plurality* or a part of *Plurality*. Now we cannot truly say that a unit is a plurality, at least if it is indivisible,[19] and in saying that it comes from a part of *Plurality* one is faced with many other difficulties; for (a) each part must be either indivisible,[20] or a plurality (in which case the unit will be divisible),[21] and then the elements will not be the *One* and *Plurality* (for each unit will not come from *Plurality* and the *One*), and (b) the thinker who says this does nothing more than posit another number, for *Plurality* will be a number of indivisibles.

Again, we must also inquire from the thinkers[22] who speak in this

manner whether the Numbers are finite or infinite. It seems that at the
25   beginning there was a finite *Plurality*,[23] and from this and the *One* were
generated a finite number of units; but *Plurality Itself* is distinct from
Infinite Plurality.[24] What kind of *Plurality*, then, in addition to the *One*,
is the element?[25] Similarly, one might also inquire about the *Point* and
the element from which these thinkers[26] generate Magnitudes; for at
30   least the *Point* is not the only one point. From what, then, is each of
the other points generated? Certainly not from some *Interval*[27] and the
Point Itself?[28] But the parts of an interval cannot even be indivisible
like those of plurality whose parts are units; for a number is composed
of indivisibles but a magnitude is not.
35   All these and other such difficulties, then, make it evident that Numbers and Magnitudes cannot exist separately. What is more, the dis-
1086*a*   agreement among the leading thinkers concerning Numbers is a sign
that it is the falsity of the alleged facts which brings about this confusion
in their positions. For those[29] who posit only the Mathematical Objects
as existing apart from sensible things, perceiving the difficulties about
5   the Forms and their fictitiousness, abandoned the Numbers as Ideas
and posited Mathematical Numbers. Those who wished to posit the
Forms and at the same time the Numbers,[30] not seeing how, if one posits
the same principles, Mathematical Numbers can exist in addition to the
Numbers as Ideas, posited both the Ideas and Mathematical Numbers
10   as being the same Numbers in formula, although the Mathematical
Numbers are in fact done away with; for they put forward hypotheses
which are peculiar to themselves but not mathematical.[31] The first
thinker,[32] who posited the existence of the Forms as Numbers and also
the Mathematical Objects, separated the two for a good reason.[33] Thus,
it turns out that all of these thinkers are right in some respect, but on the
whole they are not right.[34] And they themselves admit that their state-
15   ments are not the same but contrary to each other. The cause of this is
the fact that their hypotheses and principles are false. It is difficult to
speak well from bad materials,[35] for, according to Epicharmus, "As soon
as 'tis said, 'tis seen to be wrong."[36]
        Concerning numbers, we have gone over the *difficulties* and settled
them sufficiently; for he who is convinced would be yet more convinced
20   by additional arguments, but he who is not convinced would come no
nearer to conviction.
        Concerning the first principles and the first causes and elements, what
is said by those who limit themselves only to sensible substances has
been partly stated in the *Physics*[37] and partly does not belong to our
25   present inquiry; but what is said by those who assert that there exist
other substances besides the sensible substances needs to be investigated
next after what has just been discussed.[38]
        Since, then, some thinkers say that the Ideas and the Numbers are

234

such substances, and that the elements of these are the elements and principles of things, we must inquire what these thinkers say and how they say it.

30 Those[39] who posit only Numbers which are Mathematical must be examined later,[40] but regarding those who posit the Ideas, we might attend to the manner in which they express themselves and at the same time to the *difficulties* they are facing. For they posit the Ideas as being universal substances and at the same time as separate and as indi-

35 viduals.[41] That this is impossible has already been discussed before.[42] Those who say that the Ideas are universal combined these two beliefs[43] about Ideas because they did not posit the Ideas as being the same substances as the sensible substances. They thought that the individuals

1086b among sensible things are in a state of flux and that none of them is permanent, but that the universal exists apart from these and is something distinct from them. As we said earlier, Socrates began thinking in this direction because of his inquiry into definitions; however, he did

5 not separate these from the individuals, and he thought rightly in not doing so. This is brought out by the facts; for without the universal it is not possible to acquire *knowledge,* but the separation of the universal from the individuals is the cause of the difficulties that arise with regard to the Ideas. The exponents of the Ideas, however, thinking that, if indeed there are to be any substances besides the sensible and ever-changing ones, they must exist separately, had no others to put forward

10 but the so-called "universal substances"; and so the universal substances turn out to be of about the same nature as the individual substances. This in itself, then, would be one of the difficulties we have stated.

10

Let us now turn to a point which presents some *difficulty* for both

15 those who posit the Ideas and those who do not,[1] and which has been taken up at the beginning in the discussion of the *difficulties.*[2]

If anyone does not posit the substances[3] to be separate, and in the manner in which individual things are said to be separate, he will be eliminating substances in the sense which we mean by the term "sub-

20 stance". But if he posits substances to be separate, how will he posit their elements and principles? If he posits them as individuals and not as universal, (1) there will be as many things as there are elements,[4] (2) and the elements will not be *knowable.*[5] For (1) let the syllables in speech be substances, and the letters of syllables be the elements of

25 substances. Then there must be only one BA and only one of each of the other syllables, if indeed these are not universal and the same in kind

but each is to be numerically one and be a *this* and not have a common
name (besides, each thing which exists as Itself is posited as being only
one[6]); and if this is so with the syllables, so is it also with the elements
of which each syllable consists.[7] Hence, there will not be more than one
A and not more than one of each of the other letters, and this follows
30   from the same argument by which no two syllables are the same. But
if this is so, there will be no other things besides the letters, but only the
letters. Moreover, (2) the elements will not be *knowable;* for they are not
universal, but *knowledge* is of universals. This is clear from demonstra-
35   tions and definitions; for there is no syllogism of the fact that this
triangle[8] has its angles equal to two right angles unless every triangle
has its angles equal to two right angles, nor of the fact that this man is
an animal unless every man is an animal.

1087a   But if the principles are universal, or even if the substances composed
of these are also universal, non-substances will be prior[9] to substances;
for the universal is not a substance, and the elements and the principles[10]
will be universal, but both the elements and the principles are prior to
that of which they are the principles and elements.
5   All these, then, are reasonable consequences, when these thinkers
posit the Ideas as out of elements and also claim that apart from the
substances which have the same form there exists one Idea which is
separate and unique.
Now if, as for example in the case of the elements of speech, nothing
prevents the existence of many A's and B's even if there is no A-Itself
10   and B-Itself apart from the many A's and B's, then in view of this there
can be an infinite number of similar syllables. Of the positions stated,
the one, namely, "Since all *knowledge* is universal, the principles of
things are necessarily universal and are not separated substances" contains a *difficulty* of the highest degree, but this statement is in one
15   sense true and in another not true. For *"knowledge"*, like *"knowing"*,
has two meanings, one exists in potentiality and the other in *actuality.*
Potentiality, like matter, being universal and indefinite, is concerned
with the universal and the indefinite; but *actuality,* being definite and
a *this,* is concerned with some definite thing and some *this.*[11] But it is
20   by accident that sight sees color universally, and this is in view of the
fact that this color, which sight sees, is a color [universally taken];[12] and
likewise, *this* A, which the grammarian investigates, is an A [univer-
sally taken]. For if the principles are of necessity universal, what comes
from them must also be universal, as in demonstrations;[13] and if this
is so, nothing can be separate or a substance. But it is clear that there
25   is a sense in which *knowledge* is universal and a sense in which it is not.

Book N

1

Concerning this substance,[1] then, let the foregoing account suffice.
Now as in the objects of physics, so also in the case of immovable
substances all thinkers posit the principles as being contraries. If, then,
nothing can be prior[2] to the principle of all things, it would be impossible
for the principle to be something else and still be a principle. That is, if,
for example, one were to say that whiteness is a principle not qua
something else but qua whiteness, and yet say that whiteness is an
attribute of a subject (in which case we would have some other thing
which is white), then that other thing would be prior to whiteness.[3]
But all generated things are generated from contraries in the presence
of a subject; a subject, then, must exist for contraries most of all. Thus,
all contraries are attributes of a subject and none of them is separable.[4]
But just as appearance has it, that nothing is contrary to a substance, so
does argument confirm it. None of the contraries, then, is a principle
independent of all, but something else is.[5]

But these thinkers posit one of the contraries as being matter, some[6]
saying that this is the *Unequal*, which is the contrary of the *One* or the
Equal, as if this were the nature of plurality, and others[7] saying that
it is *Plurality*, which is the contrary of *One*.[8] For, according to the former, Numbers are generated from the *Unequal Dyad*, or the *Great* and
Small, but according to the latter, from *Plurality*; and according to both,
they are generated by a substance, the *One*. For even he who says that
the *Unequal* and the *One* are the elements, and that the *Unequal* is the
Dyad, which consists of the *Great* and *Small*, speaks of the *Unequal* or
the *Great* and *Small* as being one but does not state definitely that it is
one in formula, but not numerically.[9]

Again, they do not even describe well the principles, which they call
"elements"; for some speak of the *Great* and *Small* along with the *One*
as the three elements of Numbers, the first two as matter[10] and the *One*
as *form*; others speak of the *Many* and *Few*,[11] in view of the fact that

236

greatness and smallness are by nature more *proper* to magnitude; and others[12] speak of what is more universally predicated of these, *Excess* and *Deficiency*. However, these positions do not differ at all, so to speak,
20   with respect to some of the consequences, but only with respect to logical difficulties which these thinkers are trying to avoid, because it is also logical demonstrations which they use.[13] There is, however, this exception: the argument which favors *Excess* and *Deficiency* as the principles and not the *Great* and the *Small* also favors that Number be generated from the elements before Two is generated; for in each case
25   the first is more universal than the second.[14] As it is, they assert the one but not the other.[15]

Other thinkers oppose the *Other* or the *Another* to the *One*,[16] and still others[17] oppose *Plurality* to the *One*. But if things, according to the intention of these thinkers, are composed of contraries, and of unity either no contrary exists, or, if there is to be any, plurality is the con-
30   trary,[18] and if the unequal is opposed to the equal, the other to the same, and the another to the selfsame, then those who oppose the *One* to *Plurality* have the best claim to be saying something.[19]

But even these are not stating things adequately. For the *One* will be few; for plurality is opposed to fewness, and the many to the few.[20] Evidently "one" signifies a measure.[21] And in every case there is some
35   distinct underlying subject; for example, in the musical scale a quarter-tone; in magnitude a finger or a foot or some other such thing; and in rhythm a beat or a syllable. Similarly, in weight there is some definite
1088a unit of weight, and in the same way in all cases, some quality in qualities, some quantity in quantities (and the measure is indivisible, with respect to kind in one case,[22] with respect to sensation in the other case[23]); so that the one is not by itself a substance of some one thing.[24] And this is
5   also according to formula; for "one" signifies a measure of some plurality,[25] and "a number" signifies a measured plurality or a plurality of measures. Therefore, it is also with good reason that unity is not a number; for neither is a measure measures,[26] but a measure is a principle,[27] and so is unity. But the measure must be something which is the same in all; for example, if the measure is a horse, the things measured are
10   horses, and if it is a man, then they are men. And if the things measured are a man, a horse, and a god, then the measure is perhaps an animal,[28] and their number will be a number of animals. But if the things measured are a man and white and walking, there is scarcely a number of them because they can all belong to a subject which is the same and numerically one; however, their number will be a number of genera or of something else with a name of this sort.[29]

15   Those who posit the *Unequal* as something which is one, and the *Dyad* as something indefinite consisting of the *Great* and *Small*, say

what is very far from what is commonly thought and what is possible. For (a) these are *attributes* or accidents, like the even and odd, the smooth and rough, and the straight and curved, rather than underlying subjects of numbers and of magnitudes (the many and few[30] of numbers, and the great and small of magnitudes).

20 In addition to this error, (b) the great and the small and all other such are of necessity relations (and of all the categories a relation is least of all a nature or a substance and is posterior to quality and quan-
25 tity[31]); and this relation is an *attribute* of quantity, as we said, and not matter, if indeed there is something else distinct from relation which underlies a relation in general or any of its parts or kinds.[32] For there is nothing great or small, much or little, or, in general, a relation to something else which is not something other [than a relation] that is much or little or great or small or related to something else. A sign that a relation
30 is least of all a substance and a being is the fact that of a relation alone is there no generation nor destruction nor motion, while there is increase and decrease with respect to quantity, alteration with respect to quality, locomotion with respect to place, and unqualified generation and destruction with respect to a substance. But there is no generation or destruction or motion with respect to a relation; for without being
35 moved, a thing may be at one time greater and at another less or equal, if that to which it is related is moved with respect to quantity.[33]

1088b Also, (c) the matter of each thing, and so of a substance, must be potentially that to which it changes, but a relation is neither potentially a substance nor *actually*. Accordingly, it is absurd, or rather impossible, to posit non-substance as an element of and prior[34] to substance; for all the other categories are posterior.

5 Finally, (d) the elements are not predicates of the things of which they are elements, but the much and the little are predicates both separately and together of numbers,[35] and so are the long and the short of lines, and the wide and the narrow of planes.[36] If indeed there is a plurality which is always few, for example, two (for if two were many,
10 one would be few[37]), there will also be a plurality which is unqualifiedly many; for example, ten will be unqualifiedly many if there is no greater plurality,[38] or else ten thousand.[39] Accordingly, in what manner will a number be composed of the Many and the Few? For either both ought to be predicates of each number or none; but in fact only one of them is a predicate.[40]

2

15 We must inquire in general if it is possible for eternal beings to consist of elements. If it is possible, they will have matter; for every thing which is made of elements is a composite. If that which is composed

of elements must be generable[1] from these elements, whether it existed
eternally or was generated, and that which is generated is generated
from that which is potentially that which will be generated (for it could
not be in the process of generation nor have become something from
that which did not have this potentiality), and that which is possible
20   may be *actualized* or may not, then, just as a number[2] or any other thing
which has matter may not be, however always it may have existed[3] (as
in the case of that which is a day old or any number of years old, which
may not be), so even that whose existence in time had no limit may not
25   be. As we had occasion to discuss elsewhere,[4] then, such things[5] cannot
be eternal, if indeed that which may not exist is not eternal. If that which
we have just stated is universally true, namely, that no substance is
eternal unless it is an *actuality*,[6] and if the elements of substances are
matter, an eternal substance can have no elements of which it consists.
There are some who, besides the *One*, posit the *Indefinite Dyad* as
30   an element, but they object to the *Unequal* with good reason, because
of the impossibilities that follow.[7] But these are exempt from only those
objections which of necessity arise by positing as an element the *Unequal* and as a relation; but all the objections which follow apart from
this doctrine must be faced also by these thinkers, whether they posit
35   the Ideas which are Numbers or the Mathematical Numbers as consisting of those elements.[8]
1089a   There are many *reasons* which led these thinkers off to these causes,[9]
but most of all the fact that they raised the problem in a primitive
fashion. For they thought that all things would be one, *Being* itself,
unless they refuted or did not wish to go along with the saying of
Parmenides:

For never will this be proved, that things which are not, exist.

5   Hence they thought it necessary to show that nonbeing[10] exists; for if
things are to be many, they are made in this way, out of being and
something else.[11]
But, first, if "being" has many senses (for it means a substance, or a
quality, or a quantity, or any of the other categories), what kind of being
10   will all beings be one if nonbeing is not to exist? Will it be the substances, or the affections, or, similarly, any of the others? And will the
"*this*" and the "such" and the "so-much" and the others, each of which
signifies something which is one, all of them be one?[12] But it is absurd,
or rather impossible, that there should be just one nature[13] which be-
15   comes the cause of the existence of a *this*, and of a such, and of a
so-much, and of a whereness.
Secondly, of what kind of not-being and being are things composed?
For "not-being", too, has many senses, just as "being" has; and "not-man"
signifies being a not-*this*, "not-straight"[14] signifies being a not-such, and

"not-three-cubits-long" signifies being a not-so-much. Of what kind of being and not-being, then, are composed the things which are many? This thinker[15] has in mind the false and calls this nature "not-being", and from this and being he generates the plurality of things. And this is why it used to be said that something false must be assumed, just as the geometricians assume the line which they draw to be a foot long when it is not. But this cannot be so; for neither do geometers assume a falsehood (for no false premise enters into the syllogism[16]), nor are things generated or destroyed from nonbeing of this kind.[17] But since "non-being" in its various cases has as many meanings as there are categories, and besides these it signifies what is false and also what is potential, it is from this last[18] that generation proceeds; and so a man is generated from what is not a man but is potentially a man, and the white is generated from what is not white but is potentially white, and the situation is similar whether one thing is generated or many.

But the inquiry of these thinkers seems to be, how being, in the sense of a substance, is many; for the things that are generated for them are numbers and lines and bodies.[19] Yet, in their inquiry into how things are many, it is absurd to seek only the whatness of things, but not their qualities or quantities. For neither the *Indefinite Dyad* nor the *Great* and the *Small* is the cause of the existence of two whites or of many colors or flavors or shapes.[20] For if the one or the other were the cause, these, too, would be numbers or units. But if they had considered these other categories, they might have seen the cause of plurality even in substances; for the cause is either the same or analogous.[21]

It is because of this deviation[22] that, in seeking the opposite[23] of *Being* and of *Unity* so as to generate things from *Being* and *Unity* and this opposite, they assumed the relative or the *Unequal*,[24] which is neither the contrary nor the denial[25] of *Being* or of *Unity*, and which is one nature of being just as whatness or quality is. And they should have also inquired how it is that there are many relations and not just one. As it is, they inquire how there are many units besides the first *One*, but not how there are many unequals besides the *Unequal*.[26] Yet they use and speak of the *Great* and *Small*, *Many* and *Few*, from which *Numbers* are generated, and *Long* and *Short*, from which lines are generated, and *Wide* and *Narrow*, from which planes are generated, and also *Deep* and *Shallow*, from which volumes are generated. And they speak of still more kinds of relations; then what will be the cause of the plurality of these relations?[27]

To repeat, then, it is necessary to assume for each case that which exists potentially; and he who took this position has further stated what that is which is potentially a *this* and a substance, but is not a being by itself, namely, that it is a relative (as if he had said a quality), which is neither a potentiality for a unity or a being nor a denial of unity or of

being but is one kind of being.[28] But he should have gone much further, as we said, and should have asked how it is that things are many, not restricting his inquiry within the same category and asking, for example, how it is that there are many substances, or many qualities, but inquiring how it is that there are many beings; for some beings are substances, some are affections, some are relations.[29] And in the case of these other
25   categories there is also something else that needs attention in connection with the problem of how things are many, for it is because these categories are not separable, and also in view of the fact that the underlying subject becomes many and is many, that there are many qualities and many quantities; and so there must be in each genus some matter, though this cannot be separate from substance.[30] However, in the case
30   of a *this*, there is a reason in asking how there are many instances of it, if something is not to be both a *this* and also a nature of such a kind.[31] But this is rather that other problem, namely, how there are many substances in *actuality* and not just one.[32] Moreover, if a *this* and a quantity are not the same,[33] still they do not state how and why there are many beings,[34] but only how there are many quantities.[35] For "Num-
35   ber" in each case signifies a quantity; and a "unit", if not a measure, signifies something indivisible with respect to quantity.[36] So, if a quan-
1090a tity is distinct from whatness, we are not told of what whatness consists nor how it is many; but if quantity and whatness are the same, he who takes this position is faced with many contrary beliefs.[37]

One might also press this inquiry concerning Numbers: What will convince us that they exist? Now, for the thinker[38] who posits the Ideas,
5   Numbers provide some cause for existing things, that is, if each Number is some Idea, and if an Idea is the cause of existing things in some way or other; and let us assume this for them. But with regard to him[39] who does not consider Numbers in this manner (because he observes inherent objections in the Ideas and so because of these objections he
10   does not posit Ideas as Numbers) but posits Mathematical Numbers, we may inquire, what will convince us that such Numbers exist,[40] and of what use will these be to the other things? Neither does he who posits such Numbers say that they are of use to anything (although he says that these Numbers exist as natures by themselves), nor do these Numbers appear to be the causes of anything; yet the propositions of arith-
15   meticians will all belong to the sensible objects as well, as we said before.[41]

3

Those[1] who posit that Ideas exist and that they are Numbers, by the method of exhibiting each[2] apart from the many and taking it to be

some one thing, at least try to state how this exists and why it exists.[3]
Since, however, these statements are neither necessary nor possible,[4]

20 one should deny that because of them Numbers exist. As for the Pythagoreans, because they observed that many *attributes* of numbers belong
to sensible bodies, they posited that things are numbers, not that numbers exist separately, but that things are composed of numbers. But why,
one may ask? According to them, it is in view of the fact that the *at-*

25 *tributes* of numbers exist in musical notes and in the heavens and in
many other things.[5] As for those[6] who say that only Mathematical Numbers exist, they cannot according to their hypotheses say any such
thing,[7] but they said that no sciences can exist of sensible things. But
we, as before,[8] say that sciences of sensible things exist; and it is also

30 clear that mathematical objects do not exist separately, for if they were
separated, their *attributes* would not belong to bodies. Now with respect
to this point the Pythagoreans are not open to objections;[9] but in positing
that physical bodies are composed of numbers, and so that things which
are heavy or light are composed of things which are neither heavy nor
light, they seem to be speaking of another heaven and of other bodies

35 but not of the sensible ones.[10] Those[11] who posit separate Numbers, in
view of their belief that the axioms are not of sensible things and also
in view of the fact that mathematical statements are true and please

1090*b* the soul, believe that such Numbers exist and exist separately; and similar remarks may be made concerning Mathematical Magnitudes. It is
clear, then, that the contrary argument[12] will make contrary statements;
and these thinkers must solve the *difficulty* just raised, namely, why it
is that, if Mathematical Objects do not exist in sensible things, their
attributes do exist in them.

5 There are some who, from the fact that a point is a limit or an ex-
tremity of a line, a line of a plane, and a plane of a solid, think that it is
necessary for such natures to exist.[13] We should then examine also this
argument and see if it is not rather weak. Now (1) such extremities are

10 not substances, but rather all of these are limits; otherwise, since even
of walking and in general of motion there is a limit, this would then be
a *this* and a substance, which is absurd. But (2) even if they are substances, they will all be *substances*[14] of these sensible things, for the
argument of these thinkers started from its application to sensible things.
Why, then, should such limits exist separately?

Again, without taking it lightly, we may press this difficulty regarding

15 all Numbers and Mathematical Objects: those of them which are prior
contribute nothing to those which are posterior; for if Numbers did
not exist, Magnitudes nonetheless would exist according to those[15] who
say that only Mathematical Objects exist, and if these did not exist,
soul and sensible bodies would still exist. But to judge from the ob-

20   served facts, nature does not seem to be a series of episodes, like a bad
        tragedy. Those who posit the Ideas,[16] however, avoid this difficulty;
        for they generate Magnitudes from matter and Numbers thus: Lines
        from Two,[17] Planes from (perhaps) Three, Solids from Four or from
        other Numbers (for it makes no difference). But will these Magnitudes
25   be Ideas, or what is their manner of existence,[18] and what do they con-
        tribute to things?[19] They contribute nothing, just as the Mathematical
        Objects[20] contribute nothing. What is more, no theorem will be true of
        them, unless one wishes to change the principles of mathematics and
30   posit some other peculiar doctrines.[21] But it is not hard to take any
        chance hypotheses and add more to them and draw conclusions. These
        thinkers, then, are in error in trying to unite the Mathematical Objects
        with the Ideas.

            Those[22] who were first to posit two kinds of Numbers, that of Forms
        and also the Mathematical Numbers, neither said nor could say how
35   Mathematical Numbers exist or from what principles they are com-
        posed.[23] For they place them between Numbers as Forms and sensible
        numbers. For if they consist of the *Great* and *Small*, they will be the
1091*a* same as those of the Ideas. But from what other Great and Small, seeing
        that he [Plato] must also generate Magnitudes?[24] If he mentions an-
        other material, he will be positing more than one element;[25] and if the
        principle is some Unity distinct in each case,[26] there will be something
        common to these two unities. And so we might inquire (a) how there
        can be many Unities, and (b) how at the same time there can be, accord-
5   ing to this thinker, no generation of a Number other than that from the
        One and the *Indefinite Dyad*.[27] All these are unreasonable, and they
        conflict both with themselves and with what is reasonable, and these
        thinkers seem to resort to the long rigmarole of Simonides;[28] for they
        end with a long rigmarole when they have nothing sound to say, as
10   slaves do. The elements themselves, the *Great* and the *Small*, appear to
        resist loudly when dragged against their nature; for they can in no way
        generate all the Numbers, except Two and powers of Two.[29]

            It is also absurd, or rather one of the impossible things, to posit the
        generation of eternal things. There should be no doubt whether the
15   Pythagoreans do so or not; for they plainly say that when the *One* had
        been constructed, whether out of planes or out of surface or out of seed
        or out of something which they find difficult to say,[30] immediately the
        nearest part of the *Infinite* was drawn in and was bounded by the
        Limit.[31] But since they are constructing the universe and wish to speak
        physically about objects, it is just that we should examine them some-
20   what from the point of view of physics[32] and leave them out of the
        present inquiry; for we are seeking the principles of immovable things,
        and such things are the Numbers whose generation should be examined.

4

They say that there is no generation of the odd, so clearly there is generation of the even;[1] and some thinkers[2] say that the first even Number[3] is generated from the *Unequals*, the *Great* and *Small*, when these are equalized. Accordingly, the inequality of the *Great* and *Small* must exist before their equalization. If they had been always equalized, they would not have been unequal before their equalization; for of that which exists always there is nothing before. So it is evident that they posit the generation of Numbers not for the sake of investigating the truth.[4]

There is a *difficulty*, and a credit to him who solves it, how the elements and principles are related to the good and the noble; and the *difficulty* is this: whether there is in the principles and elements something like what we mean by the good itself and the best.itself, or whether this is not so, but these are later in generation.

The theologians[5] seem to agree with some modern thinkers[6] who say that this is not so but that the good and the noble appeared after the nature of things progressed. And they say this to avoid a real difficulty which confronts those[7] who say, as some do, that the *One* is a principle. The difficulty arises not because they posit the good as belonging to the principle,[8] but because it is the *One* that they posit as a principle, and a principle in the sense of an element,[9] and because they generate Numbers from the *One*. In this respect, the early poets agree in saying that the good belongs not to those who were first, as, for example, to *Night* and *Heavens*, or to *Chaos*, or to *Ocean*, but to *Zeus*, in so far as he is a king and a ruler. These poets, however, are inclined to make such statements because the rulers of things are changing, although those of them who speak in a mixed and not completely mythical fashion posit the first generator as the best, as Pherecydes and some others do, and also as the Magi and some of the later wise men such as Empedocles and Anaxagoras, of whom the first posits *Friendship* as an element, and the second posits *Intelligence* as a principle. Of those who posit the existence of immovable substances, some say that the *One Itself* is the *Good Itself;*[10] but they thought the *substance* of the *Good* to be, most of all, the *One*.

The *difficulty*, then, is this: which of the two accounts ought to be given?[11] It would be strange if self-sufficiency and preservation belonged not primarily as a good to that which is first and eternal and self-sufficient. Moreover, this principle is indestructible and self-sufficient because it is good and not because of something else.[12] So, there

25

30

35

1091*b*

5

10

15

20   is good reason in truly saying that the principle is of this sort; but to
say that this principle is the *One* or, if not this, an element, and an element in Numbers, is impossible. For many difficulties result; and to
avoid these difficulties, those[13] who agree that the *One* is a first principle
and an element, but in Mathematical Numbers, abandoned the position
25   that the *One* is good.[14] For otherwise, every unit becomes something
which is fully a good,[15] and there will be a great abundance of goods.
Moreover, if the Forms are Numbers, every Form will be something
which is fully a good.[16] But let one posit Ideas of whatever he wishes.
If he does so only of what is good, the Ideas will not be substances;[17]
30   and if he does so of substances as well, all the animals and the plants
and whatever participates in the Ideas will be good.[18]

These absurdities then follow, and it also follows that the contrary
element, whether this is *Plurality* or the *Unequal* or the *Great* and *Small*,
is the *Bad Itself*. It is indeed on account of this that one thinker[19]
avoided attaching the good to the *One*, for, since generation is from
35   contraries, the nature of *Plurality* would of necessity be bad. Others,[20]
however, say that the *Unequal* is the nature of the *Bad.* It follows, then,
that all things participate in the *Bad* except one,[21] the *One Itself,* that
1092a   the Numbers participate in the latter[22] more purely than Magnitudes
do,[23] that the *Bad* is the space or receptacle of the *Good,*[24] and that it
participates in and wants that which is destructive; for one contrary
is destructive of the other contrary.[25] And if, as we were saying, it is
in fact matter that is potentially each thing, for example, the matter of
5   actual fire is that which is potentially fire, the *Bad* would be that which
is potentially *Good.*[26]

All these, then, are consequences from the following: These thinkers
posit every principle to be an element,[27] they posit the principles as
contraries,[28] they posit the *One* as a principle,[29] and they posit as first
substances the Numbers both as separate and as Forms.[30]

5

If, then, impossibilities result in this way both by not assigning the
10   good to the principles and by assigning it to them, it is clear that
neither the principles nor the first substances have been stated well.
Nor has anyone the right belief if he likens the principles of all that
exists to those of animals and plants (where generation always proceeds
from the indefinite and the incomplete to the more complete) and says,
because of this, that it is the same also for the first principles, and con-
15   sequently that the *One Itself* is not even a being.[1] For even in animals

and plants generation of the incomplete proceeds from principles which are complete; for it is a man that begets a man, and it is not the seed that is first.[2]

It is also absurd to generate place at the same time as Mathematical Solids (for the place of each individual[3] is proper to itself, and so these are separate in place, but the mathematical objects are not in place[4]), and to say that these will be in some place, but not to say what place is.[5]

Those who say that things are from the elements, and that of the things which are generated Numbers are first, should have distinguished the senses in which something is said *to be from* something else and should then have stated in what sense a Number is from the principles. Is it by blending?[6] But not everything can be made by blending;[7] and that which is made is distinct, and then the *One* will neither be separate nor a distinct nature.[8] But they wish it to be so.[9] Is it by composition, then, like a syllable? But then the elements must have position, and he who conceives a Number must conceive the *One* and *Plurality* separately. And then a Number will be this, a *Unit* and *Plurality*, or the *One* and the *Unequal*.[10] And since to be *from* objects is, in one sense, to be from objects which are constituents in the thing, but in another sense it is to be from objects which are not constituents in the thing,[11] in what sense does a Number come from the elements? It is not possible for a thing to be from objects which are constituents except for those things of which there is generation. Does a Number come from the elements as from seed? But no part can come out of that which is indivisible.[12] Does a Number come, then, from the elements as from a contrary which does not persist? But things which exist in this manner exist also from something else which persists. Accordingly, since one thinker posits the *One* as the contrary of *Plurality*, and another posits it as the contrary of the *Unequal*, using the *One* as the *Equal*, a Number must come from elements as if from contraries. There will be, then, something else which persists, and from this as well as from one of the contraries a Number exists or is generated.[13]

Again, why is it that in the other cases every thing which comes from a contrary or which has contraries[14] is destroyed, even if it comes totally from a contrary,[15] but a Number is not destroyed?[16] Nothing is said about this. Yet whether present or not, the contrary destroys it, as *Strife* destroys the *Blend*; but it should not, for it is not contrary to it.[17]

Nor is it stated definitely in which sense Numbers are the causes of substances and of existence, whether (a) in the sense of boundaries (as points are of magnitudes, and as Eurytus used to assign a certain number to a certain thing, for example, this number to a man and that

number to a horse, like those[18] who were arranging numbers in the shape of a triangle or of a square and in this manner were producing by the use of pebbles likenesses of the *shapes* of plants), or (b) as a
15   ratio or a harmony of Numbers, as in a man and also in each of the others?[19] As for the affections, such as whiteness and sweetness and heat, in what manner are they Numbers?[20] It is clear that Numbers are neither substances nor causes of the *shape* of things; for it is the ratio that will be the *substance* of things, but Numbers will be the matter. For example, the *substance* of flesh or of bone will be a number in this manner, three parts of fire to two parts of earth.[21] And a number,
20   whatever it may be, is always of something, for example, of parts of fire, or of parts of earth, or of units; but the *substance* will be the ratio of so many parts of this to so many parts of that in the blend, and this is no longer a number but a ratio of numbers forming a blend, whether these numbers are corporeal or of any other kind.[22] A Number, then, whether a Number in general or a Number whose parts are just units, is neither a cause in the sense as that which acts, nor as matter, nor as
25   a formula or a form of things. Nor is it a cause in the sense of final cause.[23]

6

One might also raise the question as to what the good is which comes from Numbers by the fact that things in a blend are expressed in numerical ratio, whether one that is easily calculable or as an odd number.[1] As a matter of fact, a honey-blend[2] is no more healthy if it is blended in a proportion *thrice three;*[3] on the contrary, it would be more beneficial if it were diluted in no numerical ratio[4] than if it were strong
30   in a numerical ratio.

Again, ratios of blends are expressed by placing numbers in a relation and not as mere numbers; for example, three in relation to two, not thrice two.[5] For a multiple and that of which it is the multiple must be in the
35   same genus.[6] Thus, the product ABC must be measured by A, and DEF by D,[7] and so in every case, each product must be measured by the same
1093*a*   unit. Therefore, it cannot be the case that BECF is the number of fire, or that twice three is the number of water.[8]

Now if all things of necessity have number in common, it will be necessary for many things to be the same and for the number of some one thing to be the same as that of some other thing.[9] But is this the cause[10] of the thing, and is it through this that the thing exists, or is it
5   not clear? For example, there is a number of the locomotions of the Sun, and also of those of the Moon,[11] and of the life and also the prime

of life of each animal. What prevents some of them from being square, others from being cube or equal, still others from being double? Nothing prevents this; and if all things had number in common, they would be within the range of these kinds of number, and different things might fall under the same number.[12] So, if certain things happened to have the same number, then by having the same kind of number they would be the same[13] as one another; for instance, the Sun and the Moon would be the same. But why should numbers be causes? There are seven vowels, seven strings in the scale, seven Pleiades, seven is the age at which animals lose their teeth (at least some do, though some do not), and seven heroes who attacked Thebes. Is it then because of the nature of such a number that the heroes were seven or that the Pleiades consists of seven stars, or rather, in the first case, because of the seven gates or for some other cause[14] and, in the second, because we count them in this manner, just as some count the Bear as twelve while others as more than twelve?[15] They even say that Ξ, Ψ, and Z are concords, and that, in view of the fact that there are three concords, the double consonants are also three.[16] The fact that there might be many more such does not concern them; for one might use a single letter for the combination ΓΡ.[17] If it is a fact that each of these three consonants, but no others, are twice the remaining consonants, and if the cause of this is that, as there are three parts of the mouth,[18] just one letter from each part is coupled with Σ, then it is because of this that there are only three double consonants and not in view of the fact that there are three concords. As a matter of fact, there are more than three concords, but in the case of the consonants considered, no more than three can be double the remaining.

These thinkers are indeed like the early Homeric scholars who saw small similarities but overlooked great ones. Some still say many such things; for example, that of the middle notes[19] the one is nine and the other is eight, and that the epic line is seventeen, equal to the sum of those two notes, and has nine syllables on the right but eight on the left;[20] and also, that the interval in the alphabet from A to Ω is equal to that from the lowest note of a flute to the highest,[21] and that its number is equal to that of the whole system of the universe. It should be observed that no one would have any difficulty in stating or finding such similarities in eternal things, seeing that they exist also in destructible things.

But the natures which are praised in numbers, and their contraries, and the mathematical attributes in general, in the manner they are described and are posited as causes of nature by some thinkers, seem to vanish if we examine them in this manner; for not one of them is a cause in any of the senses described in the first principles.[22] But these

thinkers posit it as evident that goodness exists, that oddness, straightness, equality, and the powers of certain numbers are in the column of the beautiful[23] (for they say that seasons are at the same time such-and-
15   such numbers), and that all other attributes which they collect from mathematical theorems have this power. But these seem to be coincidences; for they are attributes,[24] although *proper* to each other.[25] And
20   they are one by analogy; thus, as straightness is in length, so is planeness in width, perhaps oddness in number, and whiteness in color.

Moreover, the Numbers as Forms are not the causes of those in harmony and those of other such things. For equal numbers of the latter differ in kind from each other, since their units differ. So, at least because of this, Forms should not be posited.[26]
25   These, then, are consequences which follow, and yet more may be added. The fact that these thinkers find much trouble in generating Numbers and can in no way form a consistent system is a sure sign of the fact that mathematical objects are not separate from nor the principles of sensible objects, as some say they are.

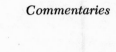
Commentaries

Commentaries

The references given in the Commentaries and in the Glossary are to the standard pages (sections) and lines according to Bekker's edition of Aristotle's works (Berlin, 1831). In particular, pages 980a21–1093b29 cover the whole of the *Metaphysics,* and these pages (and lines) appear as such in the margins of the translation. The Bekker pages covering each of Aristotle's works are as follows:

Categories: 1a1–15b33.
Nature of Propositions (De Interpretatione): 16a1–24b9.
Prior Analytics: 24a10–70b38.
Posterior Analytics: 71a1–100b17.
Topics: 100a18–164b19.
Sophistical Refutations: 164a20–184b8.
Physics: 184a10–267b26.
On the Heavens: 268a1–313b23.
On Generation and Destruction: 314a1–338b19.
Meteorology: 338a20–390b22.
On the Universe, To Alexander: 391a1–401b29.
On the Soul: 402a1–435b25.
On Sensation and Sensibles: 436a1–449a31.
On Memory and Recollection: 449b1–453b11.
On Sleep and Wakefulness: 453b11–458a32.
On Dreams: 458a33–462b11.
On Divination from Dreams: 462b12–464b18.
On Longevity and Shortness of Life: 464b19–467b9.
On Youth, Old Age, Life, and Death: 467b10–470b5.
On Respiration: 470b6–480b30.
On Breath: 481a1–486b4.
A Treatise On Animals: 486a5–638b37.
On Parts of Animals: 639a1–697b30.
On Motion of Animals: 698a1–704b3.

On Locomotion of Animals: 704a4–714b23.
On Generation of Animals: 715a1–789b20.
On Colors: 791a1–799b20.
On Objects of Hearing: 800a1–804b39.
Physiognomy: 805a1–814b9.
On Plants: 815a10–830b4.
On Reported Marvels: 830a5–847b10.
Mechanics: 847a11–858b31.
Problems: 859a1–967b27.
On Indivisible Lines: 968a1–972b33.
Positions and Names of Winds: 973a1–b25.
On Xenophanes, Zeno, and Gorgias: 974a1–980b21.
Metaphysics: 980a21–1093b29.
Nichomachean Ethics: 1094a1–1181b23.
Great Ethics: 1181a24–1213b30.
Eudemean Ethics: 1214a1–1249b25.
On Virtues and Vices: 1249a26–1251b37.
Politics: 1252a1–1342b34.
Household Management: 1343a1–1353b27.
Rhetoric: 1354a1–1420b4.
Rhetoric for Alexander: 1420a5–1447b7.
Poetics: 1447a8–1462b18.

Book A

1

1. The term "understanding" means knowing through the causes (194b18–20, 981a24–30, 983a25–6). The qualification "by nature" excludes men who, defective at birth or for some other *reason*, do not desire understanding (134a5–11, 199b14–8).

2. Just as seeing, which is superior to the other sensations in giving us knowledge, is liked for its own sake, so is understanding, which is superior to, say, sensations. So by analogy, seeing, which is desired for its own sake, is a sign of the desire to understand for its own sake. On the superiority of sight see 436b18–437a18.

3. An alternative to "appearances" is "imagination", and imagination presupposes sensations.

4. Judgment is of that which can be otherwise, that is, of that which may or may not come to be or be true (1139a6–15); in practical matters, it is prudence if true, and the opposite if false. Evidently, men have the power of judging.

5. That is, from memory as a material cause, for memory is only a necessary condition.

6. "The same thing" refers to an individual; for example, Socrates, or his acting in a certain manner.

7. The seeming similarity lies in this: An experience has such a form as this, "x is B," where x is an individual, but in science or art we have such a form as this, "all A is B." Cf. 981a7–12. If x is B, y is B, z is B, etc., one may infer "all A is B" if x, y, z, etc. are A's, just as in his many memories of "x is B" he infers that it is the same x in all of them. For example, let x = phlegmatic Socrates, y = phlegmatic Callias, etc., A = phlegmatic, B = curable with such-and-such medicine.

8. That is, experience as a material cause only.

9. Gorgias, 448C, 462B.

10. As a material cause only.

11. "Theory" here signifies art or universal knowledge. One may acquire it through experience, or by teaching (in which case he need not have the corresponding experience).

12. Callias is necessarily a man, but a man is by accident Callias since he may be Socrates or someone else. Further, to cure a universal man in actuality is to cure every existing man; moreover, the doctor certainly does not cure the universal as it exists in the soul since this is knowledge. Again, he does not cure the essence of Socrates, for this stays the same, but disease (which is an accident of Callias).

13. "The *why*" means the cause, inasmuch as it is the true answer to the question, "Why?"

14. Practice is a matter of imitating and requires no universal and causal knowledge, or very little of it, as in the case of placing bricks accurately in a certain way, or swinging a golf club effectively.

15. Perhaps the sciences concerned with giving pleasure refer to the arts of amusing and entertaining others, not necessarily the artists themselves. The mathematical sciences need not give pleasure to others, but the pursuit of them for their own sake is pleasant.

16. The others are prudence, wisdom, intellect (1139b14–1142a30).

17. A productive science, such as making steel, is for the sake of something else, steel, but a theoretical science is chosen for its own sake; so the latter is better, for a good end is better than the means to that end.

2

1. For example, such *knowledge* of an individual thing would be of the fact that the individual is subject to the law of contradiction or that it must be *known* or understood through its definition.

2. For example, carpentry is for the sake of something else: the chairs produced—and these for the sake of comfortable sitting.

3. That is, he knows universally or what is common, although not

the individuals or what is proper to them; or he knows potentially (86a22–30).

4. The unit, which is a principle in arithmetic, is just indivisible; but the point, which is the corresponding principle in geometry, is indivisible and, in addition, has position (87a29–37).

5. A productive science is what we usually call "an applied science". For example, engineering, architecture, carpentry, shipbuilding, steelmaking. It is knowledge borrowed from theoretical sciences, such as mathematics or physics or chemistry, and applied on materials of one kind or another in order to produce something.

6. The term φρόνησις usually means prudence for Aristotle. Perhaps he is using it here in a sense used by others before him, such as thinking or thought or wisdom or *knowledge*.

7. A free man is contrasted with a slave. One who lives for his own sake and not for the sake of others need not disregard the good of others; a tyrant who is free may disregard it; but a virtuous man who is free, because of his virtue, will not in his relations to others disregard what is good for them, and because of this he will be more happy.

8. That is, men of great intellectual capacity would be unfortunate if denied by God the right to exercise that capacity in the pursuit of wisdom or philosophy.

9. Jealousy is a vice, and no vice is an attribute of God.

10. An instrumental science is not for its own sake but is necessary for the sake of something else. Carpentry is for the sake of making shoes, and shoes for the sake of wearing them. Here, the reference may be for the necessities of life, such as food, etc. Thus, the instrumental sciences are for the sake of philosophy or wisdom.

3

1. "The first causes" here refers to the causes generically taken; that is, essence, matter, source which begins motion, final cause, and attributes of them.

2. "The first cause of each thing" refers to the specific first cause (or causes), which is (or are) a special case of the generic causes.

3. "The *substance*" signifies the form or the whatness, and it extends to all categories. Thus, there is a whatness of a man, of a triangle, of virtue, etc., each signified by a definition (1017b21–22, 1025b30–32, 1030a21–32, 1037a33–b3).

4. That is, one of the *why's*.

5. The kind of formula meant is usually a definition, whose parts are indefinable.

6. The end of generation is the form; for example, in the generation of a statue it is its shape, and in the generation from seed it is the form of a tree, or the form in the animal born. An example of the end of mo-

tion would be a drive to the ball park for the sake of the enjoyment in watching the game.

7. 194b16–195b30.

8. "First" here means ultimate. For example, in the case of water, not hydrogen and oxygen, but protons and electrons and other such, if these cannot be broken down further.

9. He is only altered; that is, changed with respect to quality.

10. He may mean the heat in animals, which take in food (which is moist), and so keep on being warm.

11. "Prior" in the sense that water consists of air and not conversely, just as hydrogen was once thought to consist of electrons and protons but not conversely.

12. Infinite in kind is meant (302b10–24), and if in kind, then certainly in number.

13. Water and fire are examples given by Aristotle, but Anaxagoras excluded these as well as air and earth from being homogeneous (302a28–302b5, 314a24–29).

14. A moving cause is meant.

15. That is, aware of the problem of a cause of change, they posited its denial.

16. 188a19–22, 330b13–15, 986b27–987a2.

17. Referring probably to Empedocles and some others.

18. The contrary nature here is the nature of resting or causing rest.

19. Referring in particular to the good or the noble in things, or the final cause.

20. An alternative to "noble" is "beautiful".

21. *Chance* and luck are posterior in being to what exists or happens always or for the most part, and so they cannot be the causes here (198a2–13).

4

1. This corresponds to *desire,* not to desire.

2. Apparently there is no reference in the extant works.

3. Alternatives to "noble" and "base" are "beauty" and "ugliness."

4. 194b16–195b30, 198a14–b9.

5. "Neither adequately" may refer to the fact that *Friendship* and *Strife,* although appearing to be final causes, are presented more like moving causes, and so they are not doing what they are supposed to do. The lack of consistency, from the sentences that follow, is this: *Friendship* is supposed to bring things together; but in so doing, it separates each part from its own kind.

6. That is, principles of combining and of separating, respectively.

7. Fire has the nature to move, the others have the nature to rest.

8. These thinkers are not using "nonbeing" in the sense of non-existence; the opposition of nonbeing to being here is a contrariety, so that both the *Full* and the *Void* are taken as existing.

9. These *attributes*, as principles, are changeless, but all other attributes can change.

10. The individual shapes of the elements are changeless and principles; but *Order* and *Position* are generic principles of things, that is, the things must have some order and position, although their particular order and position may vary (275b29–32, 325b17–19).

5

1. The term "a number" throughout this book will mean a plurality of units, or, according to present mathematicians, a natural number, excluding 1. The idea that the Greeks had a narrow conception of number is not quite true. Real or directional numbers were known to Aristotle, although he would use a different phrase to name them. The term ποσόν (= "quantity") is very wide in meaning and is somewhat close to our term "number".

2. "By nature first" here means prior in existence to the other mathematical entities. For example, assuming hydrogen to be composed of protons and electrons, the latter are prior in existence to hydrogen; for, if hydrogen exists, protons and electrons must exist, but not conversely (1019a1–4, 14a29–35).

3. Justice was defined as a square number, probably the number 4, perhaps in view of the fact that the two equal factors treat each other alike (987a19–27, 1132b21–23, 1182a11–14).

4. Probably the unit 1, or perhaps the number 2. Because the smaller numbers are prior in existence to the greater, they were considered more important and nearer to the principles of all things, and both the soul and the intellect were likewise considered.

5. Perhaps the number 7, according to some commentators, since some human and natural events were observed to occur every (or at the end of the) seventh unit of time, such as the cutting of teeth seven months after birth (1093a13–16).

6. In an octave, for example, the length ratio is 1:2.

7. By "every nature in numbers" he means probably this: a number which is odd (like 5), even (like 6), prime (like 7), composite (like 6), a square (like 4), a cube (this is 8; probably they did not consider higher powers), a perfect (this is 6, since its factors add to 6, for $1 + 2 + 3 = 6$), oblong (like 6, with two unequal factors), and perhaps others.

8. 293a20.

9. Perhaps affections are taken as temporary but possessions as permanent attributes.

10. Perhaps because when added to a number the result is sometimes an odd and sometimes an even number, or because both even and odd

numbers are composed of units, or because the *One* is composed of both the *Odd* and the *Even*. Logic among the Pythagoreans, of course, was not strong (987b29–33).

11. These are the ten pairs of contraries, which are the principles.

12. Pythagoreans and Alcmaion.

13. All their terms which signify principles are given as adjectives or derivatives rather than as nouns or attributes, for example, "moving" rather than "motion". Since the Pythagoreans failed to make distinctions and made all things out of numbers, perhaps the derivative term would be more appropriate. Thus, "moving" lies somehow between "motion" and "body in motion".

14. Their logic, through lack of distinctions and other failures, was weak (191a23–191b34).

15. That is, they did not attack the problems of physical reality, as for example, the problem of change, for they did away with change.

16. That is, one in kind, such as *Water*, or *Air*.

17. That is, 'one' as a predicate, rather than as a material thing (in the case of Melissus). Thus, the nature or essence of 'one' as a predicate would be something finite. There may be infinite instances of 'one' or an infinite magnitude of it, yet one definition, which is finite. The pertinency to the inquiry lies in the fact that 'one' as a predicate indicates the formal cause, but as a material thing it indicates a material cause.

18. 184b15–186a3.

19. The Pythagoreans.

20. "In the same manner" may refer to the fact that the principles are (a) two contraries, or (b) two, matter and form (985b29–31, 986a15–7), and perhaps also to the fact that they spoke somewhat vaguely, especially about the formal cause. Elsewhere, a moving principle is vaguely or slightly indicated (203a10–2).

21. That is, they put forward mathematical principles as the principles of all things.

22. That is, starting from the principles (*Infinite, Finite, the One*), the first number which can be a double is 2.

23. Thus, according to them, four is justice, and also a solid.

6

1. That is, the philosophies of the Pythagoreans and others.

2. Pythagoreans.

3. The terms "Forms" and "Ideas" denote the same things. Perhaps "Ideas" indicates a contrast as against "sensibles", while "Forms" signifies a permanence or nature or cause in the case of Ideas in relation to the sensibles which are caused by and participate in the Ideas but are in a state of flux.

4. Since Plato considers mathematics a science, its objects according to his assumption must be immovable (987b6–7); and since theorems in

that science often include two or more objects of the same kind (for example, in theorems of congruence, two triangles of the same form are used, and in arithmetic one may add or multiply equal numbers, as in $2+2=4$), Plato posits a plurality of such objects, which must therefore differ from the Ideas.

5. For Aristotle, "one" is a predicate of a subject which has some nature; for example, that which is one may be an apple, or a man, or a line, or a color, etc., but it is not just oneness without something underlying it. For the Pythagoreans and Plato, oneness is a subject or a substance, and so it exists by itself and not like redness which is an attribute of a body or a surface (1053b25–1054a19).

6. Logical inquiries would be inquiries not about the things themselves but about terms, definitions, proposition, reasonings, etc., which are universal and which somehow refer to or are predicated of objects; and they are related to our knowledge of things.

7. The term πρώτων refers to first Numbers, or else to prime Numbers. As Heinze points out, it may have been miscopied from περιττῶν, which refers to odd numbers. Three interpretations arise: (1) odd Numbers; (2) first Numbers; (3) prime Numbers. I prefer (1); for, since the function of the *Dyad* is to double the Form received, any even Number, such as Ten, can readily be generated when the *Dyad* receives Five, if Plato's principles are granted. The second interpretation, in which the first Numbers are the Forms, is possible but not as plausible; for, the numbers to be generated would be the Mathematical or the sensible, and these numbers cannot be as readily generated. The third interpretation is highly improbable; for, it is easier to generate some prime Numbers, such as Three, than some composite, such as Nine, assuming Plato's method of generating them (1084a3–7).

8. If it is the whole *Dyad* that receives the *One* or a Number to double what it receives, then Aristotle's objection is good; but if only part of the *Dyad* does so, then Plato can meet Aristotle's objection. Of course, we have no information as to what Plato actually said, and to assume that the *Dyad* is a whole with parts, or is one, would spell trouble for Plato.

9. For Plato and Aristotle, the male supplies the form, the female supplies the matter.

10. The final cause appears lightly or accidentally in Plato, that is, not as *that for the sake of which* something is or changes, as Aristotle would have it.

7

1. 194b16–195b30.
2. Pythagoreans.
3. Thales, Anaximenes, Diogenes, Hippasus, Heraclitus.
4. Empedocles.

5. Anaxagoras.

6. Parmenides, perhaps Hesiod (984b23–31).

7. Platonists.

8. Thus, for the Platonists, the *One* or *Being* would be good as a formal cause rather than as a final cause.

9. That is, not as that for the sake of which, but in the sense that, for example, the mover happens to be good; for, the mover need not be good, or it may be good, or it may be good and not be the moving cause of something else, and in this way it is by accident a final cause. And to use the term "good" without assigning to it its usual meaning is to use it accidentally.

8

1. These thinkers speak inadequately, for attributes, such as color, shape, and length, although existing in corporeal things, are incorporeal; and the elements of these are not material things or bodies.

2. Any motion or change requires a mover, and this cause was left out.

3. They left out the formal cause.

4. One thing is a principle of another because it is in some sense prior, but these thinkers, in saying that fire, or air, or water is a principle, did so without searching for any priority in the manner in which these elements are generated from each other. For example, water comes from hydrogen and oxygen, and these from water, the former by combination, the latter by separation, but the latter are prior in existence and so are principles of the former.

5. If something is regarded as an element or a principle without an examination into priority, but by chance, then earth has as much right as the others.

6. That is, the complete is prior to the incomplete; man is prior to seed. It may be added, man is prior to seed, just as the mover is prior to what is moved qua moved.

7. Aristotle suggests (1) and (2) as types of priority to be used in searching for causes. In this particular case, (1) leads to fire as a principle, (2) leads to earth.

8. If fire changes into something else, it is destroyed, and so it is not a principle; for, a material principle is indestructible (994b6–9, 1000b23–28).

9. 305a33–306b2.

10. "Rightly" probably refers to Empedocles' statements in relation to facts or truth, and "reasonably" in relation to logical consistency or truth (985a23–29).

11. If cold is a principle, it cannot become hot, for it will then be destroyed; moreover, if it can be affected, it will be a composite of matter and form and not a principle. Further, if the cold becomes hot, there

is some other underlying principle which is now cold and now hot, and this is matter, but Empedocles denies such a principle.

12. One blends material elements, not such elements with attributes. One cannot blend water, length, color, and position.

13. Attributes and accidents always exist in a subject and cannot exist by themselves.

14. In other words, in spite of his errors, Anaxagoras seemed to have been thinking of a form and a moving cause, which he called "the *One*", and of matter or potentiality (the *Other* or the *Blend*).

15. Mathematical objects, arrived at by removing in thought the principles of motion and whatever is sensible, are immovable in their nature (1077b17–34), although objects of astronomy (stars, Sun, Moon, etc.) have motion.

16. 1091a13–18.

17. Non-sensible or intelligible beings are probably meant.

18. They leave out the moving cause as a principle.

19. The heavenly bodies were usually believed to be carried rather than to move by themselves about the Earth.

20. Light and heavy bodies differ; hence there are differences in their corresponding principles.

21. The argument about light and heavy bodies applies equally to mathematical and physical bodies. The same applies to fire, earth, etc.

22. If numbers and their attributes are causes of what exists and is generated, and if the numbers of this world are the only things that exist, then the existing things would be causes of themselves and what is generated.

23. Plato says that Numbers (or Ideas) are the causes of numbers (these are the sensible things), and thus he avoids the Pythagorean position that a thing is a cause of itself.

9

1. In 1078b36, "equal to or not less" is replaced by "greater"; and "these" probably refers to the number of species, but not to individuals. Thus, corresponding to men, animals, and colors there would be as Ideas, Man Himself, Animal Itself, and Color Itself. If equilateral, isosceles, and scalene are the only species (of triangles), there would be not only the corresponding Ideas but also the Idea Triangle.

2. Attributes are meant, since there are species and genera of them. For example, color, whiteness, justice, power, etc.

3. Sensible and destructible things around us are meant.

4. Such as the Sun, Moon, stars, etc.

5. Referring to Plato and his school, of which Aristotle at the time was a member, although not in agreement with the doctrine of Ideas.

6. This may refer to productive sciences, for whose objects no Ideas exist according to Plato (991b6–7, 1070a18–21). If there are Ideas of

the objects of every science, then there should be Ideas also of the objects of productive sciences.

7. These may be such objects as not-man, not-white, etc., since "not-man" and the like are universal terms.

8. For Aristotle, thinking is impossible without images, and we can think about what has perished by means of the image we have of it. But then, there will be Ideas of what may not exist.

9. The word "we" may refer to the Platonists, and in Plato's *Phaedo* Equality as an Idea is posited; it does not refer to Aristotle's own position, in view of 1079a11–13 and of the fact that a relation as an attribute must exist in something else.

10. To know something as a double, which is a relative, such as 8, you must refer it to something else, 4; but to know a quantity, such as a circle, or a substance, such as a man, no outside reference is needed. In general, what is relative cannot be known or exist by itself without reference to something else.

11. The *third man* argument may be this: If a man and the Idea Man are alike, there is something common to both, and this would be a third object or Idea, and prior in existence to both (Plato's *Parmenides*, 132–133). This may go on indefinitely.

12. Refers to the principles, in particular, to the *Dyad*, composed of the *Great* and the *Small* (the material principle).

13. Refers to the Platonists.

14. For, "a number" is more universal than "a dyad" or "two", and so a number would be prior in existence and in *knowledge* to a dyad or to two; yet they posit as a material principle the *Dyad*, and further, Two is generated first and not Number.

15. The *Great* and the *Small*, parts of the *Dyad* somehow, are posited as principles, yet that which is great or small must be a quantity and cannot exist or be known as great or small except in relation to some other quantity, but a quantity can exist or be known without reference to the great or the small. Hence, a quantity is prior in existence and in *knowledge* to smallness or greatness. But they posit the *Great* and the *Small* as principles.

16. In particular, their belief that Ideas are substances.

17. That is, qua a substance; for, to participate in an Idea is to participate in it as a substance and not to participate only in some attribute of it. So, what participates in an Idea must be a substance. But redness is not a substance, yet it participates in Redness Itself which is an Idea and so a substance.

18. Besides, if the double participates in Double Itself (which is eternal), eternality is in Double Itself essentially, but it is accidentally in the double since the double is destructible; but while participating in Double Itself which is a substance, the double should be a substance (but as a fact, it is not).

19. The Greek should probably be: ὥστ᾽ ἔσται οὐσίας τὰ εἴδη (οὐσίας be-

ing genitive), or, ὥστ᾽ ἔσται οὐσιῶν τὰ εἴδη, or, ὥσται εἰ ἔσται οὐσία τὰ εἴδη, ταὐτὰ τε ἐνταῦθα οὐσίαν σημαίνει κἀκεῖ.

20. The eternal Two's are the Mathematical Two's.

21. The heavenly objects, such as the Sun, stars, etc., which are assumed to be eternal.

22. There would be no *knowledge* even of the eternals among the sensibles, if the Ideas as their *substances* are not in them.

23. It is absurd to think that the *substance* of a thing is not in that thing, just as it is absurd to think that the shape which is the form of a statue is not in that statue.

24. Whiteness is an attribute, and so inseparable from a substance; it is not a body or a substance that can be blended with something else.

25. Aristotle is probably using "to copy" here like "to participate in" or "to come to be by participating in", as a particular from an Idea in the case of Plato.

26. Thus, an eternal Socrates, like a destructible man resembling Socrates, would neither be the cause of the individual Socrates, nor be in him.

27. For, a man is an instance of Man Himself, of Two-footed, of Animal, etc.

28. A genus is to its species like a pattern to its copies, a sort of one–many relation; hence, Man Himself is a pattern to its copies, the individual men, but a copy to Animal Itself, which is its genus among the Ideas (the same logical relations are assumed to exist among the Ideas as among the sensibles). But this is absurd, for Ideas are not regarded as copies by the Platonists.

29. Referring to the Platonists.

30. That is, if houses and rings are generated without any help from Forms (and the Platonists admit this), why do we need Forms for the generation of men, plants, and the like? Besides, Socrates would not have been born had his father (as mover) not acted, even if the Idea Man is eternal.

31. If the sensibles participate in the Forms, and the Forms are Numbers, then the sensibles should be numbers. This seems absurd.

32. If Numbers have something in common with numbers, this alone does not make Numbers, even if eternal, the causes of the latter, and for the same reasons as stated earlier.

33. The term "ratio" is not limited to two numbers. Thus 2:3:5:7 would be a ratio, if a mixture or blend has four distinct elements.

34. For example, if a man is the ratio 2:3:5:7 of fire, earth, water, and air, respectively, then 2 is two parts of fire and not of earth or of something else, and likewise for 3, 5, and 7. But this ratio would be a copy of a pattern, the Form, which is Man Himself; hence, this Form

will be the Ratio 2:3:5:7, in which 2, 3, 5, 7 will not be just Numbers, but Numbers whose parts differ in their matter, as in man, otherwise, it will not be a ratio but a sum of comparable units (and this is just a number).

35. If Man Himself is the Ratio 2:3:5:7, then in a sense he may be a Number, namely, 17 ($= 2 + 3 + 5 + 7$), if there are 17 parts in all. This would correspond to saying that a man has 17 bodily parts. But "17 bodily parts" is a generic term and will not state completely the essence of a man. The same argument applies to Man Himself. Thus, Man Himself may be a Number, but he is more than that, namely, a Ratio of Numbers differing in their Units.

36. In arithmetic, units do not differ. Thus, an actual number may become a part of another and so lose its actual existence; but how can a Form become a part of another Form if it has separate existence and is immovable? If sensibles are addible and are also imitations of Forms, also Forms should be addible, and this would make Forms changeable.

37. The Forms.

38. For example, if all Units were alike, one Form would be either greater or less than another; a Unit would not be unique (for Plato, no two things are the same among the Forms); if Five is Horse and Eight is Pig, then Horse would be part of Pig, and likewise among the sensibles, etc. Many other absurdities follow if the Units differ. Book M discusses the difficulties at greater length.

39. Something that Plato himself posited. Units are just indivisible, without qualities, quantity, etc.

40. Plato posits only two principles, *One* as form, the *Dyad* as matter. As for the manner of generation, if the *Dyad* receives the *One*, Two is generated; if it receives a Number, a double Number is generated; if the *One* is added to an even Number, an odd Number is generated. No other principles are posited and no other manner of generation is stated. Then how and from what principles can Mathematical Numbers and the other Intermediate Objects be generated (1084a3–7)?

41. The meaning may be this: Two is generated when the *Dyad* (*Great* and *Small*) received (or was acted upon by) the *One*. Then Two is made out of the *Dyad* or a part of it, and so is each Unit in Two. But if the *Dyad* is in a sense two, the *Great* and *Small*, how can each Unit in Two be indivisible? Moreover, the *Dyad* is somehow two, so this exists before Two is generated.

42. A number has some unity if it is to be one. What kind of unity has a Number, that is, what causes it to be one and not just a plurality? Is it by continuity, by being glued together, or what? Plato did not specify. If no cause of unity exists, no Idea exists, for the Units are separate.

43. That is, on the assumption that the Units or the Ones differ, there is something different that underlies each Unit or each One (like fire in one case, earth in another, water, and air for Empedocles), and it is these underlying things that are the principles and the substances and not the *One* or the *Unit*; hence, *One* or a Unit or a Number are attributes of something else (like fire, water, etc.) and not substances, and "One" has many senses. Thus, the *One*, if it is a principle, will have to be spelled out, and it will turn out to be different things that underlie it, like fire, air, etc. (1053b9–1054a19).

44. If the *Long* and *Short, Wide* and *Narrow, Deep* and *Shallow*, are the material principles of lines, planes, and bodies, respectively, what happened to the *Great* and *Small?* If the latter is a genus of the others, still the others cannot be reduced to the *Great* and *Small*, for the differentiae of a species is a new principle and not reducible to the genus; for example, a man is more than an animal, and his rationality is something new (998b17–31). The lines, planes, and bodies he considers may be among the Ideas, or the Mathematical Objects, or even the sensibles; for, the objection applies to all alike.

45. The *Long* and *Short* is a principle, and so is the *Wide* and *Narrow*, and thus each cannot be reduced to the other. Hence, if the plane is generated from the *Wide* and *Narrow* alone, it cannot have lines, since these have the *Long* and *Short* as their material principle. But this is not so, for planes can have lines.

46. Similarly, a solid will have neither planes nor lines; and further, none of these magnitudes has a number, and so they could not be numbered, for a number has as its material principle the *Many* and *Few*, which is distinct from and not reducible to the other principles. Yet magnitudes have a number or can be numbered.

47. The assumption here is: If the *Wide* is a genus of the *Deep*, what is generated from the former is a genus of what is generated from the latter.

48. The Platonists mentioned no material principle for points, whether those (Points) among the the Mathematical Objects or those among the sensibles.

49. Though Plato used the phrase "principle of a line" for the point, he could not have meant the material or the formal principle of a line because he already had other principles for a line.

50. If indivisible lines instead of points are posited, such lines still have points at their ends, and so points reappear once more, and indivisible lines are somehow divisible. Thus, if such lines are proved to exist, points in the original sense of "point" are likewise proved to exist and be distinct from indivisible lines.

51. The cause referred to is the final cause, and this may be happiness,

or pleasure, or some other form to be found in nature in general where action takes place.

52. In the *Republic:* 533, it is said that mathematics should be studied for the sake of something else, dialectics; so if dialectics is prior or superior, mathematical objects cannot be prior to those of dialectics.

53. The terms "great" and "small" signify attributes, and it is not attributes but what underlies them that is matter or has matter. Moreover, mathematical matter exists in objects with physical matter, and not conversely, so physical matter is prior in existence or in formula.

54. 201b16–21, *Timaeus:* 52–53, 57–58.

55. The material principle of a Form is the *Great* and *Small,* which is motion; so the Forms, having this principle, should be moving or capable of it.

56. If the Forms are motionless, and the sensibles are copies of the Forms, where do the sensibles get their motion from, or, what cause moves them?

57. A moving cause is necessary in physics, and if the Platonists have no such cause, physics is impossible.

58. That is, the *substance* of each thing is Unity.

59. It might be argued that 'man' is the form of each man, 'animal' the form of each species of 'animal', etc., and so rising to the ultimate, that *Oneness* is the form of all things, and that the *Dyad,* which is the material principle, is the cause of the plurality of things. But is 'one' a genus? If a man is defined as a biped animal, the genus 'animal' is not necessarily predicated of bipedness, nor is bipedness an animal. But if 'one' were assumed to be a genus, its differentia would be necessarily one. So 'one' is not a genus (998b22–27).

60. If Ideas are Numbers, and a Number with the *Dyad* or with the *One* always gives rise to another Number (1084a3–7), how will we ever get to the Magnitudes?

61. The Platonists might say that they are like the Ideas, and related to the Mathematical Magnitudes as Numbers are related to Mathematical Numbers, that is, as causes to effects. But this assumption leads to other difficulties. And if Numbers are the causes of sensibles, what function do Magnitudes have?

62. Assuming that Magnitudes have been generated, they cannot be Ideas since they are not Numbers; for example, Triangle is not a Number. Moreover, Triangle is unique, but among the Mathematical Objects there are many triangles of the same kind. Further, if the Mathematical Triangles are not destructible, certainly Triangle is not (the assumption here is, a Number : Mathematical Numbers :: Triangle : Mathematical Triangles, and the antecedents are causes of the consequents). Thus, Magnitudes are a fourth genus of things, since they are

not Ideas or Mathematical Objects or sensibles, and they seem to lie between the Ideas and the Mathematical Objects.

63. If "being" has many senses, then of which being are they seeking the elements? Moreover, although there are elements in the definition of things within every category, this is not so in the case of material elements; for, acting, being acted upon, quality, etc., are not composed of material elements, and these thinkers assume that they are composed of such elements.

64. The argument now seems to turn not to coming to know the elements of all things directly, but to learning them from others. This, of course, is more hopeless for those who posit only one science (76a16–25). Hence, experience with each genus of things is necessary, since each genus has, besides the generic principles, additional principles.

65. For Plato, dialectic is that science (*Republic:* 533), and similarly for all those who, without distinguishing the various senses of "being", posit the same principles for all things.

66. Plato thinks that *knowledge* is innate at birth, but only recall is required to bring it out (*Meno:* 81, *Phaedo:* 72). Aristotle rejects this on the principle that we are not aware of such knowledge.

67. If there is only one science, he who *knows* its elements can *know* anything whatsoever, in particular, a given color, even if he were born blind. But such a man cannot know a color (193a4–9).

10

1. 194b16–195b30.

2. They used the right names, but not quite with the proper meanings and the attributes that follow.

3. The term "new" may mean unfamiliar or strange; "just beginning" may refer to what Aristotle says elsewhere, namely, that the beginning or principle of anything is the most difficult (183b22–26).

4. In other words, Empedocles first posits the four elements as the substances of things, which may be regarded as the material causes, but in speaking of the ratio as the *substance* of a thing, he is speaking vaguely of the essence or the formal cause.

Book α

1

1. Perhaps the analogy here is, truth : door :: a certain part of truth : a certain part of the door. The latter two parts of the proportion are both

difficult as compared to the first two parts, which are attained partially; for one does not get the whole truth nor hit the whole door, but some chance part of it. Examples of parts of the whole truth would be: The fact that there are causes and principles, the principle of contradiction, the existence of change, and other such universal statements.

2. The cause of this difficulty is in us if our powers of knowledge are lacking, or limited, or not mature yet, and it is in the facts if these are in their nature difficult to understand, whether they be material or immaterial, abstract or complex.

3. These are the principles and causes of all things which are furthest removed from the senses but most known in their nature (71b33–72a5, 184a16–b14).

4. No mention is made of a productive science, perhaps because its end, a product which is instrumental or to be used for something else, is further from the final cause, while the end of a theoretical or a practical science is a final cause or an end in itself.

5. That is, truth is used by a practical science not as an end in itself but as a means to something else or for something temporary which itself is an end in itself; for example, ethical truth for the sake of virtuous activity.

6. To use other examples, the cause of the divisibility of a straight line is not its straightness, not its one-dimensionality, but its continuity or its being a quantity; and the cause of 180° in an isosceles right triangle is not its being isosceles or right, but its triangularity.

7. As with being, so with truth; for, although being and truth imply each other, being is somehow the cause of truth (which is an affection of the soul), but not conversely (14b10–22).

8. For example, the truth of "this triangle has 180°" is temporary, for the individual triangle is destructible, and so is the corresponding truth. But the truth "Whatever is a triangle has 180°" is eternal. Thus, since the form of an individual is the cause of the corresponding temporary truth, and since the eternal is more true than the temporary, the principles of eternal forms or things are most true.

2

1. If one thing is a cause of another, in any of the four senses of "cause", the question arises whether there is a first cause, that is, an object which cannot be caused by another object.

2. A modern example in series is: water comes from water molecules, a water molecule from hydrogen and oxygen, hydrogen from electrons, protons, etc. Is there an end, or, are there ultimate particles or ultimate matter? For Aristotle, there is an end.

3. The view of Empedocles is used simply as an illustration.

4. For Aristotle, happiness is the ultimate final cause of walking.

5. For example, if x is an individual bronze right triangle, then it

has 180°. What is the cause of its having 180°? Consider this series: triangle, right triangle, x. Certainly the cause is not x, and not quite the right triangle (for it can have 180° without being right), but triangularity. Its being made of bronze or its being right are irrelevant to its having 180°.

6. If "it" within the parentheses refers to the middle term, this may be one or many middle terms, or else, finite or (hypothetically) infinite in number; but if it refers to the last term, such as x (= individual bronze right triangle), then x may be taken as one or many or infinite, since the individuals are potentially infinite. Probably the former is the case.

7. That is, infinite as a series in which there is order.

8. That is, if A_1 were the cause as essence of A, A_2 of A_1, A_3 of A_2, and so on ad infinitum, the series A_1, A_2, A_3, ... are all alike intermediate except A; and if there is no end to A_1, A_2, A_3, ..., then there is no first cause and so no unqualified cause of A; for the intermediates are qualified causes, caused by something prior.

9. The terms "coming to be", "generation", and "becoming" are used synonymously for idiomatic purposes.

10. When water becomes air, water is destroyed; when air becomes water, air is destroyed. The process is reversible and in each case one substance is destroyed and another is generated. But when a boy becomes an adult there is no generation from one substance to another, but that which is incomplete is becoming complete. Similarly, if a learner becomes a scientist, both are the same substance, a man; and no substance is destroyed. The change here is one of quality, science, which is added to the learner.

11. A boy finally becomes something, an adult, and the process stops; and when water and air change back and forth, only two things are involved, and these are not infinite.

12. The ultimate material cause is meant.

13. This is the generation indicated in lines 994a3–5.

14. I delete the word μὴ (= "not") in 994b8. However, if kept, then the translation, to be in accordance with Aristotle's meaning, should be: "otherwise, since generation does not proceed upwards to infinity, it would be necessary, when something is generated with the destruction of something else, for that which is first (in the sense *that from which*) not to be eternal". Of course, according to the assumption, it must be eternal. But if the word μὴ (= "not") in line 994b8 is omitted, then we have the translation as given. Both these alternatives make sense.

Using a modern example, the argument is this: If water consists of hydrogen and oxygen, and each of the latter consists of protons and electrons, which are the first from the top not consisting of anything else, then when water is formed by the destruction of hydrogen and oxygen, or vice versa, there is always something ultimate which is coming to be something else, and this is protons and electrons (if these are ultimate), which are eternal. In general, if X becomes Y, and X is made out of x_1, x_1 out of x_2, x_2 out of x_3, ..., x_{n-1} out of x_n, and x_n is first from the top, then when X is destroyed yielding Y, it may be that x_i, where $i < n$, is also destroyed (in which case the x's prior to x_i are also destroyed), but x_n is not destroyed; for, if x_i is being destroyed, there must be a later x out of which it is made and which is coming to be something else, and x_n is the last. Here, each of X, x_1, x_2, . . . , x_n, may be particles of more than one kind, or matter of more than one kind.

15. The argument, very condensed in the Greek, seems to be: If D_1, D_2, D_3, . . . are definitions of an essence, each of them longer than the preceding, then to say that each D is a definition to a higher degree than a preceding D implies that it is closer to a last D which is first in the sense that it is the definition in the highest degree. But an infinite series eliminates the possibility of such a D. To say that D_2 is longer than D_1 is to say that at least one term in D_1 is replaced by more than one term in D_2. For example, if D_1 stands for "an odd natural number", then D_2 might stand for "a natural number not divisible into two equal parts".

16. Perhaps these are the indemonstrable premises, which are first causes, or even the ultimate indefinables in the definition of a thing.

17. Perhaps the term "to know" here means to apprehend the principles of the thing itself, or else, to *understand* the indefinable terms, as in the case of a triangle. If a triangle had an infinite number of parts, a conception of them in a finite time would be impossible. These parts do not include the properties stated in the theorems which are derived, but only those stated in the definition. This kind of knowledge is called "knowledge by nature".

18. The infinite by addition is meant, which never ends, that is, when something is always added without stopping.

19. A finite line is not a sum of discrete parts, like a number; and we cannot have a conception of it by always dividing the infinitely divisible parts. But we can think of the line as one and as finite without the necessity of thinking of the potentially infinite number of its parts.

20. That is, the infinitely divisible line, though finite in length.

21. Perhaps the Greek is corrupt in this and the next sentence. If not, perhaps an interpretation of this sentence is: The matter of a moving body must also be conceived in this way; for, qua a magnitude, it is infinitely divisible but finite as a solid and so similar to the line already considered.

22. That is, actually infinite.

23. This may be interpreted thus: An infinite object must be so only potentially, by addition or by division, and the conception of it as such necessitates a finite essence or definition of infinity; for example, that "to be infinite is to be divisible without an end", and this definition has a finite number of terms.

3

1. Perhaps the part within the brackets does not belong here but was erroneously inserted. On the other hand, the paragraph distin-

guishes the method in mathematics as regards accuracy from that in physics, and, by implication, it may suggest a method for the science we are seeking, philosophy, or a method of determining whether it is one science or more than one which investigates the first causes and principles (this is the first of the problems in Book B that follows, 995b4–6).

Book B

The fourteen problems listed in 995b4–996a17 are generically stated, and then discussed dialectically. The answers given include answers arising from subsidiary problems, some of which may come under more than one generic problem, and so may their answers. Some problems are so raised as to presuppose an answer to another problem. For example, problems (2) and (5) assume that philosophy is somehow concerned with substances, and consequently with the kinds of substances and other related matters.

All problems except (13), along with a less elaborate and systematic discussion of them, appear almost identically in K, 1059a18–1060b30, which was probably an earlier draft.

(1) Discussed: 996a18–b26.
     Answered: A, 980a21–993a27; α, 993a30–994b31; Γ, 1003a21–32; K, 1060b31–1061b33.
(2) Discussed: 996b26–997a15.
     Answered: Γ, 1005a19–1012b31; K, 1061b34–1063b35.
(3) Discussed: 997a15–25.
     Answered: E, 1025b3–1026a32; K, 1063b36–1064b14.
(4) Discussed: 997a34–998a19.
     Answered: Λ, 1069a18–1076a4; M, N, 1076a8–1093b29.
(5) Discussed: 997a25–34.
     Answered: Γ, 1003a33–1005a18; most of Δ, 1012b34–1025a34; E, 1026a33–1028a6; Z, 1032a12–1038a35; Θ, 1051a34–1052a11; I, 1052a15–1059a14; K, 1060b31–1061b33, 1064b15–1069a14.
(6) Discussed: 998a20–b14.
     Answered: Δ, 1012b34–1013a23.
(7) Discussed: 998b14–999a23.
     Answered: Z, 1037b8–1039a23.
(8) Discussed: 999a24–b24.
     Answered: Z, 1028a10–1032a11, 1041a6–b33; H, 1042a3–1045b23.
(9) Discussed: 999b24–1000a4, 1002b12–34.
     Answered: Λ, 1070a31–1071b2.
(10) Discussed: 1000a5–1001a3.

Answered: α, 994a1–b31; Z, 1032a12–1036a25; Λ, 1069a18–
1073a13.
(11) Discussed: 1001a4–b25.
Answered: Z, 1040b5–1041a5; I, 1053b9–1054a19.
(12) Discussed: 1003a5–17.
Answered: Z, 1038b1–1040b4.
(13) Discussed: 1002b32–1003a5.
Answered: H, 1042a3–1045b23; Θ, 1045b27–1051a33.
(14) Discussed: 1001b26–1002b11.
Answered: M, N, 1076a8–1093b29.

1

1. Principles and causes considered in Book A. The problem here, assumed in Book A, is whether only one science or more than one should discuss the various causes.

2. The term "substances" here is used dialectically, since its various senses must still be considered; and perhaps it includes *substances,* if these are studied generically, as in Books Z and H.

3. Plato and his followers.

4. Just as substances have essential attributes, so the latter, too, have attributes. For example, magnitude is an attribute of a physical substance, divisibility ad infinitum is an attribute of a magnitude. The example given here is: a given contrary is so opposed to one contrary only. The contrary of white is black, of oddness it is evenness, etc.

5. Perhaps the parts as matter are meant, such as those of a substance or of a quantity (1036a9–12); or else, the parts as matter and form. At this stage, the problem is dialectical, and distinctions are needed.

6. A proximate genus is also called "a species" or "ultimate species".

7. The form or essence (without the matter) is meant.

8. Or, separate. For Aristotle, some forms are separate or separable, such as God and the active intellect of a man, but the form of, say, a cat is not, except in thought or as a whatness or a definition.

9. In a bronze statue, for example, its form would be predicated of the bronze, which is the matter of the statue. Matter as such has no attribute (1029a20–1) and is unknowable, so "to be predicated of" here is used in the sense of "to actualize", or "to be attached to", or "to be with", or something of this sort.

10. By "definite in number" is meant finite in number and all distinct; by "definite in kind" is meant finite in kind but many or even infinite for each kind.

11. Hippasus and Heraclitus.

12. Thales.

13. Anaximenes and Diogenes of Apollonia.

14. Assuming that they exist potentially or *actually.*

15. For example, God exists as form or actuality but without matter, but in motion there is matter.

16. For the Pythagoreans and the Platonists, they are substances; for the Pythagoreans they are not separate from sensible things, since they are the things themselves.

2

The discussion of each problem is calculated to give both sides, pros and cons, by the use of dialectical or even sophistical premises or arguments, that is, premises or arguments accepted by all or most people, or by all or most learned people, or by some group of people, etc. A dialectical premise may be scientific.

1. The assumption here is that contraries come under the same science; for example, black and white come under the science of colors, motion and rest under physics, equality and inequality under mathematics (14a15–25, 427b5–6).

2. To shelter people or animals or materials.

3. 982a8–19.

4. That is, "x is white" gives us more knowledge about x than "x is not a number", for the latter is too indefinite and negative; and more knowledge is nearer to understanding than less knowledge.

5. That is, the definition of a man gives us knowledge about a man to the highest degree; a statement such as "a man can run" or "a man is heavier than an apple" gives us little knowledge about him.

6. Only of substances is there a whatness in its full sense. But in a qualified sense, there is a whatness and a *substance* of a quality and of a quantity and of the others; and in these cases, too, the whatness gives us knowledge in the highest degree. For example, the definition of a triangle, "a three-sided plane figure", gives us such knowledge, and such a statement as "a triangle has an area" or "a triangle has boundaries" gives us little knowledge about the triangle.

7. That is, in addition to the causes or the principles of substances (995b6–10).

8. That is, attributes demonstrated of the subject in that science.

9. "From something" refers to axioms and indemonstrable premises; "about something" refers to the subject of the science, for example, triangles and circles in geometry; "of something" refers to the attributes demonstrated, for example, the incommensurability of the diagonal with the side of a square, and the equality of the base angles in an isosceles triangle.

10. This would be Plato's position. Aristotle differs.

11. The word "doctrines" here signifies the axioms or demonstrative principles, also called "common doctrines".

12. One interpretation is: a subject belongs to one science, the axioms also to one science, but the latter science may or may not be distinct

from the former. This comes under problem (2), not yet resolved (996b26–997a15). A hint is given in 76a37–b2, 77a22–8.

13. An alternative to "substances" is *"substances"*. Of course, the discussion of problems here is dialectical.

14. For Aristotle, God and the other pure forms, which move the spheres, are immaterial and non-sensible.

15. Plato and his followers.

16. Referring to the Platonists while he was a member, but excluding himself.

17. In A, 987a29–988a17.

18. Sensible objects like men, horses, etc., are by nature destructible. But destructible and indestructible objects differ widely in kind; hence, the absurdity of positing eternal Man as being the same in kind as a sensible man (1058b26–1059a14).

19. That is, a Heaven besides the sensible heaven and Heaven Itself.

20. The sensible heaven is in its nature movable, for the material things in it are movable and are investigated also as such; so the Heaven among the Intermediate Objects should likewise be movable to be a heaven; but the Intermediate Objects are posited as immovable.

21. The dialectical argument is: If science is knowledge, and knowledge is of that which exists, then if what exists is destroyed, no knowledge and so no science of it exists. Is geodesy, then, about eternal objects? The Platonists have no room for it among eternal objects.

22. Protagoras may have pointed out that a ruler actually touches a circle not at a point but at a line. As for the stars in astronomy, perhaps they are posited as points for convenience.

23. Probably they took this position to avoid the objection to the claim that Ideas are apart from and yet *substances* of sensible things.

24. The argument may be that stated in lines 997b26–8. There is also this possibility: If the Intermediate Objects are in the sensibles because they are substances or the causes of them, so are the Forms, since these must be also in the Intermediate Objects for the same reason.

25. But the Intermediate Objects are posited as immovable.

3

1. Of written language, the letters would be the principles; of spoken language, the syllables, or else the letters.

2. These would be the theorems which, relatively speaking, are demonstrated in the beginning of a science, and which are presupposed by all or most demonstrations of later theorems; or else, the kinds of syllogisms which are as if forms of mathematical demonstrations.

3. So far, the constituents or material parts or causes are put forward as being the principles or elements. The phrase "how the parts were put together" suggests the formal cause.

4. Of course, the differentia are also principles, but this is not so

evident at this stage (998a30–1). Besides, the genus is in a sense prior to the differentia; for example, 'animal' is prior in existence to 'rationality' or to 'biped'.

5. Here, it is the parts or some parts of a definition that are put forward as elements and principles, especially the genus, and these suggest the formal cause. Aristotle does not mention the differentiae here, which are also parts of a definition, perhaps because he was giving the Platonic position whose tendency is to go to the highest genus and discard the differentiae as principles and elements.

6. By "formula" here Aristotle may mean either the definition of a thing, or what is signified by it, its essence.

7. In the first case, we have genus and differentia; in the second, matter and form in the thing. There is a difference.

8. Of an individual isosceles triangle, for example, the first genus might be "surface", the last perhaps "isosceles triangle". We say "perhaps" because of 1054a35–b3.

9. If a man is defined as a rational animal, rationality cannot be an animal or a man. For, if animality were in rationality, then "animal" in "rational animal" would be superfluous, or it would be twice in "rational animal", or "man" and "rationality" would be the same. But rationality adds something distinct to animality and does not duplicate it. And if "a man" were a predicate of "rationality", the latter would be a species and not a differentia, and "an animal", which is a predicate of "a man", would also be a predicate of it. Thus, both genus and differentia must be principles of and not analysable into the species (144a36–b11). So, assuming that "being" (or "unity") to be a genus and "X" a differentia of it, since X must be a being, the genus "being" would be a predicate of its differentia or what this differentia signifies, and this cannot be so.

10. For example, if "quantity" is an ultimate genus, then by adding successively differentiae we obtain, say, "magnitude", "plane", "polygon", "quadrilateral", etc. as genera lying between "quantity" and the last one which is called "a species".

11. This refers to the species, which is no further divisible into lower species.

12. If form is a principle to a higher degree than matter, and a differentia is to its genus as form is to matter, this analogy suggests that a differentia is a principle more than its genus (1016a24–28, 1024a36–b9, 1038a5–9, 1045a33–35, 1058a21–25).

13. The term "infinite" means also a great number (1066a37).

14. The wider the genus, the greater the number of differentiae. For example, there are more differentiae to "an animal" than to "a terrestrial animal", for the former includes also sea animals.

15. Priority in existence is meant. What is indivisible in quantity, such as an individual man (*qua* a substance), is also indivisible in species, but not conversely, since the indivisible in species is divisible into individuals with respect to quantity. Thus, the indivisible in species is prior in existence to the indivisible in quantity.

16. That is, the species.

17. Even the Platonists might be inclined to agree with this; for they generate first Two from their principles, then Three, etc., but not Number as such or universally taken, yet they should have generated Number first, if Number were prior to Two and to the rest (414b21–24, 1080b11–12).

18. For the Pythagoreans and the Platonists, the reduction of things to mathematical objects and their principles makes mathematical genera prior in existence and in definition to, and also causes of, the other genera. Thus, the relation of genus to species with respect to priority in the case of the other genera of things follows the relation in the case of mathematical objects.

19. Priority in time among individuals exists, but this is not the kind of priority meant since it is not important among destructible objects; and if by "indivisible" he means ultimate species, perhaps here, too, there is no priority in existence, as in the case of horses and dogs (14b33–9).

20. Within a genus, say that of numbers, the genus is prior both in existence and in definition to any of its species; for, if three exists, a number exists, but not conversely, and three is defined in terms of "number" but not conversely. Thus, the genus should be a principle to a higher degree than any of its species. If so, the ultimate genera should be the principles.

4

1. The lowest genera are the indivisible species.

2. 998a20–999a23.

3. The term "predicate" here does not quite have its usual meaning; it means: *it is with*, or, *it gives form to*, or, *it actualizes*. For example, we may say that the shape of a statue is a predicate of bronze.

4. The question may be general, referring to universals or to the Ideas or to pure forms, like God. The phrase "or in none?" may seem superfluous in view of the hypothesis "if it exists", but it need not be; for, it indicates that pure forms, or Ideas (hypothetically), may be posited as existing without being the same as or similar to the sensibles in any way. The phrase "apart from them in all cases" implies the existence of forms somehow the same as or similar to the respective kinds of sensibles.

5. This dialectical argument leaves no room for abstraction from sensible objects and for *knowledge* as something potential (1087a10–25), for knowledge would be restricted to sensation.

6. Unless "sensible things" excludes celestial bodies, this may be a dialectical argument posited by some natural philosophers who regarded even celestial bodies as destructible.

7. To assume that no thing is eternal is to assume generation of everything (Aristotle does not mention motion here because a thing may

always move and still be eternal as a substance; for example, the Sun for Aristotle), but to assume generation is to assume ungenerable or eternal prime matter (994a3–5, 994b6–9); and generation from nothing is ruled out.

8. Having refuted "nothing is eternal", Aristotle now turns to "nothing is immovable". By definition, a generation has an end, and this is a form in the thing which has been generated, or some attribute in things whose motion came to an end, and these are immovable while they exist in the composite; and both forms and attributes are immovable anyway (1033b5–8, 1044b21–24, 1067b9–11, 1069b35–1070a4). This dialectical argument leaves out the eternal motion of the heavenly bodies.

9. The dialectical argument may be: since matter cannot exist without form, it cannot be prior to it; so if matter exists because it is ungenerated, form must certainly exist for the same reason; or else, if matter becomes a certain form, there must be a mover of the same form which causes this.

10. This is in line with those Platonists who say that no Ideas or Forms exist for products of art.

11. By "one" he means one in species, but Plato takes the position that Man Himself, numerically one (so Aristotle understands it), is the *substance* of all men. But men are numerically many, so how can Man Himself, numerically one (and indivisible, or at least undivided), be in numerically many men? The assumption is: The *substance* of a thing cannot exist apart from that thing.

12. That is, if no two principles were the same in kind. For example, if there were numerically only one letter "e" in the alphabet, it would be impossible to have the term "seek", since this uses two such letters.

13. That is, finite in number, and no two of them the same in kind.

14. Apparently, a repeated tasting of nectar and ambrosia is indicated here in order to maintain an eternal existence; and the implication is, if the repeated tasting is not maintained, the gods will not be immortal because they need food. Thus, the gods were once destructible, but they can be eternal by repeated tasting. On the other hand, what can be eternal must be eternal, and what must be eternal can never be or have been destructible (203b30, 281a28–283b22, 337a34–338b19, 1058b26–1059a14).

15. That is, *Friendship*, which is the principle which causes things to be one (1001a12–15).

16. Apparently, *God* is the *One*, or *Friendship*, or the whole universe when united by *Friendship*.

17. The Greek word is φρόνιμος, whose usual meaning is: prudent. But here it probably means *knowing* or wise or something of this sort.

18. An alternative to "*Strife*" is "strife".

19. Since *God* has no *Strife*, he has none of the things caused by *Strife* and so he cannot know such things, for like is known by like.

20. Prior in existence.

21. If A, which is posited as a principle, is destructible, then it is

composed of, say, B and C. But then A cannot be a principle, for B and C are prior in existence to A. So, either B and C are the principles, or the ultimate constituents of B and C are principles, and in both cases the principles would have to be indestructible; and to assume that no ultimate constituents of B and C exist is to assume that no principles at all exist anyway.

22. The argument is: If we assume that there exist destructible principles, since what is destructible will at some time in the future be destroyed, there will be a time when no destructible things composed of such principles will exist. Such a situation is denied by Aristotle. (283a24–28)

23. That is, one set of principles for destructible things, another for indestructible things. For example, Plato posits the *One* and the *Great* and *Small* for both destructible (sensibles) and indestructible objects (Ideas and Intermediate Objects).

24. That is, is unity a substance as Socrates is a substance, without something else underlying unity just as nothing underlies Socrates, or is there some other underlying nature of which unity is only an attribute? For example, redness is an underlying nature, and oneness is only an attribute of redness, for redness or a red color is one; and it may likewise be that what is called "one" must always be some other underlying nature, for example, a sound, a line, a stone, water, etc.

25. Whether "being" and "unity" have the same meaning for those who regard them as principles seems to be left undecided here by Aristotle. For him they do not have the same meaning, although whatever is one is a being, and conversely (1003b22–24, 1054a13–19, 1061a17–18).

26. For example, for Empedocles, that which is one is *Earth*, or *Water*, or *Fire*, or *Air*, so that one unity may differ from another in kind; but this is not the case for the Pythagoreans.

27. The dialectical argument may be: Let X be any other universal; then, since X is a unity or a being, and unity or being is not a substance, X is not a substance.

28. The dialectical argument is: Since a number is a plurality of units, and each of these is regarded as just a unity with nothing else underlying it, if each such unity is not a substance, the plurality of units cannot be a substance. And if such a plurality is assumed to be somehow unified (although there is a difficulty if it is), still it is not a substance if it is regarded as a unity.

29. The dialectical argument may be: If unity itself exists, nothing else exists and all things are one; for if other things exist, a number of things exists, and a number, being distinct from unity itself, is not a substance and so does not exist. Thus, only being itself (or unity itself) exists.

30. 1001a24–27.

31. By "another unity" he means a number, an object distinct in kind from unity itself. The argument is: Since another unity, which is a number, is distinct from unity itself, if only unity itself is a substance or a

being, a number cannot be unity itself or a substance or a being, and so it must be a non-unity-itself or a nonbeing; for if the whole universe is numerically only one thing (according to Parmenides), then only unity itself exists, and if numerically many, then each of them is a unity itself, so there is no room for a number since a number is assumed to be a unified plurality, a kind of unity distinct from unity itself.

32. For example, when the straight line AB falls on an equal straight line CD so that AB lies outside CD, the resulting line is greater than CD, but when AB falls on CD so as to coincide with it, the result is not greater than CD.

33. That is, for the existence of something indivisible.

34. The difficulty is: If unity itself is indivisible and the only substance, whether numerically one or many, how can a magnitude be formed from such unities, if an addition of them increases a number but not a magnitude. For Aristotle, a line cannot consist of a number of indivisible points, whether finite or infinite (that is, a denumerable infinite) (231a21–b20).

35. For example, this is the material principle for the Platonists, named "the *Dyad*" or "*Inequality*" or "the *Great* and *Small*".

36. The Platonists leave this unexplained, since from their principles only Numbers can be generated (1084a3–7).

5

1. Mathematical solids are probably meant, as σῶμα was sometimes used in this sense.

2. For example, a motion is an attribute, and as such it must exist not by itself but in a body when in motion; but a body can exist without being in motion.

3. "A *this*" signifies something which is numerically one or undivided and exists separately by itself and can be exhibited, like an individual man, a book, a watch, etc. By contrast, an attribute, such as fever or redness, exists in something else, in a man or a body (3b10–13).

4. The dialectical assumption is: What is prior in definition to, or what is a boundary of, something is also prior in existence to it and hence prior as a principle or nearer to a principle. Thus, a triangle is defined in terms of or bounded by straight lines and so cannot exist without them, but not conversely. The assumption is not necessarily true (1077a36–b4).

5. Pythagoreans and Platonists.

6. This is the position of Plato and his followers.

7. For Aristotle, a division of a body, which is a surface, is like an attribute of the body and so posterior in existence to it (1077a24–b14).

8. Referring to the shape of the statue of Hermes before it was made by the sculptor, for that shape is somehow in the stone, potentially.

9. That is, the surface which divides the cube into two halves.

10. For, a cube may be divided into two parts, and two new congruent surfaces appear.

11. The process of generation or of destruction of a substance is not instantaneous but takes time.

12. 241a6–26, 1044b21–29, 1174b12–14.

13. From what sort of material is a point generated? Obviously, from none.

6

1. Lines 1002b12–32 are part of problem (4). Perhaps it has been postponed because it presupposes problem (9).

2. Referring to the Platonists, while Aristotle was a member.

3. For one thing, they are immovable and eternal (987b14–18).

4. For example, there are only twenty-six kinds of letters (material principles) in the English language, but numerically there are many a's, many b's, etc.

5. That is, if it is necessary to have a definite number of principles, numerically finite and all distinct, this would require to posit objects of another kind, such as the Forms; for example, Man Himself to correspond to all men, and so on with the rest.

6. 999b24–1000a4.

7. That is, whether they exist *actually*.

8. The cause as form or as *actuality* is meant.

9. For example, if a house exists, its materials (which are its potentiality) exist, but not conversely; so potentiality here seems to be prior in existence to *actuality*. And if the principles exist *actually*, they would not be principles since the potentiality for them would be prior in existence.

10. That is, it is possible for no being in actuality to exist at all.

11. In other words, what is not an actual being may be not only the impossible, like a number 5 which is even, but also potentiality, like the materials which may become a house.

12. That is, if each is one numerically and separate.

13. Perhaps prior in knowledge is meant; for, so the dialectical argument seems to be, we cannot know individuals unless we know first the universal principles which are predicated of these individuals.

Book Γ

1

1. For example, arithmetic and geometry investigate the attributes of numbers and magnitudes, respectively, and these come under quantity, which itself is a part of being.

2. The contrast between "accidentally" and "qua" seems to be that between an accidental cause and an essential cause. For example, an isosceles triangle has its angles equal to two right angles not qua isosceles triangle nor qua isosceles, but qua a triangle. But a triangle is accidentally isosceles (it need not be so).

3. There are causes in every genus of being, so the investigation of the first or highest causes does not belong to a science of any specific genus of being but to the science of being universally. The causes meant are the four causes, their existence, nature, and their attributes, generically or analogically considered. Thus, the investigation of essence, definition, material elements, prime mover, etc., would belong to the science of being qua being, which is first philosophy.

2

1. This is a substance, which is separate.

2. For example, the terms "ethical", "political", "mathematical".

3. An *attribute,* such as color, exists in a substance and not by itself; it is an aspect of a substance, a partial being, so to say, not a being in the full sense. A substance, in contrast, is said to be a being in the full sense; it is not an aspect of anything but is separate, as a man or a statue.

4. For example, an embryo or seed becomes a man, which is a substance, and bronze becomes a statue.

5. For example, all species of animals have a common nature, and qua animals all are investigated by zoology, the science of animals.

6. For example, in defining the *healthy,* such as a healthy body or a healthy instrument, "health" appears as a part of the definition of it, although "health" is not a genus in it; so what is defined is in some sense named according to health.

7. By "first" he means first in existence, in definition, and in time, and this is a substance. For example, sickness is an attribute, and it cannot exist unless it does so in a substance, but a substance need not have sickness (1028a31–4); and since a name is a sign of a thing, a thing should be named and defined in the manner it exists. Thus, health or the healthy should include in its definition the body. Book Z discusses this.

8. This does not mean that the philosopher investigates the properties of every kind of being, such as those of quantity, for example, but it does mean that it is the philosopher's job to investigate how many kinds of being there are, what their nature is, how they exist, what their principles are, and other such problems; for these problems do not belong to a specific science. But some science must consider these, and this science is philosophy.

9. In modern terminology, "being" and "unity" have the same denotation but different connotations. More strictly, whatever is a being

is also one, and conversely, but to be a being is not to be unity. By "formula" he does not here mean a definition, but rather a description proper to the thing, for neither being nor unity are definable. A definition is a formula, but not conversely.

10. That is, if being and unity had the same formula, then certainly that which is one would also be a being and conversely; moreover, there would not even be a problem since the two would not be distinguishable except in name.

11. When Socrates is born, his unity and his being or nature simultaneously come to be, and when he dies, they are simultaneously destroyed.

12. That is, not denotatively distinct.

13. Referring to the *substance* of a thing in any category. In this way, also a color would be a being and one. The *substance* of a thing is the cause of its unity; for example, the soul in the case of a man.

14. Matter, for example, being indefinite and without form, would not be one or a being if it were not for the form or *substance* which is with it, so to say.

15. For example, sameness is unity in *substance,* likeness is unity in quality, etc., so these are kinds of unity (1021a11–12).

16. Probably a lost treatise. See also 1054a30.

17. An alternative to "substances" is *"substances"*; and in this sense, quantities are *substances,* investigated by mathematics, and physical *substances* are investigated by physics.

18. See Comm. 7. Priority in sciences follows priority in their subjects. Of the latter, the prime movers are first, then come the moving substances whose changes somehow depend on the prime movers, then the mathematical *substances* which somehow exist in physical substances.

19. Universal mathematics treats of all quantities qua quantities by analogy, without considering their differences, whether discrete or continuous; and in it are to be found such terms as equality, inequality, ratio, proportion, etc. This is first in mathematics, that is, first in knowledge. Then there are arithmetic and geometry. There are also species of geometry, geometry of lines, and of surfaces, and of solids (74a17–25, 76a37–b2, 1026a25–27, 1061b17–25, 1064b8–9). Philosophy, too, is concerned with the nature and principles of each kind of being, such as immaterial substances, material substances (both eternal and perishable), quantity as such, etc. By "immediate" he means that each of these kinds is an ultimate genus (998b22–7).

20. Denial and privation are kinds of opposition (1018a20–38, 11b15–14a14).

21. As the Greek text stands, it makes no sense; but if οὖν is replaced by οὐ (= "no"), what follows seems to be in accord with Aristotle's thought, and we have translated in the latter sense.

22. That is, the denial of unity is just its absence. For example, if Socrates is dead, then "Socrates is not one" is true, and here we have

simply a denial of "Socrates is one" or of the unity of Socrates (13b27–35); from this denial no subject is indicated which might be either a plurality (rather than a unity) or something other than Socrates.

23. For example, are magnitudes and numbers one in *substance?* No, they are not one, but they are other (or distinct), and otherness is the privation of sameness (or oneness in *substance*), since they are in distinct and not in the same species of quantity; and both species are assumed as existing, each with a differentia, so there is a nature underlying (224a2–15). Or else, the opposition of one to plurality here is a privation, for there is an underlying subject in both. Whether unity is the privation of plurality, or plurality the privation of unity, is not clear. Lines 1054a20–9 favor the former, lines 1004a9–20 seem to favor the latter. Perhaps the former is a privation with respect to sensation, the latter by being posterior in existence. The opposition between unity and plurality is a privation.

24. The kinds of unity are sameness (unity in *substance*), likeness (unity in quality), equality (unity in quantity), and the corresponding privations are otherness (plurality in *substance*), unlikeness (plurality in quality), inequality (plurality in quantity).

25. 1018a12, 1055a3–5.

26. For example, the term "different" is analogously predicated of substances and of quantities.

27. For example, in straight lines equality in length may be a predicate of lines AB and CD; but we may also say that two straight rods are equal. Now rods are not straight lines or lengths, but they possess lengths, and so they are said to be equal secondarily and not primarily, that is, because of their lengths.

28. An alternative to "substance" is *"substance"*. This distinction applies also to the corresponding problem raised in 995b18–27, although as a dialectical problem it may be considered as requiring further definiteness.

29. 995b18–27.

30. Prior in existence (or time), definition, and knowledge (1028a30–b2).

31. For example, two is few without qualification; it is the smallest number. However, five is few relative to ten, but many relative to two.

32. By "solids without weight" here he means solids investigated by geometry; solids with weight, or bodies, would be accidental or secondary quantities, to which primary quantities would be applicable.

33. The term "genus" here is used in a wider and loose sense; it signifies the various senses of "being". Aristotle often would rather borrow a known term and use it in a wider or narrower sense than invent a new term. See also 1024a29–b16.

34. The philosopher pursues philosophy for the sake of knowledge and, in virtue of his capacity, also has some knowledge of its objects;

the sophist does so for the sake of money and reputation, or for the sake of winning an argument; the dialectician only tries to find philosophic truths from commonly accepted opinions (171b3–172b8, 100a25–101a4).

35. That which is at rest remains one and the same, but that which changes is becoming many.

36. Or, the *Finite* and the *Infinite*. These are the Pythagoreans.

37. The *Odd* is indivisible and so has unity, the *Limit* gives unity to a thing, *Friendship* unites things into one, etc. The *Even* is divisible and hence many, the *Unlimited* is infinite and hence many, *Strife* keeps things apart and hence many, etc.

38. Aristotle does not hold that all things are composed of contraries as their matter; he only argues dialectically, using commonly accepted opinions of previous philosophers to show that the study of contraries belongs to philosophy. The phrase "composed of contraries" is also used for what is between contraries, like grey, which is partly black and partly white and so composed of contraries in that sense.

39. He is referring to "being" or "unity", which is not univocal, even if its primary sense is a substance and the other senses are related to it by being attributes of it, etc.

40. For Plato, the *One* is both universal and separate, and it is a nature in itself and not, say, like whiteness, which is an attribute of a subject (a body).

41. A geometer may investigate them qua a philosopher; or, like a dialectician, he may investigate or use them by making initial hypotheses, but then he will have hypothetical knowledge of them and not *knowledge* like that of the philosopher.

42. The whole of Book Δ is a part of the answer to this problem.

3

1. These are the logical axioms. See also Book Κ, Sec. 4, Comm. 1.

2. An alternative to "substances" is *"substances"*, and this alternative seems better in view of the next sentence.

3. For example, universal mathematics will use these axioms only for quantities, arithmetic only for numbers, etc. A quantity or a number is a being, and the axioms of being are axioms of every instance of being.

4. That is, about the whole of being or about all beings, for they thought that only physical things exist.

5. The prime mover and the other immaterial substances are meant, or at least, included. The expression "investigates universally" includes both primary beings (which are separate, whether material or immaterial) and qualified beings (attributes). Such *universal* investigation will be analogical and not univocal, for "being" is not univocal.

6. Referring to Antisthenes and other uneducated thinkers, who

demand a demonstration of everything, unaware of the fact that the very first starting points of demonstration are indemonstrable axioms and premises (72b5–35, 1006a5–8).

7. Or, *substances;* for, qualified beings are also included.

8. For example, for physics these would be the very first principles of physics, and likewise for mathematics; and in each science, such are the axioms without which nothing can be known in that science (72a14–8).

9. Most known or knowable in its nature (or by nature) is meant, not known to us, for the latter is confused knowledge and rather of particulars.

10. If it is hypothetical, one may be mistaken about it and have no certain belief about it, and so it cannot be the most certain.

11. Lines 1005a19–b17 seem to indicate that the principle of contradiction applies to all being; but no reference is made to nonbeing. Now if "A" signifies a nonbeing, both "A is B" and "A is not B" cannot be true at the same time, and one of them must be true, as is also indicated in 16a30–3 and 16b12–5. However, the statement of the principle does not specify only being, so that the term τὸ αὐτό, which is literally translated as "the same" and which I translate as "the same object", is probably intended to signify either a being or a nonbeing. However, there is this difficulty: If "A" signifies a nonbeing, A is not one, for being and unity follow each other (1003b22–5), and so in "A is B" or "A is not B" we do not have one subject of which "B" is affirmed or denied. To say "A" has one meaning is not to say that it signifies one thing, except by hypothesis or accidentally; and it is in this hypothetical or accidental sense that we use "an object" to signify something as if it was one. Perhaps the same remarks apply to the predicate "B" in "A is B" and "A is not B".

12. This is a principle about all things, not only about thoughts as some logicians think.

13. For example, if a stone is half-way immersed in water, is it or is it not immersed in water? Part of it is and part is not, so if by "the stone" one means the whole stone, the answer is "No", and if one means a part of the stone, a specification of that part will make the answer obvious. In a way, the phrase "in the same respect" would take care of any possible specification.

14. Heraclitus himself would not have believed what he said, had he understood what he said.

15. Concerning what contrary opinions are, see 23a27–24b9. It is just as impossible for a man to have contrary opinions concerning the same thing at the same time and in the same respect as for 5 to be both odd and even. See also 1011b15–22. He considers only contrary opinions as an example, but the same applies to any contrary beliefs, or else, an alternative to "opinion" is "doctrine", since δόξα has more than one sense.

16. Perhaps referring to theorems which are demonstrated by a reduction to the impossible, that is, to a situation in which A is B and is not B at the same time.

17. All other axioms assume this principle. For example, in mathematics, "the whole is greater than the part" assumes that it is impossible for the whole to be and not to be greater than the part. Thus "the whole is not greater than the part" is excluded because it is false.

4

1. Probably some Sophists, among others.

2. Heraclitus and his followers (1010a10; 1012a24, 34), Empedocles (1009b15), Anaxagoras (1009a27, b25), Democritus (1009a27, b11, 15).

3. 1005b22–32.

4. To ask for a demonstration of everything is to ask for the impossible: for, since one will ask for a demonstration of every premiss posited, the process will go on to infinity, and so no demonstration of anything is thus possible.

5. But if these thinkers posit the possibility of demonstration, they must posit as indemonstrable some principles or premises from which our principle is demonstrated; yet they posit nothing.

6. That is, qua not saying anything.

7. It is assumed, here, that a demonstration by refutation is not a species of a demonstration, although the term "demonstration" appears in the former expression.

8. To beg the question is to assume at the start as true that which one is to prove as true, or as false that which he is to prove as false.

9. For example, if X denies the truth of the proposition P but at the same time assumes its truth in his arguments, one can refute his denial by pointing out his assumption of P's truth.

10. In argument, or communication in general, the meaning of a proposition is presupposed before one can discuss or determine its truth or falsity.

11. If X grants that the proposition P has one definite meaning, then he admits that P does not both mean and not mean something; hence, though openly denying the principle of contradiction, at least in this case he assumes it (that it is impossible to be and not to be at the same time, etc.).

12. That is, both so and not so, at the same time, etc. Aristotle often omits repeating the qualifications; but they are taken as understood.

13. Knowledge of one thing is prior in time to knowledge of many things.

14. To be predicated of one thing is not the same as to have one meaning. Of Socrates we may predicate "white", "philosopher", "snub-nosed", etc.; but each of these predicates has a different meaning; but of an instance of whiteness only "whiteness" or its formula is a predicate

as its essence. If this distinction is not kept in mind, fallacies such as the following result: Socrates is a man; but Socrates is white, and being white is not being a man; hence Socrates is not a man. Also, Socrates is a man, and white, and musical, etc.; so all these, and in fact everything, is one (for if Socrates is not black, there will be something musical which is black, etc., so since Socrates is musical, he is also black). In modern parlance, connotation is distinct from denotation.

15. Terms have meaning by convention; so just as "a garment" and "a coat" may have the same meaning, so one may decide to use by convention "to be" and "not to be" with the same meaning. But the principle of contradiction is concerned with facts and not with conventions, so these two terms are posited at the start as differing in meaning.

16. Perhaps what Aristotle is doing here is to proceed from terms, differing in appearance but having the same meaning, to what would then follow: the oneness of consequent meanings; but the supposition is false, since "to be" and "not to be", followed by "a man", which has one meaning, do not have the same meaning.

17. "To be a not-man" and "not to be a man" differ. In the proposition "X is a not-man", if true, X is assumed to exist; but in "X is not a man", if true, X does not necessarily exist. The latter proposition merely denies the unity of a human X, whether X exists or not.

18. In some cases, although to be a man is not to be white, X may be both a man and white, as in the case of an individual white man; but in no case can X be both a man and a not-man, for not-man is the privation of man.

19. See above, Comm. 14.

20. An alternative to "accidents" is "attributes", since accidents are not the only attributes which may belong to a man.

21. That is, if X is a man, and also X is Y_i (where $i = 1, 2, 3, \ldots$), if to be an Y_i is not to be a man, the confusion stated in Comm. 14 would lead one to say that X is not a man a countless number of times.

22. A substance, like a man, is separate; an essence, like that of whiteness, is inseparable from a body, although it may be a subject having some other attribute, as when we say that this whiteness is brilliant. If substances and essences are denied, no science is possible; for "A is not A" would be true of anything.

23. The word "just" probably modifies a substance, but not any *substance* or essence; what is just a substance is not an attribute of something else, as in the case of Socrates.

24. Refers to "the essence of a man".

25. In other words, a man is a subject, and he has necessary attributes, such as mortality, and also accidental attributes, such as sickness. But this distinction is lost if essences are denied; for one would then say alike truly that a man is not mortal and also that he is not sick.

26. An alternative: "there would be no subject of which something

would be universally a predicate. For example, "mortality" or "animality" would not be always a predicate of a man, or "oddness" of five. Greek texts differ.

27. If everything is present in something else, there is no substance (which is separate and so not present in anything).

28. An alternative to "accidental" is "attributive", and likewise for the term "accident" which follows repeatedly.

29. 1017a7–22.

30. That is, B is an accident of subject A, C is an accident of B, D is an accident of C, etc. Accidents do not necessarily form a unity, for they can exist apart from each other, though in substances.

31. Whiteness is an accident of Socrates by being present (although it need not be) in Socrates; but the musical is an accident of the white by the fact that both are present in the same subject, say, Socrates. So in both cases, a subject is presupposed.

32. For example, it is a term, such as "a man", that signifies a substance, but it is the thing itself, the man, who is a substance.

33. Namely, that what seems to a man to be true, this is true; and since contradictories, and contraries, etc., seem to different persons to be true of a subject, all things would be true of it.

34. That is, no thing exists actually by itself, for all things are blended into something indefinite or indeterminate.

35. The argument may also be stated thus: Since to say "a man is a man" is more true than to say "a man is a trireme", then since "a man is not a man" is more opposite than "a man is a trireme", if "a man is not a man" is true, then certainly "a man is a trireme" is true. And if "a man is not a man" is true, even if to be a man belongs to a man, then certainly "a man is not a trireme" is true, since trireme does not even belong to a man.

36. If these thinkers allow as true instances of both "A is B" and "A is not B" to be true, even the principle of the excluded middle (either p or not p) may be denied; for p may be denied, not p may be denied, and the combination (p and not p, or, p or not p) may be denied.

37. That is, there will be some permanent nonbeing in these cases in which the denial is true but not the assertion. For example, if "A is not B" is true but "A is B" is not true, then AB will be permanently a nonbeing, as in the case of an odd eight.

38. It is not clear to which opposite assertion he is referring. If, from (2), for any A and B, "A is B" is true and implies the truth of "A is not B", but the truth of "A is not B" does not always imply that of "A is B", then we have a contradiction; for if, for some A_1 and B_1, "A_1 is not B_1" is true but "A_1 is B_1" is not, this contradicts the initial assumption that "A is B" is true for any A and B.

Perhaps by "more known" he means more *understood*; for "nonbeing" is *understood* through "being", and "A is not B" presupposes "A is B" for its *understanding* (86b30–6), just as "A does not exist" presupposes for its *understanding* "A exists". And if one thing is more *understood* than another, this is definite, so not everything is so and not so.

39. That is, if X_1 is saying these things, he is also not saying them. Moreover, X (universally taken) both exists and does not exist, and so X_1 both exists and does not exist. And if X_1 does not exist, how can he talk or think?

40. 1006b15–7, 1007a4–7.

41. That is, if for any X and Y we can say that it is a Z and it is not a Z, for every Z, then X and Y and all the rest, having the same predicates, will be the same.

42. That is, if A is speaking truly, and also not truly, then he is speaking falsely, for not to speak truly is to speak falsely; or else he admits as true the fact that he speaks falsely.

43. Namely, that they posit as a principle both the assertion and the denial, so to use a contrary principle is to pit a principle against a principle and not to disprove one by means of the other.

44. How can a thing have a nature if that nature is also denied of it?

45. Namely, that something is definitely more true than something else. But these thinkers would even attach to this its denial, for they would rather believe the two joined together than any of the two separately.

46. For, according to them, both a man and a plant alike think and do not think.

47. Aristotle now attacks the doctrine by showing that these thinkers do not behave in accordance with it. Thus, by behaving in one way rather than in another, they definitely believe the former to be better than the latter; and if they talk to a man but not to a stone, they definitely believe the former to be a man, but not the latter. But behavior in one or a definite way usually follows belief in one or a definite way. So, not everything is believed to be so and not so.

48. If A is nearer to C than B is to C, then C must exist if A is to be nearer to it. For example, if A's distance from C is less than B's is, then C must exist.

49. There may be a doubt in some cases. If A is whiter than B, or more just than B, does perfect whiteness or justice exist? It may be possible for it to exist, or it may exist in thought or as a definition.

5

1. For Protagoras, man is the measure of things; so what appears to a man to be is what actually exists.

2. That is, relatively to those who have opposite opinions.

3. That is, if being cannot be generated from nonbeing. Thus, if a man is now healthy and now sick, and if each cannot come from nonbeing, both health and sickness, and likewise for other contraries, must be in the man.

4. They are right in the sense that the matter in a thing is both contraries, but potentially and not actually; they are mistaken in the sense that, though potentially both, it is not actually both.

5. It can be generated from that nonbeing (and this is a not-being) which exists as potentiality or matter, but not from pure nothing or an impossibility; for generation requires an underlying subject.

6. Matter is a being in the sense of potentially a being, and is a nonbeing (here, a not-being) in the sense that it is not an actual being (1017a35–b9).

7. According to St. Thomas Aquinas, this is God, who possesses no contraries and is not generable or destructible or in motion. An attribute or a form qua such, too, possesses none of these, as whiteness for example, and the same applies to prime matter qua such (1069b35–1070a4).

8. In contrast, Epicharmus may have said that the statement of Xenophanes is true but does not seem to be; for Xenophanes posited the *One* as immovable, while things do appear to change (974a1–15).

9. The word "altogether" refers to the changing of an attribute entirely or as a whole; the word "in every way" refers to such a change of every attribute of a thing.

10. While one is speaking about a thing, the thing has changed; but in pointing a finger, one indicates the continuous change which really takes place.

11. It takes time to step into the river once; but, according to Cratylus, during this time it is not the same river.

12. For example, if the white object is changing to black, it first arrives at an intermediate stage, say grey; and up to this stage it has kept that part of white which is in the grey, and from this stage till it becomes black it will keep that part of black which is in the grey.

13. The term ὑπάρξει should probably be ὑπάρχει.

14. This is the subject which stays the same, and which is at least prime matter (994a1–b31).

15. Ultimately, this is the prime mover, which always exists and beyond which there is no other mover.

16. One meaning of "quality" is form (1020b13–7), which is meant or included here.

17. To know a man is not to know, for example, what he weighs exactly, but to know his form in general; and we do know that he has weight, but we need not know his exact weight. A man is still a man as he changes in some respects, which Aristotle calls "accidental".

18. 1009a36–8.

19. If a thing always has and has not every attribute, it will not be changing.

20. An alternative to "sensation" is "power of sensation".

21. For example, sight sees colors and only colors, and truly (418a7–16, 427b11–3, 428b18–9).

22. Appearance goes beyond sensation. Sensation is of colors, and

it is true; but in sensing the Sun, one may think that it is a foot in diameter. Thus, its diameter *appears* to be a foot long. In general, judgments concerning quantities and the other common sensibles may be mistaken (418a7–25, 425a13–30, 428b22–5, 442b4–10).

23. Sweetness is non-proper to sight, but proper to taste; and taste is closer to smell than to sight (440b28–30, 443b7–12).

24. When sight sees white (that is, something which is wholly so), it does not at the same time see some other color which is not white, nor is it not seeing white.

25. That is, the wine may change, or the sense of taste may be defective later for some reason, but the essence or nature (or *substance*) of sweetness does not change.

26. For example, five will not necessarily be odd for these thinkers, just as the essence of five according to them may not be the same.

27. To be sensible is to be capable of being sensed; so if no object with a power of sensation can exist, no sensible object can exist either. Aristotle denies this, for if all animals are destroyed, things for him still exist.

28. That is, qua sensible.

29. That which causes (as a mover) a sensation is prior in existence to that sensation. For example, a colored object may exist even if no one sees it; but if one sees a color, there exists a colored object which causes this sensation.

30. Seeing and being seen occur at the same time and are relative to each other; and in general, a sensation is actualized when a sensible object qua sensible is actualized. But a sensible qua an object and qua a possible mover may exist before the sensation of it (7b15–8a12, 1021a26–b3).

6

1. Probably referring to the doctrine that that is true which appears to be so, or that everything is relative.

2. Perhaps referring to the fact that, by acting in one way rather than in another, they are not really convinced of these doctrines, as was indicated in 1010b9–14.

3. In a demonstration, by "that which has no reason" he means an indemonstrable premise, such as an axiom or a definition or a hypothesis.

4. For example, to *know* 10 as a double, you must *know* it as such in relation to something else, to 5; for the double qua double exists in relation to something else. But a circle qua a circle does not exist in relation to something else (unless in the sense that it is inseparable from something), and it can be *known* by itself (or in virtue of itself). Further, if every thing must be *known* in relation to something outside of it, an infinite regress results, and *knowledge* (even partial *knowledge*) is impossible.

5. For example, the Sun appears a foot in diameter, but its being a foot in diameter is not a fact if its magnitude does not depend upon its appearance to me. Perhaps it is assumed in their argument that only what appears may be true (or false), so what appears is identified by these thinkers with what is true or what is fact. I am using "true" or "a fact", depending on whether an appearance is taken (a) to be of something else (just as a belief is of something believed) or (b) to be of itself or by itself. Of course, Aristotle here argues only dialectically.

6. That is, relative to someone having that appearance.

7. For if an appearance just exists, it cannot be relative to the possessor of it.

8. For example, it may appear to sight but not to taste, or it may appear with respect to one attribute but not with respect to another.

9. If these qualifications are added, then at least in this sense what appears is true but not false, so at least in this sense the principle of contradiction is true. One may say that what appears is true and false, but not to the same person; besides, nothing would appear as false to anyone, and falsity would disappear, and there would be no point in arguing if everyone thinks truly.

10. The modern doctrine "to be is to be perceived" seems no different, or not much so, from the doctrine of these thinkers.

11. That is, without anyone sensing or thinking about it.

12. For example, if X gives birth to Y, the father of Y is to the son of X as a relative to the correlative; it is a one-one correspondence. The expression "something definite" may include the fact that either X or Y may have more than one part, but that the whole is definite. Thus, we may have "father of p and q", but then "children of X"; and so one relative would correspond to just one correlative.

13. I am using "think" instead of "opine" here, with no loss in the force of the argument.

14. That is, the same in essence.

15. That is, if a relative is distinct in essence from its correlative, and if the object of thought is a man, then the thinking object cannot be a man, which is absurd.

16. And so, either the thinking object, assumed to be numerically and in essence one, will be an infinite number of kinds of things, some of which are contradictory, or else all these things will be one in essence and numerically. This is absurd or impossible.

17. If X and Y are contraries, and if X belongs to A, then no intermediate between X and Y can belong to A, and certainly Y cannot belong to A; and if Y is a privation of X, and a privation is a kind of denial, then Y must be denied of A when X is affirmed of A. The primary contraries are meant; e.g., whiteness and blackness.

18. That is, X may be partly black and partly white; but if it is partly black, it is black in a qualified way; or X may be potentially black and white, but *actually* neither (it may be grey).

19. For example, A may be *actually* (and so without qualification) white; but in being at the same time potentially black, it is black in a qualified way.

7

1. The term could be "object", if qualified as Comm. 11, Sec. 3, of this Book, although "subject" may be taken in a correspondingly wide sense.

2. Truth and falsity are defined in the same way for beliefs (16a9–13, 1027b18–27, 1051a34–b9).

3. That is, a statement is limited by definition to what is and to what is not; it does not apply to such object which both is and is not or which neither is nor is not. A literal translation is: "But neither being is said to be or not to be, nor nonbeing", but perhaps this requires interpretation.

4. He considers two hypotheses of what might be between being and nonbeing in order to discuss what might be between two contradictories.

5. For example, to change from a man to a horse through an intermediate is impossible.

6. For its definition, see 226b23–6, 1068b27–9; also, see 1057a18–36.

7. For, if grey changes into white, grey is still not-white and is not something which is neither white nor not-white.

8. By "object of *thought*" he probably means a fact or its opposite, e.g., a wise Socrates or a stupid Socrates; by "intelligible object" perhaps he means something with parts, which may or may not exist, such as a triangle, or a triangle consisting of indivisible magnitudes so-and-so placed together.

9. Generation is a change from nonbeing to being, destruction from being to nonbeing. If X were between being and nonbeing, what kind of change would that from X to being (or to nonbeing) or that from being (or nonbeing) to X be?

10. That is, if to every two opposites A and non-A an intermediate $\bar{A}$ is added, there will be a 50% increase. But $\bar{A}$ has its own opposite, non-$\bar{A}$; then there will be an intermediate of these, say $\bar{\bar{A}}$. The process goes to infinity.

11. Of course, no such *substance* can exist, so "*substance*" here is used dialectically or hypothetically.

12. 159b30–5, 185b19–25.

13. If, for Anaxagoras, only the *Blend* and *Intelligence* exist, then every statement of the form "the *Blend* is X" would be false, first, because X would be a material part and not an attribute of the *Blend* (and besides, the *Blend* would not be X, just as a man is neither blood nor bones), and second, because if all were blended, "X is Y" would be false even if Y were an attribute (such as white) in the *Blend* (203a19–28, 989a30–b19).

8

1. This commensurability is always non-existent, and of necessity so.

2. That is, every statement.

3. 1010a7–15, 1012a26–9.

4. 1006a18–25.

5. If A cannot both be and not be, assuming that either it is or it is not, and if "A is" is true when A is, and "A is not" is true when A is not, but "A is not" is false when A is, and "A is" is false when A is not, then each of the latter falsities is the denial of a truth ("A is" in the second case is the denial of "A is not", for "A is" has the same meaning as "A is not not A"), so if there is a false statement, there is also a true one.

6. Perhaps referring to objects. If so, we have the principle of the excluded middle for objects, that is, either A is or A is not; and then from the definition of truth and falsity it follows that contradictory statements cannot be both true at the same time.

7. Referring to the one-sided statements of the opponents, that all statements are true, or that all are false.

8. He who says that every A is true would also include "not every A is true" as true; and the same applies to "every A is false".

9. Such positions were probably taken as a guard against the *common objection* mentioned.

10. Namely, the statement "every statement is false".

11. That is, if he who says "every A is false" adds that only his own statement is true, it nevertheless follows that additional statements will be true, namely, " "every A is false" is true", " " "every A is false" is true" is true", etc. And he who says that "not every A is true" is the only false statement is also faced with admitting as false "every A is true" is false", etc.

12. The conclusion, then, is: the statement "he who says "all things are at rest" exists" is sometimes true and sometimes false, so this statement is not always at rest.

13. It is not clear to what he is referring. If all things move always in every respect, then no statement about what so moves is true at some interval of time, and so every such statement is false. But this is impossible, because "all things so move" is regarded as true, and also because of 1012b17–8. Perhaps there is another interpretation.

14. The subject that changes with respect to something must remain the same. This may be prime matter, or a substance. Thus, when Socrates gets sick from being healthy, Socrates qua Socrates is still the same; he is still a man.

15. The first or outer sphere is always in motion, so that not all things are sometimes in motion or sometimes at rest; and the first mover, or God, who moves this sphere, is always immovable. He considers these at length in Book Λ and in the *Physics*.

Book Δ

The entire Book Δ forms a part of the answer to the fifth problem in Book B (995b18–27). In 1003a33–1005a18 Aristotle says that it is the philosopher's task to investigate both substances and their attributes; in Book Δ he proceeds to state what these are (1004b25–6). Further investigation of these will come later.

1

1. What is first and the principle of a thing would be what is logically first, and such would be too abstract for children to learn. For example, the mathematical definition of continuity would be too abstract for a ten-year old (71b33–72a5).

2. This is Aristotle's position (455b35–6a6, 468b28–31).

3. The father and mother are the moving principles of the baby but are not constituent parts of the baby.

4. The principles of knowledge meant here are what we might call "logically first", and these are the indemonstrable hypotheses and definitions, which are the first premises of what is demonstrated (72a7–24). Aristotle does not mention the axioms here; it may be because the axioms are not premises but principles *by means of which* conclusions are demonstrated *from* premises (77a10–13, 88a36–b3, b27–29). Or else, he may be using "hypotheses" in a wider sense than usual, in which case the axioms would be included.

5. He does not mean that "a cause" and "a principle" have the same meaning, but that the two terms have the same denotation; that is, what is a cause is a principle, and conversely.

6. In a man, for example, his form and matter are in him, and so is the final cause, say his happiness; but the moving principles (his parents) are not.

7. "Nature" has many senses. Here it probably means the cause or principle as form (1014b16–1015a19). By "element" he probably means the matter or material cause.

8. *Thought* and *choice* are given as examples of moving principles.

9. If by *"substance"* he means the cause as form, then "nature" in Comm. 7 above would mean the matter in physical substances. However, by "a *substance* and a final cause" he may mean a form which in generation is the final cause, as the form of a house or a man born.

10. For the difference between the good and the noble, see 1078a31–b6, 1248b16–37, 1366a33–6.

2

1. A material part of the thing is meant.

2. The formula of the essence as it exists in the mind or in writing

cannot be the form as it exists in the thing, so "formula" may mean the form or structure of the thing, so to say. Or else, if the word is τούτου instead of τοῦτο in 1013a–27, as some texts have it, then the translation becomes: "the form and the pattern, and the formula of the essence is of this, . . .". It may be that both causes are meant to be included, as existing in the thing and also in the mind, the first as cause of the thing, the second as cause of knowledge.

3. Perhaps he means the term "a number", not a number, in view of "and the parts in that formula".

4. For example, this may be a force (in the modern sense) which slows up a motion to a stop.

5. If A is done for the sake of B, B for the sake of C, and C is the end, then B is the proximate final cause of A but C is the ultimate final cause of A, and both A and B are said to be for the sake of C.

6. That is, the absence of the pilot.

7. By "hypotheses" he may mean the premises; if not, then probably the first unproved premises. If the premises are unproved, they are first or ultimate material causes; if proved, they are proximate.

8. The hypotheses are, in a manner of speaking, the materials from which a conclusion is formed.

9. Referring to the syllables, manufactured articles, bodies, etc., each of which is a composite.

10. Evidently, the so-called "material cause" or "matter" is not restricted to physical or sensible matter; for neither the letters of the syllable (universally taken) are such, nor the elements or the genus of a definition, nor the so-called "intelligible matter" in quantity (1036a9–12, 1036b35, 1045a33–5).

11. By "the other" he means the other constituent of each composite, and this is the form or essence. For example, the order of the letters in the case of a syllable, the shape in the case of a manufactured article, etc.

12. Perhaps by "whole" here he does not mean the unity of matter and form, such as the whole bronze statue, but that (the wholeness, so to say) which makes the thing a whole, and this is the form or the cause of unity (1023b29–36). The form itself may be a kind of a whole with parts, as in the case of the soul of a man.

13. The term "the end" is wide enough to include both the good and the apparent good (the latter may be evil or bad, yet it exists and must be considered).

14. Perhaps prior in existence is meant (which could be prior also in other ways, as in definition or in time), but whether the example given (an artist is prior in existence to a doctor) exemplifies this priority or no example of it is given here, is not clear. If A is the moving cause of B, and B the moving cause of C, then A is prior to B as a moving cause. For example, let A = art of building, B = builder, C = house. This example is given in the discussion of causes in the *Physics* (195b21–5), and perhaps this is the kind of priority meant, or this more than the

other; for in this the causes themselves are considered, but in the other, the genus and species are considered, and these are related to knowledge. But again, any kind of priority may be meant.

15. By "includes" he probably means the kind of inclusion which relates the genus and the species. For example, the "artist" includes the "doctor", and "a number" includes "two"; thus, the genus includes the species.

16. The moving cause of a statue must be a sculptor, but it may or may not be Polyclitus; so Polyclitus is an accidental moving cause of a statue. Perhaps "a statue" is taken universally, for of a definite statue only Polyclitus may be the cause.

17. The white or the musical are more remote as moving accidental causes of the statue than Polyclitus, for they are in turn accidents of Polyclitus.

18. Perhaps the term "essential", which he usually uses elsewhere, would be an alternative (196b24–8).

19. The term "portrait" is here used as a genus of "a statue".

20. By "this bronze" and "bronze" and "matter" here he refers to the materials manufactured by an art (metallurgy, for example) prior to their being shaped into something useful (194a32–b8).

3

1. The term "first" means ultimate. Thus, if bodies are composed of protons, electrons, etc., which cannot be further divided or reduced to anything else, they would be first and so the elements of bodies.

2. Water was then believed to be homogeneous by many thinkers.

3. A part of a syllable is a letter, which is first or ultimate.

4. For example, a cent in U.S. currency, or a nail, or a brick.

5. It is in this sense that the syllogism "All A is B, all B is C, so all A is C" is an element, for it belongs as a form, so to say, to many instances. See also 121b11–4, 151b18–20, 1403a17–9.

6. That is, elements. The Pythagoreans, Platonists, Speusippus, and others are meant.

7. For Plato, these would be 'One' or 'Being'; for Aristotle, the categories: 'quantity', 'quality', 'relation', and the rest, for there is no definition of them.

8. That is, "formula" in the sense of definition.

9. For example, if the differentia of 'quantity' are 'discrete' and 'continuous', what is continuous is a quantity, but what is a quantity need not be continuous.

4

1. The terms φύσις (= "nature") and φύεσθαι (= "to grow") have the same root.

2. In plants, perhaps this would be the seed, and in birds, the egg. By "first constituent" he means the proximate and not the ultimate constituent, for the latter might be earth and water and the like.

3. This is the moving cause or principle.

4. For example, if flesh and bone are grown together, though they are continuous and so their limits are one, to be bone is not to be flesh. For the meaning of "quality", see 1020a33–b1.

5. This is the material cause of a natural thing. The term "first" means proximate as used for the bronze of a statue or the wood of a bed, but ultimate as used for fire or earth or the like (1015a7–10).

6. This is the form or *shape*, which excludes the material principle, as the shape of a statue or the soul of a man.

7. A composite of natures in the sense (4) and (5), that is, a composite of matter and form in the senses stated.

8. The term "water" here is used hypothetically (as Thales did) to indicate ultimate matter.

9. At the end of generation, the object in the process of generation has taken on a form, and the end of the generation is this form.

10. This sense of "nature" extends to all categories. Thus, in quality, one speaks of the nature of philosophy (983a21), in quantity, one speaks of the nature of time (218a31) or of a triangle.

11. The force of this argument seems to be: first, all A was called "B"; later, the meaning of "A" was so extended as to be identical with that of "B".

12. The moving cause of a natural generation is a form, and the end of an object while in the process of natural generation is to attain or take on a form.

13. The interpretation of this last sentence appears difficult. Perhaps it is this: If the form of a man is the moving principle, then it is certainly actual in the man, and this form may be in activity or dormant (potential); but the moving principle may be only a part of that form, such as the art of building, or *choice*, and as a part, it too exists potentially in the whole form (414b29–33, 432a15–433b30).

5

1. Force is an external cause, and the compulsory is that which acts or is acted upon by force, or can act or can be acted upon by force. Thus, the compulsory (that which acts by force) is a composite, so to say, having force as its form or as an attribute.

2. Preventing and obstructing differ probably in this: what is prevented is not allowed to begin, what is obstructed is not allowed to continue or to be completed.

3. *Choice* exists in men only among animals; tendency exists also in inanimate objects, as stones which tend towards the center of the universe.

4. That is, on the part of that which is compelled.

5. Referring to the good or life or existence, which makes certain things necessary.

6. Perhaps what is meant is that the demonstrated conclusion is necessary, and the cause (or necessity) of it is the premises.

7. Demonstration without qualification is defined in *Posterior Analytics* (71b9–72b4). Such a demonstration cannot be hypothetical or *ad hominem,* but it is possible by the *per impossibile* method.

8. By "first premises" he means indemonstrable, so that no other premises are prior to them in the sense that they are the causes of what is demonstrated; and these first premises cannot be otherwise, that is, they are necessarily true.

9. Thus, of conclusions which are necessarily true (for example, if n is a natural number, "$(2n+1)^2 - (2n-1)^2$ is a multiple of 8" is a necessarily true conclusion), the first premises are the causes, but these premises have no other causes, and it is *they* that are the causes of other necessary truths.

10. That which is simple has no parts, so it is not subject to composition and decomposition or to generation and destruction, for what is generated or destroyed not by accident is not simple, as a man or a statue.

11. This refers, for one thing, to the prime movers, and these are eternal, immovable, and simple; and there is nothing compulsory for them or against their nature, for if they could change when compelled, they would act now in one way and now in another, but then their nature would not be simple, or, if they change, they have matter and a form or a contrary, and so they cannot be simple. In a sense, first necessary principles are simple; for they are necessary and cannot be otherwise, and they are not caused; and such is the principle of contradiction and the necessary premises which are indemonstrable.

6

1. In saying that Coriscus and the musical are one by accident, the term "one" indicates that it is in fact one thing numerically which is both Coriscus and musical, and "by accident" indicates that Coriscus need not be musical, for he is still Coriscus if he loses his musicality.

2. A universal name need not be a genus, as for example, "one", or the differentia "straight".

3. The phrase "by accident" refers to the relation of the musical to a man, for what is a man need not be musical, but an individual man must be a man.

4. Or as a species. Sometimes Aristotle uses "genus" in a sense so as to include the species (1018b5–6). Moreover, the *substance* of Coriscus is in him, but the species "man" is universal, and if anywhere, in the soul as knowledge.

5. A habit, such as generosity, is difficult to displace; an affection, such as sickness or blushing, easily comes and goes.

6. In the case of a fagot, perhaps "contiguity" is the right term (227a6–23).

7. Perhaps this is so because art imitates nature, or because in some sense it is by convention or by human force that some things are made one, whereas what is one by nature is one in virtue of itself and not because of something outside.

8. This is not a definition of continuity but a property, and it is a property (so it seems) of solid continuous things, for non-solid continuous things can also move in part, as the hand of a man while the other parts are resting (227a10–13, 1016a9–10).

9. A straight line must move as a whole, for if it moves about one of its points, say B, all of it moves except B; but B is not a part of the line but only a limit or a division present in the line. Similarly, a line is not a part of a plane in which it is present. Thus, such a line (or a plane, or a solid) moves as a whole and not part of it at one time and part at another time (220a18–20).

10. By "things" here he means parts, or potential things.

11. For example, the line ABC, in which the parts AB and BC are straight lines forming an angle.

12. That is, one part of the leg may be moving while another part is resting.

13. By "a simultaneous motion" he means one motion as explained in 1016a6. If ABC moves about AB, AB is resting while BC is moving; but if it moves about, say, AC, the whole line ABC is moving. The motion of lines, however, is accidental; for, only bodies move, and lines move by being in bodies as attributes (1067b9–11).

14. For example, samples of wine from the same bottle would be one to sight or to taste.

15. The term "first" refers to the ultimate genus, such as the genus of liquids, but "last" refers to the ultimate species or kinds.

16. Wine is one, and water is one, but water and wine are two and not one.

17. Perhaps this is taken hypothetically, and this view was held by some; but his own view is complex and has many qualifications.

18. This sense of "one" is in a sense like the preceding, or analogous to it. Just as physical matter underlies different sensible qualities, so a genus somehow underlies the various differentiae.

19. For example, if A is the genus of the species X and Y, X the genus of the species x_1, x_2, etc., and Y the genus of y_1, y_2, etc., then any two x's (such as x_1 and x_2) are said to be the same A but not the same X, and any two y's (such as y_1 and y_2) are said to be the same A but not the same Y.

20. Such a formula is a definition.

21. That is, a formula qua a number of concepts (for example, genus and differentia) or parts of speech is divisible, but the essence signified by it is indivisible qua essence.

22. The ultimate species are meant. For example, if "scalene triangle"

is an ultimate species, then it is indivisible in the way stated. Thus, scalene triangles, whether small or large, are one in species, just as Socrates, whether he gains or loses weight, is one in formula.

23. Just as the ultimate species of substances are beings in the highest degree above all, so they are indivisible (or are one as stated) in the highest degree. If one thinks of each part of a substance at different times, then he does not think of the substance itself as one at any of those times, and so he does not think of the substance as one at all; and the same applies to "different places" and "different formulae".

24. This sense of "one" combines two previous senses, one by continuity and one in kind or in formula. For example, a piece of earth such as a rock is one by continuity, but one would hardly regard it as one in kind as he would regard a man; for part of a rock is still a rock, but part of a man is not a man. So a rock is like matter, or close to it, and its shape or form may vary and so is accidental to it (1040b5–8).

25. That is, the whole circular line, which we commonly call "circumference" or "circle".

26. That is, "one" in any of the preceding senses. Here, however, the one is further taken as a measure and a principle, without which a number cannot exist or be known, for a number is a number of ones or of units.

27. Probably a surface is meant. The term ἐπίπεδον has been used in these two senses.

28. An alternative to "according to species" is "according to kind". The term "kind" is wider than "species", but the same Greek word is used for both meanings.

29. That is, the underlying subject, like Socrates.

30. It is not clear whether "one in genus" refers to an ultimate genus (= a category, such as quantity, or quality, etc.) or to any genus of an ultimate species. In both cases, it is a matter of definition; the second alternative is more inclusive, but lines 1016b35–1017a1 suggest the first alternative.

31. Straightness and planeness are one by analogy, for straightness is to a line as planeness is to a surface. Similarly, sight is to the body as intellect is to the soul; and equality is to numbers as equality is to lines. Thus, "equality" is an analogous and not a univocal term (76a37–41, 1093b17–21, 1096b27–9).

32. Socrates is one numerically and also in species; Socrates and Plato are one in species but two numerically.

7

1. An alternative to "The term 'being' is used" is: "Things are said to be".

2. An accidental being is a being which is an accidental composite of two things.

3. The expression "the not-white is" is a sort of incomplete form

of "the not-white is a thing", and this is like "the musical is a man"; for just as the musical is an attribute of the man, so the privation not-white is a sort of attribute of the thing (assuming the thing exists and it is not white).

4. The word "is" in all these cases refers to the subject, of which the other or the others are attributes.

5. The various ways of predication are the kinds of predicates taken without reference to the subject. Thus, in "A is B", the part "is B" or "B" is a predicate. Linguistically, "is B" is often combined into one word, as for example "is walking" is combined into "walks", etc. In one sense, "whatness" is applied not only to substances but also to any *substance*. Thus, if one wishes to speak of the whiteness of an object and says "it is whiteness" or "it is a color", the terms "whiteness" and "a color" which he uses express the whatness of what he wishes to speak, yet they signify a quality as terms. And if one calls a line "straight", then this term signifies a quality (within the genus of quantity) of the line, yet the line is a quantity (103b27–39).

6. That is, true to say or to think that Socrates is musical.

7. That is, false to say, or to think, etc.

8. The line is a *substance* in one sense of "substance" (1017b17–20); moreover, if the potential line (or Hermes, in the case of the marble) is actualized, the original is destroyed, but not so in the case of that which sees or knows or rests potentially.

9. Book Θ, 1045b27–1051a33.

8

1. Generically, the simple bodies are earth, water, air, fire, ether; specifically, they are the species of these (268b26–29, 392a5–9).

2. The Sun, Moon, stars, etc. (1028b8–13, 1042a7–11).

3. This is the form of a body (the latter is a composite of matter and form, and each of these is a constituent of the composite).

4. This meaning of "substance" is close to the previous meaning; later, Aristotle will refute its application to planes, lines, points, and numbers as separable or separate substances, although they are *substances* in a qualified sense.

5. Platonists, Pythagoreans, Speusippus.

6. An alternative to "limit" is "define", and this is close to Plato's position.

7. This sense of "substance" is wide. Thus, we may speak of the *substance* of a man, or of a triangle, or of redness, or of things in other categories, and the definition "three-sided plane figure" signifies the *substance* of a triangle.

8. That is, two main senses.

9. What this ultimate subject happens to be, whether ultimate matter or a composite or something else, is to be investigated later, in Book Z.

10. That is, separable in formula or definition, for the form of an animal such as a horse is inseparable in existence. Perhaps the term "separable" is left hanging here, for the sake of agreeing with other thinkers, but with the intention of qualifying it later after further investigation into things.

9

1. The senses of "the same" by accident correspond to those of "one" by accident (1015b16–27).
2. That is, because of the fact that sameness here is accidental and not essential, and of the fact that what is accidental happens sometimes and not always.
3. That is, truly said.
4. Sameness is a relation of two things, as when we say "A is the same as B", but it is not necessarily so with oneness, as when we say "Socrates is one".
5. An alternative to "are affected" is "have been affected". An affection is a species of quality, admitting the more or the less, and can be easily acquired or lost by some subjects. For example, heat, blushing, sickness.
6. A quality need not be an affection, as in the case of the color of snow, a virtue, hotness in fire, etc.
7. Why is equality left out here? Perhaps because sameness is closest to substance, which is one primarily, and likeness, as an attribute of quality, is closer to substance than equality, which is an attribute of quantity. However, equality is considered in 1021a8–12.

10

1. That is, from which and to which things change; for example, black and white, not-man and man, bad and good, etc.
2. Grey is as if a blend of black and white, which are contraries; that is, it is somehow made out of these two, and lies between black and white. Thus, not only black and white, but also grey and white are said to be opposed, for they cannot belong to the same thing at the same time, etc.
3. For example, justice and injustice; the one is a virtue and so a good, the other a vice and so a bad, and good and bad are different genera (14a19–25). Different genera need not be in different categories.
4. For example, cowardice and rashness, blackness and whiteness in the genus "color".
5. Idiocy and wisdom in men, blackness and whiteness in a body or a surface.
6. Such for example are disease and health, which come under medical science.
7. Under the category "whereness" (or "in place"), the center of the

universe and its outer surface differ most without qualification, but the lowest and highest part of a tree differ most but only relatively because the lowest is nearest to the center and the highest is nearest to the outer surface of the universe.

8. That is, they can have contraries although they do not have them (perhaps by nature, as in the case of offspring which later acquire contrary attributes).

9. Fire can heat or is actually heating something, ice can cool or is cooling something, and likewise in the case of being affected or the capability of being affected.

10. Just as "one" and "being" have many senses, though all related to a primary sense, so "sameness" and "otherness" and "contrariety" have many senses. Thus, the odd and the even are contraries, and so are blackness and whiteness, yet they are called "contraries" not in the same sense but by analogy; for contrariety in the one case is in number, in the other it is in color, and numbers and colors come under distinct categories.

11. If X is the genus of A and B, and B the genus of b_1 and b_2, then A and B are other in kind, and so are A and b_1; but B and b_1 are not other in kind.

12. In the preceding, b_1 and b_2, or A and B, would be other in kind.

13. For example, water and earth are other in kind, for moisture and dryness are contraries and appear in the *substance* of water and earth respectively. An alternative to "contrariety" is "contrast".

14. Contraries in the primary sense are the first five types indicated.

15. The phrase "indivisible in genus" here probably means the thing cannot be subdivided as a genus is subdivided; perhaps "indivisible into other species" would be better.

16. Those things have the same *substance* or definition, or come under the same species, but they have accidents which are contraries. For example, hot and cold water, sick and healthy pigs, black and white men.

11

Priority and posteriority are discussed also in 14a26–b23.

1. The terms "nearer" and "farther" are not limited to quantity but extend analogously to all categories. Thus, if the white is taken as a principle (in quality), the light grey is prior to the dark grey and so is nearer to the white.

2. For Aristotle, the center and outer surface of the universe are definite and changeless, and as such they are principles by nature or without qualification. However, relative to the surface of the Earth (or some other place) there are the prior and posterior with respect to up and down; and if we posit as a principle some attribute in a man, such as justice for some reason, then the more just is prior to the less just man.

3. An alternative to "nearer" is "prior", and this is what other trans-

lators are using. Neither term appears in the Greek, although one of these two terms is implied; but I find it difficult to interpret "prior". If a man initiates an order, and the boy transmits it to somebody else or moves something else, then the boy is prior to the other person or object, and the man is a mover without qualification since no one moves him. Other interpretations are possible. By "first mover" he does not necessarily mean the prime mover or God.

4. Example (a) comes under the category of whereness, (b) under that of whenness, (c) under that of action, (d) under quality (power here is a quality), and (e) can be in any genus depending on what the formula is.

5. According to formula, all the indefinables, whether the ultimate genera or the ultimate differentiae, are prior without qualification for Aristotle. However, for the sake of the learner (1013a1–4), the things closer to sensation are prior in a qualified sense; thus, for very young learners, a sensible body is prior to a mathematical solid (71b33–72a5, 184a16–b14), since the latter is more abstract; and one may begin a science with undefined terms which may be definable, and then proceed to define the rest, but such terms are taken as principles in a qualified sense, for they can be defined.

The undefined terms in high school plane geometry, either most or all, would be principles in a qualified sense. According to Aristotle, an ideal science, that is, one in which all the first terms are indefinable and all knowledge is through the first causes, is very difficult (76a26–30).

6. Sensations are prior in time to universals, for the latter are acquired by abstraction from the former; similarly, the less universal is prior in time to the more universal.

7. An alternative to "accident" is "attribute".

8. We cannot *know* what a musical man is, or that X is a musical man, or the meaning of "a musical man", unless we *know* what musical is.

9. Musicality is an attribute which cannot exist separately, for it must be in a subject; but a subject can exist separately, as a man, and he need not be musical.

10. It is assumed here, but discussed elsewhere, that lines are prior in definition to surfaces.

11. An underlying subject need not be a substance; for example, straightness is an attribute of a line, and the latter is a subject relative to the former. But a line is a quantity, and so an attribute relative to a surface, and this relative to a body, which is a substance.

12. Perhaps the meaning is this: While the whole line (or any whole with parts) has actual existence, half of it does not have such existence (although it has another kind of existence, namely, potential), and so since the whole can have such existence without the part having it, the whole is prior to the part with respect to such existence. On the other

hand, the part has potential existence, and so it *can* be while the whole need not be; and this happens when the whole is cut into halves. For then the part actually exists while the whole does not so exist. In other words, the part has the potentiality of actual existence at a time when the whole does not have it, and so with respect to such potentiality the part is prior.

13. That is, priority in existence, in the sense of actual and potential.

14. That is, they can exist actually while the parts do not so exist. But, one may say, the part actually exists as a part; but this is a misuse of the word "actually", for then both part and whole would exist actually, and the distinction between their kinds of existence would be lost.

15. That is, similarly for senses (1), (2), and (3). For example, while the prior event is actually existing, the posterior is not; actual knowledge of musicality can exist without actual knowledge of a musical man; and actual knowledge of straightness can exist without actual knowledge of planeness. (We often define a plane surface in terms of a straight line, but not conversely, for otherwise we would have a circular definition.)

12

1. For idiomatic purposes, the word δύναμις is translated as "potency", "power", "capacity", "ability", "capability", or "potentiality". Likewise, δυνατόν is translated as "capable", "able", or "possible", and its opposite as "incapable", "unable", or "impossible".

2. That is, the principle of being acted upon, either well or according to *choice*. This sense differs from sense (2) in this, that while a thing in sense (2) can be moved or changed (whether in any way or for the better), in this sense it is disposed to change for the better. For example, one man may be curable with difficulty or with average means, but another may be easily curable or completely because of some potency or principle in his nature.

3. The capable is that which has a potency; for example, the doctor is capable in view of the fact that he has the medical art (which is a potency). But that which has such a potency is a substance, like the doctor.

4. What brings about rest has a principle of changing another (from motion to rest) and not necessarily of moving another.

5. Perhaps the term ἄλλο (= "another") should be ἄλλῳ (= "by another"), although both would give the same meaning if the sentence is translated properly in each case.

6. That is, so affected as to be destroyed.

7. That is, capable of being affected.

8. That is, deprived of something by which it would resist being so affected.

9. That is, it will mean *having something*, but not univocally, for it will have two senses: *having a possession,* and *not having* (or, being deprived of) *a possession.*

10. This amounts to having a potency which resists the destruction of the thing. This potency is potency in sense (5).

11. In other words, a thing is capable in any of the preceding senses either if it is capable just as stated without qualification, or with the qualification that it has the potency of acting or of being affected well.

12. In this sense, "incapable of seeing" is predicated equally of blind men and of stones.

13. A child is incapable of begetting in the sense that he is *not yet* capable but he will be later; in the case of a man, he is incapable temporarily for some reason, such as being sick; a eunuch is permanently incapable, although by nature he should be capable, for he lost that capability because it was removed and cannot be replaced.

14. That is, the contrary of "it cannot be" is "it must be", for these two are furthest apart. What is possible lies somehow between what is always and what is never.

15. More than that, it is necessarily false; and this is what he means.

16. The Greek text reads ἐναντίον, which means contrary, but this he cannot mean; it should be "contradictory", for the contrary of the impossible is the necessary (1019b23–6).

17. The contrary of "it is possible to be" is "it is possible not to be", and each implies the other. Perhaps "subcontrary" is better.

18. Perhaps "true but not of necessity" would be better, although the one implies the other.

19. The dialectical argument may be: what is, is possible, for if impossible (principle of excluded middle), "what is" would be false. However, this leads to the following difficulty (unless we assume "possible" here to have a different meaning): what is necessary also exists, what exists is possible to be, what is possible to be is also possible not to be; hence, what necessarily exists is also possible not to exist, and this is a contradiction.

20. Perhaps "X may be true" means: Although X is not necessarily true, no contradiction arises if X is posited as true (32a18–20).

21. For example, in a square of unit side, the diagonal is a *power* with respect to the side. In Greek, this means that the area whose side is the diagonal is commensurate with the area of the square. In general, A is a power relative to B if A^2 and B^2 are measurable by a common unit. For example, $\sqrt{2}$ is a power relative to 1 or to $\sqrt{7}$.

22. That is, "possible" and "impossible" as used in the preceding paragraph apply to propositions (in the mind, or as spoken or written) and to geometry, but not to what has or has not a potency as formulated earlier.

23. This is potency in sense (1).

24. Perhaps "of changing another thing" rather than "of change in another thing" is better, for this would indicate the moving cause more explicitly.

13

1. "Quantity" is a category, and so indefinable; so this must be considered not as a definition but as an explanatory formula, or a property. One may note the metaphysical terms in that formula.

2. "Either" is used when a quantity, such as 2, is divided into two parts, but "each" when divided into more than two parts.

3. That is, the constituents are not matter and form, but parts as matter which, after division, are actual unities. For example, after division, such are the parts of a body, and of a line or a surface, and of a number.

4. The sense of "dimension" here is somewhat wider than that of "perpendicular direction". A surface need not be plane to be divided in two dimensions.

5. The terms "a body" and "a solid" are often used synonymously.

6. That is, it is present as a genus, for it might also be present otherwise.

7. By "*attribute*" here he means what may or may not be truly said of a quantity, by "possession", what must be. Thus, "fewness" may or may not be a predicate of 20, for 20 is few relative to 1,000 but not few relative to 3. But in a triangle, two right angles is a possession, for the sum of the angles must be equal to two right angles.

8. The terms "much", "little", and the others that follow appear as derivative terms, but as signifying attributes they should be given as nouns, such as "muchness", "littleness", "longness", "shortness", etc.

9. For example, 2 is a small number in virtue of itself, as there is no lesser number (220a27), and the magnitude of the universe is likewise great, as there is no greater magnitude (207b15–21); but 20 is great (or greater) in relation to 5, and small in relation to 1,000.

10. For example, we speak of great and small honors, but honor is a quality (1308b13–14).

11. For example, whiteness is in a surface, which is a quantity (1022a16–17), and that which is musical may be a body.

12. If body X moves from A to C, then just as the distance AC is divisible, say into AB and BC, so is the motion into that from A to B, and that from B to C. As for time, if one circular motion of the universe about the earth is taken as a unit, which we may call "a day", then ten such motions would be a number of motions, or time.

Motion is also divisible in another way, with respect to the moving body. Just as body X is divisible into parts, say P and Q and R, so there is a motion of P, a motion of Q, and a motion of R (234b21–27).

14

Qualities are discussed also in the Categories, 8b25–11b7.

1. That is, the *substance* or essence of a thing in any category.

2. "Non-angular" is not the complete differentia of a circle; it is given here only as an illustration, or as part of the complete differentia. The same applies to the differentia of a man or a horse.

3. Aristotle is thinking of the Pythagoreans and Plato's school.

4. The term "composite" here is used in the mathematical sense.

5. The terms "one-dimensional", "plane", and "solid", are predicates of lines, surfaces, and solids, respectively, and they are predicates of numbers (prime, composite with two factors, and composite with three factors, respectively) only by imitation. Thus, "a plane number" means a number with two factors only, such as 15, which is 3 times 5.

6. Perhaps the meaning is this: Although six is measured also by 2, and by 3, 2 and 3 are in no way a part of the *substance* of six; for, six has a unity of its own. It is a quantity, but it is also *such* a quantity; and "*such*" (whatever this may be) indicates its differentia or quality.

7. That is, quality in sense (2).

8. For Aristotle, mathematical *substances* are not in motion; but for some others, like the Pythagoreans and the later Plato, sensible objects are numbers and in motion. Here, Aristotle leaves the issue unsettled, but he settles it in Book M.

9. Two kinds of qualities are indicated, affections and differentiae of motion, and the latter exist when the former are actualized. For example, cowardice exists in a cowardly man even when sleeping, but the actual running away is a motion, the differentia of which is a quality.

10. The highest good among animals is happiness, a certain kind of *chosen* activity which can exist only in men and is an end in itself.

15

Relative terms (or relations) are discussed also in 6a36–8b24, and in 1056b3–1057a17.

1. This last sense is the most general, a sort of genus of all the others.

2. That is, the number 2. The double of 5 is 10. Thus, given a number (or the unit itself), its double is definite. The relation here is 2 : 1, which is definite, although the two numbers so related need not be definite, unless one of them is.

3. The multiple of a unit may be 3, or 4, or etc.

4. The numerical relation of a superparticular to its subparticular is the ratio $(n + 1) : n$, where n is a whole number. For example, relative to 8 there are many superparticulars, such as 9 and 10 and 12, in the ratio 9 : 8 and 5 : 4 and 3 : 2, respectively.

5. The ratio of that which exceeds to that which is exceeded (the greater : the less) may not be as a number to a number, as in the case

of the diagonal to the side of a square, which are incommensurable magnitudes. That which exceeds to that which is exceeded need not be stated as a ratio; for it may be stated by indicating by how much the first exceeds the second.

6. Moderns might wonder why the equals, like the double and the half, do not come under a ratio, that is, 1 : 1. Such a ratio is a technical device and not a philosophical distinction; it is like calling a unit "a number" instead of "a measure" or "principle of a number". Modern mathematicians wrongly criticize the ancient Greeks for saying that *one* is not a number; the Greeks were not using "number" in the same sense, and operationally they were applying the axioms to units as well as to numbers.

7. This is the unity which is considered as a unit–a principle and a measure of a number. What can be a measure is a thing and so has unity.

8. He may be referring to a work that is lost. The objects of mathematics are immovable, for they result by removing in thought the principles of motion from physical things. Thus, such objects have no potencies which can be *actualized;* but possible relations among them are found by the activity of thought (1051a21–33, 1077b17–1078a31).

9. To know 6 as a double, one must also know that of which it is the double, namely, 3; and similarly for 3 as a half; and to know that which can heat as such, one must also know that it can heat something which can be heated. Thus, in the whatness of such relatives, reference must be made to something else. In the case of knowledge, although its whatness must make reference to the object known, the whatness of that object (of a triangle, for example) does not make reference to the knowledge of it. A color is similarly related to its sensation. Further, an object may exist without its knowledge, and a color without its sensation, but not conversely.

Some objections may be raised. Like a color, 6 itself is a nature but is not a relative, and so is 3; and what can heat is a substance, like fire, and similarly for that which can be heated. However, perhaps unlike the sensible, which is a color and so a nature under a genus other than "relation", sensation does not seem to be a thing under some other genus. Is it not a quality? Knowledge is considered to be a disposition or a habit, and these are qualities (8b25–29, 11a20–38). But can any knowledge, like that of a triangle, be defined without reference to the triangle? The triangle, on the other hand, can be defined without reference to the knowledge of it.

The account on relatives here differs a little from that given in the *Categories* (6a36–8b24).

10. In stating the whatness of sight, we do not say "sight is of that of which it is the sight". This is true as a statement, but it is circular as a definition, and so it does not state the whatness.

11. It appears that the term "science" by itself signifies a relative, but

that "science of health", which includes the object to which science refers, signifies a power which is a quality. Thus, a genus and its species
need not be under the same category. There seems to be a problem
(11a20–38).

12. The distinction here is between a subject and an attibute of it.
Thus, just as the derivative term "white" signifies a subject (a body)
with whiteness, so "the equal" signifies a quantity, say a square, with
an equality (when related to a rectangle with equal area for example).
Perhaps we should call the equal "a relative", and equality "a relation".

16

1. Perfection with respect to the quantity of parts is indicated in
sense (1).

2. Perfection of power or quality is indicated in sense (2).

3. The term "magnitude" here is metaphorically used (1020a23–6).

4. This sense seems to apply to the actuality or activity of a power,
if this is good. For example, the perfection of a man is not complete
virtue but the exercise of it, which is happiness.

5. The term τέλειον (= "perfect") and τελευτή (= "death") have
τέλος (= "the end") as their root.

17

1. Of a triangle, the first part is its three sides, of a line it is its end-
points, and of a time, it is its first and last moment.

2. In going somewhere to collect the debt, collecting the debt is the
end, and in walking to the park to watch a game, watching the game is
the end.

3. Perhaps the shape of a man is a limit but not a principle, if it does
not appear in his definition which indicates all four causes or principles.

18

1. Other synonyms are: "that with respect to which", "that according to which", "that in which", "that by which", "essentially".

2. Color is also said to be in the body, but the first thing is the
surface (which is in the body) and not the body in which color resides;
that is, it is in virtue of the surface that color is in the body.

3. This sense is idiomatic in Greek.

4. The definition of a man as "two-footed animal", perhaps current
at the time, is given as an illustration; it is not Aristotle's definition.

5. This includes the properties. For example, two right angles belong to a triangle in virtue of itself; and capability of learning grammar belongs to man in virtue of himself, for no other animal has such
capability.

6. For, being apart from the rest, it has attributes which are not

possessed by anything else. In English, the phrase "by itself" here is more idiomatic than "in virtue of itself".

19

1. For example, we may speak of the disposition of the universe with respect to its parts (spheres).
2. For example, the king is prior to all in a kingdom, then comes his immediate subordinate, etc.
3. For example, the order of the parts of the soul are vegetative, sensitive, rational, if priority of existence is the principle, but the reverse, if priority of dignity or of *substance* is the principle.
4. The term "position" here is used in a wide sense, perhaps analogously; it is not restricted to place.

20

1. The word "has" here means wears, not just owns, for if the garment is in the closet, there is no having.
2. The argument is this: Let A be that which has, B be that which is had, and H the having between A and B. If H can be had, let A (or something else) have H. Then there is a having, say H_1, between A and H. Similarly, there is an H_2 between A and H_1. This goes on to infinity.
3. For example, health is a disposition of a man in himself, but physical strength is a disposition which he has in relation to heavy objects.
4. For example, quickness in thinking or mathematical ability is a disposition of a part of the soul, the rational part or a part of the rational part.

21

1. For example, in the case of sickness, the alteration towards sickness is said to be an affection, and the existence or *actuality* of that sickness is also said to be an affection.
2. Aristotle does not mention the *actualities;* so either they are included although not mentioned, or the phrase "Of the latter" refers only to the alterations in (2).
3. Nothing is said here about the other meaning of the term πάθος, that is, of *attribute*.

22

Privation is discussed also in 12a26–13b27, 1046a31–35, 1055a33–b29.
1. The word "or" has the force of "and/or".
2. In the Greek, "*un*" and "*in*" and "*im*" and "*less*" are rendered by the prefix "*a*".

3. This is because he is not deprived of all goodness or badness but only of some.

23

"To have" is also discussed in the *Categories*, 15b17–33.

1. That is, as a subject (in a wide sense) has an attribute or form.

2. Each part is a part of the whole, but the liquid is not a part of the vessel unless "vessel" includes in its meaning the liquid; so in a sense there is a difference, unless by "whole" he means the form (as he occasionally uses the term in this sense).

3. This may refer to Empedocles and some others, who say that the fast circular motion of the heavens prevents it from falling to the earth (284a24–26, 295a16–19).

4. For example, the water in a vessel is continuous, but it would be dispersed if the vessel breaks.

5. That is, in general, if A *has* B, then B *is in* A.

24

For further discussion of "to be from something" see 724a17–30, 994a22–b3, 1044a23–25, 1092a23–35.

1. I shall also use "to come from", "to be made out of", "to be formed from", "to be composed of", and "to be by" as translations of ἔκ τινος εἶναι.

2. That is, the highest material genus.

3. This is Plato's position (*Timaeus* 58D) and in some sense Aristotle's (382b28).

4. In generation, matter takes on a form, and the result is a composite; in destruction, the form is lost and the result is the parts as matter.

5. That is, from "two-footed" as well as from "animal".

6. The concept of man comes from other concepts as parts just as the definition of a man has parts, and the syllable (as well as its definition) comes from its letters (1034b25).

7. In the statue which is a composite, the bronze is sensible matter; but the letters in a syllable are analogously called "matter", and so is "animal" from which as matter (or something indeterminate) comes "man".

8. The principles of such changes are matter and the contraries (or, matter, form, and privation). See 188a19–192b4.

25

The senses of "a part" are considered also in 1034b32-1035b7.

1. Perhaps "in some sense" is used to indicate that two is not a part of three in sense (2).

2. For example, each of the factors of 30 (such as 1, 2, 3, 5, etc.) but not 30 itself, is in this sense a part of 30.

3. This is not quantitative division; "division" has more than one meaning.

4. If just the form of the bronze cube is taken as a whole, then an angle of that form (the cubical shape) or of a square face of it is a part of that form or of the square face.

5. For example, "animal" is a part of "man".

6. It is a part in sense (3).

26

1. The phrase "some one thing" may mean either that (a) each of what is contained is one, or (b) each of what is contained comes under one and the same genus. The example given typifies (b).

2. The wider meaning of "animal" includes God (122b12–4, 1088a10–1). Perhaps "living being" is better, but plants are excluded.

3. Can that which is one by continuity be actually many? Two men glued together are one by continuity, but actually two substances; they are actually two by nature, but continuously one by art or something like it. This is indicated by the sentence which follows.

4. That is, possible in different respects, as the ensuing examples show.

5. For example, "all men are mortal" means that each man is mortal.

27

1. This is a continuous whole and so has magnitude.

2. If one or more units are removed, the number is destroyed and a different number results.

3. Five is divisible into two and three as its parts, and these are unlike.

4. A main part is such that its removal destroys the *substance* of the whole.

5. For what results cannot hold the liquid, and so it is no longer a cup.

6. The term φαλακρός usually means bald, and sometimes it means shaven; here it probably means shaven, for this seems to be more in accord with what preceded.

We may summarize the formula thus: A mutilated thing is one which is a continuous whole with unlike parts, having lost one or more parts which cannot grow again but which did not change the *substance* of the thing. The term "whole" in this formula includes the fact that the parts have position, for the term "whole" is used here in sense (3).

28

1. An alternative to "a continuous generation of things" may be: "things whose generation is continuous".

2. More accurately, "A race (in the first sense) named after their first mover". Of course, this mover himself had a mover, but *he* is the mover of those named after him.

3. For (according to Aristotle), the male supplies the form, and the female the matter (988a2–7, 1044a34–5).

4. The term "genus" here signifies the underlying subject of the thing itself, but in the next sense, sense (4), it signifies a certain term in the whatness, whether this term be vocal, written, or a concept in the mind.

5. A genus in senses (3) and (4) acts as underlying subject or matter, but analogously.

6. By "first" he probably means the ultimate or most generic, but univocally generic.

7. "To analyze" here means probably "to have" or "to lead back". Thus, a square is analyzed into a quadrilateral (as its genus), and both into a plane or a surface as their ultimate genus. Not so with "whiteness" and "a number", for they come, say, under "quality" and "quantity", which are unanalyzable categories.

8. Evidently, from what has been said, "genus" in "other in genus" is not restricted to a category. This is the wider sense of "genus".

9. 1017a24–27.

29

1. The phrase "a false fact" in a sense (a) is like "a dead man" (21a21–24); for just as a dead man is not a man, neither is a false fact a fact. It is nonbeing, and in two ways: first, like what we may call "a number which is both odd and even", which can never be; second, like what is signified by "Socrates sits at such-and-such a time", when he is actually standing. In other words, a false fact is an alleged unity of two objects, but no such unity exists.

2. In sense (b), a false fact is a fact or a being, but not what it appears to be; for example, a statue of Socrates may be painted so realistically that it is easily mistaken for Socrates, and Socrates may or may not exist.

3. The term "formula" here may signify a definition or a proposition, whether spoken, written, or in the soul.

4. A formula by itself may have only the potentiality of being true or false; it is when applied to something that it is actually true or false. The phrase "qua false" probably indicates that it is actually applied to a certain thing, but falsely.

5. This formula would be the definition (1031a11–14), which is unique for each thing.

6. Such a formula would be a proposition or its equivalent. If we say "Socrates is musical", it is a proposition; if we say that "musical Socrates" is a predicate of Socrates, then "musical Socrates" is the equivalent. Of Socrates, there are many formulae such as "musical Socrates", for Socrates has many attributes.

7. Such formula would be false regardless of the thing to which it

is applied, like the formula "a number which is both odd and even", which formula always signifies nonbeing.

8. That is, since a formula can be false in senses 2(a) and 2(b), Antisthenes was naive on both counts.

9. For example, when we say "Socrates sits" when he is standing.

10. When a thing is called by a false formula in sense 2(b).

11. This refutes Antisthenes by showing that a thing can be truly called not only by its definition, but also by an attribute or a property; for also "double of 4" is a predicate and so a formula of 8.

12. One might tell a falsehood by *choice* to prevent a calamity, but this is not telling a falsehood for its own sake.

13. Perhaps "readily or by *choice*" is implied, for one may create a false impression by accident.

14. Such a man is able to speak both truly and falsely; hence, the argument goes, he is both true and false.

30

1. That is, it comes from the latter as from a moving cause, and after the latter in the temporal sense. For Aristotle, night comes after day of necessity, and the prime mover causes motion of necessity.

2. That is, the accident belongs to the subject not qua the subject's nature or what the subject *chose* to do, but because (a moving cause) of the storm or the pirates, and causes such as the latter are indefinite in the sense that they are not of one kind.

3. Such attributes may be properties which follow from the thing's nature, or properties of some genus of that thing. In the case of the two right angles, we have a property of the triangle, but the equality of the external angles to four right angles is just an attribute of the triangle, for it can also belong to a quadrilateral and to some other figures.

4. The use of "may" rather than "must" is justified by such cases as capability of learning grammar for men. A defect at birth or a mental injury later may prevent one from learning grammar, even if this is a property of a man by nature. But a triangle of necessity has its angles equal to two right angles, and in general, what exists eternally or is immovable has attributes which are eternal.

5. In many places, such as in *Posterior Analytics,* 71a1–100b17, and elsewhere.

Book E

1

1. These are the theoretical sciences, whose end is *knowledge* for its own sake.

2. The practical and productive sciences require *thought* or *knowledge* to some extent, but this is for the sake of individual *action* or production of individual objects.

3. A science is more accurate (a) if it requires fewer principles (fewer as against additional), or (b) if its terms are more abstract, whether these be more universal, as "quantity" is more universal than "magnitude" (and in this case the science of quantity is said to be more accurate than that of magnitude), or whether they are obtained by isolating in thought what is combined in reality, as a surface is isolated from a solid or a body (and in this case the science of surfaces is said to be more accurate than that of solids or of bodies), or (c) if it is concerned with the facts and their causes, as against the facts alone. See 87a31–37, 982a25–28, 1078a9–28.

4. When completeness is lost, by the omission of causes or distinctions or of whatever makes a science complete, the result is what he calls "a simplified science".

5. The study of unqualified being is the same as that of a part of being qua being. For example, the attributes of a square qua quadrilateral are identical with the properties of a quadrilateral, and the attributes of a quantity (which is a part of being) qua being are identical with those of being qua being.

6. For example, sensation in the science of colors, hypothesis in arithmetic or geometry (76a31–36).

7. The induction is this: just as these sciences do not demonstrate the whatness or the *substance* of their subject, so no other science does; but there is another way of revealing, though not demonstrating, these.

8. Examples of a productive science are the science of making cars, or chairs, or steel, or houses; and of a practical science, ethics and politics.

9. The moving principle is meant.

10. That which is done is not something outside the man, like a car or a chair, but an *action,* which is in the man himself, and an *action* is *chosen;* and what is *chosen* is an *action.*

11. The end of a theoretical science is *knowledge* for its own sake, of a productive science it is knowledge for the sake of things produced, and of a practical science it is knowledge for the sake of *action* (993b19–23, 1140a1–23).

12. These are physical substances qua in motion.

13. Of course, physical substances are separate. But *"substance"* applies to the form of such substances and also to the essence of physical attributes, and all these cannot be separated from or be defined without sensible matter. The term "non-separable" may also mean non-separable from sensible matter.

14. The study of most of the soul comes under physics. In animals, the parts of the soul do not exist apart from sensible matter, and these parts are also in men. It is only the active intellect in men that can exist apart (403a16–28, 413b24–27, 736b27–29, 1070a24–27).

15. These are arithmetic and geometry, but not astronomy, optics, or harmonics (194a7–12, 997b15–21), and their objects are investigated qua separate in thought.

16. These are physical substances, which have matter and are separable or separate.

17. Or separate. The composite substances (matter and form) are meant.

18. Quantities qua such are immovable but, somehow, in physical substances. The term "some immovable things" excludes the objects of astronomy, optics, etc., and the word "perhaps" suggests that the problem will be discussed and settled later, in Books M and N.

19. First or highest causes are meant (994a1–b31).

20. These are the immovable movers, which move the spheres (1072a19–1073b17).

21. The Sun, Moon, stars, etc.

22. "Theology" comes from θεῖος (= "divine") and λόγος (= "the study of"). So it means the study of divine things.

23. What is here regarded as divine is eternal and honorable.

24. 981b27–982a3, 982b24–983a11.

25. The term "universal" here signifies a science whose objects are in distinct genera, or even in distinct categories; and in this case their treatment would be analogical, as in the case of logic and universal mathematics.

26. Geometry is concerned with magnitudes, astronomy with divine bodies in the heavens; universal mathematics, on the other hand, is concerned with all quantities, but analogically. The axiom "Equals result if equals are added to equals" is one by analogy, for lines must be added to lines, surfaces to surfaces, numbers to numbers, etc. (76a37–b2).

27. Perhaps he means this: by being first, it is universal in the manner in which universal mathematics, which is prior (at least in *knowledge*), is universal.

28. At first, this science would investigate also the senses of "being" or of "*substance*", their relations if any, and what belongs to all beings universally but in an analogical sense. Such, for example, would be the investigation of essence, definition, contrariety, and the like, and in this respect it would be like universal mathematics. See Comm. 7 in Book K, Section 7, 1064b13.

2

1. 1017a7–b9.

2. For example, one triangle may be of bronze, another wooden, a third to the right of some object; but these are accidental to the triangle. The geometer investigates the attributes belonging to the triangle qua triangle.

3. This problem is not geometrical, and the geometer may investigate this problem qua a philosopher, but then he is by accident a philosopher.

4. *Sophist,* 254A.

5. If they are the same, then what is musical should be grammatical; but the musical is not always grammatical. If distinct, then the musical cannot be grammatical; but sometimes it is. Hence, a paradox. Similarly for Coriscus and musical Coriscus. Other paradoxes arise if distinctions are confused.

6. It is easy to manufacture many sophistical arguments here, but the one hinted is not fully stated.

7. Perhaps the meaning is this: If A is accidentally B, then A is followed by B only occasionally, and since most of the time the sequence AB (this is accidental being) does not exist, AB is somewhat close to nonbeing.

8. If A and B are contraries, and S the subject, it is S which is becoming B from A. For example, it is a man who becomes grammatical from ungrammatical. If the musical becomes grammatical, it is by accident, for it is the man and not the musical that is becoming grammatical. There is a gradual change in the man from being ungrammatical to being grammatical; but the musical does not change, for attributes as such do not change. Thus, the change from the musical to the musical and grammatical is sudden (4a10–b19).

9. If event A happens for the most part, it follows that sometimes A does not happen; so its happening for the most part causes (perhaps as a formal cause) its occasional non-happening (which is an accident).

10. That is, the kind of food which the doctor prescribes for the sick.

11. In some of them it is art, in others it is nature. Nature sometimes fails, and then art imitates nature, so to speak, as in health.

12. That is, matter is a material cause.

13. The facts confirm this. Also, if there exist events which happen for the most part, then sometimes they do not so happen, and what fails to happen only sometimes is by definition accidental.

14. God is eternal, the motion of the heavens is eternal, the angle bisectors of a triangle always meet at a point, etc.

15. 1071b3–1074b14.

16. If "A is B" is true for the most part, and if one knows definitely the conditions (let us call them "C") under which "A is not B" is true, then "AB(C)" (= "A is B, when C is not") and "AB(C)" (= "A is not B, when C is") are always true. If the C's for all cases at all times are known by someone, perhaps God, then is accidental being eliminated? Evidently, AB still happens sometimes, and by definition it is an accident; so the fact that AB(C) happens always does not destroy the accidental nature of AB. Of course, we prefer to know AB(C) and AB(C) as happening always rather than AB as happening for the most part, but this is another matter. But, we should add, C is not necessarily something simple; it may vary from individual to individual and may perhaps be infinite; it is connected with what goes by the name of "the initial conditions" of our world. Thus, "AB(C)", and also "AB(C)", is equivocal and may not even

be expressible or knowable, but "AB for the most part" is knowable. For example, if A cures men suffering from B for the most part, the conditions under which A will not cure may be variable and a great many, and "C" has the form of "C_1 or C_2 or C_3 or . . .".

3

Accidental causation and chance are discussed at length in the *Physics*, 195b31–198a13.

1. If every B is caused by an A of necessity, then B is not an accident; and neither is A, for A itself is likewise caused. This is so for every case. So everything exists of necessity. But this is not so. Hence, not every cause if of necessity. Such causes come into existence and pass out of existence instantaneously; they are not in the process of becoming or of being destroyed.

2. One may deny this, for a time interval is infinitely divisible. On the other hand, an effect B cannot be caused by a sequence of causes ad infinitum (994a1–b31), so there must be a first cause, and this exists at some moment, whether past, present, or future (and in this case the effect must be in the future).

3. The presence of contraries in the human body necessitates its destruction at some future time, but the manner of its destruction varies and is caused by accidents.

4

1. The combinations and divisions here are those of the soul; they are affections of the soul or of thought. As symbols of these, they take on the form of vocal or written propositions, such as "A is B" or "A is not B". But these are posterior to and for the sake of the former (16a3–13, 1028a1).

2. For example, in thinking that Socrates is sitting, we are thinking of sitting Socrates as one thing, not now of Socrates and then of sitting.

3. 1011b25–28, 1051a34–b17.

4. For example, in *thinking* that seven is odd, such *thought* is true. But this presupposes that we have a thought of seven and also of oddness; and each of these thoughts is not of things combined or divided, and so it is neither true nor false. Accurately speaking, we either have a thought of seven or we do not have it, and to say that there is truth when we have it is to use "truth" in another sense.

5. 1051a34–1052a11.

6. The subject here may be under any category.

7. The term "whatness" refers to the definition or to a genus of the thing. For example, one may give the definition of three, or say that it is an odd number or just a number.

8. Things as such should be considered first, for they are prior in

existence and in definition to thoughts and accidents. A thought is about a thing or things, and not all things are thoughts; and an accident, such as sick Socrates, presupposes sickness as such and Socrates as such, which are not accidents.

Book Z

1

1. 1017a7–b9.

2. The whatness of a thing is contrasted with its quality, or its quantity, or its place, etc.; and we know the thing to a higher degree or more fully if we know its whatness than if we know its quantity or its quality or etc. For example, we know a thing more or more fully if we call it "a man" than if we call it "heavy". The term "a *this*" signifies an obvious unity and separateness of the thing. For example, a man is obviously one and is separate, but his color or height or motion does not appear to have these attributes.

3. The term "three cubits long" indicates a quantity, as distinguished from a quality indicated by "good" or "bad".

4. That is, if unity and separateness belong to being, then since walking and sitting and health seem to lack unity and separateness, one may wonder whether they are beings at all, or beings in the same sense.

5. The term "that which sits" or "sitter" includes in its meaning a substance, although without specifying it.

6. That is, the others, if existing at all, exist in substances as aspects or parts or attributes, and if substances did not exist, neither would they. For example, if Socrates is sick, his sickness is an attribute of him; but he may exist without being sick.

7. Using an analogy or proportion, a qualified being is to a being without qualification as a part is to a whole, or as what is partial to what is full. For example, the height of a man is a sort of part or aspect of the whole man.

8. This is priority in time. If sickness (which is an attribute) exists, a substance must exist, but the converse is not necessarily true. In time, an attribute never comes to exist before the substance in which it exists, but the converse may be true (260b16–19, 1019a1–6).

9. A formula or definition must signify what is defined; so if to understand an attribute is to know it as something which exists in or is caused by a substance, then the formula or definition of that substance must be included in that of the attribute.

10. This priority of knowledge is with respect to the degree or fullness of knowing something. To say that X is a man is to have more or fuller knowledge of X than to say that X is white.

11. Even of what is not a substance, in asking "What is a triangle?", for example, we know more if we are told "It is a three-sided plane figure", which signifies its whatness, than if we are told "It has altitudes", which is a possession, or if we are told "Its area is smaller than that of the square on its largest side", which is a relation.

12. For Parmenides or Zeno, it is one in number; for Thales, it is one in kind (983b20).

13. For Empedocles, it is four in kind (984a8).

14. For Anaxagoras, it is infinite in kind (984a11–16).

2

1. These may be Pythagoreans (some or all), or Platonists (some or all), or both. See 1002a4–12, 1090b5–8.

2. Physical philosophers, and perhaps the Pythagoreans (989b29–990a5, 1002a8–11).

3. Platonists, Speusippus, perhaps others.

4. That is, many in kind.

5. 1075b37–1076a4, 1076a21–22.

6. Xenocrates and his followers. 1086a5–10, 1090b20–32.

7. Non-sensible substances do not exist apart from sensible substances, according to Eudoxus (991a14–18, 1079b18–22).

3

1. Surfaces and lines and points and numbers are also said by some to be substances (1017b17–21); however, this sense of "substance" is excluded here but will be considered in Books M and N.

2. Or *substance.*

3. That is, the subject is not said of something else essentially, for it may be said of something else accidentally, as in the accidental predication "This is Socrates" and "The white is Socrates".

4. X may be a subject relative to Y but an attribute relative to Z. Thus, whiteness is a subject relative to color but it itself is an attribute of a body. But the subject, as he has defined it, is not in anything else, and so it is the starting-point of predication.

5. That is, the material of the statue, excluding its *form.*

6. Evidently, "*form*" and "form" here seem to be used synonymously.

7. Of the kinds of priority (1018b11–1019a14), the one meant is not indicated here, although Aristotle said something earlier (1028a32–3). Perhaps priority in formula or in *knowledge* or in both is meant, since Aristotle is concerned with the meaning of "substance" and our *knowledge* of what is signified; but priority in existence is also possible. In any of the senses, if form is prior to matter, it would be prior also to the composite. For example, form can exist without matter, as in the prime mover, but matter is always with some form. Of course, his inquiry into these is dialectical at this stage.

8. The statement is not specific enough; it is somewhat like the formula of an element (1052b7–15).

9. Just as color belongs primarily to a surface, and living primarily to a soul, so geometrical quantities belong primarily to bodies, and bodies by being separate are substances to a higher degree.

10. Its being is just a potency of taking on those others.

11. The word "predicate", if applied both to a substance and to matter as the subject, is not univocally used, but probably analogously. In "Socrates is white", Socrates is the subject, and both Socrates and whiteness come under a category, so one category is a predicate of another; but in "*substance* is a predicate of matter", matter does not come under any category at all.

12. Whether by "substance" here he means the form or the composite is not clear. Perhaps he means the form, or *substance*, which is distinct from matter but exists with matter as if a predicate of it. The argument may be just dialectical.

13. The denials referred to here are probably privations like those stated in 1022b32–36. In a sense, such privations are possessions (1019b6–10); or else, privations and possessions are two contraries under a category. Since matter does not come under a category but is only a potentiality for both, it does not have qua matter by itself a possession or its privation. So, although "matter is not A" is true, where A comes under a category, "matter is not-A" is false, since not-A is a privation. Further, if matter qua matter were not-A, then when it takes on A it would have both A and not-A (qua matter), and this is impossible. An alternative to "accidentally" is "as an attribute".

14. Certainly the *composite* is separate and a *this;* as for the form, it is more of a *this* and more separate or separable than matter, although this requires investigation. For one thing, the form is separable in thought and definable (193b3–5, 1042a26–31, 1070a13–18). The existence of separate forms will be considered in 1071b3–1076a4.

15. Being a composite of two principles, matter and form, it is (for one thing) posterior in *knowledge* or in formula to each of them.

16. For one thing, it is evident by analogy (191a7–12).

17. The term "substances" here means essences or forms. Since the discussion now turns to essences, and essences are more known to us in sensible things than as separate by themselves (the eternal movers), and since knowledge proceeds from what is better known to us to what is better known by nature (that is, the order desired is psychological rather than logical), essences which exist in sensible objects will be considered first.

18. Perhaps this is what seems to be good, or good for a certain time, or place, or good in some narrow sense. But that which is good in general is that which leads to virtue and so to happiness.

19. For example, to know a book slightly is to know its color and size, without knowledge of its contents. But then, what is known is accidental and close to nonbeing.

4

1. 1028b33–36. From what has just been said, "essence" would seem to mean form.

2. By "logical remarks" he probably means what is said about essence, whether dialectically or by way of introducing essence.

3. In other words, what the thing is in itself, or when stated by itself. Thus, accidents and properties are excluded from the essence, although they may belong to the thing having that essence.

4. "To be a surface" and "the essence of a surface" are used synonymously. In general, "to be" and "the essence of" will have the same meaning when followed by the same term.

5. The two examples given help one understand what essence is not. Socrates is still Socrates whether he is musical or not; so such an accident is no part of his essence. Neither is the essence of a surface the same as that of a color, even if a surface is always colored. Evidence of this is the fact that the two concepts "color" and "surface" are regarded as distinct. In general, to understand "A is in B", in which A is no part of B, we must first understand "B" in itself; moreover, the essence of B has no other cause as form (1022a32–35), but if A is in B, A has a cause, since it is in B or exists because of B. So the essence is a cause (as form, and so not caused as such by something else), and also a principle (to know it, one starts from it). The assumption seems to be, then, that "essence" and "definition", as causes, are like "being", and they are used both primarily and in a qualified sense.

6. The term "essence" in "the essence of whiteness" is used in a qualified sense; this will be considered later.

7. Motion as such does not come under a category, but in motion there is acting and being acted upon; and it is perhaps these that are meant (120b26–7).

8. In "a white man", the term "white" modifies "a man", and though a man exists by himself and not in another, whiteness does not so exist but exists in another thing. So a white man is a mixed unity and not simple, and it does not seem to fit the formula of essence given in 1029b13–4.

9. That is, it is not something composite which includes, for example, things from two categories, like whiteness and a man, but is only a *this* (a substance).

10. In "a white animal", the term "white", which is said of (or modifies) "animal", is a derivative term, from "whiteness", which is in the category of quality, and it is not like the differentia "rational" in "rational animal". See also Comm. 14 in this Section.

11. Evidently, the *Iliad* is a formula, for, by definition, a formula has parts each of which has significance (16b26–8).

12. That is, something which is first and a principle; something which is not itself divisible in kind nor said of something else (and this is a substance).

13. If essence belongs only to what is a *this,* and this would be un-qualified essence, then it is restricted to a species in the category of sub-stance. If not restricted, it will belong to all categories, but in a manner similar to the way in which being belongs to all categories.

But is not a species said of (or predicated of) the individual? But the individual is species plus accidents, and if it is *known* through the species, then the species is somehow in the individual (or better, in the individuals, since it does not exist apart from them). Now a species, for example 'man', may mean (a) the concept of a man, which exists in the soul as *knowledge,* or (b) what that concept signifies in an individual man, and this is the form of a man which is in the individual. That form, unlike whiteness, is not in something else, unless "in" is used in the sense in which a form is in matter or with matter. Thus, that form is predicated of the individual not in the same sense as whiteness is predicated of a man.

14. It is not stated what participates in what. Perhaps he means that the genus does not participate in the differentia (1037b11–21). In the case of an attribute, perhaps he means in the sense that color is an attribute of a surface, or in the sense that a demonstrated attribute be-longs to a thing. And in the case of an accident, as in a sick man, sickness is an accident of a man.

Let "a pale man" be the formula of a cloak, and "rational animal" that of a man. Why is there an essence of a man but not of a cloak? But the same man may be now pale and now not pale, now sick and now healthy, whereas the same animal cannot be now rational and now not-rational (let "rational" here be defined as "capable by nature of stating universal truths or falsehoods"), otherwise he would become a dog or a horse or some other animal. Rationality and animality in a thing (a man) come into being simultaneously, and they cease to be likewise; so they form an indivisible unity. But a man may cease to be pale or healthy and still be a man.

15. A simplified formula of a philosopher may be "a man who knows philosophy"; a more accurate formula may be "a rational animal with adequate *knowledge* of the first principles and causes of things".

16. To substances, for they are separate.

17. To things under the categories other than that of substance.

18. Besides its whatness, we may also ask of a color how it is related to something else, or how brilliant it is, or where it exists, etc.

19. Aristotle was quite aware that language and grammar may mis-lead people, and those who think that he was influenced by the limi-tations of Greek grammar and language are certainly mistaken.

20. For example, if A cannot be B, then what is signified by "A is B" is unknowable, but what is signified by "It cannot be known that A is B" is knowable or known (1402a6–7).

21. That is, things under the other categories.

22. A primary essence, that of a substance, and secondarily of things under the other categories.

23. The events signified by the *Iliad* are one by temporal continuity.

24. Perhaps "contiguity" is more accurate for things bound together (227a6–26, 1016a5–6, 1069a1–2).

25. Aristotle often leaves the list of categories incomplete.

5

1. The term "concavity" in its usual and general sense signifies an attribute of a line or a surface, just as "whiteness" signifies an attribute of a surface (or a body). But "concave" as used in the present context has probably a narrow sense, applicable only to noses, just like the term "aquiline".

2. In understanding oddness or stating its formula, a number must be understood or stated, respectively; and similarly for male, greater, and the like. But whiteness, although it requires a surface (or a body) in the *knowledge* of it or its formula, does not require a man. Thus, oddness may be defined: "indivisibility of a number into two equal numbers", and the term "number" appears in that definition.

3. 1030a17–b13.

4. Since by hypothesis (lines 1030b28–29) the meanings of "snub nose" and "concave nose" are the same, substitution of the former for the latter in "a concave nose nose" just obtained will yield "a snub nose nose"; and using "concave nose" for "snub" again, we get "a concave nose nose nose", etc.

5. For, female (or femaleness) is an instance of quality, just referred to, just as oddness is.

6. 1030a17–b13.

6

1. The terms "thing" and "essence" are not limited to substances alone but signify things in any category.

2. Does he mean the same in species or numerically or both? If in species, Plato would be the same as Socrates, and if numerically, Plato may be the same as the white; and this is not his meaning. It is the same, then, both numerically and in species (or its definition). Thus, the accidents belonging to Plato are not included in his essence; he would still be Plato, had he eaten beans rather than meat.

3. For example, this is useful for the inquiry whether universals exist apart from individuals or not (1039a24–b19) and whether the parts of a thing do or do not enter into its definition (1034b20–1037a20). For Plato, *knowledge* is of universals; so, if to *know* a thing is to *know* its essence, and essences or universals exist apart from individuals, the latter have no essences in them or are no essences and so cannot be *known* in any way, whether potentially or in actuality (1087a10–25).

4. This may be stated in two ways; if Socrates is the thing, he may be called "white Socrates" or "white".

5. As people say, the assumption made is this: a man is the same

as a white man, or generally, X is the same as PX, where P is an accident of X. But if X is also QX (the man may be also musical), then PX would be the same as QX; so if, universally, the essence of Y were the same as Y, the essence of PX and that of QX would be the same, and so the essence of P and that of Q would be the same. For example, the essence of white and that of musical would be the same, and this is not the case. This, of course, is a dialectical argument.

6. An alternative translation is: "Or, it is necessary for accidental being not to be the same as its essence".

7. Alternatives to "white" and "musical" here are "whiteness" and "musicality". The term λευκόν has two meanings, white and whiteness (1031b22–26).

8. For example, from the definition: "An even number is a number divisible into two equal numbers or units", it follows that to be even is to be divisible into two equal numbers or units.

9. For example, if Socrates is what you wish to consider, then he is stated as "Socrates", and if it is his whiteness, then you say "this white-ness", which happens to be in Socrates. Perhaps the meaning of "by itself" is this, a thing in a category, whether separate or inseparable, is considered or stated by itself and not as modifying something or as being in something or with something or as related to something.

10. For Plato, Ideas are prior in existence as well as in *knowledge* to sensible individuals, and although Tree Itself is the *substance* of a sensible tree, there is nothing prior to Tree Itself (except its principles, the *One* and the *Dyad*); consequently, Tree Itself and its essence are the same (numerically as well as in definition), and to *know* the essence of Tree Itself is to *know* the Tree Itself.

11. The term "Good" is also used as an abbreviation of "Good Itself"; likewise for all Ideas.

12. That is, if the Ideas were distinct and separate from their essences.

13. That is, no science of Ideas, for there is science only of essences, but the Ideas are not essences.

14. That is, the essences would not be beings, since beings, for Plato, are only the sensibles, the Mathematical Objects, and the Ideas.

15. That is, the two exist apart, like Socrates and Plato, and Socrates is not Plato.

16. For Plato, *One* is the first principle of all things as form alone; and if its essence were distinct and separate and prior, then *One* would not be the first principle.

17. That is, neither will the essence of X be X, where X may be any thing whatsoever. Of course, to say that the essence of being is not a being is to deny also its existence, and this would be absurd.

18. Perhaps the word μή (= "not") should be omitted; and if so, the translation would be: "Moreover, if the essence of good belongs to something, this will not be good (or, may not be good)". Accordingly,

this would follow: a subject has the essence of good and yet it is not (or may not be) good; and this seems absurd. According to the translation as given, the meaning may be this: if to be an X or to be called "X" a thing must have the essence of X, then if the essence of Good exists apart from the Good, the Good will not be good.

19. Numerically as well as in definition (which signifies the essence).

20. An alternative to "beautiful" is "noble".

21. Perhaps by "primary" he means things which are stated as subjects (such as whiteness, a triangle, justice, etc.) and are not composites, whether accidental (like a white man) or named accidentally (as when Socrates is named "white") or composites of subject and attribute (like "odd number").

22. If a thing and its essence are one, we can *know* it directly, and recourse to the Ideas is not necessary.

23. If, for Plato, *knowledge* is of Forms, of which no others are prior, then since *knowledge* is of essences and a Form and its essence are one numerically and in definition, and since Forms are always by themselves and not with other attributes or accidents (unlike Socrates who is now sick and now well), a Form and its essence have more reason to be the same than a sensible and its essence.

24. Probably referring to sensible individuals. If Ideas are separate and are the *substances* of sensibles, then if a sensible does not have the corresponding Idea it cannot be a *substance* (or a substance, which has a *substance* or essence).

25. That is, they would exist by being in the corresponding sensible subjects and would not be separate, and hence not substances.

26. Perhaps by "one" he means one numerically, and by "the same" he means the same in definition.

27. An alternative to "by accident" is "in virtue of an attribute". Perhaps the meaning is this: a thing and its essence are inseparable, both in existence and in thought. An accident may disappear but the thing remains, and any other attribute, such as a demonstrable property, is distinguishable in thought.

28. He may be referring to the examples considered, which may even include the Ideas which were hypothetically considered.

29. An alternative to "accidentally" is "with an attribute", or "by an attribute".

30. If "white" means whiteness (an attribute, considered by itself), then whiteness and its essence are one and the same; but if it means a man indirectly or a white man, then this is not the case, for the subject is stated by an accident or attribute.

31. That is, the primary things, as stated earlier (1031b14).

32. That is, numerically one.

33. Perhaps this is given as evidence rather than as a proof or a demonstration for the sameness in definition, as the use of "for" instead of "because" indicates; for, two things may always be one numerically

though not the same in definition, as convexity and concavity in a line, and the road from A to B and that from B to A (433b22–25, 1066a30–4).

7

1. The break from essence to generation may be only apparent. A reference to this part seems to be indicated in 1039b20–21. As St. Thomas Aquinas says, having shown what essence is, that it exists in the thing itself, and that through it the thing is known, there is still the problem of whether or how it is generated in generable or sensible things. Perhaps it will be also shown that Plato's Ideas are not needed for the generation of sensible things. On the other hand, the summaries in 1037a21–b7 and 1042a4–22 seem to indicate that this part is out of place.

2. For example, when properly placed in soil, the seed begins to germinate by itself; and the moving cause in such a thing is in the thing moved.

3. For example, of a house, its moving cause is outside, in the art existing in the architect's mind.

4. These come to be when nature fails, as in a monstrosity, or when the object intended does not come about but something else does, or the latter comes about when not intended, as kicking a stone and finding a coin under it (195b31–198a13).

5. The moving cause.

6. The material cause or matter.

7. That is, each of the categories with respect to which there is non-accidental change. Thus, relation is excluded. If a substance is generated, the generation is called "simple" or "unqualified", but if a thing under another category, it is called "qualified". Likewise for destruction (225a12–20).

8. By "*this*" he may mean the composite of matter and form, which is a substance, or just the form which comes to be in the substance.

9. Thus, "nature" has two meanings, the matter or the form of sensible non-artificial things; and the form may also be a moving cause (1014b16–1015a19).

10. The form of the parent is the same in species as the form of the child.

11. Productions by a power may be those requiring no art and very little *thought*, as breaking rocks with a given instrument, cutting wood with a saw, digging a hole to plant, and productions by *thought* may require some knowledge and little or no art, as cutting a wooden rod into 3 equal parts, and constructing a semi-circular board.

12. For example, a sick man feeling cold may rub himself, and the heat from rubbing may cause him to get well, but accidentally, for he is not a doctor although a doctor would have done this by art. Similarly, by nature some lower forms of animals are generated from seed, but

(for Aristotle) they are also generated by the action of the Sun or the heavens on certain soils (569a10–21, 732b11–14, 761b23–26).

13. 1032b23–30, 1034a9–21.

14. By "form in the soul" he means, not the form as existing in the thing, but the *knowledge* or formula of it which is in the soul.

15. By "first *substance*" he means the lowest species or form (of the work produced) not predicable of a still lower species.

16. That is, the formula of sickness in the soul exists thus: "absence of health in a body"; hence, "health" is included in the formula of sickness.

17. He says "in a sense", for, literally, health is generated from the formula or *knowledge* of health in the soul, and similarly in the case of a house. The term "essence" has two meanings, the form, as it exists in the thing, and the formula or *knowledge* of it, as it exists in the soul. By "immaterial *substance*" he means essence in the latter sense.

18. As it exists in the soul.

19. Thus, healing is caused by the doctor through his art, or by chance. In the latter case, the chance cause does without art what the doctor will do, and let us say that this is rubbing; but such a cause may vary, for it may be the patient who rubs himself because he feels cold, or someone else to relieve the pain in the patient's body, etc. According to Aristotle, then, medicine is a productive science.

20. That is, assuming this to be a part of health, missing in the sick man.

21. If a house is to be, stones (or whatever the materials are) must be bought or made; if this, money is needed; if this, it must be borrowed, etc. The last thing (in time) that must be present in the production of a house, then, is stones. But while warmth in health is a part in one sense, say as an attribute of or as a moving cause in the definition of health, stones and bricks are a part as sensible matter in the house.

22. This may be the saying that being does not come from nonbeing (974a2–3, 1062b24–6).

23. That is, it is this matter to which the moving cause introduces a form, and what results is a *composite*.

24. The formula "bronze sphere" or "such-and-such a figure, made of bronze" includes the sensible matter. On the other hand, if "bronze" is left out, seeing that a sphere can exist apart from bronze (as in a wooden sphere) and is not like the snub nose, still the formula "such-and-such a figure" has "figure" as its genus, and the genus is like matter (intelligible matter) in the definition; so even here there is matter by analogy (1016a24–28, 1024b6–9, 1045a33–35). Now the sphere as form is not generated out of any matter but now it exists and now it does not, and it is in a sense generated by a 'sphere', or better, by the formula or knowledge of a sphere existing in the artist as a mover (1044b21–29).

25. Or "that-en", as in "wooden". Other variations exist; for example, from "bronze" as a noun, we have "brazen" or "bronze" as an adjective. The term "brazen" by itself signifies the matter but without reference

to a shape, for the shape is signified by the modified term "sphere" in "brazen sphere".

26. That is, a man remains a man during the change, and as such he is a subject and, in a sense, like matter; and from being sick the man comes to be well, and so sickness is no more. So we have a man who is healthy, but not a sick man who is healthy.

27. In saying "the bronze becomes a brazen sphere", "bronze" signifies matter in some shape, usually left nameless, since there is much variation in it; and this shape is like sickness (a privation) in a man, from which the man became healthy. Likewise for bricks and timber in the case of a house, and the rest.

28. The term "wood" here, like "a sick man", signifies matter or a subject but with some *shape*.

29. The qualification needed here would be some nameless shape in the wood, for the change would be from this shape to the shape of a statue.

8

1. 1033a8–10.

2. The subject or matter here is to be considered without the form, so the bronze must be considered without the shape it may chance to have.

3. One makes a round bronze, or the bronze (as subject only, without its privation) to be round, but one does not make the bronze (as subject only) or roundness.

4. 1033a25–6.

5. The word "that" refers to the bronze sphere, and the bronze sphere is a sphere.

6. If he were to make the sphere by itself out of X and Y (matter and form), then since Y is a form like the sphere, Y itself is something that could be made out of, say, X_1 and Y_1, and Y_1 could be made in the same manner, etc. ad infinitum.

7. He seems to repeat himself, but this is not so; for here he may be referring not to a form as existing in matter, but to a form which some thinkers believe to exist by itself as separate, like the Idea Sphere for Plato.

8. An essence (in the thing itself) is a form.

9. That is, the essence of a sphere (or formula) as it exists in the soul as art and a moving cause.

10. Although the genus "figure" of a sphere is like matter in its formula or definition, this does not preexist like the matter bronze in which a form can be produced. So it is the whole such-and-such a figure that is produced in the subject bronze; for the sphere as a unit is a form, although as an object to be understood it has parts or a formula.

11. Sensible matter is meant.

12. One part is matter and another is form.

13. Probably the word πλίνθους in 1033b20–1 should be πλινθίνους or πλινθίνας, for, like the material spheres, he is thinking of the brick houses and not just the bricks.

14. For Aristotle, separate forms, such as God and the other heavenly movers, are not generable at all.

15. In sensibles which may change, a form is with matter; and since many subjects can have a form of the same kind, it is called "such". It is contrasted with a *this,* which is separate, like an individual man.

16. An alternative to "definite" is "bounded". Anyway, a separate thing is indicated, like a house or a bronze sphere.

17. Perhaps it is more accurate to say "a *such* this from a this", where "this" signifies the subject alone, not including the form put into it.

18. An alternative translation is: "and when this becomes generated, it is *such*"; that is, after the generation, the subject that persists takes on a form.

19. He is referring to the forms of sensible or generable objects.

20. Referring to the Forms, which are posited as the causes of sensible forms.

21. Plato's Forms were posited to be the causes of sensible objects, both as moving causes and as the forms of them; and if they are useless in both ways, their existence as separate substances is highly doubtful. Now what is generated is a *composite,* and it is generated from matter or a subject and also by a *composite,* and after the generation, the form introduced is in that matter or subject and not outside. But for Plato, the Forms as moving causes are without matter; and as the forms of the individuals, they are not in them but exist by themselves.

22. That is, the father and the son are numerically distinct, but the same in form or species.

9

1. The word "which" may refer to the generation, or to matter. If to the former, then evidently the matter or subject is part of the thing generated. If to the latter, then part of the thing generated may exist in various ways, for "matter" here signifies not prime matter but a subject with attributes; it may be bricks as mere materials in the case of a house, or a seed having in itself a moving cause which causes it to develop into a tree, or a sick body having powers which may generate heat or other changes in the body and so cause health directly or indirectly.

2. Without support, bricks move only down, fire only up.

3. For example, a house cannot be built without the art, but health can come to be without the art.

4. A sick man may accidentally so act as to cause his health (even if he has no art); or he may lie on a hot bed, and the heat from this (which is outside of him) may cause the heat needed by his body to bring about health. And it may be only a part of the body or of the external agent that so acts to bring about health.

5. That is, by the art as it exists in the soul; and this is the house in some sense, that is, it is the knowledge of the essence of the house.

6. That is, if we say "by the intellect", then the house is generated by a part of the intellect, and this part is the art of a house.

7. More literally, the knowledge of that form.

8. A part with the same name must be distinguished from a part in some sense having the same name. In the example that follows, the latter would be the art of health in the intellect, but the former would be the heat in the body, which is either health or a part of health or etc.

9. This is the proximate first cause, as the heat induced in the body, which is health, or a part of health, or followed by, etc., as stated next.

10. For example, in the production of health (if not by chance) or of a house, the whatness of these exists as art in the intellect, and it is from this art that motion first begins.

11. It is generated from a horse and an ass, or, from what these may be called by a common name next to their species.

12. For Aristotle, some lower forms of living things can come into existence (for example, from decayed matter, etc.) without the seed. So he allows for some generation by chance.

13. These would probably be the higher forms of life, such as men.

14. That is, not generated as something separate, nor from any matter.

15. By "primary form" he probably means in each category the ultimate species which comes to be in a subject. For example, if a body changes to green from some other color, then greenness would be the primary form taken on by that body. The term "form" here is used in its wide sense, that is, it signifies the primary contraries or primary privation and possession in generations.

16. The term "bronze" here means a metal of a certain kind, with matter and form (the form being not the outward shape, but the kind of metal). Thus, if silver is changed to bronze by art, there is matter or a subject (other than silver) which underlies the change and becomes bronze, and the generation is one of substance.

17. The form, in the case of the bronze sphere, must preexist in the soul as art.

18. For example, if the change is one of increase by nature, as the air heated, the moving cause may be a substance, say fire, and the air is potentially larger; and if by art, then it is the quantitative form in the intellect (or the knowledge of that form) which is a quantity only in a sense, as stated before.

10

1. There is this problem: In what sense is "part" here used? The term "straight" is a part of "straight line", but straightness is not a part of a straight line in the same sense as half that line is a part of the whole

line. The distinctions come out as he answers the question raised, so we may consider his statement here as somewhat dialectical.

2. An acute angle is usually defined as "an angle less than a right angle", and a finger as "such-and-such a part of an animal with such-and-such function"; so the whole is prior in formula or in definition to the part.

3. Evidently the living body is prior in existence to the finger, for it can exist without the finger, while without the living body the finger is dead and so is equivocally called "a finger". But in the case of the acute angle this does not seem to be so, unless it is defined qua a part of the right, in which case the right must preexist, otherwise the acute would not be a part. In either case, his statement that the whole is prior in existence to the part is still true, although one may not regard the acute as a part of the right angle (even if it is less than a right angle).

4. 1023b15–17.

5. This form is the outward shape, the material not included.

6. An alternative to "should" is "can", though less probable. The term "statue" may signify the form, or the *composite,* but is never used for the matter alone. Moreover, if the matter varies, it is still the same statue, but not if the form varies. Thus, it seems that it is a statue in virtue of its form.

7. For example, a circle is never defined in terms of two semicircles, whether these be individuals or universally stated.

8. Are not the letters parts of the syllable as matter, like the two semicircles of a circle? But the semicircle is defined in terms of a circle; not so, in the case of the letters. Further, just as the shape itself of a statue has parts with position, which do not include the bronze or whatever the matter may be, so is the syllable related to the letters.

9. For example, as in the case of a coin. When the form of a circle is actualized in an individual, there must be individual segments as parts or matter upon which this form is actualized, but there need not be bronze. Hence, the segments are nearer to the form than the bronze is.

10. If X is destroyed, there is matter or a subject underlying this change; but the form or *substance* of that which changes has no matter, and so it cannot be destroyed, except accidentally, that is, if the composite is destroyed.

11. For example, the formula of the snub will contain that of flesh, but the formula of concavity will not.

12. For example, the saw is a composite, and it cannot be made from any matter; so its definition must include the kind of matter appropriate to it.

13. The material principles.

14. God and the other movers are not destroyed at all; the form of a statue is destroyed accidentally, as stated above in Comm. 10.

15. An individual circle is meant, like that of an existing coin (assuming it has the form of a circle); and it may be reduced to segments by breaking the coin into parts, each of which is a segment of that circle (by "circle" he means the plane bounded by the circumference).

16. Socrates has both a proper name, "Socrates", and common names, like "man" which is a predicate also of others; but it is pointless to use proper names for individual circles, apples, and the like.

17. He is speaking of the formula of the form here. He says "some of them", since some part may not be prior in definition or existence but simultaneous with the form, as in the case of the ultimate differentia. Thus, if a magnitude is a continuous quantity, magnitude and continuity are simultaneous, but a quantity is prior in definition and in existence to a magnitude.

18. By "not divisible into" he means: does not have as a part.

19. The acute angle is a material part of the right angle, so the latter must be viewed as a *composite* of matter and form. Hence, since the acute is defined in terms of the right (as a *composite*), and the latter in terms of the right angle (only as form), the acute must be defined in terms of the right (as form only). The example of the finger is more evident.

20. Qua parts of the whole thing, they are posterior both in definition and in existence.

21. In translating lines 1035b14–22, I have tried to reconstruct the argument on the basis of thought and consistency, for, perhaps there is some corruption in those lines.

22. That is, of the living body.

23. Sensation is essential to the soul of an animal; and so, each such part must include sensation in its definition.

24. According to St. Thomas Aquinas, if sight (a part of the form) is lost, the composite (for example, a blind man) may still exist. So, such part is not necessarily prior.

25. That is, the living body.

26. After division, these are no longer living parts, but only matter, like dead fingers, dead feet, etc.

27. As matter (dead parts), they are prior in existence, but as living parts, they are posterior in formula and in existence.

28. That is, neither prior nor posterior. For example, if rationality (the *substance* or form or part of it of a man) were in the brain, then the brain would be such a part.

29. Perhaps he is using "formula" in the sense of form.

30. Perhaps this is the essence of the composite qua composite, signified by the definition of, say, a man ("a rational animal", or something of this sort).

31. For example, in the case of the soul of a man, sensation would be such a part.

32. For example, in the case of a man, his foot (when alive).

33. For example, this would be the surface of an individual circle, for such surface (without its color) cannot be sensed by any of the five senses; it is a common sensible, known (or inferred, if you wish) by common sensation, 425a13–b11.

34. Perhaps thought by common sensation, for they are individuals. For example, we sense the color of the surface of a circle directly, and by common sensation we think directly (or we sense commonly, if you wish) the individual circle (without its color).

35. In other words, when we are not observing them directly, we cannot be sure whether they exist or not, and any knowledge of them under this condition will have to be by means of universal terms, if the individuals still exist. It is such kind of knowledge that we get of individuals, for example, when we do not see them or never see them but hear about them from others through speech (by the use of universal terms).

36. He may mean ultimate matter, which these individuals have, for their proximate matter may somehow be known, as in a bronze statue, whose bronze is a *composite* of prime matter and form.

37. These examples as stated are not ultimate matter, but *composites* of matter and form and other attributes. If they change with respect to form, there is matter or a subject underlying the change, but if with respect to an attribute only (a quantity, or a quality, or a place), the *composite* of matter and form is the subject. The matter or subject underlying the change is said to be movable or sensible or physical. But intelligible matter is mathematical or quantitative matter (for example, the continuum, without a form), and this is qualified matter and immovable.

38. That is, prior in definition and in existence to an individual acute angle or to an individual bronze acute angle. See Comm. 3, above.

39. For example, both an animal and its soul are prior in existence and in formula to a material part of an animal or an individual animal, e.g. to a leg.

11

1. By "separable from X" he does not mean that a circle can exist by itself, but that it can exist in another kind of subject, say, in Y.

2. That is, since it is possible for some forms to exist always in matter of the same kind.

3. For example, the continuity of a (finite) straight line for these thinkers is like the flesh and bones in the case of a man, or the bronze in the case of the circle; therefore, it should be omitted in the definition. What remains now is the two bounding points, whose position may also be omitted for the same reason. If so, we are left with the form of two points, and this is two units, or two for the Pythagoreans, and Two for some Platonists.

4. If the Forms are Numbers for the later Platonists, and if Two is

the form of individual two's and Line the form of individual lines, where Line may be in the so-called "fourth" genus of things (992b13–18), then is Line a Number (Two), or is it a *composite* of Two and the *Dyad?* Both alternatives lead to difficulties.

5. The form of a line does not appear to be that of a two; and the Pythagoreans are not right in saying that 4 is the form of both justice and friendship, and perhaps of other things, too (987a19–27).

6. If the Platonists are to be consistent, then for them there is only one form of all things, the *One*. For, Two and the other Numbers, as well as all other things, are generated from the *One* as form and the *Dyad* as matter; and since the *Dyad* is no part of the form of a thing, only the *One* is the cause as form and also the form of all things. Thus, all things would be one in form, though many numerically.

7. An alternative to "surely" is "perhaps".

8. As sensible and movable, a man and an animal and their definitions must include the necessary physical parts, even if the matter of these need not or should not be specified as flesh and bones and the like (1036b3–7).

9. For example, such would be the individual circle of an individual coin; for, just as this coin is a *this*, so its individual circle is in a sense (in a qualified way) a *this*.

10. That is, unlike whiteness, which is an attribute of a subject such as Socrates or sugar, the soul is not an attribute of something else, except in the sense that it is with matter or a body (1037b1–4). He says "first", for, in predicating one thing of another, one *begins* with something which is not predicated of (or is not an attribute of) something else; and the soul of each specific animal is first in this sense, if we exclude the special meaning of "a predicate" (the sense in which "form" is a predicate of matter).

11. That is, the *composite* of this soul and this body (or, this individual thing).

12. The term "a man" or "an animal", which signifies a *composite* of soul and body, universally taken (1037a6–7).

13. Referring to the *Great* and *Small* of the Platonists, to *Plurality* of Speusippus, to the *Infinite* of the Pythagoreans, and the like.

14. Such as the *One* and the Numbers of Plato.

15. Books M and N (1076a8–1093b29), and perhaps Book Λ (1069a18–1076a4).

16. Perhaps "also" should come after "for it is", for the discussion of form in physical substance is in a way preliminary to the discussion of prime matter and of the prime immovable mover and the other immovable movers.

17. That is, the form of physical substances.

18. 193b6–8.

19. A more literal alternative to "why" is "through what"; and what is signified by this is the cause of unity, which is the form of the thing (which is a whole with parts).

20. 1037b8–1038a35, 1045a7–b23.
21. 1029b1–1030b13.
22. 1034b20–1037a20.
23. This seems to contradict lines 1036b22–32. However, he is considering there whether a man can exist as a soul apart from body, and whether a definition of a man or an animal (perhaps qua a *composite*) can be given without any material parts. Also, "matter" here may mean a certain kind of matter, and a form may be independent of it, or, just matter indefinitely taken.
24. 1030b14–1031a14.
25. 1031a15–1032a11.
26. An alternative to "by accident" is "in the sense that one is an attribute [not a part of the essence] of the other".

12

1. 92a27–33.
2. Perhaps "this" refers to the formula "a two-footed animal"; if so, then the question is still clear, for a many-termed formula is said to be one if it signifies one thing (one essentially, not by accident).
3. If existing, they are distinct, and the two exist apart and are many.
4. The term "affected" suggests that λευκός may not mean white. Other meanings of λευκός are: pale, light, weak, joyful, gay, pleasant.
5. A white man shares in whiteness; but a genus does not share in a differentia, for if it did, it should share alike in all and not just in one. But the differentiae are contrary, partly or wholly (1018a25–27), and no thing can have contraries simultaneously. One may object: a man does not share in whiteness or blackness, just as he does not in two-footedness or four-footedness, so why the difference? Of course, two-footedness and the others are limited to the animals, but whiteness and the like are not, and the latter are infinite, so to say, but the former are limited; also, the latter may come and go, but the former come and go together with the animal. A man retains his differentia and cannot become a dog, but he can change with respect to the so-called "accidents".
6. Whether he means a unity of all things, or of just those present in the thing, is not clear. Perhaps it makes no difference, since he wishes to rule out accidental unities.
7. The assumption is: the elements of a definition are said to be one if together they signify one *substance*.
8. This is taken just as an illustration, for "living thing" is prior in definition to "animal" and so a genus of it. The same applies to the differentiae given.
9. That is, a genus must exist with some one differentia and not by itself with none; for example, a triangle must be either equilateral, or isosceles, or scalene.

10. For example, like the bronze which exists as matter in the statue, for it must have also a form; and the same applies to a genus.

11. An alternative to "and" is "or".

12. Somehow, the genus has been left out of the definition. Perhaps "definition" has two senses, one which includes the genus (considered as matter, so to say), and the other without it. The analogy may be this: just as the essence or *substance* of (say) a man is his soul or form, so the *substance* or definition (without the genus) of the formula of a man (this formula is a sort of *composite,* genus and differentia, or matter and form) is without the genus or matter of that formula. This is only a hypothesis.

13. Otherwise, there are infinite subdivisions, since the accidents are infinite; and besides, the distinction between genus and differentia is left out, or between matter and form, or between what is wider and narrower in predication. Further, just as animals may be subdivided into black, yellow, etc., so yellow things may be subdivided into animals, minerals, vegetables, etc., and the principle of proper subdivision is destroyed.

14. That is, "clovenness" is a differentia of "footedness", so that what is cloven is also footed, just as what is straight is also a line; but what is wingless is not necessarily footed. One may ask: Is "footedness" related to "cloven-footedness" as genus to species, or as matter to form? But "footedness" is a (first) differentia of "animal". Perhaps a differentia, by analogy, is a sort of a genus to its own differentiae.

15. He seems to include the genus here, although he leaves it out in lines 1038a19–20.

16. That is, as many as the number of sub-differentiations.

17. And there is a countless number of such accidental subdivisions.

18. The *substance* or form of a thing, as in the cubeness of a bronze cube for example, is conceived as a whole or as a unit and not first one part, then another, etc.

13

1. This actuality is the form of a sensible substance.

2. The Platonists.

3. 1031a15–1032a11.

4. This is not necessarily a definition of a universal but a dialectical formula, one commonly accepted. So the attack on the Platonists starts from this. If a definition were given, the Platonists might question it.

5. For, if of all, seeing that it belongs to all, it would not be peculiar to just one thing.

6. If it is to belong to just one, then to belong to all at the same time would mean, in view of the formula of a universal, that all are numerically one, just as Socrates and the gadfly of Athens and the philosopher of Athens who drank the hemlock are numerically one and have just one *substance.*

7. By "one" he means numerically one.

8. An alternative to "a substance" is "a *substance*". If so, then even if a *substance* (or a form) is with matter, it is not predicated of a subject which is a *this* in the way in which a universal is so predicated (as "man" of Socrates, and of Plato, etc.).

9. That is, as something peculiar to just one thing, as an essence is.

10. He probably means an individual man and an individual horse; both of these have animality, and this has the same formula for both. An alternative to "in a substance" is "in a *substance*".

11. If everything in a *substance* had a formula, there would be no indefinables and an infinite regress would result.

12. Namely, the universal.

13. For example, of some part, if not of the whole individual man.

14. Here, man = the essence or *substance* of an individual man.

15. If this universal is the *substance* of some part of an individual man, it would be peculiar to that part and so cannot also be the *substance* of other parts in other individuals.

16. The preceding argument assumes that an individual substance is composed of parts which are themselves substances. This assumption is now strengthened. The parts into which a substance can be resolved are prior, and as such they cannot be qualities (the universals are thought to be qualities, 1003a7–9) or any inseparable attributes.

17. The texts have γενέσει (= "in generation"); perhaps it should be γνώσει (= "in knowledge"), since "in generation" would be equivalent to "in time", which has already been stated.

18. For example, 'animal', which is the *substance* of some part of Socrates. So, it will be in that part and in Socrates; or, there will be at least two *substances* in Socrates, 'animal' and the *substance* of Socrates. There are other alternatives of interpretation and translation of the Greek text.

19. Referring to 'man' or any other such thing (as an individual).

20. That is, it exists neither as something separate (as some say the Ideas do) nor in more than one thing. For Aristotle, a universal, qua existing, is in the soul of an individual man.

21. The term "belong" here is technical; it means, not something present in the thing as a material part or as an inseparable attribute, but something which is predicated of a thing, like a term.

22. This may be any predicate, whether signifying a substance, like the predicate "man", or an attribute, like "line", 3b10–23.

23. If both Socrates and the universal 'man' were substances, both would have something in common, say 'Man', and so a third object arises, the *third man*, which is also a universal and a substance. Likewise, there would arise a fourth, a fifth, etc.

24. That is, one in actuality.

25. By "double line" he means the actual finite line, which is twice as long as each of its potentially existing halves.

26. That is, if the line is cut in half, it no longer exists actually, and then we have two existing lines, which were formerly parts of (or potentially existing in) a line.

27. That is, it cannot consist of substances existing in actuality; and if they exist potentially, they are not substances but parts as matter.

28. For Democritus, indivisible magnitudes are always substances (in actuality); so no two of them can become one, for if so, each of the two would then exist potentially and not be a substance (in actuality).

29. That is, if it is composed neither of universals which are non-substances nor of substances in actuality, it cannot be composed of any-, thing and so it is simple.

30. 1031a11–14.

31. 1039b20–1040b4, 1045a7–b23.

14

1. An alternative to "substances" is *"substances"*, for Ideas according to Plato are the forms of sensible things. However, "substances" will also do, because various relations of genus to species are dialectically considered here, not to speak of the fact that Ideas are generated from the *One* as form and the *Dyad* as matter and so have both matter and form.

2. That is, they so posit them among the Ideas.

3. For since, in view of the fact that "man" is predicated of many similars, Man Himself is so posited, so, in view of the fact that "animal" is predicated of "man" and "horse" etc., Animal (or Animal Itself) should be so posited.

4. That is, one numerically.

5. If it is numerically one, but in many, it should be divided from itself. See *Parmenides* 131.

6. If, in order to have Man, Animal has to be with Biped, then, to have also Horse, Animal will have to be with Four-footed, and likewise with Eight-footed, etc. But this Animal is numerically one and the same. So it will have contraries or it will be with contraries at the same time, which is absurd.

7. If Animal is not with Biped, nor with Four-footed or with any of the others, then it exists only by itself. If so, Man cannot exist, for in him there will have to be Animal and Biped; and "some animals are biped" will have to be false, since if it were true, the existence of biped animals would necessitate that of the Idea Man or the Idea Biped Animal.

8. Two things may also form a unity in any of these ways. For one thing, the parts of any such unity must have position, and therefore place, but for Plato the Ideas are not in place (203a8–9, 209b33–210a2).

9. The term "infinity" here means: a great number. See 1066a36–7.

10. For example, there is Animal in Man, Animal in Horse, etc., and these Animals are numerically distinct, and all are substances (or *substances,* since they are just Forms for Plato); but they posit Animal as unique.

15

1. Perhaps by "formula" he means the form alone as existing in the thing, although one might consider as an alternative the formula which exists universally as knowledge in the soul.

2. The formula (whichever alternative one may choose in Comm. 1, above), not having sensible matter, cannot be generated; now it exists and now it does not, and it comes into existence or goes out of it instantaneously, like any attribute of a *composite,* and such things are immovable (1033a24–b19, 1044b21–29, 1067b9–11).

3. Perhaps by "the essence of this house" he means the individual *composite,* or else an individual form which is put in certain materials, but not that form apart from any matter; as for such an individual form, now it exists and now it does not, for such forms are generable and destructible only in a sense.

4. 1033a24–1034a8.

5. Destructible substances are meant, not the eternal (like the Sun).

6. And if scientific, then of what necessarily is.

7. One is said to be disposed to ignorance of the fact that A is (or A is not), if he believes that A is not (or A is); but if he has no thought at all about A, then he is said to be negatively ignorant of it (79b23–28).

8. Does he mean simple necessity, or hypothetical, or any of the two? For example, God and the Sun and other such exist of necessity (for Aristotle); but there is also hypothetical necessity, for example, if A is to be, then B must be (if a triangle is defined as so-and-so, then it must have such-and-such attributes; and if a man is to exist, there must be a moving cause of him). Of course, generation always exists (now of this, now of that), and so do triangles (at least potentially), but an individual like Socrates or this house does not. So perhaps both necessities are meant.

9. If he means *knowledge* of the individuals in question, then it is such knowledge of them in *actuality,* while they are observed, for "*knowledge*" has two senses (1087a15–25).

10. If the formula of the species of the thing in question is meant, then it cannot be a definition of the thing, since the thing is destructible; and it cannot be the formula of just that thing anyway, for it would have to contain individual attributes (e.g. this place, this time, etc.), and these are accidental to a thing which may change such attributes and still have its essence. A formula is universal (1035b33–1036a1).

11. Perhaps "tries to define" is better, or "gives some formula as a definition of".

12. That is, not qua an individual, since a definition is of what exists.

13. Plato might say that an Idea, unlike a sensible or a destructible individual, possesses no accidental attributes; and as such and as eternal, it is definable. But other difficulties arise, as is shown next.

14. If the definition of an Idea has new names and each (or any one) of these is unknown, then the definition remains meaningless; and if each of these signifies an Idea (which is an individual), it can only be known by direct knowledge of that Idea, (which appears impossible). Other difficulties arise.

15. I do not follow logically the literal meaning of lines 14–22; the interpretations or alternatives that follow may not be the ones Aristotle had in mind.

16. An alternative to "belong" is "may belong".

17. An alternative to "both" is "each separately".

18. If "each separately" is right in Comm. 17, above, one interpretation is: (a) "two-footed animal" is a predicate of some animals, such as men (if they exist), and also of some others, such as hens. Another is: (b) since Man is Animal, if Animal is not Two-footed, also Man is not Two-footed (or Two-footed Animal). Hence, Animal is Two-footed Animal; and likewise, Two-footed is Two-footed Animal. Another is: (c) just as Man is the *substance* of and exists apart from men, and what is an essential predicate of a man is certainly of Man (who is the cause of a man) among the Ideas, so a predicate of Man is a predicate of Animal which is likewise related to Man. There may be other alternatives.

But if "both" is right, then, since Man and Animal and Two-footed are all Ideas and so distinct, just as "two-footed animal" is a predicate of Man, so it is of the composite of Animal and Two-footed, that is, of Two-footed Animal; hence, it is not a predicate of only one thing. There may be other alternatives.

19. He has in mind the Ideas, and three arguments follow: with respect to priority, composition of parts, and separateness.

20. Perhaps prior in existence is meant, or in definition, or both.

21. An alternative to "and" is "or".

22. This is Aristotle's position, but not Plato's; for, if Animal is not separate from Man and Horse and the others, neither would these (and also Animal) be from the corresponding individuals, nor would the universal exist apart from the individuals.

23. The necessity, as indicated by "necessary" in line 19, may be this: while men or hens need not exist, in which case "two-footed animal" may not be a predicate of many things, Man and Hen must exist, so "two-footed animal" must be a predicate of more than one thing.

24. What belongs to what is caused does so to what causes it (its *substance*, or Idea for Plato), and the cause is prior in existence to what is caused. So, if Animal or Two-footed is similarly related to Man, a predicate of the latter is a predicate of the former.

25. Aristotle considers the possibility, which he would regard as absurd, that an Idea is composed of Ideas, for example, that Man is a composite of Animal and Two-footed, since this seems to follow if a man is a two-footed animal and if Plato's universals are not inseparable but exist separately.

26. There is Animal Itself as a separate Idea, and Animal as a part in Man and Horse and the others; so "animal" or "Animal" would be a predicate of many things and not just one. This would give rise to another universal, say, "*Animal*", like the *third man* argument.

27. If Animal Itself and Animal in Man are distinct in *substance*, then there will be unique Ideas each having only one predicate, and such Ideas cannot be *known* through common or universal terms, but if at all, directly. This is untenable both in itself, and also on Platonic principles (such as Plato's assertion that Ideas are shared by individuals and perhaps also by less universal Ideas which are posterior in existence, as Animal is shared by Man).

28. That is, at night.

29. That is, according to their definition.

30. That is, it would be absurd to define the Sun by using such attributes (perhaps accidental) rather than by mentioning its nature as a substance.

31. That is, a definition of Idea Itself as an individual. Evidently, such a definition would and should be applicable to all Ideas, since Man and Animal and the rest are Ideas, and so it would be a common predicate or attribute.

An alternative to "Idea" is "an Idea of these", referring to Cleon or Socrates.

16

1. Qua parts, they exist potentially, and if separated, each may be one by continuity, but such unity is not by nature like that of a man or a tree or the Sun or a house (with a purpose), but rather by accident.

2. These have no definite form or unity; a volume of air, for example, is easily deformed and becomes now one by contact and now many, and it is also homogeneous.

3. For example, a tree is an organic unity of the elements.

4. An alternative to "and" is "or".

5. According to some translators, "those" refers to the parts of the soul (413b10–24) and not to the material parts. On the other hand, Aristotle in this Section is only considering whether material parts and predicates of substances are substances or not.

6. Referring to monstrosities, like siamese twins and other unnatural growths (773a2–29).

7. Like being, unity belongs to all things, but the *substance* of each thing belongs only to that thing; hence, contrary to Plato, unity or

being or a universal or what is common cannot be the *substance* of what is numerically one.

8. A principle (and likewise for an element or a cause) qua a principle is of a thing, and so it is a relative or a relation, and as such it is not a substance; but qua a nature, it may be the *substance* of the thing (if it is its form) or it may not (if it is its matter or an outside mover or a final cause). But to know the thing completely, so to say, we do ask for all its principles.

9. For a substance is one or has unity, at least its own unity if not another's; but a principle or an element or a cause, qua a relative, is hardly a nature or a substance (1088a22–35), and qua what it is itself, it may not even have unity, as in the case of matter, and if it has a unity, it may not be that of the thing of which it is a principle or a cause, like the unity of the outside mover.

10. If to itself, it is just a form, like God; otherwise, it is the *substance* of a *composite,* like the soul of a man.

11. Perhaps "in many ways" is generic, meaning in many things, or in many places, and perhaps something else. The Greek πολλαχῇ is usually translated as "in many places".

12. If it exists as one numerically, it does so in the soul, but as such (a predicate) it does not exist in the things of which it is predicated.

13. Qua a substance, a Form must be an individual and separate, and if so, it cannot be in many individuals.

14. That is, an Idea has the same form as, but without the matter and/or accidents of, each destructible thing bearing the same name.

15. They use "Itself" perhaps in order to eliminate matter and accidents and consider the form by itself.

16. God and the other movers exist of necessity, even if our knowledge of them is meagre. To say that God is a mover and separate and leads a pleasant life, etc., is not to state his essence, and to say that He is Intellect and a substance is perhaps to state his essence analogically and incompletely.

17. Discussed in lines 1040b16–1041a3.

18. Discussed in 1040b5–16, indicated in 1039a14–17.

17

1. The expressions "what" and "what kind" probably require distinct answers. Since a substance is considered to be a principle and a cause, perhaps the answer to the first is "essence", which is a principle, and that of the second is "a cause" through which, let us say, the bricks are a house or a house has being, and/or which unifies the bricks into one thing. Or perhaps, the first is "essence", and the second is "a cause" as stated and perhaps also a "principle" (that is, a starting-point, but not

in the sense of an element), since also "a principle" merely qualifies the essence and does not state, so to say, the whatness of an essence, as in the case of a principle as a mover. There are other alternatives.

2. God and the other movers, for they are essences or forms.

3. In the case of existence, say of Socrates, inquiry into nothing would be inquiring why Socrates is Socrates; in the case of fact, as when the Moon is eclipsed, such inquiry would be inquiring why an eclipsed Moon is an eclipsed Moon. Inquiry into the *why* of a fact or an existence presupposes the fact or the existence. For example, to ask why the Moon is eclipsed presupposes the fact that the Moon is eclipsed (89b23–35).

4. This is what is now called the "Law of Identity", "A is A".

5. An alternative to "answer" is "formula" or "reason".

6. That is, "a thing is itself" or "a thing is indivisible from itself".

7. Perhaps another way of putting it is: "Through what are these materials a house?" Evidently, through the form or essence.

8. Perhaps "logically" refers to the kind of cause sought without going outside into physics where final and moving causes are also sought but attending only to what is given verbally, and this is the fact, for example, that these materials are a house, and such a fact requires an essence as a cause.

9. In Comm. 7, above, the cause as essence is sought; but other causes may also be sought, such as "By what?", which is an inquiry into the moving cause, or, "For what?", which seeks the final cause. The latter two exist in generations, but the last (final cause) may also exist not in generations. Thus, man has a final cause (happiness) while existing, and so does God who always exists, and no generation enters here. However, no such cause exists in a triangle.

10. For example, bricks must have something (a form), or must be something (a house).

11. By "this" he means the form, which is the soul in the case of a man, and the shape in the case of a house.

12. Such are those which are not *composites* of matter and form, and they are known, if at all, by the intellect. They are the indefinables.

13. That is, the syllable has its letters as matter and also an essence or a *substance* as a form which unifies the letters and causes the syllable to be one.

14. If that additional something were an element, then the syllable would be three elements but still lacking unity, etc.

15. If it were many elements, then the syllable would still be many and so would lack unity.

16. It is a cause not in the sense of an element (for an element is also a cause, but as matter), but as form.

17. It is the cause as form, and it is first in the sense of proximate and in the thing (for one might think that only a part of this form is that cause, for example, the vegetative soul as the form of a man, or that

more than this form is that cause, for example, when one gives the form with some accidents).

18. He is discussing sensible and destructible substances here.

19. That is, a principle as form, for an element is a principle as matter.

Book H

1

1. 1025b3–1026a32, 1028a10–b7.
2. 1028b8–15, 1040b5–16.
3. 1028b15–27.
4. 1028b33–1029a34, 1041a6–b33.
5. 1029b1–1032a11, 1037b8–1038a35, 1039b20–1040b4.
6. 1034b20–1037b7.
7. 1038b1–1039b19, 1040b16–1041a5.
8. Books M and N: 1076a8–1093b29.
9. That is, matter is that which, not being separate by itself, has now one form and now another (or is potentially a *this* or *that*). The *"this"* may refer to the form which it takes on and by which it is called, as indicated by what follows; or it might refer to the *composite*.
10. Such would be the prime mover and man's active intellect (413b24–7, 430a10–23, 1072a19–1073a13, 1074b15–1075a10). For the prime mover, "separable" would mean separate without qualification; for man's intellect, it would mean separable if it is in the individual, but separate when the individual does not exist.
11. Such would be the form of a house or of a horse, and this is separable in formula, but not in actuality since it must exist with matter.
12. More accurately, change in quantity is meant.
13. Perhaps what is meant, more literally, is: that which (this is matter) is a *this* when with a form, but later is a subject with the privation of that form. The privation may be another form.
14. By "follow" perhaps he means: what can change with respect to substance can also change with respect to quality and quantity and place.
15. For example, the heavenly bodies, such as the Sun, Moon, and stars which change with respect to place are indestructible and ungenerable (1044b7–8, 1069b25–6). He says "one or two", for these bodies also *appear* to change in quality, as the Moon when in different positions; and here he leaves this an open issue, but in 270a12–35 he says that such bodies do not alter.
16. 225a12–20.

2

1. 985b4–19.

2. If he means substance instead of *substance,* he is using the term hypothetically; for none of the differentiae mentioned in the preceding paragraph is a substance.

3. They come under the categories other than substance.

4. From what follows, "combined" seems to mean: existing with matter, or a subject. Thus the analogy in the case of a substance and calm is, *actuality* : matter :: smoothness : sea.

5. For example, if calm is defined as smoothness in the sea, smoothness is closer to *actuality* than the sea is, for the sea is matter relative to smoothness. Of course, smoothness is a qualified *actuality,* if an *actuality* at all, just as a quantity is a qualified being.

6. That is, distinct in genus. For example, wood, water, and sound are distinct generically, and so are the *actualities* (in a qualified sense) of a threshold, a calm, and a symphony.

7. That is, since distinct matter is followed by distinct *actuality,* and matter and *actuality* are themselves distinct, some use only the matter in defining, others only the *actuality,* others both. Of course, the use of matter only is not right, for the same matter can take on different forms or *actualities.* The sea may be still or in motion.

3

1. Pythagoreans and Platonists (1036b12–20).

2. This is probably the composite of matter and form. If so, then "an animal" is related to an animal (which includes both matter and form) by signifying either the whole of it, or a part of it (its form). This is in a sense analogous to "being", unqualified and qualified (1003a33–b10).

3. He may be referring to the inquiry concerning the manner in which things should be defined, whether with or without matter, as in physics and mathematics (193b22–194a27, 1025b25–1026a6, 1036a26–1037a20, 1064a19–28).

4. If the thing is just a form.

5. The combination of a thing is its form, and as such it is not a constituent as matter.

6. Here he rejects the hypothesis that the combination as such (which is a form) is identical with or includes the materials which are combined. He could also have rejected another possible hypothesis, namely, that the combination is a distinct element as matter. This he suggests in line 12, where he says "and this is neither an element".

7. That is, if the *actuality* of the threshold is its position.

8. Perhaps the term "wood of such-and-such a form", which excludes position, would be better than "threshold", for the latter includes posi-

tion, which is the *actuality;* but if "threshold" signifies the position as well, the statement is still true, for the position as such does not include matter, but the threshold does.

9. More literally, the threshold as a composite of position and some material has position (a form) as one of its constituents.

10. He considers this hypothetically, for two-footedness is often regarded as a differentia, and this is not matter (1038a5–9, 18–21).

11. If he means substance (unqualified *actuality*) rather than *substance,* the argument still holds (1034b7–19, 1033b5–10, 1044b21–6). The prime mover would be an example of such a substance, which is eternal.

12. 1033a24–b26.

13. By *"this"* he means the composite, and the meaning of "to make a *this"* is given in 1033a31–4.

14. Namely, from matter and form (1033b5–19).

15. The *actuality* or *substance* of a house or utensil may not be a substance (unqualified essence) but an attribute caused in a natural thing by art.

16. That is, the essence or form of a natural thing like an animal or a tree (1014b35–1015a5, 1015a13–5).

17. That is, composite of matter and form.

18. Those parts, each of which is no longer a composite. Perhaps he means the matter and form of a thing, although there is still the problem of whether each of these has parts, as the cube of a cubical bronze.

19. For example, in the formula "spherical bronze", the bronze is like matter and the sphere like *shape;* and the sphere is attributed to the bronze, or "spherical" modifies "bronze".

20. The parts of a substance are not like the units of a number; for the units are homogeneous and are like matter, and there is also a form which gives unity to a number, but the parts of a substance, such as matter and form if these are indivisible, for example, are neither homogeneous nor both matter.

21. A definition, given in ultimate indefinable terms, is a number of such terms.

22. 994b16–24.

23. A number is by definition finite, for the infinite exists only potentially (202b30–208a23).

24. For example, "an odd number" and "an odd prime number" do not have the same meaning.

25. If a Number for Plato has unity, this is something other than its units, namely, its essence or form, and its units are its matter; but Numbers are posited as the Forms of things, and the cause of unity in a Number is not given.

26. In a definition, its genus is like matter and its differentia like form (1038a5–9), and the latter gives unity to the definition.

27. Each actuality is a form and is one, and one actuality differs from another, for example, the soul of a man from that of a tree; but all units of a number are undifferentiated and exist as matter.

28. Individuals admit of the more and the less with respect to their accidents because of their matter. For example, one may be more or less white, weigh more or less, be taller or shorter, be more or less virtuous, etc.

29. That is, substances in the sense of actuality as well as in the sense of matter and form.

30. This does not seem to be a complete summary of Book H up to now, if it is so intended.

4

1. The primary constituent meant here is probably the prime matter, and this is indestructible, ungenerable, just potentiality. The primary constituents as separate or separable may refer to the four material elements: air, fire, water, earth. There is no indication that Aristotle posits more than one kind of prime matter, as his definition of it shows (1029a20–1).

2. He may mean, for example, that perhaps the bitter and the sweet come from the same matter (not necessarily prime matter) in the sense that though their proximate matter is the same, their difference may be caused by different moving causes. A modern example would be isomers.

3. Using a modern example, we may say that water (H_2O) comes from hydrogen and oxygen, or, from electrons, protons, etc.

4. Material principles are meant. Now X may come from Y (a) if Y is in the process of becoming and finally becomes X, *or* (b) if Y decomposes into Z (which may be more than one element) and then Z becomes X when acted upon by a mover. The first is a change from the incomplete to the complete, the second is a generation of something by the destruction of another, as water from air (994a19–b3).
There is an alternative translation, to which corresponds an alternative interpretation. This translation from line 1044a22 is: "and it comes from the bile if it is decomposed into its first [material] principle, which is the bile. For one thing may come from a second in two ways, either when the second is earlier on the way to generation, or when the first is decomposed into its principle". So, to say that X comes from Y in the second way is to say that Y is the ultimate matter of X.

5. As a statue from bronze or silver.

6. In the generation of a man, the final cause of the subject which is in the process of being generated is the taking on of a form or essence, which is the soul in this case. After generation is completed, then man's final cause is his happiness. So his essence can be a cause both as form and as final cause, but from two points of view, generation and existence, respectively.

7. 268b11–270b31.

8. For example, the celestial bodies, such as the Sun and the stars, are neither destructible nor generable, so either they have no matter (for matter can take on now one form and now another), or "matter" will have two senses; and if the latter, then their matter can change only

with respect to place but not with respect to essence. Such bodies, then, are simple, for if composite, they would be generable and destructible. See Comm. 7, above.

9. The moving cause is meant.

10. Just as the primary part is sought and not the whole animal as the subject of sleep, so the primary affection is sought of that part if immobility is not the primary affection.

5

1. The term "form" here is wide; it extends to all categories, as is evident by the term "whiteness" which is mentioned.

2. 1002a32–b11, 1033a24–b26, 1034b7–16, 1060b17–19, 1069b35–1070a4, 1174b9–13.

3. What is generated is a composite of physical matter and form, as when a man is born, or a composite of a physical substance and an attribute (not the Sun, or stars, etc.), as when Socrates becomes dark or musical or sick.

4. What is generated is a light man, from a man as matter or subject and darkness, and lightness comes to him by a moving cause (1070a4–8); but lightness itself is not generated since it is not a composite of matter and form, and it comes *from* darkness in the sense that it comes *after* darkness, just as the darkness of night comes from the light of day (1023b5–11).

5. Physical matter is meant.

6. Wine is water with form, vinegar results when wine is deprived of its form.

7. He does not mean that destruction is accidental to wine or a living animal, for these are necessarily destructible. He may mean that destructions are accidental to the form which results. It is water, the matter of wine, which becomes vinegar, and the matter of a living body which becomes a corpse; and wine becomes vinegar just as day becomes night, in the sense that after day there is night.

8. Of course, to do so, a moving cause is needed.

6

1. 1044a2–6.

2. A formula is said to be one if it signifies one thing, and many if many. This is just a matter of definition.

3. Plato and followers.

4. Plato posits Man, Biped, and Animal as three distinct Ideas. If the latter two Ideas taken together as a whole make up Man, then the first Idea (= Man) is superfluous; but then what makes those two Ideas one and not two? If Man is not Biped + Animal, how can we truly say that a man is a biped animal if individuals among sensibles imitate Ideas?

5. That is, if 'animal' is matter and 'biped' is *form*, a "biped animal"

is one idea and of one thing; 'animality' is like matter, not yet specified as 'biped', or 'four-footed', or 'winged', or what not. In general, the unity of a genus and a differentia as one concept is the problem. It is the *actuality* or form which gives unity to the composite of matter and form.

6. The analogy is, genus : differentia :: sensible matter : sensible form. Thus "matter" is analogously a predicate of a genus and of sensible matter.

7. "What causes" here means what is the *moving* cause, not the cause as *form*. Thus, a moving cause puts a *form* on matter; but when this is done, the *actuality* is the cause as *form* or essence and of unity in the composite of matter and *form*.

8. The word "each" probably refers to matter and to the composite. That which causes (gives *actuality* and unity) a potential sphere (which is matter) to be a sphere (the composite) is the *actuality* or essence; that which *is* the cause (as *actuality*) of the composite is the essence or *form*.

9. Sensible matter is matter that underlies sensible qualities and can change, such as water, etc. Intelligible matter applies to the genus of a concept and to mathematical matter.

10. He does not give the complete definition of a circle; but for the sake of illustration, 'figure' is the genus or matter, 'plane' is the differentia or *actuality*.

11. As a category, 'a quality' is indefinable, and so not a composite of a genus and a differentia; hence it has no matter at all; and so it is an indivisible unity and a being. And 'unity' and 'being' are not genera of distinct categories but are analogous predicates of them (998b22–27). Similarly, the prime mover (God) is in no way a composite of matter and form and so not definable; he is indivisibly one and a being, and primarily so.

12. In other words, they have no matter which might need an *actuality* to become one or a being; they are themselves unities and beings.

13. A triangular bronze is not a composite of a triangle and a bronze in the sense that these two can be separated and exist apart and also be combined. Every instance of bronze has some shape, and every shape is with some matter, and bronze is to triangle as matter to *actuality*. Even if bronze and triangle could be combined, still something else would be needed to hold them together, some *actuality* (1041b4–33).

Book Θ

1

1. Books Z and H, 1028a10–1045b23.
2. 1028a10–b7.
3. 1017a7–b9, 1026a33–b2.

4. 1019a15–1020a6.

5. See Book Δ, Sec. 12, Comm. 21.

6. That is, related to potencies of one kind, the primary.

7. That is, the latter formulae include those of the former, but all those of the former have the formula of the primary potency, hence the formula of the primary potency is in all the formulae of the others.

8. If we consider that which can be acted upon only by itself, it has a potency of being acted upon; for example, a wooden chair can be burned, and this potency (the wood) is a principle in the chair. Likewise, heat is a potency of acting and a principle in fire, and the art of building is a potency in a man. On the other hand, the potency of acting is impossible without that which can be acted upon by it, and the action of that which acts on that which is acted upon is one and indivisible; that is, while the one is acting, the other is simultaneously being acted upon. Thus, there is one action but there are two aspects of that action, just as there is one road between A and B but the direction from A to B is different from that from B to A.

9. That which acts does so on another, and that which is acted upon is so acted upon by another; and if A acts on A itself, where A is a composite, then it is one part of A that acts on another part of A. Heat does not act on itself, wood does not burn by itself but does so by a mover; and if a man heals himself, it is his art, which is a part of himself, that acts upon another part of himself, his body.

10. By "with respect to the same thing" he means, for example, that if sight is a potency, then the contrary of this is the privation of sight and not of something else.

11. In this sense, a stone as well as a man may be said to be deprived of sight.

12. In this sense, a man may be said to be deprived of sight, but a stone is not said to be deprived of (or to have) sight.

2

1. Referring to potencies.

2. The soul has also nonrational potencies, such as those of seeing, hearing, digesting, etc.

3. Reason makes known the privation of a thing in an object by denying the possession of that thing.

4. For example, medicine is for the sake of health rather than of sickness, although for some other *reason,* such as research or even a bad *reason,* it may produce sickness.

5. This applies to practical sciences as well.

6. By "essentially" here he may mean *for the sake of* (1022a19–33), or else, *primarily.*

7. If medicine causes disease, it is either accidentally or for the sake of (or primarily for) knowledge or some other *reason,* but ultimately for the sake of health. For example, in experiments, diseases are caused in living things ultimately for the sake of health.

8. In the case of health, for example, reason is of health as well as of its privation, and so it is a sort of composite (not in the sense that reason is both healthy and sick, since this is impossible), one part of it being about health and the other about sickness; and such a potency can produce now the one and now the other, but not both at the same time and in the same respect.

9. Not at the same time but at different times, etc.

10. The artist, by means of the principle of motion in the soul (which is desire or *choice*, 1048a10–15), which principle selects now the one and now the other part of reason, produces in a thing now one of two contraries and now the other.

11. For example, a doctor can produce health or disease in a body (which is a thing having no reason qua body).

3

1. "To be able" or "can" here means to have a potency.

2. These are the materials which may be changed by the artist into works of art; and materials which can be changed by the artist always exist.

3. Two absurdities follow from the Megarian thesis and the premises just given. (a) When the artist stops acting qua artist, he immediately forgets his art, or loses it through some affection or lapse of time; (b) when he immediately starts building again, he has the art without having acquired it, for according to the Megarians he did not have it a minute earlier.

4. Man is the measure of what exists. So, if to be is to be sensed, and if X is sensed by A but not by B, then X both exists and does not exist (1009a6–1011b22).

5. That is, when they close their eyes.

6. It follows from the meaning of "incapable" that what is incapable (without qualification) will never be.

7. If motion is possible, then some A will sometime change to B; but then A will have a potency of becoming B prior to its change, and such potency is denied by the Megarians.

8. The term "may" must not be confused with "capable" which follows; the former applies to, let us say, the assumption that the thing is something, a logical possibility so to say, but "capable" means that the thing has a potency of being so. The one is sometimes called "logical possibility"; the other, "real possibility" or "potency", or something of this sort.

9. Or in general, generation and destruction are possible; and the example of walking, which follows, indicates that the other changes (motions) are also possible.

10. Capability of sitting is something which the thing has, whether it sits or not, whether it desires or is ordered or is assumed or whether chairs are available for it to sit or not. But "may" probably refers to

something additional besides capability, such as the things mentioned (desire to sit, etc.).

11. For example, nothing impossible follows if a man is assumed sitting, but the impossible follows, if five is assumed to be even.

12. The Greek term for *actuality* (ἐνέργεια) suggests motion or activity, as against their opposites; but the term for actuality (ἐντελέχεια) suggests existence or perfection as against the opposites of these latter. Aristotle seems to use both synonymously.

4

1. Namely, nothing impossible follows if a thing is assumed to have what it is capable of having (1047a24–6).

2. What Aristotle is saying amounts to a denial that everything is possible, for otherwise the impossible would be eliminated.

3. Perhaps by "without taking into account" he means *by excluding*, or something of the sort.

4. By "not possible" he means *impossible*. If it is not necessary for A to be possible, it may be actual, or necessary, or impossible.

5

1. 1105a17–b18, 1049b33–1050a2.

2. In living things, such are the powers of nutrition, growth, sensing, etc.

3. For example, fire can only heat the object in contact, not freeze it.

4. For example, a doctor can produce health as well as disease.

6

1. 1045b27–1048a24.

2. A potency merely to move another or be moved by another, regardless how, is a potency without qualification; a potency *in some manner* is a qualified potency, such as a potency of moving another *well*.

3. Not everything is definable; and there are principles and attributes of being qua being which are indefinable, such as *actuality* and potentiality.

4. The following serial analogy may also illustrate the meaning. *actuality* : potentiality :: shape (of a statue) : bronze :: form : matter :: seeing ; sight (without the seeing) :: motion : body (without the motion)

5. That is, if "to see" means to have the potency of seeing, it is possible for that which has the potency to be *actually* seeing without qualification. But the infinite as something potential cannot become an *actual* infinite, although there can be *actual* and finite *knowledge* (or

formula, or definition) of the infinite as potential. For example, the definition of an infinitely divisible line may be: "a line which is divisible without an end," and this formula is finite.

6. *Actuality* in the infinite is the never ending process of division or addition; but such process, in view of the fact that it never comes to an end, exists potentially. Thus, *actuality* and potentiality exist together, so to say, in the infinite, as in the case of motion; but there is a difference. There is a beginning and an end in motion, which can therefore be complete; but there is no end to the process of division or addition in the case of the infinite (200b12–208a23).

7. That is, actions which begin and end, as contrasted with an endless division in the case of infinity. Perhaps he is using πρᾶξις dialectically.

8. He is using "end" here as *final cause* or *that for the sake of which.*

9. That is, what is an end and an *action* is an action which exists or is pursued for its own sake.

10. Seeing is here taken as an end in itself, as when we watch a beautiful painting, not as a means to an end, as when we go to the next room to see whether the book sought is there. Similarly with prudent acts and thinking.

11. He is probably referring to the kind of thinking which is pursued for its own sake, for some thinking may occur for other causes, such as for the sake of getting money, escaping, taking revenge, etc.

12. If we take any successive intervals of happiness, I_1 and I_2, then I_1 is an end in itself, not a means to I_2 or something else; and we can truly say during I_2 both that we were happy (during I_1) and that we are now happy (during I_2).

13. That is, one can truly say this at time T_2, since there is an earlier T_1 during which he has seen.

14. By "kind" he refers to the fact that *actuality* is an end in itself or complete in each of its parts.

7

1. See later, 1049a11–7.

2. 1032b21–6.

3. The sick body. Thus, if the doctor wishes and acts, and the body is healable, and nothing outside prevents the doctor's acting on the body, then healing results. Perhaps by "nothing outside prevents" he refers to no shortage of drugs, help, instruments, etc., and no interference by other agents.

4. This phrase may be referring to the externals which might hinder the generation of the house.

5. That is, the moving cause.

6. In health and a house, which are products of art, the moving cause of what is potentially healthy or a house is art, which is external; but in what is generated by nature, the moving cause is in that which is poten-

tially something else, as in the case of seed, which has the moving cause in itself.

7. "By itself" in the sense of a moving cause, acting on the matter in which it exists, like a doctor healing himself.

8. Combine with the female material part.

9. Its moving cause.

10. That is, prior to this the seed needs another moving principle, the male who must deposit it; and it needs the material principle in the female.

11. An alternative expression is: "that-y" as in "stony", and perhaps others. Each language has its own variety.

12. The series earth, air, and fire is taken to illustrate his point and does not represent his view as to the truth of this sequence.

13. Greek texts vary. Some would be translated thus: "then fire is primary matter as a *this* and a substance". If so, then this matter is not the prime matter indicated in 1029a20–6. From the lines that follow, this alternative is less probable.

14. An alternative translation (because of differences in texts) is: "For that of which something is predicated or the underlying subject is differentiated by being or not being a *this*." If the translation as we gave it is correct, then evidently "wooden" and "musical" and other such terms appear to be universal and not signifying a *this*, while the subject (the box or a man) is a *this*. If the alternative translation is correct, then while a man as an underlying subject of the musical is a *this*, the wood, which is the underlying subject or matter of a box, is not a *this*.

15. For the usage of "predicate", see Book Z, Sec. 3, Comm. 11.

16. The principle here is: If certain things, though distinct in some ways, have something in common (*indefiniteness* in this case), this should be indicated linguistically.

17. An alternative to "affections" is "*attributes*".

8

1. 1018b9–1019a14.

2. For example, a man has a moving principle in himself, for he can move by himself, and fire moves qua fire or the hot (192b8–193b21).

3. A power is defined in terms of, or known by, the corresponding activity (or *actuality*); but power and activity are distinct, for the power may be present without the corresponding activity, as when an artist is asleep. For example, if carpentry is defined as the power of making wooden articles, evidently, "the making of wooden articles" is present in that definition and signifies an activity. Similarly for any potentiality.

4. In other words, the seed is potentially a tree and is prior in time to what it will *actually* be; but the seed was caused by another tree which existed *actually* prior to the seed. Thus, if A is potentially a B, there is always a B prior in time to A. By "a first mover" he means a

proximate mover; for example, such mover of Socrates would be his father.

5. "From something" signifies the material cause or potentiality, "by something" the moving cause. So, if A is a potentiality for a B, there must be another B in *actuality* which acts as a moving cause if A is to become a B (1032a12–1034a8). In the case of the materials of a house, it is not an actual house that must preexist but the art or knowledge of the form of a house, and this must preexist in the artist as a moving cause.

6. The sophistical argument seems to be: Let S be the first thing A did scientifically. Then prior to S, A had no science; hence, A did S scientifically without having acquired science.

7. 236b19–237b22. If X moves from A to E, at some instant within the motion AE, say at C, it has partly moved, for example, the partial motion AC.

8. If X learns to play, and he performs A_1 for the first time well, it is by accident and not by art. It is by repetition of performing A_1 well that he gains by degrees the art of performing A_1 well. Moreover, there are many A's which constitute the whole art. Thus, the art which is a power is gained part by part, numerically as well as by degrees; and this takes place after the successful repetitions, which are the *actualities* here (1105a17–26).

9. That is, posterior in time, or later in time.

10. By "prior in substance" [or "prior in *substance*"] here he may mean a substance to a higher degree, for it has a form or has it to a higher degree, while what precedes in time does not yet have it (seed relative to man) or does not have it completely (child relative to adult). An alternative to "substance" is "*substance*", and in this case *actuality* is prior to potentiality since a form may exist without potentiality, as in the prime mover, but potentiality (whether matter or a power like art) cannot exist without being with a form.

11. The argument is: What is being generated is potentiality, and it is being generated for the sake of a principle and an end, and this is an *actuality* (a form in the case of seed, a complete form in the case of a child, an activity in the case of sight).

12. As when high school students work out original problems, an activity which prepares them for research. This is somewhat like learning an art, as above in Comm. 8.

13. For example, learning may be acquired merely for its own sake, or for the sake of application, or for teaching, but not for research.

14. To say that something is a potency (or exists potentially) implies that it is a potency for something else. As a potency, then, matter is in a sense relative to what it will be or may be or acquire (194b8–9). Thus, universally, matter is a potency of possessing a form.

15. An alternative to "in a form" may be "with a form".

16. Motion here may be an immediate end, not an ultimate end.

For example, the power of running is for the sake of running, and this for the sake of something else; and the art of building for building something, namely, a house, and this for the sake of shelter.

17. "Nature" here may signify physical matter (1014b26–35), whose end is to take on a form; and it may also signify a physical form (1014b35–6), whose end is the exercise of that form, as in the case of the soul, whose end is living or happiness (412a3–28, 1050a34–b3), or in the case of medical art, whose end is healing.

18. According to Alexander, this statue was such that it was difficult to tell whether its form was the outer surface or was within some transparent mediium enclosing the statue.

19. An alternative is: "For the end is performance, and performance is an *actuality*."

20. The term ἐντελέχεια might be translated literally as "an end possessed by something" or, "the possession of an end by or in something". Thus, since "*actuality*", derived from "performance", signifies something which is an end, the term ἐνέργεια points to ἐντελέχεια. As for their meaning, Aristotle seems to use these two terms synonymously (201a3–202b29, 1065b5–1066a34).

21. Except accidentally, as when one goes to see whether the food is done or whether someone is at the door.

22. In the former case, seeing is the end and is final; in the latter, the act of building is for the sake of the house and it is in (and inseparable from) what is being built (202a13–b22). So, if the house is the end, then the act of building is closer to that end than the potency of building and so it is an end to a higher degree than that potency. The house itself is for the sake of use, which is the final end.

23. Of course, if the action of the mover on what is moved is by contact, both the mover and the thing moved are in motion; but while the motion of the latter results in, say, a house, that of the mover need not affect the primary moving cause (e.g. art). The materials become a house, but the artist remains an artist.

24. An alternative term would be "living". Happiness is living well, and so it is a final cause in the sense that it is best.

25. This will be considered in 1071b3–1073a13.

26. This is priority in existence (1019a1–6). Of course, a substance is prior in existence to its attributes. Earlier, priority in substance was discussed with respect to a potency and the *actuality* of that same potency. Now priority in substance (or existence) is discussed with respect to things with and things without a potency.

27. For example, in the case of quality, a man may lose his health or his sickness (this is qualified destruction), and so, when healthy Socrates becomes sick, healthy Socrates is destroyed, but in a qualified sense.

28. For example, a man may lose his form (he may die).

29. The Sun is still a Sun in the day as well as in the night, and what is potential in it is place, for the Sun is now here and now there. So it is destructible with respect to place and has matter with respect to

place, but with respect to its *substance* it has no matter and is not destructible.

30. That is, they are always in *actuality* with respect to their *substance*. And so, since they exist even if things in potency may not exist, but not conversely, they are prior in substance (in existence) to them.

31. Things which exist of necessity are either eternal, such as the prime mover and the stars, or hypothetical, such as incommensurable diagonals (for a diagonal cannot be commensurable with the side). In the first case, if what has potentiality exists, like Socrates, then the prime mover exists, but not conversely; in the second, if Socrates is sick (he is potentially sick and well), he has the nutritive power (or any property of man), but not conversely. So, in both cases, *actuality* is prior in existence to potentiality (22b29–23a26).

32. Motion, an *actuality* of the potential qua potential (201a9–15), is added here perhaps because it is a sort of mixture of *actuality* and potentiality but can be eternal as well as temporary. The same applies to an object eternally in motion. The motion of the stars, for example, is eternal, not potential (that is, it is not possible for it to stop), and the stars in motion have no potentiality for rest, though they do have qualified potentiality (for different places); so they have qualified matter, that is, matter as potentiality only for different places.

33. That is, in the sense of physical matter capable of motion as well as of rest, as in the physical things on this Earth, not in the sense of qualified matter, as that in the Sun or stars.

34. That is, there is always change in destructible things which, though not numerically eternal, are in kind eternal. A man of necessity has a power to learn, whether it be Socrates during time T_1, or one of his descendants during time T_2; and water and air always change back and forth, for there are eternal movers which cause this (336a15–338b19).

35. Probably the passive as well as the active potencies in destructible things.

36. Such as the medical art, which can heal as well as make sick.

37. For example, if fire is near A, it heats A, if not, not; and, to heat and not to heat are contradictories.

38. That is, potencies. Since science is a potency, if there is an Idea of science, Science Itself, then there should also be an Idea of the *actuality* of science (this is an Idea of scientific thinking), and it should be prior in view of what has been said. No such is posited by Plato; and if he did, he would be positing an Idea which is in *actuality* or in motion while at the same time he regards Ideas as immovable (113a24–32, 1076b39–1077a9).

9

1. The potentialities considered here seem to be those to whose *actualities* goodness and badness are attributed, and such potentialities are capable of contraries.

2. While it is a potentiality, it has neither one nor the other contrary *actually* (and so it is neither good nor bad *actually*), and as a potentiality for something, it is a potentiality for both contraries alike (and so for both good and bad).

3. That is, what is *actually* good is better than what is potentially both, or neutral, or even potentially good.

4. Badness is not an *actuality* existing by itself but an *actuality* of what was potentially bad. So the bad is a subject with badness as its *actuality*, and the potentiality of what is bad existed before it became bad.

5. First principles and eternal things have no potentiality, for what is potential may not exist while eternal things must exist (337b35–338a3). Hence such things cannot be defective or corruptible, and therefore bad. Thus there exists no *Bad Itself* as an Idea, and Plato is not right in positing the *Indefinite Dyad*, which is the first material principle, as bad (988a14–5, 1075a34–6, 1091b30–2; *Republic* 476A; *Theaetetus* 176E; *Laws* 896E).

6. The term "demonstration" here includes both the fact and its causes, not only the fact. Thus, "The sum of the angles of a triangle are equal to two right angles" is not a demonstration, since it signifies only the fact. By "dividing" perhaps he means dividing in thought or by thought, or dividing an individual which typifies universally all possible cases.

7. Referring to the divisions. Whether a potentiality should be called "good", when it is alike a potentiality for both contraries, is a disputed point. Perhaps the text is corrupt and should read: ὅτι δέ βελτίων καί τιμιωτέρα τῆς δυνάμεως ἡ σπουδαία ἐνέργεια.

8. The Greek translates into: "it would be at once clear." So "it" may refer to the cause or to the theorem.

9. That is, any angle E.

10. The sum of the base angles of triangle ADC is equal to the sum of the angles 1 and 2, for all four angles are equal since triangles ABD and CBD are isosceles; moreover, the sum of the angles of a triangle is two right angles. Hence the sum of angles 1 and 2, or the angle D, is one right angle.

11. Referring to the theorem that all angles inscribed in the same arc (here it is the semicircular arc) are equal. Thus, angles D and E are equal. We have, then: E is equal to D, D is half the sum of $A + D + C$, half the sum is a right angle, hence E is (or is equal to) a right angle.

12. Thinking, an *actuality*, causes (as a moving cause) the potential to become *actual* by dividing. There are two *actualities*: thinking as a moving cause, and the *actuality* it produces in the potential figure by dividing. The formal cause in the theorem is in the latter *actuality*.

13. This is thinking, the moving cause. Evidently demonstration (or deduction) requires this cause; for it is this cause that selects premises, arranges them, divides what is potential if this is needed to select premises, etc. Thus, nothing follows from a number of premises if think-

ing does not add something to them. To select the premises is itself not easy. Substitutions are often *disguised minor premises*. For example, we deduce $0 + A = A$ from $A + 0 = A$ and $A + B = B + A$ by substituting 0 for B in the second axiom and then using the first axiom, and the axiom "things equal to the same thing are equal to each other". Assuming here that A and B are any numbers, such substitution amounts to the premise (not explicitly stated) that 0 is a number. Similarly, if pq or $p \supset q$ or any other such is substituted for p, such substitution amounts to a minor premise, namely, that pq or $p \supset q$ is an instance of p. Anyway, such substitutions do not appear in the initial set of axioms, and yet they are needed. In general, the premises in a system are many times greater than those usually given nowadays in an axiom set because of the additional minor premises which are required. This fact was clearly known by Aristotle (71a17–29).

14. This is the diagram after division, relative to which the diagram before division exists potentially.

10

1. It is not clear whether these are contraries of potentiality and *actuality* or of the categories, or of both, whenever contraries exist. There are contraries of potentiality (1046a29–31) as well as within a category (such as black and white).

2. The statement "being in the most proper sense is the true and the false" seems to contradict 1027b29–33. There, "truth" and "falsity" signify attributes of thoughts and statements, while here they may be used in a wider sense so as to be predicated also of things as well (1051b33–5), that is, assuming the word ἐπὶ ($=$ "concerning") in the next line is used in a wide sense so as to include the sense in 1051b33–5.

3. Alternatives to "concerning" are "about" and "which depends on".

4. He will first consider truth and falsity as attributes of beliefs and of the corresponding propositions.

5. This amounts to what may be called the "realistic" position of Aristotle. Things are prior in existence to our thoughts of them, and truth or falsity of the latter depend on the corresponding union or separation of the former.

6. As will be seen, potentiality is the cause of contrariety in some of these.

7. For example, "Socrates sits" is sometimes true and sometimes false.

8. Necessary unions are meant, such as equality as an attribute of vertical angles, and necessary separations, such as the diagonal of a square and its commensurability with the side of that square.

9. Examples of incomposites are a triangle, a point, whiteness, a man, and any essence, in the general sense of that term. These may be definable (as a triangle) or not (as quality). Although a definition is a composite, yet it is a whatness of one thing, unlike a white man which

is not definable except by addition (1029b1–1031a14). "To be" or "not to be" for composites means that two things are united or not united respectively. But there is no union or separation if there is only one thing; and so neither can thought regard two things as united or as separate. Consequently, "to be" and "not to be", as well as "truth" and "falsity", will not have the same meanings for them.

10. That is, truth concerning an incomposite is defined as the apprehension of it, or as getting a concept of it. The term "truth" as an attribute of thought, then, has two senses, but not entirely unrelated, for in both cases there is knowledge; in one case it is of one thing as undivided, in the other it is of the union or separateness of two things as they are, and the latter knowledge presupposes the former.

11. When two things are united or divided, thought can consider them either as united or as divided, and so it can be either true or false; but if there is only one thing, thought can either apprehend it or not apprehend it, and not to apprehend it is to be ignorant of it. Perhaps the reason why Aristotle does not use "falsity" synonymously with "ignorance" here is that, while in falsity one has the two concepts and does something to them, although erroneously, in the case of one thing a man does not even have a concept to use erroneously in any way.

12. For example, one may have a concept of heaviness, but he may misapply it when he thinks that a given object is heavy. Thus he is mistaken not about the whatness of heaviness but about whether that whatness belongs or does not belong to a given object; and such mistakes happen sometimes (accidentally).

13. Such substances are not composites of matter and form; they are just forms or *actualities*, like the prime mover.

14. Greek texts differ. An alternative and perhaps less likely translation is: "But we do inquire about the whatness of them, whether they are such-and-such or not".

15. These are different meanings of "truth" and "falsity", but they are related to the corresponding ones which exist in thought or statements. For example, the equality of base angles in an isosceles triangle is truth in this sense and is signified by the corresponding true belief or statement; but a diagonal of a square commensurate with its side is a falsity in this sense, for no such thing exists, that is, we have non-being (1024b17–21).

16. Besides a unity of two things, which is called a "truth" in the second sense, we speak also of a thing by itself, such as the prime mover, a point, etc. We are then concerned not with a unity of two things but with one thing, and here we do not say that the thing is true (for example, that a point or God is true), but only that it exists, or does not exist; and "truth" about such a thing is only used in the sense of the conception of the thing, as stated earlier. And if we do not conceive it, we do not say that we have a false conception of it but only that we are ignorant of it. But unlike blindness, which by definition deprives one of ever seeing, one who is ignorant of a thing may conceive it later.

17. For example, 'a number' is immovable, but it is a genus; and

some numbers are odd but others even. The term "immovable thing" refers to a thing generically taken, and the various species of it have contrariety.

18. The term "numerically one" applies also to an ultimate species of immovable things; for here there is no contrariety under a species, since a species is indivisible into lower species, and properties of such a species are eternal.

Book I

1

1. 1015b16–1017a6.

2. That is, just continuous, without any restrictions or regardless of the cause.

3. 1016a5–17.

4. The moving cause of the unity of these is outside, a man or his art.

5. Locomotion is prior in existence to the other kinds of motion (260a20–261a26).

6. Of locomotions, the circular is prior in existence to the others (261b27–265b16).

7. The celestial sphere, or the celestial bodies (especially the spherical).

8. For example, if the conception of a triangle takes one second, in no part of that second has the triangle been conceived. But if a triangle and a square have been conceived in time T, then it is possible for the triangle to have been conceived in a part of T.

9. What is indivisible in kind (not to be confused with the indivisible in species) may be indivisible in species or genus.

10. For example, all triangles qua triangles have one and the same formula, let us say "a three-sided plane figure", and all of them are known as such by one concept or formula.

11. This is the essence or form (1041a6–b33).

12. Substantial forms are prior to the other forms (1028a32–3).

13. Just as an animal may be (or, is potentially) a man, or a dog, or etc., so what is one may be an individual, or a universal, or something continuous by nature, etc. However, "an animal" has one univocal meaning, but the meaning of "one", like that of "an element" or "a principle", is one by analogy (1016b31–1017a3).

14. This is the position of Hippasus and Heraclitus, given just as an illustration.

15. The Pythagorean position, and in a sense that of Plato.

16. In raising the question, "What are the elements of things?", one has to know first what the term "element" means, otherwise the question is meaningless; afterwards, it is a matter of investigation to deter-

mine what sort of things or what natures are qualified to be truly called "elements".

17. If by a number, then that number is a measure but not the first measure; for the number itself is known by a unit or a one, and this latter is a principle as it is not known by something else within the genus of number. Thus, that by which, as first or a principle, a number is known is the one. For example, the one in five horses is a horse or one horse.

18. In English, we have the two terms "weight" and "heaviness" to bring out the two meanings, but in Greek only the term βάρος is used. Similarly, τάχος has two meanings, speed and swiftness (or high speed).

19. What about a fraction of a foot, such as ¼ of a foot? But such a part in the statement "¼ of a foot" is defined and known in terms of one foot, and so one foot is still a principle; and if the ratio of the two magnitudes is considered, then this is 1:4, and the measure is no longer the foot but a smaller magnitude. Thus, for the Greeks, the fraction ¼ has meaning only if the original measure is a magnitude and so divisible qua magnitude, and in such a case the numerator, which is 1, becomes the new measure. In other words, our theory of fractions assumes continuity, or else it is a theory of ratios of whole numbers, like that of the Greeks.

20. This is the principle in arithmetic, where the unit is indivisible in every respect and so one cannot take a part away from it nor add a part to it to make a new unit.

21. Since every magnitude is infinitely divisible, no unit of magnitude has the accuracy of the unit in a number; but for psychological reasons, to know the greatness or extent of a given magnitude, we choose such a magnitude as a unit which we can recognize by the senses with the least percentage of error.

22. A simple motion would be a primary motion (this is locomotion) along a simple line (a straight line or a circular line).

23. This is an attribute of fastest motion and not a definition.

24. Since Aristotle defines time in terms of motion (219b1–3), then uniformity and fastest-ness for him become attributes of motion and not of time.

25. We may use as a unit one motion of the heavens around the Earth, and call this "a day", which is easily recognizable, or we may use a part of it as a unit. Thus, two days will be the time of two such motions. Then the time of a given motion is the number of such units of that motion, assuming that the limits of the given motion (if this motion is other than the motion of the heavens) coincide with the corresponding limits of the heavenly motion whose time is the same as the time of the given motion.

26. For example, what is one in time is a motion, and in music it is a quarter-tone, and these two are distinct.

27. Perhaps because the two were not easily distinguishable by hearing, as St. Thomas Aquinas suggests. If so, then like the moderns,

Aristotle is using quantitative methods where a quality (hearing) fails psychologically to yield distinctions. The two quarter-tones may be those distinguished by Aristotle's pupil Aristoxenus, namely, the enharmonic (or ¼ of a tone) and the chromatic (⅓ of a tone).

28. These may be the twenty-four distinct letters, or else, the two kinds of syllables, long and short (4b32–4).

29. One interpretation may be: If a unit measures the diagonal exactly, it cannot so measure the side but a distinct unit must be taken, and similarly for any two magnitudes. Another interpretation may be: Two distinct units are needed to measure each of any two magnitudes, such as the diagonal and the side of a square. For example, in a square of side 10 feet, we have 10 and $10\sqrt{2}$ as lengths. The side is measured by a foot 10 times, the diagonal is measured 14 times with a remainder, for $10\sqrt{2} = 14 + x$, where $x = 10\sqrt{2} - 14 = $ less than one foot. So x, or $x/2$, or $x/5$, or x/n may be taken as the other unit, and then $10\sqrt{2}$ is measurable by the foot and that other unit. Another interpretation may be: All magnitudes of the same kind can be measured by two units. Of course, this cannot be, for 10, $\sqrt{2}$, and $\sqrt[3]{2}$ cannot be so measured. Other interpretations are possible. I am inclined to accept the first interpretation.

30. For example, a number is divided only with respect to quantity, for it is divided into undifferentiated units; but if the units differ, then the kinds of units should be stated. For example, the letters of the alphabet are different kinds of units.

31. Such a unit comes closest to being psychologically indivisible, although it is actually divisible since it is a magnitude.

32. An alternative to "perhaps" is "equally", to be inserted near the end of the sentence after "is".

33. Again, Aristotle guards himself against being taken in by language. One may say: "If the measure of magnitudes is a magnitude, etc., then that of numbers is a number." Now "a number" and "units" have the same meaning; but the term "a number" is singular and gives the appearance of being a unit, while "units" does not do this but is like "magnitudes" in relation to a magnitude which is the unit.

34. The apparent similarity is this: Just as a number is known by a unit, which is a measure, so the knowable or sensible is known by knowledge or sensation, which some mistakenly call "a measure".

35. Although truth in the soul and the corresponding fact imply each other, the fact is the cause of the corresponding truth and not conversely (14b10–22). And since the cause is a measure, the fact is a measure of the corresponding truth, and not conversely.

36. "Quality" here means differentia of a substance (1020a33–b1), and this is the same as "kind", which Aristotle uses previously in 1053a20.

37. "Either simply or qua one" may mean: either in all respects or in a certain respect. An arithmetical unit is indivisible in all respects,

and so is a point. However, a triangle is divisible qua a magnitude, though indivisible in thought.

2

1. 1001a4–b25.
2. Empedocles, 985a21–31, 1001a12–15.
3. Anaximenes, Diogenes, 984a5.
4. Anaximander, 203b13–5.
5. 1038b1–1039a23.
6. 998b23–6.
7. That is, we should inquire what unity is as a nature, or what is that of which "one" is a predicate.
8. Just as the primary one is a substance, so the primary one within colors would be the primary color, which is white.
9. The triangle is the primary rectilinear figure, potentially present in all the other rectilinear figures (414b19–32).
10. As we would say, denotatively but not connotatively; that is, if X is a being, then it is one, and conversely, but to be one is not to be a being.
11. No new concept is added to "Socrates" by using "one Socrates", for they have the same meaning.
12. The term "oneness" is not univocal but analogical, like "medical" or "healthy" (1003a33–b15), and the nature which underlies oneness varies from category to category, and even from species to species.

3

1. Here, the terms "divisible" and "indivisible" are used in the generic sense, but in the lines that immediately follow they are used in a specific sense. See *Glossary*.
2. That is, of the indivisible and the divisible, the former is opposed as being the privation of the divisible.
3. The kinds of opposites are: contradictories, relatives, contraries, privation and possession. Evidently, one and many are not relatives or contradictories, for unity need not be related to something else, and what is not one may be nothing. They are opposed as privation and possession not in every sense but as contraries, for the latter come under the former (1022b22–1023a7, 1055a3–b29), and there is something underlying the one and the many.
4. Probably a lost work on contraries, mentioned by Alexander and listed in the catalogues of Diogenes Laertius and Hesychius.
5. This may be named by accidents, like "the musical" and "the sick" when predicated of the same individual.
6. This would be of the indivisible or lowest species predicable of many individuals. For example, "man" is a species, but not "animal".

7. That is, numerically many.

8. Apparently, equality in quantity for Aristotle is a necessary condition if many quantities are to come under one ultimate species.

9. A composite *substance* has matter and form, but its matter is not necessarily sensible. It may be intelligible, like the surface of a square.

10. That is, if we call two unequal squares the same, they would be so with a qualification, namely, with respect to the definition of a square but not the quantity of surface.

11. For example, qualities such as colors admit of variation of degree, and colors may be similar.

12. Tin and silver are in more respects the same than distinct, and this is similarity without qualification; gold and fire are similar with respect to their color, which is an obvious attribute.

13. This probably refers to sameness in sense (1), so that two things are the same if numerically one, but distinct if numerically two.

14. They may be distinct in their matter, or formula, or both. Thus you and your neighbor are the same in formula (you are both men) but numerically distinct.

15. Corresponding to sameness in sense (3), two unequal straight lines are distinct, and so are two unequal squares, for, in each case, the formulas of the first *substance* (and these include the area) are not one.

16. Namely, because of the fact that what is the same or distinct must be a being and one. "Unity" and "plurality" are predicates of beings, each of which is one, and since "sameness" and "otherness" come under "unity" and "plurality", respectively, they too are such predicates.

17. For example, "a circle-square is other than 5" is false, but "a circle-square is not the same as 5" is true. By "a circle-square" we mean an object which is both a circle and a square; of course, no such can exist.

18. For example, a color and 5 differ in genus, for "genus" is that which is the same and with respect to which they differ; but 5 and 3 differ in species. But a cause is distinct from 5, for both are beings but "difference" does not apply to them, since a cause does not fall under a unique genus.

19. Referring to the contraries.

20. Instead of "the same in genus", "the same in kind" may be used, for some texts have the term γένει, but others the term εἴδει; and both make sense. But "the same in species" is false.

21. 1024b9–16.

4

1. The terms "more", "less", and "greatest" are not restricted in meaning to quantities but are analogously used for other things (1020a23–6).

2. If A and B differ in genus, they cannot differ more or less in genus; for they are not comparable and there is no motion from the one to the other, and so contrariety in the sense of greatest difference does not apply.

3. What has been shown here is that the greatest difference is also a complete difference. The root of τέλειος (= "complete") is τέλος (= "end").

4. Since, in general, the greatest difference is complete difference, to each sense of "the greatest difference" corresponds a sense of "complete difference". Such senses may be: analogous, primary and secondary, and other modes such as those in 1018a31–5.

5. The argument is: An interval can have only two extremes, which we call "contraries"; so a contrary can have only one contrary.

6. Perhaps the meaning here is: the other definitions which are given of contraries are predicates of and coextensive with the definition just given of contraries. Strictly, of a thing there is just one definition, and a definition as such is neither true nor false.

7. That is, there is no difference admitting the more and the less, and so the greatest difference; for differences among genera are not comparable (1055a6–7).

8. The definition of contraries as "things which differ most in the same genus" is equivalent to "things whose difference is greatest", for "in the same genus" does not add anything since things in different genera are not comparable anyway.

9. This is the third definition given in 1018a28–9.

10. This is the fourth definition in 1018a29–30.

11. If a privation is not complete, as when one is deprived only of one eye, or when a thing has an intermediate color and so is deprived of whiteness, then the difference is not the greatest.

12. By "other contraries" he means those which are called "contraries" according to the primary ones. For example, if whitness and blackness are primary, then a white subject is contrary to a black subject, but secondarily, and what is acquired or lost may be the subjects which have the primary contraries. Evidently blackness and whiteness would be primary, for both the black and white subjects are composite, each containing a primary contrary. Similarly, the acquisitions (or losses) of two primary contraries are secondarily called "contraries", in view of the primary contraries which are acquired.

13. Privation and possession are meant. As in the case of the terms "a contrary" and "contrariety", so "privation" signifies sometimes one of the extremes and sometimes both, but in Greek there is only one term.

14. If A is *black*, then it is *not white*, but if it is *not white*, then it does not follow that it is *black*. So what is *not white*, which is a contradictory, is prior in existence to what is *black*, which is a contrary. Aristotle uses "contradictory" to mean both the propositions which are so called and

also the terms, such as "white" and "not white", or what these signify.

15. For example, whether A is a being or not a being, either A is *B* or A is *not B*, and there is no middle. But A may be neither white nor black, or neither sick nor healthy, and in general, if $\bar{B}$ is the contrary of B, then both "A is B" and "A is $\bar{B}$" may be false.

16. In general, to get a privative expression from the contradictory "A is not B", we limit A to what is a being, thus excluding nonbeing, and we further specify *not B* in some determinate way. For example, A may be a body, B may be whiteness; and then *not B* would be some other color.

17. 1022b22–1023a7.

18. For example, if A is a thing but not a quantity, then both "A is equal to B" and "A is unequal to B" are false; so A is neither equal nor unequal to B, and so there is something intermediate, so to say. Likewise, justice is neither white nor black, for it is not a color or a body. But if A and B are lines, then A is either equal to B, or unequal to B, and no intermediate exists.

19. For example, it may be deprived partially, or in the sense in which justice is said to be deprived of whiteness.

20. The word "deprived" here means "does not have something".

21. A baby just born cannot see, but we do not say that it is blind or deprived of sight.

22. In this sense, one is blind if sight is lost in both eyes, not just one; and one is sick if the whole body is sick, not just a part.

23. A baby is neither good nor bad; for it does not yet have powers of deliberation which are necessary for virtue or vice.

24. For whiteness and blackness, it is surface; for oddness and evenness, it is numbers; for sickness and health, it is a living body. But contraries like one and many, and good and bad, are in all categories (1096a19–29).

5

1. In other words, the terms "came" and "did not come", which are opposites, are assumed to be predicated of Cleon and Socrates, one of each; or else, by hypothesis, only one of "Cleon came" and "Socrates came" is true. And it is with this in mind that we ask whether Cleon or Socrates came.

2. That is, the disjunctive "whether" would apply to "both" or "just one of them", an instance of "one" and "many", or else, to "both" and "not both", an instance of contradiction; and both are opposites.

3. There is no more reason for it to be contrary to one rather than to the other, whichever this may be. So it cannot be contrary either to the greater, or to the less; that is, it cannot be contrary to just one of them. And it cannot be contrary to both, for there is only one contrary to it.

4. The "unequal" is as much an attribute of the greater as of the less; and if so, the equal would be contrary to two things, or to both the unequal and the greater, etc.

5. That is, to both the greater and the less taken as a pair or a unit.

6. For Plato, the first principle as form is the *One* or the *Equal,* and the first principle as matter is the *Dyad,* which he called also "the *Unequal*" and "the *Great* and *Small*" (1087b4–12).

7. This is impossible whether the greater and the less are considered as a unit, or taken separately.

8. Plainly stated, this amounts to the following: No contrary is an intermediate, and this also follows from the definition of contrariety. For if A and B were contraries, and B an intermediate, then the interval AB would not be complete. If A and B are contraries, it is something else, say C, that is an intermediate between A and B, and it is the interval AB which contains that of AC or of CB.

9. The equal is opposed as a relative only to its equal, and it is not opposed to the great and the small as a contrary, as stated above. So the only opposites remaining are denial and privation.

10. That is, the equal, the greater, and the less are all included in the expression "whether A or B", where "A" means *equal,* and "B" means *greater or less.*

11. The Greek text, literally translated, reads "It is of necessity not a privation;". But this makes no sense or is contrary to Aristotle's thought. I think the word οὐ (= "not") should be ἔστι (= "there is"). The meaning intended is clear: If the greater and the less are to be opposed by the equal, we must stay in the same genus, quantity, and we can only do so by denying the greater and the less, not without qualification or entirely (for then what is neither greater nor less might be a quality which cannot be equal, or even a nonbeing), but in a qualified way, that is, privatively or staying within the genus of quantity. Our position is confirmed also by what follows.

12. In the expression "privative denial" the word "denial" means just a denial, but "privative" limits this denial to the same genus. Now the equal is exactly this; for, it *is not* greater or less, and it is a *quantity.*

13. It is between, because it is not an extreme and is in the same genus.

14. 1096a19–29. This is the subject which is partly good and partly bad, but not that which can be neither the one nor the other; and the subject is distinct in a distinct category.

15. That which is neither white nor black as a privative denial can at least be named generically, for it is a color, whether grey or yellow or something else; but that which is neither good nor bad is not in any definite genus. Thus, the former is definite to a higher degree than the latter, for it is limited to colors; but still it is not unique, for the equal is unique, while what is neither black nor white may be yellow or red or some other color.

16. A shoe and a hand are not species under the same genus, and the denial of the two cannot be in a definite genus and so cannot be privative.

6

1. That is, since to an opposite there corresponds only one opposite, the one is numerically the same as the little or few. But this is impossible, for what is little or few need not be one; for two is also few.

2. Since two is double of one but the double is a multiple, and since the multiple is many and the many are opposed to the few, two will be opposed to the few, and this few can only be unity. But this cannot be, as before; besides, two itself is few, and indeed without qualification.

3. Just as numbers are divisible, so are liquids and gases or whatever takes the shape of a container; so the terms "many" and "much" seem to have the same meaning (or else denote the same thing), and likewise for "little" and "few", and they are all pluralities. Of course, the arguments are somewhat dialectical.

4. If, as just shown, the one is few or little, and the much and the little are in plurality what the long and short are in length, then the one will be a plurality.

5. Water and 5 are divisible, but with some difference; for water is indefinitely divisible, but 5 is divisible definitely into ultimate units, five units.

6. Perhaps he means what is discretely divisible, not like a continuum.

7. In relation to 5, 1,000 is a plurality in excess. It is more difficult to exemplify an excessive plurality without qualification, if numbers go on to infinity potentially. If, as some thinkers advocated, 10 is the greatest number (1073a18–21, 1084a12–3), then 10 will be such a plurality; or, in some field where there is a mean plurality, as in a family, a family with 20 children will be such a plurality. In magnitudes, that of the universe is the greatest, and so it is a magnitude in excess without qualification. The expressions "in excess" and "deficient" are opposed like the terms "great" and "small", as when we speak of great and small numbers.

8. The usage of "little" rather than "few" here may mean that unlike "much" and "many", "little" and "few" were synonymously used for magnitudes and numbers by most people.

9. Relative to 20, 4 is a deficient plurality; but 2 is a deficient plurality without qualification, for it is the least plurality and it can be a deficient plurality only, whether relatively or not.

10. That is, regardless of whether the number is excessive or deficient. In sense (a) "many" and "few" (or "little") are like differentiae or species of "plurality". In sense (b), "many" is a predicate of both many and few as used in sense (a), and as such it is like a genus of them; so, if opposed at all, it would be opposed as "a number" to "the one" (or the

"measurable" to the "measure"). It is assumed here that "opposite", "contrary" and the like are predicates of things as well as of the terms signifying the things, primarily of the former, secondarily of the latter.

11. He states the measured first rather than the measure in view of the fact that it is the former that is related to the latter and not conversely. He could have said "the measure, and the measured or measurable". See 1021a29–b3.

12. That is, as first plurality, but qua just a plurality. Perhaps by "first" he means prior in existence to all others, or nearest to the one or the measure; at any rate, it is the least plurality.

13. Some commentators object to Aristotle's correction of "in smallness". But was the meaning of "the infinite" such that it could be applied to what we nowadays might call "infinitely small" or "infinitesimal"?

14. 1021a26–b3.

15. That is, in the sense of being few or a deficient plurality.

16. Not strictly a genus, for plurality as such is not in any category, but in the sense that "plurality" is a wider predicate than "number".

17. This is to be taken as an undemonstrated property, relevant to the problem here, and not as a definition. One may notice the *metaphysical* nature of the terms employed in that formula.

18. The term "one" here does not mean a unit or a measure, but whatever is one under any category. Thus, a point is one, and indivisible; 5 is one (for it has a unity), but is divisible.

19. The *knowable* is prior in existence to *knowledge*, like the unit to a number, or the measure to the measurable. Thus, things exist whether we know them or not. But if we know X, then X exists, for by definition *knowledge* is of that which exists. *Knowledge* is potential of what exists potentially (and this is universal knowledge), and *actual* if it is of the *actually* existing, as of the Moon and the stars and the motion of the first heaven.

20. Not everything divisible or divided is a number, for no common measure may exist (except an accidental measure), as in whiteness and length and God (1088a11–4).

7

1. This is the thesis to be shown, and the primary concern is to show that the intermediate differentiae consist of the primary contraries. From this it will follow that an intermediate species is composed of those contraries and the genus.

2. Non-substantial change is from a contrary, and such contraries are in the same genus (224b26–225b9).

3. If the white changes to a sphere, it does so accidentally, that is, qua non-spherical (whatever shape this may be) which is by accident white, and not qua white.

4. The term "privation" here means the two opposites taken together, usually called "privation and possession".

5. Contraries qua contraries are relatives, for a contrary is a contrary of something, of its contrary; for example, black as a contrary is the contrary of white (1056b34–6).

6. The *knowledge* of something is a quality in the soul; but what is *known* may be in any category, such as a triangle or a star.

7. This is the equal. The great, the small, and the equal are all quantities, and so in the same genus.

8. Privatives need not be discussed, for complete privations are contraries, and other privatives are secondary—or between contraries (1022b22–1023a7, 1046b14–5, 1055a33–b11).

9. The definitions of blackness and whiteness are hypothetically taken, perhaps from Plato (Timaeus 67E). Let A be a genus (such as 'color'), X and Z its contrary differentiae (such as 'piercing' and 'compressing'), AX and AZ the corresponding species ('whiteness' and 'blackness'), and AY any intermediate between AX and AZ. Now, also the species AX and AZ are called "contrary" (1018a25–35). So AX and AZ have a genus in them, and this is A; but X and Z have no genus in them, and it is because of these that AX and AZ possess contrariety and are called "contraries". So X and Z are the prior contraries; that is, they are prior as causes, and prior in *knowledge* or definition.

10. That is, AX and AZ are contrary to a higher degree than AX and AY, or AY and AZ.

11. That is, Y is distinct from X and from Z.

12. That is, unlike AX and AZ, which have A as their genus, X and Z by themselves do not have that genus (although they are differentiae of a genus).

13. He is speaking of the differentiae under a genus, whether contrary or not. So the question is: Is Y an incomposite or not, and if not, of what incomposites is it a composite?

14. That is, X has nothing of Z, and conversely; and both are incomposites, and therefore principles.

15. That is, there is a motion from a contrary to what is called "an intermediate."

16. That is, Y is partly piercing and partly compressing, and it is closer to Z than X is, and closer to X than Z is; for if it were entirely distinct, it would be an incomposite, or composed of other incomposites (but of which, if not of X and Z?), and in either case the term "closer" in relation to X and Z would not apply to it. Further, to say that a color is almost white is to say that it has much of X and little of something else (of Z), and such colors evidently exist.

17. This refers to AX, AY, and AZ. Just as Y is between X and Z, so AY is said to be between AX and AZ. Moreover, AX is a composite of A and X, AZ of A and Z, and AY of A and of Y, where Y is part of X and part of Z. The term "contrary" is a predicate also of AX and of AZ, and "intermediate" is of AY.

18. That is, AY is a composite of A, X, and Z.

19. If he means the primary contraries and the corresponding inter-

mediates, then "consist of" is the proper translation; but if he includes both primary and secondary, then "composed of", which is wider than "consist of", should be used. See Comm. 1 of this Section.

8

1. "Animal" would be accidentally differentiated as "black" and "white", for it is of "color" that the latter are essential differentiae.

2. 1016a24–8, 1024b6–9.

3. That is, animality must be distinct not in the sense that "animality" is equivocal, but in virtue of having one differentia in one species and another in another.

4. A contrast is not necessarily a complete difference; and in this sense, there is a contrast between white and grey.

5. 1057a18–b4. This is not any contrariety, such as unity and plurality, but one within a genus.

6. Perhaps he is using "different in species" synonymously with "other in species".

7. An alternative of "exist together" is "exist at the same time".

8. Since the differentia of grey is a mixture of that of white and that of black, are not these contraries existing together at the same time in grey? Partly, yes; wholly, no. It is like an object painted partly black and partly white. Is it black, or white? Neither. But it is *partly black,* and *partly white,* and this is not black and white.

9. By "indivisible" he probably means: no longer differentiable. This applies to the ultimate species.

10. That is, in the subdivision of a genus into its species.

11. The intermediate genera are meant, and these lie between the ultimate genus (such as 'quantity', which is a category) and the last species which is indivisible into lower species.

12. These are the last species.

13. A genus, like matter, is potentially each of its species but actually none. So, it can be potentially the same in species as or distinct in species from a given species of it; but actually, no species of it is the same in species as or distinct in species from it, just as no matter is the same in species as or distinct in species from a form.

14. For example, a triangle differs in genus from white, for the former is in quantity and the latter in quality.

15. In what way is "difference" distinct from "contrast"? Now things are different if, being distinct, they are the same in some respect or if they are other with respect to something. But the term "contrast" ($= \dot{\epsilon}\nu\alpha\nu\tau\acute{\iota}\omega\sigma\iota\varsigma$) is derived from the term "contrariety" ($= \dot{\epsilon}\nu\alpha\nu\tau\iota\acute{o}\tau\eta\varsigma$), and it indicates that this otherness is an otherness in contraries. That is, if A and B show contrast, then A and B may be contrary species, like white and black, and so the differentiae of A and B would be primary contraries; or else, A may be a contrary and B an intermediate, or both A and B distinct intermediates, and in the first case, B has part of the other

contrary but A does not, but in the second, the amounts of the primary contraries differ in A and B. In any case, the interval from A to B is an interval between or within contraries.

9

1. Blackness and whiteness are not essential differences of animals; they are in surfaces of physical bodies in general.

2. The phrase "less *proper*" is dialectical, intending to indicate that although whiteness and blackness exist in animals, they are *proper attributes* of a wider genus than that of animals. Strictly, "not *proper*" is the accurate term, but this would also apply to what is not an *attribute* of animals.

3. Perhaps the term should be ἐναντιώσεις (= "contrasts").

4. The name would then signify an accidental unity (1015b16–34, 1029b22–1030a17).

5. That which makes Socrates distinct from Callias is the distinct individual body, not the species, and the distinctions that arise in them are distinctions qua distinct bodies or distinctions in their matter.

6. "This" may refer to the formula or to the species, and the species can no longer be subdivided into lower species.

7. Perhaps the definition of man is meant.

8. Whiteness is in Callias not qua a man; hence it is an accident to a man, universally taken.

9. Likewise, bronze or wood is an accident of a circle.

10. Perhaps the sense is this: There is matter in the formulae of a man and a pigeon. Such matter is in the formula of a species, as feathers for the pigeon, since it must be capable of flying. Such material difference comes from the species, but whiteness does not, since flying does not need whiteness. So, in some sense, certain matter differentiates one species from another, namely, that which appears in the formula of the species.

11. That is, in their definition, "animal" must appear.

12. The word "their" refers to the animals.

10

1. The indestructible may be defined as that which is incapable of being acted upon so as not to exist (without qualification). See 280b25–34, 1019a26–7.

2. An alternative to "for a privation is a definite incapacity" is "for an incapacity is a definite privation".

3. This is a thesis to be shown. We may add, since indestructibility is a privation of being changeable into nonbeing from being, and being and nonbeing are not species with a genus, and since destructibility belongs to many species, as in animals, destructibility and indestructibility must be distinct in genus and not in species.

4. As in men, who may be white and black (1058b3–5).

5. That is, when some men are white and some black, both coming under the universal "man".

6. Not in the sense in which a Negro is black, but in the sense in which a white man becomes dark or black by exposure to the Sun or by some other cause.

7. What is black may become white; but what is destructible cannot be or even become indestructible, and vice versa.

8. Referring to destructibility and indestructibility, the primary opposites or contraries.

9. Man Himself would be indestructible and an individual man would be destructible; so that these contraries, which belong to things necessarily and are distinct in genus, would belong to the same species and do so accidentally. This is impossible.

Book K

1

1. 981a27–993a27.

2. Certainly the first causes are not contraries; for example, essence is not the contrary of final cause. Besides, there are four causes, but only two parts to a contrariety.

3. The same problem is raised in 995b4–6 and discussed in 996a18–b26.

4. For example, both physics and geometry are alike demonstrative sciences, so each has as much right to examine the principles of demonstration.

5. A somewhat similar problem is raised in 995b6–10 and discussed in 996b26–997a15.

6. Also raised in 995b10–13 and discussed in 997a15–25. By "all substances" he means all kinds, sensible as well as non-sensible, destructible as well as indestructible; and a substance may be a *substance,* and so in any category.

7. If "substance" is univocally predicated of all, perhaps there should be one science; and if substances differ radically, as destructible and indestructible do, or as quantities and qualities do qua *substances,* perhaps there should be many sciences. Additional arguments may be used for and against.

8. Also raised in 995b18–27 and discussed in 997a25–34.

9. That is, prior in knowledge, in existence, and also indemonstrable. An alternative to *"substances"* is "substances" in this paragraph.

10. 194b16–195b36.

11. This is a dialectical argument, not Aristotle's position. The implication here is that wisdom would consider immovable rather than movable substances.

12. Namely, nonsensible substances which are immovable. A somewhat similar problem is raised in 995b13–8 and discussed in 997a34–998a19.

13. The Platonists posit the Forms as being immovable and first in existence, and then the Mathematical Objects as coming after the Forms; Speusippus posits only the Mathematical Objects.

14. Discussed in 990a33–993a10.

15. Referring to sensible quantities.

16. Just as the Mathematical Objects are posited as a third set of immovable objects, so a similar set should be posited besides the Form of Man and individual men, a similar set besides the Forms for colors and the individual colors, and so on with all the other genera of objects for which Forms are posited.

17. Straight lines and circles and the rest as defined by the mathematician do not seem to exist in sensible objects (997b34–998a6). So perhaps they do exist apart from sensible objects.

18. Wisdom should deal with prior objects, and these exist as separate and eternal, but mathematical objects are inseparable from sensible objects, and further, the latter are destructible. What, then, does wisdom deal with, if it is to be *knowledge* which is certain and of eternal objects?

19. This problem as raised here does not appear in the problems raised in 995b4–996a17. A related problem there is raised in 996a12–5 and discussed in 1001b26–1002b11.

20. Considered in 1077b14–1078a31.

21. These would be the individuals.

22. Also raised in 995b27–31, and discussed in 998a20–999a23.

23. No genus is a predicate of a differentia of that genus; so if 'being' and 'unity' were genera, since a differentia is one and a being, "unity" and "being" would be predicates of it. Hence, unity and being are not genera, and so not principles.

24. These are the ultimate species; for example, that of men.

25. The genus is prior in existence to each of its species, and a principle is prior in existence to that of which it is a principle. For example, a straight line is a principle and an element of a triangle; for if a triangle exists, so does a straight line, but not conversely.

26. But not conversely (understood).

2

1. For example, these might be the universals, and these were called "Ideas" by Plato, "Mathematical Objects" by Speusippus, etc.

2. The problem raised as a whole in lines 1060a3–27 is also raised in 995b31–6 and discussed in 999a24–b24; however, the part in 1060a19–24 is peculiar to Book K, and the discussion in 999b5–16 is peculiar to Book B.

3. And qua infinite, they cannot be known, and besides, they are de-

structible; but science is (or should be) of the eternal and cannot be of the infinite (for this cannot be traversed in a finite time).

4. These, as against the individuals, may be finite and so known.

5. He may be referring to 1059b31–8.

6. The problem now is general, for something other than the individuals is not limited to species and genera (or Plato's Ideas) but may be Anaxagoras' *Intelligence,* or Empedocles' *Friendship,* or Aristotle's prime mover.

7. The question is especially directed to the Platonists, who posit Ideas for men and horses and the like but not for houses, utensils, etc. But are not all of these destructible?

8. This unreasonableness is partly considered in 990a33–991b9.

9. Qua actual, the form is a being to a higher degree than matter. Besides, if matter exists, so does form, but the converse may not be true (and for Aristotle it is not); matter as separate and by itself does not exist.

10. Also raised in 996a2–4 and discussed in 1000a5–1001a3.

11. A difference in the objects coming under two eternal principles should necessitate a difference in the eternal principles themselves. For Aristotle, pure form or God is one such principle; prime matter, which can be many things and a cause of destructibility in a thing, is another.

12. In other words, a principle qua such cannot be destructible, and if such an object is assumed destructible, then it necessitates either an infinite regress, which is denied in Book *a,* or an indestructible principle, which leads us back to the same problem.

13. The problem in 1060a36–b12 is also raised in 996a4–9 and discussed in 1001a4–b25.

14. For example, whiteness is a being and is one, yet it is inseparable from a body; and a substance is prior in existence to an attribute of it.

15. For example, whiteness and a motion and a relation and the like will be substances, since each is a being; but this is not the case.

16. Although five and other composites have being, there may be a difficulty as to whether each of them is one or many. Of course, the problem is dialectical at this stage, so at least some inseparable things have unity. For Aristotle, being and unity are convertible (1003b22–34, 1054a13–9).

17. The Platonists are meant. The Pythagoreans are excluded, for they generate only numbers; and it is not clear whether Speusippus is included, for he uses other principles also.

18. By "composite" he does not mean the contrary of prime, but merely a number with a plurality of material parts (units).

19. An alternative to "*One*" is "one". Difficulties arise in either case. Thus, if *One* is a principle because each thing has unity and is also a substance, then "*One*" would be a predicate of Two, and so Two, by being *One,* would be a principle, and its *substance* would be *One,* which is not the case for the Platonists. And if, in saying "Two has unity", the terms "*One*" and "unity" do not have the same meaning, how are these terms

related, and why posit the *One* as a principle? If the *One* and unity have something in common, this would be prior in existence to the *One* and so a principle to a higher degree.

20. Also raised in 996a12–5 and discussed in 1001b26–1002b11.

21. For the early Plato, the primary Lines and Surfaces and the like are Ideas, from which are generated Mathematical Lines and the rest. For the later Plato or the Platonists, who identify Ideas with Numbers, they are among the *after-Ideas*. For Speusippus, who rejects the Ideas, they are among the Mathematical Objects. Other Platonists generate Lines from the *Short* and *Long* as matter, Planes from the *Wide* and *Narrow*, Solids from the *Deep* and *Shallow* (992a10–20).

22. A limit or division exists in that which is limited or has been divided and so is not separable from it.

23. An alternative to "point" is "*Point*", which signifies the principle of Magnitudes for Speusippus, and from which the other Points among the Mathematical Objects are generated. In either case, the points which are generated by these thinkers are posited as substances (1028b21–4, 1085a31–4).

24. A substance which is generated has matter and form. How can a point have matter and so be generated, if it is a division and so like an attribute (1002a28–b11, 1044b21–9, 240b8–241a26)?

25. Also raised in 996a9–10 and discussed in 1003a5–17.

26. For example, arithmetic is not concerned with these two individual apples, but with the number two universally taken, which indicates suchness or such-and-such a thing. Since all universal propositions, which signify the objects of a science, have only universal terms as principles, and these terms signify universals, the principles with which a science is concerned cannot be substances because these are individuals and separate.

27. That is, a form.

28. The assumption is that every *composite* is destructible, and so its form is not eternal.

29. Plato and Aristotle agree in the case of a house, but not in all other cases; for Aristotle, the form of a house is not separable.

30. Also raised in 996a1–2 and discussed in 999b24–1000a4.

3

1. In a way, Section 1 gives the answer to the problem raised in 1059a20–3. The corresponding answer in Book Γ, 1003a21–1005a18, is somewhat longer.

2. This being is a substance, which is separate or by itself, like a man or the Moon.

3. For example, a man is clearly one, but his color or height or motion is an aspect of his unity, or else each of them is one in a qualified or partial manner; otherwise, the man would be both one and many.

4. In one sense, primary contraries are, so to say, unmixed contraries, and so they are principles. For example, whiteness and blackness are such, but grey is not; and neither is a black thing or a white thing, for each of these is mixed with a subject, a body. The primary contraries of being are, of course, the most universal; and as such, they are primary also in the sense of prior in existence. For example, unity and plurality are prior in existence to sameness in species and difference in species.

5. To be one is to be indivisible somehow; but to be a being is to be some nature, like a quality or a quantity or a substance. As we would say, their connotation is distinct, but they denote the same things.

6. The definition of the generic sense of "justice" is given here (1129b11–1130a13).

7. For example, if a man disobeys only traffiic laws, generically he is neither just nor unjust, for he still obeys other laws, but is somewhere between. However, he is unjust with respect to traffic laws, if such injustice be a species no longer divisible into lower species.

8. As indicated later, he is referring to geometrical objects and to the geometrician.

9. For one thing, geometrical objects are abstracted from sensible qualities; but the investigation of those objects qua continuous may also be generic in the sense that it does not specify whether continuity is in one, two, or three dimensions, although continuity does not exist apart from one or two or three dimensions. It would be like studying men but only qua animals, or more generally, qua physical substances, or even qua substances. Lines 1004a–9 are a better statement of the analogy than lines 1061a28–b3, and this seems to indicate that Book K is an earlier version.

10. 1059a20–3, 1059a26–9.

4

1. This axiom is common to all quantities, but only to quantities and not to other beings. Hence, it is not as universal as the principle of contradiction or of the excluded middle. However, since the philosopher is concerned with each sense of "being", and one such sense is quantity, then the first axioms of quantities, too, might be his concern. This axiom of quantities is neither mentioned by name nor discussed in the problems in Book B, for the statements in that Book are concerned with the syllogistic axioms about all beings (995a8–10, 996b26–997a15). In Book Γ, too, Aristotle discusses only the syllogistic axioms (1005a19–1012b31), although the phrase "the so-called mathematical axioms" in 1005a20 may include the axioms about all quantities but as being secondary in nature or subordinate to the syllogistic axioms (1005b33–4).

2. For example, the arithmetician is concerned only with numbers, so he is not concerned with the axioms for all quantities but only as-

sumes them. No mention is made here, as is made later and elsewhere (74a17–25, 1026a25–7, 1064b8–9), about universal mathematics. Universal axioms concerning quantities would seem to be like universal axioms concerning movable objects in physics, and so universal mathematics and universal physics would seem to be alike parts of wisdom or of philosophy (1061b32–3).

3. Numbers qua numbers are a part of being, but it is not clear here whether by "a part of being" he includes quantities as such, although one sense of "being" is quantity. Anyway, if by "attributes" here he means the properties demonstrated for all quantities, then certainly these are the concern of the universal mathematician and not of the philosopher.

4. That is, not qua in motion or qua having some specific nature.

5. By "parts of wisdom" here he probably means what is specific, as against what is generic, not in the sense that the objects of physics and mathematics are investigated by first philosophy, except for their principles. Scientifically, the study of the more generic should precede that of the less generic.

5

1. The proposition "A is" is to be taken in a generic sense so as to include qualified as well as unqualified existence. Thus "Socrates is white" signifies a qualified existence or predication, but "Socrates exists" an unqualified one. Similarly for "A is not".

2. This principle, qua a principle, cannot be demonstrated, and qua the most known by nature and the most certain, it cannot depend on a prior principle.

3. Lines 1062a2–5 correspond to lines 1006a5–18.

4. Lines 1062a5–20 correspond to lines 1006a18–1007a20.

5. He who asserts the opposites of any thing would find it impossible to restrict a term to one meaning, for he will assert and deny that meaning at the same time; so discourse with him would be impossible (1006a31–b10).

6. Perhaps by "name" he means any expression, even a proposition.

7. Lines 1062a20–3 leave much to be supplied; they may correspond to lines 1006b11–34. Whether "necessary" applies to the fact signified, like the incommensurability of the diagonal of a square with its side, or to the necessity that a fact be signified when the corresponding true proposition is made, is not clear from what little is said; perhaps the latter.

8. An alternative to "not a man" is "a not-man".

9. An alternative to "not a horse" is "a not-horse".

10. Lines 1062a23–30 correspond to 1007b18–1008a2. Dialectically, "not a horse" is a truer predicate of a man than "not a man" is; and if so, then "a horse" should be a less true predicate of him than "a man". But for these thinkers "a horse" and "not a horse" are alike true predicates

of him; and so he who allows contradictories to be simultaneously true turns out to be a horse, and likewise stupid, and the like.

11. The point in these qualified demonstrations seems to be this: to draw the opponent into a position of saying something but denying its opposite, thus showing him that he does not really believe that contradictories are simultaneously true.

12. Lines 1062a31–5 somewhat correspond to lines 1005b23–6.

13. Lines 1062a36–b7 correspond to lines 1008a4–7, and 1062b7–9 to 1012b11–8.

14. In other words, if "it is possible for A to be and not to be . . ." is true, it is also false. Aristotle here equates the falsity of "it is possible . . ." to the truth of the statement "it is not possible . . .".

15. For example, just as "A is B" is no more true than "A is not B", so "it is not the case that A is B and also not B" is no more true than "it is the case that A is B and also not B".

16. From the doctrine which makes all contradictories or all propositions true, he now turns to the one making them all false. But this doctrine, if true, would make itself false (a case of theory of types here).

17. That is, true statements which are not also false, or false statements which are not also true.

6

1. Lines 1062b12–24 correspond to lines 1009a6–16, 22–30.

2. 187a20–b7. Anaxagoras, Democritus, etc.

3. Lines 1062b24–33 correspond somewhat to lines 1009a30–8.

4. That is, if the subject did not have both the not-white and the white prior to the change into the not-white, this not-white would be generated out of nothing or nonbeing; and this goes against their hypothesis that being is not generated from nonbeing.

5. 189a11–192b4.

6. Lines 1062b33–1063a10 correspond mainly to lines 1010b1–26.

7. Lines 1063a10–7 correspond to lines 1010a25–32.

8. Perhaps γενέσθαι is better than γίγνεσθαι.

9. For example, there is Socrates, the subject, and also health and sickness, the two contraries. If the motion is to a sick Socrates, Socrates must be first in health, not just be Socrates without health, then in some intermediate state, and finally in sickness. So these three stages of Socrates must differ if there is to be motion. But if contradictories were alike true of them, they would be the same, and then even motion would disappear.

10. 261a31–b26.

11. That is, a composite substance (matter and form) exists in actuality because of its form or differentia (1020a33–b1), which is definite, not because of any specific quantity of it, as this is often changing.

12. Lines 1063a22–8 correspond to lines 1010a22–5.

13. Lines 1063a28–35 correspond to lines 1008b12–27.

14. How would we differ from the sick, if both the sick and the healthy were alike in always changing?

15. To think that things appear differently to the sick is to admit that it is the same things which appear so to them, after they changed from healthy to sick. But to admit that these things are the same is to admit they have not changed; and if they are not the same, then the basis upon which the sick and the healthy are *judged* is eliminated.

16. If we are distinguished from the sick by being well, then there is something which remains with us, namely, health.

17. That is, they are unable even by themselves to think out things.

18. Such men would challenge or question any statement, demonstrable or indemonstrable; hence, discussion with them is useless.

19. Lines 1063b7–16 correspond to lines 1009a16–22 and 1011a3–16.

20. Lines 1063b17–9 correspond to lines 1011b17–22. One of two contraries is a denial of the other contrary within a genus; hence, it is a denial of the other contrary.

21. By an "intermediate" he means something between contradictories; for example, that which is neither A nor non-A. In the example given he limits predication to a contrary, like white or black. A somewhat stronger argument would be needed for grey or some other color.

22. Lines 1063b19–24 correspond, though perhaps weakly, to lines 1011b23–1012a24.

23. 1012a24–8, 1062a31–4. Lines 1063b24–35 correspond to lines 1012a24–b31.

24. If the *Blend* has everything actually and as separate, then it will be black as well as white, etc.

25. For, if he speaks truly, then not all statements can be false.

26. That is, if all statements are true, this would include the statement "all statements are false"; and if the latter is true, then false statements exist. Hence, a contradiction.

7

1. This Section (lines 1063b36–1064b14) corresponds to Section 1 of Book E (lines 1025b3–1026a32) and answers 1059a26–9.

2. The principles of moving and of being moved are in the physical objects themselves.

3. The end of a theoretical science is truth, not production or *action*.

4. 1071b3–1073a13.

5. Theology is the study of what is divine; and this is eternal and most honorable.

6. The phrases "the study of being qua being" and "the study of a separate and immovable substance" do not have the same meaning. So this question arises: Is philosophy (or theology) concerned with both?

7. Is Aristotle using "universal" as meaning prior (whether in existence or in some other manner) or is he saying that it is prior and consequently universal? The latter seems to be the case. His statement

about the mathematical sciences seems to indicate this, for there is universality there, too, but analogical, as in the case of being. The axiom "If equals are added to equals . . ." is analogously true for the various kinds of quantities, and the principle of contradiction is analogously true for the kinds of being. Similarly for essence, definition, and the like (1005a19–b1, 76a37–b2, 1026a23–32, and Comms. 26, 27, and 28 in Book E, Section 1.

8

1. Lines 1064b15–1065a26 correspond (though less completely) to lines 1026a33–1028a6 in Book E.

2. Perhaps the argument is this: If he became musical and grammatical at the instant t, prior to t he was not musical and grammatical; hence, he was not one or the other but was becoming the combination of both. But he was musical; hence, the paradox. The fallacy is evident.

3. *Sophist*, 254A.

4. 1026b29. In demonstrations, since the premises are true, the conclusions are of necessity true (or, it is impossible for them not to be true).

5. That is, not sought by first philosophy.

6. For example, by nature the seed of an oak tree becomes an oak tree.

7. Those which are generated through *thought* or *choice*.

8. For example, the cause of finding a coin may be the search for a purse, or the digging, or kicking the stone out of the way, etc. In an individual case, such as the finding of a coin at a given time and place, the cause as luck is unique and definite, but the finding of a coin by luck, taken universally, has no definite cause.

9. The meaning may be this: An accidental cause, taken universally, is not a cause of events of a definite kind.

10. From 1206b30–1207b19 and 1425a20–1 it appears that "good fortune" and "misfortune" signify the causes and not the effects, but this is not always clear.

11. This is what Anaxagoras postulates; but Aristotle might be referring to the prime mover, although it makes no difference here.

12. Luck : chance :: *Intelligence* : nature.

9

1. For example, if Socrates exists and is healthy, he and his health exist *actually*. The prime mover, being only a form, always exists as *actuality* only (1076b26–30). Prime matter exists only as potentiality. Bricks, having *shape*, exist *actually*, but they are also potentially a house. But when a thing moves from one place to another, though motion is an *actuality*, it is of the thing with respect to its place as potential, for while in motion, the thing has no *actual* place yet.

2. The implication is: Motion is not a category or in any category.

3. In 1068a8–16 he excludes the possibility of essential change with respect to some categories, such as that of relation, for example.

4. That is, the process of building, which is a change.

5. Aristotle uses the term "movable" not as a part of the definition, but perhaps for the sake of the reader. The definition is given in 1065b16. Greek texts differ, and there may be some corruption. I suggest this: ἡ δὴ τοῦ δυνάμει ὄντος ἐντελέχεια, ὅταν ἐνεργῇ οὐχ ᾗ αὐτὸ ἀλλ᾽ ᾗ κινητόν, κίνησις ἔστιν.

6. That is, something other than bronze.

7. A color is in the body which has it; but to be visible is to be somehow related to that which sees in the presence of an *actualized* medium, for a color may not be seen in darkness (418a26–b3).

8. He seems to be using "genus" in a wider sense, not restricted to the categories; for "*actuality*" is not one of the categories, although it may be used as if a genus, so to say (1024b9–13).

9. The Platonists used these terms.

10. An unqualified *actuality* is a category, either a *this*, or a quantity, or etc. But motion as an *actuality* is qualified; it is incomplete *actuality*, and it is of the potential and not of any category (although it is of the potential with respect to a category).

11. The mover.

12. If that *actuality* is unrelated to the mover, what causes it in the moved? Qua not a mover, the mover is causing no motion; but qua a mover (in *actuality*), it is causing it, but it does so *in* the thing moved. Whether the mover is itself moved (qua other) makes no difference. See 202a13–b22.

10

1. That is, just as redness is neither odd nor even, since it is not a number to which one of these two contraries must belong, so it is neither finite nor the contrary of finiteness, since it is not something (a quantity is meant) to which one of these contraries (or an intermediate, in other cases) may belong. In this sense, "infinite" signifies, not the contrary, but that contradictory of finiteness which is not a contrary.

2. That is, almost without an end, or is traversed with much difficulty. In this sense, Aristotle sometimes uses "infinite" to mean a great number.

3. In this sense it is somehow a quantity.

4. If line AB is divided at C, AC may then be subtracted from AB. In the *Physics*, 204a7, he uses "by division" instead of "by subtraction", seeing that division must also take place if something is to be subtracted.

5. A number may increase by the endless addition of one unit after another. A given line AB may be diminished by taking half of it, then half of what remains, and so on endlessly. In the latter case, what has been taken away may also be added endlessly, so that there will be an

endless addition as well as an endless subtraction; and time, as continuous, is infinitely divisible, and it is infinite by addition, since there is more and more of it to be taken.

6. A better alternative to "and sensible" is "from sensible things", as stated in 204a8–9. The Pythagoreans and Plato posited the infinite as a substance by itself (203a1–16).

7. A substance qua a substance is indivisible, as in the case of a man. There is no such thing as half a man, except metaphorically, and a man is divisible qua a magnitude, for he has a body which has magnitude.

8. In that sense, infinite would be a contradictory but not the contrary of finiteness. It would be like calling a man non-even or non-odd or both, since he is not a number.

9. Even if numbers and magnitudes do exist as substances, still the infinite as an *attribute* of them would be inseparable. But if they are themselves inseparable, the infinite is inseparable even more so.

10. An alternative to "as an attribute" is "accidentally".

11. An element is not an attribute but a part, like matter; for example, a brick of a house, and a unit in a number.

12. Just as a part of air, which is a substance and separate, is air, so would a part of the infinite be. So, if the infinite is a non-sensible substance, and so without sensible matter, but is an *actuality*, then if it is posited as divisible, a part of it, too, will be infinite.

13. And in that case it will be divisible not qua infinite and a substance, but qua having magnitude and an attribute, as air is.

14. He now proceeds to the intended meaning, which is or is related to a quantity.

15. For quantity is an attribute of a substance; or else, "infinite" is a derivative term, which is a predicate of a quantity but is derived from "infinity" which signifies an attribute, like the term "unjust".

16. The principles posited by Anaximenes and the Pythagoreans, respectively. This is a dialectical concession.

17. Finite in kind is probably meant, like air, water, fire, and earth.

18. He assumes "infinite" to mean a magnitude in the direction of the great without an end. So if, for example, the element which has heat as its contrary were infinite in magnitude, then, regardless of the ratio of heat to cold with respect to their power, it would destroy the contrary (coldness) of the other element, and so also that element itself. It is assumed that any two elements have at least one contrariety, whether heat and cold, moist and dry, or some other, so that the infinite element would destroy in turn each of the finite elements.

19. If all elements were infinite, it would follow from the definition of the infinite given here that all would occupy the same space, and this is impossible. Aristotle is not considering partial infinites, such as the space in each octant in a Cartesian system.

20. 203a3–15.

21. What we observe is resolution into one or more of the four elements and not into a more elementary thing called "infinite", and if an element changes, it changes to another element, i.e. water changes to air.

22. It has already been shown that if one element is infinite, nothing else would exist.

23. The argument may be this: If all is fire, nothing contrary to fire or the hot would exist to change fire into something else.

24. If a change is from one contrary to another, as from a hot object to a cold object, how can any element which has a contrary come from the *One* which has no contrary principle in it at all?

25. Place is defined as the inner motionless boundary of a containing object; for example, the inner surface of a can of tomatoes (208a27–213a11).

26. The natural place for earth is the same for a part or the whole of it; it is a surface (perhaps spherical) near the center of the universe (perhaps below the surface of the Earth, since water is farther from the center than earth is).

27. Perhaps the reason (not stated) for the two alternatives is this: Just as a finite homogeneous body (like a stone) either moves or rests as a whole, so does the infinite body. But while a finite body in motion changes its place and so rests when it reaches its place, the infinite body, whether in motion or at rest, does not change its place relative to something else (there are no different places for it) but is at the same state at time t_1 as at any later time t_2. So it always rests or always moves. It may be added, the proper place of each part of a body exists potentially, so even if the part of a body moves relative to another part, still it does not move relative to the place of the whole.

28. Motion requires distinct places; but if an infinite body exists, such places cannot exist, and so motion from one place to another or rest at one place rather than at another cannot exist. And since a part of it is homogeneous with any other part and with the whole, there is as much reason for it to move in one direction as in another, or to rest at one place as at another (here, "place" may be taken dialectically to mean the place proper to a part); so it either moves in all directions (the term "direction" may not even have meaning in the case of an infinite body) or rests at all places. All this is impossible.

29. Referring to the whole bodily universe, which would be one by contact.

30. And in that case, there will be many kinds of bodies.

31. That is, finite in kind. The magnitude of each kind is assumed finite.

32. That is, infinite in extent. Apparently, he rules out finiteness in kind, with each kind infinite in extent, perhaps because for him what is infinite is infinite in all directions, and only one body can be infinite in

this way; but he seems to allow such an infinite to surround a finite body, perhaps just hypothetically, or for dialectical purposes.

33. An infinite fire, which surrounds a finite earth or water, will destroy the latter and cause it to become fire. Then all will be fire, but this is impossible.

34. That is, infinite in kind but each kind being a finite body; and also simple, like air, and having as such a place proper to itself, like the center of the universe for earth.

35. An actual infinite cannot exist, so neither the elements nor their corresponding places are infinite. Further, the places are evidently finite, and knowledge of an infinity of elements is impossible. See Comm. 36 below.

36. Apparently, he excludes the Sun, Moon, and the other sensible heavenly bodies, perhaps because they are without qualities and unalterable and so are sensible only accidentally. Anyway, the heavenly bodies are neither heavy nor light and so move around a circle and not up or down (269b18–270a35). So again, since bodies moving up or down are surrounded by the heavenly bodies, their places must be finite.

37. That is, how could one locate, say, the center, or any place, or how can one discover differences in places if there is no principle or starting-point in the infinite, as there is, say, in a sphere (either the center, or the outer surface)?

38. 205b31–34, 208b11–25.

39. The potential infinite is meant.

40. In the order of priority (in definition or in *substance*), we have magnitude, motion, and time; for time is an attribute of motion and also defined in terms of motion, and motion is similarly related to a body which has magnitude.

11

1. An alternative to "accidentally" is "as an attribute". Both make sense, but the latter is wider.

2. For example, the white moves, if the white is a man and he moves the table. Comm. 1 above applies here too.

3. The term "form" here is used perhaps in the sense of opposites and intermediates which are gained and lost when a subject is moved.

4. Both these are qualities; in general, all forms and attributes are immovable. Only that which has physical matter is primarily movable, and the heavenly bodies (with respect to place only).

5. Contradictories here would be from being to not-being (destruction), and also from not-being to being (generation).

6. The term "may" here signifies logical alternatives, not possibilities. Some logical alternatives are impossible, but what is possible is not impossible.

7. For example, what is signified by "a man" and not by "a not-man".

8. For example, there is no change from the not-white to the not-black, for a thing, like a point or a triangle, may be immovable and yet be both.

9. For example, a change from a not-man to a man, or from not-air to air.

10. For example, from not-white to white, and from not-in-the-Lyceum to in-the-Lyceum.

11. This may be nonbeing in the sense of falsity, as it exists in the soul; or else, he may mean truth or/and falsity in the soul. (Of course, truth and falsity in the soul do not move). If it is nonbeing in the sense of a false fact, like an odd 4, this too does not move.

12. What exists potentially and is not a *this* is opposed to what is a *this* (unqualified being). For example, prime matter qua such cannot move (1029a20–23). What moves must be a subject nameable by a category, even if this is privative, as when the black (body) moves.

13. The not-white is qualified not-being; and though some not-whites do not move (a triangle, a thought), others do move accidentally (a man may be not-white, also a yellow body, since "not-white" is a predicate of each) but not qua not-white.

14. Whether Socrates or any non-existent comes under unqualified not-being or not, is not clear. Anyway, what does not exist cannot move, and what is eternal, like prime matter, cannot move qua such.

15. Rest and motion are contraries; so what cannot by nature be in motion cannot by nature be at rest, and conversely.

16. From A to not-A, or from not-A to A, where the subject A is a substance.

17. The term "contrary" here (and also "intermediate") signifies probably a *composite,* a subject with its primary contrary (these as principles). For example, a white body, sick Socrates, etc. This is one of its meanings (1018a31–32).

18. Though correctly translated, the term "toothless" means without teeth, and so linguistically it does not seem to be an affirmative term.

12

1. 3b24–32.

2. John may be taller than Tom today, but shorter than Tom two years hence, although he retains the same height.

3. That is, from one kind of change to another kind of change.

4. That is, change from being to not-being, or vice-versa; and in general, change into contradictories, as stated in Comm. 16 of Section 11 of this Book.

5. In motion, the body remains the same in *substance.* Socrates is Socrates, whether healthy or sick.

6. Change is from contraries or from contradictories.

7. If becoming sick were one contrary, becoming healthy would be the other, just as black is the contrary of white.

8. That is, a man.

9. I cannot quite unravel the arguments in lines 1068a33–b15. There are some spotty differences in texts. I have translated literally, but since the arguments are too concentrated, perhaps knowledge of the arguments may necessitate some alteration in the translation.

10. In "a change of a change", by "the former" he means the first term "a change".

11. Perhaps the argument is this: If X becomes Y, then it is no longer X when it reaches Y or afterwards; and Y is the contrary or contradictory of X (for example, black vs. white, and man vs. not-man). Likewise if X = becoming, then Y = being destroyed, for the opposite of becoming is being destroyed. Thus, if a becoming becomes, when the process terminates it comes to be a process of destruction (or a process of being destroyed), which is the contrary of becoming.

12. For example, a sick man becomes a healthy man, and the man or his body is the subject that remains. The sick man and the healthy man are *composites* of subject and contrary, but if something becomes a motion, motion is not a *composite*, and there is no subject which, while remaining, becomes motion.

13. 1020a33–b1.

14. For example, the attributes; for these are immovable in a sense similar to that in which the voice is invisible (= not visible, which is the contradictory and not the contrary of the visible).

15. For example, it may be prevented by force from being moved.

16. Thus, whiteness and a line and the other attributes can neither move nor be at rest.

17. For example, if the coffee is in the cup, which is in the room, its primary place is said to be the inner surface of the cup; and it is said to be in the room secondarily and not primarily (208a27–213a11).

18. As a noun, the term "intermediate" will be used, but as a preposition, the word "between" will be used.

19. By "after" he does not necessarily mean right after or directly after. Thus, both 2 and 10 come after 1.

20. Both the principle and what follows it are taken as being of the same kind or genus. For example, what is succeeded by a house is a house, and the starting point or principle is also a house.

21. Of course, nothing at all may exist between the two, and one may touch the other, like two successive touching bricks.

22. For example, if one house succeeds another, a tree may exist between the two houses.

23. That is, a thing of the same kind or genus.

24. That is, the opposites proper to change are contraries and contradictories; relatives are excluded.

25. That is, prior in definition to the others, and also in existence.

26. The Greek words for "touch", "contact", and "contiguous" are cognates.

27. Either a line, or other points.

Book Λ

1

1. If it is a whole consisting of material parts (1023b26–7, 32–36), then substance is prior in existence and in nature or definition, as the heart (or whatever the part in which the soul first comes to be) in a thing generated (735a23–6); and if it is a whole as a universal (1023b29–32), like "being", then again substance is prior in existence (probably this is not his meaning).

2. That is, a succession in which there is no second unless there is a first part, as in the numbers 1, 2, 3, etc., in which 2 does not exist unless a unit exists, potentially or actually (1003a33–b10).

3. And in general they are attributes of substances and inseparable from them. Thus, if sickness exists, it does so in a substance, but that substance may exist without being sick. Usually, Aristotle does not exhaust the list of categories.

4. That is, beings in the unqualified sense.

5. The term "not-white" and the like can be predicates of what exists, for what is black, or yellow, or etc., is not-white. See 1017a18–19.

6. An alternative to "are more inclined to . . . substances" is "posit the universals as substances to a higher degree".

7. That is, their inquiry is directed to expressions or things spoken, such as terms, genera, formulae, and definitions of things. For example, "being" is the most universal predicate; hence, they would say, "being" or Being is the most elementary or most substantial because it is found in all things. Plato's inquiry was of this kind.

8. They directed their attention to the things themselves as natures rather than to statements about them.

9. The Sun, Moon, stars, etc.

10. Eternal but non-sensible.

11. For example, Plato.

12. For example, Xenocrates.

13. For example, Speusippus.

14. That is, qua movable. Aristotle's universal discussion of matter, form, cause, definition, etc. in the *Metaphysics* shows that sensible substances qua being are investigated first by philosophy and not by physics.

15. And so, it is not from every nonwhite that there can be a change

to white; otherwise, also voice, being nonwhite, could change to white.

16. It is not the attribute blackness or redness that changes to whiteness; it is the body that becomes white from being black or otherwise colored.

2

1. This is not a new paragraph, since the thought is continuous with what preceded.

2. Aristotle often uses also "underlying subject" instead of "matter". In formula, however, the two are distinct; to be matter is to be a potentiality of taking on this or that, but to be a subject is to be that which persists in a change or that of which something is an attribute.

3. This is a change with respect to substance or *substance*.

4. Evidently, in unqualified generation and destruction, form and privation of form are also considered here as contraries.

5. That is, while remaining the same as subject, matter loses one contrary but gains another.

6. For example, not only from the nonwhite as a privation is the white said to be generated, but also from the subject (a body) which is potentially white. If specified, this nonwhite is not-white, and this is black or some intermediate color like red, each of which is an attribute.

7. This is the *Blend* (of all things), also called *"Other"*, as matter or material cause, which was acted upon by *Intelligence* (989a30–b21).

8. For example, a saw is not made from wood, nor vinegar from iron. Of course, there is the problem whether the ultimate matter of all kinds of matter is the same or not. If water, air, fire, and earth change into each other, then there is an ultimate matter which underlies them and is the same for all; and the formula for matter, being unique, seems to confirm this (1029a20–1).

9. For Aristotle, the Moon and the Sun and the stars are indestructible, yet they do change from place to place; so they have matter whose potentiality is limited to different places only.

10. (a) Negations such as not-whiteness, non-oddness, etc.; (b) non-existents, such as Socrates (if dead) and a number which is both odd and even; (c) matter or a subject which can take on a form (in its wide sense). See 1051a34–b5, 1089a26–31.

11. It is not from any matter or subject that a saw is made, but from a metal, not from wood.

12. That is, a great many.

13. That is, of one kind, such as the *Blend* referred to earlier.

14. The assumption here is: Since *Intelligence* is simple, as a mover it acts only in one way; and since also the *Blend* as matter is undifferentiated, what results when *Intelligence* acts on the *Blend* must be either one thing or many things of the same kind. But a variety of things are generated and exist.

3

1. In all the Greek versions, this and the next paragraph are very sketchily presented and are probably corrupt in spots. The translation given here is guided by consistency in thought.

2. By "ultimate matter" he means prime matter (192a22–34), and by "ultimate form" he means the proximate form, such as roundness and the soul. In general, no attribute or form is generable (1033b5–8, 1043b13–16, 1044b21–24), and this includes the prime mover (God).

3. The proximate mover is meant; the art in the case of a house, the father in the case of a son.

4. This may be proximate, as the bronze when a bronze statue is generated, or ultimate, if water changes to air (assuming the matter common to these two is ultimate).

5. The term "form" here is wide; it includes substantial form, like the soul, and attributes which come and go in a change, like whiteness and roundness.

6. And if bronze as a substance is generated, there is matter (and form) in it, and the same may be said of this matter; but there must be a stop ultimately (994a3–5).

7. This is the *composite* of matter and form, using "form" as above in Comm. 5.

8. Artificial substances or works of art, like a statue.

9. A moving principle, which is not, for example, in the house generated.

10. If fire goes up, the moving principle is in fire itself, its form. Likewise, a man moves himself; and the seed, when properly placed, moves itself into a tree or a man (1049a13–17).

11. In general, worms are generated by worms of the same kind; but when generated by chance, the chance causes (and it is probably these that he calls "privations", since they lack the form of a worm) act in the same manner as worms do to generate worms. It is likewise with health; for this is generated either by the medical art (*thought* is used here), or by luck, when some chance agent acts the way the art would act, though this agent lacks (is deprived of) the art (1034a9–b7).

12. What appears is the body (as matter) of a man, not his form or soul.

13. That is, the matter or subject possesses the form, or the form is in the matter or subject, and by "nature" he means the form. The term *"this"* here seems to signify something nameable in some category.

14. This is the form generated by art or the form of an animal (not a man, for the active intellect of a man is separable).

15. Of course, the art is separable from the house, though not from the soul (we exclude the symbols corresponding to art which exist, say, in a book, or even as substances such as shaped wooden letters).

16. Whether these are forms in the things generated by art (in a

house, or a statue, etc.) or the art itself (in the soul), now they exist and now they do not, and they are inseparable, the former from the things themselves and the latter from the soul.

17. Not all, but in the case of a man; and not all his soul, but only the active intellect (430a22–3).

18. Of natural substances around us, animals are of the highest degree substances; and of these, men are highest.

19. He means the form of a thing generated (using "form" in its wide sense, as above in Comm. 5), not the formula as it exists in the soul.

20. The mover usually exists prior to what it can cause, but what is caused exists at the same time as the thing in which it exists qua caused. For example, health and the healthy man (not just the man) are simultaneously generated.

21. That is, in a man.

22. If it is an individual man that begets an individual man, and the art in his soul that generates health and other products of art, then Plato's Ideas are useless as movers of things generated; and if health and the sphere and the soul come to be at the same time as the *composites* of which they are the forms, then again these forms cannot be eternal Ideas, nor can the Ideas be the forms of these *composites*. By "the formula of health" he means the formula as it exists in the soul as art, and this is the moving cause of health which is produced in a body.

4

1. He shortens the arguments that follow by using substances and only relations, instead of substances and all the other categories, for there is no loss in the effect by so shortening the arguments.

2. For if the elements were the same for all, substances and the others would come from these same elements, since the latter are prior in existence; but the categories have nothing in common, and so their principles and elements cannot be the same.

3. The elements of a substance cannot be relations, for these would then be prior in existence to substances; but relations are inseparable from substances and are attributes of them (1038b23–29). Nor can a relation be composed of substances, for such a composite would be a substance or have matter. As in the case of a relation, so in the case of any other category, the arguments are the same.

4. This condensed argument may amount to something like this: Since BA cannot be the same as B or as A, if all things (substances and the other categories) had the same elements, they would be composites, but not of substances or of any other category. The elements, then, cannot come under any category. But they must, for what else can they be?

As for unity and being, which are posited by Plato and others, and which are the most universal and so intelligible and not sensible, if they are distinct elements, since unity is a being and conversely, unity would have being as well as be unity, and so it would not be an element. Besides, if being is an element, since a composite is a being, it would follow that a composite is an element.

5. Form and privation as contraries ("form" is used in a wide sense).

6. For example, the proximate matter for the form of a saw is iron (or some other metal), not a material principle of iron itself.

7. Thus, in one sense, a surface and air are distinct principles in distinct genera, but in another, they are the same analogously and as such they are called "matter".

8. Principles are causes and conversely (1003b22–24), elements are principles but not conversely, for an element of a thing must be in the thing.

9. That is, the proximate cause.

10. Since man begets man, the form of the mover and of what is generated is the same in kind; but the form of the house in the soul is not the same in kind as the form of the house itself, for the one exists as knowledge, the other in the house. In both cases, however, the causes are numerically four (final cause excluded), but in kind they may be three or four.

The four causes here do not coincide with the usual four causes. The final cause is omitted, and the formal cause is split into two, form and privation. Three of them, matter, form, and privation, are principles of motion as discussed in the *Physics* (188a19–191a22), but sensible and changeable substances are also discussed in first philosophy, though from another point of view. The moving principle is introduced here because this Book is leading to the prime mover. Why, then, is final cause omitted now, if it is present in God, whose life is the most pleasant?

11. The prime mover or God.

5

1. The translation (confirmed by the term ταῦτα in 1071a34–5 and by 1071a35–6) is correct if the term is ταὐτά in line 1071a1; but then, perhaps by "causes" he means causes of existence (1043a2–3, 1071a34–5), since physical matter as a material cause of a substance is not such a cause of an attribute (1070b19–21). But if the term is ταῦτα, then the translation should be "and because of this, these (= substances) are the causes of all things"; and again, he means causes of existence or prior in existence.

2. Referring to the causes present in substances (= elements, which are matter, and form or privation) if the translation should be as given; otherwise, referring to what are analogously called "substances" (matter, form). He says "perhaps", for perhaps he is inclined to consider

inanimate physical bodies as matter or close to matter (1040b5–10), or perhaps there is a *difficulty* in viewing the will as a substance.

3. In lines 1071a6–17 Aristotle gives the distinct ways in which *actuality* and potentiality exist. For one thing, what exists potentially (matter) may have a given *actuality* (a form) or may not.

4. An *actuality* may exist as separable (eternally separate, as God, or separable, as man's active intellect), or as an inseparable form and a principle (the soul of a horse), or as a privation (as darkness in a dark medium), and these are causes as forms or the privations of forms (in a way, privations are forms, 193b19–20); but what exists potentially is a cause as matter. In general, *actuality* and potentiality are causes.

5. The father as a moving cause may be potentially or *actually* such a cause, and likewise for the Sun and the *oblique course;* but the former is a proximate moving cause, while each of the latter is a remote moving cause; in addition, the father has the same form as the son, while each of the other moving causes does not have the same form. The *oblique course* (this is the ellipse) through which the Sun moves, being now near and now far from the Earth, causes in some sense now generation and now destruction of the sensible bodies around us.

6. By "primary" he probably means the proximate, or else the prior in existence (the individuals and not the universals, for the latter cannot exist apart from the former).

7. By "principles" he probably means those from which something is generated; for example, of a son, the father as a mover or the form he imparts and also the matter in the mother.

8. By "primary" he means proximate; for example, the father, not the Sun or the *oblique course.*

9. The matter; for example, that which is in the mother (1049b19–26).

10. He may be referring to Plato, who posits universals (Ideas) as the principles of individuals.

11. The moving principle is meant, but the same applies to the other principles, since the form and matter of a thing exist in that thing.

12. That is, the kinds of being. See the meaning of *"substance".*

13. All four causes.

14. The causes in the thing: matter, form, privation.

15. That is, an answer is possible if the term "principle" or "element" is used in an analogous sense; for example, in the case of the elements, one may analogously say that they are matter, form, privation.

16. Substances are causes in the sense that they are prior in existence to the others.

17. This is the ultimate cause as mover, God.

18. That is, proximate, either as individual, or universally taken but as ultimate species.

19. The contrary "the white" has more than one sense; it may mean

whiteness (the form or attribute), or the *composite* of whiteness and the subject in which it is, or etc. (1018a25–35).

6

1. 1069a30–1.

2. 1028a31–b2.

3. That is, it is impossible for no motion to exist at all. The motions of some individual bodies are generated and destroyed, but accidentally, for it is the body that gains or loses motion. See 250b11–254b6.

4. One argument may be: If time is a certain attribute of motion (219b1–10) and motion is eternal, so is time. Another (dialectical argument) may be: If time has a beginning, then there is no prior or *before* such beginning; so both statements "Before the beginning of time nothing existed" and "Something existed *before* . . ." are false.

5. The position of some thinkers (218a33–b1).

6. This is Aristotle's position (219b1–10).

7. 261a27–265a12. The motions which are not locomotions proceed from contraries at which the body must rest.

8. For Aristotle, it is a principle that motion necessitates a moving cause.

9. Plato's Forms are not moving causes (988b1–6).

10. Referring perhaps to the Mathematical Objects or to other posited eternal objects to which no eternally active moving cause is assigned.

11. It is the nature of a potency to be sometimes in *actuality* and sometimes not.

12. For if with matter, they are destructible, and so they cannot be eternal movers. But the Sun and stars are eternal and eternally in motion.

13. Prior in existence (or in nature, or in *substance*) is meant (1019a2–4).

14. This seems to be a dialectical conclusion: What is potentially a substance need not exist *actually;* and if so, no impossibility follows by assuming its non-*actuality*. But if no *actual* substances exist, nothing else can, and so it is possible for nothing to exist. But the assumption that nothing can or will exist is impossible, for then there would be nothing in *actuality* to bring anything into existence, etc.

15. If only *Night* (which is only potentiality, 1069b20–24, 1091b4–6) existed, there was no moving cause in *actuality* to act on it, and so *Night* would exist eternally. The same applies to the *Blend (All things were together),* for this is like matter or potentiality.

16. That is, as a moving cause.

17. The seeds and the semen have the power of causing motion and will do so under certain conditions.

18. For Leucippus, the material elements are always in motion; and

for Plato, they were always in haphazard motion, until they were ordered by a mover *(Timaeus,* 30). Motion is an activity, although incomplete.

19. Probably the moving cause is meant, although the final cause is also possible. Plato did indicate a final and a moving cause (Timaeus, 30), but apparently Leucippus did not.

20. There are many kinds of motion, and these thinkers did not specify (300b8–19).

21. For example, by nature or by force, and if, for example, it is loco-motion, whether circular or straight.

22. That is, why it moves in this manner or in that manner.

23. That is, prior to all in existence. Locomotion is prior to the others, and of locomotion, the circular is prior; and this can be eternal, and it is, but the others are not, as in the case of a motion from a contrary to a contrary.

24. That is, the disordered elements existed first, then the soul was generated *(Timaeus:* 30) at the same time as the heaven; but the soul as a self-moving object is eternal and ungenerable *(Phaedrus:* 245–6, *Laws,* 894–6). This is inconsistent.

25. 1049b4–1051a3.

26. By "in cycles" he may mean what takes time but is even, though repeated continually, like the even motion of the fixed stars; and by "in some other way", he may mean what is repeated, but with uneven parts, as in the elliptic orbit of the Sun which, because of the differences in its distance from the Earth, causes now generation and now destruction.

27. He is probably referring to the outermost sphere of the fixed stars, which is in motion always in the same way and by such motion moves the inner spheres; or else, he is referring to the prime mover or God, who is simple and so moves the outermost sphere always in the same way.

28. For example, the mover (an *actuality)* which moves the Sun would move it evenly or in the same way, if there were nothing else to interfere. But the prime mover (God) does interfere (but indirectly, by moving the outermost sphere, which in turn moves the inner sphere). Hence, the uneven motion of the Sun is caused by two different movers whose activities are distinct. An illustration may help. Let a point start moving along an infinite straight line, which begins at point A, with a constant speed from point A, and let the line, with A as center, move in a plane with constant angular speed. Then the point describes a spiral. Each motion is constant and even, but the moving point shows differ-ences because of the different kinds of motion; and along the spiral one may notice both aspects, the circular and the constantly increasing distance from A (336a15–b9).

According to St. Thomas Aquinas, the Sun by itself acts always in different ways. If so, there would be the problem of how the unmoved mover, who acts directly on the Sun or its sphere, could act always in different ways and yet be simple.

7

1. 1017b26–8.

2. If this nonbeing is not-being (1069b18–24), it is potentiality which still requires a mover; and if it is not not-being, that is, if it is the impossible or the false (as an alleged fact but not a fact) or pure nothingness, all agree that no generation from such is possible (314a6–13, 974a2-3, 977b21–2, etc.).

3. The outermost sphere of the fixed stars (first heaven) is assumed as something observed to move around the stationary Earth.

4. That is, it is assumed as contributing to the motions of the inner spheres (1072a10–8).

5. Referring to the outermost sphere here.

6. Otherwise, there will be an infinite regress, which is ruled out (256a4–b27, 994a5–7).

7. This is the prime mover, or God.

8. 432a15–434a21.

9. That is, in each genus, the primary object of desire is identical with the primary intelligible object. Perhaps by "primary" he means first in goodness or nobility, or best (1012b34–1013a23).

10. Since *desire* by itself may or may not be right, its object *appears* to be noble, that is, it may or may not be noble. Here, Aristotle may be restricting by contrast the terms "*desire*" and "wish", the first to what seems but is not noble, the second to what is noble by the right wish or the *primary* wish (see above, Comm. 9).

11. The term "seems", like "desire", may be used as a genus of "appears" and "is", thus signifying some kind of thinking, whether imagining or believing (427b27–9). Since what appears noble either is or is not noble, and that which is noble is better than and so also prior to that which is not noble, the primary object of what appears to be noble is noble and so is identical with the primary object of wish or right wish in each genus. Hence, the primary object of desire is identical with the primary intelligible object in each genus (see above, Comm. 9).

12. What is intelligible in virtue of itself here, as against what is intelligible not in virtue of itself, is a being, as against a nonbeing or a not-being. For example, the good as against the bad, whiteness as against blackness, etc.; for blackness is intelligible not in virtue of itself, since it is intelligible in virtue of whiteness (as the contrary or the privation of whiteness). In general, to know any nonbeing, such as a privation or a false fact, you must know it by means of the corresponding being.

13. Substances exist by themselves and are known without reference to something else; but attributes are in substances and the understanding of them must include their reference to something else. Thus, substances are prior or first in existence and in *knowledge*. And of substances, that which is simple is prior and so first, for the composite cannot exist or be *known* without the simple, but not conversely; and

especially if the simple exists as an *actuality*, for qua simple and without potentiality it is indestructible and ungenerable and so eternal, while composites may or may not exist and so may or may not be *known* (71b25–6).

14. What is one may be a composite, as a man, who may or may not exist; but what is simple (for example, God) and a substance has no potentiality for not existing, and so it exists always.

15. Is that which is chosen for its own sake contrasted with that which is not so chosen? If so, the latter may be that which is chosen for the sake of something else, or that which is avoided, or any of these two. What is chosen for its own sake (in *action*) may be a parallel to what appears to be noble (in thinking), and so it may or may not be good or noble.

16. Since what is chosen for its own sake is what is desired, and what is desired is what appears noble or is noble, just as the primary object of desire is identical with the primary intelligible object (in each genus), so the primary object chosen for its own sake is identical with the best object, which is the noble.

17. He says "by analogy", for "good" and "noble" have analogous meanings in the various categories (1096a19–b29).

18. For example, if a man does or produces something, perhaps by "for some thing" he means the man himself or his happiness, since *action* is for the sake of happiness, and perhaps by "that for the sake of which" he means something not yet existing or outside of him, as a house, or health, or a baby generated, or God.

19. For Ross, "exist" = "exist in the sphere of immovable things", and such final cause would be the second kind as above, in Comm. 18, which applies to, say, God, but the first kind to, say, movable things, such as a house or a man. For St. Thomas Aquinas, the second kind has prior existence and may be in the realm of immovable things, as the center of the universe which is immovable and prior in existence to the motion of heavy bodies, which by moving towards the center tend to participate in something immovable; but the first kind does not exist actually but only in the intention of the agent, and may exist later, as health, which does not yet exist in the patient but only as medical art, and which exists only in movable things, such as men (194a28–36, 415a26–b7, 742a19–b12). I find it difficult to interpret Aristotle's meaning, except to say what I did above in Comm. 18.

20. This is the circular and even motion of the outermost heaven.

21. The heavenly bodies, though eternal, change with respect to place.

22. That is, just as *actuality*, with no potentiality at all.

23. Locomotion is prior in existence to the other motions (260a26–b29, 1073a12).

24. Such motion is the closest to Him, for it is eternal and even and has the least change or variation.

25. 1015a20–b15.

26. 982b19–983a11, 1177a12–1178a8.

27. Because we are *composites* of matter and form, and so destructible.

28. First actuality and second actuality exist in such destructibles and *composites* as men, who can be now asleep and now awake (412a19–28), but not in God who is simple; but if at all, then His actuality is the second, or by analogy so. So, perhaps also pleasure and *activity* are indistinguishable in Him or analogously attributed to Him, though distinguishable in us.

29. These are akin to the second actuality.

30. These are less vivid, as if between the first and second actualities, and so their pleasure, caused by their vividness so to say, is not as great.

31. The meaning seems to be: the final cause of thinking, if not impeded in any way, is of the best subject of which it is capable of thinking. But the best thinking in man is not as good as that in God, because of man's limitations.

32. Since the Intellect (= God or the prime mover) is just activity, and this is thinking and the best thinking, and this is of the best object of thought, which is the Intellect itself, the Intellect must be thinking of Himself.

33. The word "becomes" is used metaphorically; "is" may be better.

34. Since the intelligible object here is the Intellect itself, and this object qua intelligible does not exist apart from the Intellect (as in universal scientific knowledge), the two are the same, at least numerically, so to say. Perhaps even more, since the Intellect is simple (see above, Comm. 28).

35. In a man, this is the potential intellect.

36. After receiving the intelligible object, the intellect now is no longer potential to it but actually possesses it. In God, however, there is no becoming or motion but only the same *actuality*, so His thinking is no motion or becoming but an eternal possession and contemplation of the object of His thought.

37. But even if the intellect possesses its object, a man may not be contemplating it, as when he is asleep or not thinking it. Thus, contemplating the object is better than just having it but being dormant.

38. That is, when we are actually contemplating the best object of which we are capable.

39. That is, if God's pleasure is greater or of a higher quality than ours.

40. In a man, the second *actuality* of the intellect is the best part of his life; but in God, His *actuality* is simple, and this is eternal and can only be something analogous to the second *actuality*, for there is no potentiality in Him.

41. Prior in time, *substance,* and definition; for a man is prior to his seed which will become another man.

42. What has magnitude has matter, but God has no matter, for He

is just *actuality* or form and is one and simple (not simple like water, for this has matter and so has parts). See 266a10–267b26.

43. 204a8–206a8.

44. 260a26–b29. Since God has no matter, He cannot move with respect to place; and since no thing can be affected or altered unless it (or a part of it) can move with respect to place, God cannot be affected or altered.

45. An alternative to "why these facts are so" is: "why these attributes belong to Him (that is, to God)".

8

1. 206b27–33, 1083b36–1084a13, 1084a29–32.

2. The prime mover which moves the outermost sphere.

3. It has no magnitude; hence, it cannot be moved in virtue of itself. It is not an attribute, like whiteness in Socrates, nor a substance in some place, like a man in a boat; so, it cannot be moved accidentally (211a17–23, 1067b1–4). An alternative to "accidentally" is "with respect to an attribute". Thus, neither His nature nor any of His attributes can change.

4. The motion of the outermost sphere.

5. It is one, that is, not a composite motion like those of the inner spheres which move in virtue of themselves or by their own movers and are also moved by the outer spheres.

6. These locomotions are different from the first; they are motions of spheres with different axes of rotation and each has its own unmoved mover.

7. 261b27–266a9, 268b11–269b17, 286a3–290b11.

8. The cause, when causing, exists at the same time as the effect, when this is being caused (95a10–24). Hence, if something is caused by something else to be moved eternally, the moving cause exists and moves eternally.

9. As a moving cause, it is of course prior (1018b20–26); and as being an *actuality* without any potency, and also as being better and more honorable, it is also prior (1049b4–1051a21).

10. What moves a substance eternally is not an attribute (this would have to be in a substance anyway), but a substance.

11. 1073a5–11.

12. Namely, those of the spheres.

13. More accurately, arithmetic and geometry are concerned with numbers and magnitudes, respectively, which are attributes of substances in general; but astronomy is concerned with the mathematical attributes of the heavenly bodies (such as stars) in particular, which are sensible but eternal. Eternal substances qua substances are also the concern of philosophy. Hence, of the mathematical sciences, astronomy is closest to philosophy.

14. It is moved by its mover and also by other spheres.

15. References concerning details of the astronomical theories that

follow are in the *Commentaries on Aristotle's Metaphysics,* by Ross
(Clarendon Press, 1924, Vol. II, pp. 384–94).

16. Referring probably to the locomotion of a sphere.

17. Referring probably to unmoved movers.

18. Referring probably to the spheres, which carry the stars.

19. For the sake of the stars.

20. The argument may be something like this: The unmoved substances are by nature eternal movers, and one for each sphere; so such
substances are equal to the moving spheres, whose number may be
obtained by the observed stars which they carry for their own sake (for
in divine things nothing is done in vain).

21. That is, if there were many heavens specifically the same.

22. By "principle" he means the prime mover of each heaven.

23. That is, things of the same species.

24. The prime mover has no matter. So if many such existed, then
being just actualities, they would be in no way distinguishable. Aristotle
assumes this to be impossible; for he believes that if many things of one
species exist, since they cannot be distinguished by their form, they
must be distinguished by something else, by a potency or matter which
they must have in order to be counted as many by the same specific
measure.

25. Referring to the sphere moved by a prime mover.

26. But since the spheres of this universe are many, are not the immovable movers many, as it was already shown? On the other hand,
since the locomotions of those spheres are distinct, so are the movers in
their essence; each of the movers is like a distinct species.

9

1. In a man, for example, his essence (a soul) is distinct from his
thinking, which is an activity of the soul, and it is the soul or part of it
that causes his thinking.

2. As such, it can cause activity and so can exist now with activity
and now without it, like the human soul or intellect.

3. In a man, the soul qua potency alone is not the best, for it is not
as good as when accompanied by its activity of thinking. Likewise for
The Intellect, assuming He is a potency and His activity is distinct from
that potency.

4. That is, as a potency.

5. That is, just the activity of thinking, without potency.

6. The assumption, then, is: it is better to think of what is better,
and so best of what is best; for the better the object of thought, the better
the thought.

7. If He does so change, He cannot be the best possible (see above,
Comm. 5).

8. What changes from one contrary to another or to an intermediate
is in motion; further, motion is an incomplete *actuality,* and as such it

cannot be as good as a complete *actuality* which has goodness and completeness in all its parts (1048b18–34).

9. God and Thinking are numerically the same, but "Thinking" signifies Him as activity rather than as potency. Likewise, He is called "prime mover" by being the first moving cause of all, and He is called "Intellect" in answer to the question "What kind of substance is He?"

10. If He were a potency, then by that very nature He would be subject to change from one contrary to another, for example, from activity to inactivity and conversely; so to be continuously in activity for a long time would be against its nature and would require an effort, and to be always so would even be impossible, since what can be eternally is eternally or must be eternally, for "A is possible" among eternals also means A exists or A necessarily exists (22b29–23a18, 203b30, 337b35–338a2).

11. The argument is perhaps this: Since the Intellect does not move (lines 26–7), He always thinks of the same thing; since the better the object of thought, the better the thought (lines 23–6), Thinking must think of the best object if He is to be the best; if Thinking were to think of something else (say, X) and not of Himself, then His thinking of X would be better than His thinking of Thinking, X as an object of thought would be better than Thinking as an object of thought, and so X as an object would be better than Thinking as an object. But Thinking is the best of all things. Hence, Thinking thinks of Thinking. Here, Thinking = God = Intellect.

12. That is, the essence or definition of thinking is not the same as that of the object of thought.

13. Are they the same in essence, or rather numerically?

14. As existing in the soul; so is the object of a theoretical science, for it does not exist outside of the soul, but the knowledge of it is universal and exists, so to say, in potentiality with respect to individual objects (1087a15–19). So, universal knowledge and its object are one (numerically).

15. Or Thinking and His object, since the discussion here is concerned ultimately with The Intellect.

16. Now that the object of Thinking is Thinking, is Thinking a composite?

17. But it cannot change, as shown in 1074b25–27.

18. Qua a form, the human intellect is indivisible; and if it is one with its object and the latter is indivisible (for example, what is indefinable is such), then again it is indivisible.

19. Referring to the intellect.

20. He may be referring to the axioms, or to the whatness of things, both of which are principles but composites; for example, the principle of contradiction, or the definition of a triangle (84b37–85a1, 100b5–17, 1140b31–1141a8).

21. Its goodness lies in thinking not a part but the whole of a com-

posite as a unity, and not in a part of the time taken to think but in the whole time taken.

22. But thinking is indivisible and simple, He is of Himself, and He is changeless. Hence, Thinking is the thinking of Himself through all eternity. Moreover, being simple and thinking of Himself every instant, so to say, goodness and pleasure is in Him during any part of time, so to say, like happiness in men (1048b18–36).

10

1. That is, like Good Itself in the case of Plato.

2. What kind of cause does "because" indicate? For one thing, the general causes the order as a mover of it, for it is he who puts order in the army. Again, the general is more honorable and so deserves more than any soldier, and without him the soldiers would attain no good and even perish. So, perhaps both causes are indicated. If such is the case in an army, in which both the general and the soldiers are of the same species, it would be more so in the case of God and the things caused by him, in which the species (if "species" is the correct term) are even radically distinct.

3. For example, the simple elements for the sake of plants, these for the lower animals, these for men, etc. But is it not bad for animals to be butchered by men? On the other hand, is this not better than if men (of greater worth) did not exist at all, if their existence depends on these animals? 1256b15–22.

4. The following proportion may facilitate the meaning: head of household : wife and sons : slaves, etc. :: God : other movers and heavenly bodies : destructible objects.

5. A division of labor, so to say, whereby each of a number of distinct things acts according to its nature, and for the good of the whole.

6. For example, God is not composed of contraries, and what is so composed must also have matter.

7. A contrary acts upon matter, not on a contrary (189b9–19, 335b29–31).

8. By positing matter as a subject in which a contrary exists.

9. Plato and followers (1088b28–33, 1089a35–b8, 1091b35–7).

10. Speusippus (1087b4–9).

11. The *Unequal* and *Plurality* (or the *Many*) were also called "*Badness Itself*" or "*Badness*". Since all things, including the heavenly bodies, come from the *One* and from *Badness*, they participate in Badness or have badness. Only *One* has no *Badness* (or is not bad at all) 988a14–5.

12. The Pythagoreans and Speusippus (1072b30–4).

13. For example, God.

14. Empedocles posits *Friendship* as the good (a final cause) but uses it rather as a mover and as matter. Further, what is (or can be) both matter and a mover is a composite of matter and form (for, a mover is

or has a form, as a man who can move things and also be, as matter, a soldier in an army; but he is neither prime matter nor a prime mover, and so not a first principle), and so *Friendship* as such a composite cannot be a first principle. Does goodness belong to *Friendship*, then, qua a mover or qua matter?

15. Perhaps because an eternal principle cannot be bad (1051a4–21).

16. But it appears that health as art (as existing in the soul) still exists as a mover and for the sake of something else, namely, health which is to be induced in a body.

17. For, he spoke of the principles as being somehow contraries, good and bad (988a14–7).

18. For Aristotle, matter (which can be or become more than one thing) is a principle of destructible but not of indestructible things. The eternal movers are just forms; and the Moon, Sun, and stars are eternal in *substance* and possess matter only in a qualified sense, that is, they are changeable only with respect to place (1042b5–6, 1050b13–8).

19. Parmenides, Xenophanes, Melissus (986b10–30).

20. For Aristotle, the movers cause it (1072a9–18).

21. If these are matter and form, they need an eternal mover; if they are contraries, these do not always move, for a potency, which is prior to motion, must underlie them.

22. That is, if the principles are contraries, matter or potentiality underlies them; and this matter is prior to either contrary, for matter is always there with either contrary, while the other contrary is not there. But what has matter is not an eternal mover, and if it is in motion, eternally or otherwise, it needs a mover, as in the case of the spheres and in destructible things.

23. If the Forms are separate from sensibles, how can they be movers of them? And if they are immovable and so act always in the same way, how can they sometimes generate things and sometimes destroy them? So, another mover of other movers are needed.

24. Perhaps the argument runs thus: If, for these thinkers, the highest principle has a contrary, then just as knowledge and ignorance, which are contraries, are respectively of being and of nonbeing (*Republic*, 477–8), which are contraries, so there will be a contrary to wisdom, whose object (God, or *Friendship*, or etc.) is first and most honorable. But there is nothing contrary to wisdom because there is no contrary to what is first; and if there were such, then it would have matter, which would be potentially now this object and now its contrary, for example, now *Friendship* and now *Strife*, or now the prime mover and now its contrary (and this is impossible, for *Friendship* does not become *Strife*, and neither of them has matter).

25. An eternal and immovable moving principle is probably meant. If so, there will be no orderly and eternal locomotion of the heavenly objects; and there will be no generation, if there is no more than one such (1072a10–8); and the absence of an immovable mover necessitates an infinity of movers, which is impossible.

26. Perhaps as final causes, as objects desired or loved; for they cannot be material causes, they are not posited as eternal moving causes (for otherwise, Two would be generating Fours continuously), and they are not formal causes if they are not in the sensibles.

27. He is referring to the Ideas or Numbers. As forms participated in, they are not continuous; as matter, no number of their units can form a magnitude; and as movers, they cannot make what is continuous (1084a2–7).

28. He is probably referring to the contrary principle posited by these thinkers as being also a mover. A primary contrary, such as whiteness, exists with matter; and the white object as a *composite* may not exist. And if the white object is a mover, it cannot always move, for it moves in virtue of its primary contrary (whiteness) which may be lost, and not in virtue of its matter.

29. Perhaps he is referring to things with eternal actuality, such as the stars, Moon, prime mover, spheres, etc., which will not exist if the principle or principles of things are contraries as given in the previous note.

30. They should not posit the principles as contraries, and they should posit them as *actualities* or forms, if they are to be eternal movers.

31. In things generated, the moving cause puts the form in matter and so generates a thing which is one. But if one asks "In virtue of what is an existing thing one?", the answer is "In virtue of its form."

32. Things generated from distinct principles cannot be related to or affected by each other, for if they can, additional principles will be necessary (and such are not posited by Speusippus). But there is one universe, and things do, as we say, "rub shoulders against each other". For example, though magnitudes are not numbers, they can be numbered if, say, six triangles exist. So "number" is a predicate of these magnitudes; likewise, a line can be numbered by a unit line, and as such it can be, let us say, five feet in length.

33. Homer's *Iliad*, ii, 204.

Book M

1

1. 188a19–193b21.
2. 1028a10–1052a11.
3. Plato and his followers (987b14–18).
4. Xenocrates and his followers.
5. Speusippus and followers. The Pythagoreans do not posit such objects as existing apart from sensible objects.
6. 1076a38–1078b6.

7. 1078b7–1080a11.

8. Lost Works, for greater audiences.

9. This inquiry will consider also the Pythagoreans.

10. 998a7–19, perhaps a school of thinkers of minor importance. In a certain sense also the Pythagoreans. The first school, which is meant here, posits the mathematical objects as distinct from but in sensible objects; the Pythagoreans say that the sensible things are the numbers themselves. Thus, "in the sensible things" has two senses. There is a third possible sense, namely, as attributes of sensible things, but this is brought out by "they exist in some other manner." This is Aristotle's position.

11. Plato, Speusippus, Xenocrates.

2

1. 998a7–19. This is the first doctrine, Comm. 10 of the previous Section.

2. That is, not only the genus of mathematical objects, but the other genera of things as well, for example, whiteness and relations and such powers as the art of healing and hotness in fire (997b12–998a9).

3. A sensible body is probably meant. If such a body is divided, so will the mathematical body in it, and in the same way; hence, a mathematical body would be destructible. Moreover, such division leads ultimately to the division at a point or of a point, and a point according to their doctrine is an indivisible substance, not a limit of something else.

4. There are two objections to their doctrine here. (a) The presence of mathematical objects in sensible things is redundant, for their division does not disturb the division of sensible things. (b) How can mathematical objects in sensible things be divided if they are posited as immovable?

5. Plato, Speusippus, and Xenocrates posit a separate existence of Mathematical Objects.

6. Corresponding to each universal name which is applied to sensibles there is an Idea which is prior in existence and separate. So, there is an Idea of a point and of a line and of a plane as well as of a solid.

7. That is, separate from that solid, and also prior in existence (understood) to those, respectively, in the solid. The points, lines, and planes in the immovable mathematical solids are inseparable, so others which are prior and separate are needed.

8. For Plato, all Mathematical Objects are substances; and incomposite or less composite substances are prior in existence to the composite or more composite, respectively. For example, if a house exists, so do bricks (or whatever the material), but not conversely. Moreover, just as the *One* (the formal principle) is prior in existence to Two (for, the

One acts on the material principle, the *Dyad,* to produce Two), and the Idea Man is likewise prior to Socrates, so with Mathematical Objects. Evidently, then, a plane would be less composite than a solid, a line than a plane, and a point than a line.

9. And also separate from (understood).

10. The terms "separate" and "by themselves" have the same meaning (1022a35–6).

11. That is, the solids which are prior to the sensible solids.

12. There seem to be more sets of lines and points than stated: seven sets of lines, fifteen sets of points. However, this does not disturb the effectiveness of the argument. See my *Aristotle's Philosophy of Mathematics* (University of Chicago Press, 1952, pp. 200–2).

13. This is posited by Plato. Prior in existence is meant. Since there is priority of existence in the distinct sets of points (and of lines, and of planes), one set of points cannot be assumed as identical in nature to another set. So, a science of points (or of lines, or of planes) cannot be concerned with all of the sets.

14. A point is one, and so it is a unit; but a unit need not be a point. Hence, a unit is prior in existence to a point. Similarly, an individual man is one, the Idea Man is one, etc., and we shall have distinct sets of units and numbers, as in the case of planes, lines, and points; and the units of one set cannot be identical with those of the other sets, just as in the case of points, lines, and planes. Moreover, sensible objects are much greater in kind and in number than mathematical objects as usually understood; hence, the distinct sets of mathematical units (and so, of numbers) in this case would be far greater than the sets of points, lines, etc. The term "infinite" here means very large (1066a37).

15. 995b13–8, 997b12–24.

16. If, for example, motion is a necessary attribute of some parts of the heaven, such as of the Sun and the stars, how can there be Ideas of them if Ideas are immovable?

17. The objects of astronomy, optics, and harmonics have more reason to be called "mathematical" than any others. But they are sensible. So, if there are Ideas (and/or Intermediates) of them, so must there be of the other sensible objects.

18. For example, such are propositions about all quantities, or all magnitudes, etc., like "Equal quantities from equal quantities leave equal quantities as remainders", and theorems concerning proportion, like "Of magnitudes, if A is commensurable with B but incommensurable with C, then C is incommensurable with B and with $A + B$.". There should be an Idea of Quantity as such, and also of Magnitude and of Number as such (74a17–25, 1026a25–27, 1064b8–9, 1096a17–19).

19. The Intermediates are posited as being species of Numbers, Lines, Planes, etc., as evidenced by the way Plato generates them from his principles, but not Quantities as such or even Numbers and Magnitudes as such (1084b2–6, 1096a17–19). So, since there are propositions

about quantities as such (and even about magnitudes and numbers as such) and the latter are not among the Intermediates (nor among the Ideas, since Ideas are not the objects of a mathematical science; for the Idea Two is unique, whereas "$2+2=4$" and the like require many twos, etc., so, many twos are posited among the Intermediates, 987b14–18), and since a quantity is prior in existence to a number and to specific numbers and to specific magnitudes (and a magnitude to a specific magnitude such as a line, etc.), Quantities and Magnitudes and Numbers as such, if objects of a science, must form a class between the Ideas and the Intermediates. No such class is posited by Plato and the others.

20. And also immovable and eternal (understood).

21. That is, prior in existence and in substance according to their doctrine.

22. For these thinkers, the order of generation of magnitudes from their principles is: point, line, plane (or surface), solid. Even so, a solid is complete, and that which is complete is a substance to a higher degree and prior in existence, as a father in relation to his son and the mover in relation to the moved.

23. A living thing has a form, and unity. The lifeless, like earth and water, is like matter; it disintegrates easily, or it is divisible easily, or it is like a heap (1040b5–10).

24. The whole soul would be the cause of the unity of the body in the lower animals; in man, not the whole soul, since the intellect does not contribute in keeping the body together.

25. For example, glue or an attribute of it (1015b36–1016a4).

26. For example, a line has parts, whether these be indivisible lines, as some say, or points; but if these parts are substances (not attributes) and separable, what holds them together?

27. For these thinkers, too, generation from principles proceeds this way; and Speusippus admits that the last in generation is more complete (1072b30–4), and so prior in substance (and this would go against the priority of their principles).

28. An alternative to "axiom" is "claim".

29. There are only three dimensions, and a body is three-dimensional (268a1–13).

30. We observe bodies as being separate and so as substances somehow; but positing points and lines and planes as substances, and especially as capable of being put together to form bodies, contradicts observation.

31. In the definition of a cube, for example, we must include points and lines and planes, but not conversely.

32. That is, not always together.

33. For example, neither is whiteness prior in existence to a white man, nor is a white man posterior in existence to the whiteness in him.

34. Shown in 1076a38–b11.

35. That is, they exist not by themselves but in something else, in substances or bodies as attributes. This is Aristotle's position.

3

1. That is, divisible into indivisibles (units) in the case of numbers, or else, investigated not as divisible but with respect to other attributes, such as equality, ratio, etc.

2. That is, just as there are propositions about quantities in general which do not consider these quantities as continuous or as discrete, but leave these attributes out and consider only divisibility in quantities, so there are propositions about sensible magnitudes which leave out sensible attributes and consider only continuity in sensible magnitudes.

3. For example, men and rocks may be considered only qua moving, and the whatness of a man or of a rock and the attributes or properties that follow from it may be left out entirely.

4. An alternative to "moving" is "motion". No such thing is separate from an object, for motion is something inseparable from a substance or a body (this is an objection against Plato's Idea of Motion as something separate).

5. This is an objection against those who regard mathematical objects as substances but in sensible bodies, in which case two bodies or substances would be in the same place (991a14–8).

6. That is, propositions of only the planes in sensible bodies, and the same applies to lengths, etc.

7. Whether divisible qua magnitudes (in general) or qua quantities is not stated; but in each case an abstraction from a specific magnitude is made. It is probably qua magnitudes, for what comes after it, the indivisible in position, is a point, and a point exists in a magnitude.

8. This is a unit, for this is the result when position is taken away.

9. The term "motion" would be more appropriate than "the moving".

10. They are concerned with nonsensible attributes but of sensible things.

11. That is, femininity or masculinity is an *attribute* of an animal and not something existing apart from an animal.

12. The corresponding objects of three sciences here are: a body (magnitude + motion), a magnitude (no motion), a unit (neither magnitude nor motion).

13. Of motions, locomotion is prior in existence and in time to the others, that is, to alteration, increase, and decrease, and also to generation; and of locomotions, the circular and straight are simple motions, but the circular is prior in existence to the straight (243a6–10, 260a20–b33, 265a13–18, 268b17–20, 1072b8–10). Since the circular is curved, and this admits the more and the less, but the straight does not and so is more simple, the straight appears to be prior in knowledge to the circular. So the circle is defined in terms of a straight line, but not con-

versely. Thus, by "primary motion" Aristotle may mean either all locomotions, or the primary locomotions; and if the latter, then either the
simple motions (circular and straight), or the straight (since exact knowledge is of the prior in knowledge).

14. Since the even is prior in definition to, and therefore simpler than,
the uneven, the even primary motions are the simplest.

15. These *proper attributes* are not properties. Properties of sight or
sound are attributes belonging to sight or sound qua sight or sound;
but *proper* attributes may be in another genus and yet belong to them
(necessarily or for the most part). For example, the equality of the
angles of incidence and reflection belongs to the path of a reflected ray,
and the length ratio of 2:1 belongs to a string emitting a sound and its
octave, respectively (other things being equal). *Proper* attributes may
be axioms or theorems, and modern science is largely concerned with
these. Aristotle was well aware of the existence of such attributes
(78b34–79a16), which are investigated by mixed sciences, such as astronomy, optics, mechanics, and harmonics.

16. Not as existing separately, but as something to be investigated
apart from or without reference to that of which it is an attribute or
with which it exists. Perhaps the term "distinguishable" brings out this
fact.

17. The meaning in Greek (perhaps corrupt) is not clear. Perhaps it
is something like this: the attributes of a man qua a solid are the same
even if a man qua a substance is indivisible; for if he dies, his unity
and substance are destroyed but the attributes of the body qua a solid
are still there. The divisibility is true of him qua a solid, not qua a man.

18. Primary being is actuality or substance. If a substance has quantity, this is not its actuality, and quantitative parts in such a substance
are intelligible matter and the concern of mathematics (1036a9–12).

19. An alternative to "beautiful" is "noble". Perhaps the latter is a
genus of the former.

20. For example, Aristippus (996a32–b1).

21. Since beauty is in symmetry, order, and definiteness, and the
latter and their properties are investigated by mathematics, mathematicians are concerned with the beautiful even if the term "beauty" does
not appear in their vocabulary.

22. Whether such work was never written, or written but lost, is not
definitely known. A book on mathematics by Aristotle, in which beauty
may have been discussed, is listed in the catalogues of Diogenes Laertius
and of Hesychius, but the reliability of these catalogues has been questioned by some scholars.

4

Most of this chapter is repeated from Book A, so the commentaries are
referred to the corresponding ones in Book A.

1. Plato and followers, his early doctrine.

2. By definition, science or *knowledge* is of that which always exists.

3. 194a20–1, 642a24–31.

4. See Book A, Sec. 5, Comm. 5.

5. See Book A, Sec. 5, Comm. 3.

6. Probably defined as the number 5, for $5 = 2 + 3$ (where perhaps 2 stands for female and 3 for male).

7. The term "formulae" here means definitions.

8. As is often done is Plato's *Dialogues*, it is possible, even without definitions, to prove something thus: Let A be a thing, X an attribute in question. If Y, Z, etc., are admitted to be attributes of A and if other facts are also admitted, then by assuming that A is X, along with what is admitted, one may arrive at a contradiction by the use of axioms of logic.

9. That is, Socrates posited universals and definitions as being about sensible things.

10. This amounts to saying that there is an Idea corresponding to every universal term, such as "a man", "a triangle", "a color", etc.

11. See Book A, Sec. 9, Comm. 1. The text may be translated also thus: "For, in seeking . . . , which are more numerous, so to say, than the forms (or species) of the individual sensibles."

12. See Book A, Sec. 9, Comm. 2.

13. See Book A, Sec. 9, Comm. 3.

14. See Book A, Sec. 9, Comm. 4.

15. See Book A, Sec. 9, Comm. 6.

16. See Book A, Sec. 9, Comm. 7.

17. See Book A, Sec. 9, Comm. 8.

18. See Book A, Sec. 9, Comms. 9 and 10.

19. See Book A, Sec. 9, Comm. 11.

20. See Book A, Sec. 9, Comm. 12.

21. See Book A, Sec. 9, Comm. 14. An alternative to "*Dyad*" is "Two".

22. The *Great* and *Small* are relations, yet they are principles (first in existence) from which Two and the other Numbers (which are substances according to Plato) are generated.

23. See Book A, Sec. 9, Comm. 15.

24. We can have a concept of a triangle, a color, etc., and these are not substances; and they are also objects of a science.

25. In particular, their belief that Ideas are substances.

26. See Book A, Sec. 9, Comm. 17.

27. See Book A, Sec. 9, Comm. 18.

28. See Book A, Sec. 9, Comm. 19.

29. That is, according to their position, since Redness Itself is a substance, a sensible red color should also be a substance; but it is a quality, and also inseparable from a body, and hence an attribute.

30. These are the Mathematical Twos, not Ideas.

31. For example, if Man Himself and a man have nothing in common, why posit Man Himself? And what would "Man Himself" mean?

32. For example, there is three-sidedness, a figure, and a triangle; and a triangle is defined as a three-sided figure. Among the Ideas, we have Three-sidedness Itself, Figure Itself, and Triangle Itself. Should Triangle Itself, then, be defined as Three-sided Figure Itself, or Three-sided Itself Figure Itself, or Three-sided Itself Figure? Further, just as "figure" is the genus of a triangle and a quadrilateral, so Itself should be the genus of Triangle Itself and Quadrilateral Itself. But no Idea of Itself is posited; and such Idea should be prior in existence.

5

1. Such as the Sun, stars, Moon, etc., which are assumed eternal.

2. Not the Forms? What moves these sensibles?

3. See Book A, Sec. 9, Comm. 22.

4. An Idea is unique. For example, Man Himself is unique. If it were in individual men, it would be many and not one.

5. See Book A, Sec. 9, Comm. 23.

6. See Book A, Sec. 9, Comm. 24. Also, a unique Idea would be in many things, which is impossible, etc.

7. They do not come *from* Ideas as matter (Ideas are Forms), or as moving causes (Ideas are not moving causes), or any of the senses given in 1023a26–b11.

8. According to what the Platonists say, any plausible relation between the Ideas and the corresponding things leads to difficulties and contradictions.

9. See Book A, Sec. 9, Comm. 25.

10. See Book A, Sec. 9, Comm. 26.

11. See Book A, Sec. 9, Comm. 27.

12. See Book A, Sec. 9, Comm. 28.

13. The form or essence of a *composite* (of matter and form) is in that *composite*. So, how can a Form be in an individual and at the same time apart from it? Besides, being in many individuals of the same kind, it would be many and not unique.

14. That is, as formal cause.

15. That is, as moving cause.

16. That is, a sensible mover. It is Socrates' father that is the moving cause, not the Idea Man, according to observation.

17. Just as the moving cause of a house is the builder (or his art), even if no Form of a house exists, so we observe an individual to be the moving cause of another individual of the same kind; and Forms are not needed.

18. Logical arguments are those which follow from the principles posited in the *Organon*.

6

1. Pythagoreans, Platonists. By "a number" he means any specific number for the Platonists, such as Two, Three, etc. Such a number would

be a number of units, not of men or of qualities or of some other nature. Thus, numbers and units so posited would be substances, like a man, or a tree.

2. First in existence is meant. Thus, for Plato, *One* is a principle and so first in existence, then comes Two, which results when the *One* acts on the material principle (the *Indefinite Dyad*), then Three, Four, etc.

3. For example, for Plato, the units of Two are distinct from those of Three, and so Two cannot be compared with Three (that is, it is not less than Three, nor added to or subtracted from it so as to make a number (just as 1 color and 2 feet do not make 3 of anything, and 2 feet is not less than 3 pounds, etc.).

4. Incomparable units for Plato would be possible, for example, in this sense: The *One* combines with the *Indefinite Dyad* to produce a unit, call it A_1; A_1 combines with the same *Dyad* to produce, say, A_2; then likewise for A_3, etc. Such incomparable units would be, of course, distinct or different.

5. For Plato, these would be the Intermediate Numbers and units which lie betwen the Ideas and the sensibles, for Speusippus they are the Mathematical Numbers, and for the Pythagoreans they are the numbers and units which make up the sensible world.

6. First in existence after *One*.

7. For example, for Plato, Two acts on the *Indefinite Dyad* to produce Four; so, while the units in Two are of the same kind and comparable, the contribution of the *Indefinite Dyad* in producing Four would make the units of Four distinct from those of Two.

8. Alternative (4) includes all numbers coming under alternatives (1), (2), and (3). Of course, there are three other alternatives: (1) and (2) but not (3), (1) and (3) but not (2), (2) and (3) but not (1).

9. 1076a38–b11.

10. This is the Pythagorean doctrine.

11. This may be a Platonic doctrine, or one held by some Platonists; for the Ideas and the Intermediates are separated, but the sensibles, whose forms are Ideas and which share in the Ideas, may themselves be numbers. The sensibles may be destructible because they are posterior in existence and in generation and so have an excess of the *Indefinite Dyad,* which is full of motion (201b19–21, 992b1–8, *Timaeus:* 52). Lines 991b9–21 seem to indicate that Plato did not state his position about this matter explicitly.

12. This is the material principle, called the *"Infinite"* by the Pythagoreans, the *"Great* and *Small"* or *"Unequal"* or *"Indefinite Dyad"* by the Platonists, and *"Plurality"* by Speusippus.

13. Plato and followers (987b14–8).

14. Speusippus and followers.

15. First in existence, or prior in existence to sensible things.

16. Units in the usual sense have neither magnitude nor position.

17. Probably some Platonist of minor importance.

18. Xenocrates and followers.

19. According to lines 992b13–8, this seems to be Plato's position.

20. The Intermediates.

21. Such as Line Itself, Plane Itself, etc., which are not Ideas in the sense of Numbers, but a sort of fourth class (992b15–8). These were Ideas in the early doctrine of Plato, for Ideas at that time were not yet identified as being Numbers.

22. Speusippus and followers. The Mathematical Objects for them include both numbers and magnitudes. By "mathematical way" Aristotle means that numbers have the usual attributes assigned to them by mathematicians, such as the fact that all units are comparable.

23. Xenocrates and followers.

24. Especially that of Xenocrates (1083b1–8).

7

1. The first Numbers are the Ideas, such as Two Itself, Three Itself, etc., which are the first objects generated from the first principles (the *One* and the *Indefinite Dyad*). The Mathematical Numbers are generated later.

2. The criticism here is general and hypothetical, against any one who adopted (if this actually happened) or would adopt the doctrine that all units are comparable. For Plato and Speusippus, the mathematical numbers would be the Mathematical Numbers.

3. For example, if all units are comparable, and Three is Man Himself but Six is Horse Itself, any three units in Six will be Man Himself, and so Horse Itself will have as a part Man Himself, or Man Himself twice, which is absurd. Besides, Man Himself will not be unique (each Idea is unique according to the doctrine of Ideas), but there will be many of them. Other such absurdities follow.

4. That is, the *One* and the *Indefinite Dyad*.

5. Only the *One* and the *Indefinite Dyad* are posited as first principles. So, if all units are comparable, no unique Ideas can be generated, and so they cannot exist as unique at all. The term "Numbers" here means Numbers as Ideas, which are unique, not Mathematical Numbers.

6. Since no one said that all units are noncomparable (1080b8–9), the criticisms of this position are hypothetical and for the sake of completeness. Aristotle does not mention here (perhaps he did in a lost work) how such units, differing in priority, might be generated; but perhaps he would argue thus: the *One* acts on the *Indefinite Dyad* (or, the *Indefinite Dyad* receives the *One*, as matter receives a form) to generate the first unit; this acts on the *Indefinite Dyad* to generate the second unit; this acts likewise, etc. In this manner, given any two units, one of them would be prior in generation and in existence to the other.

7. For Plato, these coincide with the Mathematical Numbers in the Intermediates.

8. That is, the way Plato generates them (1084a2–7), so that the Dyad is prior in existence to the Triad, etc. This will be detailed in the commentary on 1084a2–7.

9. Plato stated that Two was generated when the *Unequals* (*Great and Small*) were equalized. If so, the units in *Two* cannot be noncomparable.

10. Prior in existence and generation is meant. Plato generates Two first; but if one of the units of Two is prior in generation (and in existence) to the other, it is that unit which will be generated first and not Two. Further, what about the other unit? If generated from the *One* and the material principle in the same way as the first unit, it would be comparable with it. And if it is not comparable with the first unit, it will have to be generated from that unit and the material principle, and thus it will be posterior in generation and in existence to it. No such ways of generation have been posited by the Platonists.

11. It is clear that the first unit is prior in existence and in generation to Two, but not so clear how Two is prior to the second unit, for both units are needed to make Two. However, if the second unit is generated as a material part of Two, then both that unit and Two come into existence simultaneously, Two as a Form and a whole, the unit as part of matter. But form is prior to matter in actuality (1049b4–1051a33). However, this is just a hypothesis.

12. In saying that there is a first One or unit, the implication seems to be that there is a second and a third, etc.; and the same holds when they say that there is a first Dyad or Two. Perhaps by "their principles" Aristotle means such as the uniqueness posited by Plato, which would apply even to the units of a Number; and if so, all such units should be noncomparable.

13. This is explained in the later sentence: "However, it is . . . Dyad." For one thing, if the units are noncomparable, no Dyad is possible; for the units in a number, if it is to be truly called "a number", must be comparable.

14. That is, to truly say.

15. Perhaps the meaning is this: If we are to generate numbers, and Plato does this, such generation must take place by successive addition of units. Whether numbering as stated here is given as a Platonic statement or as a generally accepted belief is not clear. We know that Aristotle was aware of two possibilities (1082b33–6). Now no number can exist with units which are noncomparable. Moreover, for Plato, the generation of the Dyad, Four, etc. is such that the units within each of them are comparable (1081a23–5). Further, he generates Three by attaching the *One* somehow to the Dyad (1084a3–7); but the *One* is not comparable with each unit of the Dyad, so Three as a Number cannot exist, and besides, the Dyad becomes a part of Three and does not exist by itself. Also, if there was a Platonic statement of numbering as initially hinted, then Three likewise becomes a part of Four; and if we consider the generation of Four from the Dyad and the *Indefinite Dyad* (explicitly stated by the Platonists), then either the Dyad becomes a part of Four, or no unit of Four is comparable with a unit of the Dyad (perhaps they did not specify which alternative they took).

16. Dyad (or Dyad Itself) is unique, but 'Dyad' is hypothetically

introduced into the argument, as a part of Four or a higher Number, and is to be distinguished from Dyad Itself. Similarly for 'Triad', 'Four', etc.

17. This argument is by analogy. If the Dyad (or Two) becomes a part of Four when received by the *Indefinite Dyad* (the material principle, 1082a13–4), then *One* should become a part of Two when *One* is received by the *Indefinite Dyad*. If so, then only one unit is generated when the *One* is received by the *Indefinite Dyad*; but the Platonists generate two units, which make up the Number Two, from the *Indefinite Dyad*. Hence, the *Indefinite Dyad* cannot be the material principle for the extra unit or the One which would be generated to make Two. But no other material principle is posited.

18. This assumes the hypothesis that there is a second Dyad besides a first, and also a third, etc. (1081b1–6).

19. Prior in generation and in existence. Also, such units would be noncomparable.

20. For the meaning of "fictitious", see 1082b2–4.

21. That is, Ten Itself is a definite and unique Number with ten units which are of a definite kind (with respect to priority and generation) and comparable; and if this Ten is divided into two 'Fives' in a definite way, the same applies to the units in each 'Five', separately.

22. According to their principles, no unit of one Number is comparable with a unit of another Number. So, each unit in one 'Five' would differ from each unit in another 'Five'.

23. The two assumptions here are: (a) All units within a Number are comparable; (b) any unit of one Number is noncomparable with any unit of another Number. So, the units of Ten Itself are comparable; but since this Ten is also composed of two 'Fives', say 5_1 and 5_2, and these two are not the same Number, their units must differ according to assumption (b). Hence, a contradiction.

24. The ten units in Ten Itself can be divided into two 'Fives' in many different ways, in fact, by the theory of Combinations, in $^{10}C_5$ or 252 ways. Any of these ways has just as much right as any other; so it is unreasonable to posit only one way. Now let a second way be into 5_3 and 5_4. Then the units in 5_3 differ from those in 5_4. Hence the Ten Itself composed of 5_1 and 5_2 cannot be the same as the Ten composed of 5_3 and 5_4. But it is the same Ten Itself. Hence, a contradiction. The same applies to Four. Of course, a division of Ten into 'Four' and 'Six' is also possible, etc.; however, one contradiction in a doctrine is sufficient to discredit it. By "two 'Dyads' " the Platonists meant those of which Four consists.

25. Two units as such form a plurality, or are matter; so, if they are to form one unity, they must have some potency in virtue of which they can be truly unified to form a Dyad or one Dyad. The unity in a white man is an accidental unity, of an attribute in a subject; that of a 'two-footed animal' is the unity of a genus and a differentia, in the sense of the form 'two-footedness' in the matter 'animal' (1030a11–4, 1037b13–

8, 1038a5–9, 1045a31–5); and there is unity by contact, position, blend, etc. (1042b15–31). But if the units in the Dyad are substances, the term "Dyad" signifies a plurality without a form and not one thing or one Idea. Again, units have no position and therefore are not in place or contact.

26. He may be referring to the fact that, on the one hand, these thinkers say that there is priority and posteriority and so a difference among the units, but on the other, they say nothing about the nature of the differences in the units but present them as just indivisible; or, perhaps he is indicating that though they have indivisibility in common, seeing that each is indivisible, this alone is no cause for their forming one unit.

27. Plato posits only one Dyad, Two Itself. But his manner of generating Numbers necessitates many 'Dyads', some prior and others posterior, and each an Idea. Thus, if it is Two Itself (or the Dyad) which, received by the *Indefinite Dyad*, makes Four, then it is each of the two 'Dyads' by itself in Four which will likewise make a 'Four', or Eight all told; so each 'Dyad' functions like an Idea. Further, Two Itself is prior in existence to each 'Dyad' in Four, and each of the latter 'Dyads' is prior in existence to each 'Dyad' in Eight.

28. Using Comm. 27 (above), just as the *One*, received by the *Indefinite Dyad*, makes the Dyad, so each unit in this Dyad, functioning like the *One* and so like an Idea, makes a 'Dyad' which is in the next Number (Four) generated, etc. So each unit is a 'One', so to say, and an Idea, and priority among the 'Ones' is similar to that among the 'Dyads'.

29. Since sensibles are copies or imitations of Ideas, just as an Idea was shown to be composed of Ideas, so with sensibles. For example, if Nine is the Idea Man, Five the Idea Mouse, and Four the Idea Ass, then a man in the sensible world will be composed of a mouse and an ass.

30. Priority and posteriority among the units generated in Plato's doctrine necessitate a difference among units, yet units as treated by mathematicians do not differ either qualitatively or quantitatively qua indivisible, and especially if they are indivisible. For example, men and horses are units qua animals, not qua magnitudes, for each animal is a substance and indivisible qua a substance; and points are indivisible in every direction, although they have position.

31. For example, if things are within the same ultimate species, equal numbers of them are the same (1054a35–b3). For example, five men are the same in *substance* as five other men, but they are not the same in *substance* as five horses, since horses and men differ, although they are equal qua animals. A problem thus arises with Plato's Numbers, whether or not Five is greater than Four, and whether or not it is equal to a 'Five' which is a part of Ten; for here we have noncomparable units, that is, units which differ in priority and so are not the same. It would be like comparing five lines with four colors or five cubes. How can a line be equal to a cube? What is their common measure? Not oneness, for "one" in the two cases is not univocal but has distinct senses.

32. Prior or posterior in existence.

33. But posterior to the Dyad Itself. So, it will be between the Dyad Itself and the Triad Itself.

34. Simultaneous in existence and in generation.

35. Perhaps he should say "not equal", which is more general, for the good and the bad, as qualities, are neither equal nor unequal, but they can be numbered as two genera (1088a11–4).

36. That is, noncomparable units, which come from different Numbers. These thinkers do not state how units differ in terms of attributes, except in priority; and though assigning them only a common attribute, indivisibility, still they posit them as noncomparable.

37. If the units of the Dyad are not comparable with those of the Triad, then the Triad is neither equal nor unequal (whether greater or less) to the Dyad. If so, then the term "Number" itself would be equivocally predicated of the Dyad, the Triad, and the rest; for it would be like predicating "a man" of Socrates, of a color, and of a motion. But if the Triad is greater than the Dyad, this necessitates comparability among their units (which they deny), and then the Dyad would be equal to any two units in the Triad. This, of course, would eliminate the priority of units in the first Numbers, which are Ideas. Also, the Triad would have 'Dyads', and there would be many 'Dyads', contrary to the uniqueness of each Idea.

38. That is, the term "number" (or "Number") would not be univocal, and the statement "The Ideas are Numbers" would be either meaningless or many statements (in each of which the term "Number" would have to be defined or somehow made clear or known).

39. 1080a23–30, 1080b11–4. Plato is included. If the units (whatever their nature) of one Number are not comparable with those of another, although "Number" would not be an appropriate term (for the term would not be univocal), the term "Idea" would. In this sense, we would have Ideas, each distinct from the others and unique in itself and a substance, but the difficulties which follow by making Ideas also Numbers would disappear.

40. That is, counting not by adding would be like naming each Idea separately, say, in the order of priority in existence and generation. For counting by adding would contradict their manner of generating Ideas from the *Indefinite Dyad* as matter (1084a3–7) and would also result in only one final Idea, a super-Idea, so to say, with parts, each of which would not be *actual* or a substance but potentially existing in that Idea.

41. The Greek mss. have ἰδέαν; it should be ἰδέας, for Aristotle wants to bring out the fact that counting by adding would result not in many Ideas but in one, something which these thinkers would like to avoid in order to have many Ideas.

42. That is, in order to posit a plurality of Ideas, they must define counting in only one way, by excluding the addition of a unit successively. But by so doing, they eliminate many facts in the science of mathematics (and in practical affairs), namely, facts which result when

counting takes place by adding (comparable) units to a number and so increasing it.

43. Perhaps the meaning is this: It is ridiculous to tie up a minor problem like that of the nature of counting to so great a problem as the one we are considering concerning the Ideas.

8

1. Probably most mathematicians at the time of Aristotle regarded units as indivisible with respect to quantity and without quality or position, and numbers as admitting of differentiae (for example, the numbers 3, 5, 8) and of being equal or unequal. Aristotle took the same position and added further requirements, such as comparability among units in numbers which admit equality and inequality, the nature and kinds of units and their dependence on the senses of "one", etc. (72a21–3, 87a35–6, 1016b17–25, 1052b9–1053a27, etc.).

2. In quantity of units, two feet are equal to two yards; but a foot and a yard differ in quantity, so two feet differ in some respects from two yards.

3. He is talking about the units in different Numbers. Plato said nothing about how they differ in virtue of their difference in their priority, and if he had made them differ in quantity, difficulties would follow.

4. An alternative to "Numbers" is "numbers".

5. Apparently, this must have been the stated position of the Platonists.

6. The function of the *Indefinite Dyad* is just to double what it receives (1082a13–5, 1083b35–6, 1084a3–7).

7. To say that one unit is prior in existence to another is to relate them and not to state how these units differ in, say, quality; it would be like stating a relation between X and Y, that X is to the right of Y, a relation from which one can gather no information as to the difference in quality between X and Y.

8. That is, as separate forms of sensible numbers or of sensible objects.

9. 1081a5–17.

10. 1081a17–b35, 1081b35–1083a17.

11. Speusippus and followers (1076a21–2).

12. The first doctrine of Plato, in which Ideas were not yet regarded as Numbers (1078b9–1080a11).

13. The later doctrine of Plato, and Xenocrates (1081b35–1083a17, 1083b1–8, 1076a19–21).

14. That is, first (or prior to all others) in existence.

15. For Speusippus, the principle of Mathematical Numbers is, as for Plato, the *One* as form, but *Plurality* as matter (1028b21–4, 1087b4–9); and the other Mathematical Numbers are generated from these.

16. For example, Plato.

17. Aristotle assumes detailed knowledge of the system of Speusippus, perhaps in a lost work; so we can only make hypotheses. Did Speusippus say that the *One* differs in essence or in any way from the other units? Whether yes or no, since the *One* needs *Plurality* as matter to generate units, the *One* must be prior in existence and perhaps distinct in essence, for, unlike the other units, it does not have *Plurality*. Moreover, if the other units are to be comparable, then they have to be generated in the same way, by a repeated action of the *One* on *Plurality;* but if it is a unit (not the *One*) which acts on *Plurality,* this unit is prior in existence to, perhaps distinct in essence from, and not comparable with the unit generated from it, etc. Again, if the *One* is simple in nature and function, it can only generate units, not a Two or other dyads, or a Three, etc. Then how would these be generated? Plato had an answer of a sort; the *One* with the *Indefinite Dyad* generates Two and only Two, Two likewise generates Four, etc., although there is some difficulty in the generation of odd Numbers (1084a4–5, 1083b28–30, 1084b13–22) and in the generation of the Mathematical Objects from the Numbers (Ideas). So, for Speusippus, if the *One* cannot generate a Dyad or other dyads, a first Dyad as a principle is needed to generate other dyads repeatedly if such dyads are to be comparable.

18. 1081b35–1083a17, and 1081a17–b35 if all units are noncomparable.

19. That is, if Numbers are separate, all alternatives for Speusippus lead to difficulties.

20. The doctrine of Xenocrates (1076a20–1, 1080b22–3).

21. These might be hypotheses of how the same objects can be both Numbers as Ideas and Numbers as Mathematical Objects; that is, hypotheses calculated to remove contradictions arising by identifying the two sets of objects. Thus, Xenocrates would be faced with three sets of difficulties; those facing Plato, those facing Speusippus, and those facing the additional contradictions arising by identifying the Ideas with the Mathematical Objects.

22. 1080b16–21.

23. That is, not separate from sensible objects.

24. That is, making numbers substances and the only substances, rather than attributes, and making them also mathematical, leads to impossibilities.

25. 315b24–317a17, 968a1–972b33.

26. If the Pythagorean numbers are the usually accepted mathematical numbers with indivisible units, then from such units no magnitude can be generated, since a magnitude is not composed of indivisibles as parts (see Comm. 25, above); and even if indivisible magnitudes were assumed to exist, an indivisible magnitude could not be a unit or a number (for units are without position, while magnitudes have position). So, in assuming units to have magnitude, the Pythagoreans implicitly deny the existence of numbers as commonly understood.

27. Aristotle's general concern is to deny the separateness of numbers and units as posited by these thinkers.

28. Plato's position is probably that each thing generated consists of both the *Great* and the *Small* (987b18–22). However, he may not have stated this clearly about each unit in a Number (1081a23–5), for equalization is possible either by give and take (of the *Great* and *Small*) or by the increase of the *Small* and diminution of the *Great*.

29. For Plato, the units within each Number are comparable. If in the Dyad, which is the first Number generated, one unit consists of the *Small* and the other of the *Great*, then the two units, being different, and in fact possessing contrariety, will not be comparable.

30. Whether the third unit in Three consists of the *Great* or of the *Small*, still there will be a lack of balance; and besides, the function of the Dyad is merely to double, not to produce a single unit. Actually, however, the Platonists avoid this difficulty, for they generate Three by placing the *One* in the middle of the two units of Two. Of course, another difficulty arises: instead of being separate and a principle, the *One* becomes a material principle and a part of Three, and likewise of Five, Seven, etc. (1084a3–7).

31. This is Plato's position (1081a23–5).

32. If each unit of Two consists of the *Great* and *Small* after these are equalized, then Two will have two units, each with two equal parts, four parts in all. But then each unit is divisible and is generated just like the Dyad (by the *One* and the *Great* and *Small*), and the Dyad would seem to have four parts; or if not, each unit is separate by itself so that the so-called "Dyad" is not one nature. Besides, such a unit, having two parts, will be like the *Dyad*, or else, like the Dyad which, according to them, has two parts or two units.

There is another difficulty or interpretation. If the *Great* can decrease and the *Small* increase in a way so as to become equal, the fact that they can be equal and so comparable necessitates that both come from the same nature. If so, the *Dyad*, or the *Great* and *Small*, cannot be two distinct natures. For example, if a small line increases and a long line decreases, both are lines (from the point of view of their matter), and so both are of one material nature. So the term "*Great* and *Small*" is misleading or inappropriate.

33. Prior in existence is meant. If the Dyad (whether as one object or two separate units) exists, one of its units exists, but not conversely; and so the unit is also prior in generation.

34. That is, one of the two units, being prior in existence, will be an Idea; and as a part of the Dyad, it will be an Idea of an Idea.

35. According to these thinkers, the Dyad is generated first, not a unit. So a unit, if generated alone at all, will have to be generated not out of the *One* and the *Indefinite Dyad*.

36. Both positions have been held (1073a18–22).

37. The number of Numbers is fixed, so they are finite, or else infinite. One could deny both a definite finitude or a definite infinitude of, say, the parts of a line, but as parts they are not separate.

38. They generate either an odd or an even Number, and an infinite

Number is neither odd nor even; hence, they do not generate an infinite Number, and so such Number cannot exist.

39. That is, Two, Four, Eight (Sixteen, etc., if Numbers go beyond Ten). Thus, when Two interunites with the *Dyad*, Four results, when Four with the *Dyad*, Eight results, and so on.

40. When the *Dyad* receives Three, Six is generated; when Five, Ten is generated, etc. An alternative to "receives" is "is interunited with".

It is probably implied here that when the *Dyad* receives an odd Number, it may double it more than once. Thus, to generate, for example, the Number 57, we may list the sequence 57, 56, 28, 14, 7, 6, 3, 2, 1, and proceed backwards. The *One* with the *Dyad* causes Two; the *One* in the middle of the units of Two causes Three; this becomes Six when received by the *Dyad;* then Seven results when the *One* is placed between the units of Six; Seven becomes in succession Fourteen, Twenty-Eight, and Fifty-Six; and the *One* placed in the middle of the units of Fifty-Six causes Fifty-Seven.

41. This may refer to their thesis that the infinite belongs to the material principle, the *Dyad* or *Great* and *Small* (329a8–17). The *One*, on the other hand, acting on the *Dyad,* gives a limit or form to what results. Thus, "infinite" cannot be a predicate of an Idea.

42. This may be the meaning: If the sensibles share in the Ideas, since there is no universal formula or definition of an infinite sensible body or object (1066b23–6), for no such exists, and since these thinkers form Ideas from universal terms or formulas or definitions, it follows that there can be no Idea (or Number) which is infinite or an Idea of something which is Infinite.

43. For example, Plato (206b27–33).

44. I define a 'Number' here as a part of a Number. For example, three units of Five is a 'Number', namely 'Three'.

45. Let us take one of the ten Numbers, say Six. Within Six the units are comparable and we may take a part of Six by taking one unit, or two, or three, or four, or five. The same applies to the other Numbers. We may also take the ten Numbers themselves as additional alternatives. Now from his biological works it is evident that Aristotle regarded the species of animals, not to mention plants and other sensible things, as greater than the possible alternatives indicated. So even this method, although yielding more than ten Ideas, still falls short in giving an adequate number of Ideas.

46. For example, if one 'Triad' in the Number Seven is taken to be the Idea Man or Man Himself, then, by the theory of Combinations, there are $^{7}C_{3}$ or 35 other instances of Man Himself in Seven.

47. The term ἄπειρος means infinite, or a great many. There are 'Triads' also in Eight, and in other Numbers, and Numbers are posited as finite in number by some but infinite by others, and for Plato a 'Triad' in Seven differs from that in Eight.

48. Aristotle would like here to distinguish Man Himself from 'Man' just as a Triad is distinguished from 'Triad'. The first is a Number; the second is a part of some larger Number, that is, it is a 'Number'.

49. That is, a 'Dyad' which is a part of Four.

50. Among the sensibles we observe not only three or four or ten objects of some kind, but also eleven and even more; and the terms "eleven", "twenty", etc., are just as universal as those which signify smaller numbers. Then why are there no Ideas of the larger numbers? Limiting the Ideas to ten goes contrary to the way in which they posit Ideas of things.

51. If no Ideas of such things (houses and manufactured articles) exist, then the *One* and the *Dyad* are not their principles or causes. Hence, additional principles are needed. So the principles which these thinkers give are not adequate. Moreover, if such things can exist or be generated from other causes and principles, which are also more evident, so can all things.

52. Each Number up to Ten Itself is generated separately, so there are ten separate Numbers; but these thinkers talk as if these Numbers taken together form a higher unity and a higher being than Ten Itself, although they generate no such unity.

53. The *One* and the *Dyad*. Motion and badness was attributed to the *Dyad*, rest and goodness to the *One* (209b11–6, 192a6–8, 306b16–9, 329a8–17, 988a14–5, 992b7–9, 1066a7–16, 1091b13–1092a8).

54. If oddness were in Three, it could not be in Five; for Five is generated when the *One* acts on the *Dyad* to produce Two, then Two acts on the *Dyad* to produce Four, and then the *One* goes between the units of Four. Thus, Three which has oddness does not participate. But if oddness is in the *One*, since all Numbers such as Three, Five, Seven, etc., need in a certain way the *One* in order to be generated, such Numbers would contain oddness and so would be odd. At least, this seems to have been the reasoning of these thinkers, although in another way all Numbers need the *One* for their generation.

55. The thinkers here are Plato, Xenocrates, and perhaps other Platonists. Perhaps the text is corrupt, but the meaning may be this: the Indivisible Line (also called "Point") is attributed to the *One*, the Divisible Line to Two, the Plane to Three, the Solid to Four (404b16–27, 992a19–22, 1036b13–9, 1043a33–4, 1090b20–9). By "then the Dyad" he may mean the Divisible Line, which was defined by some as Two (1036b12–20).

56. From what follows, by "the one" he seems to mean a unit in a Number. But since Aristotle is discussing Ideas, he is also considering how Plato was using the term "one", namely, in two senses, as an element and as a universal.

57. The sense of "prior" is considered as the discussion proceeds.

58. As a unit in a Number, it is potentially prior, since a number is divisible into units. If he is also thinking of the *One*, then this is prior in existence as a principle.

59. For Plato, universals are Forms; for Aristotle, they are predicates of many objects.

60. *Actuality* (or form) is prior to potentiality (1049b4–1051a33). An alternative to "Form" is "form".

61. By "a Number" he probably means each Number severally. Thus, the Triad is prior to any of its units, etc. (In 1096a17–9, Aristotle criticizes Plato for not having an Idea of Number as such, which according to their principles should be prior in existence to the Dyad, the Triad, and the rest; for a number, generically taken, is prior in existence to any specific number, such as three). The priority here is that of a Number to its unit, not to the *One* as a principle and something separate.

62. An acute angle is defined as an angle less than a right angle.

63. The individual house, for example, is nearer to the house as generically defined than its matter is, but this matter exists before, and the individual house is generated after. The form of a house as a formula, however, preexists in the artist's mind (the builder of the house). See also 1034b20–1037b7.

64. That is, in what sense are the Platonists using the term "one"?

65. For example, what is most generic cannot be defined and so it is indivisible. If we define two as a prime even number, and a number as a discrete quantity, quantity is no longer definable and so is indivisible in formula. Plato, confusing the many senses of "one" as a predicate, went further; thus, since for him a quantity is one, but what is one is not necessarily a quantity, or more generally, since there is oneness in each thing, he regarded the one or the *One* as the most universal principle. In such a sense he was using one as prior in (or a principle of) definition (998b17–21, 1053b9–13).

66. Perhaps the meaning is this: an element (here, the one or a unit, as matter) must preexist in order to become a part of some whole.

67. But not in the same sense of "prior", as shown earlier.

68. That is, they posit the *One*, which is a first principle in the sense of a form and a *substance* and also a cause, as the form of everything which is one; and they generate units, each of which is one and a part (as matter) of a Number, and they also make the *One* a part of Three, Five, etc.

69. For Plato this is the *One*. For Aristotle "one" has many senses, not necessarily signifying a substance.

70. For Plato, the units of one Number are distinct from (not comparable with) those of another Number. Now if each Number is to be one substance and in actuality, each of its units cannot be actually one but only potentially one or a part.

71. Either he is using "point" generically as a predicate of a unit (which has no position) as well as of a point (which has position), or these thinkers themselves were using the term in that sense. For Aristotle's sense, see 1016b24–6.

72. The Atomists; for example, Democritus.

73. That is, the unit in the sense of the *One* is prior in existence to the Dyad, for everything is one; but in the sense of a part of a Number, such as of the Dyad, it is posterior in existence to the *One*, and to the Dyad.

74. But in using "unit" in the sense of a part of a Number, such a

part is posterior in substance to that Number which is a whole and (for the Platonists) a Form.

75. An alternative to "Form" is "form".

76. For this reason, since each thing is one, they made *One* a principle as Form.

77. What is one as a form cannot be one as matter. For example, the form of a statue is one, but it is not a material part of like, say, its head.

78. Perhaps the argument is this: What is most elementary is a principle; what is without position is more elementary than what is with position; since the *One* is indivisible, and qua indivisible nothing is more elementary, and since it is also without position (and without any qualities), it must be the most elementary and so a principle.

79. For if indivisibility in definition made these thinkers posit the *One Itself* as a principle and a Form (or form), then each unit of the Dyad, by being indivisible, would be more like the indivisible *One* than like the divisible Dyad.

80. Prior in existence. What is closer as a form to the *One* should be prior in existence.

81. The *One*, acting on the *Indefinite Dyad*, generated the Dyad first and not any one of its units.

82. Perhaps the sense of the argument is this: since "one" has a single meaning for these thinkers, and since for them the Dyad is one and the Triad is one, then both make another 'Dyad' (not as a part of a Number, but a composite of Numbers, so to say). But they generate only the Dyad from the *One* and the *Indefinite Dyad* and have no other principles from which to generate this 'Dyad'.

9

1. Numbers are not continuous, so they have no ends or boundaries necessary for touching (226b18–227b2, 1068b24–5).

2. Probably succession in existence is meant. If the Numbers do not succeed the *One*, the alternative would be that units would succeed it. Thus, if one unit in the Dyad is prior in existence to the other, the first would succeed the *One*, and the Triad might succeed the second unit.

3. 992b13–8, 1080b23–5.

4. The material principle for Numbers, then, would be *Plurality* (1085a31–4, 1087b4–9, 1092a28–9). Speusippus was one who took this position.

5. Some Platonists (992a10–24, 1089b11–4). Their argument may have been something like this: Evidently, numbers differ from magnitudes; hence, also Numbers should differ from Magnitudes. But since you cannot generate a magnitude out of numbers or units, and so you would need something new to do this, therefore you would need different principles for Magnitudes. Thus, the *Great* and *Small* are genera which have species as irreducible material principles (1001b19). Plato,

of course, had only one material principle, the *Great* and *Small,* or *Dyad.*

6. The reasonable alternatives are: (a) the same principle (the *One)* as form, for the difference in the material principle will take care of the different genera of things generated; (b) one principle for Numbers (the *One)* and another for Magnitudes (the *Point),* for these two are analogous, differing in that position is an attribute of the latter; (c) one principle for Number, one for Lines, one for Planes, one for Solids. Now Plato, and Xenocrates (1028b24–7, 1090b20–32), used the *One* for everything; Speusippus used the *One* for Numbers but the *Point* for Magnitudes (1085a32–4). Those who used different material principles for different Magnitudes probably used the *Point* as the formal principle (whether others used the *One* is not known, but less likely, for they probably used a different formal principle, the *Point,* for Magnitudes just as they used different material principles for them, and for the same reason).

7. For example, since the *Long* and *Short,* and the *Wide* and *Narrow,* are principles, neither contains the other; so if only Lines are generated from the former and Planes from the latter, Planes would have no Lines in them. This is impossible.

8. The *Wide* and *Narrow* cannot have as a part the *Long* and *Short,* for if it did, it would be a composite and not a principle. So, if it is identified with the *Long* and *Short,* so will be the Plane and the Line; and in turn, so will the plane and the line among the sensibles which imitate Magnitudes.

9. Angles and Shapes and the rest are not just Lines or Planes or etc., they are new objects, not entirely reducible to Lines, Planes, etc. These thinkers probably neglected to discuss these; and if they were to discuss them, they would need additional principles.

10. These thinkers did not distinguish an *attribute* of a thing from its matter. Width and narrowness are *attributes* of a plane and not its matter, and similarly for the rest.

11. By "the one" here he means any unit in an instance of a dyad among the sensibles; and if he means the oneness of that dyad (for that dyad has unity), the argument is still valid.

12. If the *One* were in each individual unit, it would not be unique, and this is contrary to what they claim; and if it is not in such a unit, how can it be the *substance* of that unit? (For the *substance* of a thing is in that thing; for example, the soul of Socrates is in Socrates, and the shape of a statue is in that statue.)

13. Speusippus is meant.

14. *Point* : *One* :: Magnitudes : Numbers. The *Point* here is taken as form, not as matter.

15. The assumption here is: Since principles are simple, their manner of acting or of being acted upon is unique and not varying.

16. As in Comm. 8, above, either the different Magnitudes (and so the magnitudes among the sensibles) will be severed (which is impossible), or they will be identical (likewise impossible).

17. For Speusippus, this is *Plurality*, in the general sense, not a specific plurality like the *Dyad* or the *Great* and *Small* (which Plato posits). Of course, the *Dyad* is not like Two, which has two units, but has the *Great* and *Small* as its two parts, so to speak. Probably Plato did not elaborate about these parts; so finding it difficult to get at Plato's meaning, Aristotle proceeds to criticize Plato's principles by assigning to the terms which Plato used their ordinary meaning. What else can one do, if the alternative is pure guesswork?

18. 1082a20–4.

19. To say that a unit comes from the whole *Plurality* is to make the unit consist of parts and so be divisible.

20. If the unit comes from a part of *Plurality*, and that part is indivisible, then it does not come from the *One* and *Plurality* but from the *One* and a unit in *Plurality*. Further, *Plurality* would itself have units, so it would be a number (or a *Number*, if you wish, or just units). But this is not matter, and besides, they would be generating Numbers from the *One* and a *Number*, or from the *One* and units; and this was not the intention of these thinkers.

21. But if the unit comes from a part of *Plurality* which is still a *Plurality* (for example, in the sense that a part of ten may be four, and both are pluralities), then that unit will again be a composite and divisible, as above, in Comm. 19.

22. Speusippus and followers.

23. The meaning seems to be: At first, these thinkers gave the impression that *Plurality*, the material principle, was finite.

24. *Plurality Itself* is like a genus, and *Finite Plurality* and *Infinite Plurality* are like species. The three are distinct, and somewhat analogous to *Dyad, Great,* and *Small*. It makes a difference whether one posits just *Plurality*, or just one species of it, or both species, or all three; and this is analogous to positing for magnitudes just one material principle (Speusippus), or three species of it *(Long* and *Short, Wide* and *Narrow, Deep* and *Shallow)*, or all four.

25. The question, so put, suggests that no matter which position is taken, the difficulties that would follow are similar to those already considered, that is, those that follow by having a single material principle for magnitudes (in which case the species of magnitudes cannot be generated), and those that follow by having three such principles (in which case Lines, Planes, and Solids are either identical, or severed and unrelated). Aristotle does not bother to repeat or elaborate these difficulties.

26. Speusippus and followers.

27. By *"Interval"* he means some material principle for Magnitudes.

28. As above in Comm. 25, so here. The analogy is: *Point* : *Interval* : point :: *One* : *Dyad* : unit :: *One* : *Plurality* : unit. Just as for Plato a Number has units, so for Speusippus a Line or Plane or Solid should have points (aside from *Point Itself)*; and even more so, for both Plato and Speusippus posited the Mathematical Objects in such a way that there can be a science (principles and theorems) of mathematics, and in

such a science a number of things of the *same kind* are needed (for example, a number of points, a number of lines, etc.).

29. Speusippus and followers.

30. Xenocrates and followers. Mathematical Numbers are meant.

31. They try to smooth over the contradictions arising from the identification of Mathematical Numbers with Numbers as Ideas by introducing peculiar hypotheses. Nevertheless, they destroy mathematical numbers as commonly understood by mathematicians.

32. Plato.

33. He needed many things of the same kind within the Mathematical Objects so as to make possible a science of mathematics as understood by mathematicians; and he needed a single essence or form of things of the same kind (so he created a unique Form for each class of things), otherwise one would be faced with an infinitude of unrelated individuals without the possibility of *knowledge* or science.

34. That is, each had a reason, whether for having two kinds of objects, or for having one kind, or for identifying the two; but each considered only some of the *difficulties* and not all.

35. That is, the hypotheses and principles.

36. I use Ross's rendition of the quotation.

37. *Physics* 187a12–189b29, 302a10–303b8, 314a1–317a31.

38. The criticism from 1086a21 and on is not continuous with what preceded; it must have been written at another time, probably earlier.

39. Speusippus and the Pythagoreans.

40. 1090a7–b20, 1091a13–22, parts of 1076a8–1086a21, and perhaps in other lost works.

41. If they are universal, they cannot be individuals nor separate. For example, Socrates is an individual and separate but not a universal.

42. 998a20–999a23, 1003a5–17, 1038b1–1039a23.

43. That is, the belief that they are universal and the belief that they are separate and so like individuals. Their reasoning may have been like this: an Idea, of which alone there can be *knowledge,* not being a sensible and so not changing, and being the cause of many sensibles and being also participated in by them, must be universal; but existing apart from those sensibles, it is separate like an individual.

10

1. The first are Platonists, the others are Speusippus and some others.

2. 999b24–1000a4, 1003a5–17.

3. Referring to the causes, whether the Ideas or the Mathematical Objects. If they are not separate, they will not be substances in the usual sense but something else (for example, attributes), but no one wishes to eliminate substances (without which nothing else can exist). So this alternative is out.

4. The assumption is that each element is unique (that is, no two

of them are the same), for, if not, what would be generated from the elements might not be unique.

5. *Knowledge* is assumed to be universal, or of the universal.

6. Those who posit the Ideas certainly do so. There is a unique Dyad, a unique Three, etc.

7. For example, this seems to be the way in which the *Dyad*, or the *Great* and *Small*, is posited, whether or not the *One* is also to be included (they so use the *One* to generate odd Numbers, see 1084a4–5).

8. The term "this triangle" may have universal or individual meaning. Thus, it may mean an isosceles triangle or one inscribed in a semicircle, and then the term is universal; and it may also mean an individual triangle, a sensible one. In either case, the universal "every triangle has two right angles", which must be proved, is needed for the syllogism, and this syllogism is a (universal) demonstration in the first case, but a *qualified* demonstration in the second (1087a10–23). *Knowledge* here, of course, is of universal premises or conclusions, for the individual triangle is destructible; and all definitions are universal.

9. Prior in existence. But non-substances (attributes) cannot be prior in existence.

10. The term "element" refers probably to what is matter, like the *Dyad* or *Plurality*, but "principle" refers to what is a form, like the *One*.

11. Certain distinctions are needed here, if this *difficulty* concerning *actual* and potential *knowledge* is not to be *misunderstood* (as it was by Ross) and thus make us think that Aristotle is inconsistent. In saying that X has potential *knowledge* we may mean that (1) X has no *knowledge* but that he has the potentiality of having *knowledge* (when he grows, or develops, or tries, etc.). We may also mean that (2) he has acquired that *knowledge* and has it as a habit or potency, ready to use it, but he is not exercising it (because he is asleep, or listening to music, or not thinking, etc.). We may also mean that (3) he is *actually knowing* or thinking (thinking is an *actuality*), not of an *actual* individual object, but of an object universally considered (of any object), for example, not of this individual triangle but of any triangle. Thus, potential knowledge has three senses.

By the two meanings of "*knowledge*" Aristotle has in mind (a) potential knowledge in sense (3), that is, when one *actually* knows but universally, and (b) *actual knowledge* of an *actual* individual object, that is, when one *actually* knows an *actual* individual object. (Of course, one may potentially know in sense (1) or (2) an *actual* object). For example, if I now *know* that nine is a square, I have *actual* universal knowledge, but if I '*know*' that the individual X is a nine and so a square, I have *actual* '*knowledge*' of an *actual* individual object.

The object of a science is *knowledge*, which is universal knowledge; and this *knowledge* we may call "unqualified", for it is not restricted to any given *actual* object; but if restricted to a given *actual* object, we may call this *knowledge* "qualified", or just " '*Knowledge*' ". We say that unqualified *knowledge* is indefinite, and potential, in view of the fact that it is not *knowledge* of a definite or *actual* individual, and that it is potentially the '*knowledge*' of any given *actual* individual. Universal *knowledge* just acquired is like a knife just manufactured. Both are *actual* beings, but they are potential with respect to the *actual* objects to which they may be applied.

12. Essentially, seeing is of an *actual* individual color, and only thinking can be of a color universally considered.

13. Demonstrations are in science, and both the principles of demonstrations (axioms, definitions, theses, hypotheses) and the theorems are universal.

Book N

1

1. Probably referring to immovable substances, the Ideas and the Mathematical Objects.

2. Prior in existence. Thus, the *One* and the *Dyad* for Plato are prior in existence and are substances, the one as form and the other as matter, and the rest are generated from them.

3. Whiteness is an attribute and so cannot exist by itself; therefore it cannot be prior in existence to that of which it is an attribute.

4. Contraries, like whiteness and blackness, or straightness and curvature, are attributes of and so inseparable from a subject. So, they cannot be principles and prior in existence. Hence these thinkers are not right in making the principles contraries.

5. This would be a substance. Contraries are principles, i.e. of motion or of knowledge, but they exist in something else which is prior in existence and so a principle to a higher degree.

6. Platonists.

7. Speusippus.

8. Inequality, great and small, plurality, and even equality, are all attributes (worse than that, they are relations which have less being than the other categories, 1088a22–6) and not matter.

9. That is, Plato does not deny that the *Great* and *Small* are one object numerically; and what is one numerically as a principle is incomposite or simple. He could have stated definitely (or given a formula or definition) that there is one formula for the *Great* and *Small*, in which case it would be possible for that formula to signify an object which is a unity of two parts, the *Great* and also the *Small*. He did not do this.

10. If the *Great* and *Small* are two and not one, this would be inconsistent with what was just said previously, Comm. 9. So, if Aristotle is consistent, either Plato was not consistent in his statements about the *Great* and *Small*, or else it was not Plato but some Platonists who spoke of these as being two elements.

11. These are the thinkers who, seeing differences in the mathematical objects, posited different corresponding principles for them; and they may be the same who posited the *Long* and *Short, Wide* and *Narrow, Deep* and *Shallow* as material principles for lines, planes, and solids respectively (1085a7–12, 1088a17–21, 1089b11–14).

12. Like Plato, these thinkers (not mentioned by name) posit as material principles what they consider as being the most universal, thus neglecting differences in things.

13. Demonstration according to Aristotle is a certain syllogism within a science (71b9–74a3). Here, either he uses the term in a more general sense, like the term "syllogism," or he is using it because these thinkers were so using it. Perhaps his meaning here is this: these thinkers are trying to avoid inconsistencies or contradiction; as for the truth or adequacy of their assumptions, this is another matter.

14. If the more universal is to be a principle to a higher degree (for it is prior in existence in a sense; for example, an animal is prior in existence to a man), then *Excess* and *Deficiency* should be principles rather than the *Great* and *Small*, for the former are more universal; and since Plato was seeking the most universal, he should have used *Excess* and *Deficiency* as material principles and not the *Great* and *Small*, and for the same reason he should have generated Number as such before generating Two.

15. The fact that these thinkers used *Excess* and *Deficiency* instead of the *Great* and *Small* in order to avoid logical difficulties but, like Plato, generated first Two seems to indicate that they were a sect of Platonists.

16. It is not known who these thinkers are; perhaps some Pythagoreans or Platonists.

17. Speusippus and followers.

18. Aristotle takes it as a hypothesis for the sake of argument that plurality is the contrary of unity, and not necessarily as a truth. He will clarify his own position as he proceeds.

19. Probably because "unity" and "plurality" are more universal than the others. See 1054a29–32.

20. "Plurality" has more than one sense; as a contrary, it is also opposed to the few. If so, then the one would be few, and this cannot be, since the few is more than one (1056b25–8).

21. But "plurality" also means the measured, or measures; and so oneness is opposed to such plurality as the measure to the measured, and this is an opposition of one relative to another (1056b3–34). In this sense, both the measure and the measured must be of the same kind.

22. For example, the measure may be a color, or a syllable, or a virtue, or a man.

23. For example, the measure may be a foot, or a weight, or a surface (1053a2–12).

24. The one as a measure can be in any category, but not in just one category; and it is not the *substance* of any thing.

25. That is, of a plurality whose units are of the same kind or comparable; and there are various kinds.

26. The terms "number" and "measures" have the same meaning, although linguistically the first is in the singular and the second in the plural. The kind of unity signified by "measures" lies at least partly in the fact that all the parts of that plurality are of the same kind.

27. That is, the measure is a principle of measures or of a number. Knowledge of a number, such as five horses, presupposes knowledge of its unit, one horse. Thus, the measure is prior in knowledge to the measured; and it is also prior in existence.

28. The measure would be an animal if "animal" is a univocal predicate of all three. The word "perhaps" may suggest that Aristotle is aware that definitions are needed before the measure can be properly stated. A god was often regarded as an animal or a living being.

29. One might ask: "Is a man, who is white and also walks, one or three?" The subject (the man) which has the attributes is one. But if one considers the subject (a substance), and his color, and his walking, these three come under distinct genera, so one may be using a genus in general as the measure (or something of this sort) to make a number of genera possible. But the number of measures that results has an accidental unity.

30. For example, fewness is an *attribute* (not an accident) of two, since two is few without qualification, but as a relative, fewness is an accident of 20, for 20 is few relative to 100 but many relative to 3. In either case, both accidents and *attributes* are not substances either as form or as matter.

31. Only quality and quantity are mentioned here as natures, probably because these thinkers posited their principles mainly in quantative terms (Numbers, *Plurality,* the *One,* etc.), and somehow in qualitative terms (*Odd, Even,* Good, etc.). Now that which is related must ultimately be in some category other than relation. For example, the unequal must be a quantity, and so must the equal, the great (or greater), the excess, etc.; likewise, the father must be a substance, the like must be a quality, etc. So, these other categories are prior in existence to relations, and as such they are nearer to substances (or prior in substance to relations).

32. That is, the term "relation" is generic; and by "its parts or kinds" Aristotle probably means specific relations, such as inequality (the *Unequal,* for Plato), excess, greatness, etc.

33. If John is heavier than Tom today, he may not be so tomorrow if Tom increases his weight, although John remains unchanged. And John loses the relation of being heavier than Tom at an instant, not during an interval; but change requires an interval. So if we are to say that John changed by having lost the relation of being heavier than Tom, this would be an accidental change.

34. Prior in existence.

35. Six is much when related to two, but little when related to ten.

36. For example, a brick is a material element of a house, but "a brick" is not a predicate of a house, for a house is not a brick. But they make, for example, the *Long* and *Short* the material element of lines, although "long" or "short" may be a predicate of a line, whether without qualification or relative to another line.

37. "Many" and "few" here mean excess and deficiency in plurality, whether without qualification or relative to another number.

38. Aristotle has in mind those Platonists, and perhaps others, who made Ten the greatest Number (1084a12–3, 1073a17–22).

39. Whether any thinker used this as the greatest number is not known.

40. For example, since Two is generated from the *One* as form and the *Many* and *Few* as matter for these thinkers, how can Two be only few? It would then have no part of the *Many*. The same argument would apply to Ten or to 10,000 in the case of those who made these, respectively, the greatest Numbers.

2

1. That is, it must have been generated from these elements if it was generated; and if it existed eternally, then it consists of these elements.

2. Of course, he has in mind the Numbers, whether as Ideas or as Mathematical Objects, which will always exist according to these thinkers.

3. That is, whether it always existed or came into being however long ago.

4. 281a28–283b22, 1050b6–17.

5. The Ideas and the Mathematical Objects are meant here in particular.

6. That is, if it is just *actuality*, without any potentiality, such as the prime mover (God), who is simple and has no matter and so has no potentiality of not being.

7. Probably those that follow by making the material principle a relation or out of relations (1088a21–35). Perhaps these thinkers (Platonists) use the term "*Indefinite Dyad*" without identifying it with "the *Great* and *Small*," since the latter signifies a pair of relations.

8. The objections meant are those against generating eternal objects out of elements, for such objects cannot be eternal.

9. That is, the principles, such as the *One* and the *Dyad*, etc.

10. This, they thought, would be a material principle, a not-being, such as the *Indefinite Dyad*, which is neither a being nor one but is indefinite and formless and capable of becoming many things. So, it exists somehow but is close to nonexistence.

11. Since being cannot be generated from being (which already exists), if there is to be generation, something else (*Not-being*) must be posited as a principle, whether material or not, according to these thinkers.

12. This may consist of two questions: (a) Are beings all of one kind, such as substances? (b) Are they all numerically one, that is, numerically one substance? (185a20–30)

13. For example, if the *One* and the *Indefinite Dyad* are simple natures, they can cause the generation of only one kind of things, such as substances. But there are things other than substances, such as attributes.

14. The expressions "not-straight" and "not straight", like the terms "unequal" and "not equal", are not synonymous. The first is a predicate only of things within a genus, for example, of curved lines, but the second need not be restricted to any genus as a predicate, and it can even be a predicate of impossibilities, for example, of a square circle (51b25–8, 16a30–3). Similarly, when speaking of not-being, here Aristotle probably has in mind, for example, Plato's material principle, the *Dyad,* which in some sense exists (see Plato's *Sophist*).

15. Plato. See *Sophist*.

16. The line drawn on the board may not be a foot long, but it is an individual and is used as an illustration for the sake of the learner. The premises from which the geometer draws conclusions, on the other hand, are universal. For example, the premise would have a form such as this: "Every line a foot long is so-and-so". Thus, the line drawn is not signified by a premise (even if that line is exactly one foot long).

17. For example, a white thing is generated from not-white (which is another color, whether the extreme contrary which is black or a mixed contrary like red) and a subject which is potentially white.

18. That is, from what is potential, but not from what is false.

19. And all of these are posited by them as being substances.

20. For these are not substances but attributes.

21. The term "plurality" is a predicate not only of substances, but also of qualities, and of quantities, etc., and further, of kinds of being (whatness, quality, quantity, etc.). Thus, the term "cause" applied to plurality within each category may be univocal, but it is analogous if applied to different categories (1070a31–1070b21, 1071a24–1071b2).

22. Referring probably to their primitive thinking; their lack of distinguishing the kinds of being.

23. That is, nonbeing, which would be the cause of plurality.

24. Since they did not distinguish the kinds of being, it made no difference whether they picked the opposite of a substance or of some attribute, like the unequal, which is a relation.

25. The contrary of being might be not-being, for there is a sense in which potentiality or the material principle is something, a subject so to say; but the denial of being would be the nonbeing which is not not-being, for example, an impossibility, like a square circle, or a falsity, like an existing white Socrates (when he is dead), or pure nothingness. But inequality is a being and cannot be used as a material principle.

26. For Aristotle, the genus alone is not a sufficient principle from which the species are derived or generated; so, other principles are needed, such as the differentiae (998b30–1, 643a24, 1038a25–6). But

these thinkers do not posit additional principles from which may be generated the species of the unequal, such as the double, and half, and greater, and the exceeding by three, etc.

27. The implication seems to be that these thinkers posited only the *Unequal* as the material principle, but that they were either wrong in deriving the *Many* and *Few* and the *Long* and *Short* and the rest from the *Unequal* alone, or, that they said nothing as to their derivation, but just mentioned them and used them without saying that, qua distinct, they are new principles or that they require new and distinct principles for their generation. The same applies to the additional relations they spoke of.

28. The unequal, which is a relation, is not a potentiality for something but is already a kind of being.

29. The remaining categories are understood without mention. These thinkers consider the problem of a plurality of things in the same category (whether of substance or of quantity), but not the problem of a plurality of categories, that is, of many kinds of being.

30. Perhaps the meaning is this: there is plurality in a category (other than substance) which is an attribute of a substance, as is clear from the fact that a substance becomes many quantities, or many qualities, or etc.; and there is a problem of how there can be matter or potentiality for plurality in such a category, if such matter is inseparable from a substance. That is, in a physical substance there would be physical matter, mathematical matter, etc.

31. Perhaps by "a nature of such a kind" he means a being in a category other than a substance (or a *this*), or else, he means an Idea. In the first case, there is a reason in asking how there can be many instances of a *this*, for, although the problem of a plurality of categories is left out or avoided, the simplified problem of a plurality of instances of a *this* is a reasonable one. In the second case, an Idea is eternal, and what is eternal cannot be generated; so if we do not assume that which is a *this* to be also an Idea, the problem of a plurality of instances of a *this* is a reasonable one. The first alternative is suggested by what follows.

32. He may be referring to the *difficulty* of how there can be or how there can be generated from the principles a plurality of substances; or he may be referring to the problem of how there can be many instances of some given substance and not just one, that is, to such a problem as how there can be many horses and not just Horse Itself if the latter as the substance of horses would have to be in them and thus be many. Perhaps there are other alternatives.

33. That is, even if to be a *this* and to be a quantity are not the same, still they generate quantities, which are attributes and not instances of a *this* (that is, substances).

34. That is, if instances of both a *this* and of a quantity exist, we are not told why and how such different kinds of being are possible, or else, why and how there are many beings in the sense of substances rather than in the sense of quantities which are indeed inseparable.

35. The Platonists posit Ideas as Numbers; so, in positing them as separate, they consider them as substances or instances of a *this*, but in calling them "Numbers", they regard them as quantities. So either they misname the Ideas or they confuse substances with quantities.

36. As a measure, a unit or oneness would be in any category and so would extend to all of them. But for these thinkers, the *One* or a unit is posited rather as an element or principle of Numbers and so of quantities, and the other categories are left out.

37. If to be a quantity and to be a *this* (or a substance) are distinct, these thinkers posit principles for the former but not for the latter or the plurality of the latter; and if they are not distinct, the confusion of the two will give rise to many contrary beliefs. For example, Five would be odd, and also a substance of certain sensible things, and also somehow related to other things, etc.; thus, it would be many and not one; and all other attributes of Five would be also in Five and would be Ideas, and an Idea will have Ideas, etc.

38. Plato.

39. Speusippus.

40. Perhaps Aristotle is referring to the fictitious aspect of the existence of such Numbers.

41. If these Numbers are not the causes of anything, the problem of what causes things still exists; moreover, the fact that Numbers are not the causes or the *substances* of things and so are not of any use to them would make a science of Numbers useless to a science of sensibles. But arithmetic is also applicable to sensibles. Will there be two sciences of arithmetic, then? Difficulties follow, whether two such sciences are the same or different, whether partly or wholly. For Plato, arithmetic deals with Ideas, and its truth in sensibles is due to the participation of these in the Ideas.

3

1. Plato and followers.

2. That is, each Idea or Number.

3. That is, it exists separately and as a cause of certain individuals having the same name, and it is caused by the *One* and the *Dyad*.

4. Because of the impossibilities faced by Plato.

5. Of course, from this fact alone it does not follow that things are or are composed of numbers.

6. Speusippus and followers.

7. That is, that sensible things are composed of numbers.

8. 1077b17–1078a31.

9. For they say that numbers are in sensibles and that the mathematical sciences, whose objects are numbers, are concerned with sensibles.

10. If units are neither heavy nor light, and bodies are posited as composed of units, such bodies cannot be the sensible ones we know, for these are heavy or light. Their error lies in making the *One* or the

unit a substance and a nature in itself, not something analogously predicated of other natures.

11. Plato, Speusippus, Xenocrates, and minor Platonists.

12. Probably the argument against separate Numbers, posited by the Pythagoreans (1090a20–5).

13. It is not clear who these are, perhaps Pythagoreans (some or all), or Platonists (some or all), or both. See 1028b15–8, 1002a4–12. By "such natures" he means separate substances.

14. As *substances* of them, of course, they will not exist separately.

15. Speusippus and followers (1028b21–4, 1075b37–1076a4, 1085a31–4). If the principles from which Magnitudes are generated are distinct from those from which Numbers are generated, Magnitudes may exist if Numbers do not exist. But since Magnitudes may be numbered, and geometrical theorems often require a number of magnitudes (as in ratios and proportions), numbers are presupposed in geometry, and so without the existence of numbers, the objects of geometry cannot exist. Numbers, then, should be prior in existence to magnitudes, and those (Platonists) who use Numbers to generate Magnitudes are right in this respect. Thus, things are not disconnected like the episodes of a bad tragedy.

16. Platonists, including Xenocrates (perhaps not Plato's later doctrine, in which all Ideas were identified with Numbers).

17. That is, from Two and the material principle (*Indefinite Dyad*).

18. From the manner in which Plato generates things from the *One* and the *Dyad* (1084a2–7), it appears that only Ideas in the sense of Numbers can be generated, not of anything else. So Triangle Itself would be, if anything, some Number and not a Magnitude. Perhaps some Platonists, in generating Magnitudes also, did not state the manner of their generation, and the possibility of their generation as well as their manner of existence may have led to a difficulty.

19. Of course, since the Ideas are separate, they cannot be in sensible things; so, they are not the *substances* of them, and no science of sensible things is possible. According to Aristotle, such a science is possible, so the Ideas are useless.

20. Those posited by Speusippus.

21. Xenocrates identified the Ideas with the Mathematical Objects; but if there is only one Triangle, one Three, and, in general, one Idea for each species or genus of things, it would be impossible to have theorems requiring two Ideas which are the same. For example, "Two and Two make Four" and "Two Triangles are congruent if, etc. . . ." could not be theorems since there is only one Two, one Triangle, etc. In order to prove theorems, then, Xenocrates was forced to change axioms and other principles, and/or to introduce additional ones, probably artificial and unconvincing.

22. Plato's later doctrine.

23. Only Numbers as Ideas are generated (1084a2–7). So, Mathematical Numbers cannot be so generated from the *One* and the *Dyad*, and no additional principles were given for their generation; and their

manner of existence is not stated. To place them between the Ideas and the sensibles is not to state how they exist or can be generated.

24. To generate them from the *Great* and *Small* is difficult enough, but to generate also Magnitudes from them, which are among the Mathematical Objects, is even more difficult.

25. The only material principle he uses is the *Great* and *Small*.

26. That is, if the principle as form is not the *One* but some other One distinct from the *One*.

27. A difficulty will arise in many unities as principles which are forms. If the *One* is for Ideas, and another unity, say *Unity*, for Mathematical Numbers (not to speak of a third unity required for Magnitudes, if no additional material principle is used), then *One* and *Unity* will have something in common, both being at least principles and indivisible; and if so, what is common to them will be a sort of a genus, prior in existence to *One* and to *Unity* (just as an animal is prior in existence to a man or a dog), and the three unities will likewise give rise to a fourth, etc., like the *third man* argument. Other difficulties also appear. For example, if the third unity is prior in existence to the *One*, this calls for a prior generation of numbers other than the Ideas, which numbers would be prior in existence to the Ideas, etc., something which is impossible in Plato's doctrine; moreover, the *One* and *Unity* would not be principles, for the third unity, by being prior in existence and also a form, should be the form of *One* and of *Unity*.

28. Perhaps a reference to a slave in a passage by Simonides of Ceos.

29. The nature of the *Indefinite Dyad* (*Great* and *Small*) is only to double what it receives (1082a13–5). If you try to make them generate also Mathematical Numbers and sensible numbers (not to speak of Mathematical Magnitudes and sensible magnitudes), they will loudly resist because it is against their nature [only to double]. Moreover, the generation of Three, Five, Seven, etc. is also artificial, for the *Dyad* does not function according to its nature here.

30. Apparently, the Pythagoreans construct the *One* from elements, from the *Odd* (which is *Limited*) and the *Even* (which is *Unlimited* or *Infinite*), and they regard it as eternal although it is a composite (1088b14–28, 213b22–7, 204a30–4, 986a15–21, 1080b16–21). Aristotle's statement of how the *One* may have been constructed may arise from different or vague accounts given by members of the Pythagorean School.

31. The *Limit* seems to be the same as the *Limited*, from which the *One* was constructed (203a10–2). Perhaps the Pythagoreans were inaccurate or vague in their statements.

32. 203a4–208a23, 293a15–b15.

4

1. The sentence which follows seems to indicate that "they" refers to the Platonists (who constructed Numbers), some or all; but it may

also refer to the Pythagoreans, who regarded the *Odd* and *Even* as elements which are not generable. The word "even", then, may not refer to the principle *Even*. The Platonists assigned oddness to the *One*, which is not generable, but constructed all things which are even, such as Two, Four, etc. If "they" refers only to Platonists, then "odd" and "even" refer to odd Numbers and even Numbers; but Plato cannot be included, since he generates all Numbers. The reference may be to Xenocrates and his followers, or some other sect.

2. Plato and followers (1081a24–5).

3. That is, Two.

4. It is not clear which objection(s) Aristotle has in mind. If Two is eternal, it cannot have been generated; and besides, its two equal units must be eternal, and so there cannot have been a *Great* and *Small* either as prior in existence to those units or as matter from which those units were generated. Moreover, if the *Great* and the *Small* were equalized to generate Two, they are subject to change and so are not eternal; consequently they are composed of other principles which are prior in existence to them; besides, if they are comparable, the *Great* will have parts, each being a *Small*, and will thus be reducible to *Small*.

5. For example, Hesiod (1009a9–19, 1071b26–8, 984b27–9).

6. Pythagoreans, Speusippus (1072b30–4).

7. Platonists.

8. Aristotle does not object to this, for he himself posits that the prime mover, God, is a principle and is good.

9. The *One* is an element in every odd Number (1084a3–7), and since each Number has units, each of which is like the *One* and so is a good according to them, each Number is a number of goods.

10. For example, Plato.

11. That is, does the good belong to the eternal principles, or does it appear later in generation?

12. In other words, it would be strange if goodness did not belong primarily to what is eternal and self-sufficient; and if it does, then eternality and self-sufficiency belong to the principle because the principle itself is good and not because the principle has some other attribute.

13. Speusippus and followers.

14. They should have abandoned the position that the *One* is a principle and an element.

15. A unit, being like the *One* qua an element, would be fully a good. By "fully a good" Aristotle means a species or a kind of good, not in the sense of a subject which is good, but of a kind of goodness which is a quality. For the *substance* of the good is goodness, which is a quality, and Plato already said that the *substance* of the *One* is *Good Itself*.

16. Every Form or Number, being composed of units, would be a number of goods and would therefore be a good.

17. For what is just a good is a quality and not a substance.

18. And so, if the Ideas are good, there will be no Ideas of substances which are bad. This would contradict Plato's assumption that there is

an Idea corresponding to every universal term, and "bad" is a universal term, and it would also contradict observed facts.

19. Speusippus. It might also follow that a Number, consisting of units or of ones, would be good; but being a plurality, or being generated from *Plurality* as well as from the *One*, it would be bad, or else, partly good and partly bad.

20. Plato and Xenocrates.

21. Since anything, other than the *One* and the *Unequal*, is generated from these two principles, it must participate in the *Bad* and is partly bad. The *One*, of course, is fully good, for it is purely form and has no *Unequal* in it.

22. The *One Itself*.

23. For Magnitudes are generated from Numbers and from the *Unequal*, and the latter is purely *Bad;* so there is more badness in Magnitudes, sensibles, etc., than in Numbers.

24. This is another way of saying that the *Unequal* (or the *Dyad*), in the generation of things, first receives the *One*, which is *Good*.

25. The *Good* or the *Bad*, in desiring its contrary, desires that which is destructive of itself. But it is a subject that desires a contrary, and not the other contrary.

26. This would be another strange or absurd consequence; for, if *Bad Itself* is potentially something else, it can change, and so it is not a principle; or else, the *Bad* as a subject will be also *Good*.

27. For example, Plato used the *One* as an element in the generation of an odd Number (1084a2–7).

28. The first contraries are attributes, like whiteness and blackness, and not matter or substances.

29. The term "one" is a mere predicate, and it has many senses.

30. Numbers are neither substances nor forms, but only quantities and so attributes.

5

1. For it is the most incomplete of all.

2. The seed is incomplete, but it comes from a being which is complete, a man, who is prior in existence to the seed. The criticism here is especially against Speusippus.

3. By "individual" he means a body, one that has a principle of motion.

4. Mathematical objects (including solids) are attributes, and as such they are not bodies but abstracted from sensible objects which are in place in an unqualified manner or primarily. They are in sensible objects and they are in place accidentally or secondarily, in view of the fact that the bodies in which they exist are in place, and of the fact that they may be in place relatively speaking, as one triangle may be within a circle (208b22–5, 305a22–7, 989b32–3, 1026a13–5).

5. The criticism is probably against Speusippus.

6. That is, are Numbers generated by blending the elements? For the various senses of "to be from", see 1023a26–b11.

7. By definition, only bodies are blended, and so attributes cannot be blended with anything (327b17–31, 328b20–2, 447a30–b1).

8. If the *One* and (say) *Plurality* are blended, each will then be only a part of the resulting blend and will neither exist separately nor be a distinct nature in *actuality;* and the resulting blend will be distinct from the *One* and from *Plurality* and will not have "one" as a predicate.

9. That is, they wish each principle to remain distinct and separate.

10. Of course, this cannot be, for then Two would be *One* and *Plurality,* or *One* and the *Unequal* (which is not intended by these thinkers), and then many difficulties would follow. For example, the *One* has no position; the units in Two will not be comparable, etc.

11. For example, the baby comes from the father, and the latter is not a constituent or a part of the baby.

12. The reference is probably to the male sperm, which has both matter, and also a form or a potency as a moving cause which acts on the female egg. In this sense, the male sperm is divisible, and its material element is not transmitted and is no constituent in what is generated. If so, then *One,* being indivisible, can have no parts like the male sperm, and so a Number cannot come from the *One* in this sense (729b1–730a4, 730b10–24).

13. If a Number comes from *One* and *Plurality* as from a contrary (as the light comes from the heavy), either (1) the composite of *One* and *Plurality* will be that contrary (this is impossible, since unity is contrary to plurality, and so the composite cannot form one contrary), in which case another element as underlying subject must persist (no such element is posited by Speusippus), or (2) the Number will come from one of these elements (whether from *One* or from *Plurality,* but rather from *One,* since *Plurality* is posited as matter and *One* as form) and from an underlying subject which persists. If that subject is not *Plurality,* then Speusippus neglected to posit it; and if it is *Plurality,* then (a) since plurality is the contrary of unity, the underlying subject has been improperly described as a contrary, or else (b) the Number comes from a contrary (the *One*) which does not persist, in which case "one" is not a predicate of a Number (and this is not true). Other difficulties also follow. The same arguments apply to Plato's *Equal* (or *One*) and *Unequal* (*Great* and *Small,* or *Dyad*).

14. Grey has in a sense both contraries, the white and the black, for it lies between the two, which are principles of color.

15. The completely white comes totally from black, and blackness is totally absent from this white.

16. If a Number comes from contraries, it should not be eternal but destructible, like things which admit both contraries.

17. The contrary which is partially or even totally absent will destroy the subject which has the other contrary, even if it is not contrary to that subject. Thus, sickness will finally destroy a perfectly healthy animal.

18. Certain Pythagoreans. Eurytus, too, was a Pythagorean.

19. A ratio of numbers is not a number but a relation of numbers. For example, as some thought, a certain object may be defined as a ratio 5:3:2, that is, 5 parts water, 3 parts earth, 2 parts air. The same applies to a harmony.

20. Numbers are posited as substances; yet whiteness and sweetness and the like are not substances but affections. So how can Numbers be the *substances of affections?* Clearly, affections like whiteness and weight cannot take any *shape* or boundary.

21. If the ratio of Numbers is the *substance* of things, then Numbers are the matter from which ratios are formed. Thus, flesh is not a number in the usual sense, but a ratio, as above in Comm. 19.

22. But a number is a number of something, for it has parts, and each part is some nature, whether a particle of fire or of earth or a unit; for a number is a number of ones, and "one" has as many senses as there are categories. So, if flesh is a ratio of numbers, each number in that ratio has parts which are distinct in nature from those in any other number in that ratio. If all the parts of flesh were of one nature, say of fire, then flesh would be just a number of parts and not a ratio of so many parts of this to so many parts of that.

23. As described by these thinkers, then, a Number is neither a moving cause nor a final cause of things. And it is not what it is described to be, for if it is separate and a substance, it cannot be the form or *substance* of attributes since these are inseparable; and if so, Numbers are not adequate as principles of all things. If Numbers are considered as matter, they are likewise inadequate; for then there would be no principles of forms, and besides, matter does not exist without form.

6

1. The term "as an odd number" may mean either a ratio of 1 to an odd number, or of an odd number to an odd number; and "easily calculable" may mean any other ratio of a number to a number, such as 2:3, 5:8. Whether a number in a ratio may exceed 10 or not is not clear; for we have no information of what was stated by these thinkers.

2. A blend of honey and some other liquid, usually milk or water.

3. The term "thrice three", probably a Pythagorean expression, signifies here a ratio of 3 parts of honey to 3 parts of the other liquid.

4. By "in no numerical ratio" he means: not in a ratio m:n, where m and n are whole numbers. For example, $\sqrt{2}:1$ is not a numerical ratio.

5. The expression "thrice two" is not proper, for it signifies a number and not a ratio.

6. That is, 3 and 4 × 3, assuming "3" to have the same meaning in both, are numbers of things of the same kind. For example, 3 horses and four times 3 horses (= 12 horses) are numbers of horses. A number, for Aristotle, is a number of units, and these units must be of the same kind (or, the number must be measurable by the same measure). So, a

unit is not just a unit; it is a unit of something. There is an underlying subject. Like "one", "a unit" has generically as many senses as there are categories. It may be a unit of weight, or of a length, or of a substance, and so on (1052a15–1054a19).

7. In ABC, where "ABC" signifies the product A·B·C, A is taken BC times, so both A and ABC signify things in the same genus. If A is a horse (or, even a number of horses), ABC is a number of horses. Thus, A is the measure, and it is a subject in some genus; and in ABC, the product BC is of something, namely, of A's. Similarly for DEF.

8. In BECF, BC is a number, and it is of A, and EF is the number of D. So BECF is not the number of either A or of B. Neither is BECF identical with fire, nor is twice three identical with water. Whether this is Aristotle's meaning, or some other, I am not sure; but this interpretation is in accordance with his principles.

9. From what follows, by "number in common" he seems to mean that 'number' is the form or species of each thing. If so, then according to what the Pythagoreans say, or according to those who limit the Numbers to ten, or even according to those who do not limit the Numbers, things which differ in subject but have the same number would be the same in essence. Thus, a horse would be the same in essence as, say, a pig, if the essence of each is a number such as 6, or else, 5 horses would be the same in essence as 5 men, since both come under the species "five".

10. By "the cause of the thing" he probably means the cause as essence or form.

11. 1073b17–21, 32–8.

12. If all things had a number, then some things, though specifically different, might have the same number.

13. That is, the same in essence or under the same species, if the number of a thing is its cause as essence.

14. Another cause might be a final cause, such as victory, in which case seven heroes might be a minimum as a means to an end (victory).

15. The cause in the second case may be in us, not in the stars, since it is *we* who choose those stars which are to be counted as a group. The fact that some count the Bear as twelve and others as more confirms the fact that the cause is in us and not in what is counted. In other words, there is no unity in what we call "Bear", or, there is an accidental unity, namely, a relation of being counted by something outside the stars.

16. The letters Ξ, Ψ, and Z are considered as equivalent to the double consonants *cs*, *ps*, and (*th*)*s*, respectively.

17. For example, one might use a single letter for such combinations as *cr*, *pr*, *lp*, *ns*, etc. Thus, it is by convention that we use the single letters Ξ, Ψ, Z.

18. Palate, lips, teeth.

19. Ratios in length of the fourth and fifth notes relative to the fundamental note are, respectively, 9:12 and 8:12, so the length ratio of the

fourth to the fifth note is 9:8. These two notes are *midway* between the fundamental and the octave.

20. By "right" and "left" he probably means what we mean by "left" and "right", respectively.

21. As there are 24 letters in the Greek alphabet, evidently there were 24 notes to a flute.

22. He may be referring to the various senses of "cause" given in Book A or Δ.

23. An alternative to "beautiful" is "noble".

24. An alternative to "attribute" is "accident".

25. For example, 2:1 is a ratio *proper* to the lengths of the fundamental note to the octave, and also a proper ratio of 10 to 5, and also a *proper* ratio of other things; but this is an attribute or a coincidence. Further, many things are one by analogy; but they are not one in *substance*. These thinkers confuse the senses of "one".

26. The same confusion of the senses of "one" arises when Numbers as Forms are posited as causes in the sense of *substances* of differing things, such as 3 horses and 3 colors; for horses differ from colors, and the number 3 is only an attribute in each case and cannot account for the difference between a horse and a color.

Glossary

In the English-Greek Glossary, if an English term is used in many senses or has one or more synonyms, this is indicated. When convenient, we give the definition of a term, e.g. of the term "accident"; when not convenient, we usually give the reference to page and lines according to the Bekker text, as in the case of the terms "one" and "being". In some important cases, a term is slightly changed in appearance to indicate its different senses; this is done by the use of italics or an initial capital letter or both. For example, if a common name has two senses, a wide and a narrow sense, the narrow sense is usually signified by the term in italics, as in "desire" and "*desire*", "chance" and "*chance*", "knowledge" and "*knowledge*". If a term signifies a principle posited by a philosopher other than Aristotle, it is given in italics with a capital initial letter, as in the terms "*Dyad*", "*One*", "*Intelligence*", and "*Plurality*".

In the Greek-English Glossary, English synonyms used for the same Greek term are separated by a comma; for example, the translation of ἄλλο is "other" or "distinct", and the latter two terms are separated by a comma in the Glossary and are synonymously used. But if separated by a semicolon, the English terms are not synonymously used. For example, the translations of αὐτόματον are "chance" and "*chance*", and these are not synonyms. The same applies to "short" and "*Short*" for βραχύ, and to "definition" and "boundary" for ὅρος.

English-Greek

abstraction ἀφαίρεσις To abstract is to attend to a part (usually an inseparable part) of a whole, thus excluding the other part(s). For example, a geometrician abstracts continuity from a physical body, investigates the properties of continuity as such, thus leav-

449

ing motion, colors, weight, etc., out of the investigation. 1061a28–b3, 1077b2–14.

absurd   ἄτοπος

accepted opinion   ἔνδοξον   A statement regarded as true by all, or most, or the wise, and if by the wise, then by all, or most, or the most known or esteemed. Synonym: "common opinion". 100b21–3.

accident   συμβεβηκός   B is an accident of A if "A is B" is true sometimes, but not always or for the most part. For example, to be a geometrician is an accident of a man, and so is finding a coin when looking for Socrates. 1025a14–30.

according to   κατά   Synonyms: "with respect to", "in virtue of", "by virtue of". 73a27–b24, 1022a14–35.

accurate   ἀκριβής   One discipline is more accurate than another if (a) the first includes the causes of the facts to a higher degree; or, if (b) the first is of the more abstract; or, if (c) the second contains additional principles. 87a31–7, 982a25–8, 1078a9–13.

act, v.   ποεῖν   This is one of the categories, and so an ultimate genus.

act, v.   πράττειν   See "*action*". Synonym: "do".

acted upon, be   πάσχειν   This is one of the categories. 1b25–7, 1017a24–7.

action   ποίησις; sometimes: πρᾶξις, 1048b17.

action   πρᾶξις   Synonym: "conduct". An action *chosen* for its own sake with understanding and certainty and without hesitation. 1105a28–33.

active, be   ἐνεργεῖν   Synonym: "be in activity". 1045b27–1052a11.

activity   ἐνέργεια   Synonym: "*actuality*". 1045b27–1052a11; activity, be in: ἐνεργεῖν.

activity   διαγωγή   A way of living or of life, usually *chosen* for its own sake. 981b17–20, 982b22–4, 1072b14–6, 1334a11–8, 1339b17–9.

actuality   ἐντελέχεια   Probably the same as "activity".

actuality   ἐνέργεια   The same as "activity".

admire   θαυμάζειν

affected, be   πάσχειν   The same as "be acted upon".

affection   πάθος   An alterable quality or the actuality of it. 1022b15–21; affection, changing: πάθημα.

affirmation   κατάφασις   A statement signifying that something belongs to something else, e.g., such forms as "all A is B", "some A is B", "some A is not-B". 17a25.

after   μετά; ὕστερον

aim   σκοπός

air   ἀήρ   For the meaning of "air", see "water".

Air   ἀήρ   A material principle for Anaximenes and Diogenes. 984a5–7.

alleged fact   πρᾶγμα   See "fact".

alike in species or kind ὁμοειδής

all πᾶς Synonyms: "every", "total". 1024a1–10.

alteration ἀλλοίωσις Motion with respect to quality; e.g., becoming sick. 226a26–9, 270a27–30, 319b10–4.

always ἀεί Synonym: "eternally".

analogy ἀναλογία

analyze ἀναλύω

animal ζῷον (a) A living being with a power of sensation. (b) A living being with a power to know. This would include animals in sense (a), and also God. 122b12–4, 129b24–35, 413b2, 980a27–8, 1088a10–1.

apart χωρίς P is said to be apart from Q if P and Q are in different primary places. 226b21–3, 1068b26–7.

appear φαίνεσθαι To seem to be as a fact, whether through sensation or imagination or in some other way. 1010b1–9, 1024b21–4.

appearance φαντασία; outward appearance: ἰδέα.

apprehend θιγεῖν To come to know universally the indivisible or the essence, e.g., straightness, quantity, what is indefinable and predicable of many.

apprehension θίξις

argument λόγος A statement or statements aimed at convincing that something is or is not the case.

arithmetic ἀριθμητική

arrangement διακόσμησις, κόσμος

Arrangement διαθιγή According to Democritus and Leucippus, this is one of the three principles as form for all things, the others being *Contour* and *Turning*. 985b4–19, 1042b11–5.

art τέχνη This is *knowledge* of how to produce something, e.g., a bridge or a building.

assertion φάσις An assertion is a positive name or verb, which is predicated of a subject. For example, in "A is B", "B" or "is B" is an assertion of A or of "A". But "is not B" is said to be a denial of A or of "A" in "A is not B". Sometimes even a statement is called an assertion of a subject; thus, "A is B" is said to be asserted of A. 16b26–33, 17a17–20.

assumption ὑπόθεσις Synonym: "hypothesis". A statement or premise, posited without proof, which signifies that something is or is not the case. 72a14–24.

astronomy ἀστρολογία A science of heavenly bodies, such as the Sun, Moon, stars, etc., mathematically treated. 78b34–40, 194a7–12, 297a2–6, 1073b3–6.

attribute συμβεβηκός B is an attribute of A if it belongs to A as to a subject and in virtue of A but is not in the *substance* of A. For example, the equality of the three angles to two right angles is an attribute of a triangle. 1025a30–4.

attribute   πάθος   Perhaps "*attribute*" and "attribute" are synonyms. The expressions "proper *attribute*" (οἰκεῖον πάθος) and "essential *attribute*" (πάθος καθ᾽ αὑτό) are often used, each signifying that which belongs to a genus as to a subject. Thus, evenness belongs to numbers (not necessarily all), straightness to lines, contrariety and otherness to being. 997a7, 1004b5–15, 1078a7. This meaning of πάθος is not listed in lines 1022b15–21.

attribute, v.   κατηγορεῖσθαι

authoritative   κύριος

axiom   ἀξίωμα   A truth which one must have if he is to learn anything within a science. In a theoretical science, axioms are necessarily true. Axioms are used not as principles with which, but as principles from which theorems are demonstrated, that is, not as premises but as regulative principles. The principles of contradiction and of the excluded middle are axioms, and so is "Equals from equals leave equal remainders". 72a16–8, 76a37–b2, 77a26–31.

base   αἰσχρός, φαῦλος   The contrary of the noble.

be   εἶναι

be in   ἐνυπάρχειν   Synonyms: "exist in", "be present in".

beautiful   καλός

because   διά   In "A has the attribute C because of B", B is the cause of the fact that A has C. Synonym: "through".

become   γίγνεσθαι   To change from nonbeing to being, whether simply or in a qualified way. Synonym: "be generated", "come to be". See "generation". 225a12–7, 1067b21–3.

beginning   ἀρχή   Synonyms: "principle", "source", "starting-point". See "principle".

being, n.   ὄν   Synonym: "thing", "that which exists". 1017a7–b9.

Being   ὄν   A principle for some thinkers; the only existing principle for Parmenides and others.

belief   ὑπόληψις   The term is generic; it is an affection of *thought* about what is or is not the case. Its species are "*knowledge*", "opinion", "prudence", and their contraries. 427b24–7.

believe   ὑπολαμβάνω

belong   ὑπάρχειν

between, prep.   μεταξύ   B is said to be between A and C if, in going from A to C, one must by nature go through B before reaching C. Synonym: "intermediate". 226b23–31, 1057a21–6.

blend, v.   μίγνυμι   See "blend" as a noun.

blend, n.   μίξις μῖγμα   A union of bodies, readily adaptable in shape, which have acted upon and so altered each other; for example, a union of coffee and cream, not of salt and pepper. 327a30–328b32.

Blend, n. μίξις μῖγμα For Anaxagoras, this is a principle, the union of all things which existed at first as something motionless before *Intelligence* acted as a moving cause to separate the things. 250b24–6.

body σῶμα A three-dimensional physical being. For Aristotle, a body may be destructible, as a man, or indestructible, as the heavenly bodies. Sometimes it has the same meaning as "solid".

boundary πέρας, ὅρος 1022a4–13.

by ὑπό, ἐκ In the phrase "by P", P is usually a moving cause.

by itself καθ' αὑτό 1022a35–6.

by virtue of itself καθ' αὑτό See "according to".

can, v. δύνασθαι, ἐνδέχεσθαι

capable δυνατός

capability δύναμις A principle of causing motion or change in another thing or in the thing itself qua other. Synonym: "power". See "potentiality", "potency". 1045b27–1048a24.

capacity δύναμις A principle of being moved or being changed by another thing or by the thing itself qua other. See "potentiality".

carpentry τεκτονική

carry φέρειν

carrying φορά

cause αἰτία, αἴτιον, τὸ διότι 983a24–32, 1013a24–1014a25. Synonym: "why", "reason".

certainty βεβαιότης This term is applied to our state of mind about an object, not to the object itself.

chance αὐτόματον A moving cause which is accidental and hence variable or indefinite. 195b31–198a13.

chance αὐτόματον Chance which by nature has no capability of making a *choice*.

change μεταβολή This is a generic term, and its species are "generation", "destruction", and "motion". The kinds of motion are: locomotion, alteration, increase, decrease. 225a1–b9.

changing affection πάθημα Examples: anger, blushing.

changing attribute πάθημα Synonym: "changing affection".

choice αἵρεσις

choice προαίρεσις A choice of the best of the alternatives deliberated upon. 1113a1–7.

clear σαφής The term is applicable to expressions. An expression is *clear* if it has just one meaning which is known or familiar or definite.

clearly δῆλον Synonym: "it is clear".

cold, n. or adj.   ψυχρός
Cold   ψυχρόν   For Parmenides, a principle of sensibles. 986b31–7a2.
come to be   γίγνεσθαι   Same as "become".
comfort   ῥᾳστώνη
common   κοινός   The same in species or genus or by analogy. 645b20–8;
      common opinion: ἔνδοξος. Same as "accepted opinion"; commonly
      agreed: ὁμολογούμενον.
comparable   συμβλητός   Quantities A and B are said to be comparable
      if they can be added or subtracted or related to each other with
      respect to equality and inequality. For example, three and six are
      comparable, but six units and a line are not, nor a line and a
      surface.
complete   τέλειος   (a) That of which no part is outside; (b) that whose
      virtue within its genus cannot be exceeded, as a perfect doctor or
      fluteplayer. Synonym: "perfect". 1021b12–1022a3.
composite, n.   σύνολον   Composed of matter and form, or substance and
      attribute, e.g., a statue, whose parts are (let us say) bronze and
      shape, and a white man, who is a man and has whiteness. 995b34–
      5, 999a32–3, 1037a29–31, 1060b23–5, 1077b7–9.
comprehend   ἐπαΐειν   To know some important attribute (of a thing)
      other than or in addition to its causes, e.g., in the case of virtue,
      how or by what means virtue can be generated, or how a thing is
      related in important ways to other things. 1004b8–17, 1182a2–3,
      1360a30–3.
compulsory   βίαιον   That which is forced: See "force".
conceive of   νοεῖν
concept   νόημα
conclude   συμπεραίνεσθαι
conclude falsely   παραλογίζεσθαι
conclusion   συμπέρασμα
concoction   πέψις
confirm   μαρτυρεῖν
consist of   συνίστημι   To be made out of material parts, excluding the
      form.
consistent   ὁμολογούμενος
constituent   ἐνυπάρχον   A part in the thing, whether as matter or as
      form or as a part of the form. 986b4–8, 1017b14–20, 1052b9–14.
contact, n.   ἁφή   See "touch".
contemplate   θεωρεῖν   Synonyms: "investigate", "speculate", "view". This
      is an activity pursued for its own sake, and its object is *knowledge*
      or understanding.
contemplation   θεωρία   See "contemplate".
contiguous   ἐχόμενον   A is said to be contiguous to B if A succeeds and
      touches B. 227a6–7, 1069a1–2.

continuous   συνεχής   A and B are said to be continuous if their limits (not necessarily all) are one; a property of continuity is infinite divisibility. 227a10–7, 1069a5–9; 232b24–5, 268a6–7.

Contour   ρ'υσμός

contradict   ἀντιφάναι   To state the opposite or contrary of a given statement.

contradiction   ἀντίφασις   Two opposite or contrary statements taken together.

contrary   ἐναντίος   The primary meaning is: contraries are the most different in each genus; e.g., whiteness and blackness, oddness and evenness, justice and injustice. For secondary meanings, see 1018a25–35, 1055a3–b29.

contrariety   ἐναντιότης, ἐναντίωσις   Complete difference; the two contraries taken together.

contrast   ἐναντίωσις   Sometimes used as a synonym of "difference".

conviction   πίστις   Sometimes: a strong belief. Also, an attribute of a belief, admitting the more and the less. 125b28–126a2, 126b13–30, 428a19–23, 1146b24–31.

coordinate   ἅμα   See "simultaneous".

copy, n.   εἰκών

corporeal   σωματικός   Having physical matter.

Counter-Earth   ἀντίχθων   For the Pythagoreans, a body revolving around the central *Fire*. We do not see the Counter-Earth because our direction upwards is away from *Fire*, while the direction of the Counter-Earth is downward relative to us. The information as to its position is not clear, so either it is posited between the Earth and *Fire*, or *Fire* is posited between the Counter-Earth and Earth.

custom   ἔθος   A habit attained by practice, that is, by having done something many times and continually.

decrease, v.   φθίνω   To become less in quantity.

decrease, n.   φθίσις   Motion with respect to quantity, from complete to incomplete, that is, in the direction of the less. 226a29–32, 241a32–b2.

deep   βαθύς

Deep, n.   βαθύ   A material principle, along with the *Shallow*, according to some Platonists, from which solids were generated. 992a10–3, 1085a9–12, 1089b11–4.

deficiency   ἔλλειψις   This is the contrary of excess.

Deficiency   ἔλλειψις   Some thinkers posited *Excess* and *Deficiency* as the material principles from which things were generated. 1087b17–8.

definite   ὡρισμένος

definition   ὅρος, ὁρισμός; sometimes: λόγος. A formula signifying the whatness or the essence of a thing. The two Greek terms seem to be used synonymously. The term ὅρος signifies also a term in a syllogism, and also a boundary like a point in a line or a line which bounds a surface.

deliberation   βούλευσις, βουλή   An inquiry into the means, whether possible or for the most part, by which one would achieve an end. The two Greek terms often seem to be used synonymously. 1112a18–1113a15.

demonstration   ἀπόδειξις   A syllogism of what is necessarily true through its cause. 71b9–18.

denial   ἀπόφασις   A statement signifying that something does not belong to something else; for example, the forms "no A is B" and "some A is not B". The parts "not B" and "is not B" are also called "denials".

dense   πυκνός   Having its parts relatively close to each other. 10a20–2.

Dense, n.   πυκνόν   Some natural philosophers, e.g. Leucippus, posited the *Dense* and the *Rare* as the principles which caused the forms of all other things. 188a19–22, 985b10–2.

depth   βάθος

describe   διορίζειν   Synonym: "specify".

desire, v.   ὀρέγεσθαι   See "desire, n."

desire, n.   ὄρεξις   Desire is proper to the genus of animals, and its three kinds are wish, *desire*, and anger. 413b21–4, 414b1–6, 700b22, 701a33–b1, 1369a1–4.

desire, n.   ἐπιθυμία   Desire of the pleasant or of what seems to be pleasant (but is not). Used as a verb, it is: ἐπιθυμεῖν. 146b36–147a4, 414b5–6.

desiring part (of the soul)   ὀρεκτικόν

destructible   φθαρτός   Changeable from being to nonbeing.

destruction   φθορά   Change from being to nonbeing. Such a change is said to be unqualified if it is with respect to substance, as when a man dies, but it is said to be qualified if it is with respect to quality or quantity or place. 225a12–20, 1067b21–5.

dialectical   διαλεκτικός   See "dialectics".

dialectician   διαλεκτικός   See "dialectics".

dialectics   διαλεκτική   A discipline dealing effectively with any problem, whether defending or attacking a thesis, starting from commonly accepted beliefs. 100a18–b23, 101a25–8, 1004b17–26.

differ   διαφέρειν   See "differentia".

difference   διαφορά   See "differentia".

different   διάφορος   A and B are said to be different if, being the same in species or genus or by analogy, but not numerically the same, they are distinct. 1018a12–5, 1054b23–31, 1058a6–8.

differentia διαφορά If A and B are different but under the same genus, those which in their definitions make A and B distinct are said to be their differentiae.

difficult χαλεπός The contrary of easy. That which is painful or requires much time or effort or thought, etc., as in "a difficult task". 1363a23–4.

difficulty δυσκολία, δυσχέρεια In thought, a thesis is said to be difficult if it leads to apparent or actual contradictions. The terms "difficulty" and "objection" are used synonymously.

difficulty ἀπορία Uncertainty as to whether something is or is not the case, in view of arguments favoring both sides. Synonyms: "perplexity" and "problem". 145a33–b20.

discard ἀναιρεῖν Acknowledge and so abandon a principle as false or nonexistent.

discourse, v. or n. λόγος Stating or thinking, whether truly or falsely.

discuss *difficulties* διαπορεῖν Synonym: "go over the *difficulties*".

disposition διάθεσις 8b26–9a13, 1019b5, 1022b1–3.

distinct ἕτερον, ἄλλο If A and B are any beings but not the same, then they are said to be distinct or other, or that A is distinct from B, or that it is other than B. Since things may be the same either numerically, or numerically and in definition, or just in definition, things may also be distinct or other in as many ways. See "same". 1017b27—1018a19, 1054a32—b25.

distinction διαίρεσις

divine θεῖος Honorable and eternal, or almost so; godlike.

division διαίρεσις

doing πρᾶξις See "*action*".

doctrine δόξα A belief of great philosophic or scientific consequence, true or false, and usually a principle or given without proof. 987a32–4, 996b27–31.

dominant κύριος

dyad δυάς The terms "dyad" and "two" are used synonymously.

Dyad δυάς This is Two, which is a Number as an Idea for Plato, and it is the first Number which is generated from the *Dyad* and *Unity*, which are the first principles. It is also called "Dyad Itself", or "Two Itself".

Dyad δυάς For Plato, this is the material principle of all things generated. It also goes by the name "*Indefinite Dyad*".

'Dyad' δυάς Two units of a Number (as an Idea) which is distinct from (or greater than) Two; for example, two units of Five (as an Idea).

earth γῆ For its meaning, see "water".

Earth γῆ

Earth γῆ A material principle for Empedocles. 984a8–11.

easy   ῥάδιος   That which requires little time, or effort, or pain, or thought, etc. 1363a23, 1422a17–8.

element   στοιχεῖον   The first constituent in each thing. Thus, the material components which are indivisible in kind into other kinds are elements, and so are the letters of words, and the indefinable terms, and the syllogisms which are used as forms in geometrical or other demonstrations. 1014a26–b15.

eliminate   ἀναιρέω   See "discard".

end   τέλος   The term "end" is narrower in meaning than the term "extreme" (or "last") or the term "limit". 1021b25–1022a13.

equality   ἰσότης   Oneness in quantity. 1021a11–2.

equivocal   ὁμώνυμος   Having or called by the same name. A and B are said to be equivocally named if the term naming them has not the same meaning for both. For example, a man and a picture of him are equivocally called "a man", but a man and a horse are not equivocally called "an animal". 1a1–6.

err   ἁμαρτάνειν   Fail to achieve what is right.

error   ἁμαρτία

essence   τὶ ἦν εἶναι   (a) That which, being in a category, is in the thing and in virtue of which the thing remains the same and is univocally called by the same name, for example, the form of a statue, the whiteness of whatever is white insofar as it is white; (b) that in the soul (this exists as *knowledge*) by which we know a thing's essence in sense (a). 1029b1–1030b13.

essential   καθ' αὑτό   A is said to belong essentially to B if as an attribute or an *attribute* it belongs to B as to a subject by being in the whatness of B (as animality or ability to discourse is in a man) or by being provable through B (as the equality of vertical angles through the definition of vertical angles) or by being an attribute of B and definable by means of B (as oddness by means of number and straightness by means of a line). 73a28–b24, 1022a14–36.

essentially   ὅπερ

eternal   ἀΐδιος   That which exists always or necessarily, or, that which exists and is ungenerable and indestructible. 221b3–7, 282a21–3, 337b35–338a1, 1139b22–4.

eternally   ἀεί   Synonym: "always".

even (of a number)   ἄρτιος

Even   ἄρτιον   For the Pythagoreans, a material principle of things. 986a15–21.

evident   φανερός

excess   ὑπεροχή   If A exceeds B, then A is divisible into a part equal to B and an additional part. 1021a6–7.

Excess ὑπεροχή   Some thinkers posited *Excess* and *Deficiency* as the material principles of all things. 1087a17–8.

exhibit   δεικνύναι   This term is generic, having as species such terms as "demonstrate", "prove", "induce", "indicate", etc. Synonym: "show". 92a34–8.

exist   εἶναι, ὑπάρχειν

exist in   ἐνυπάρχειν   Synonyms: "be in", "be present in".

experience   ἐμπειρία   Knowledge produced by many memories of the same thing; for example, knowledge that Socrates, suffering from disease X, recovered every time he took medicine Y. 980b28–981a12.

expression   λόγος, ὄνομα   A symbol which is significant by convention; for example, a definition given vocally, or a written statement.

extreme   ἀκρότατος   For example, the extreme causes of a specific thing would be the most universal causes, not the proper causes. Thus, of a house, these would be material, formal, final, and moving causes, while the proper causes would be bricks, the specific structure, shelter, and architect or art. Synonym: "highest".

fact   ὅτι, πρᾶγμα   For example, a sick Socrates (if he is sick); the equality of the triangle's angles to two right angles; alleged fact: πρᾶγμα. This may be a fact or its contrary; thus, the expression is used as a genus of these two. For example, a sick Socrates would be an alleged fact, whether he is sick or well.

fail   ἀποτυχεῖν   The contrary of "succeed".

falsity   ψεῦδος   (a) A proposition or belief signifying that something is the case, when it is not, or that something is not, when it is. 1011b25–7, 1051b3–5. (b) That which is stated or believed as being combined, when it is not; for example, an immortal horse and a diagonal of a square commensurate with the side of the square. A falsity in this sense is a nonbeing. 1051b33–5.

few   ὀλίγα, ὀλίγον

fictitious   πλασματῶδες   That which is forced to agree with a hypothesis. 1082b1–4.

figure   σχῆμα   Synonym: "shape".

final cause   οὗ ἕνεκα   That for the sake of which something exists or is generated (the other tenses of time included). This is not limited to animals but extends to plants and to other things. 194b16–195b30, 983a24–b1, 1013a24–b28.

fine   λεπτός   That is, of particles which are small, whether without qualification or relatively, like those of fire or of air.

finite   πεπερασμένος   Synonym: "limited".

Finite, n.   πεπερασμένον   For the Pythagoreans, the *Infinite* as matter and the *Finite* as form were posited as the principles from which the other things (these being numbers) are generated. 987a13–9.

fire   πῦρ   This is a material element characterized by being hot and dry. See "water".

Fire   πῦρ   For Hippasus and Heraclitus, *Fire* is the only principle, a material principle, from which the other things are generated. 984a7–8.

first   πρῶτος   For its various kinds, see "prior". Synonym: "primary".

for, conj.   γάρ   This does not indicate a cause but rather something which confirms a cause, such as a sign or an example.

for the most part   ὡς ἐπὶ τὸ πολύ

for the sake of   ἕνεκα, ἵνα   Synonym: "final cause".

force   βία   Power of hindering (stopping from continuing) or preventing (barring from starting) something from proceeding according to its tendency.

form   εἶδος   Form is contrasted with matter, both being causes; for example, of a bronze statue, bronze is its matter and the shape its form.

form   μορφή   Synonym: *"shape"*. The terms "form" and *"form"* are probably used synonymously.

Form   εἶδος   For Plato, Forms, which are immovable and changeless, are posited as the causes of sensible or destructible things. Synonym: "Idea". 987a29–b22.

formal   εἰδηκός   Synonym: "as form". For example, "a formal principle" means a principle as form, e.g., the shape of a statue or the soul of a man.

formula   λόγος   A combination of terms; a definition or a description.

fortunate   εὐτυχής   One to whom good luck of considerable magnitude has fallen. 197a25–7.

fortune, good   εὐτυχία   Good luck of considerable magnitude. 197a25–7.

free   ἐλεύθερος   One who exists for his own sake or who is an end in himself. 982b25–8.

friendship   φιλία   1155b17–1156b35.

Friendship   φιλία   For Empedocles, a principle which causes things to come together. 984b27–985a10.

from (something)   ἐκ, ὑπό   In "A is (or is generated) from B", B may be the matter (as in "a statue is made from bronze"), or it may be the form, or both matter and form, and it may be the moving cause (in which case the synonym "by" is more frequently used). Occasionally it has the meaning of "after". 1023a26–b11.

full   πλῆρες   The contrary of empty or void.

Full   πλῆρες   For Leucippus and Democritus, the *Full* and the *Void* are the material principles from which the other things are generated. 985b4–10.

fully   ὅπερ   See "just, adv."

function   ἔργον

generally   ὅλως   Synonym: "in general", "universally".

generated, be   γίγνεσθαι   Synonyms: "become", "come to be". See "generation".

generation   γένεσις   A change from not-being to being. If the generation is to a substance, as when a baby is born, it is called "simple generation", if to an attribute, as from not-white to white, it is called "qualified generation". 225a12–7, 1067b21–3. Synonym: "becoming".

genus   γένος   In the whatness or definition of a thing, the constituent as matter or subject, to which the addition of a differentia produces a species of the same genus.

geodesy   γεωδαισία   The science of the magnitudes of the Earth and its parts.

geometrical demonstration   διάγραμμα   998a25–7, 1014a36.

geometry   γεωμετρία   The science of magnitudes. 1061a28–b3, 1143a3–4, 1355b30–1.

go over *difficulties*   διαπορεῖν   Synonym: "discuss *difficulties*".

god   θεός   An immortal animal. 122b12–4, 128b19–20.

God   θεός   The prime mover; or, the immortal animal, if only one such exists.

godlike   θεῖος   Honorable and eternal. Synonym: "divine".

good   ἀγαθόν   That which is chosen or regarded by the intellect as an end in itself or as a means to such an end. 1096a19–29, 1362a21–1363b4.

good fortune   εὐτυχία   Good luck of considerable magnitude. 197a25–7.

good physical condition   εὐεξία   This is the purpose of gymnastics or physical exercises. 113b34–6, 137a3–7.

goodness   εὖ

great   μέγας

Great, n.   μέγα   For Plato, the *Great* and *Small* is (or are) the material principle(s) of the things generated. 987b20–2.

grow   φύεσθαι

grow together   συμφύεσθαι   Things may grow together by nature, like the parts of a hand (1014b22–6), or not by nature, like siamese twins (1040b13–6).

habit   ἕξις   A disposition which is hard to displace, whether acquired, like a virtue or scientific knowledge, or natural, such as strength

or disposition to illness. 8b25–9a13, 1022b4–14. moral habit: ἦθος.
A disposition to an *action*. 1450a5–6. In a wider sense, it applies
to all animals. 487a11–2.

habit by practice ἔθος Custom, habit through practice; practice.
928b23–7, 981b5, 994b32, 1369b6–7.

happiness εὐδαιμονία A pleasant life or living according to virtue.

harmful βλαβερός The contrary of "useful". 1399b34–6.

harmonics ἁρμονική The science of sounds, mathematically treated.
1078a14–6.

harmony ἁρμονία

have ἔχειν That is, as a subject has a form or an attribute, or as a container has its contents, or as a whole has the parts. 1023a12–25.

having ἕξις The *actuality* of that which has and that which is had;
e.g., the having of a coat by a man. 1022b4–10.

having the same name ὁμώνυμος

health ὑγίεια 9a21–4, 246b4–6.

heaven οὐρανός 278b9–21.

heavy βαρύς That whose place is by nature at the center of the universe or which by nature moves towards the center. 269b23.

highest in rank ὑγεμονικώτατος

hold ἔχειν For example, as in "the tyrants hold the cities" and in "the
pillars hold the weight on them". 1023a8–25.

homogeneous ὁμοιομερής That which is the same or alike in kind as
any of its parts or ultimate parts (if the thing has such) and so any
two parts are the same or alike in kind; for example, water, air,
and fire according to many ancient thinkers, and likewise for the
units of a number. 329a3–12.

honor τιμή A sign or an external good conferred (given, bestowed,
etc.) to someone of great worth. 1123b17–21, 1361a27–39.

hot, n. or adj. θερμόν 329b24–32, 378b10–26, 388a20–4, 1070b10–5.

Hot θερμόν For Parmenides, a principle of sensibles. 986b31–7a2.

hypothesis ὑπόθεσις A premise, which is posited as true without proof
and which signifies that something is or is not the case. Synonym:
"assumption". 72a14–24.

Idea ἰδέα The Ideas were posited by Plato as existing apart from sensible things, as being the causes of those things, as being changeless, and as being the objects of *knowledge*. Synonym: "Form".
987a29–b22.

imagination φαντασία 427b27–429a9.

imitation μίμημα; μίμησις The first term signifies that which imitates
another thing; the second, the act of imitating.

immovable ἀκίνητος That which cannot by its nature be moved at all.

Hence, what is not a body is immovable, since only bodies can move. 226b10–11.

in agreement with ὁμολογούμενος Synonym: "commonly agreed".

in general ὅλως Synonym: "generally", "universally".

in itself καθ' αὑτό 1022a14–36, 1029a21–2, 24–5.

in many ways πολλαχῇ This is a generic expression, whose species are: "in many places", "in many things", "many times", etc.

in some sense πως

in the full sense ἁπλῶς Synonyms: "without qualification", "simply".

in the highest degree μάλιστα Synonyms: "most", "most of all". This term is used specifically for qualities which admit the more and the less, and analogically for other things, as when we seek to know the things which are substances most of all.

in virtue of κατά A is said to belong to B, or to C in virtue of B, if A is in the whatness or follows the whatness of B or C, or if A is defined in terms of B. Synonyms: "according to", "with respect to", "by virtue of". 73a27–b24, 1022a14–36.

inasmuch as ᾗ Synonym: "qua", "insofar as". See "qua". 73b25–74a3.

increase αὔξησις Motion with respect to quantity and in the direction of complete magnitude or of being greater. 226a29–32, 241a32–b2.

individual καθ' ἕκαστον

indivisible ἄτομος, ἀδιαίρετος

induction ἐπαγωγή

infinite, n. or adj. ἄπειρον Primarily, the infinite is in the genus of what can be gone through, but it cannot be gone through. Thus, a line is a quantity, and it cannot be gone through by successive bisection of what is left. Secondarily, "the infinite" means also (a) that which, not being a quantity, cannot be gone through, just as a line is neither virtuous nor vicious (for it is not a man), and (b) a great many, or what is difficult to go through, as when we say that the number of animals is infinite. Synonym: "unlimited". 204a2–7, 1066a35–b1.

Infinite ἄπειρον The material principle for the Pythagoreans and Plato.

innate σύμφυτος, συγγενής

inquire ζητάω Synonym: "seek".

inquiry ζήτησις

inquiry μέθοδος Systematic inquiry, as in a science. Synonym: "method".

insofar as ᾗ See "inasmuch as".

instrumental χρήσιμος Synonym: "useful". A thing is said to be useful (or instrumental) if it is for the sake of something else; for example, a spoon or money. Thus, happiness is not useful, for it is only for its own sake.

intellect   νοῦς   The part of the soul which *knows* the principles. 84b35–85a1, 100b5–17, 1140b31–1141a8, 1143a25–b17.

Intellect   νοῦς   For Aristotle, the prime mover or God.

Intelligence   νοῦς   For Anaxagoras, a moving principle and cause of things.

intelligible   νοητός

intermediate, n. or adj.   μεταξύ   Synonym: "between". B is said to be intermediate or an intermediate between A and C if, in going from A to C one must by nature go through B before reaching C. 226b23–31, 1057a21–6, 1068b27–30.

Intermediate Objects   τὰ μεταξύ   These are mathematical objects, posited by Plato as lying between the Ideas and the sensible objects. 987b14–8.

interval   διάστημα   This term is generic, not limited to quantities only.

Interval   διάστημα   A material principle assumed or posited by certain Platonists to generate magnitudes. 1085b27–34.

investigate   θεωρεῖν   Synonyms: "speculate", "contemplate". To seek universal truths for their own sake.

investigation   θεωρία   See "investigate".

joint cause   συναίτιον

judge, v.   λογίζεσθαι   To think about things which may or may not come to be. 1139a6–15.

judge, v.   κρίνειν   A genus of "to sense". For example, sight *judges* colors, the power of hearing *judges* sounds, and another power *judges* that sweetness and whiteness are distinct. Synonym, "discriminate". 111a14–20, 426b8–23.

judgment   λογισμός

judgment   κρίσις

judging power   λογιστικόν   Judging part of the soul.

just, adj.   δίκαιος

just, adv.   ὅπερ   For example, "a man" signifies just a substance, as against "a white man" which signifies a composite of a substance and an attribute, or as against "whiteness" which signifies a qualified but not a separate being.

justice   δικαιοσύνη

kind, n.   εἶδος

know   γνωρίζειν   See "knowledge".

know   ἐπίσταμαι   See *"knowledge"*.

knowable   ἐπιστητόν

known   ἐπιστητόν

knowledge   γνῶσις   This term is generic; it may be true opinion, or of what is necessarily true, or of the first principles, and it includes sensation.

knowledge   ἐπιστήμη   This is knowledge of what necessarily is, whether demonstrable or not.

lead back   ἀνάγω   Synonym: "reduce".

learn   μανθάνειν   (a) Usually, to come to know from others, and this includes books; (b) occasionally, to come to know by using knowledge. 165b32–4.

leisure   σχολή   Free time to spend as one wishes, usually in some desired activity.

length   μῆκος   The term usually means what we mean by "a line", without reference to its being finite or not. 1020a11–4. Sometimes it means a line (which we call "a finite line").

letter   στοιχεῖον   The letters of the alphabet are meant.

life   ζωή   This is a principle, namely, the actuality or form through which a thing (which we call "a living being") takes in food and grows and dies. 412a14–5.

light, adj.   λευκός   The contrary of dark.

light, adj.   κοῦφος   The contrary of heavy.

like, v.   ἀγαπάω

like, adj.   ὅμοιος   Things are said to be like if their quality is one. Synonym: "similar". 1018a15–9, 1021a11–2, 1054b3–14.

limit, v.   ὁρίζειν

limit, n.   πέρας   1022a4–13.

Limit, n.   πέρας   For the Pythagoreans, the principle as form.

limited   πεπερασμένος   Synonym: "finite".

Limited   πεπερασμένον   See "*Finite*". For the Pythagoreans, same as "*Limit*".

line   γραμμή, μῆκος (sometimes)   A limited length, or, a one-dimensional limited continuous quantity. 1016b24–9, 1020a7–14.

little   ὀλίγον

live, v.   ζῆν   413a22–b2.

living being   ζῷον   1072b29.

locomotion   φορά   Motion with respect to place. 208a31–2, 226a32–3, 1069b12–3.

long, adj.   μακρός

Long, n.   μακρόν   Some Platonists posited the *Long* and *Short* as the material principles from which the Mathematical Lines were generated. 992a10–3, 1085a9–12, 1089b11–4.

love, n.   ἔρος

Love, n.   ἔρος   *Love* was posited as the moving principle by Hesiod and Parmenides. 984b23–31.

luck   τύχη   Luck or what results from it belongs to what can deliberate, e.g., to men. See "chance", the genus of "luck". 195b31–198a13.

magnitude   μέγεθος   An infinitely divisible quantity. 1020a7–14.

main   κύριος

make   ποιεῖν   To generate something by art or *thought* or some power. 1032a25–b21.

making   ποίησις   See "make".

man   ἄνθρωπος   A human being, male or female.

man   ἀνήρ   A male human being.

many, adj., n.   πολλά, πλῆθος   The contrary of unity. Synonym: "plurality". 1004b27–9, 1054a20–1055a2; a great many: ἄπειρος; in many ways: πολλαχῇ. This expression is generic and has as its species "in many places", "in many things", "many times", etc.

mass   ὄγκος   Synonym: "volume".

master-art   ἀρχιτεκτονική   See "master-artist".

master-artist   ἀρχιτέκτων   In building a suspension bridge, for example, there is the top engineer who is the master-artist, then the manual laborer who is lowest and only takes orders, and between these there are others who both take and gives orders. 981a30–982a1.

materials   ὕλη

mathematical objects   μαθηματικά, μαθήματα

Mathematical Objects   μαθηματικά   For Plato, these are also called "Intermediate Objects" and lie between the Ideas and the sensible objects; they are immovable, eternal, and the objects of the mathematical sciences. For Speusippus, these are first in existence, eternal and immovable, and the objects of the mathematical sciences. For Xenocrates, they are the same as the Ideas.

mathematical sciences   μαθήματα

mathematical   μαθηματική

mathematics   μαθηματική

matter   ὕλη   This term is generic. If physical, it may signify prime matter which underlies a form (192a22–34, 1029a20–6, 1042a27–8), or proximate matter like wood and nails in a chair which exist potentially in the chair but can exist separately (1044a15–32), or as something between (e.g., fire and earth and water and air, if the flesh consists of these). As non-physical, the premises are said to be matter for a conclusion, the letters are matter for words, the genus is matter for the species, etc.

may, v.   ἐνδέχεσθαι

mean, v.   σημαίνειν

measure, n.   μέτρον   That by which, as first or a principle, a given quantity is known. For example, five men are known by one man as a measure, and ten feet by one foot. 1052b20–7, 1087b33–1088a14.

medical science   ἰατρική
memory   μνήμη
method   μέθοδος   Synonym: *"inquiry"*.
middle term   μέσον   If A is (or is not) a predicate of B, and also B of C, then B is called "a middle term". 25b35–6.
misfortune   δυστυχία   Bad luck of considerable magnitude. 197a25–7.
mistake   ἀπάτη   One is said to be mistaken if he thinks that A is B when A is not B, or that A is not B when A is B. 1051b17–2a4.
modify   λέγεσθαι κατά   Synonym: "said of", "predicated of".
moral habit   ἦθος   1450a5–6, 1450b8–10.
more   μᾶλλον   The term is usually used to compare qualities. Sometimes it extends to other things when no special term exists for them, as when it is said that a man is a substance to a higher degree than earth. Synonyms: "to a higher degree", "rather".
most   μάλιστα   A superlative for qualities. See "more". Synonyms: "most of all", "in the highest degree".
most   ὡς ἐπὶ τὸ πολύ   A large majority of the cases, as in "most people get well when taking such-and-such medicine".
most of all   μάλιστα   See "most".
motion   κίνησις   The actuality of potential being qua potential. The kinds of motion are locomotion, alteration, increase, and decrease. 201a10–1, 1065b16, 33, 1068a8–10.
motionless   ἀκίνητος   If what is motionless can move it is said to be at rest. Hence, rest is the contrary of motion.
mutilated   κολοβός   1042a11–28.
name   ὄνομα   Voice which is significant by convention and no part of which is significant. 16a19–20. Sometimes it is used for any expression.
narrow   στενός
Narrow, n.   στενόν   Some Platonists posited the *Narrow* and the *Wide* as the material principles from which the mathematical surfaces were generated. 992a10–3, 1085a9–12, 1089b11–4.
natural   φυσικός   Synonym: "physical". with natural ease: εὐφυῶς.
natural philosopher   φυσιολόγος   One who investigates the principles of nature or of physics.
nature   φύσις   The form of a physical object; the matter of a physical object; the principle of motion present in a physical object. Sometimes, the essence of a thing, in any category. 192b8–193b21, 1014b16–1015a19.   according to nature: κατὰ φύσιν. 192b8–193b21, 199b14–8.   by nature: φύσει. 134a5–11, 192b8–193b21, 199b14–8.
necessary   ἀναγκαῖος   The primary meaning: that which cannot be otherwise. For example, vertical angles are necessarily equal,

and they cannot be unequal. For secondary meanings, see 1015a20–b15.

necessity ἀνάγκη

need, n.   χρεία   A need is of something, not for its own sake but for something else. Thus, what is needed is the useful, which is for the sake of something else. 980a22–3, 982b24–8.

noble   καλός   That which exists or is *chosen* for its own sake and is praiseworthy, or, that which is good and pleasant, 1366a33–5.

nobly   καλῶς

nonbeing   οὐκ ὄν, μὴ ὄν   This may be the impossible, as an isosceles triangle with unequal base angles, or the potential yet not existing, as a sitting man when he is actually standing but can sit. The latter is also called "not-being".

Nonbeing   οὐκ ὄν, μὴ ὄν   For some thinkers, a principle needed to generate the plurality of things.

noncomparable   ἀσύμβλητος   The contrary of comparable. See "comparable".

nonrational   ἄλογον   Without any ability to reason; not reasoning well. 1102a32–1103a10.

not-being   οὐκ ὄν, μὴ ὄν   What can be but is not, or the potential when it does not have a given actuality, like prime matter or the bricks which are not a house.

notion   ἐννόημα

number   ἀριθμός   A plurality measured by a unit, or, a discrete quantity. This is what is nowadays called "whole number" or "cardinal number" which is greater than 1. The term closest to the modern term "number" is translated in this work as "quantity". 4b20–31, 1020a8–9, 1057a2–4, 1085b22, 1088a5–8.

Number   ἀριθμός   For the later Plato, a Number, such as Seven, is also an Idea, and it is generated ultimately from the two principles, the *One* and the *Dyad* (also called "*Indefinite Dyad*"). For Speusippus, Numbers are not Ideas, but they are first in existence and the objects of mathematics. 1075b37–1076a4, 1084a3–7, 1090b13–9.

object   This term shall signify a being or a nonbeing. There is no such term in Greek, but it is signified indirectly, as in "the thinkable", for the thinkable may be a being or a nonbeing. Occasionally, πρᾶγμα is used.

objection   δυσχέρεια, δυσκολία   An apparent or real contradiction arising from a thesis which is posited. Synonym: "difficulty".

odd (of a number)   περιττός

Odd   περιττόν   For the Pythagoreans, a principle of all things. 986a15–21.

one, adj., n.   ἕν   (a) That which is indivisible or undivided, whether numerically (e.g., Socrates and the Athenian philosopher who drank the hemlock), or in formula of a species or genus (e.g., two horses are one in species and in formula), or in kind, or by analogy. (b) A unit or measure. Synonyms: "the one", "oneness", "unity", "unit", "measure". 1015b16–1017a3, 1052a15–1054a19.

One, n.   ἕν   For Plato and others, the *One* is usually a formal principle from which other things are generated, such as Numbers and sensible objects. Synonyms: "the *One*", "*Unity*". 987a29–b22, 1084a3–7.

oneness   ἕν   Same as "one".

Oneness   ἕν   Same as "*One*".

operation   ἔργον

opinion   δόξα   A belief of what may or may not be. For example, "John is sick". 89a2–3, 100b5–7, 1039b31–1040a1, 1051b10–5; be of the opinion: δοξάζειν; common or accepted opinion: ἔνδοξος. See "accepted opinion".

opportunity   καιρός   Synonym: "right time", "proper time".

opposite   ἀντικείμενος   The main kinds are: the contradictory, the contrary, the relative, and a privation. 11b16–9, 1018a20–b8.

optics   ὀπτική   Mathematical science of light. 997b20–3, 1078a14–6.

or   ἤ; καί

order   τάξις;   set the ordering: ἐπιτάττειν.

other   ἕτερον, ἄλλο   The contrary of "same". The term applies only to beings. Thus, if A is other than B, A and B are beings. A and B may be numerically other, like Socrates and Plato, or other in species, or in genus. Thus, "difference" and "contrariety" are species of "otherness". Synonym: "distinct". 1018a9–15, 1054b14–32.

outward appearance   ἰδέα

pale   λευκός

paralogism   παραλογισμός   A conclusion falsely drawn.

part   μέρος, μόριον   1032b12–25.

participate   μετέχειν   Usually, A is said to participate in B if "B" or its definition is a predicate of A, directly or derivatively, but "A" is not a predicate of B. Plato held that sensible things participated in Ideas, but said little about the nature of participation. Synonym: "share".

pattern   παράδειγμα

peculiar   ἴδιος   Same as "proper", as against "common".

perfect   τέλειος   Same as "complete".

performance   ἔργον

perish   ἀπόλυσθαι

perplexity   ἀπορία   Same as "difficulty" or "problem".

persuasion   βία

pertinent   οἰκεῖος   Synonym: "*proper*".

philosophy   φιλοσοφία   The science of being qua being, or the science of the highest principles and causes and elements of things. 1003a21–32, 1026a10–32, 1060b31–1061b17, 1064a28–b14.

physical   φυσικός   Synonym: "natural".

physicist   φυσικός

physics   φυσική   The science of movable objects qua movable. 1025b18–21, 1061b28–30, 1064a15–6.

place   τόπος   The first inner motionless boundary of a containing body; for example, of a can of tomatoes, the inner surface of the can. 212a20–1.

plane, n.   ἐπίπεδον

plastic material   ἐκμαγεῖον

pleasure   ἡδονή   1152b1–1154b34.

plurality   πλῆθος, πολλά   Synonym: "many", as a noun. 1004b27–9, 1054a20–1055a2.

Plurality   πλῆθος   For Speusippus, this is the material principle from which Numbers are generated. 1087b4–6.

point   στιγμή, σημεῖον   That which is indivisible with respect to quantity and has position. It is limited to (spacial) magnitudes. 1016b24–6.

portrait   εἰκών

posit   τιθέναι   To lay down something, usually a principle, as existing or as being true. 72a14–24.

position   θέσις   Relative place; that which is posited. 6b2–14.

possess   ἔχειν   Synonym: "have". 1023a8–25.

possible   δυνατός   Synonyms: "potential". 1019a15–1020a6; be possible: See "can".

posterior   ὕστερος   Opposed to prior. If A is prior to B, then B is said to be posterior to A. See "prior".

potency   δύναμις   Primarily, the principle of motion or of change in another or qua other. Synonyms: "power", "potentiality", "capability". 1019a15–1020a6.

potential   δυνάμει, δυνατός

potentiality   δύναμις   Same as "potency".

potentially   δυνάμει

power   δύναμις   Same as "potency"; power of sensation: αἴσθησις.

practical   πρακτικός   The adjective corresponding to "*action*". See "*action*".

practice   ἔθος

predicate, n.   κατηγορία;   be a predicate of: κατηγορεῖσθαι.

predication   κατηγορία

premise   πρότασις

present, be . . . in, v.   παρεῖναι, ἐνεῖναι, ὑπάρχειν

primary   πρῶτος   Synonym: "first".

principle ἀρχή Synonyms: "beginning", "starting-point", "source". The first from which something is or becomes or is known. 1012b34–1013a23.

prior πρότερος P is said·to be prior to Q with respect to some principle X if P is nearer to X than Q is. For example, if X is existence, an animal is prior in existence to a man, for if a man exists, so does an animal, but not conversely, 14a26–b23, 1018b9–1019a14.

privation στέρησις (a) Not having, e.g., a sound is deprived of color, that is, it has no color. (b) Not having if by nature it should have, e.g., a blind man is deprived of sight, for qua man he should possess sight. 1022b22–1023a7.

probability εἰκός That which happens for the most part, or a statement concerning it, e.g., "the envious hate". 70a3–7.

problem ἀπορία Same as *"difficulty"*.

produce ποιεῖν Synonym: "make".

production ποίησις A change, which starts at the end of the artist's thinking and ends when he has generated a work of his art, such as health by the doctor, a bridge by the engineer, etc. In a wider sense, any generation requiring some power or thought or art. 1032a27–8, 1032b6–17.

productive ποιητικός

proper ἴδιος Synonym: "peculiar".

proper οἰκεῖος Perhaps a synonym of "proper", or else, close to it in meaning.

proper time καιρός Synonym: "right time".

property ἴδιον A property of a thing is an attribute of it which, not being in the essence of a thing belongs to it and to it alone; e.g., capability of learning grammar is by nature a property of men. The term is also used in a qualified sense; e.g., relative to cats and centipedes, two-footedness is by nature a property of men.

proposition ἀποφαντικός λόγος A statement or a combination of statements.

prove συλλογίζεσθαι To conclude truly.

proverb παροιμία

prudence φρόνησις (a) Generically (for all animals), the ability to look after one's own good, 1141a20–8. (b) Specifically (for men), a habit by means of which one can deliberate truly concerning one's conduct for a good life. 1140a24–b30.

prudent φρόνιμος See "prudence".

pure καθαρός

purging κάθαρσις

purpose οὗ ἕνεκα Same as "final cause".

qua ᾗ Synonyms: "insofar as", "inasmuch as". An attribute of C belongs to it qua B if it belongs to B but to no other genus higher than B. For example, sensation belongs to a man qua an animal, and mobility belongs to a man or a bed qua a body. 73b25–74a3.

quality   ποιόν, ποιότης   This is one of the categories. 1020a33–b25.

quantity   ποσόν   This is a category, whose primary species are numbers (which we nowadays call "whole numbers", except 1) and magnitudes (lines, surfaces, solids). There are also accidental quantities, such as time and place, and these presuppose primary quantities. 4b20–6a35, 1020a7–32.

quarter-tone   δίεσις   1053a12–6.

race   γένος

rare   μανός   Having its parts relatively at a distance from each other. 10a20–2.

Rare, n.   μανόν   For some physical philosophers, the *Rare* and the *Dense* were posited as the formal principles of things. 188a19–22, 985b10–2.

rather   μᾶλλον   See "more".

ratio   λόγος   For example, the ratio 3:2, or 5:3:2 if a thing is composed of three elements.

rational   μετὰ λόγου, λόγον ἔχειν. See "reason".

reason   λόγος   A thought or statement with parts; sometimes, if it is a cause of another thought or statement; ability to have such a thought or make such a statement, or to make universal statements.

reason   Same as "cause".

reasonable   εὔλογος   In agreement with what is commonly accepted, either by all or by most or by a given school of thought, primarily if true.

reduce   ἀνάγειν   To state in terms of ultimate principles or causes or elements.

refutation   ἔλεγχος   See "refute".

refute   ἐλέγχειν   To start from premises admitted by an opponent and prove from them a contradiction. 66b4–11, 165a2–3, 170b1–3.

relation   πρός τι   This is a category. A relation involves two things, each of which may be a composite (e.g., when A is between the pair B and C). 6a36–8b24, 1020b26–1021b11.

relative   Synonym of "relation".

reliable   κύριος

rest, n.   ἠρεμία   Privation of motion of that which by nature can be in motion. 221b12–4, 226b12–6, 1068b22–5.

right, adj.   ὀρθός   A genus of "true" and "*successful*", the first being a predicate of knowledge, the second of *actions*. 427b8–11.

right time   καιρός   Same as "proper time".

said of, be   λέγεσθαι κατά   To be predicated of.

same   ταὐτός   One in number, or kind, or *substance*, or formula. 103a6–
      39, 1017b27–1018a11, 1054a29–b3, b14–9.

science   ἐπιστήμη   Knowledge of that which cannot be otherwise, i.e.
      of what is necessarily true. Synonym: "*knowledge*".

seed   σπέρμα

seek   ζητεῖν   Synonym: "inquire".

seem   δοκεῖν   Synonym: "thought to be".

sensation   αἴσθησις; power of sensation: αἴσθησις.

sense   Synonym: "meaning".

separable   χωριστός

separate, adj.   χωρισμένος, χωριστός

separate, v.   χωρίζειν, διακρίνειν

shallow   ταπεινός

Shallow, n.   ταπεινόν   See "*Deep*".

shape   σχῆμα   Synonym: "figure".

shape   μορφή   Either a synonym of "form", or usually so. Synonym:
      "*form*".

share, v.   μετέχειν   Same as "participate".

short   βραχύς

Short, n.   βραχύ   See "*Long*".

show, v.   δεικνύναι   This term is generic, having as species such terms
      as "prove", "demonstration", "induce", "indicate", etc. Synonym:
      "exhibit". 92a34–b3.

sign, n.   σημεῖον   (See 70a); sure sign: τεκμήριον. (See 70b).

signify   σημαίνειν

similar   ὅμοιος   Same as "like".

simply   ἁπλῶς

simultaneous   ἅμα   (a) P and Q are said to be simultaneous if they are
      generated or exist at the same time, or, if the existence of any
      one of them implies the existence but is not necessarily the cause
      of the other. 14b24–32, 218a25–7, 448b19–20. (b) P and Q are
      said to be simultaneous in nature (or coordinate) if they are
      species arising from the same subdivision of a given genus, e.g.,
      odd numbers and even numbers. 14b33–15a7.

slave   δοῦλος   A man who by nature belongs to another man as a part
      does to a whole and so exists for the sake of the whole. 1254a8–17.

small   μικρός

Small, n.   μικρόν   See "*Great*".

solid   στερεόν   Usually, an immovable magnitude divisible in three di-
      mensions and resulting after the principles of motion (physical
      matter and such qualities as weight and color) have been removed
      in thought; its study belongs to geometry. Sometimes, a body.
      1004b13–5, 1016b27–8, 1077b17–30.

Solid   στερεόν   For Leucippus, a material principle of things. 985b4–10.

somewhere   ποῦ   This is a category. Synonyms: "whereness", "in a place".

sophist   σοφιστής   See "sophistry".

sophistry   σοφιστική   A discipline which appears to be wisdom or philosophy but is not. It has as its aim honor (by appearing to be philosophy), or making money, or just winning an argument. The last kind is called "eristics". 165a21–3, 171b22–34, 1004b17–9.

soul   ψυχή   The first actuality of a physical organic body. This is the form of a physical living thing. 412b4–25, 414a4–14.

sound   ψόφος

source   ἀρχή, ὅθεν, ὅθεν ἡ ἀρχή   Synonyms: "principle", "beginning", "starting-point"; source of motion: ὅθεν ἡ κίνησις. Synonym: "moving cause".

speak falsely   ψεύδεσθαι

species   εἶδος; same in species: ὁμοειδής.

specify   ὁρίζειν, διορίζειν   Synonym: "describe".

speculate   θεωρεῖν   See "contemplate".

speculation   θεωρία

starting-point   ἀρχή   Same as "principle".

statement   ἀπόφανσις   An expression signifying that something does or does not belong to something else. A statement is either true or false but not both. 17a1–24.

strife   νεῖκος

Strife   νεῖκος   For Empedocles, a principle which causes things to separate from each other. 984b27–985a10.

subject   ὑποκείμενον   This may be prime matter, or in a category, but not necessarily a substance, and it is spoken of in relation to that which belongs to it or exists in it, as straightness belongs to a straight line and physical form exists in matter. The term also signifies a part of a statement; for example, in "P is Q", the part "P", of which "Q" is said to be predicated. Synonym: "underlying subject". 1029a1–9, 1038b2–6.

substance   οὐσία   This is the generic term. It means: (a) a sensible body, physical or heavenly (Sun, Moon, etc.), which is separate, or a part of it (and this may be separable, e.g., a hand); (b) the form or essence of a being in any category, and this is called a "*substance*" (e.g., we may ask: "What is the *substance* of virtue, or of a triangle?"); (c) the subject, which is not said or predicated of another thing but of which other things may be predicated, and this may be matter or form or a *composite;* (d) some regard universals and the mathematical objects as eternal and nonsensible and separate and call them "substances" most of all. 2a11–4b19, 1017b10–26, 1028b8–1029a7.

substance οὐσία   See "substance" in sense (b).

succeed   ἐπιτυχεῖν   To achieve what one wishes. This is the contrary of "fail" (ἀποτυχεῖν).

succeed κατορθοῦν   To achieve what one wishes and what is right. This is the contrary of "err" (ἁμαρτάνειν).

succession   ἑξῆς, ἐφεξῆς   A thing is said to be successive if, being after a principle and being separate by itself in position or in kind or in some other way, there is no other thing in the same genus between it and that which it is said to succeed. 226b34–227a6, 1068b31–1069a1.

suchness   τοιόνδε   This term, in contrast to an individual, signifies a universal or a kind.

superior, be   διαφέρειν

supposition   δόγμα   Synonym: "view".

sure sign   τεκμήριον   The fact that B is an attribute of C is said to be a sure sign of the fact that A is an attribute of C, it being assumed that every B is A. For example, the fact that Dr. Jones has his Ph.D. is a sure sign that he passed his Ph.D. preliminaries. 70a3–b6.

surface   ἐπιφάνεια, ἐπίπεδον   A magnitude divisible in two dimensions. 1016b26–9.

syllogism   συλλογισμός   An expression (verbal or in *thought*) in which a statement (conclusion) follows necessarily from statements (premises) which are posited as being so. 24b8–22, 100a25–7.

system   πραγματεία   For example, Plato's philosophical system concerning Ideas.

systematic inquiry   μέθοδος   Synonym: *"inquiry"*.

teach   διδάσκειν

teachable   μαθητικός

tendency   ὁρμή

that for the sake of which   οὗ ἕνεκα   Synonym: "final cause", "purpose".

theologian   θεολόγος   One who systematically investigates divine (eternal and honorable) things.

theoretical   θεωρητική   Pertaining to truth for its own sake, as in "a theoretical science".

theory   λόγος   This is universal knowledge, usually for its own sake.

thesis   θέσις   That which is posited without demonstration as being so or as being true, and it may be a definition or a hypothesis. 72a14–24.

thing   ὄν, πρᾶγμα   Synonym: "being", and sometimes "fact".

think   νοεῖν   This term is generic, and it includes "imagine" as one of the species.

think διανοεῖν   In thought, to combine or divide, or to affirm or deny, e.g., that the diagonal is not commensurate with the side, or that vertical angles are equal.

think that δοκεῖν, οἴεσθαι Synonyms: "consider", "regard", "seem".

thinking, n. νόησις

this, n. τόδε τι This term, in contrast to a universal or a kind, signifies something separate and a substance which one can point to, but sometimes something in any category, as a color or a length or a surface.

thought, n. διάνοια See *"think"*.

through διά This word indicates a cause. For example, in "A is C through B", B is the cause of A's being a C. Synonym: "because".

time χρόνος A number of motion with respect to before and after. 217b29–220a26; right or proper time: καιρός. Synonym: "opportunity".

to a higher degree μᾶλλον Same as "more".

together ἅμα In the same place (see "place"). For example, your coffee and mine are primarily not together, for they are in different cups, but they may be secondarily together, if they are in the same room. 226b21–2, 1068b26.

total πᾶς That which does not change in nature if its parts change position. Synonym: "all". 1024a1–10.

touch, v. ἅπτεσθαι Things are said to touch if their boundaries (not necessarily all) are together, e.g., two books one on top of the other. 226b23, 323a3–6, 1068b27.

touch, n. ἀφή

transform πέπτω

traverse διεξέρχομαι To go through a quantity, e.g., a line or a number.

true ἀληθές See "truth".

truth ἀλήθεια, ἀληθές (a) A saying or *thinking* of that which is that it is, or of that which is not that it is not. 1011b25–7, 1051b3–5. (b) A composite being; for example, an isosceles triangle with base angles equal is a truth. 1051b33–4.

Turning, n. τροπή Synonym: "position". See *"Arrangement"*. 985b4–19, 1042b11–5.

two δυάς, δύο Synonym: "dyad".

Two δυάς (Synonym: "Dyad") For the later Plato, this is the first Idea which is generated from the principles, the *One* and the *Dyad*.

ugly αἰσχρός The contrary of the beautiful.

underlie ὑποκεῖσθαι A relation between a subject and an attribute or form. For example, Socrates underlies his sickness, and matter underlies form, and a line underlies its straightness.

underlying subject ὑποκείμενον The subject may be just matter, or it may be in a category, but not necessarily a substance. For example, bronze is the underlying subject of the shape of a statue, Socrates of his sitting, a line of straightness, color of whiteness, and in the case of terms, "Socrates" is the underlying subject of "his wisdom", and "line" of "curvature". Synonym: "subject".

understand   εἰδέναι   To know through the causes. 184a10–4, 194b17–20, 981a21–30, 983a25–6.

understand   συνιέναι   To know or grasp the meaning of an expression.

unfortunate   δυστυχής   One to whom bad luck of considerable magnitude has befallen. 197a25–7.

unit   μονάς   That which is indivisible in every way with respect to quantity and has no position. 1016b17–31.

Unit   μονάς   A unit of a Number. See "Number".

unity   ἕν   Same as "one".

Unity   ἕν   Same as *"One"*.

universal   καθόλου   That which by nature is predicable or belongs to many. 17a39–40, 1038b11–2. For Plato, universals are Ideas.

universally   ὅλως, καθόλου

universe   κόσμος, πᾶν   It has a spherical shape and includes all, i.e. stars, Moon, Sun, ether, physical objects, etc. 212b13–8, 285a27–32.

unlike   ἀνόμοιος   The contrary of "like". See "like".

unlimited   ἄπειρος   Same as "infinite".

Unlimited   ἄπειρος   Same as *"Infinite"*.

unreasonable   ἄλογος   The contrary of "reasonable".

use, n.   χρῆσις

useful   χρήσιμος   The useful (or instrumental) is that which exists or becomes for the sake of something else and not for its own sake, e.g., a spoon or money. Thus, the enjoyment of music, being an end in itself, is not useful. Synonym: "instrumental". 101a25–8, 742a32, 1096a7.

vice   κακία   The contrary of "virtue".

vicious   κακός   The contrary of "virtuous".

view, v.   θεωρεῖν   Synonym: "observe".

view, n.   δόγμα   Synonym: "supposition".

violence   βία   The hindering (stopping from continuing) or prevention (prohibiting from starting) of something from proceeding according to its tendency or *choice*. 1015a26–b3. Synonym: "force".

virtue   ἀρετή   Its two species are: intellectual and ethical. 1105b19–1107a27.

void   κενόν   A place (or boundary) in which there is no body at all, whether light or heavy. 208b25–7, 213a15–9, 214a2–3, 16–7.

volume   ὄγκος   Synonym: "mass".

water   ὕδωρ   As used by Aristotle, the term does not mean what we mean by "water" or "H₂O". For him, in terms of attributes, "water" means a body which is cold and moist, "fire" means a body which is hot and dry, "air" means a body which is hot and moist, and "earth" means a body which is cold and dry. These are the four material elements from which the other sensible bodies (excluding the heavenly bodies) are composed. 330a30–b7, 382b13–5, 388a29–32.

Water ὕδωρ A material principle for Thales, Empedocles. 983b20–4a9.

weight βάρος

well, adv. καλῶς

well being εὖ

whatness τὶ ἔστι A formula of what a thing is, primarily of substances, secondarily of the things in the other categories, and the existence of the thing is presupposed. 92b4–8, 93a16–20.

whenness ποτέ One of the categories. For example, an answer to the question "When?", such as "Yesterday", or "last year", signifies an instance of whenness. 1b25–2a2.

whereness ποῦ This is a category. Synonyms: "somewhere", "in a place".

white, n., adj. λευκός

why, n. διὰ τί The cause of something. Synonym: "cause".

whole ὅλος (a) That from which no natural part is absent. (b) That which contains what is contained, either (i) actually many (as a universal contains the species or the individuals of which it is a predicate), or (ii) the parts which exist potentially. (c) That in which the position of the parts makes a difference, as a whole shoe. 1023b26–1024a10.

wide πλατύς

Wide, n. πλατύ Some Platonists posited the *Wide* and the *Narrow* as the material principles from which the Mathematical Planes or Surfaces were generated. 992a10–3, 1085a9–12, 1089b11–4.

width πλάτος

wisdom σοφία Intellect and science of the most honorable things (eternal and divine). Philosophy, then, would be wisdom. In a qualified sense, there is wisdom of some part of being, e.g., of the first principles and some important theorems of physics. 1005b1–2, 1141a9–b8.

wish βούλησις Desire of the good or the apparent good (in the judging part of the soul). The object of wish is an end, not a means to an end. 1113a13–b2, 1369a1–4.

with respect to κατά Synonyms: "in virtue of", "according to", "by virtue of". 73a27–b24, 1022a14–35.

without qualification ἁπλῶς Synonym: "in the full sense", "simply".

wonder θαυμάζειν

ἀγαθόν good
ἀγαπάω like
ἀδιαίρετος indivisible
ἀεί always, eternally
ἀήρ air; *Air*
ἀ·ί·διος eternal
αἵρεσις choice
αἴσθησις sensation; power of sensation
αἰσχρός base; ugly
αἰτία, αἴτιον cause, *reason*
ἀκίνητος immovable; motionless
ἀκριβής accurate
ἀκρότατος extreme
ἀλήθεια truth
ἀληθές true; truth
ἄλλο other, distinct
ἀλλοίωσις alteration
ἄλογον unreasonable; nonrational
ἅμα together; simultaneous, at the same time; coordinate
ἁμαρτάνειν err
ἁμαρτία error
ἀναγκαῖος necessary
ἀνάγκη necessity
ἀνάγω lead back, reduce
ἀναιρέω discard, eliminate, annihilate
ἀναλογία analogy
ἀναλύω analyze
ἀνήρ *man*
ἄνθρωπος man
ἀνόμοιος unlike

ἀντικείμενος opposite
ἀντίφασις contradiction
ἀντίχθων Counter-Earth
ἀξίωμα axiom
ἀπάτη mistake
ἄπειρον infinite, unlimited; a great many; *Infinite, Unlimited*
ἁπλῶς in the full sense, without qualification, simply, in a simplified manner
ἀπόδειξις demonstration
ἀπόλλυσθαι perish
ἀπορία problem, *difficulty*, perplexity
ἀποτυχεῖν fail
ἀπόφανσις statement; proposition
ἀποφαντικός λόγος proposition
ἀπόφασις denial
ἅπτεσθαι touch
ἀρετή virtue
ἀριθμητική arithmetic
ἀριθμός number; Number
ἁρμονία harmony
ἁρμονική harmonics
ἄρτιον *Even*
ἄρτιος even (of a number)
ἀρχή principle, beginning, source, starting-point
ἀρχιτεκτονική master-art
ἀρχιτέκτων master-artist
ἀστρολογία astronony
ἀσύμβλητος noncomparable
ἄτομος indivisible, without parts; ei-

ther an individual or an ultimate
species

ἄτοπος absurd

αὔξησις increase

αὐτόματον chance; *chance*

ἀφαίρεσις abstraction

ἀφή contact, touch

βάθος depth

βαθύ deep; *Deep*

βάρος weight

βαρύς heavy

βεβαιότης certainty

βία force, violence; persuasion

βίαιον compulsory

βλαβερός harmful

βούλευσις deliberation

βουλή deliberation

βούλησις wish

βραχύ short; *Short*

γάρ for; conj.

γένεσις generation

γένος genus; race

γεωδαισία geodesy

γεωμετρία geometry

γῆ earth; Earth; *Earth*

γίγνεσθαι be generated, become,
come to be

γνωρίζειν know

γνῶσις knowledge

γραμμή line

δεικνύναι show, exhibit

δῆλον clearly

διά because, through

διὰ τί, τό *why* (n.)

διάγραμμα geometrical demonstration

διαγωγή *activity*

διάθεσις disposition

διαθιγή *Arrangement*

διαίρεσις division; distinction

διακόσμησις arrangement

διακρίνειν separate

διαλεκτική dialectics

διαλεκτικός dialectical; dialectician

διανοεῖν *think*

διάνοια *thought*

διαπορεῖν discuss or go over the *difficulties*

διάστημα interval; *Interval*

διαφέρειν differ; be superior to

διαφορά difference; differentia

διάφορος different

διδάσκειν   teach

διεξέρχομαι traverse

δίεσις quarter-tone

δικαιοσύνη justice

διορίζειν describe, specify

διότι, τό cause of a fact or of a truth

δόγμα view, supposition

δοκεῖν seem, be thought

δόξα opinion; doctrine

δοῦλος slave

δυάς two, dyad; Two, Dyad; *Dyad;*
'Dyad'

δυνάμει potential, potentially

δύνασθαι can, be able, be capable

δύναμις capacity, capability; potentiality, potency, power

δύο two

δυνατός capable, potential, possible

δυσκολία difficulty, objection

δυστυχής unfortunate

δυστυχία misfortune

δυσχέρεια difficulty, objection

ἔθος custom, practice, habit through
practice

εἰδέναι understand

εἰδηκός formal

εἶδος kind; species; form; Form

εἰκός probability

εἰκών copy; portrait

εἶναι to be, to exist

ἐκ from, by, after

καθ᾽ ἕκαστον individual (n.)

ἐκμαγεῖον plastic material

ἔλεγχος refutation

ἐλεύθερος free

ἔλλειψις deficiency; *Deficiency*

ἐμπειρία experience

ἕν one, oneness, unity; unit, measure; the *One, Unity, Oneness*

ἐναντίος contrary

ἐναντιότης contrariety
ἐναντίωσις contrariety; contrast
ἐνδέχεσθαι may; it is possible
ἔνδοξος common opinion, accepted opinion, commonly or generally accepted or admitted
ἐνεῖναι be present in
ἕνεκα for the sake of, for the purpose of
οὗ ἕνεκα final cause, purpose
ἐνέργεια *actuality*, activity
ἐνεργεῖν be active, be in activity
ἐννόημα notion
ἐντελέχεια actuality
ἐνυπάρχειν be in, exist in, be present in
ἐνυπάρχον constituent
ἑξῆς succession
ἕξις habit, having
ἐπαγωγή induction
ἐπα·ί·ειν comprehend
ἐπιθυμία *desire*
ἐπίπεδον plane (n.); surface
ἐπίσταμαι *know*
ἐπιστήμη *knowledge*, science
ἐπιστητόν *knowable; known*
ἐπιτάττειν set the ordering
ἐπιτυχεῖν succeed in
ἐπιφάνεια surface
ἔργον operation, function, performance
ἔρος love; *Love*
ἕτερος other, distinct
εὖ goodness, wellbeing
εὐδαιμονία happiness
εὐεξία good physical condition
εὔλογος reasonable
εὐτυχής fortunate
εὐτυχία good fortune
εὐφυῶς with natural ease
ἐφεξῆς succession
ἔχειν have, possess, hold
ἐχόμενος contiguous
ζῆν live
ζητεῖν seek, inquire
ζήτησις inquiry

ζωή life
ζῶον animal, living being
ᾗ qua, insofar as, inasmuch as
ἡγεμονικότατος highest in rank
ἡδονή pleasure
ἦθος moral habit
ἠρεμία rest
θαυμάζειν wonder; admire
θεῖον divine; godlike
θεολόγος theologian
θεός god; God
θερμόν hot (n. or adj.); *Hot*
θέσις position; thesis
θεωρεῖν investigate, speculate, view, contemplate
θεωρητική theoretical
θεωρία investigation, speculation, contemplation, view
θιγεῖν apprehend
θίξις apprehension
ἰατρική medical science
ἰδέα outward appearance; Idea
ἴδιον property, peculiarity
ἴδιος proper, peculiar
ἰσότης equality
καθ' αὐτός essential; by itself; in itself
καθαρός pure
κάθαρσις purging
καθ' ἕκαστον individual
καθόλου universal; universally
καί and; or
καιρός right time, proper time, opportunity
κακία vice (vs. virtue)
κακός vicious (vs. virtuous)
καλός noble; beautiful
καλῶς nobly, well
κατά with respect to, according to, in virtue of, by virtue of
κατὰ φύσιν according to nature
κατάφασις affirmation
κατηγορία predication; predicate
κατηγορεῖσθαι be a predicate of, attribute
κατορθοῦν *succeed*
κενόν void

κίνησις   motion
κοινός   common
κολοβός   mutilated
κόσμος   arrangement; universe
κοῦφον   light
κρίνειν   *judge*
κρίσις   *judgment*
κύριος   important, authoritative, main, reliable, dominant
λέγεται κατά   said of, modify
λεπτός   fine (of particles)
λευκός   white; pale; light; grey-haired
λογίζεσθαι   judge (v.)
λογισμός   judgment
λογιστικόν   judging power
λόγος   theory, reason, argument, formula, discussion, discourse, expression; ratio
μαθήματα   mathematical sciences; mathematical objects; Mathematical Objects
μαθηματικά   mathematical objects; Mathematical Objects
μαθηματική   mathematics; mathematical
μαθητικός   teachable
μακρόν   long; *Long* (n.)
μάλλιστα   most, most of all, in the highest degree
ὅτι μάλιστα   however true, however much, as much as it may be
μᾶλλον   more, rather, to a higher degree
μανθάνειν   learn
μανόν   rare; *Rare* (n.)
μαρτυρεῖν   confirm
μέγα   great; *Great* (n.)
μέγεθος   magnitude
μέθοδος   method, *inquiry* (systematic inquiry)
μέρος   part
μέσον   middle term
μετά   after
μεταβολή   change
μεταξύ   between, intermediate; Intermediate Objects
μετέχειν   share, participate

μέτρον   measure
μὴ ὄν   nonbeing; not-being
μῆκος   length; line
μῖγμα   blend; *Blend*
μίγνυμι   blend
μικρόν   small; *Small* (n.)
μίμημα   imitation (n.)
μίμησις   imitation (act of)
μίξις   blend; *Blend*
μνήμη   memory
μονάς   unit; Unit
μόριον   part
μορφή   *form, shape*
νεῖκος   strife; *Strife*
νοεῖν   think, conceive of
νόημα   concept
νόησις   thinking
νοητός   intelligible
νοῦς   intellect; Intellect; *Intelligence*
ὄγκος   volume, mass
ὅθεν   source, that from which
ὅθεν ἡ ἀρχή   source
ὅθεν ἡ κίνησις   source of motion
οἴεσθαι   consider, regard, think that
οἰκεῖος   *proper*, pertinent
ὀλίγα, ὀλίγον   few, little
ὅλος   whole
ὅλως   in general, generally, universally
ὁμοειδής   the same or alike in species or in kind
ὁμοιομερής   homogeneous
ὅμοιος   similar, like
ὁμολογούμενος   consistent, in agreement with, commonly agreed
ὁμώνυμος   equivocal; having the same name
ὄν   being, thing; *Being*
ὄνομα   name; expression
ὅπερ   just, essentially, fully, full
ὀπτική   optics
ὀρέγεσθαι   desire (v.)
ὄρεξις   desire (n.)
ὀρεκτικόν   desiring part (of soul)
ὀρθός   right
ὁρίζειν   limit, specify
ὁρισμός   definition

ὁρμή   tendency
ὅρος   definition; boundary
ὅτι, τό   fact
οὗ ἕνεκα   final cause, purpose, that for the sake of which
οὐκ ὄν   nonbeing; not-being; *Nonbeing*
οὐρανός   heaven
οὐσία   substance; *substance*
πάθημα   changing affection or attribute
πάθος   affection; *attribute*
πᾶν, τό   universe
παράδειγμα   pattern
παραλογίζομαι   conclude falsely
παραλογισμός   paralogism
παρεῖναι   be present in
παροιμία   proverb
πᾶς   all, every, total
πάσχειν   be acted upon, be affected
πεπερασμένον   finite, limited; *Finite* (n.), *Limited*
πέπτειν   transform
πέρας   limit; boundary; *Limit*
περιττόν   *Odd*
περιττός   odd (of a number); intellectually eminent
πέψις   concoction
πίστις   conviction
πλασματῶδες   ficticious
πλάτος   width
πλατύ   wide; *Wide* (n.)
πλῆθος   plurality, many; *Plurality*
πλῆρες   full; *Full* (n.)
ποιεῖν   act, produce, make; posit
ποίησις   action, making, production
ποιητικός   productive
ποιόν   quality
ποιότης   quality
πολλά   many, plurality
πολλαχῇ   in many ways
ποσόν   quantity
ποτέ   whenness
ποῦ   whereness, somewhere, in a place
πρᾶγμα   thing, fact; alleged fact
πραγματεία   system

πρακτικός   practical
πρᾶξις   *action*, doing; action (sometimes)
πράττειν   *act*, do
προαιρέω   *choose*
προαίρεσις   *choice*
πρός τι   relation, relative (n.)
πρότασις   premise
πρότερος   prior, remote, earlier
πρῶτος   first, primary
πυκνόν   dense; *Dense* (n.)
πῦρ   fire; *Fire*
πως   in some sense
ῥάδιος   easy
ῥαστώνη   comfort
ῥυσμός   *Contour*
σαφής   *clear*
σημαίνειν   signify, mean
σημεῖον   sign; point
σκοπός   aim
σοφία   wisdom
σοφιστής   sophist
σοφιστική   sophistry
σπέρμα   seed
στενόν   narrow; *Narrow* (n.)
στερεόν   solid; body (occasionally); *Solid*
στέρησις   privation
στιγμή   point
στοιχεῖον   element; letter
συγγενής   of the same rank or genus; innate
συλλογίζεσθαι   prove
συλλογισμός   syllogism
συμβεβηκός   accident; attribute
συμβλητός   comparable
συμπέρασμα   conclusion
συμπεραίνεσθαι   conclude
σύμφυσις   a growing together
σύμφυτος   innate
συναίτιον   joint cause
συνεχής   continuous
συνιέναι   *understand*
συνίστημι   consist of
σύνολον   *composite* (n.)
σχῆμα   shape, figure
σχολή   leisure

σῶμα body; solid
σωματικός corporeal
τάξις order
ταπεινόν shallow; *Shallow* (n.)
ταὐτός same
τεκμήριον sure sign
τεκτονική carpentry
τέλειος complete, perfect
τέλος end
τέχνη art
τὶ ἔστι whatness
τὶ ἦν εἶναι essence
τιθέναι posit
τιμή honor
τόδε τι a *this*
τοιόνδε suchness
τόπος place
τροπή *Turning*
τύχη luck
ὑγίεια health
ὕδωρ water; *Water*
ὕλη matter, materials
ὑπάρχειν belong, be present in; exist
ὑπεροχή excess; *Excess*
ὑπό by; from
ὑπόθεσις hypothesis, assumption
ὑποκείμενον subject, underlying subject
ὑποκεῖσθαι underlie
ὑπολαμβάνειν believe
ὑπόληψις belief
ὕστερος posterior, after
φαίνεσθαι appear
φανερός evident
φαντασία imagination, appearance

φάσις assertion
φαῦλος base
φέρειν carry
φθαρτός destructible
φθίνω decrease, v.
φθίσις decrease, n.
φθορά destruction
φιλία friendship; *Friendship*
φιλοσοφία philosophy
φορά locomotion; carrying
φρόνησις prudence
φρόνιμος prudent
φύεσθαι grow
φύσει by nature
φυσική physics
φυσικός physical, natural; physicist
φυσιολόγος natural philosopher
φύσις nature
χαλεπός difficult
χρεία need
χρήσιμος useful, instrumental
χρῆσις use
χρόνος time
χωρίς apart
χωρισμένος separate
χωριστός separable; separate
ψεύδεσθαι speak falsely
ψεῦδος falsity
ψόφος sound
ψυχή soul
ψυχρόν *Cold*
ψυχρός cold
ὡρισμένος definite
ὡς ἐπὶ τό πολύ most, for the most part

accident:
  A of B, two senses, 62
  cause of, 105
  definition, 100-101
  generable without process of generation, 106
  nature of, 104-106, 187
  no definite cause of, 106, 188
  no generation or destruction of, 104
  no science of, 104, 187
according to: *see* in virtue of
accuracy:
  definition, 14
  not always desirable, 38
accurate: prior in formula and simpler, 217
action:
  as complete and an end in itself, 152-53
  definition, 152-53
activity: as end in itself, 13
actuality:
  and actuality, 149, 155
  good, better than potentiality, 157
  one by analogy, 151-52
  prior to potentiality, 154-57
  superior to potentiality, 156
  taught by induction, 151-52
  vs. motion or generation, 152-53, 155-56
  whatness of, 151-52
adhere by nature: definition, 77
affection: senses, 94-95
Air: see Anaximenes, Diogenes
Alcmaion: principles, as contraries, 21
all: definition, 98
alteration: definition, 198
analogy: in each category, 249

analytics: no education in, 58, 59
Anaxagoras:
  actuality, prior, 203
  all are together, 62, 65
  Blend, as principle, criticism, 27-78, 71, 198
  everything is false, 71, 185
  excluded middle exists, 71, 185
  good, assigned to first principle, 244
  Intelligence: 27
    cause of order, 18
    good as mover, 211
    used artificially, 19
  principles, infinite and homogeneous, 17
  things are as believed, 66
Anaximander: *Blend,* 198
Anaximenes:
  Air, a material principle, 17
  causes, formal, *Dense* and *Rare,* 20
angle:
  acute, definition, 123
  right, prior in definition to acute, 230
animal: sensation, a property, 12
Antisthenes:
  every statement is true, 100
  whatness, indefinable, 141
apart: definition, 195
appearance: not sensation, 67
Archytas: substance, as matter and form, 139
Aristippus: contemptuous of mathematics, 41
Aristotle:
  credits predecessors, 16, 35
  realist, 68

arithmetic: subject of, 207
art:
cause included, 13
found and lost many times, 209
generation by, with thinking and making, 117
kinds, 147
moving principle, 147
primarily of one contrary, 147-48
same as contraries, 147-48
universal presupposed, 12, 13
astronomy:
of mathematical sciences, closest to philosophy, 207
subject, 44
attribute:
A of B, not infinite upwards, 62
A of B, two senses, 62
definition, 100
formula of, has that of substance, 108-109, 146
immovable, 193
attribute: usage, 201
axiom:
of being, by the philosopher, 58
of being, most certain, 58-59
of being, necessary for understanding, 58
of being, not a hypothesis, 58
of being, principle of all other axioms, 59
of mathematics, by the mathematician, 181
of mathematics, by the philosopher, 181
of physics, by the physicist, 181

badness: not separate from things, 157
bee: hearing, deprived of, 12
beginning: *see* principle
being:
accidental, cause of, 105
accidental, no definite cause of, 106, 188
accidental, no science of, 104, 187
actual, 83
as truth, 82, 106-107, 158
axioms of, by philosopher, 58
by attribution, 82
cause of truth, 158
changeable, imitates the indestructible, 157
clearer to us, close to nonbeing, 111
contrariety in, 180
convertible with unity, 55, 180
distinct in essence from unity, 55
does not add to unity, 164
essential, 82
eternal, not bad or in error, 157
eternal, not out of elements, 238-39
from not-being, 65, 183

incomposite, 159
independent of sensation, 68
indestructible, not potential, 156
kinds, 55
known to us, close to nonbeing, 111
main sense, 107
necessary, for the most part, accidental, 105
necessary, not potential, 156
not a genus, 45, 177
not an element, 200
not a substance, 133-34
not equivocal, 54-55
not from nonbeing, 65, 183
potential, 83
potential, conditions for actual, 153-54
potential, destructible, 156
senses, 104, 108, 239
senses, related, 54-55, 179-80
simple, truth or falsity of, 159
whether a substance, 49-51
beings: all in motion or immovable, criticism, 72
between: definition, 195
blend: not of attributes, 27
Blend: criticism, 27-28, 62, 65
body:
definition, 81, 89
finite, has finite power, 206
formula of, 191
has potentially any figure, 51
heavenly, eternal, not potential, 156
by nature: definition, 77

Callippus: spheres, number of, 207-208
capable: senses, 87-88
category:
has no matter, 144
immediately a unity and a being, 144
indefinable, 76, 144
list of, 82, 194
cause:
actual, simultaneous with effect, 76
analogous, 200, 202
coextensive with principle, 55
convertible with principle, 73, 200-201
distinct in essence from principle, 55
first, eternal, 103
investigation, whether by one science, 41-42
joint, 78
list, 16
modes of, 75-76
not a *substance,* 133-34
not contrary, 41
potential, not always simultaneous with effect, 76

primary, indestructible, 37
primary, necessary, 36-38
proximate should be given, 142
senses of, 74-76
chance: in work of art, 117-18
change:
  as many as categories, 189
  kinds, 193
  not of change, 194-95
  principles of, three, 197-98
  senses, 192-93
circle: same as its essence, 124
Collection of Contraries: 55
complete:
  a species of "extreme", 92
  senses, 92-93
composite:
  cause of unity of, 143-45
  definition, 179, 216
  usage, 46, 47
comprehend: causes included, 13
compulsory: 78
contiguous: definition, 196
continuous:
  definition, 196
  not out of indivisibles, 212, 216
contradiction:
  definition, 171
  primary opposition, 167
  principle of, 58-59, 182
  principle of, by philosopher, 58
  principle of, if denied, all are one, 62
contraries:
  as principles, by all predecessors, 57
  Collection of, 55
  not in same thing, 70
  not simultaneous, 185
  primary, not affected, 27
contrary:
  analogous, 85
  definition, 166-67, 173
  discussion, 166-68
  has only one contrary, 166
  primary, a privation, 167-68
  secondarily used, 85
  senses, 85, 166-67
  under same genus or category, 173
  with respect to place, definition, 195
conviction: by argument, sometimes useless, 65, 185, 233
Cratylus: speech falsifies fact, 67
custom: strong, 38

decrease: definition, 198
definition:
  a number, in a sense, 141
  cause of unity in, 143-45

has unity, 141
matter and form in, 144
not infinite, 37
not of a sensible individual, 131-32
of a thing, unique, 45
of necessary only, 131-32
parts in, 128
parts of, in relation to parts of thing, 121-24
parts, only differentiae, 128
primarily of substances, 113
principle of syllogism, 219
unity in, cause, 127-29
universal and of the form, 125
Democritus:
  Blend, 65, 198
  causes, formal, *Shape, Order, Position,* 20
  causes, material, *Full* and *Void, Being* and *Nonbeing,* 20
  definition, lightly touched, 218-19
  Full and *Void,* 65
  matter, one kind only, 138
  one, not actually many, 130
  substance, as indivisible magnitude, 130
  truth is nonexistent or inscrutable, 66
demonstration:
  by refutation, 59, 182-83
  impossible of all, 59
  not of a sensible individual, 131-32
  of necessary only, 131-32
denial: not a predicate of matter, 110
depth: definition, 89
desirable: as an immovable mover, 204
desire: of the apparent noble, 204
destructibility: a necessary attribute, 174-75
destructible: distinct in genus from inde-structible, 174-75
destruction: definition, 193, 198
dialectics:
  aim, 57
  appears to be philosophy, 57
  nonexistent before Plato, 24
  possible without definition, 219
  subject, 40, 57, 181
difference: 165-66
  attribute of, 165-66
  species of, 84
different: senses, 84
differentia:
  a principle, 45
  as quality, 89-90
  definition, 172-73
difficulty: in things or in us, 35
Diogenes:
  Air, a material principle, 17
  causes, formal, *Dense* and *Rare,* 20

disposition: senses of, 94
distinct: *see* other
divine: implies honorable, 16
doctor: cures only the potentially healthy, 153
doctrines: one-sided, criticism, 71-72, 185
Dyad:
    generated first, 231
    not as universal as Number, 237
    units of, by equalization of *Unequals*, 224, 228
Dyad:
    an attribute, criticism, 237-38
    function, to double, 225, 227, 229

Earth: a material principle for Empedocles, Parmenides, 17, 22
eclipse: cause of, 142
education: in analytics, lack of, 58, 59
effect: not infinite, 36-37
Egypt: first in mathematical arts, 13-14
element:
    analogous, 200, 202
    by analogy, three, 200-201
    definition, 76
    not a *substance*, 133-34
    not same as principle, 200-201
    not same for all beings, 200
    senses, 76
    senses, not distinguished by others, 33
    whether a genus or a constituent, 44-46
    whether existing potentially, 53
Empedocles:
    actuality, prior, 203
    Blend, 198
    causes, material, used as only two, 20
    causes, moving, *Friendship* and *Strife,* 19
    causes, moving, used inconsistently, 19-20
    essence as ratio, 34
    four material principles, 17
    Friendship and *Strife,* criticism, 48-49
    Friendship, good, as matter and as mover, 211
    God, not wisest, 48
    good, assigned to first principle, 244
    knowledge changes with habits of men, 66
    nature, only as form, 77
    One, as *Friendship,* 50
    principles, material, four elements, criticism, 27
    Strife, indestructible, 211
Epicharmus: false principle yields false conclusions, 233
equal:
    contradictory of, 167

definition, 91
how opposed to greater and less, 168-69
essence:
    as form only, 140
    as one, 55, 133, 143-44
    formula of, a definition, 112
    formula of, logical, 111
    if generable or destructible, not in process, 140
    in the soul, 117
    no generation or destruction of, 131-32
    of a composite, 113-14
    primarily of substances, 113
    same as things, 114-16
essentially: senses of, 89
eternal:
    matter in, qualified, 198
    not bad or in error, 157
    not out of elements, 238-39
    principle of truth, 184
    ungenerable, 243
Eudoxus:
    Ideas, in things, 30, 220-21
    spheres, number of, 207
Eurytus: numbers, causes as point boundaries of things, 246-47
every: definition, 98
excess: usage, 138, 139
Excess: more universal than *Great* or *Plurality,* 237
excess and deficiency: within quantity, 90-91
excluded middle: principle of, 70-71
existence:
    primary and secondary, 112
    unqualified and qualified, 112
experience:
    definition, 12
    generation of, 12
    in *action,* sometimes better than art, 13
    knowledge of fact, 13
    knowledge of the individual, 13
expression: should correspond to facts, 112

facts: lead men to truth, 18
false:
    as nonbeing, 99-100, 159
    definition, 70
    in geometry, not in premises, 240
    not same as impossible, 150
    senses, 99-100
female: same in species as male, 173-74
few: definition, 169-70
fictitious: definition, 226
figure: any, potentially in a body, 51
final cause:
    destroyed by infinity, 37

in immovables, 204-205
not caused by chance, 18
primary, necessary, 36
two kinds, 204-205
finger:
    definition of, 123
    equivocal if dead, 123-24
Fire: see Heraclitus, Hippasus, Parmenides
flash: not part of form of a man, 125
for the most part: cause of accident, 105
force: definition, 78
form:
    a *this*, 199
    as cause, primary, necessary, 36
    if generable or destructible, not in proc-
        ess, 140-41
    immovable, 193
    no generation of, 119, 199
    not more or less, 141
    whether separate, 46-48
    without matter, only of one thing, 208
Form: not a moving cause, 203
formal cause: primary, necessary, 36
formula: false, 100
Four: generation of, 225
free: definition, 15
from:
    in generation, 118
    senses, 96-97

general: better than order in army, 210
generation:
    and destruction, ultimate moving causes
        of, 203-204
    by art, with thinking and making, 117
    by chance as by art, 120-21
    definition, 193, 198
    discussion, 116-20
    kinds, 116
    not from nonbeing, 65, 183
    of a *composite* only, 138
genus:
    as a measure, 237
    as matter, 128
    definition, 172
    not a predicate of a differentia, 45
    range, 128
    senses, 99
    subdivision, method of, 128
geodesy: subject of, 44
geometrical demonstration: 76
    elements of, 45
geometry:
    subject, not of contraries or of being, 57
    subject of, 180-81, 207
God:
    activity of, 209-10

discussion of, 209-10
good:
    in universe, 210-12
    not same as noble, 218
good fortune: definition, 188
grammar:
    a science, 55
    subject of, 55
great:
    and small, proper to magnitudes, 236-37,
        238
    metaphorically used, 89
Great and *Small:* forced to do the impos-
    sible, 243

habit: senses, 94
harmonics: subject of, 217
have: senses of, 95-96
having: *see* habit
healthy: senses, related, 54, 180
heat: moving principle, 147
heaven: one only, 208
Heraclitus:
    all can become fire, 191
    everything is and is not, 71, 185
    everything is true, 71, 185
    extreme doctrine of, 67, 185
    Fire, a material principle, 17
    vs. principle of contradiction, 59, 182-83,
        185
Hermes:
    statue of, by Pauson, 155
    statue of, potentially in stone, 51
Hermotimus: *Intelligence,* cause of order,
    18
Hesiod:
    Chaos, first principle, 19
    final and moving causes, 19
    Love, a moving principle, 19
    principles, gods, 48
Hippasus: *Fire,* a material principle, 17
Hippias: a *knowing* man is both true and
    false, 100
Hippo: shallow in thought, 17
hope: cause of pleasure of, 205
house:
    causes of, 41
    form, inseparable, 47, 140-41, 179, 199
    form of, a qualified substance, 139
    form of, perhaps not a substance, 140-41

Idea:
    as universal, not a substance, 134
    definition of, criticism, 130-31, 132-33
    distinct in genus from thing, so non-
        existent, 175
    not a moving cause, 199, 203

Idea—*Cont.*
  out of Ideas, 226
  useless in generation of a form in a *composite,* 119-20
Ideas:
  as individuals, *unknowable,* 234-35
  as Numbers, criticism, 223-27, 228-33
  badness, assigned to *Unequal,* criticism, 245
  good, criticism, 245
  not sharing in sensibles, 115
  possible reason for being posited, 52-53
identity: principle of, 134
ignorance: of simple being, 159
immaterial: as just being, 145
immovable: senses of, 195
impossible: definition, 88
in: senses of, 96
in virtue of: senses of, 93-94
incapability: senses of, 88
incapable: senses of, 88
increase: definition, 198
indefinable: has no matter, 144
indestructibility: a necessary attribute, 174-75
individual: indefinable, 132-33
indivisible: senses of, 46
infinite:
  essence of, finite, 37
  not one nature, 192
  potential only, 152
  senses of, 190
intellect:
  active, separable, 199
  cause of desire, 204
  prior to chance, 188
Intellect:
  activity of, 209-10
  discussion of, 209-10
Intelligence:
  cause of order, 18
  prior to chance, 188
  see also, Anaxagoras
intelligible: as an immovable mover, 204
intermediate:
  definition, 171, 195
  out of contraries, 171-72
  see also between
Intermediate Objects:
  criticism, 44
  in sensibles, 44
interval:
  from A to B, not from B to A, 190
  from one to two, 190

joint cause: example, 78

know: potentially or actually, 83
knowledge:
  generation of, 12
  highest, of eternal, 36
  not a measure of things, 162-63
  not innate, 33
  of a thing, through definition, 45
  through form, 67
knowledge:
  best, abstract, 217-18
  causal, 35-36
  for the sake of understanding, 15
  highest, of eternal, 36
  measured rather than measure, 170
  of essence, 115
  of whatness better than of attribute, 41-42
  same as *known* object, sometimes, 210

language: must correspond to facts, 112
laws: through custom, childish, 38
learning:
  definition, 12
  from what is clearer to us, 111
  how best, 73
  how possible, 155
length: definition, 89
Leucippus:
  causes, formal, *Shape, Order, Position,* 20, 138
  causes, material, *Full* and *Void, Being* and *Nonbeing,* 20
  motion, eternal, 203
  motion, prior, 203
like:
  definition, 91
  senses of, 84, 165
limit:
  a genus of "principle", 93
  a species of "extreme", 93
  of magnitude, as substance, criticism, 242
  senses of, 93
line:
  as section or division or limit, 179
  definition, 81, 89
  division or limit of a surface, 51-52
  not out of points, 50
  sensible, not straight, 44
  straight, not ultimate species, 165
  ultimate species of, 165
Line: defined as Two, criticism, 125
locomotion:
  definition, 198
  prior to other changes, 138
  the only eternal motion, 202

luck:
  an accidental cause, 188
  good, definition, 188
Lycophron: communion as cause of unity,
  144

Magi: good, assigned to first principle, 244
magnitude:
  abstracted from sensibles, 180-81
  definition, 89
  inseparable, 179
  not from indivisibles, 212, 216
  one, primarily, 160
man:
  causes of, 142
  definition, with matter, 126
  free, necessarily ordered, 210
  moving causes of, 201
manual worker:
  acts through practice, 13
  knows no causes, 13
many:
  of one species, have matter, 208
  primarily, 81
  senses of, 82
mathematical arts: first in Egypt, 13-14
mathematical objects:
  exist materially, 218
  immovable, 28
  inseparable, 214-16
  not with sensibles, 214
  separable in thought, 216-18
  universal, not separate, 215, 216
  whether substances, 51-52
Mathematical Objects: same as Intermediate Objects
mathematician: always demands accuracy,
  38
mathematics:
  a theoretical science, 103
  as philosophy, 103
  deals with the good and the noble, 218
  final cause in, 218
  no final cause in, 41
  part of philosophy, 182
  parts of, ordered, as in philosophy, 55
  subject, 180-81
  subject, immovable, 186
  subject, inseparable, 186
  subject, some qua immovable, 103
  universal, 187
  universal, like philosophy, 103
matter:
  as potentiality, 147
  changes, with respect to something, 198,
    199
  definition, 110

first, as separate, 153
in each genus, 241
in eternals, qualified, 198
intelligible, 124, 144
many kinds, 198
not a moving cause, 18, 203
not a *this*, 137
prime, necessary, 36
prime, not a moving principle, 147
prime, ungenerable, 47, 199
prime, whether unique, 141-42
privation not an attribute of, 110
proximate, middle, ultimate, 141-42
relation to contraries, 143
relation to generation and destruction,
  143
sensible, 124, 144
unknowable, 124
with respect to place only, 138, 142
meaning: *see* significance
measure:
  definition, 161
  in all categories, 161
  in magnitudes, 161-62
  numerically many, 162
mechanics: subject of, 217
medical: senses, related, 54, 180
Megarians: potency and actuality the same,
  criticism, 148-49
Melissus:
  immature, 22
  principle, only one, material, immovable,
    infinite, 22
memory:
  cause of prudence, 12
  pleasure in, cause of, 205
misfortune: definition, 188
mistake: definition, 159
moment:
  destructible, but not in time, 52
  division or limit of time, 52
  generable, but not in time, 52
motion:
  as many as categories, 189
  definition, 189
  eternal, 202
  eternal, not potential, 156
  eternal, only locomotion, 202
  even, 162
  kinds, 194
  not infinite, 47
  not of motion, 194-95
  ungenerable, 202
  vs. *actuality*, 152-53
mover:
  immovable, discussion, 202-206
  immovable, many, 206-208
  senses of, 193

mover—*Cont.*
  same in species, in a sense, as in thing
    moved, 120, 154-55
mover, prime:
  activity of, 205, 209-10
  an *actuality*, 203
  has no parts, 206
  immovable, 72
  immovable, essentially and attributively,
    206
  moves all, 201
  only one, 208
  separate from sensibles, 206
moving cause:
  primary, necessary, 36
  prior or simultaneous, 199
  same in name, 199
moving principle: immovable, 147
much:
  and little, proper to numbers, 238
  definition, 169-70
multiplication: meaning, 247
mutilated: definition, 98-99

nature:
  a moving principle in the thing itself, 154
  as substance, 77-78
  prior to chance, 188
  senses, 77-78
necessary:
  definition, 78
  meaning, 61
  senses of, 78-79
  simple, 79
nectar: and gods, 48
noble:
  kinds, 218
  not caused by chance, 18
  not same as good, 218
nonbeing:
  a being, in a sense, 55
  as *desirable*, 149
  as falsity, 82-83
  as thinkable, 149
  cannot become being, 65, 183
  exists qualifiedly, as nonbeing, 112
  sameness and otherness not attributes of,
    165
  senses of, 198, 239-40
number:
  a substance only like a definition, 141
  definition, 89
  essential attributes, 56-57
  has unity, 130, 141
  not the *substance* of things, 247-48
  of substance, not a unity, 225-26
  unit of, comparable, 223, 224

Number:
  a substance only like a definition, 141
  as form of a thing, criticism, 125
  generation, criticism, 246
  not cause of good, 247
numbering: two kinds, 227

Oceanus: father of generation, 17
one:
  according to first *substance*, 165
  as a measure, 161
  as a measure of genera, 237
  as a mere predicate, 163
  as measure, a nature underlying it, 237
  as same or equal or like, 91
  by analogy, 81
  by attribution, 79
  by continuity, 79-80
  by continuity, if a whole, 81
  contrariety in, 180
  contrary of plurality, 164
  convertible with being, 55, 163, 164, 180
  distinct in essence from being, 55
  does not add to being, 164
  essence of, 161
  essence of, as principle of number, 81
  essentially, 79-82
  in formula, 80
  in genus, 80, 81
  in kind, 81
  in kind of subject, 80
  in thought, 80
  kinds, 55, 164
  not a genus, 45, 177
  not a nature in itself, 163-64
  not a number, 237
  not a relation, 200
  not a single nature, 81
  not a substance, 200
  not a *substance*, 133-4
  not an element, 200
  not generable, 179
  not same as simple, 204
  numerically, 81, 165
  numerically, definition, 47
  only if a whole, 81
  opposed to many as measure, 170
  opposed to plurality, 56
  primarily, 81
  qua undivided, 80-81
  secondarily, 81
  senses of, 79-82, 113, 160
  underlying nature of, 163-64
  whether a substance, 49-51
One:
  as the immovable universe, 18
  Other, as a contrary, 237

see also Empedocles, Parmenides, Plato,
    Pythagoreans, Xenophanes
one-sided doctrines: criticism, 71-72, 185
opinion:
    definition, 158-59
    of what may or may not be, 132
opposite: senses of, 84-85
opposites: by one science, 56
optics: subject of, 217
order:
    cause, nonsensible, 212
    in universe, 210-12
other:
    analogously used, 85
    contrary of same, 165
    in species, definition, 172, 173
    in species or kind, 85
    only of being, 165
    opposite of same, 84
    senses of, 84, 165
other in genus: senses of, 99
Other and *One:* as contraries, 237
out of: *see* from

Parmenides:
    being, unique, 22, 48
    causes, two, 18
    knowledge, as physical disposition of
        body, 66
    Love, as final and moving cause, 19
    nonbeing, not existing, 22, 48
    One, as immovable, 18
    only being exists, 239
    principle, one only, formal, immovable,
        finite, 22
    principles, of sensibles, *Hot (Fire)* and
        Cold (Earth), 22
part:
    as measure, 97
    senses of, 97
participation: not clarified by Platonists,
    144
Pauson: statue of Hermes, 155
perfect: *see* complete
Pherecydes: good, assigned to first princi-
    ple, 244
philosophizing: starts in wonder, 15
philosophy:
    as mathematics by Platonists, 32-33
    as science of truth, 35
    first, also demonstrative, 137
    first, prior to physics and mathematics,
        103
    first, subject, eternal, immovable, sepa-
        rate, 103
    first, whether universal or of one nature,
        103-104

for relativists, chasing birds, 66
    free, 15
    investigates kinds of being, 55
    no contrary of, 211-12
    parts of, ordered, 55
    parts of, ordered, as in mathematics, 55
    subject, 54-57, 179-81, 186
    subject, separate and also universal, 187
    three in number, 55, 103
Phrynis: and Timotheus, 35
physics:
    a theoretical science, 102, 186
    as philosophy, 103
    as wisdom, 58
    definition in, with matter, 103, 186
    part of philosophy, 182
    second philosophy, 126
    subject, 102-103, 126, 181, 186
    subject, also corporeal soul, 103
    subject, mostly inseparable, 102-103
    whether first philosophy, 103-104
place: six kinds, 192
plane: definition, 81
Plato: 23-25, 218-27
    badness, assigned to *Unequals*, criticism,
        245
    being, as just substance, 49-50
    causes, only matter and whatness used,
        24
    definition, not of sensibles, 23
    definition, of Ideas only, 23
    Dyad, from equalizing the *Unequals*,
        223, 228, 244
    Dyad, generated first, 231
    Dyad, as *Great* and *Small*, 24
    Dyad, as one, 236
    Dyad, as one matter for many things,
        criticism, 24
    Dyad, function, to double, 225, 227,
        229
    Dyad, useful for easy generation of Num-
        bers, 24
    element, senses not distinguished, 33
    final cause, neglected, 32
    final cause, somewhat assigned to *One*
        and *Dyad*, 25
    form of things, the *One*, 24
    Forms, as causes of all others, 24
    Forms, as formal causes of things, 24
    Forms, as many as by nature, 199
    Forms, as Numbers, 24
    Forms, from *Great* and *Small*, share in
        One, 24
    fourth genus of things, 33
Great and *Small*, as matter, 24
    Ideas, as both patterns and copies, 30,
        221

Plato—*Cont.*
  Ideas, as causes of existence and generation, 31, 221
  Ideas, as Numbers, 233
  Ideas, as Numbers, criticism, 31-32
  Ideas, criticism, 29-34
  Ideas, exceed sensibles in kind, 29, 219
  Ideas, not of number, quantity, etc., 29, 219
  Ideas, not of relations, 29, 219
  Ideas, not of works of art, 31, 221
  Ideas, should be of substances only, 29-30, 220
  Ideas, universal and individual, 234
  indivisible lines, 32
  influenced by Cratylus, 23
  influenced by Heraclitus, 23, 218
  influenced by Pythagoreans, 23
  inquiry, dialectical, 24
  inquiry, logical, not of things themselves, 24
  Intermediate Objects, 24
  Intermediate Objects, generation of, criticism, 243
  Intermediate Objects, separate, criticism, 214-16
  Intermediate Objects, vs. Forms, 24
  Intermediate Objects, vs. sensibles, 24
  Itself, an Idea, 220
  Mathematical Objects, *see* Intermediate Objects
  matter of things, *Great* and *Small*, 24
  motion, eternal, 203
  moving causes, neglected, 32
  Numbers, apart from sensibles, 24
  Numbers, generation of, 229, 236
  Numbers, generation of, criticism, 246
  Numbers, noncomparable, 228
  Numbers, ten, more unified than Ten, 230
  Numbers, units in, criticism, 228-29
  One, a nature or substance, 163
  One, as both element and form, 230-31
  One, as formal cause of Forms, 24
  One, as just substance, 24, 49-50
  One, as *substance* of things, 40
  participation, a poetic metaphor, 30, 32, 221
  participation, not explained, 24
  Phaedo, Ideas as causes of existence and becoming, 31, 221
  philosophy, as mathematics, 32-33
  physics, discarded, 32-33
  point, a geometrical supposition, 32
  point, as an indivisible line, 32
  prior, in substance, 86
  sensibles, named after Ideas, 23
  sensibles, share in Forms, 23

  sophistry, subject, accidental being, 187
  sophistry, subject, nonbeing, 104
  soul, self-moving mover, generation of, 203
  substance, three kinds, 109
  third man, 29, 30, 130, 219
  Three, generation of, 228-29
  Two, from *Great* and *Small* when equalized, 223, 228, 244
  Unequal, as one, 236
  units, criticism, 228-29
  Unity, a nature or substance, 163
Platonists:
  eternal things, two genera, 222
  good, assigned to *One*, 244
  Great and *Small*, kinds, criticism, 32
  Ideas, ten or infinite, 206
  Magnitudes, generation of, criticism, 231-32
  Mathematical Magnitudes, 223
  Number, finite or infinite, criticism, 229-30
  quantity, prior to quality, 227
  substance, immovable, two kinds, 213
plurality:
  a genus-like of number, 170
  contrary of unity, 164
  definition, 89
  opposed to one, 56
  opposite of one, senses, 170-71
  prior in formula to unity, 164
  species of, 164-65
poets:
  good, later in generation, 244
  often lie, 15
point:
  as section or division or limit, 179
  definition, 81
  division or limit of line, 51-52
  not generable, 179
possible:
  definition, 149
  meaning, 150
  not eternal, 156
  senses of, 88
posterior:
  in generation, prior in *substance*, 155
  see also prior
potency: *see* potentiality
potentiality:
  conditions for actual being, 153-54
  in geometry, equivocals, 88, 146
  in soul, as mover, kinds, 150
  moving, kinds, 147
  nonrational, of one contrary only, 147, 150-51
  not of something eternal, 156

primary, definition, 88-89
range of, 146
rational, same of contraries, 147-48, 150-
    51
senses of, 87-89, 146-47, 151-52
power: *see* potentiality
predecessors:
    being, from nonbeing, by some, 211
    contributions of, 35
    principles, as contraries, criticism, 210-11,
        236-49
    principles, as essence, 25
    principles, as final cause, 25-26
    principles, as matter, 25
    principles, as movers, 25
predication: *substance* of matter, 110
premiss: as matter for conclusion, 75
principle:
    a species of "limit", 93
    analogous, 200
    as only material, inadequate, 26
    as only one physical element, inadequate,
        26-27
    convertible with cause, 55, 73, 200-201
    definition, 73
    distinct in essence from cause, 55
    first, good, 244-45
    not a *substance*, 133-34
    not same as element, 200-201
    not same for all being, 200
    primary, indestructible, 37
    senses of, 73-74
    whether a genus or a constituent, 44-46
principles:
    as distinct physical elements, impossible,
        27
    contraries, by all predecessors, 57
    demonstrative, definition, 42
    demonstrative, example, 42
    demonstrative, most universal, 42
    demonstrative, principles of all, 42
    demonstrative, whether by one science,
        42
    exist necessarily, 36-38
    of destructibles, whether destructible, 49
    of destructibles, whether the same as of
        indestructibles, 48-49
    of syllogism, *see* axioms of being
    whether universal or individual, 53
prior:
    definition, 85
    if in things, their genus is not separate,
        46
    in actuality, 86-87
    in formula, 216
    in formula, not necessarily in substance,
        216
    in nature, 86
    in substance, definition, 86, 216
    in substance, not necessarily in formula,
        216
    potentially, 86-87
    senses of, 85-87
privation:
    a possession in a sense, 88
    in a subject, 56
    most generic, unity and plurality, 168
    not a predicate of matter, 110
    senses of, 95, 147, 167-68
    wider than contrariety, 167-68
problems:
    discussion necessary, 39
    list, 39-40
    often difficult to state or discuss, 40
production:
    definition, 117
    kinds, 117
    moving cause, kinds, 102
Protagoras:
    all are one, 62
    all things are true and false, 64-65,
        183
    critic of geometry, 44
    man, a measure of things, 163
prudence: as *knowledge*, 15
Pythagoreans: 20-21
    best, not in principle, 205
    Counter-Earth, 21
    criticism of, 228
    definition, in terms of number, 219
    definition, predicable of many kinds, 23
    definitions, superficial, 23
    Even, as *Infinite*, 21
    generation from principles, 243
    heaven, a harmony and a number, 21
    imitation, not explained, 24
    imitation, of numbers, by things, 23-24
    number, as matter and attributes of
        things, 21
    number, elements of, 21
    number, insensibles, 242
    Odd, as *Finite*, 21
    One, as just substance, 24, 49-50
    One, from *Odd* and *Even*, 21
    One, *substance* of things, 40
    principles, as matter only, 21-22
    principles, as *Odd* and *Even*, 21
    principles, as substances, and of things,
        23
    principles, not physical, criticism, 28-29
    principles, ten contrarieties, 21
    sensibles, out of units, criticism, 242
    things, as numbers, 24
    things, from numbers only, 222-23

Pythagoreans—*Cont.*
  unit, has magnitude, 223
  unity, a nature or substance, 163

quality:
  prior to quantity, 197
  senses of, 89-90
quantities:
  destructible but not in time, 52
  generable but not in time, 52
  whether substances, 51-52
quantity:
  abstracted from sensibles, 180-81
  attributes of, metaphorically used, 89
  by attribution, 89
  definition, 89
  essential, 89
  more indefinite than quality, 184
quarter-tone: two kinds, 162

race: senses, 99
Rare: *see* Leucippus
realism: 68
refutation: either of thought or of expres-
    sion, 65
relation:
  cause of relative, 92
  definition, 91-92
  least a nature, 238
  no contrary of, 194
  no generation or destruction of, 238
  posterior to other categories, 238
  senses of, 90-92
  two kinds, 91-92
relativism: inconsistent, 69-70

same:
  a kind of oneness, 84, 91
  analogously used, 85
  by attribution, 83-84
  contrary of other, 165
  definition, 91
  essentially, 84
  in genus, 80
  in species, definition, 173
  in species or kind, 85
  senses of, 83-84, 165
science:
  about one genus, 55, 167
  accepts whatness by hypothesis or sen-
    sation, 186
  accurate, 14
  discovered and lost many times, 209
  indemonstrable, example, 45
  not of accident, 105
  of necessary or for the most part, 105, 187
  of things related to one nature, 55

potential and actual, 235
  practical, aims at *action*, 35
  practical, principle in doer, 186
  productive, principle in producer, 186
  the same for whatness and existence, 102
  theoretical, aims at truth, 35
  theoretical, preferable to others, 103
  theoretical, three genera, 103, 186
  two senses, 235
  universal, 235
seed:
  as a moving cause, 75
  not necessary for generation, 117, 121
semicircle: definition, 123
sensation:
  cause, moving, outside, 68
  knowledge of individual, 13
  lack of, cancels corresponding knowl-
    edge, 33-34
  not of sensation, 68
  of one genus, 55
  of proper object, true, 67
  posterior to its object, 68
  power of, authoritative in knowledge of
    individuals, 13
  property of animal, 12
sensibles: of indefinite nature, 66
sight:
  causes knowledge most, 12
  of powers of sensation, liked most, 12
significance:
  prior to syllogism, 59-60, 182
  uniqueness of, 60, 182
similar: *see* like
Simonides: "long rigmarole", 243
simple: not same as one, 204
sleep: causes of, 142-43
Socrates:
  definitions, 23, 218-19
  definitions and induction, 219
  ethical matters, but not nature, 23, 218-
    19
  universals, 23, 218-19
  universals, not separate from sensibles,
    219, 234
Solid: *see* Leucippus
sophistry:
  aim, 57
  appears to be philosophy, 57
  subject, 181
  subject, accidental being, 104, 187
  subject, being, 57
soul:
  corporeal, by physics, 103
  same as its essence, 124
source: *see* principle
species: not a predicate of its differentia, 45

speed: two senses, 161
Speusippus: 232-33
  best, not in principle, 205
  eternal objects, only Mathematical Objects, 222, 223, 227-28
  good, not in principles, 245, 246
  Interval, as matter, criticism, 233
  Numbers, generation of, 236
  Numbers, generation of, criticism, 246
  Numbers, useless for sensibles, 241
  place, generated simultaneously with Mathematical Objects, 246
  Plurality, as matter, criticism, 232
  Point, as form, criticism, 233
  principles, many, criticism, 212
  principles, unrelated, criticism, 242-43
  sensibles, no science of, 242
  substance, immovable, Mathematical Objects only, 213
  substance, kinds, 109
spheres: number of, 208
square: ultimate species of, 165
squaring: definition, 42
starting-point: *see* principle
statements:
  all true, all false, criticism, 71-72
  manner of, should conform to fact, 112
  self-refuting, criticism, 72
Styx: as *Water,* a principle, 17
subject:
  as a *this* or separate, 153
  definition, 110
  kinds, 110, 129
  not a moving cause, 18
substance:
  as potentiality or matter, 133
  eternal, changeable in place or quality, 156
  kinds, 109
  no contrary of, 194, 236
  prior in time, formula, knowledge, 108-109, 146
  senses of, 83, 110, 137
  whether by one science, 42-43
  whether only sensible, 43-44
substance:
  analogous, 139
  as nature, 77-78
  cause of unity and being of a *composite,* 134-36
  first, 165
  if generable or destructible, not in process, 140
  not a separate substance, 163
  not an element as matter, 135-36
  not apart from thing, 31
  only of things by nature, 140-41

  parts of, no order, 128-29
succession: definition, 195-96
Sun: changeable in place or quality, 156
surface:
  as section or division or limit, 179
  definition, 89
  division or limit of a body, 51-52
syllogism: principles of, *see* axioms of being

teacher: aim of, 155
teaching: requires understanding, 13, 14-15
ten: a complete number, 21
Tethys: father of generation, 17
Thales: *Water,* as a material principle, 17
that in virtue of: as separate, 94
theologians:
  generate things from *Night,* 203, 204
  good, by some, later in generation, 244
theorem:
  about triangles, discovery of, 157-58
  geometrical, discovery by *actuality,* 157-58
thinking: cause of desire, 204
third man: 29, 30, 130, 219
this: 83
  as a category, 189
thought: not of simples or whatness, 107
time:
  eternal, 202
  ungenerable, 202
Timotheus: lyric poetry, 35
together: definition, 195
total: definition, 98
touch: definition, 195
triangle: a measure of polygons, 164
truth:
  as being, 159
  cause of, being, 158
  definition, 70
  for relativists, chasing birds, 66
  if more or less, then absolute truth exists, 64
two: little, without qualification, 238
Two: *see* Dyad

underlying subject: *see* subject
understand: definition, 13, 16
understanding: implies ability to teach, 13, 14-15
unequal: privation of equal, 167
Unequal: see Dyad, Plato
unit:
  definition, 81, 241
  no quality or quantity in, 226, 227
unity: *see* one
universal:
  definition, 129

universal—*Cont.*
    known sometimes without experience, 13
    most, most distant from sensation, 14
    not a *substance,* 129-30, 133-34
    not a *this,* 53
    not always a genus, 33
    whether existing, 46-48
universe:
    cause of order in, nonsensible, 212
    good in, 210-12
    order in, 210-12
unlike:
    opposite of like, 84
    senses of, 165
use: an end in itself, 155

water: homogeneous, 76
Water: see Empedocles, Thales
wear: matter a cause of, 156
weight: two senses, 161
whatness:
    beginning of syllogism, 121, 219
    indemonstrable, 43, 102, 186
    of categories other than substance, 109
    senses of, 112
whether: indicates an opposition, 168
white: two senses of, 115

whole:
    a species of unity, 98
    as universal, 97-98
    three senses, 97-98
width: definition, 89
wisdom:
    a science, 14
    a science of principles, 176
    about first causes and principles, 14
    causes included, 13
    no contrary of, 211-12
wise: attributes of, 14
wish: of the noble, 204
with respect to: *see* in virtue of
wonder: beginning of understanding, 16

Xenocrates:
    Ideas, same as Mathematical Objects, 213, 223, 233
    indivisible Magnitudes, 223
    Magnitudes, from *Dyad* and Numbers, criticism, 243
    substance, kinds, 109
    thesis about Numbers, worst, 228
Xenophanes: principle, *One,* God, 22
    immature, 22

Zeno: indivisible, not existing, 50